The International Handbook of Collaborative Learning

Collaborative learning has become an increasingly important part of education, but the research supporting it is distributed across a wide variety of fields including social, cognitive, developmental, and educational psychology, instructional design, the learning sciences, educational technology, socio-cultural studies, and computer-supported collaborative learning. The goal of this book is to integrate theory and research across these diverse fields of study and, thereby, to further our understanding of collaborative learning and its instructional applications. The book is structured into the following four sections: 1) Theoretical Foundations 2) Research Methodologies 3) Instructional Approaches and Issues, and 4) Technology. Key features include the following:

Comprehensive and Global — This is the first book to provide a comprehensive review of the widely scattered research on collaborative learning, including the contributions of many international authors.

Cross-Disciplinary — The field of collaborative learning is highly interdisciplinary, drawing scholars from psychology, computer science, mathematics education, science education, and educational technology. Within psychology, the book brings together perspectives from cognitive, social, and developmental psychology as well as from the cross-disciplinary field of the learning sciences.

Chapter Structure — To ensure consistency across the book, authors have organized their chapters around integrative themes and issues. Each chapter author summarizes the accumulated literature related to their chapter topic and identifies the strengths and weaknesses of the supporting evidence.

Strong Methodology — Each chapter within the extensive methodology section describes a specific methodology, its underlying assumptions, and provides examples of its application.

This book is appropriate for researchers and graduate level instructors in educational psychology, learning sciences, cognitive psychology, social psychology, computer science, educational technology, teacher education, and the academic libraries serving them. It is also appropriate as a graduate level textbook in collaborative learning, computer-supported collaborative learning, cognition and instruction, educational technology, and learning sciences.

Cindy E, Hmelo-Silver (Rutgers University) is co-editor of the *Journal of the Learning Sciences* and has been active in the Computer-supported Collaborative Learning Community.

Clark A. Chinn (Rutgers University) edited the Computer Supported Collaborative Learning 2007 Conference Proceedings. He is editor of *Educational Psychologist.*

Carol K. K. Chan (University of Hong Kong) is associate editor of the *International Journal of Computer-Supported Collaborative Learning.*

Angela M. O'Donnell (Rutgers University) was recently recognized by the AERA Cooperative Learning Special Interest Group as Outstanding Researcher in Cooperative Learning.

Educational Psychology Handbook Series

The International Handbook of Collaborative Learning
Edited by Cindy E. Hmelo-Silver, Clark A. Chinn, Carol K. K. Chan, Angela M. O'Donnell

Handbook of Self-Regulation of Learning and Performance
Edited by Barry J. Zimmerman, Dale H. Schunk

Handbook of Research on Learning and Instruction
Edited by Patricia A. Alexander, Richard E. Mayer

International Handbook of Research on Conceptual Change
Edited by Stella Vosniadou

Handbook of Moral and Character Education
Edited by Larry P. Nucci, Darcia Narvaez

The International Handbook of Collaborative Learning

Edited by

Cindy E. Hmelo-Silver, Clark A. Chinn,
Carol K. K. Chan, and Angela M. O'Donnell

Routledge
Taylor & Francis Group
NEW YORK AND LONDON

First published 2013
by Routledge
711 Third Avenue, New York, NY 10017

Simultaneously published in the UK
by Routledge
2 Park Square, Milton Park, Abingdon, Oxon OX14 4RN

Routledge is an imprint of the Taylor & Francis Group, an informa business

Library of Congress Cataloging in Publication Data
The international handbook of collaborative learning / Edited by Cindy E. Hmelo-Silver, Clark A. Chinn, Carol Chan, and Angela M. O'Donnell.
pages cm. — (Educational psychology handbook series)
Includes bibliographical references and index.
1. Group work in education—Cross-cultural studies. I. Hmelo-Silver, Cindy E. editor of compilation.
LB1032.I524 2012
371.39'5—dc23
2012017121

ISBN: 978-0-415-80573-5 (hbk)
ISBN: 978-0-415-80574-2 (pbk)
ISBN: 978-0-203-83729-0 (ebk)

Typeset in Minion
by EvS Communication Networx, Inc.

Printed and bound in the United States of America
by Edwards Brothers, Inc.

CONTENTS

LIST OF CONTRIBUTORS

Richard C. Anderson, University of Illinois at Urbana-Champaign, US
Adrian F. Ashman, University of Queensland, Australia
Brigid J.S. Barron, Stanford University, US
Katerine Bielaczyc, Clark University, US
Carol K.K.Chan, University of Hong Kong, Hong Kong
Clark A. Chinn, Rutgers University, US
Douglas B. Clark, Vanderbilt University, US
Allan Collins, Northwestern University, US
Lindsay L. Cornelius, University of Washington, US
Ulrike Cress, Knowledge Media Research Center, Tübingen, Germany
Vanessa P. Dennen, Florida State University, US
Christina DeSimone, University of Ottawa, Canada
Nicole DiDonato, Montclair State University, US
Hebbah El-Moslimany, Rutgers University, US
Randi A. Engle, University of California, Berkeley, US
Gijsbert Erkens, Utrecht University, The Netherlands
Deborah A. Fields, University of Pennsylvania
Frank Fischer, University of Munich, Germany
Robyn M. Gillies, University of Queensland, Australia
Susan Golbeck, Rutgers University, US
Allyson F. Hadwin, University of Victoria, Australia
Kai Hakkarainen, University of Turku, Finland
Leslie R. Herrenkohl, University of Washington, US
Friedrich Wilhelm Hesse, Knowledge Media Research Center, Tübingen, Germany
Christopher Hoadley, New York University, US

Cindy Hmelo-Silver, Rutgers University, US
Iris Howley, Carnegie Mellon University, US
Jeroen Janssen, Utrecht University, The Netherlands
Heisawn Jeong, Hallym University, Korea
Yasmin B. Kafai, University of Pennsylvania, US
Kaijn Kangas, University of Helsinki, Finland
Manu Kapur, National Institute of Education, Singapore
Paul A. Kirschner, Open University, The Netherlands
Ingo Kollar, University of Munich, Germany
Timothy Koschmann, Southern Illinois University, US
Lisa Linnenbrink-Garcia, Duke University, US
Chee-Kit Looi, National Institute of Education, Singapore
Elijah Mayfield, Carnegie Mellon University, US
Brian Miller, University of Illinois at Urbana-Champaign, US
Angela M. O'Donnell, Rutgers University, US
Sami Paavola, University of Helsinki, Finland
Roy Pea, Stanford University, US
Nancy E. Perry, University of British Columbia, Canada
Sadhana Puntambekar, University of Wisconsin-Madison, US
Toni Kempler Rogat, Rutgers University, US
Carolyn Penstein Rosé, Carnegie Mellon University, US
R. Keith Sawyer, Washington University in St. Louis, US
Pirita Seitamaa-Hakkarainen, University of Helsinki, Finland
Shlomo Sharan, Tel Aviv University, Israel
Yael Sharan, GRIP-Group Investigation Projects
Yanjie Song, National Institute of Education, Singapore
Gary Stahl, Drexel University, US
Karsten Stegmann, University of Munich, Germany
Jingjing Sun, University of Illinois at Urbana-Champaign, US
Ivy Geok-chin Tan, Nanyang Technological University, Singapore
Jan Van Aalst, University of Hong Kong, Hong Kong
Noreen M. Webb, University of California, Los Angeles, US
Christof Wecker, University of Munich, Germany
Armin Weinberger, Saarland University, Germany
Philip H. Winne, Simon Fraser University, Canada
Jenna Wolfstone-Hay, University of Washington, US
Lung-Hsiang Wong, National Institute of Education, Singapore
Xiaoying Wu, University of Illinois at Urbana-Champaign, US
Jianwei Zhang, University at Albany, State University of New York, US
Jan Zottmann, University of Munich, Germany

FOREWORD

Whether in school or out of school; whether in face to face or virtual environments; and, whether in performance of a teacher-orchestrated or a self-selected task, positive interdependence in the form of cooperative learning remains foundational to the educational experience. That is a premise that has been widely accepted by educators and educational researchers for decades, as well as by those involved in human learning and performance within a wide array of disciplines—from business to medicine or from computer programming to mathematical problem solving. That collaborative learning is basic to human growth and development is likewise a belief shared by the editors of and contributors to the *Handbook of Collaborative Learning*. Although their theoretical orientations may vary to some extent, while the particular language or attributes they use to conceptualize cooperative learning may differ to a certain degree, and while the specific contexts for the research they report may contrast, all those involved in this important project are consistent in their valuing of cooperative learning as a positive mechanism for human growth and development.

Despite the long-espoused benefits of peer-to-peer cooperation within academic contexts, there is still much to know about the nature and forms of effective cooperative learning both from the perspective of the researcher and the teacher, as the editors of this Handbook have made most evident. For those engaged in research on cooperative learning, for instance, it is essential to become up-to-date on the more recent studies of cooperative learning undertaken not solely in the United States or in realm of curriculum but also in other countries and within other domains and disciplines of inquiry not as often investigated. Thus, we find contributions by scholars from across the globe populating this comprehensive volume; scholars who help bring the notion of cooperation into the international arena and into the 21st century. This is especially true with regard to the area of technology and collaborative learning (CL) or computer-supported collaborative learning (CSCL) environments. The focus on computer-involved or computer-supported cooperation in this work already distinguishes it from prior volumes devoted to cooperative or collaborative learning.

Another distinguishing feature of the *Handbook* is its thoughtful detailing of research methodologies that can be applied to the study of cooperative learning and to the analysis of its potential contributions to academic development. The consideration of the established and emergent research methodologies allows for a particularly broad and deep investigation of cooperative learning and its documented effects. However, the examination of new or effective methodologies is not restricted to research designs or data analyses. Rather, the contributors to this work also overview various pedagogical techniques or instructional interventions that promote or entail positive interdependence among students. Indeed, it is rare to find such a balance between research and practice within the pages of a scholarly volume and it is precisely due to this research–practice synergy that the *Handbook of Cooperative Learning* is an indispensable addition to the library of any educator who employs cooperative learning in his or her own teaching or who focuses on cooperative learning in his or her program of research.

As the editor for the Taylor and Francis series on the *Psychological Foundations of Teaching and Learning*, I am honored to have such a timely and comprehensive book within the series. Further, as the editors for this *Handbook*, Cindy Hmelo-Silver, Clark Chinn, Carol Chan, and Angela O'Donnell have once again demonstrated their expertise on the subject of cooperative learning. They have also succeeded in bringing together an equally impressive group of recognized scholars who cast a piercing, multidisciplinary light on positive interdependence, which allows others to see cooperative learning with new eyes.

Cooperative learning has likely been part of the human educational experience throughout history, from the gathering of mentors and mentees in forums or agoras of ancient cities to the online learning communities of contemporary societies. Despite its long and rich history, a number of questions related to cooperative learning remain. For instance, when and how does positive interdependence arise from human interactions around shared problems or tasks, what methods or techniques can be used to promote academic cooperation, and what modes of inquiry can be appropriately applied to unearth the learning and development that result from such student-to-student interactions? These are precisely the questions that the *Handbook of Collaborative Learning* can help to answer. Thus, those who apply cooperation techniques in their teaching or pursue the study of cooperative learning are well advised to listen to the lessons captured within the pages of this comprehensive, contemporary, and contributory volume.

Patricia A. Alexander
Series Editor
Psychological Foundations of Teaching and Learning

INTRODUCTION: WHAT IS COLLABORATIVE LEARNING?

An Overview

ANGELA M. O'DONNELL AND CINDY E. HMELO-SILVER
Rutgers University

Collaborative learning has become an increasingly important part of education, but the research on collaborative learning is distributed across a variety of literatures including social, cognitive, developmental, educational psychology, instructional design, the learning sciences, educational technology, sociocultural research, social psychology, sociology, and computer-supported collaborative learning. Although these fields overlap, researchers and practitioners do not necessarily read outside their own disciplines. As the study of collaborative learning continues to expand, there is a need for an interdisciplinary research agenda with sharing of theoretical and methodological perspectives. The goal of this volume is to integrate theory and research findings across these communities of scholars to forward our understanding of collaborative learning.

The motivations to create this book include an effort to integrate the scattered nature of the work on collaborative learning which is distributed across many disciplines and represented in a large number of journals. Much of the original work on cooperative learning was done in North America (e.g., Johnson & Johnson, 1989; Slavin, 1996) or in Israel (Sharan & Sharan, 1992). However, there is a burgeoning literature from a variety of countries that explores issues related to collaborative learning; another goal of this handbook is to reflect the increasingly international flavor of the research. Thus, it greatly expands the consideration of models of collaborative learning, evaluations of their effectiveness, methodologies for evaluating success, and ideas for moving forward with a productive research agenda.

The overarching purpose of this handbook is to document the current state of research on collaborative learning. To accomplish this, the book (a) describes the theoretical foundations of collaborative learning, (b) discusses methodologies for studying collaborative learning, (c) provides examples of instructional approaches and issues, and (d) addresses issues with respect to technology and collaborative learning, focusing especially on computer-supported collaborative learning. These four topics form the four sections of the book. The contents of the book reflect the diversity of interests in collaborative learning. Researchers from 9 countries on four continents are represented in the book and this diversity of contribution marks a new interdisciplinary approach to the study of collaborative learning.

What is collaborative learning? How is it distinguished from cooperation? Damon and Phelps (1989) distinguished between three forms of peer learning: peer tutoring, cooperative learning, and collaborative learning. The main characteristics distinguishing these three approaches were the dimensions of equality and mutuality of influence. Peer tutoring typically involves an unequal relationship between a tutor and a tutee, the former being more knowledgeable than the latter about the content that is the subject of the tutorial interaction. There is little in the way of mutuality of influence. The tutee is less likely to influence the tutor than vice versa. The power of the participants in this kind of tutorial interaction is not equal. According to Damon and Phelps, cooperative learning can be high in equality but low on mutuality whereas collaborative learning may be high on both. The Damon and Phelps article was written from the perspective of developmental psychology and does not capture the range of techniques and variables that distinguish between forms of cooperative and collaborative learning. A developmental psychological perspective is only one of many lenses by which collaborative or cooperative learning can be viewed. For the purposes of this volume, we will use the terms *cooperative learning* and *collaborative learning* interchangeably with an emphasis on mutual influence and equality of participation.

We begin with theoretical overviews as these theoretical perspectives shape the kinds of research methodologies used and instructional approaches adopted. The section on methodology will provide a comprehensive review of methodological approaches and tools that can be used by researchers. The section on instructional approaches and issues discusses a broad range of methods, reflecting different theoretical perspectives with a strong research base. It also addresses critical issues such as motivation and assessment. Research from the very rapidly growing field of computer-supported collaborative learning is addressed in the final section.

PERSPECTIVES ON PEER LEARNING

There are a variety of ways to conceptualize collaborative learning and these varied perspectives have implications for key decisions one makes in forming groups for the purposes of academic performance, problem solving, or other task performance. The first section of the book addresses some of the differences in perspective among approaches to collaborative learning. Among the decisions to be made by teachers include deciding on the size of the group, whether it should be heterogeneous or homogeneous in composition with respect to variables such as ability, race, and ethnicity, whether the tasks should be structured or minimally structured or whether rewards should be used. Slavin (1996) distinguished between a number of perspectives on collaborative peer learning. The perspectives he discusses include a social motivational perspective, a social cohesion perspective, two developmental perspectives influenced by Piaget and Vygotsky respectively, and cognitive elaboration perspectives (O'Donnell & O'Kelly, 1994).

Most people have worked in groups, helped another student with schoolwork, received help with schoolwork, or had some experience with tutoring. All these experiences involve peers working together to improve some aspect of academic performance. Another benefit of peer learning is greater interaction and respect among diverse students. For example, when peers are engaged in peer assisted learning strategies this can result in improved social outcomes for students with learning disabilities (Fuchs, Fuchs, Mathes, & Martinez, 2002). Peer learning is often recommended as a teaching strategy, and both students and teachers can respond well to its use. Many state and national curriculum standards include recommendations about the use of groups and other peer learning situations to enhance critical thinking, conceptual understanding, and other higher order skills. Students often enjoy interacting with one another. Teachers frequently find that the presence of other students can serve as a key instructional resource. Acceptance by peers is linked to many positive outcomes in school, such as satisfaction with school, improved academic performance, and positive beliefs about academic competence. The use of collaborative and cooperative learning in classrooms has the potential to provide the social and emotional support students need from their peers (Hymel, Bowker, & Woody, 1993; Wentzel, 1994; Wentzel & Asher, 1995; Wentzel, Battle, & Looney, 2001).

Many of the original theories of cooperative learning were strongly influenced by social-psychological principles (Deutsch, 1949). The general principle underlying these theories is that of interdependence (Johnson & Johnson, 1991). Interdependence is one example of a goal structure that guides interaction in a group. Interdependence is a condition in which group members' goal accomplishments are linked together. Thus, if one is to succeed in accomplishing one's goals, others in one's group must also accomplish their goals. For one person to succeed in accomplishing his or her goals, other members of the group must be successful too: this is a condition of positive interdependence. Two social psychological approaches arose from this perspective on collaborative learning. According to social-motivational theory, positive interdependence is created among members of a group by orchestrating the availability of rewards or recognition to encourage cooperation and collaboration. Thus, students work together to jointly gain rewards. Deutsch's theory (1949) suggests that cooperation and competition are two sides of the same coin, a view that was later supported by Johnson and Johnson (1991). In a competitive context, when one individual accomplishes his or her goals, other participants cannot do so. This is called negative interdependence. For example, when one individual wins a track race, it means that others cannot succeed in accomplishing their goals. In a cooperative context, in contrast, no one can accomplish his or her goals unless everyone does. The success of the group is dependent on everyone in the group succeeding. A relay team is an example of a cooperatively interdependent group. No one on the team succeeds unless everyone does. If one individual drops the baton, all team members fail.

Two different approaches have been taken to creating the kind of interdependence that is necessary for a cooperative group: the social-motivational perspective and the social cohesion perspective. A social-motivational approach to creating interdependence relies on the use of rewards or recognition for group productivity. Techniques derived from this perspective include teams-games-tournaments (TGT; De Vries & Edwards, 1973); team-accelerated instruction (TAI; Slavin, 1984); cooperative integrated reading and composition (CIRC; Madden, Slavin, & Stevens, 1986); and student teams achievement division (STAD; Slavin, 1986). The assumptions on which these techniques are based are that students will be motivated to work together and help one another because the group as a whole will be rewarded or will receive recognition. Thus, if one person is not working to help the group, the whole group suffers. Interdependence is created by the use of rewards or the promise of recognition. STAD is one of the most thoroughly researched cooperative learning techniques (Slavin, 1996).

Rewards or recognition are given to teams with high levels of achievement. Again, teachers must decide how many teams to reward or recognize and how to do so. Although there is cooperation among members of a group, the groups compete with other groups in the class. Within the group, however, there is the opportunity for mutuality of influence and equality of interaction. The use of individual accountability mechanisms is an effort to ensure equal participation. Each student is responsible for his or her performance and points are awarded to a team based on improvement in performance. A weakness of STAD is that it focuses on lower level cognitive objectives. Because students use prepared answer sheets to respond to their peers' efforts to answer questions, the cognitive levels of the tasks may remain quite low, focusing on factual recall and basic comprehension rather than on higher level abilities. Most of the specific collaborative learning contexts described in this volume aim for higher order outcomes on the part of students.

A second social psychological approach depends on creating interdependence through social cohesion. From this perspective, students are motivated to help one another succeed because they care about one another. Students are motivated to help one another because they wish to see one another succeed. David and Roger Johnson, directors of the Center for Cooperative Learning at the University of Minnesota, have conducted research on cooperative learning techniques since the 1970s. They developed the technique known as Learning Together (Johnson & Johnson, 1991).

Effective cooperative learning has five basic elements (Johnson & Johnson, 1991): positive interdependence; face-to-face promotive interaction in which students promote one another's cognitive and affective skills within a group context; individual accountability in which each individual is held accountable for the work of the group thus encouraging personal responsibility; interpersonal and small-group skills; and group processing. In Learning Together, a great deal of attention is given to the role of social skills. However, students may need quite a bit of help in developing and displaying the appropriate social skills. Students come to classes with histories of experience with one another and depending on their previous experience, they may not exhibit the kinds of social skills needed for the more open-ended tasks involved in Learning Together. In using Learning Together, a teacher selects a lesson and identifies objectives both for the content and for social skills. The teacher must make a number of important decisions about the size of each group, and which students make up a group. He or she must ensure that adequate materials are available and that students are assigned particular roles within the group. The use of assigned roles helps students navigate the ambiguity of the more open-ended tasks involved in a technique such as Learning Together. The teacher explains the task to the students and establishes positive interdependence among group members. One function of assigning roles within the group is to maintain that interdependence as students work together. The teacher must also establish criteria for evaluating the success of the group and develop a strategy for ensuring that each individual in the group is accountable for his or her performance. As the students work together on the task, the teacher needs to monitor their interactions and note any evidence of expected behaviors (e.g., providing encouragement to others). He or she will comment on effective uses of particular social skills. An important element of this particular approach is the group debriefing that occurs when the task is completed. Students analyze what things they did well and identify areas in need of improvement.

The tasks on which children work using Learning Together can be complex, requiring students to coordinate their efforts in pursuit of a single goal, to monitor progress toward that goal, and to redirect their efforts if necessary. These are advanced cognitive skills, and if students do not also have good social skills and know how to disagree and question the direction of the group, many kinds of interpersonal issues can arise.

Social psychological perspectives on peer learning do not directly address cognitive processes. A basic assumption of such techniques is that if students are motivated, good things will result and appropriate and effective cognitive processes will be deployed. It is true that motivation is an important element of effective learning. However, "will without skill" is unlikely to lead to successful outcomes. As Rogat, Linnebrink-Garcia, and DiDonato (chapter 14 this volume) note, collaborative learning environments can pose significant challenges to motivation and engagement. Under such circumstances, it is unlikely that effective cognitive processing will occur.

Social psychological perspectives on peer collaboration as described here are not well represented in this particular volume. Descriptions of these approaches and the research associated with documenting the effective use of collaborative learning techniques influenced by these perspectives are widely available (e.g., Slavin, 1996). This volume sought to go beyond the outcomes from these structured techniques to consider how higher order learning outcomes can be accomplished by the use of collaborative learning strategies.

COGNITIVE-ELABORATION PERSPECTIVES

Cognitive-elaboration approaches to peer learning are based on an information-processing approach. From this perspective, peer interaction is used to amplify, or cognitively elaborate, the performance of basic information-processing activities such as encoding, activation of schemas, rehearsal, metacognition, and retrieval. Encoding involves actively processing incoming information. Students with prior knowledge of a topic are more likely to encode new information effectively because they can link it to information that they already understand. Teachers can help students encode information more effectively by reminding them of what they already know that connects to the new content or helping them activate existing schemas or organized sets of knowledge about the topic. Schemas are the basic cognitive structures for organizing information. By practicing or rehearsing the information, students process it more deeply, making it easier to retrieve the information later. Performing these activities in the presence of peers will result in deeper processing and more active engagement (O'Donnell, Dansereau, Hythecker, et al., 1987). The presence of a peer can help students stay on task, and feedback provided by a peer can help students decide when they need to check their understanding of the content they are trying to explain (O'Donnell & Dansereau, 1992).

Noreen Webb's work also stems from a cognitive-elaboration perspective (1989, 1991, 1992). Much of her work focuses on student learning of mathematics. Webb has explored the effects of various types of groupings on achievement (i.e., heterogeneous, homogeneous, female-dominated, male-dominated). Webb's groups are more open-ended than the dyads that use scripted cooperation. The students decide how to participate, although training in how to do so is usually provided. Students are taught how to seek help and get explanations of the content. Webb and her colleagues found that students who participate actively in a group learn more than students who are passive; those who provide explanations achieve more than those who do not; and higher quality explanations are associated with higher levels of achievement (Webb, 1989, 1991, 1992). High-level explanations are expressions of deeper processing and elaboration of content, and may aid in restructuring existing knowledge.

Webb (chapter 1 this volume) describes the key cognitive processes that are the focus of an information processing approach to collaborative learning. Both the theory and empirical evidence provide strong support for the activity of collaborative learning in engaging learners in constructive processing here. In this perspective, the focus is on the individual knowledge gains as a result of participating in collaboration. Webb notes that the information processing perspective is compatible and even synergistic with other perspectives.

COGNITIVE-DEVELOPMENTAL PERSPECTIVES

Both Piagetian and Vygotskian theories provide a foundation for understanding collaborative learning that focuses on development. They differ, however, in the emphasis on individual cognitive processes or social processes. The three theoretical perspectives described earlier (social motivational, social cohesion, and cognitive elaboration) all depend in part on Piagetian or Vygotskian theories. Both Piaget and Vygotsky stressed a constructivist approach to teaching and learning that involves both individual and social processes. A constructivist perspective suggests that individuals create meaning using their prior understandings to make sense of new experience and construct new understandings. The developmental perspective takes into consideration how children's knowledge develops as a result of social interaction (Golbeck & El-Moslimany, chapter 2 this volume). Moreover, Golbeck and El-Moslimany consider how children's ways of collaboration change over time.

Piagetian Theory

Piaget developed a constructivist theory of cognitive development in which a child forms new conceptual structures as a result of interactions with his or her environment. Cognitive growth occurs through the process of adaptation. Conceptual development proceeds through the processes of assimilation (a process in which an outside event is brought into one's way of thinking) and accommodation (a process in which low-level schemas are transformed into higher level schemas). Modifications to existing cognitive structures occur when a structure is changed in some way as a result of experiencing new objects or events. The individual seeks equilibrium or balance in the cognitive system, and when this balance is disrupted, he or she seeks to restore equilibrium. The disequilibrium experienced fuels the effort to restore balance. Peers may provide opportunities for others to experience cognitive disequilibrium or cognitive conflict. For example, students may disagree about the solution of a problem or even about the representation of a problem. Through discussions and other activities such as experiments or other hands-on activities, they may restore cognitive equilibrium by arriving at new understandings as they work together.

Conceptual change teaching seeks to challenge students' existing concepts so as to create cognitive disequilibrium. Providing students with evidence that contradicts students' initial beliefs will require them to modify cognitive structures on the basis of new information. Through this process of adaptation, students build new cognitive structures.

A general approach to instruction that emerges from this notion is that the teacher first elicits students' expectations about a phenomenon, and then gives them opportunities to test their predictions, uncover contradictory evidence, and contrast their expectations with their experiences (Neale, Smith, & Johnson, 1990). Teachers need to create conditions in which students are responsive to the data they gather. For example, in preparing for a unit of instruction on light and shadow, students might be asked to predict where their shadows will fall as they turn their bodies in the sunlight. Some students may respond with the expectation that their shadows will appear in front of their bodies. The teacher can challenge this expectation by providing experiences that contradict it. In this case, if the children are positioned sideways to the sun, their shadows will appear at their sides. The teacher needs to remind them that their predictions about what would happen were different from what actually happened. He or she must then ask them to think about why their predictions were not accurate. At the same time, the teacher should be aware that even though the contradictory information is available, students will not necessarily experience it as creating cognitive conflict. In fact, the new experience or information may simply be assimilated into a prior concept with little change in existing cognitive structures.

The intent of this strategy is first to make students aware of their beliefs, then to create cognitive conflict by presenting contradictory experiences. A key element here is the development of awareness of beliefs. Without such awareness, the disconnect between one's expectations and what occurs may not be noticed. The goal is to have the students take in (assimilate) the new information, then restructure (accommodate) their existing cognitive structures as a result. However, this general approach to instruction may not always work. Accommodation is only one of many possible outcomes that may result when contradictions are presented (De Lisi & Golbeck, 1999). Students may ignore the contradiction between what they expected and what occurred, or they may believe that the actual event is what they anticipated. Chinn and Brewer (1993) showed that students rarely respond effectively to data that contradict their beliefs. In the example of the children's shadows discussed above, it is best to have other children trace the shadows so that there is an observable record of the event and different interpretations of the events can be discussed.

Through a combination of predictions, observations, and efforts to reconcile differences, children may experience conceptual change. From a Piagetian perspective, cognitive structures develop as a result of this process of cognitive conflict and subsequent restoration of cognitive equilibrium. It is important to keep in mind that, although a teacher may believe that students have experienced cognitive conflict because she has arranged what appear to be contradictory experiences, it does not necessarily follow that they have experienced such conflict. Chinn and Brewer (1993) and De Lisi and Golbeck (1999) describe a variety of responses that children might have to information that conflicts with their existing knowledge. Processes such as cognitive disequilibrium and restoring balance to the cognitive system could also occur in social-motivational, social-cohesion, and cognitive-elaboration approaches to peer learning.

Piaget's work has important implications for cooperative and collaborative learning, mainly because of his ideas about peer influence (De Lisi & Golbeck, 1999). According to Piaget, children are more likely to develop cognitively in contexts in which peers have equal power and all have opportunities to influence one another. In tutoring contexts, participants do not have equal power. When adults work with children, there is an inevitable power structure that is likely to result in children complying with the adult. The risk is that children will simply accept what the more powerful, authoritative adult says without experiencing cognitive conflicts or examining existing beliefs. Even when peers work together without an adult present in the group, power relations may not be equal. Certain children may have more status and power as a function of perceived ability, popularity, and other characteristics, such as gender or race. Children with high status typically have more influence over the interactions that occur in the group. They tend to say more, offer explanations, and provide answers to questions asked by children with lower status. Other children may simply go along with the ideas of these high-status children.

Vygotskian Theory

A second approach to understanding collaboration is associated with Vygotskian theory. Vygotsky's perspective on development includes both cultural–societal and individual components. According to Vygotsky (1978), there is a dialectical relationship between the child and the cultural environment: "In the process of development, the child not only masters the items of cultural experience but the habits and forms of cultural behavior, the cultural methods of reasoning" (Vygotsky, 1929, p. 415). Although the social environment provides models of performance and skill, children must still master the skills for themselves. Moshman (1982) refers to this mutual influence between the individual and the environment as dialectical constructivism; in this view, knowledge lies in the continual interaction between the individual and the environment. He contrasts this type of constructivism with that of endogenous constructivism which is more Piagetian in nature and exogenous constructivism which is more akin to information processing.

The characteristics of a student's environment are very important. According to Hogan and Tudge (1999), "The presence or absence of certain types of institutions (e.g., schools), technologies, and semiotic tools (e.g., pens or computers) as well as variations in the values, beliefs, and practices of different cultural groups are interdependent with differences in ways in which children's development proceeds" (p. 41). An example of an effort to provide an environment that is conducive to positive development is the Head Start program. It was founded to improve the quality of the environments available to young children so that their cognitive development could be enhanced. The characteristics of the learner are also important, because traits such as motivation, work ethic, and curiosity affect the degree to which learners work to master the skills they need to participate in their community.

A second key idea concerns what Vygotsky termed the *zone of proximal development*. According to Vygotsky, the zone of proximal development is a level of competence on a task in which the student cannot yet master the task on his or her own but can perform the task with appropriate guidance and support from a more capable partner. Assistance comes from a more competent child or adult who can recognize the learner's current level of functioning and the kind of performance that might be possible, and provide appropriate support. Cognitive development occurs as the child internalizes the processes that take place in the course of interacting with a more competent adult or peer. The child's cognitive structures are reorganized, and in later interactions the child may show evidence of having developed new cognitive structures by explaining his or her thinking or actions.

From a Vygotskian perspective, pairing an adult with a child is most likely to promote cognitive growth. The adult may be expected to have some skill in recognizing the child's current level of functioning and adjusting instruction to support the child's efforts. Webb (1991) noted that the kind of help a learner receives must match his or her needs. One might reasonably expect adults to provide more effectively the level of help needed by a learner in comparison to a peer. The zone of proximal development is jointly established by the participants (Hogan & Tudge, 1999) and is best accomplished when one partner is aware of the other's current level of functioning and is able to prompt, hint, or otherwise scaffold or support the other partner's developing competence. Students may have difficulties in providing appropriate levels of help for one another. Webb and Farivar (1994) found that middle school students could be taught how to solicit help.

If adults are not available, more competent peers can support the learning of a less competent student. However, peers need assistance in providing the appropriate level of help. Person and Graesser (1999) have shown, for example, that naïve tutors are not very good at identifying the tutee's current level of functioning and scaffolding the tutee's efforts so that his or her performance improves. Webb and Farivar (1994) have clearly shown that it is difficult to train young students to identify or act within another learner's zone of proximal development. However, King and her colleagues (King, Staffieri, & Adelgais, 1998) show that with appropriate instructional support, peers can respond effectively to one another's efforts.

Hakkarainen, Paavola, Kangas, and Seitamaa-Hakkarainen (chapter 3 this volume) present the sociocultural perspective on collaborative learning. This perspective is informed by Vygotsky's views of how the individual interacts with the social world. In contrast with the information processing and Piagetian cognitive development perspectives, sociocultural theorists focus on the importance of participation in social practices of knowledge creation. They extend this to the trialogical approach that emphasizes social practices with shared objects. Stahl (chapter 4 this volume) looks to the underlying theoretical basis for computer-supported collaborative learning (CSCL) and argues that it is in the small group that is where the action is in CSCL, and therefore is the appropriate unit of study. Different theoretical perspectives lead to the range of research methods that are described in section II of this volume and have different implications for instructional designs, described in sections III and IV.

Collaborative learning environments are complex and are studied with a range of sophisticated research methods. These methods are both quantitative (Cress & Hesse, chapter 5 this volume; Janssen, Cress, Erkens, & Kirschner, chapter 6 this volume) and qualitative (Sawyer, chapter 7 this volume; Koschmann, chapter 8 this volume). One of the difficulties of the fragmented nature of the study of collaborative processes has been the lack of shared methodologies, Thus, we see different disciplines applying the methodologies of their discipline to the study of collaboration without due reference to the innovations in analysis that may be made in other areas of study. This section of the volume is critically important in laying out a variety of methodologies from which many disciplines can benefit. For example, researchers in education may not be knowledgeable about social network analysis which allows a researcher to track the influence of various individuals in a group. This section of the volume opens up many opportunities for cross-fertilization of methodologies across disciplines in the service of understanding the nature of effective collaborative learning, Many approaches to analysis may involve combinations of methods (Jeong, chapter 9 this volume; Howley, Mayfield, & Rosé, chapter 10 this volume; Barron, Pea, & Engle, chapter 11 this volume; Puntambekar, chapter 12 this volume). Cress and Hesse (chapter 5) note that a hallmark of quantitative analysis is being able to make and test predictions about both learning processes and learning outcomes of individuals, interaction processes among group members, and learning outcomes of groups as well as the interrelationship among these factors. Many datasets used in collaborative learning have data that are hierarchically nested and violate the assumptions of standard inferential statistics; Janssen et al. discuss the multilevel analysis methods for addressing this issue in chapter 6.

Many collaborative learning studies use strictly qualitative techniques for data analysis. As Sawyer (chapter 7 this volume) notes, qualitative methods have many advantages for studying the naturally occurring activities in small groups, in particular the emergent characteristics of groups. Koschmann (chapter 8 this volume) describes a specific qualitative method, conversation analysis, to describe talk-in-interaction. Puntambekar (chapter 12 this volume) considers how a mix of methodologies can be used to answer complementary research questions. The remaining chapters in this section talk about specific approaches to analyzing collaboration that are somewhat agnostic to the qualitative–quantitative distinction. Jeong's chapter on verbal analysis speaks to techniques derived from a cognitive science approach to analyzing knowledge representation and cognitive processes that have been extended to include social processes (chapter 9 this volume). The approach outlined emphasizes being able to classify utterances into codes that can then be quantified. Jeong rightly notes that the verbal data analysis approach is a tool in a toolbox of methodologies that can be used to analyze collaborative learning. Similarly, Barron et al. (chapter 11 this volume) suggests that video analysis can be an integral part of a range of research designs. Theoretical commitments drive the ways that video and verbal data analysis methods are employed. Barron et al. (chapter 11) provide recommendations for research practices that support video analysis. Howley et al. (chapter 10 this volume) bring the constructs from linguistic analysis to the study of collaborative learning. These constructs include the ability to study how reasoning processes are displayed through language as it can be used to examine multiple levels of social processes that are part and parcel of learning conversations. These approaches vary as to their levels of theoretical commitments and what counts as evidence of learning. One theme that runs throughout this section is the focus on the appropriate unit of analysis and what it should be. More information processing-oriented theories tend to be more concerned with the individual unit of analysis whereas other approaches focus on the group as the appropriate unit of study. Different methods are more or less suited for particular units of analysis but as several of the chapters have noted, there are often reasons to look across these different units.

Many aspects of collaborative learning are reflected in the range of issues that are important for the design of CL environments. As Rogat, Linnenbrink-Garcia, and DiDonato (chapter 14 this volume) observe, an assumption of CL environments is that they will promote motivation and engagement, but these environments can also provide challenges to student motivation as they must deal with the increased complexity of dealing with collaboration. They argue that we need methodologies that will allow us to study the effects of shared motivational contexts. These methodologies should allow understanding of change over time. Bielaczyc, Kapur, and Collins (chapter 13 this volume) present a model of creating communities of learners that tries to reconceptualize educational practice and requires a real change in the roles of teachers and students, a theme that cuts through many collaborative learning innovations (e.g., Hmelo-Silver & DeSimone, chapter 21 this volume; Chan, chapter 25 this volume). Communities of learner models seek to foster both development of critical thinking skills as well as deep disciplinary understanding through engagement in consequential tasks. Bielaczyc et al. note the challenges needed to change the classroom culture to support such a model. One change is that the students need to assume responsibility for their learning. This is consistent with Miller, Sun, Wu, and Anderson's (chapter 15 this volume) observations of how learners can take on group leadership (see also Gressick & Derry, 2010; Hmelo-Silver, Katic, Nagarajan, & Chernobilsky, et al., 2007). They argue that leadership is characterized as reciprocal social processes in which one individual can help guide collaborative groups. Consistent with the approach of community of learners and knowledge building, groups that have a focus on collective improvement are productive in the long term, but Miller et al. also note that it is important for students to lead in ways that don't dominate (much like the soft leaders approach described in Hmelo-Silver et al., 2007). Another important challenge for collaborative learning is assessment. Like leadership, assessment is another opportunity for students to exert agency through peer and self-assessment in collaborative learning (van Aalst, chapter 16 this volume). Ashman and Gillies (chapter 17 this volume) address the elephant in many classrooms: can collaborative learning be used with diverse learners? In their review of the research, collaborative learning appears promising for students with learning difficulties but the results for students with social and emotional disorders are a little more mixed. In the latter population, groups must be carefully structured and students may need opportunities to learn social skills (including the regular education students). They note that teachers must be prepared to implement collaborative learning well for diverse populations of learners.

Many designs reflect the importance of a range of disciplinary roots. These principles are instantiated in many of the specific designs described in section III. Chinn and Clark (chapter 18 this volume) discuss the role of collaborative argumentation in the classroom. One reason for the importance of collaborative argumentation is its connection to specific disciplinary practices that require claims to be substantiated by evidentiary norms of particular disciplines. As a form of collaborative discourse, argumentation supports learning critical thinking and deep content understanding. However, collaborative argumentation in the classroom requires scaffolding to be productive as Chinn and Clark demonstrate. Moreover, Cornelius, Herrenkohl, and Wolfstone-Hay (chapter 19 this volume) argue for the importance of considering disciplinary norms in considering how to scaffold student learning and organize instruction, in particular, in considering appropriate kinds of discourse. Cornelius et al. suggest that one way of accomplishing this is through the consideration of disciplinary "rights and responsibilities" in choosing the discipline-specific tools that can foster productive collaboration. For example, they report a study in which they assigned different intellectual roles to students in science and history that reflected the norms of inquiry in those disciplines. Nonetheless, despite these disciplinary differences, having common participant structures may help provide routines that transcend disciplinary boundaries.

Several chapters provide examples of participant structures that support collaborative learning. Group Investigation (GI; Sharan, Sharan, & Tan, chapter 20 this volume) builds on the ideas of Dewey and Piaget in recognizing the importance of social factors in inquiry. Sharan et al. make clear the important role of teachers in structuring cooperative groups and promoting productive group norms. GI is organized around driving research questions that emphasize shared agency in planning, conducting, and evaluating their investigations. Another instructional model for collaborative learning is problem-based learning (PBL; Hmelo-Silver & DeSimone, chapter 21 this volume). Like GI, PBL is focused on facilitated collaborative inquiry. Rather than a driving question, PBL is focused on ill-structured problems and has a particular emphasis on promoting skills for self-regulated learning. Hmelo-Silver and DeSimone provide examples of how PBL might be adapted for different contexts and the kinds of scaffolds that can be used, some of which include a role for technology.

Technology plays an increased role in CL, reflected in the growing field of computer-supported collaborative learning (CSCL). Designing technology for CSCL is particularly challenging as Dennen and Hoadley note (chapter 22 this volume). Designers must consider not only the technology but also the different forms of group interaction with and around the technology, including the larger activities within which the technology is situated and the technology itself. They also note that theory only provides limited guidance in dealing with the complexity of CSCL environments. Fischer, Kollar, Stegmann, Wecker, Zottman, and Weinberger (chapter 23 this volume) note the importance of structuring interaction at both macro and micro levels. They argue that using scripts in CSCL empowers learners. They also argue that sometimes scripts should problematize what is being learned to encourage learners to engage in deeper cognitive processing. One issue to be considered is how scripts can be made adaptable for different learners and learning situations (and this seems to be an area where technology has a natural role).

CSCL designs build on what we know about collaborative learning but they also require that new possibilities be envisioned, and nowhere is this more salient than in the design of mobile CSCL technologies. Looi, Wong, and Song (chapter 24 this volume) note that mobile CSCL allows learning to be ubiquitous and to take advantage of the places where learners are—thus extending learning over time and space. The physical characteristics of different mobile devices provide affordances (and constraints) for collaboration in situ. Because these devices are ubiquitous, they can provide opportunities for extended engagement in CSCL, but Looi et al. also note the importance of the tasks developed to take advantage of this CSCL technology. Many of the learning tasks designed for mobile CSCL build on ideas of distributed cognition. Another important affordance of mobile technology is the capacity to bridge formal and informal learning. Looi et al. are cautious as they note the paucity of high quality research in the area of mobile CSCL.

An increasingly influential theoretical and pedagogical approach to CSCL is Knowledge Building (Chan, chapter 25 this volume). This approach draws from the practices of scientists and researchers who have a goal of collectively improving a community's knowledge. This approach stresses agency for the participants in choosing their research goals and addresses the "soft skills" of collaboration and creative work with knowledge (Fischer & Sugimoto, 2006; Scardamalia & Bereiter, 2006). Central to this design, as Chan notes, has been the CSCL tool, Knowledge Forum (Scardamalia & Bereiter, 2006) where participants can maintain a database of community knowledge and discourse. An important feature of Knowledge Forum is the Analytic Tool Kit, a suite of assessment tools, which can support formative assessment for teachers as well as provide data for researchers studying knowledge building. This chapter lays out the principles for knowledge building that can support productive CSCL. This is perhaps one of the most widely studied CSCL approaches, which is being used on an international scale. The unit of analysis for knowledge building is really a collective unit but there is also evidence of benefits for individual learners (Chan, chapter 25 this volume). Nonetheless, it can be a challenging model to implement, in particular in building social norms needed to sustain the kind of knowledge work that this model calls for (Hakkarainen, 2009). Developing these "knowledge practices" is an important area for future research.

Working with knowledge or collaboratively at any level places additional demands for metacognitive skill. Winne, Hadwin, and Perry (chapter 26 this volume) move from considering solo metacognition to considering shared and other regulation that come into play in CSCL environments as metacognition becomes socially shared. Moreover, the nature of CSCL can allow students' metacognitive knowledge and skills to become visible, which can provide opportunities for formative feedback. As Winne et al. note, much of the metacognitive support comes from teachers and peers. They pose the challenge for CSCL research to develop "software systems to support metacognition and collaboration in ways that parallel or extend what effective teachers and competent peers do." Making use of the trace data that are available in CSCL systems is a start to being able to support metacognition in such systems.

An important part of collaborative learning happens outside of school as Kafai and Fields (chapter 27 this volume) demonstrate in their discussion of virtual youth communities. A key aspect of such communities is that the participants have opportunities to choose what activities they participate in and the extent of their participation. Such informal spaces are an important middle ground between home and school and offer opportunities for different kinds of interactions with peers or mentors than might be found in a more formal setting. They present examples of two such communities: Whyville and Scratch. They demonstrate how peer helping is an important practice in these communities and ways in which these informal settings become sites for knowledge building. These take the form of "cheat" sites where youth can share hints about the virtual worlds, wikis, and other community forums. For example, Kafai and Fields have found that collaboration plays an important part in the development of these cheat sites. Collaboration and participation in these sites can be quite variable, as they illustrated in their example of the Scratch programming community. One mode of collaboration is remixing of different programs and modifying code (though participants had various views as to whether that was cheating or building on others' work. The dynamic nature of these virtual communities makes them hard to study. It is hard to know what the appropriate unit of analysis is, and with the community in flux, it may be that collective knowledge is the only possible unit in these massive communities. Moreover, we need to better understand collaboration that happens across multiple spaces, both the physical and the virtual and how knowledge diffuses within and between spaces. Such communities are quite different from the formal settings where most of the other chapters focus. Kafai and Fields suggest the need for connective ethnography to study these virtual spaces and the communities that interact in them, making use of a range of data sources to understand collaboration in these settings.

Finally, central to collaboration, particularly that enabled by technology, is the role of culture. Zhang (chapter 28 this volume) brings the role of culture in technology-mediated collaboration to the foreground. Zhang notes the importance of considering the nature of cultural norms, whether it is culture writ large, as in an international collaboration, or we would add, writ small, as in trying to bring more student-centered norms into educational systems which may have been more teacher-centered. As Zhang notes, collaboration and learning are inherently cultural activities, and we need to understand these preexisting cultural practices and norms in designing collaborative learning environments. Several studies demonstrate that cross-cultural collaborations can help teachers and learners reflect on their assumptions about learning. These can also provide opportunities for the development of intercultural competence—important in an increasingly globalized world (Friedman, 2007).

ACKNOWLEDGMENTS

We gratefully acknowledge the assistance of Courtney Farrugia and Rebecca DiGiglio. We are especially grateful to Kristiana Monterosso for her help in finishing up this long book project.

REFERENCES

Chinn, C. A., & Brewer, W. F. (1993). The role of anomalous data in knowledge acquisition: A theoretical framework and implications for science instruction. *Review of Educational Research, 63,* 1–49.

Damon, W., & Phelps, E. (1989). Critical distinctions among three approaches to peer education. *International Journal of Educational Research, 13*(1), 9–19.

De Lisi, R., & Golbeck, S. (1999). Implications of Piagetian theory for peer learning. In A. M. O'Donnell & A. King (Eds.), *Cognitive perspectives on peer learning* (pp. 3–37). Mahwah, NJ: Erlbaum.

Deutsch, M. (1949). A theory of cooperation and competition. *Human Relations, 2,* 129–152.

De Vries, D. L., & Edwards, K. J. (1973). Learning games and student teams: Their effects on classroom process. *American Educational Research Journal, 10,* 307–318.

Fischer, G., & Sugimoto, M. (2006). Supporting self-directed learners and learning communities with socio-technical environments. *Research and Practice in Technology Enhanced Learning Environments, 1*(1), 31–64.

Friedman, T. L. (2007). *The world is flat.* New York: Farrar, Straus & Giroux.

Fuchs, D., Fuchs, L. S., Mathes, P. G., & Martinez, E. A. (2002). Preliminary evidence on the social standing of students with learning disabilities in PALS and no-PALS classrooms. *Learning Disabilities Research, 17*(4), 205–215.

Gressick, J., & Derry, S. J. (2010). Distributed leadership in online groups. International *Journal of Computer Supported Collaborative Learning, 5,* 211–236.

Hakkarainen, K. (2009). A knowledge practice perspective on technology-mediated learning. *International Journal of Computer Supported Collaborative Learning, 4,* 213–231.

Hmelo-Silver, C. E., Katic, E., Nagarajan, A., & Chernobilsky, E. (2007). Soft leaders, hard artifacts, and the groups we rarely see: Using video to understand peer-learning processes. In R. Goldman, R. D. Pea, B. J. S. Barron, & S. J. Derry (Eds.), *Video research in the learning sciences* (pp. 255–270). Mahwah NJ: Erlbaum.

Hogan, D. M., & Tudge, J. R. H. (1999). Implications of Vygotsky's theory of peer learning. In M. O'Donnell & A. King (Eds.), *Cognitive perspectives on peer learning* (pp. 39–65). Mahwah, NJ: Erlbaum.

Hymel, S., Bowker, A., & Woody, E. (1993). Aggressive versus withdrawn unpopular children: Variations in peer and self-perceptions in multiple domains. *Child Development, 64,* 879–896.

Johnson, D. W., & Johnson, R. T. (1989). *Cooperation and competition: Theory and research.* Edina, MN: Interaction Book.

Johnson, D. W., & Johnson, R. T. (1991). *Learning together and alone: Cooperative, competitive, and individualistic learning.* Englewood Cliffs, NJ: Prentice Hall.

King, A., Staffieri, A., & Adelgais, A. (1998). Mutual peer tutoring: Effects of structured tutorial interaction to scaffold peer learning. *Journal of Educational Psychology, 90,* 134–152.

Madden, N. A., Slavin, R. E., & Stevens, R. J. (1986). *Cooperative integrated reading and comparison: Teacher's manual.* Baltimore, MD: Johns Hopkins University, Center for Research on Elementary and Middle Schools.

Moshman, D. (1982). Exogenous, endogenous, and dialectical constructivism. *Developmental Review, 2,* 371–384.

Neale, D. C., Smith, D., & Johnson, V. G. (1990). Implementing conceptual change teaching in primary science. *Elementary School Journal, 91,* 109–131.

O'Donnell, A. M., & Dansereau, D. F. (1992). Scripted cooperation in student dyads: A method for analyzing and enhancing academic learning and performance. In R. Hertz-Lazarowitz & N. Miller (Eds.), *Interaction in cooperative groups: The theoretical anatomy of group learning* (pp. 120–141). New York: Cambridge University Press.

O'Donnell, A. M., Dansereau, D. F., Hythecker, V. I., Larson, C. O., Skaggs, L., & Young, M. D. (1987). The effects of monitoring on cooperative learning. *Journal of Experimental Education, 54,* 169–173.

O'Donnell, A. M., & O'Kelly, J. O. (1994). Learning from peers: Beyond the rhetoric of positive results. *Educational Psychology Review, 6,* 321–349.

Person, N. K., & Graesser, A. C. (1999). Evolution of discourse during cross-age tutoring. In A. M. O'Donnell & A. King (Eds.), *Cognitive perspectives on peer learning* (pp. 69–86). Mahwah, NJ: Erlbaum.

Scardamalia, M., & Bereiter, C. (2006). Knowledge building: Theory, pedagogy, and technology. In R. K. Sawyers (Ed.), *Cambridge handbook of the learning sciences* (pp. 97–115). New York: Cambridge University Press.

Sharan, Y., & Sharan, S. (1992). *Expanding cooperative learning through group investigation.* New York: Teacher's College Press.

Slavin, R. E. (1984). Combining cooperative learning and individualized instruction: Effects on students' mathematics achievement, attitudes, and behaviors. *Elementary School Journal, 84,* 409–422.

Slavin, R. E. (1986). *Using student team learning* (3rd ed.). Baltimore, MD: Johns Hopkins University Press

Slavin, R. E. (1996). Research on cooperative learning and achievement: What we know, what we need to know. *Contemporary Educational Psychology, 21,* 43–69.

Vygotsky, L. S. (1929). The problem of the cultural development of the child. *Journal of Genetic Psychology, 36,* 415–434.

Vygotsky, L. S. (1978). *Mind in society: The development of higher psychological processes.* Cambridge, MA: Harvard University Press.

Webb, N. M. (1989). Peer interaction and learning in small groups. *International Review of Educational Research, 13,* 21–40.

Webb, N. M. (1991). Task-related verbal interaction and mathematics learning in small groups. *Journal of Research in Mathematics Education, 22,* 366–269.

Webb, N. M. (1992). Testing a theoretical model of student interaction and learning in small groups. In R. Hertz-Lazarowitz & N. Miller (Eds.), *Interaction in cooperative groups: The theoretical anatomy of group learning* (pp. 102–119). New York: Cambridge University Press.

Webb, N. M., & Farivar, S. (1994). Promoting helping behavior in cooperative groups in middle school mathematics. *American Educational Research Journal, 31,* 369–395.

Wentzel, K. R. (1994). Relations of social goal pursuit to social acceptance, classroom behavior, and perceived social support. *Journal of Educational Psychology, 86,* 173–182.

Wentzel, K. R., & Asher, S. R. (1995). Academic lives of neglected, rejected, popular, and controversial children. *Child Development, 66,* 754–763.

Wentzel, K. R., Battle, A., & Looney, L. (2001, April). *Classroom support in middle school: Contributions of teachers and peers.* Paper presented at the annual meeting of the American Educational Research Association, Seattle, WA.

I
Theoretical Approaches

1

INFORMATION PROCESSING APPROACHES TO COLLABORATIVE LEARNING

NOREEN M. WEBB

University of California, Los Angeles

The potential of small-group collaboration to promote student learning is recognized by educators, researchers, and policy-makers alike. Confirmatory research evidence began appearing decades ago (e.g., meta-analyses by Johnson, Maruyama, Johnson, Nelson, & Skon, 1981; Slavin, 1983a,b). Since then much research has focused on clarifying the mechanisms by which working with peers produces positive learning outcomes. This chapter addresses the question from an information-processing perspective; that is, how students can learn by actively processing information while collaborating with others. In particular, this chapter focuses on the relationship between the dialogue among students and processes tied to cognitive change. The first part of this chapter describes the overt communication processes and internal cognitive processes that may be associated with positive learning outcomes. The second section describes debilitating processes that might prevent learning. The final section describes approaches that have been used to promote beneficial processes and inhibit detrimental processes.

MECHANISMS THAT MAY PROMOTE LEARNING

A number of overt communication processes during collaboration may trigger internal cognitive processes that are associated with learning. During group collaboration, students may present their ideas, and thereby convey information to others (e.g., when solving a problem, completing a task, or summarizing material); they may explain to their group mates to help the latter understand the material or learn how to complete the task; or they may justify their ideas in response to challenges, questions, disagreements, or perceived conflicts or discrepancies. Both the speakers and the listeners involved in these overt communication processes can learn by engaging in a number of internal cognitive processes. First, students may activate and strengthen their understanding of material they have already learned. Second, they may fill in gaps in their understanding, thus repairing mental models that may be correct globally but are fragmented or incomplete with gaps of missing knowledge (Chi, 2000). Third, they may correct misconceptions in what Chi (2000) terms flawed mental models, which may include local mistakes or global inaccuracies. In all of these internal processes, learners actively construct their own learning by generating new relationships among pieces of information they already know, by linking new information to information they have previously learned, and by changing their thinking in light of new information they encounter (cf. Wittrock, 1990).

Both preparing to present ideas and presenting the ideas may promote learning on the speaker's part. In the process of *formulating* an explanation or idea to be presented, students must transform what they know into communication that is relevant, coherent, complete, and accurate so that others can understand it. During this preparation, students may rehearse information they already know; identify the salient features of the problem or task; prioritize, reorganize, and clarify information to make it more coherent; see new relationships and build new connections between pieces of information or concepts; generate multiple ways of representing information and make explicit the links among different representations; monitor their own understanding and develop a metacognitive awareness of their own misconceptions or gaps in understanding—and seek new information to correct those misconceptions or fill in gaps in their understanding; and strengthen connections between new information and previously learned information, all of which may help these students to develop new perspectives and deeper understanding (Bargh & Schul, 1980). *Presenting* ideas may elicit many of the same processes, especially when the presentation exposes contradictions or incompleteness of ideas that are recognized by the explainer or are pointed out by others.

To communicate most effectively, those presenting material or explaining to others must take into account the level of understanding and extent of knowledge of their listeners. Having to tailor explanations to listeners' comprehension may push speakers to construct more elaborate conceptualizations than they would otherwise do (Chi, 2000). First, *anticipating* the listener's level of comprehension may promote such activity on the part of the explainer (Benware & Deci, 1984). Second, *responding* to evidence of listeners' comprehension (e.g., as conveyed through listeners' questions) may force explainers to generate revised or novel explanations (Roscoe & Chi, 2007).

Listeners may engage in processes analogous to those carried out by presenters. When comparing their own knowledge with what is being presented, listeners may recognize and fill in gaps in their own knowledge, recognize and correct misconceptions, see contradictions that cause them to seek new information (e.g., by asking questions), and generate new connections between their own ideas, or between their own and others' ideas. They may generate self-explanations that help them internalize principles, construct specific inference rules for solving the problem, and repair imperfect mental models (Chi, 2000; Chi & Bassock, 1989; Chi, Bassock, Lewis, Reimann, & Glaser, 1989). To promote learning, then, listening must be active. The benefits will accrue when learners *apply* the information received to try to solve the problem or carry out the task themselves (Vedder, 1985).

Presenting and listening to information shared during the context of peer collaboration may be especially effective compared to other contexts such as explaining to or listening to adults (e.g., teachers), because peers share a similar language and can translate difficult vocabulary and expressions into language that fellow students can understand (Noddings, 1985). Moreover, learning material at the same time as other students may help them tune into each other's misconceptions, so they may give more relevant explanations than adults can (Vedder, 1985). And learners can control the pace of group discussion to better understand information and explanations offered.

The information-processing perspective on learning in collaborative groups is not independent of other theoretical perspectives discussed in this volume. First, for example, in sociocognitive conflict theory based on a Piagetian perspective (Piaget, 1932), conflict arises when there is a perceived contradiction between the learner's existing understanding and what the learner experiences in the course of interacting with others. Learners may respond to this perceived contradiction and disturbance to their mental equilibrium by taking into account their own perspectives while considering others' incompatible viewpoints, reexamining and questioning their own ideas and beliefs, seeking additional information to reconcile the conflicting viewpoints, and trying out new ideas (De Lisi & Golbeck, 1999; Forman & Cazden, 1985). They may carry out these processes as a result of hearing contradictory information or opinions, or through confronting others' ideas and justifying their own positions.

Second, in sociocultural theory based on a Vygotskian perspective (Vygotsky, 1978), through a process sometimes called scaffolding or guided participation, a more skilled person enables a less competent person to carry out a task that the latter could not perform without assistance. By actively listening to the more competent person, explaining what he has heard, and applying the new information to the task at hand, the less-proficient student can practice, develop, and internalize skills so that they become part of his individual repertoire.

Third, in a perspective that may be termed *coconstruction of knowledge*, students contribute different pieces of information or build upon others' explanations to jointly create a complete idea or solution (Hatano, 1993). By acknowledging, clarifying, correcting, adding to, building upon, and connecting each other's ideas and suggestions, students may collaboratively build and internalize knowledge and problem-solving strategies that no group member has at the start (Hogan, Nastasi, & Pressley, 2000).

Empirical Evidence

Indirect evidence about the mechanisms in collaborative settings that may promote learning comes from correlational research linking explanations and learning outcomes. The strong relationship between explaining and achievement in collaborative groups has been well documented (Webb & Palincsar, 1996; more recently by Howe et al., 2007; Veenman, Denessen, van den Akker, & van der Rijt, 2005). Moreover, giving complex explanations (e.g., reasons elaborated with further evidence) has been shown to be more strongly related with learning outcomes than giving less complex explanations (e.g., simple reasons; Chinn, O'Donnell, & Jinks, 2000). Tutoring studies also corroborate the importance for tutor learning of giving elaborated explanations, such as conceptual explanations (e.g., discussing how an answer does or does not make sense; Fuchs et al., 1997), and explanations that integrate concepts and draw upon prior knowledge to generate new inferences (e.g., generating novel examples and analogies; Roscoe & Chi, 2008).

In contrast to the positive relationship between giving explanations and learning outcomes, research on the relationship between receiving explanations and achievement is inconsistent (Webb & Palincsar, 1996). In support of Vedder's (1985) hypothesis that in order for receiving explanations to be effective, students must have and use the opportunity for practice by attempting to apply the explanation received to the problem at hand, engaging in constructive activity after receiving an explanation (e.g., reworking the problem, paraphrasing the solution strategy) has been found to be positively related to achievement, whereas receiving or hearing an explanation without carrying out constructive activity is not (Webb & Mastergeorge, 2003; Webb, Troper, & Fall, 1995).

More direct evidence about mechanisms that promote learning comes from analyzing collaborative dialogues for indications that students are engaging in the cognitive processes described above. For example, Roscoe and Chi's (2008) coding of explaining episodes in which students explained to other students about the basic structure, location, and function of the human eye revealed instances of students drawing upon their prior knowledge and making additional new connections with prior knowledge, generating novel examples and analogies, generating new inferences that went beyond the text material they were studying, rethinking their ideas, and repairing perceived errors and misconceptions. Explainers' metacognitive statements were especially useful for signaling when students were making new connections and building their understanding (e.g., "This is something that I didn't really get before"; Roscoe & Chi, 2007, p. 336). Other analyses of group discussions show how the group's challenge of an explainer's incomplete or incorrect ideas may cause the explainer to reexamine her prior knowledge, to formulate and test predictions based on her incorrect mental model, and to use information provided by her peers in response to her predictions to revise her ideas (e.g., a student revising her overly general concept of camouflage as an animal defense mechanism to a more accurate understanding that an animal will change its color to match only those in its natural background; Brown, Campione, Webber, & McGilly, 1992, pp. 177–178).

DEBILITATING PROCESSES

Despite the potential benefits of collaborative work, researchers have documented a number of debilitating processes that inhibit positive outcomes. Students may fail to share elaborated explanations, may not seek help when they need it, may disengage from interaction or suppress other students' participation, may engage in too much conflict or avoid it altogether, may not coordinate their communication, and may engage in negative social-emotional behavior that impedes group functioning.

Failure to Provide Elaborated Explanations

The tendency of students to present ideas with little elaboration is well documented (e.g., Galton, Hargreaves, Comber, Wall, & Pell, 1999; Meloth & Deering, 1999). For example, when tutoring their peers, students tend to restate, paraphrase, or summarize text information with little elaboration (a "knowledge-telling bias"; Roscoe & Chi, 2008), unless they are trained to give elaborations (e.g., King, Staffieri, & Adelgais, 1998). Untrained tutors may provide elaborated explanations (e.g., creating analogies, drawing inferences, making new connections) only when their tutees ask deep questions about content not provided explicitly in the text (Roscoe & Chi, 2008). In some cases, the lack of elaboration may be due to students modeling their communications on teacher discourse that consists of giving unlabeled calculations, procedures, and answers to mathematics problems instead of labeled explanations or explanations of mathematical concepts (Webb, Nemer, & Ing, 2006).

Failure to Seek and Obtain Effective Help

Some listeners may be students who are having difficulty with the material and need help. They may not be able to correct their misconceptions or fill in gaps in their understanding if they fail to seek help when they need it and fail to obtain effective help when they do seek it. Students may fail to seek help for many reasons (Nelson-Le Gall, 1992). Students may lack the metacognitive skills necessary to monitor their own comprehension and so may not realize that they don't understand the material or can't perform the task without assistance, or they may watch their teammates solve a problem or accomplish a task and assume that they can do it too.

Even if students are aware that they need help, they may decide not to seek it for fear of being judged incompetent and undesirable as a work mate, they may not want to feel indebted to those giving the help, they not want to be seen as dependent upon others, or they may not believe they are self-efficacious—that they can do well in school and can control learning through their own efforts (Newman, 1998; Schunk, 1989). A reluctance to seek help may be associated with a performance-goal or relative-ability-goal orientation, in which students are focused on looking good compared to others, performing better than others, being publicly recognized for their superior performance, and having others judge their competence positively (Ryan, Pintrich, & Midgley, 2001). These students are especially concerned about how others view them and will avoid help seeking because they feel it signals a lack of competence. (Students with a mastery-goal orientation, in contrast, are focused on learning, improving their progress, and mastering the task, and, because they are less focused on external evaluation, help seeking does not threaten their self-perceptions about their abilities.) Similarly, students who are concerned with their social status (especially if they don't feel socially competent) may avoid help seeking because it exposes them to evaluation and scrutiny by others and threatens their self-worth (Ryan et al., 2001).

Students may believe that help-seeking is undesirable as a result of classroom norms that call for students to remain quiet and work alone, or classroom norms that value performance over learning, or sex-typed norms that view help-seeking as more appropriate for females than males. Or they may have received antagonistic or unsatisfactory responses to previous help-seeking attempts. Students may also believe that no one in the group has the competence or resources to help, or that they themselves lack the competence to benefit from help provided.

When students do seek help, they may select helpers who are nice or kind, or who have high status, rather than those who have task-relevant skills (Nelson-Le Gall, 1992). Or students may not have effective strategies for eliciting help. In particular, the kinds of questions students ask often have important consequences for the kinds of responses they receive. Requests for elaborated help that are explicit, precise, and direct, and targeted to a specific aspect of the problem or task are more likely to elicit explanations than unfocused questions or general statements of confusion (Webb & Palincsar, 1996). Asking precise questions makes it easier for other group members to identify the student's misconceptions or nature of their confusion and to formulate appropriate and precise responses. Detailed requests for explanations may also signal to the group that the help-seeker is motivated to learn how to solve the problem, already has at least some understanding of the problem that enabled him to pinpoint a specific area of uncertainty, and will profit from the explanations provided, making it more likely that the group will put forth the effort to provide elaborated help (Webb, Nemer, & Ing, 2006).

Asking precise questions may have still another benefit for the help-seeker. The act of articulating a specific question (e.g., putting words to a confusion) may help the questioner to organize and integrate his thinking in new ways that lead to improved understanding (Roscoe & Chi, 2007).

In contrast to specific questions, general questions ("How do you do this?") or general declarations of confusion ("I don't get it") leave potential help-givers with little clue about what the help-seeker does not understand. Such help-seeking behavior may also signal to the group that the help-seeker lacks ability or motivation to work or learn, especially when students seek help before expending any discernible effort on the task. Help-givers may be unwilling to work hard to generate explanations if they perceive that the help-seeker lacks the competence to be able to understand or use them, or is depending on others to do the work for him.

Even if groups are willing to help, they may not have the skills to provide effective explanations. Help-givers may be confused or have misconceptions themselves, may not be able to translate their thinking into appropriate or understandable language, may not be willing or able to use examples and language familiar to the help-seeker, may not provide enough detail or detail relevant to the help-seeker's particular difficulty, may not be able to identify the help-seeker's problem, or may have difficulty integrating what they know with the help-seeker's misconceptions (Ellis & Rogoff, 1982).

Because help-givers tend not to test whether their explanations are effective for the help-seeker, for example, by asking the help-seeker to recapitulate the explanation, practice the problem, or apply it to other problems (Fuchs et al., 1997; Ross & Cousins, 1995), help-seekers must take responsibility themselves for ascertaining whether the help they receive is beneficial for improving their understanding. Help-seekers can make it more likely that they will obtain effective help and gain understanding if they persist in asking questions, for example, by repeating their questions, paraphrasing them, prefacing their question with a description of the parts of the problem they do not understand; insist on being given explanations (instead of calculations or answers); reject group members' attempts to dictate the solution; resist group members' invitations or commands to copy their papers; and apply help they receive to determine whether it allows them to solve the problem on their own without assistance (Webb & Mastergeorge, 2003).

Failure to seek help is not only detrimental for those who need help but may also be a missed opportunity for other students to benefit from being questioned. Responding to peers' questions may force students to clarify confusing explanations, or to resolve contradictions or incompleteness in their explanations, leading to improved understanding (Roscoe & Chi, 2007). Moreover, deep questions (those that require reasoning and application of knowledge) may stimulate knowledge-building on the part of explainers in ways that shallow questions about basic facts do not; for example, "How does that [the structure of the blind spot] affect your vision?" vs. "The blind spot is where all the nerves are located?" (Roscoe & Chi, 2008, p. 341).

Suppressed Participation

Students wishing to participate actively in group collaboration don't always have opportunities to do so. Personality characteristics may explain some effects such as extroverted, outgoing, and energetic members doing most of the talking and dominating group work. Status characteristics may also determine relative influence in the group (Cohen & Lotan, 1995). High-status students, especially those with high academic standing or peer status characteristics (perceived attractiveness or popularity), tend to be more active and influential than low-status individuals; while low-status individuals tend to be less assertive and more anxious, talk less, give fewer suggestions and less information, and ask fewer questions than high-status individuals. Interviews of low-achieving students working in groups with high-achieving students have revealed their frustration with having their ideas ignored, being left behind by the speed with which others solved problems or completed tasks, and being left out of decision-making processes (King, 1993). Social characteristics, such as gender or race, may also operate as status characteristics in heterogeneous small groups, with boys and White students being more active than girls and students of color. Even artificially created status differences, such as classifying students' competence on the basis of fictitious test scores (Dembo & McAuliffe, 1987) can create imbalances in individual participation and influence, with students designated as "high status" dominating group interactions and being perceived as more capable than "low status" students.

Whereas some students may be shut out of interactions, other students may choose not to participate. Students may engage in social loafing, or diffusion of responsibility, which arises when one or more group members sit back and let others do the work, possibly because they believe that their efforts can't or won't be identified or are dispensable. This free rider effect may turn into a sucker effect when the group members who complete all of the work discover that they had been taken for a free ride and start to contribute less to the group work in order to avoid being a sucker (Salomon & Globerson, 1989).

Students who choose not to be involved or who are excluded from group interaction will not experience the benefits of active participation described in the previous sections. And the students who do participate will not benefit from the knowledge and perspectives of the passive students, and may even lead the group off track by pursuing the wrong task or suggesting incorrect solutions that are not challenged.

Too Little or Too Much Cognitive Conflict

Although students can learn by resolving discrepancies in ideas, too little or too much conflict can be detrimental (Bearison, Magzamen, & Filardo, 1986). Infrequent conflict may reflect suppression of disagreements, or pseudoconsensus or pseudoagreement, in which students minimize disagreements or pretend they don't exist. Because disagreements may be seen as threatening group members' self-image, students may avoid disagreement to maintain positive social relationships (Chiu & Khoo, 2003). In these cases, incorrect ideas may persist and go unchallenged. Too much conflict, on the other hand, may prevent group members from seeking new information to resolve their disagreements. If they spend all of their time arguing they may never develop new insights, especially if their aim is to win the argument regardless if they are right or wrong.

Lack of Coordination

Opportunities to benefit from information being shared in the collaborative group may be lost when group members do not coordinate their communication. Lack of coordination of group members' efforts and participation can impede both group functioning and individual learning (Barron, 2000). Low levels of attention to, and uptake of, group members' suggestions may inhibit group progress on a task, even when those suggestions are correct and potentially productive. In uncoordinated conversations, students advocate and repeat their own positions and ideas, ignore others' suggestions, reject others' proposals without elaboration or justification, and interrupt others or talk over them. When students do not pay attention to what others say, they cannot learn from their suggestions. Barron (2000) documented a number of ways in which students may fail to attend to others' suggestions. Students may engage in "skip connecting" in which they do not acknowledge or reference what another speaker has just said, but instead reassert what they had said previously. They may also reject a suggestion or idea out of hand, without any rationale for why it was incorrect or inappropriate. Or they may refuse to yield the floor to other speakers by continuing to talk without making eye contact with others.

In highly coordinated groups, in contrast, members acknowledge each other's ideas, repeat others' suggestions, and elaborate on others' proposals. Speakers' turns are tightly connected, with group members paying close attention and responding to what other members do and say, giving space for others' contributions, and monitoring how the unfolding contributions relate to the problem-solving goal. Proposals are directly linked to the prior conversation, are acknowledged and discussed, are not ignored, and are not rejected without reasons being given (Barron, 2000). Repeating others' ideas, asking questions about them, and elaborating on them are important components of active listening. These communication behaviors may help listeners test their own understanding of the ideas being proposed, help them identify what they find confusing or unconvincing, may help them evaluate the ideas for accuracy and completeness, and may provide a foundation to help them link the new information to what they already know and generate new inferences or connections they had not previously seen.

Negative Socioemotional Processes

Negative socioemotional processes, such as rudeness, hostility, and unresponsiveness, can also impede group members' participation. Rudeness (especially rude criticisms of others' ideas, such as "You're wrong," compared to the more polite criticism: "If 6 is multiplied by 2, we don't get 10") may cause students to withhold correct information and disagree with correct suggestions posed by others, with negative effects on the quality of groups' solutions to problems (Chiu & Khoo, 2003, p. 507) and correspondingly, with reduced opportunities for group members to learn. Such processes can also suppress help-seeking, especially when students are insulted when they seek help, receive sarcastic responses, or have their requests rejected or ignored. Students who carry out negative behavior may themselves have their requests for help rejected (Webb & Mastergeorge, 2003).

APPROACHES TO PROMOTING BENEFICIAL PROCESSES AND INHIBITING DETRIMENTAL PROCESSES

Simply asking students to collaborate will not ensure that they will engage in productive dialogue. Therefore, researchers have designed and tested a number of approaches for maximizing the chances that beneficial processes will occur while preventing detrimental processes, as well as investigating factors that may influence the quality of group dialogue. This section addresses how students may be prepared for collaborative work, how group work itself can be structured to require certain student behavior, how teachers may intervene with collaborative groups, and how teacher discourse in the classroom more generally may influence student–student dialogue.

Preparation for Collaborative Work

A number of activities may take place before students begin their collaboration. Teachers can build students' communication skills, arrange group membership to encourage productive communication, and design group tasks that support high-quality dialogue.

Instructing Students in Communication, Explaining, or Reasoning Skills. Instruction in communication, explaining, or group reasoning skills is a primary component of many small-group learning programs, and produces positive effects on the depth of collaborative group discussions and, often, group performance and student achievement. For example, preparation in communications skills is a central feature of the Social Pedagogic Research into Group work (SPRinG) program designed to help teachers create inclusive and supportive classrooms (Baines, Blatchford, et al., 2008; see also Baines, Blatchford, & Chowne, 2007; Blatchford, Baines, Rubie-Davies, Bassett, & Chowne, 2006). Students receive instruction in taking turns speaking; engaging in active listening; asking and answering questions; making and asking for suggestions; expressing and requesting ideas and opinions; brainstorming suggestions, ideas, and opinions; giving and asking for help; giving and asking for explanations; explaining and evaluating ideas; arguing and counterarguing; using persuasive talk; and summarizing conversations.

Many other programs also train students in similar constellations of communication skills. Some teach students to actively listen to each other, to provide constructive feedback for each other's suggestions and ideas, to encourage all group members to contribute to the group task, to try to understand other group members' perspectives, and to monitor and evaluate the progress of the group (e.g., Gillies, 2003, 2004). Others focus on joint group activity such as jointly analyzing problems, comparing possible explanations, and making joint decisions), and help students learn how to share all relevant suggestions and information, provide reasons to justify assertions, opinions, and suggestions, ask for reasons, listen to others attentively, discuss alternatives before making decisions, and accept and respond to constructive challenges (Mercer, Dawes, Wegerif, & Sams, 2004; Rojas-Drummond & Mercer, 2003). Some training programs include specific activities designed to improve students' explanation-giving and help-seeking skills (e.g., giving explanations rather than answers, asking clear and precise questions; Veenman et al., 2005).

Still other programs focus on teaching principles of argumentation as a way of developing students' reasoning skills. Students may receive instruction on the definition, purpose, and uses of arguments, as well as the parts of arguments, the position, the reasons supporting the position, the supporting facts, the objections that might be raised, and the responses to the objections (Reznitskaya, Anderson, & Kuo, 2007). Or they may be taught how to carry out argumentation processes such as providing reasons and evidence for and against positions, challenging others with counterarguments, and weighing reasons and evidence (Chinn, Anderson, & Waggoner, 2001).

Assigning Students to Groups. Also under the teacher's control is how to compose groups. Most often compared empirically are group compositions in terms of the gender and ability mix of groups (Webb & Palincsar, 1996), but results are not sufficiently clear-cut to produce recommendations for teachers about optimal groupings. Moreover, as some studies have demonstrated, whether a particular group composition is optimal for its members depends on the group processes that ensue, and similar groupings may produce different processes and, consequently, different outcomes for students. For example, in an investigation of why high-ability students performed better in homogeneous than in heterogeneous ability groups (as had been reported by Webb, Nemer, Chizhik, & Sugrue, 1998), Webb, Nemer, and Zuniga (2002) found that high-ability students in some heterogeneous groups performed very well whereas high-ability students in other heterogeneous groups did not. Outcomes for high-ability students corresponded to the quality of their groups' functioning, rather than to the composition of the group, such as the level of help that high-ability students received, the level of contributions they made, and whether their group engaged in negative socioemotional behavior. Such results suggest that manipulating group composition cannot by itself guarantee optimal participation; teachers may more productively focus on ways to maximize group functioning for all students such as preparing students for collaborative work (as described above), and structuring group interaction (as described below).

Constructing the Group-Work Task. To encourage the participation of all group members, Cohen (1994b) recommended that teachers give groups complex tasks or open-ended problems without clear-cut answers or that require procedures that cannot be completed very well by a single individual and that utilize the combined expertise of everyone in the group. Such tasks encourage groups to recognize the multiple skills and perspectives needed in order to complete the task, and to value the different contributions that each student makes. Tasks or problems that can be completed by one student with the requisite skills, on the other hand, are more likely to limit the participation of students without those skills.

In a series of studies that supported Cohen's views, Chizhik and colleagues (Chizhik, 2001; Chizhik, Alexander, Chizhik, & Goodman, 2003) compared group collaboration and learning on open-ended or ill-structured tasks (e.g., designing a swimming pool and estimating its volume) versus single-answer or well-structured tasks (e.g., calculating the volume of a swimming pool with given dimensions). These studies showed smaller differences in participation rates between high-status and low-status group members (whether artificially assigned status scores or social characteristics such as ethnic background) with ill-structured than with well-structured tasks.

Other research, however, raises questions about the correspondence between task type and patterns of participation within groups. Esmonde (2009) showed that groups might interpret the same task in different ways, with some groups approaching the task as if following a procedure in which one student was expert and could direct other group members, and other groups approaching the same task as a problem to solve in which all students collaborated. One task, for example, was a group quiz (e.g., a mathematics quiz asking groups to determine the number of cakes a dessert shop should bake to maximize profits, subject to certain constraints). Esmonde described the interaction in some groups as asymmetrical in which some students who positioned themselves as "experts" taught "novices" and the novices deferred to the experts. In other groups, the interaction was more symmetrical, with no students positioned as experts or novices, and all students asking for and providing help and jointly collaborating. Esmonde's results suggest that groups' beliefs about group members' relative expertise and groups' perceptions about whether the task can be completed by a small number of experts are important predictors of group participation patterns beyond how a teacher conceives the task initially.

Structuring Collaborative Work: Requiring Students to Carry Out Specific Activities or Adopt Specific Roles

Some collaborative learning approaches structure group interaction in specific ways to improve the quality and depth of discussion. Features of these methods include requiring groups to carry out certain strategies or activities, assigning students to play certain roles, or both. Research finds that these approaches have positive effects on the nature of group collaboration, on group task performance, and, often, on student achievement.

Explanation Prompts. Some peer-learning approaches give students specific prompts in order to encourage them to engage in high-level discourse about the task. Students are given written prompts to help them to construct explanations, to find patterns in experiment results, to justify answers and beliefs, to relate prior learning to the task at hand, and to use as well as distinguish between "scientific" and "everyday" definitions and explanations (Coleman, 1998; Palincsar, Anderson, & David, 1993). Coleman (1998, pp. 406–412) gave the following examples of explanation prompts: "Explain why you believe that your answer is correct or wrong. Can you compare how you used to think about this with how you think about it now? How does your explanation compare with the scientific definitions that we learned in class? Is this explanation a scientific definition or an everyday definition?"

In Mevarech and Kramarski's (1997) metacognitive questioning method, groups answer questions to enhance their mathematical reasoning. Comprehension questions ("What is the problem/task all about?") help students reflect on problems before solving them; strategic questions ("Why is this strategy/tactic/principle most appropriate for solving the problem/task?") prompt students to propose and explain problem-solving strategies; and connection questions ("How is this problem/task different from/similar to what you have already solved? Explain why") prompt students to find similarities and differences between current and past problems they have solved or tasks they have completed (Mevarech & Kramarski, 2003, p. 469).

Reciprocal Questioning. In reciprocal questioning, students are trained to ask each other high-level questions about the material to help them monitor their own and each other's comprehension as well as to encourage students to describe and elaborate on their thinking (Fantuzzo, Riggio, Connelly, & Dimeff, 1989). For example, students may be given "how" and "why" question stems to guide their discussions of text, such as, "Why is … important? How are … and … similar?" (King, 1992, p. 113). Or students may be given questions to help them coconstruct and explain strategies for solving problems, such as "What is the problem?"; "What do we know about the problem so far?"; "What information is given to us?"; and "What is our plan?" (King, 1999, p. 101). Similarly, Fuchs, Fuchs, Kazdan, and Allen's (1999) students were trained to ask each other questions that begin with who, what, when, where, why, or how.

Structured Controversy. In order to promote the benefits that can arise when students try to resolve conflicting ideas, Johnson and Johnson (1995) built controversy into the group's task by subdividing groups into teams and requiring the teams to master material on different sides of an issue (e.g., should there be more or fewer regulations governing hazardous waste disposal), to present their views to the other team, to switch roles and repeat the process, and then to synthesize the two positions. Compared with groups required to seek concurrence by working cooperatively and compromising, groups required to discuss opposing ideas often carried out more high-level discussion of the material and less description of the facts and information; they also showed higher achievement.

Cognitive Role Specialization. Students can be required to adopt specific roles so that they will carry out particular cognitive activities. Students may be assigned such roles as recaller (also called learning leader or summarizer) and listener (also called active listener, learning listener, or listener/facilitator; Hythecker, Dansereau, & Rocklin, 1988; Yager, Johnson, & Johnson, 1985), which can be incorporated into scripts for groups to follow (O'Donnell, 1999). The recaller summarizes the material and the listener is responsible for detecting errors, identifying omissions, and seeking clarification. Students then work together to elaborate on the material; they change roles for the next part of the task. In a variation of this scripted cooperation approach, Lambiotte et al. (1987) suggested that instead of the summarizer and listener studying the same material, students should study and teach each other different material. Lambiotte et al. hypothesized that listeners in this situation will be more likely to ask questions of clarification (because they have not already studied the material), and summarizers will be forced to organize the material more effectively and clearly, and to remember it better to present it to others (because they cannot assume that others have knowledge about the material). Finally, students in both roles will worry less about how others will evaluate their questions and summaries, and can focus better on the task.

Students can also be trained to engage in reciprocal peer tutoring, in which students playing the tutor role model strategies such as summarizing text as well as how to give explanations, corrections, and feedback about other students' work. To promote high-level discourse during paired discussions, teachers can train tutors to give highly elaborated conceptual rather than algorithmic explanations to their partners (e.g., using real-life examples, discussing why an answer does or does not make sense; Fuchs et al., 1997). Reflecting the importance of the activity of the help-receiver, some peer tutoring models guide the tutor in helping the *tutee* to give high-level explanations (King, 1999). The tutor asks questions designed to encourage the tutee to provide explanations of the material, asks further questions to push the tutee to elaborate upon or justify her or his explanations as well as to correct incomplete or incorrect explanations, and asks questions to push tutees to make connections among ideas and to link new material to their prior knowledge.

It should be noted that "teacher" and "learner" role specialization was a feature of some of the earliest cooperative learning methods. In the *Jigsaw* (Aronson, Blaney, Stephan, Sikes, & Snapp, 1978) classroom, students are assigned responsibility for mastering a portion of the material (and discussing that material with other students assigned the same topic) and then for teaching their topic to the other members of their groups. In *Group Investigation* (Sharan & Hertz-Lazarowitz, 1980), in which students carry out research on their piece of a group project and then come together as a team to integrate their findings and plan their class presentations, students are involved in teaching their own project pieces to the group and in learning from their peers about the remaining portions of the project.

Reciprocal Teaching. In reciprocal teaching, students carry out certain strategies designed to improve their comprehension of the text, including generating questions about the text they have read, clarifying what they don't understand, summarizing the text, and generating predictions (Brown & Palincsar, 1989; Palincsar & Brown, 1984; Palincsar & Herrenkohl, 1999). The teacher has an explicit role during group work to help students become proficient in these strategies. Teachers initially take the leadership in small groups, explaining the strategies and modeling their use in making sense of the text. Then teachers ask students to demonstrate the strategies, but give them considerable support. For example, in order to help a student generate questions to ask her group mates, the teacher might probe what information the student gleaned from the text and help the student phrase a specific question using that information. The teacher gradually assumes the less active role of coach, giving students feedback and encouraging them. Students then carry out the text-comprehension strategies in their small groups.

Group Processing. Some social psychologists maintain that groups will function most effectively if they discuss their group's interaction and how they might improve it, sometimes called "group processing." Such discussions may help groups identify, understand, and solve general communication problems (e.g., lack of student participation, disruptive or bullying behavior) and may reinforce student collaboration (Johnson, Johnson, & Holubec, 1988). Gillies (2007) suggested sample checklists and activities that teachers and students can use in order to evaluate group processes. Ross (1995) added another group processing component. In addition to having groups complete and discuss a self-appraisal instrument, Ross provided groups with feedback about their group functioning in the form of five-page excerpts of the transcripts of their conversations, and transcript scores that rated their levels of requesting help, of giving help, and of being on task. Ross observed that groups gave more help (in terms of procedures, explanations, acknowledgments, and evaluations of each other's work) after they received this feedback than before.

Activities of the Teacher during Collaborative Work

Altering Expectations and Status Relationships. Students don't always participate actively in groups. While personality characteristics may explain why some students participate more actively than others (extroverted, outgoing, and energetic members may talk the most), researchers have also found that status characteristics can produce inequities in participation by determining relative activity and influence in the group (Cohen & Lotan, 1995; Mulryan, 1992, 1995). High-status students, especially those with high academic standing or peer status characteristics (perceived attractiveness or popularity), tend to be more active and influential than low-status individuals; while low-status individuals tend to be less assertive and more anxious, to talk less, and to give fewer suggestions and less information than high-status individuals (e.g., Bianchini, 1997, 1999; Esmonde, 2009). Individuals' characteristics, such as gender or race, may also operate as status characteristics in heterogeneous small groups, with boys and White students often being more active than girls and Black students (for some specific examples of the dominance of boys over girls and high-achievers over low-achievers, see Baxter, Woodward, & Olson, 2001; King, 1993; Mulryan, 1992, 1995). Even artificially created status differences (such as classifying students' competence on the basis of fictitious test scores) can alter group members' participation and influence. Dembo and McAuliffe (1987) found that, regardless of actual competence and ability to give help, students designated as "high status" dominated group interaction, were more influential, and were perceived to be more capable than "low-status" students.

To prevent low-status students from being marginalized in group interaction, Cohen and colleagues (e.g., 1995) developed two status interventions based on broadening the notions of status and student competence. In the multiple ability treatment, the teacher raises students' awareness of the multiple skills necessary to accomplish a task. The teacher discusses with students the multiple abilities needed to solve complex problems (e.g., visual thinking, intuitive thinking, and reasoning) and stresses the fact that no single student possesses all of the needed abilities but that all students have some of them. In the second treatment, teachers assign competence to low-status students by observing groups at work to spot instances of low-status students exhibiting intellectual abilities relevant to the task, publicly identifying the contributions, and commenting on the importance and value of them. Cohen and Lotan noted that, as high-status persons, teachers' evaluations have a strong influence on students' beliefs about their own and others' competence. To carry out these interventions, a teacher must have a deep and comprehensive understanding of the multiple competencies relevant to the task and must be a very astute observer to look for abilities that may not be noticed by students in the group. For example, Cohen and Lotan described how teachers might observe the work of quiet students to pick out accurate, informative, or creative work that they are doing, bring it to the group's attention, and encourage the group to listen to the quiet students describe and explain their work.

These approaches have shown success in reducing the relationship between status (based on, for example, language background, ethnicity, race, socioeconomic status, or academic ability) and behavior in small groups (Cohen & Lotan, 1997). The more frequently teachers talk about the multiple abilities needed for a task (and the fact that no one has all of the abilities), as well as comment on the value of low-status students' contributions, the more low-status students participate, and the smaller the gap between high-status and low-status students' participation rates.

Other Teacher Interventions with Small Groups. Many prominent cooperative learning researchers and theorists advise teachers to monitor small-group progress and to intervene when groups seem to be functioning ineffectively (e.g., Johnson & Johnson, 2008). Conditions calling for teacher intervention may include: when no group member can answer the question, when students exhibit problems communicating with each other, when students dominate group work without allowing true dialogue, and when students fail to provide reasons for their opinions and ideas (Ding, Li, Piccolo, & Kulm, 2007; Tolmie et al., 2005).

Cohen (1994a) proposed several guidelines for how teachers should intervene, including asking open-ended questions to redirect groups' discussions and telling students they all need to be able to explain what the task is about. Cohen cautioned teachers to carefully listen to group discussions so that they can form hypotheses about the groups' difficulties before deciding on what questions to ask or suggestions to make. She argued that students are more likely to initiate ideas and to take responsibility for their discussions if teachers provide little direct supervision (such as guiding students through tasks, or answering individual student's questions before the group has attempted to work collectively to solve a problem). Any help that teachers do provide should be based on careful observations of group progress and not meant to supplant group efforts. It is important that guidance provided, such as pointing out key aspects of the task, checking for students' understanding of what the problem is asking, and filling in missing parts of students' knowledge, does not constitute the teacher doing the task for the group or directing them in how to carry out the task, but rather is intended to help groups to negotiate the task (Cohen, 1994a).

Research on the impact of teacher interventions on collaborative activity and student learning largely supports her recommendations. The first theme supported by research concerns the benefits of teachers listening to students' interaction and then providing indirect guidance to help them elaborate their thinking. One set of studies showed that pushing students to explain their thinking and probing their ideas while minimizing direct instruction about how to complete the task or solve the problem promoted student explanation and achievement. Hogan, Nastasi, and Pressley (2000) found that asking a variety of questions meant to elicit the details of students' thinking about how to create a mental model of the nature of matter (e.g., asking students to describe their initial thinking, to elaborate on specific points they made in their initial explanation, and to clarify the language they used) was beneficial for the complexity of scientific reasoning that groups attained (e.g., how well students' ideas were supported and explained; the logical coherence of their thinking), especially when groups were not prone to engage in high-level reasoning when the teacher was not present. When teachers did make statements, they were repetitions or restatements of *students'* ideas, and were intended to clarify students' suggestions or to emphasize certain aspects of students' proposals rather than to tell students how to carry out the task. Similarly, Webb, Franke, De, et al. (2009) found positive effects from intense probing of students' ideas. The teacher intervention that nearly always produced more student explaining, and often resulted in groups giving correct and complete explanations about how to solve the problem, was teachers probing student thinking so that students gave further details about their problem-solving strategies beyond their initial explanations. Moreover, probing students' explanations was most likely to result in additional student explaining (especially correct and complete explanations) when teachers used the details of students' strategies given in initial explanations to drive their probing questions, when teachers persisted in asking questions in order to push students to clarify the ambiguous aspects of their explanations, and when teachers did not interject their own thinking (or their own assumptions about what students were thinking) into their probing questions.

Gillies (2004) reported similar results in a study in which some teachers were trained to engage in the kinds of probing interventions described above. These teachers were instructed to ask students probing and clarifying questions ("Can you tell me a little more about what you're intending to do here?"), acknowledge and validate students' ideas ("I can see you've worked really hard to find out how these items are related. I wonder what you could do now to identify a key category they can all fit into?"), identify discrepancies in students' work and clarify the options they may take ("I wonder how you can include … when you've already mentioned …?"), and offer suggestions in a tentative fashion ("I wonder if you've considered doing it this way?"; Gillies, 2004, p. 260). Compared to teachers who did not receive training in these specific communication skills but were instructed only to set and discuss ground rules for cooperative group discussions (e.g., sharing information, giving reasons, challenging others, considering alternatives before making decisions), the specially trained teachers asked more questions, especially to ascertain students' ideas and strategies, and carried out more mediated-learning behaviors (e.g., challenging students to provide reasons, highlighting inconsistencies in student thinking, prompting students to focus on particular issues, asking tentative questions to suggest alternative perspectives; see Gillies, 2006). Their students provided more detailed explanations, more often expanded on other students' suggestions, asked each other more questions, and exhibited greater learning than did the students of the teachers who did not receive the specific training.

The second theme supported by recent research is the detrimental effect of providing direct instruction to collaborative groups, especially when teachers provide suggestions before evaluating students' progress on the problem or task. In Chiu's (2004) study, the explicitness of teachers' help (on a 4-point scale that included no help, focusing student attention on certain concepts or aspects of the problem, explaining a concept or a part of the problem, and giving the solution procedure) was negatively related to students being on task immediately after the teacher's intervention and to groups' performance on that problem. As Chiu explained, one explanation for this result was that teachers who gave explicit help and issued many directives tended not to evaluate the group's ideas before intervening. As an example, a teacher did not inquire about the group's work and so missed the group's misinterpretation of a problem, told the group the steps to carry out to solve the problem (but did not stay with the group to ensure that the students could solve the problem correctly), and the group failed to make further progress after the teacher left. As this episode shows, when teachers do not have, and do not seek, information about the group's ideas, their options for how to provide help are limited. Another unintended consequence of providing explicit content-related help may be decreased student engagement. In Dekker and Elshout-Mohr's (2004) study, the teacher providing detailed instruction often communicated with just one student (typically the student who asked the teacher for help) and other students tended to drop out of further conversations.

There is some evidence that providing direct instruction might be effective *if* teachers tie their help to student thinking. Meloth and Deering (1999) described several instances of explicit teacher guidance that did not reduce productive discussion, including giving brief, direct explanations of key concepts, briefly explaining what students were supposed to learn, and providing examples of how groups could locate or apply information. After these teacher interventions, students provided further elaboration of their thinking and made new suggestions. In these cases, teachers had asked questions to determine the groups' need for information or guidance, including soliciting details of students' ideas, and so the teacher guidance was closely tied to the group discussions. This same study suggested that teacher direct instruction that is not closely tied to student thinking may not have a deleterious effect under one condition; namely, when groups are proceeding well and are confident in their approach to the task or problem. When teachers interrupted such group collaborations to make suggestions without having heard the groups' discussions, these groups simply disregarded the teachers' suggestions and returned to their conversations.

Teachers' Discourse with the Whole Class

The nature of teacher discourse with students in the context of whole-class instruction and the norms teachers negotiate with the class about expected interpersonal exchanges may also influence group collaboration, especially the extent to which students explain their thinking and try to learn from others.

It is well known that teacher discourse, especially their questioning practices, plays an important role in limiting or enhancing students' opportunities for participation during whole-class discussion (Cazden, 2001). Recitation-style discourse (Nystrand & Gamoran, 1991) in which teachers ask students questions and evaluate their responses in a rapid-fire sequence of questions and answers with little or no wait time (Black, Harrison, Lee, Marshall, & Wiliam, 2002; Turner et al., 2002) places limits on student discourse, especially when teacher queries consist of short-answer, low-level questions that require students to recall facts, rules, and procedures (Ai, 2002; Galton et al., 1999; Graesser & Person, 1994). In contrast, high-level teacher questions that require students to draw inferences and synthesize ideas (Hiebert & Wearne, 1993; Wood, 1998), encourage students to provide justifications for their work (Boaler, 1997), and create opportunities for argumentation that promote student explaining, listening, and evaluation of each other's ideas and arguments (Forman, Larreamendy-Joerns, Stein, & Brown, 1998).

Emerging research suggests that these patterns of teacher discourse in the whole class, especially the extent to which teachers press students to explain their thinking, are also important for the depth of students' discussion in collaborative groups. That is, the patterns of behavior that students exhibit during whole-class discussions carry over to their small-group collaborations. In mathematics classrooms in which teachers press students to explain beyond their initial descriptions or explanations of their problem-solving strategies, students are likely to use mathematical arguments to explain why and how their solutions work, to justify their choice of problem-solving strategy, as well as to arrive at a mutual understanding about solutions (Kazemi & Stipek, 2001; Webb, Frank, Ing, et al., 2008). Such pushing of students to explain their thinking may include asking students to justify every step in their procedure, asking specific questions about why students chose particular approaches or how they obtained their intermediate results, asking for clarification of steps in procedures even when solutions are correct, and to demonstrate procedures in different ways or using different representations (e.g., verbal descriptions, diagrams, fractions). In literature classrooms in which teachers push students to help interpret the story and ask them questions in order to encourage them to elaborate on their ideas and to generalize from the text, students in small groups engage in deep reasoning. They generalize from the text instead of describing facts or giving literal interpretations, elaborate on their ideas, and frequently ask each other to explain their reasoning (Smagorinsky & Fly, 1993).

When teachers assume responsibility for doing most of the work during whole-class instruction, students may show little initiative to explain their thinking during collaborative group work. In mathematics classrooms, when teachers set up the steps in the mathematics problems and ask students only to provide the results of specific calculations that the teachers themselves pose, students in their group work may correspondingly provide low-level information such as answers, calculations, and procedural descriptions instead of explanations, and not inquire about their peers' thinking (Webb, Nemer, & Ing, 2006). In literature classrooms, when teachers assume responsibility for interpreting the text and do not often ask students to contribute, small-group discussions may largely consist of students giving brief interpretations of the text without elaborating on their suggestions (Smagorinsky & Fly, 1993).

Teacher discourse during whole-class instruction (especially whether they ask students to explain their thinking) sends signals about the desirability of explaining and challenging others to explain and justify their thinking versus passively accepting others' transmitted knowledge. Teachers can also carry out specific activities with the whole class to mutually construct classroom norms for student engagement. Yackel and colleagues (Yackel, Cobb, & Wood, 1991; Yackel, Cobb, Wood, Wheatley, & Merkel, 1990) described strategies that teachers may use to develop norms around student explanations. Teachers can invent scenarios or use specific situations that arise spontaneously during group work (e.g., one student completing the activities without his partners' being able to understand his solutions or being able to construct their own solutions) as springboards for whole-class discussions about students' responsibilities during group work, such as their obligations to create and explain their own meaningful problem-solving approaches, and to probe and challenge other students' thinking and solutions. Negotiating norms for active student participation can also head off debilitating processes such as social loafing or diffusion (Salomon & Globerson, 1989). Emphasizing students' responsibilities to explain, defend, and evaluate their own and others' thinking (Turner et al., 2002) may also encourage them to ask for help from their peers when they need it, and to engage in more effective help-seeking.

CONCLUSION

Research on collaborative dialogue and student learning has revealed important links between group processes and students' learning outcomes. In many cases, these results have been used in the design of specific collaborative learning approaches, with encouraging results for student learning. Much remains to be learned, however, about how collaborating with peers produces changes in student thinking and understanding. Carrying out detailed analyses of the interaction among students, especially at a sufficiently fine-grained level to detect changes in student thinking, promises to increase our understanding of how students learn in collaborative settings as well as the conditions that either promote or inhibit student learning in collaborative groups.

REFERENCES

Ai, X. (2002). *District mathematics plan evaluation: 2001–2002 Evaluation report* (Planning, Assessment, and Research Division Publication No. 142). Los Angeles, CA: Los Angeles Unified School District.

Aronson, E., Blaney, N., Stephan, C., Sikes, J., & Snapp, M. (1978). *The jigsaw classroom*. Beverly Hills, CA: Sage.

Baines, E., Blatchford, P., & Chowne, A. (2007). Improving the effectiveness of collaborative group work in primary schools: Effects on science attainment. *British Educational Research Journal, 33,* 663–680.

Baines, E., Blatchford, P., Kutnick, P., with Chowne, A., Ota, C., & Berdondini, L. (2008). *Promoting effective group work in the classroom*. London: Routledge.

Bargh, J. A., & Schul, Y. (1980). On the cognitive benefits of teaching. *Journal of Educational Psychology, 72,* 593–604.

Barron, B. (2000). Achieving coordination in collaborative problem-solving groups. *Journal of the Learning Sciences, 9*(4), 403–436.

Baxter, J. A., Woodward, J., & Olson, D. (2001). Effects of reform-based mathematics instruction on low achievers in five third-grade classrooms. *Elementary School Journal, 101,* 529–547.

Bearison, D. J., Magzamen, S., & Filardo E. K. (1986). Socio-conflict and cognitive growth in young children. *Merrill-Palmer Quarterly, 32,* 51–72.

Benware, C. A., & Deci, E. L. (1984). Quality of learning with an active versus passive motivational set. *American Educational Research Journal, 21,* 755–765.

Bianchini, J. A. (1997). Where knowledge construction, equity, and context intersect: Student learning of science in small groups. *Journal of Research in Science Teaching, 34,* 1039–1065.

Bianchini, J. A. (1999). From here to equity: The influence of status on student access to and understanding of science. *Science Education, 83,* 577–601.

Black, P. J., Harrison, C., Lee, C., Marshall, B., & Wiliam, D. (2002). *Working inside the black box: Assessment for learning in the classroom*. London: King's College London, School of Education.

Blatchford, P., Baines, E., Rubie-Davies, C., Bassett, P., & Chowne, A. (2006). The effect of a new approach to group work on pupil–pupil and teacher–pupil interactions. *Journal of Educational Psychology, 98*, 750–765.

Boaler, J. (1997) *Experiencing school mathematics*. Milton Keynes, England: Open University Press.

Brown, A. L., Campione, J. C., Webber, L. S., & McGilly, K. (1992). Interactive learning environments: A new look at assessment and instruction. In B. Gifford & M. C. O'Connor (Eds.), *Changing assessments: Alternative views of aptitude, achievement, and instruction* (pp. 121–211). Boston, MA: Kluwer Academic.

Brown, A. L., & Palinscar, A. S. (1989). Guided, cooperative learning, and individual knowledge acquisition. In L. B. Resnick (Ed.) *Knowing, learning, and instruction: Essays in honor of Robert Glaser* (pp. 393–451). Hillsdale, NJ: Erlbaum.

Cazden, C. B. (2001). *Classroom discourse* (2nd ed.). Portsmouth, NH: Heinemann.

Chi, M. T. H. (2000). Self-explaining expository texts: The dual processes of generating inferences and repairing mental models. In R. Glaser (Ed.), *Advances in instructional psychology: Educational design and cognitive science* (pp. 161–238). Hillsdale, NJ: Erlbaum.

Chi, M. T. H., & Bassock, M. (1989). Learning from examples via self-explanations. In L. B. Resnick (Ed.), *Knowing, learning, and instruction: Essays in honor of Robert Glaser* (pp. 251–282). Hillsdale, NJ: Erlbaum.

Chi, M. T. H., Bassock, M. Lewis, M. Reimann, P., & Glaser, R. (1989). Self-explanations: How students study and use examples in learning to solve problems. *Cognitive Science, 13*, 145–182.

Chinn, C. A., Anderson, R. C., & Waggoner, M. A. (2001). Patterns of discourse in two kinds of literature discussion. *Reading Research Quarterly, 36*, 378–411.

Chinn, C. A., O'Donnell, A. M., & Jinks, T. S. (2000). The structure of discourse in collaborative learning. *The Journal of Experimental Education, 69*, 77–97.

Chiu, M. M. (2004). Adapting teacher interventions to student needs during cooperative learning: How to improve student problem solving and time on-task. *American Educational Research Journal, 41*, 365–399.

Chiu, M. M., & Khoo, L. (2003). Rudeness and status effects during group problem solving: Do they bias evaluations and reduce the likelihood of correct solutions? *Journal of Educational Psychology, 95*, 506–523.

Chizhik, A. W. (2001). Equity and status in group collaboration: Learning through explanations depends on task characteristics. *Social Psychology of Education, 5*, 179–200.

Chizhik, A. W., Alexander, M. G., Chizhik, E. W., & Goodman, J. A. (2003). The rise and fall of power and prestige orders: Influence of task structure. *Social Psychology Quarterly, 66*, 303–317.

Cohen, E. G. (1994a). *Designing groupwork* (2nd ed.). New York: Teachers College Press.

Cohen, E. G. (1994b). Restructuring the classroom: Conditions for productive small groups. *Review of Educational Research, 64*, 1–35.

Cohen, E. G., & Lotan, R. A. (1995). Producing equal-status interaction in the heterogeneous classroom. *American Educational Research Journal, 32*, 99–120.

Cohen, E. G., & Lotan, R. A. (Eds.). (1997). *Working for equity in heterogeneous classrooms: Sociological theory in practice*. New York: Teachers College Press.

Coleman, E. B. (1998). Using explanatory knowledge during collaborative problem solving in science. *Journal of the Learning Sciences, 7*, 387–427.

Dekker, R., & Elshout-Mohr, M. (2004). Teacher interventions aimed at mathematical level raising during collaborative learning. *Educational Studies in Mathematics, 56*, 39–65.

De Lisi, R., & Golbeck, S. L. (1999). Implications of Piagetian theory for peer learning. In A. M. O'Donnell & A. King (Eds.), *Cognitive perspectives on peer learning* (pp. 3–38). Mahwah, NJ: Erlbaum.

Dembo, M. H., & McAuliffe, T. J. (1987). Effects of perceived ability and grade status on social interaction and influence in cooperative groups. *Journal of Educational Psychology, 79*, 415–423.

Ding, M., Li, X., Piccolo, D., & Kulm, G. (2007). Teacher interventions in cooperative-learning mathematics classes. *Journal of Educational Research, 100*, 162–175.

Ellis, S., & Rogoff, B. (1982). The strategies and efficacy of child vs. adult teachers. *Child Development, 53*, 730–735.

Esmonde, I. (2009). Mathematics learning in groups: Analyzing equity in two cooperative activity structures. *Journal of the Learning Sciences, 18*(2), 247–284.

Fantuzzo, J. W., Riggio, R. E., Connelly, S., & Dimeff, L. A. (1989). Effects of reciprocal peer tutoring on academic achievement and psychological adjustment: A component analysis. *Journal of Educational Psychology, 81*, 173–177.

Forman, E. A., & Cazden, C. B. (1985). Exploring Vygotskian perspectives in education: The cognitive value of peer interaction. In J. V. Wertsch (Ed.), *Culture, communication, and cognition: Vygotskian perspectives* (pp. 323–347). New York: Cambridge University Press.

Forman, E. A., Larreamendy-Joerns, J., Stein, M. K., & Brown, C. (1998). "You're going to want to find out which and prove it": Collective argumentation in mathematics classrooms. *Learning and Instruction, 8*(6), 527–548.

Fuchs, L. S., Fuchs, D., Hamlett, C. L., Phillips, N. B., Karns, K., & Dutka, S. (1997). Enhancing students' helping behavior during peer-mediated instruction with conceptual mathematical explanations. *Elementary School Journal, 97,* 223–249.

Fuchs, L. S., Fuchs, D., Kazdan, S., & Allen, S. (1999). Effects of peer-assisted learning strategies in reading with and without training in elaborated help giving. *Elementary School Journal, 99,* 201–219.

Galton, M., Hargreaves, L., Comber, C., Wall, D., & Pell, T. (1999). Changes in patterns of teacher interaction in primary classrooms: 1976–96. *British Educational Research Journal, 25,* 23–37.

Gillies, R. M. (2003). Structuring cooperative group work in classrooms. *International Journal of Educational Research, 39,* 35–49.

Gillies, R. M. (2004). The effects of communication training on teachers' and students' verbal behaviours during cooperative learning. *International Journal of Educational Research, 41,* 257–279.

Gillies, R. M. (2006). Ten Australian teachers' discourse and reported pedagogical practices during cooperative learning. *Elementary School Journal, 106,* 429–451.

Gillies, R. M. (2007). *Cooperative learning.* Los Angeles, CA: Sage.

Graesser, A. C., & Person, N. K. (1994). Question asking during tutoring. *American Educational Research Journal, 31,* 104–137.

Hatano, G. (1993). Time to merge Vygotskian and constructivist conceptions of knowledge acquisition. In E. A. Forman, N. Minick, & C. A. Stone (Eds.), *Contexts for learning: Sociocultural dynamics in children's development* (pp. 153–166). New York: Oxford University Press.

Hiebert, J., & Wearne, D. (1993). Instructional tasks, classroom discourse, and students' learning in second-grade arithmetic. *American Educational Research Journal, 30,* 393–425.

Hogan, K. Nastasi, B. K., & Pressley, M. (2000). Discourse patterns and collaborative scientific reasoning in peer and teacher-guided discussions. *Cognition and Instruction, 17,* 379–432.

Howe, C., Tolmie, A., Thurston, A., Topping, K., Christie, D., Livingston, K., … Donaldson, C. (2007). Group work in elementary science: Towards organisational principles for supporting pupil learning. *Learning and Instruction, 17,* 549–563.

Hythecker, V. I., Dansereau, D. F., & Rocklin, T. R. (1988). An analysis of the processes influencing the structured dyadic learning environment. *Educational Psychologist, 23,* 23–27.

Johnson, D. W., & Johnson, R. T. (1995). *Creative controversy: Intellectual challenge in the classroom.* Edina, MN: Interaction.

Johnson, D. W., & Johnson, R. T. (2008). Social interdependence theory and cooperative learning: The teacher's role. In R. M. Gillies, A. Ashman, & J. Terwel (Eds.), *The teacher's role in implementing cooperative learning in the classroom* (pp. 9–36). New York: Springer.

Johnson, D. W., Johnson, R. T., & Holubec, E. J. (1988). *Cooperation in the classroom* (Rev. ed.). Edina, MN: Interaction.

Johnson, D., Maruyama, G., Johnson, R., Nelson, D., & Skon, L. (1981). Effects of cooperative, competitive, and individualistic goal structures on achievement: A meta-analysis. *Psychological Bulletin, 89,* 47–62.

Kazemi, E., & Stipek, D. (2001). Promoting conceptual thinking in four upper-elementary mathematics classrooms. *Elementary School Journal, 102,* 59–80.

King, A. (1992). Facilitating elaborative learning through guided student-generated questioning. *Educational Psychologist, 27,* 111–126.

King, A. (1999). Discourse patterns for mediating peer learning. In A. M. O'Donnell & A. King (Eds.), *Cognitive perspectives on peer learning* (pp. 87–116). Mahwah, NJ: Erlbaum.

King, A., Staffieri, A., & Adelgais, A. (1998). Mutual peer tutoring: Effects of structuring tutorial interaction to scaffold peer learning. *Journal of Educational Psychology, 90,* 134–152.

King, L. H. (1993). High and low achievers' perceptions and cooperative learning in two small groups. *The Elementary School Journal, 93,* 399–416.

Lambiotte, J. G., Dansereau, D. F., O'Donnell, A. M., Young, M. D., Skaggs, L. P., Hall, R. H., & Rocklin, T. R. (1987). Manipulating cooperative scripts for teaching and learning. *Journal of Educational Psychology, 79,* 424–430.

Meloth, M. S., & Deering, P. D. (1999). The role of the teacher in promoting cognitive processing during collaborative learning. In A. M. O'Donnell & A. King (Eds.), *Cognitive perspectives on peer learning* (pp. 235–256). Hillsdale, NJ: Erlbaum.

Mercer, N., Dawes, L., Wegerif, R., & Sams, C. (2004). Reasoning as a scientist: Ways of helping children to use language to learn science. *British Educational Research Journal, 30,* 359–377.

Mevarech, Z. R., & Kramarski, B. (2003). The effects of metacognitive training versus worked-out examples on students' mathematical reasoning. *British Journal of Educational Psychology, 73,* 449–471.

Mevarech, Z. R., & Kramarski, B. (1997). IMPROVE: A multidimensional method for teaching mathematics in heterogeneous classrooms. *American Educational Research Journal, 34*, 365–394.

Mulryan, C. M. (1992). Student passivity during cooperative small groups in mathematics. *Journal of Educational Research, 85*, 261–273.

Mulryan, C. M. (1995). Fifth and sixth graders' involvement and participation in cooperative small groups in mathematics. *The Elementary School Journal, 95*, 297–310.

Nelson-Le Gall, S. (1992). Children's instrumental help-seeking: Its role in the social acquisition and construction of knowledge. In R. Hertz-Lazarowitz & N. Miller (Eds.), *Interaction in cooperative groups: The theoretical anatomy of group learning* (pp. 49–68). New York: Cambridge University Press.

Newman, R. S. (1998). Students' help seeking during problem solving: Influences of personal and contextual achievement goals. *Journal of Educational Psychology, 90*, 644–658.

Noddings, N. (1985). Small groups as a setting for research on mathematical problem solving. In E. A. Silver (Ed.), *Teaching and learning mathematical problem solving* (pp. 345–360). Hillsdale, NJ: Erlbaum.

Nystrand, M., & Gamoran, A. (1991). Student engagement: When recitation becomes conversation. In H. C. Waxman & H. J. Walberg (Eds.), *Effective teaching: Current research* (pp. 257–276). Berkeley, CA: McCutchan.

O'Donnell, A. M. (1999). Structuring dyadic interaction through scripted cooperation. In A. M. O'Donnell & A. King (Eds.), *Cognitive perspectives on peer learning* (pp. 179–196). Mahwah, NJ: Erlbaum.

Palincsar, A. S., Anderson, C., & David, Y. M. (1993). Pursuing scientific literacy in the middle grades through collaborative problem solving. *Elementary School Journal, 93*, 643–658.

Palincsar, A. S., & Brown, A. L. (1984). Reciprocal teaching of comprehension fostering and monitoring activities. *Cognition and Instruction, 1*, 117–175.

Palincsar, A. S., & Herrenkohl, L. R. (1999). Designing collaborative contexts: Lessons from three research programs. In A. M. O'Donnell & A. King (Eds.), *Cognitive perspectives on peer learning* (pp. 151–178). Mahwah, NJ: Erlbaum.

Piaget, J. (1932). *The language and thought of the child* (2nd. ed.). London: Routledge & Kegan Paul.

Reznitskaya, A., Anderson, R. C., & Kuo, L-J. (2007). Teaching and learning argumentation. *Elementary School Journal, 107*, 449–472.

Rojas-Drummond, S., & Mercer, N. (2003). Scaffolding the development of effective collaboration and learning. *International Journal of Educational Research, 39*, 99–111.

Roscoe, R. D., & Chi, M. T. H. (2007). Understanding tutor leaning: Knowledge-building and knowledge-telling in peer tutors' explanations and questions. *Review of Educational Research, 77*, 534–574.

Roscoe, R. D., & Chi, M. T. H. (2008). Tutor learning: The role of explaining and responding to questions. *Instructional Science, 36*, 321–350.

Ross, J. A. (1995). Effects of feedback on student behavior in cooperative learning groups in a Grade 7 math class. *Elementary School Journal, 96*, 125–143.

Ross, J. A., & Cousins, J. B. (1995). Impact of explanation seeking on student achievement and attitudes. *Journal of Educational Research, 89*, 109–117.

Ryan, A. M., Pintrich, P. R., & Midgley, C. (2001). Avoiding seeking help in the classroom: Who and why? *Educational Psychology Review, 13*, 93–114.

Salomon, G., & Globerson, T. (1989). When teams do not function the way they ought to. *International Journal of Educational Research, 13*, 89–99.

Schunk, D. H. (1989). Social cognitive theory and self-regulated learning. In B. J. Zimmerman & D. H. Schunk (Eds.), *Self-regulated learning and academic achievement: Theory, research, and practice* (pp. 83–110). New York: Springer-Verlag.

Sharan, S., & Hertz-Lazarowitz, R. (1980). A group-investigation method of cooperative learning in the classroom. In S. Sharan, P. Hare, C. D. Webb, & R. Hertz-Lazarowitz (Eds.), *Cooperation in education* (pp. 14–46). Provo, Utah: Brigham Young University Press.

Slavin, R. (1983a). When does cooperative learning increase student achievement? *Psychological Bulletin, 94*, 429–445.

Slavin. R. (1983b). *Cooperative learning*. New York: Longman.

Smagorinski, P., & Fly, P. K. (1993). The social environment of the classroom: A Vygotskian perspective on small group process. *Communication Education, 42*, 159–171.

Tolmie, A., Thomson, J. A., Foot, H. C., Whelan, K., Morrison, S., & McLaren, B. (2005). The effects of adult guidance and peer discussion on the development of children's representations: Evidence from the training of pedestrian skills. *British Journal of Educational Psychology, 96*, 181–204.

Turner, J. C., Midgley, C., Meyer, D. K., Gheen, M., Anderman, E., Kang, Y., & Patrick, H. (2002). The classroom environment and students' reports of avoidance strategies in mathematics: A multimethod study. *Journal of Educational Psychology, 94*, 88–106.

Vedder, P. (1985). *Cooperative learning: A study on processes and effects of cooperation between primary school children.* Westerhaven, Groningen, Netherlands: Rijkuniversiteit Groningen.

Veenman, S., Denessen, E., van den Akker, A., & van der Rijt, J. (2005). Effects of a cooperative learning program on the elaborations of students during help seeking and help giving. *American Educational Research Journal, 42,* 115–151.

Vygotsky, L. S. (1978). *Mind in society: The development of higher psychological processes* (M. Cole, V. John-Steiner, S. Scribner, & E. Souberman, Eds. & Trans.). Cambridge, MA: Harvard University Press.

Webb, N. M., Franke, M. L., De, T., Chan, A. G., Freund, D., Shein, P., & Melkonian, D. K. (2009). Teachers' instructional practices and small-group dialogue. *Cambridge Journal of Education, 39,* 49–70.

Webb, N. M., Franke, M. L., Ing, M., Chan, A., De, T., Freund, D., & Battey, D. (2008). The role of teacher instructional practices in student collaboration. *Contemporary Educational Psychology, 33,* 360–381.

Webb, N. M., Ing, M., Nemer, K. M., & Kersting, N. (2006). Help seeking in cooperative learning groups. In R. S. Newman & S. A. Karabenick (Eds.), *Help seeking in academic settings: Goals, groups and contexts* (pp. 45–88). Mahwah, NJ: Erlbaum.

Webb, N. M., & Mastergeorge, A. M. (2003). The development of students' learning in peer-directed small groups. *Cognition and Instruction, 21,* 361–428.

Webb, N. M., Nemer, K. M., Chizhik, A., & Sugrue, B. (1998). Equity issues in collaborative group assessment: Group composition and performance. *American Educational Research Journal, 35,* 607–651.

Webb, N. M., Nemer, K. M., & Ing, M. (2006). Small-group reflections: Parallels between teacher discourse and student behavior in peer-directed groups. *Journal of the Learning Sciences, 15*(1), 63–119.

Webb, N. M., Nemer, K. M., & Zuniga, S. (2002). Short circuits or superconductors? Effects of group composition on high-achieving students' science performance. *American Educational Research Journal, 39,* 943–989.

Webb, N. M., & Palincsar, A. S. (1996). Group processes in the classroom. In D. Berliner & R. Calfee (Eds.), *Handbook of educational psychology* (pp. 841–873). New York: Macmillan.

Webb, N. M., Troper, J. D., & Fall, R. (1995). Constructive activity and learning in collaborative small groups. *Journal of Educational Psychology, 87,* 406–423.

Wittrock, M. C. (1990). Generative processes of comprehension. *Educational Psychologist, 24,* 345–376.

Wood, T. (1998). Funneling or focusing? Alternative patterns of communication in mathematics class. In H. Steinbring, M. G. Bartolini-Bussi, & A. Sierpinska (Eds.), *Language and communication in the mathematics classroom* (pp. 167–178). Reston, VA: National Council of Teachers of Mathematics.

Yackel, E., Cobb, P., & Wood, T. (1991). Small-group interactions as a source of learning opportunities in second-grade mathematics. *Journal for Research in Mathematics Education, 22,* 390–408.

Yackel, E., Cobb, P., Wood, T., Wheatley, G., & Merkel, G. (1990). The importance of social interaction in children's construction of mathematical knowledge. In T. J. Cooney & C. R. Hirsch (Eds.), *Teaching and learning mathematics in the 1990s* (pp. 12–21). Reston, VA: National Council of Teachers of Mathematics.

Yager, S., Johnson, D. W., & Johnson, R. T. (1985). Oral discussion, group-to-individual transfer, and achievement in cooperative learning groups. *Journal of Educational Psychology, 77,* 60–66.

2

DEVELOPMENTAL APPROACHES TO COLLABORATIVE LEARNING

SUSAN L. GOLBECK AND HEBBAH EL-MOSLIMANY

Rutgers University

We have been charged with presenting a developmental perspective on collaborative learning. A developmental scientist assumes that to understand human thought and behavior, it's necessary to understand its origins and history within the life-course of the individual. This view directs us to look for the roots of collaboration in infancy and to expect that it will be radically transformed over the course of childhood, and beyond. Developmental outcomes are influenced by diverse interacting factors from the immediate context, such as the family and caregivers, as well as the larger cultural setting. A developmental perspective also suggests that characteristics of the child must be considered. Children change as a result of the reactions they provoke from other people in the environment (see Sameroff, 2009).

In the *Psychology of Intelligence*, Piaget said, "The human being is immersed right from birth in a social environment which affects him just as much as his physical environment" (Piaget, 1950/1973, p. 156). While Piaget wrote relatively little about social learning, other developmentalists have elaborated (see Bruner, 1985; Gauvain, 2001; Rogoff, 2003; Tomasello, 2009). Collaborative learning begins within a system of social and cultural learning. When two individuals share a focus on some aspect of the external world they establish intersubjectivity (Trevarthen, 1988). Through processes of mutual attention and communication a shared understanding is achieved. For example, such a "shared understanding" is evident in infancy, when mother and child play peek-a-boo (see Bruner & Sherwood, 1976) and the infant initiates an action to regain the mother's attention. Forms of shared activity will change dramatically over the life-course (Vygotsky, 1978) but they will always be characterized by a shared focus and understanding.

Tomasello and colleagues (Tomasello, 2009; Tomasello, Kruger, & Ratner, 1993) argue that imitation is the earliest, most primitive form of learning with another individual. Infants can learn through imitation. Babies spontaneously imitate the actions of others (Meltzoff & Moore, 1989). Imitation does not seem to require any reflective awareness since it can occur without the actor's or the model's awareness. A second form of social learning is instruction. Learning by instruction is more complex and mutual than learning by imitation. Learning by instruction involves a learner and another individual who assumes the role of teacher. It begins informally, before schooling, usually with a parent. Roles are specified and activity is intentional but the roles are not balanced (Tomasello, 2009; Ziv & Frye, 2004). A third form of social learning is collaboration, which involves cooperation. It involves joint activity that is balanced. Ideally, all participants have an opportunity to be the leader and also the follower (see Tomasello, Kruger, & Ratner, 1993). The origins of collaboration are found early in development but mature forms are not seen until years later. What accounts for the transformations in patterns of social learning and when does true cooperation and "mature" collaborative learning begin? We will explore these issues in the remainder of the chapter.

WORLDVIEWS AND EPISTEMOLOGIES

Any inquiry into the development of learning begins with assumptions about what it means to learn, how knowledge is acquired, and how individuals coordinate this understanding. Much of the research (see O'Donnell & King, 1999) can be aligned with one of three broad traditions or paradigms described below. Each has its own epistemology, intellectual history, and empirical traditions (see Brown & Smith, 2002; Case 1996; Miller, 2011). These epistemological frameworks provide an initial orientation to such questions as: (a) What is the source of new knowledge? (b) What is the difference between learning and development? (c) What motivates the learner? (d) What changes and how does this change occur (learning or development) in both the short term (microgenetic) and the long term (ontogenetically)? (e) What contexts (social and other) are of special interest in research? (f) What are the most important learning and developmental outcomes?

The Empiricists

The first tradition has been characterized as an "empiricist" or a "traditional learning theory" perspective. The epistemological roots of this framework are found in British empiricism, as articulated by Locke (1696/1989) and Hume (1748/1955). This epistemology posits that knowledge of the world is acquired by a process in which the sensory organs first detect stimuli in the external world, and the mind then detects the customary patterns or conjunctions in stimuli that are contiguous in space and time. Researchers of young children's learning working from this perspective define their tasks to be: to describe the processes by which new stimuli are discriminated and encoded (also called perceptual learning); to describe the way in which patterns among stimuli are detected (also called cognitive learning); and finally to describe the processes by which new knowledge is accessed, tested, and used in other contexts (also called transfer) (Case, 1996). Learning and development are seen as synonymous and are often characterized in a linear fashion; a slow, gradual accrual. This approach to learning has also been characterized as "mechanistic" and "reductionist" (Overton, 2002). When it is applied to learning in real world contexts, the focus is often upon the ways in which different learning environments offer opportunities for different levels of stimulation and direct instruction. Also of concern are the organization and sequencing of experiences within the environment, opportunities for appropriate reinforcement, and rewards for specific responses. Research conducted from this perspective typically makes use of experimental designs in an effort to control the context and eliminate sources of variance that would confound conclusions regarding the variables under study. It is assumed that cognitive processes can be directly observed, or inferred from behavior.

From this perspective, learning with other people through collaboration presents a special learning context or environment, with a distinctive set of environmental inputs or stimuli. The environment also offers a rich source of naturally occurring rewards, which support and enhance learning. Peers are motivating to children and they can maximize children's attention to a problem. Social contexts can naturally support learning strategies that have been established to be effective in the laboratory on individual basis. Peers can enhance the interest children will show in a problem and provide abundant reinforcement across a variety of different behavioral measures.

The Rationalists (or Constructivists)

A second tradition can be characterized as a "rationalist" and constructivist perspective. This tradition is quite different from the first. It follows from the work of Kant and his transcendental philosophy. Kant (1796/1961) suggested that knowledge is acquired by a process in which an organization is imposed by the human mind on experience and the sensory data the mind detects. This is quite different from the sensory detection described by the empiricists. Kant posited mental concepts that organize experience. Such knowledge included space, time, causality, and number and he argued that these preexisting concepts were essential for making sense of sensory experiences. Furthermore, these concepts such as original number concepts, space, and time are not "extracted" from sensory experience. The human mind comes equipped with such understanding. These preexisting concepts were "a priori" knowledge in Kant's view (see Case, Griffin, & Kelly, 2001).

Early researchers working from within this view approached children's learning by focusing upon the underlying organization of children's learning which were referred to as structures or schemes. They argued that children were equipped at birth with some of these (e.g., a reflex scheme and propensity to adapt that scheme). The researcher's task then was to document and to explain changes in these schemes or structures over time.

Piaget was the best known scientist following in this tradition (Piaget, 1936/1952). He used the model of evolutionary biology in his work and he developed an elaborate theory to account for the full range of competencies that children develop in each of Kant's categories. These funtions as the general organizing frameworks or structures that underpin the stages of thought (Case et al., 2001). Higher level structures were seen as constructed by the differentiation and coordination of two or more lower level structures via a process in which children's independent mental activity (not association and not direct instruction) played the major role. Independent mental activities that were particularly critical were those involved in independent exploration, play, problem solving, and reflection (Piaget, 1950/1973). From this perspective, all individuals sharing similar experiences in similar environments construct similar conceptual sequences of thought as their knowledge is evidenced in a stagelike sequence. What varies is the "rate" at which concepts develop. Rich experience in a particular area might lead to progress at a slightly faster pace.

In the later phases of his work, Piaget intensified his focus on the processes by which learning and development occur and downplayed the aspects of his theory concerning stages and stage progressions. However, the assumptions regarding the biological model of change and adaptation to the environment remained constant. Child initiated activities such as play, exploration, problem solving, and reflection as opposed to direct instruction and reinforcement of desired responses are central for children's learning. Knowledge develops in part as a result of biologically based schemes which become transformed through interaction with the physical and social environment.

With regard to collaboration, the constructivist framework emphasizes the role of the individual child's understanding and how that understanding evolves as a result of social interactions. Piaget studied children's understanding of social rules and morality. He relied upon direct observations of children's game playing complemented with interviews of the children. For example, after observing children's actual group play in the school yard, he probed their ideas about the game's rules. He proposed variations in the rules and asked whether or not those changes would be acceptable and why (Piaget, 1932/1965). Importantly, he always asked children to explain their reasoning on a topic. Such "clinical" interviews, along with observations of children working on various problems were at the heart of Piaget's methodology (for an in-depth discussion of Piaget's theory and peer learning see DeLisi & Golbeck, 1999.)

Piaget argued that social experience plays an important role in cognitive growth and change (Piaget, 1985). He focused on the role of social interaction for "decentering" of the thinking (Piaget, 1950/1973). Social interaction, he argued, can lead the child to reexamine personally held ideas and opinions. While Piaget himself did not conduct much of this work, his students have applied his framework to reach an understanding of the social world. In particular, it has been argued that interactions between peers are an especially potent source of disequilibration and ultimately cognitive change (Ames & Murray, 1982). Discussion, debate, and dialogue with another is one way cognitive change can occur. This will be discussed later in the chapter.

Sociohistoric (Social Constructivist) Approach

The third tradition is the sociohistoric interpretation of Hegel's epistemology. This was further elaborated by modern continental philosophers (see Case et al., 2001; Kaufmann, 1980). From this perspective knowledge does not originate in the knower or the object, nor between the interaction of the structures of the subject and the structure of the objective world. Rather, the primary origin of knowledge is in the social and material history of the culture of which the knower is a part and the tools, concepts, and symbol systems that the culture has developed for interacting with the environment. Radically different from the other approaches, this perspective begins with an analysis of the social and cultural contexts in which human societies find themselves. This includes the technology and practices any particular society has devised for dealing with problems and the conceptual frameworks, forms of discourse and the symbols system that support all of these. Then, one must study how these are transmitted or passed down from one generation to the next. "The essential motor of cognitive development is the initiation into a community in which knowledge is accessed, created, and shared via particular forms of technology and discourse" (Case et al., 2001, p. 20).

The work of Vygotsky is the best known in psychology and education within this tradition. Vygotsky's theory posits that thinking must be studied within the context of both its biological and cultural evolution. Studies of thinking most likely should include ethnographic methods and other methods from anthropology as well as those used by evolutionary biologists. Vygotsky argued that the most important features of human beings as a species are that they have developed language, they fashion their own tools, and they transmit their discoveries from one generation to the next by way of cultural institutions such as schools (Vygotsky, 1978). It follows that a critical aspect of children's development is their acquisition of language (at about 2 years of age). Language enables the child to master the conceptual frameworks, forms of discourse, and higher mental systems that are embodied in and transmitted by the cultural institutions, such as schools. The acquisition and use of language is more important than general exposure to stimulation, independent exploration, play, and reflection.

A full analysis of development entails an analysis of the larger context in which the child and his family are situated. Culture and work are essential features of this context. As noted earlier, cognitive development is viewed as the initiation of the child into the community and the culture. Contemporary researchers have identified specific processes that are important for this initiation. With adult guidance, children appropriate the knowledge of the community and move gradually to roles of increasing independence and responsibility (Rogoff, 2003, p. 282). Collaboration is always a part of learning. Knowledge begins in a sort of collaboration, or at least as the result of some collaboration in culture. Over the course of childhood and adulthood the learner moves from the periphery to the center; from the role of apprentice to the role of expert or master. Knowledge begins in the external dyadic interaction and only gradually becomes internalized as thought.

In Sum

Although any study of collaborative learning must begin with assumptions about the learner, the context, the meaning of learning and development, and the optimal methods for scientific inquiry, contemporary research reflects a blending of these three worldviews. Research over the last two decades has shown that no single theory, nor even a single paradigm, is adequate for understanding the development and emergence of collaborative learning skills and competencies. Increasingly, researchers are searching for new ways to integrate ideas across the perspectives described here (see Gauvain, 2001 for an excellent overview). In the next section we examine the development of children's collaborative learning with other people (adults, especially parents and peers) through a discussion of collaborative problem solving.

PROBLEM SOLVING AND DEVELOPMENT

We have approached collaborative learning through a discussion of problem solving in a social context. Problem solving, according to Gauvain (2001, p. 139) is the identification of an action goal and the delineation of steps or means to reach the goal.

We explore two types of problem solving in a social context: (a) adult (often parent) and child problem solving and (b) peer problem solving. Our intention is to demonstrate that both are critical components of a developmental perspective on collaborative learning. They can be tied together ontogenetically since parent–child interactions always precede peer interactions. In addition, the cognitive skills that support and contribute to the ability to engage in successful collaborations with peers begin in infancy and early childhood. These include language, play, an awareness of other minds, or a "theory of mind," and an understanding of the teaching role. Most of these cognitive activities are first seen in supportive interactions between parent (or other caring adult) and child. The adult supports and guides the interaction, sometimes consciously and other times without conscious awareness. Adults "collaborate" with children to help them develop the skills they will need to work with others later on. After helping children build the foundations, adults "step aside" and allow children to use these skills on their own with peers.

Adult–Child Problem Solving

Sociocultural psychologists contend that shared intentional action, or joint problem solving, is at the core of the socialization process (Bruner, 1985). Such a socialization process is the central theme of the sociohistoric approach to human development. A variety of behaviors are used by adults to enlist children's participation in joint problem solving. These include modeling, instructing, scaffolding, and guided participation. (Children use these same behaviors when they attempt to involve peers in activities.) Through shared activities with adults, or more capable others, children learn about and practice the problem solving skills noted above.

Adults often interact with children in specific ways that support their learning and enhance their likelihood of success with a problem (Rogoff, 2003). Components of a variety of emerging problem solving skills including encoding, strategy acquisition and choice, and content knowledge all seem to benefit from this kind of social interaction. This structure has been described using the metaphor of a scaffold (Stone, 1998; Wood, Bruner, & Ross, 1976). Importantly, the scaffold is constantly shifting to match the situation; it is reduced and eventually disappears as the child masters the task or problem at hand. Examples of this process in parent–child interactions can be seen from infancy through adolescence (see Rogoff, 1990; Gauvain, 2001 for excellent overviews).

In a classic study of preschoolers and their mothers, Wood, Bruner, and Ross (1976) asked mothers and their 3- to 5-year-old children to work together to complete a complex three-dimensional block puzzle. In general, mothers adjusted their assistance to the child permitting the child to work as independently as possible while also helping her or him experience success and a sense of accomplishment. While not conscious of doing so, the mothers had created a "scaffold" for their children. This scaffolding maximized the likelihood of success but also permitted the children to actively assume responsibility.

Another example of mother and child jointly working on a problem is provided by Freund (1990). She experimentally manipulated parent participation in the task to directly test the effect of mother's participation in the activity. Children aged 3 and 5 years helped a puppet move his furniture into his new house—basically a sorting task in which dollhouse furniture was sorted into a living room, kitchen, and so on. Children were pretested to assess their independent level of success on the task. Then, half the children interacted with their mothers on easy and difficult versions of the task. The latter had more rooms and more objects. The experimenter instructed the mothers to help their children but not explicitly teach them. The other half of the children spent this time working on the tasks by themselves rather than with their mothers. In a posttest the children performed the task on their own. The children who worked on the problem with their mothers performed at a more advanced level on the posttest than children who worked on their own, even though all the children had been given the correct solution by the experimenter.

As Miller (2011) notes in her discussion of Freund's study, the mothers adjusted their behavior in a variety of ways to match the child's cognitive level. They gave more specific content (such as, "the stove goes in a kitchen") to the 3-year-olds rather than the 5-year-olds. They provided more general help, such as planning and keeping the goal in mind (e.g., "Let's make the kitchen and then the bedroom?") to the 5-year-olds. They seemed to adapt their behavior to their children's needs, talking more to the 3-year-olds than the 5-year-olds. Mothers also talked more when the task was difficult; they generally acted in the way advocated by Vygotsky to move their children through a "zone of proximal development." Dyads showed intersubjectivity and use of shared past experience in statements such as, "Where is the refrigerator in our house?" And, children also contributed to the exchange by actively attempting to solve the problems and adjusting their behavior in response to feedback from their mothers.

The research literature offers many examples of such problem solving assistance from adults, especially mothers, to children. Guberman and Gearhart (1999) showed mothers' support for early counting skill. In a different content domain, Rigney and Callanan (2011) identified patterns in parent–child conversations about animals at a marine science center, illustrating the relationship between parents' talk and children's tendency to draw distinctions between typical and atypical animals.

Teachers also provide scaffolds in their interactions with children. In several studies with 3- and 4-year-olds, Golbeck and colleagues (Golbeck, 1995; Golbeck, Rand, & Soundy, 1988) demonstrated that various sorts of scaffolding supported young children's success in creating a scale model arrangement of their classroom. Highlighting correspondences between symbolic artifacts and their referents, exploring through play, discussions about everyday use, and gesture all facilitated children's success. Many other examples can be found in recent studies of instructional practices in early childhood and elementary classrooms (O'Donnell & King, 1999).

Much of the adult–child talk in the studies just described includes explanations generated by both children and adults. Explanations seem to be an important component in any collaborative learning situation. Explanations facilitate communication among collaborators and the problem solving process. Persuading another of one's point of view entails the presentation of an argument and offering an explanation. Typically children ask questions which generate explanations from adults but adults also provide opportunities for children to engage in such talk. Rittle-Johnson and colleagues (Rittle-Johnson, 2006; Rittle-Johnson, Saylor, & Swygert, 2008) examined self-explanations of a correct solution strategy in multiple classification problems with preschoolers and their mothers. Four- and 5-year-olds solved the problems, received accuracy feedback, and were prompted to explain the correct solutions to their moms, to explain the solutions to themselves, or to repeat the solutions. Generating explanations (to either self or to mother) improved problem solving accuracy at posttest. Explaining to mother led to greatest problem-solving transfer.

Parent–child problem solving continues to support children's development throughout childhood. Work by Gauvain and Perez (2005) illustrates this continued engagement of parents as guiding collaborators. In their longitudinal research, Gauvain and Perez show that parental expectations and practices about children's planning are related to children's planning at home and at school and both expectations and practices shift over time as children become older. Furthermore, there were cultural variations in these patterns.

SUMMARY: ADULT SUPPORT AS A FOUNDATION FOR COLLABORATIVE LEARNING.

Adults provide a preparation for collaborating in the world of peers: (a) by helping children engage in social knowledge building experiences, (b) by practicing skills that will help them learn, and (c) by building an early sense of teacher–learner roles within the social world. These complement the emerging social, language, and cognitive skills children are establishing during infancy and early childhood. It is noteworthy that these processes are embedded in a larger cultural context. The way that parents support their children is shaped by cultural setting and values. The interactions described in the studies above are highly verbal. Such explicit and implicit instruction is typical of European American dyads. Different types of interactions occur in other cultural contexts. For example, Rogoff (2003) reports that mothers in India and Guatemala rarely instructed children verbally. They transmitted information *in* rather than *out of* context and they relied extensively on nonverbal communication and cues. Cultural differences have also been identified by Howes and colleagues in their studies of rural Mexican families and California families (Farver & Howes, 1993; Howes, Guerra, & Zucker, 2008). Parents respond quite differently to children's play across settings with American parents becoming more actively engaged while Mexican families view play as the domain of children. While adults engage children in other activities, they do not participate in play. This work underscores the importance of examining the larger cultural context of specific adult–child interactions.

PROBLEM SOLVING WITH PEERS

Peer collaborations differ from parent–child ones in many ways. They offer new opportunities and present new challenges. Rather than always being the novice working with an expert adult, in peer learning situations children can have roles of equal knowledge status. They must learn how to present their ideas and how to critique the ideas of peers. They can become more skilled and comfortable challenging an idea that is different from their own and conversely, learn how to defend their beliefs when challenged (Azmitia, 1998). Interactions with peers enable children to learn about other people's perspectives and needs.

Peer situations are structured by a different set of attachment relationships than parent–child interactions. Parent–child attachments are intense and not easy to walk away from. This is not the case with peers. Children have much more freedom to leave a peer if they are unhappy with the social interaction (Hartup, 1996). Parents also protect children from problems in collaboration. Parents adjust problems to meet children's needs and shelter children from difficult challenges.

Studies with Preschoolers

Children begin learning from peers as soon as they have access to them. In Western society, children encounter peers in child care or preschool and intensive peer interactions typically begin in this context (Tobin, Wu, & Davidson, 1989). Corsaro (1985) has documented the development of a social community in preschool. He shows how this process unfolds among preschool children as they enter school and develop a classroom community. Through his close observations of children playing in the dramatic play area of the classroom, he identifies examples of conflicts and resolutions to conflicts among children, many of which center around ways to adapt a play scenario to include new children. (e.g., a child is refused entry to the group as "the father" but he is allowed in if he assumes the role of "the dog").

Preschoolers show some evidence of benefitting from peers in more traditional sorts of problem solving tasks. Azmitia (1998) showed that 4-year-olds learned from a peer, especially if the peer was more of an expert on the task. She showed that children who worked with another child performed better on a block building task than did children who worked alone. But, successful preschoolers did not engage in conflict or discussion with their peer partner. Instead, they seemed to use the peer as a model, imitating successful strategies. In follow-up work, Azmitia and Montgomery (1993) examined other tasks in which young children benefited from proximity to peers. Findings from this early work showed that preschoolers do not negotiate on block building problems in the way adults do nor do they support each other the way adults do with children.

Unlike Azmitia's work on traditional problem solving in structured situations, studies of collaboration in preschoolers' play show a different picture of young children's emergent skills in collaboration. Play is a valuable and "safe" context for exploring collaboration. Garvey (1990) notes that play is a particularly useful way to explore these processes because in the world of pretend, if conflicts cannot be resolved, the play narrative or activity can easily shift. It is not bound by the same constraints as problem solving in the physical world.

Several studies of play in preschool have examined negotiations between play partners (Leaper, 1991). While the focus of this work was not on problem solving per se, the research procedures included observations of pairs of children playing with different kinds of toys associated with rich sociodramatic play and pretend. Evidence of cooperation was based upon explicit negotiations of pretend. Negotiations of pretend were scored as collaborative, obliging, controlling, or withdrawing. Caulfield (Caulfield, 2002; Caulfield & Golbeck, 2003) reports that for both boys and girls, approximately 60% of the pretend acts showed the collaboration between the play partners. Using a similar measure with different play materials, Eberly and Golbeck (2004) also identified numerous incidents of collaborative negotiations among preschoolers using Leaper's measure. These and other studies (see Goncu & Gaskins, 2006; Howes, Guerra, & Zucker, 2008; Paley, 1988) support the notion that children do more than simply imitate each other's actions, as suggested by the Azmitia study earlier. Preschoolers can and do collaborate in their play as they create and enact pretend narratives and play scenarios. They negotiate actions and roles in these and a significant portion of those negotiations are collaborative. Preschoolers engage each other in discussion and debate what will happen next in the play scenario.

CHILDREN OF SCHOOL AGE: SOCIOCOGNITIVE CONFLICT AND KNOWLEDGE CHANGE

A different issue in collaboration emerges among elementary school aged children; the ability to discuss and reflect upon problems and their solutions. From the perspective of neo-Piagetian scholars an important source of intellectual change is the joint exploration of conflicting ideas among peers (Ames & Murray, 1982; Duveen & Psaltis, 2008; Perret-Clermont, 1980). Through discussion with peers the individual recognizes discrepancies and inconsistencies in his own thinking and this can eventually result in knowledge change. Indeed, discussion with others is central to both a neo-Piagetian as well as a neo-Vygotskian sociocultural view.

From a constructivist point of view, over time and repeated encounters with contradictory ideas, the child's thinking evolves in the direction of more advanced understanding. Importantly, cognitive change is only one of several responses to disconfirming experiences. Simple exposure to another person's ideas does not mean that cognitive change will occur. Research suggests that characteristics of the participants, the quality of the interaction, and prior knowledge are all important. This notion of conflict has been characterized as a process of intermental conflict (or external social conflict) that provokes intramental conflict (conflict within the mind of the knower) (see DeLisi & Golbeck, 1999 for a full discussion of these ideas).

There is a sizable literature that explores the effects of discussion and debate among peers and its influence on children's reasoning. Many of these studies use problems drawn from earlier research in cognitive development for which the overall developmental trajectory is well documented. Such problems include Piagetian conservation tasks (Ames & Murray, 1982), spatial concepts (Golbeck, 1998; Golbeck & Sinagra, 2000), formal reasoning (Dimant & Bearison, 1991; Forman & Cazden, 1998), moral dilemmas (Kruger, 1992), and abstract logical reasoning (Moshman & Geil, 1998). These studies have generally, but not always, supported the notion that children and adolescents can benefit from discussion with peers, although the findings are not always as clear as one might like. Certain types of interaction between peers are important. For example, Bearison and colleagues have argued that statements that reflect transformations and extensions of the partners talk are especially important.

Another approach to examining sociocognitive conflict calls for evaluating the role of social feedback in comparison to other types of feedback (e.g. from direct exploration of the physical world). Druyan (2001) and Levin and Druyan (1993) examined Piaget's equilibration model by comparing different types of conflict and their implications for change in a lablike setting. They attempted to induce cognitive change in prekindergarten, third, and fifth grade children. Children were pretested individually on a balance beam problem and assigned to one of several conditions that varied the type of conflicting information presented. Four types of conflict between an internal and an external factor were examined. Physical conflict entailed confronting the child's response with correct visual or kinesthetic feedback. The social conflict entailed confronting the child with verbal feedback from either a child or an adult. Results from their study that used the balance beam showed that peer conflict provoked cognitive growth but only among the fifth grade children.

Other researchers have more directly pitted the neo-Piagetian perspective and the sociocultural perspective against each other to examine the effects of peer collaboration (see Light & Littleton, 1999). From a sociocultural perspective, unlike the neo-Piagetian perspective, knowledge creation is like a conversation, a joint construction, cocreated by participants. Knowledge does not reside with either individual but is created socially. With regard to peer interaction and cognitive change, the sociocultural stance focuses on different learning mechanisms. Greater emphasis is placed upon modeling and imitation of peers along with knowledge acquired through informal instruction including language. Knowledge change is a more fully externalized joint process (see Forman & Cazden, 1998; Hogan & Tudge, 1999; Tudge, 1992 for further discussion).

The sociocultural view and the cognitive developmental view can also make different predictions about learning after the shared collaborative experience. Fawcett and Gardner (2005) examined the effects of peer based collaborative learning on 7-year-old children's problem solving skill by studying the influence of knowledge status as well as the use of explanatory language. Children were paired with peers of similar or different problem solving ability on the basis of pretesting, or, alternatively were assigned to a control condition where they worked independently. To examine the role of language and communication, dyads were assigned to either a "talk" condition or to a "no talk" condition. The greatest change was expected among the lower ability children assigned to work with higher ability peers, who were instructed to talk and to provide an explanation. The problems concerned card sorts. Results showed that low ability children working with a high ability peer improved from pre- to posttest compared with all other conditions. Children working with a peer of same or lesser ability, or working independently, did not show improvements. The authors also note that high ability children tended to regress from pre- to posttest in all conditions except those working with a low achieving peer in the talk condition. Children who were required to talk about their card sort with their partner improved more than those pairs where talk was minimized. Fawcett and Gardner argue for the integration of insights from both a Piagetian cognitive developmental equilibration model and the Vygotskian sociocultural model. Findings regarding the value of working with a peer of more advanced cognitive standing are consistent with Vygotsky's theory. They emphasize that specific features of verbal explanations and talk were critical for any collaborative effect. In their study, cognitive change required joint and shared discussion. And, the pattern of regressions within the high group also suggests that the instructive talk of the high group to the low group actually served to support knowledge development among both members of the dyad.

A second point of divergence between the cognitive developmental and the sociocultural views concerns the relationship between short term and long term change. From the sociocultural perspective it is difficult to explain improvement or change within the "individual mind" that occurs after the collaborative experience has ended, as, for example, when children's performance on a task improves between the first posttest and a delayed posttest because new understanding is a cocreation.

Howe and colleagues examined this issue in a series of studies of children engaged in collaborative group work with physical science type problems (Howe, 2009; Howe, McWilliam, & Cross, 2005; Howe, Tolmie, Greer, & Mackenzie, 1995). Howe reexamined data from several studies she had completed over the last decade (Howe, 2009). She had already demonstrated that collaborative problem solving was related to positive cognitive change in at least some situations. In her studies, children had been assigned to small groups with instructional activities. The group experience was followed by an immediate posttest. Several weeks later a delayed posttest was presented. However, in the original work she had not examined the dialogue during the collaborative problem solving so this was the focus of the new analysis. A close analysis of the discussions occurring within the collaborating groups of 8- to 12-year-olds across the three independent studies noted earlier was conducted. The studies focused on motion and speed, temperature, and flotation, respectively. Discussion during the problem solving was coded to capture the critical characteristics of the group dialogue. Joint construction and contradiction were considered in terms of the specific factors relevant to the solution for each set of problems (movement, cooling. and flotation). The analysis, which also controlled for pretest performance, showed a relationship between contradiction during discussion and delayed posttest scores. There was also a relationship between joint constructions and performance within the group as well as on the immediate posttest.

Several features of this study are valuable. Tracking children over time, with the delayed posttest, the use of familiar problems, and pretesting and posttesting individually are all important features of this set of studies. The focus on contradiction and change in reasoning in these children is very much in line with a neo-Piagetian analysis of the sort described by Druyan (2001). Finally, it is essential to analyze dialogue during problem solving in relation to later outcomes (Bearison, Magzamen & Filardo, 1986). The findings here are at least partially consistent with other studies of collaborative learning in middle childhood (Chambers, 1995; Daiute & Dalton, 1993; Forman & Cazden, 1998; Phelps & Damon, 1989).

FUTURE DIRECTIONS

There are many studies in the literature that build upon both a cognitive developmental, Piagetian, framework (see Light & Littleton, 1998; Murray, 1983) as well as more socioculturally oriented approaches (see Hogan & Tudge, 1999; Rogoff, 2003; Tudge, 1992; Tudge, Winteroff, & Hogan, 1996—space has precluded a full discussion of the first framework, the empiricist approach). But, these two conceptual orientations, one rooted in a constructivist, rationalist perspective and the other rooted in a sociocultural frame, reflect some inherent contradictions. The former focuses on an individual knower, learning and developing within a social and physical context. Change is conceptualized in terms of the individual mind and it is assumed that it is possible to study the mind separate from context. On the other hand, the later perspective always focuses on a social group. The individual emerges from the group. Change is always relative to other individuals within the context. This tension permeates all the literature on the development of collaborative problem solving. Fortunately, a focus on transactions during problem solving provides an avenue for bridging approaches. A concern with the ways participants in a group (or a dyad) simultaneously influence their partners in a bidirectional way is common to both (perhaps all three) perspectives.

Several new areas of inquiry seem especially promising for understanding the development of collaborative learning skills and collaborative problem solving among children. We will briefly mention three; children's use of explanations, children's understanding of teaching, and children's negotiation skills.

Explanations

As noted above, explanations are frequently a part of problem solving interactions in the peer collaborations described above and the study of explanations is an integral part of many different topic areas in philosophy, psychology, and education (e.g., Callanan & Jipson, 2001; Ploetzner, Dillenbourg, Preier, & Traum, 1999). As noted above, recent research in cognitive change has shown that explanations, both self and other generated, that are repeated by the child lead to change. Wellman and Lagattuta (2004) explore the relationship between theory of mind, teaching, and explanations. They argue that children's explanations are central to children's developing theories of mind and that, "they are a part of the mechanism for development in this domain." Siegler (2002) has reported on a set of studies that examined explanations generated by learners as vehicle for instruction. He notes that children benefited even when they had not originally generated the explanation.

Children's Understanding of Teaching

Children's understanding of teaching is a second area holding promise for understanding collaborative learning. Teaching here refers to an awareness of being a knowledge and information source as well as acting as an instructor. An understanding of teaching as a distinct role is present in very young children (Ashley & Tomasello, 1998; Davis-Unger & Unger, 2008). This suggests an awareness of complementary roles in a social situation in which one person is a learner and the other a leader. Awareness of the other's mind, knowledge sharing, and teaching are all complementary cognitive activities in this situation (LeBlanc & Bearison, 2004; Ziv, Solomon, & Frye, 2008). This work can have implications for understanding mixed age as well as peer tutoring, teaching, and collaboration (Maynard, 2004).

Negotiation Strategies

A final promising area of inquiry is the development of negotiation strategies in children. As we noted above, children's play provides an example of how this might be done (Dunn, 2008; Howes, Guerra, & Zucker, 2008; Leaper, 1991). Close observation of children in problem solving situations, followed over time (microgenetically), would reveal how children create and share ideas with peers and move from negotiation in play to more content oriented problem solving tasks. Linking this inquiry closely with the content of instruction, as well as assessments of children's knowledge independently as well as inside the problem solving situations would be very useful for educators as well as researchers.

CONCLUSIONS

We have explored a developmental approach to collaborative learning by overviewing three broad theoretical/epistemological orientations and considering some illustrative research in problem solving. We have tried to make the case that parents and other caring adults play a critical role in helping children learn to collaborate through their own activities with their children. When children are very young, collaborations are with adults. Early peer collaborations begin by preschool, especially in play. The research shows that by the time children are in elementary school, peers serve a powerful role in children's intellectual growth as well as their social development. Beyond this description of development, we have tried to demonstrate the value of developmental theory for understanding processes of learning with peers more broadly. Contemporary research illustrates a dynamic and colorful blending of conceptual perspectives drawn from a richly textured theory base in human development.

REFERENCES

Ames, G., & Murray, F. (1982). When two wrongs make a right: Promoting cognitive change by social conflict. *Developmental Psychology, 18,* 894–897.

Ashley, J., & Tomasello, M (1998). Cooperative problem solving and teaching in preschoolers. *Social Development, 7,* 143–163.

Azmitia, M. (1998). Peer interactive minds: Developmental, theoretical and methodological issues. In D. Faulkner, K. Littleton, & M. Woodhead (Eds.), *Learning relationships in the classroom* (pp. 207–234). London: Routledge.

Azmitia, M., & Montgomery, R. (1993). Friendship, transactive dialogues, and the development of scientific reasoning. *Social Development, 93,* 202–221.

Bearison, D., Magzamen, S., & Filardo, E. (1986). Socio-cognitive conflict and cognitive growth in young children. *Merrill-Palmer Quarterly, 32,* 51–72.

Brown, T., & Smith, L. (2002). (Eds.). *Reductionism and the development of knowledge.* Mahwah, NJ: Erlbaum.

Bruner, J. S. (1985). Vygotsky: A historical and conceptual perspective. In J. Wertsch (Ed.), *Culture, communication and cognition: Vygotskian perspectives* (pp. 21–34). Cambridge, England: Cambridge University Press.

Bruner, J. S., & Sherwood, V. (1976). Early rule structure: The case of "peekaboo." In R. Harre (Ed.), *Life sentences* (pp. 55–62). London: Wiley.

Callanan, M., & Jipson, J. (2001). Explanatory conversations and young children's developing scientific literacy. In K. Crowley, C. D. Schun, & T. Okada (Eds.), *Designing for science: Implications for every day, classroom and professional settings* (pp. 21–49). Mahwah, NJ: Erlbaum.

Case, R. (1996). Changing views of knowledge and their impact on educational research and practice. In D. Olson & N. Torrance (Eds.), *The handbook of education and human development* (pp. 75–99). Malden MA: Blackwell.

Case, R., Griffin, S., & Kelly, W. (2001). Socioeconomic differences in children's early cognitive development and their readiness for schooling. In S. Golbeck (Ed.), *Psychological perspectives on early childhood education* (pp. 37–63). Mahwah, NJ: Erlbaum.

Caulfield, M. (2002). *The influence of war play theme on cooperation and affective meaning in preschoolers' pretend play.* Doctoral dissertation submitted to the Graduate School of Education, Rutgers University.

Caulfield, M., & Golbeck, S. (2003, April). *The influence of play theme on cooperation and affective meaning in preschoolers' pretend play.* Paper presented at the Biennial Meetings of the Society for Research in Child Development, Tampa, FL.

Chambers, S. M. (1995). Age, prior opinions, and peer interactions in opinion restructuring. *Child Development, 66,* 178–192.

Corsaro, W. M. (1985). *Friendship and peer culture in the early years.* Norwood, NJ: Ablex.

Daiute, C., & Dalton, B. (1993). Collaboration between children learning to write: Can novices be masters? *Cognition and Instruction, 10,* 281–333.

Davis-Unger, A., & Carlson, S. (2008). Development of teaching skills and relations to theory of mind in preschoolers. *Journal of Cognition & Development. 9,* 26–45.

DeLisi, R., & Golbeck, S. (1999). Implications of Piaget's theory for peer learning. In A. M. O'Donnell & A. King (Eds.), *Learning through cooperation: Cognitive perspectives on peer learning* (pp. 3–37). Mahwah, NJ: Erlbaum.

Dimant, R., & Bearison, D. (1991). Development of formal reasoning during successive peer interactions. *Developmental Psychology, 27*(2), 277–284.

Druyan, S. (2001). A comparison of four types of cognitive conflict and their effect on cognitive development. *International Journal of Behavioral Development, 25*(3), 226–236.

Dunn, J. (2008). Relationships and children's discovery of mind. In U. Muller, J. Carpendale, N. Budwig, & B. Sokol (Eds.), *Social life and social knowledge* (pp. 171–182). New York: Erlbaum.

Duveen, G., & Psaltis, C. (2008). The constructive role of asymmetry in social interaction. In U. Muller, J. Carpendale, N. Budwig, & B. Sokol (Eds.), *Social life and social knowledge* (pp. 183–204). New York: Erlbaum.

Eberly, J., & Golbeck, S. (2004). Blocks, building and mathematics: Influences of task format and gender of play partners among preschoolers. *Social Contexts of Early Education and Play: Advances in Early Education and Day Care, 13,* 39–54.

Farver, J., & Howes, C. (1993). Cultural differences in American and Mexican mother–child pretend play. *Merrill-Palmer Quarterly, 39,* 344–358.

Fawcett, L. M., & Garton, A. F. (2005). The effects of peer collaboration on children's problem solving ability. *British Journal of Educational Psychology, 75,* 157–169.

Forman, E., & Cazden, C. (1998). Exploring Vygotskian perspectives in education: The cognitive value of peer interaction. In D. Faulkner, K. Littleton, & M. Woodhead (Eds.), *Learning relationships in the classroom* (pp. 189–206). London: Routledge.

Freund, L. (1990). Maternal regulation of children's problem-solving behavior and its impact on children's performance. *Child Development, 61,* 113–126.

Garvey, C. (1990). *Play.* Cambridge, MA: Harvard University Press.

Gauvain, M. (2001). *The social context of cognitive development.* New York: Guilford.

Gauvain, M., & Perez, S. M. (2005). Parent–child participation in planning children's activities outside of school in European American and Latino families. *Child Development, 76*, 371–383.

Golbeck, S. (1995). The social context of young children's spatial representations: Recreating the world with blocks, drawings and models. *Advances in Early Education and Child Care, 7*, 213–250.

Golbeck, S. (1998). Peer collaboration and children's representation of the horizontal surface of liquid. *Journal of Applied Developmental Psychology, 19*, 571–592.

Golbeck, S., Rand, M. K., & Soundy, C. (1988). Constructing a model of a large-scale space with the space in view: Effects of guidance and cognitive restructuring in preschoolers. *Merrill-Palmer Quarterly, 32*, 187–203.

Golbeck, S., & Sinagra, K. (2000). Effects of gender and collaboration on college students' performance on a Piagetian spatial task. *Journal of Experimental Education, 69*, 22–31.

Goncu, A., & Gaskins, S. (2006). (Eds.). *Play and development: Evolutionary, sociocultural and functional perspectives.* Mahwah, NJ: Erlbaum.

Guberman, S. R., & Gearhardt, M. (1999). Cultural aspects of young children's mathematical knowledge. *Child Development, 67*, 1609–1623.

Hartup, W. W. (1996). The company they keep: Friendships and their developmental significance. *Child Development, 67*, 1-13.

Hogan, D. M., & Tudge, J. (1999). Implications of Vygotsky's theory for peer learning. In A. O'Donnell & A. King (Eds.), *Cognitive perspectives on peer learning* (pp. 39–66). Mahwah, NJ: Erlbaum.

Howe, C. (2009). Collaborative group work in middle childhood: Joint construction, unresolved contradiction and the growth of knowledge. *Human Development, 52*, 215–223.

Howe, C., McWilliam, D., & Cross, G. (2005). Chance favours only the prepared mind: Incubation and the delayed effects of peer collaboration. *British Journal of Psychology, 96*, 67–93

Howe, C., Tolmie, A., Greer, K., & Mackenzie, M. (1995). Peer collaboration and growth in physics: Task influences on children's understanding of heating and cooling. *Cognition & Instruction, 13*(4), 483–503.

Howes, C., Guerra, A., & Zucker, E. (2008). Migrating from Mexico and sharing pretend with peers in the United States. *Merrill Palmer Quarterly, 54*, 255–288.

Hume, D. (1955). *An inquiry concerning human understanding.* New York: Bobbs-Merrill. (Original work published 1748)

Kant, I. (1961). *Critique of pure reason.* Garden City, NY: Doubleday Anchor. (Original work published 1796)

Kaufmann, W. (1980). *Discovering the mind: Goethe, Kant and Hegel.* New York: McGraw Hill.

Kruger, A. C. (1992). The effect of peer and adult–child transactive discussions on moral reasoning. *Merrill-Palmer Quarterly, 38*(2), 191–211.

Leaper, C. (1991). Influence and involvement in children's discourse: Age, gender and partner effects. *Child Development, 62*, 797–811.

LeBlanc, G., & Bearison, D. J. (2004). Teaching and learning as a bi-directional activity: Investigating dyadic interactions between child teachers and child learners. *Cognitive Development, 19*, 499–515.

Levin, I., & Druyan, S. (1993). When sociocognitive transaction among peers fails: The case of misconceptions in science. *Child Development, 64*, 1571–1591.

Light, P., & Littleton, K. (1999). *Social process in children's learning.* Cambridge, England: Cambridge University Press.

Locke, J. (1989). *Essay concerning human understanding.* London: Clarendon Press. (Original work published in 1796)

Maynard, A. (2004). Cultures of teaching in childhood: Formal schooling and Maya sibling teaching at home. *Cognitive Development, 19*, 517–535.

Meltzoff, A. N., & Moore, M. K. (1989). Imitation in newborn infants: Exploring the range of gestures imitated and the underlying mechanisms. *Developmental Psychology, 25*, 954–962.

Miller, P. H. (2011). *Theories of developmental psychology* (5th ed.). New York: Worth.

Moshman, D., & Geil, M. (1998). Collaborative reasoning: Evidence for collective rationality. *Thinking and Reasoning, 4*, 231–248.

Murray, F. (1983). Equilibration as cognitive conflict. *Developmental Review*, 3, 54-61.

O'Donnell, A., & King, A. (Eds.). (1999). *Cognitive perspectives on peer learning.* Mahwah, NJ: Erlbaum.

Overton, W. (2002). Understanding, explanation and reductionism: Finding a cure for Cartesian anxiety. In T. Brown & L. Smith (Eds.), *Reductionism and the development of knowledge* (pp. 29–52). Mahwah, NJ: Erlbaum.

Paley, V. (1988). *Bad guys don't have birthdays: Fantasy play at four.* Chicago, IL: University of Chicago Press.

Perret-Clermont, A.-N. (1980). *Social interaction and cognitive development in children.* London: Academic Press.

Phelps, E., & Damon, W. (1989). Problem solving with equals: Peer collaboration as a context for learning mathematics and spatial concepts. *Journal of Educational Psychology, 81*(4), 639–646.

Piaget, J. (1952). *The origins of intelligence in children.* New York: International Universities Press. (Original work published 1936)
Piaget, J. (1965). *The moral judgment of the child.* New York: Free Press. (Original work published 1932)
Piaget, J. (1973). Social factors in intellectual development. In *Psychology of intelligence.* Totowa, NJ: Littlefield & Adams. (Original work published 1950)
Piaget, J. (1985). *The equilibration of cognitive structures: The central problem of intellectual development.* Chicago, IL: University of Chicago Press. (Original work published 1975)
Ploetzner, R., Dillenbourg, P., Preier, M., & Traum, D. (1999). Learning by explaining to oneself and to others. In P. Dillenbourg (Ed.), *Collaborative learning: Cognitive and computational approaches* (pp. 103–121). Amsterdam, Netherlands: Pergamon.
Rigney, J., & Callanan, M. (2011). Patterns of parent child conversations about animals at a marine science center. *Cognitive Development, 26,* 155–171.
Rittle-Johnson, B. (2006). Promoting transfer: The effects of direct instruction and self-explanation. *Child Development, 77,* 1–15.
Rittle-Johnson, B., Saylor, M., & Swygert, K. E. (2008). Learning from explaining: Does it matter if mom is listening? *Journal of Experimental Child Psychology, 100,* 215–224.
Rogoff, B. (1990). *Apprenticeship in thinking: Cognitive development in social context.* New York: Oxford University Press.
Rogoff, B. (2003). *The cultural nature of human development.* New York: Oxford University Press.
Sameroff, A. (Ed.). (2009). *The transactional model of development: How children and contexts shape each other.* Washington, DC: American Psychological Association.
Siegler, R. S. (2002). Microgenetic studies of self-explanation. In N. Grannot & J. Parziale (Eds.), *Microdevelopment: A process oriented perspective for studying development and learning* (pp. 31–58). Cambridge, England: Cambridge University Press.
Stone, A. (1998). What is missing in the metaphor of scaffolding? In D. Faulkner, K. Littleton, & M. Woodhead (Eds.), *Learning relationships in the classroom* (pp. 156–168). London: Routledge.
Tobin, J., Wu, D., & Davidson, D. (1989). *Preschool in three cultures.* New Haven, CT: Yale University Press.
Tomasello, M. (2009). *Why we cooperate.* Cambridge MA: MIT Press.
Tomasello, M., Kruger, A. C., & Ratner, H. H. (1993). Cultural learning. *Behavior & Brain Sciences, 16,* 495–552.
Trevarthen, C. (1988). Universal co-operative motives: How infants begin to know the language and culture of their parents. In G. Jahoda & I. M. Lewis (Eds.), *Acquiring culture: Cross cultural studies in child development* (pp. 37–90). London: Croon Helm.
Tudge, J. (1992). Processes and consequences of peer collaboration: A Vygtoskian analysis. *Child Development, 63,* 1364–1379.
Tudge, J., Winteroff, P. A., & Hogan, D. M. (1996). The cognitive consequences of collaboration and feedback. *Child Development, 67,* 2892–2909.
Vygotsky, L. S. (1978). *Mind in society: The development of higher psychological processes.* Cambridge, MA: Harvard University Press.
Wellman, H. M., & Lagattuta, K. H. (2004). Theory of mind for learning and teaching: the nature and role of explanation. *Cognitive Development, 19,* 479–497.
Wood, D., Bruner, J., & Ross, G. (1976). The role of tutoring in problem solving. *Journal of Child Psychology and Psychiatry, 17,* 89–100.
Ziv, M., & Frye, D. (2004). Children's understanding of teaching: The role of knowledge and belief. *Cognitive Development, 19,* 457–477.
Ziv, M., Solomon, A., & Frye, D. (2008). Young children's recognition of the intentionality of teaching. *Child Development, 79*(5), 1237–1256.

3

SOCIOCULTURAL PERSPECTIVES ON COLLABORATIVE LEARNING

Toward Collaborative Knowledge Creation

KAI HAKKARAINEN

University of Turku

SAMI PAAVOLA, KAIJU KANGAS, AND PIRITA SEITAMAA-HAKKARAINEN

University of Helsinki

INTRODUCTION

The term *sociocultural approaches to learning* is quite widely used. It refers especially to approaches which have been influenced by L. S. Vygotsky's (1978) seminal work on understanding human development and learning. Vygotsky and his coworkers' texts, and later interpretations and developments (e.g., Cole, 1996; Engeström, 1987) have had a great influence on our understanding of human learning. Although sociocultural approaches are widely adopted, they still challenge many deeply rooted preconceptions of learning and human development. The basic locus of human learning is social interactions, cultural practices, and reciprocal personal and social transformations rather than individuals and individuals' minds. Within sociocultural approaches the meaning of language and semiotic mediation is often emphasized as a basis for understanding human activities.

In this chapter, we are *not* trying to give an overview of different ways of interpreting the sociocultural approach. Instead, we concisely analyze a distinction that we maintain cuts across many sociocultural approaches; that is, a distinction between approaches that emphasize participation and social interaction and those that emphasize collaborative knowledge creation. First we introduce the idea of three basic metaphors of learning; that is, as individualistically oriented acquisition, as participation, and as collaborative knowledge creation. Then we analyze some basic elements important for the knowledge creation approaches. Finally, we delineate a "trialogical" approach to learning which focuses on those activities where people are organizing their work to develop shared artifacts and practices. While our approach emerges from studying technology mediated collaborative learning in institutional education, we maintain that it applies more generally to collaborative learning in a variety of settings, such as business and government entities devoted to research or development of products, processes, and technologies.

THREE APPROACHES TO COLLABORATIVE LEARNING

There appear to be three prominent approaches to learning within the domain of learning theories; the knowledge acquisition metaphor, the participation metaphor, and the knowledge creation metaphor. The *knowledge acquisition metaphor* examines knowledge as a property or characteristic of an individual mind (Sfard, 1998). The acquisition metaphor may be based on the traditional assumption of the transmission of knowledge to the student, or, as Sfard emphasizes, also an active and "constructive" (but individual) process. Acquisition approaches emphasize individual learning, but they can be applied also in collaborative learning (CL). CL is then interpreted as a peer-interactive process that facilitates (or sometimes hinders) an individual's personal learning, belief revision, and conceptual change by, for example, provoking cognitive conflicts (Mugny & Doise, 1978). Collaboration, however, does not in itself play a foundational role in this kind of learning although collaboration between individuals is an essential part of this type of approach. An alternative approach, according to Sfard (1998), is the *participation metaphor* for learning, which examines learning as a process of growing up and socializing in a community, and learning to function according to its socially negotiated norms (Brown, Collins, & Duguid, 1989; Lave & Wenger, 1991). From the participatory perspective, learning is the process of growing to become a full member of a community, in which there gradually occurs a shift from peripheral to full participation. From this perspective, knowledge is not a thing in the world itself or within the mind of an individual, it is simply an aspect of cultural practices (Brown, Collins, & Duguid, 1989; Lave & Wenger, 1991). Rather than the focus being, for example, on a body of knowledge in the traditional sense, the emphasis is on interaction, shared practices of meaning making (knowing), and learning from joint problem solving efforts. Collaborative activities involve intensive intersubjective interactions and shared meaning making (Stahl, 2006).

We maintain that besides these two metaphors, a third metaphor of learning is needed as a basis for theory and empirical investigation of collaborative learning. We call it the *knowledge creation metaphor* (Hakkarainen, Palonen, Paavola, & Lehtinen, 2004; Paavola, Lipponen, & Hakkarainen, 2004). This metaphor suggests, that despite clear differences, several theories of collaborative learning have a common aim of explicating collaborative processes involved in the creation or development of something new. As representative theorists of the knowledge creation metaphor, we ourselves have analyzed especially Bereiter's (2002) knowledge building, Engeström's (1987) expansive learning, and Nonaka and Takeuchi's (1995) organizational knowledge creation (Paavola et al., 2004). These theories have clear affinities with theories representing the participation metaphor of learning but still diverge from them in respect of being explicitly focused on addressing collaborative work for creating or developing novel things as a central aspect of collaborative learning. The knowledge creation metaphor is not meant to be a specific theory of collaborative learning, but more like an umbrella term for otherwise quite different theories and approaches to collaborative learning. Many sociocultural approaches have elements both from the participation and the knowledge creation metaphor of learning.

A forerunner of knowledge creation is the theory of knowledge building, and we have ourselves tried to see connections between this theory (that emphasizes development of ideas together) and the cultural-historical activity theory (emphasizing collaboration around practical issues). Knowledge building is a pedagogical approach that is focused on transforming school classes to inquiry communities focused on improving their shared ideas understood as conceptual artifacts with the assistance of collaborative technologies (Scardamalia & Bereiter, 2006). While knowledge building clearly represents the knowledge creation metaphor it would benefit by being more anchored in social practices and material artifacts emphasized by activity theory and practice theories, which lie at the base of knowledge creation approaches. Activity theory builds on the idea that human activities are mediated by artifacts, used and modified by succeeding generations of human beings, and grounded in practical, everyday activities (Cole, 1996, pp. 108–110). Praxis and cultural artifacts are developed in interaction with one another in historically situated and evolving processes. Human activity, especially knowledge creation activities, is "object-oriented" (Engeström, 1987; Knorr Cetina, 2001) meaning that collaboration is organized around long-term efforts to develop shared, tangible objects, such as articles, models, and practices. It appears that activity theory could be advanced by a more comprehensive account of sustained epistemic mediation (i.e., work with various kinds of artifacts where knowledge is emphasized) involved in technology-mediated learning; collaborative learning entails that even elementary school children are engaged in deliberate construction of knowledge artifacts (texts, graphs, models, concepts, etc.) as psychological tools for remediating their activities (Vygotsky, 1978). Rather than being mainly guided to discuss and share their opinions of the issues and themes inquired, they are deliberately engaged in crystallizing, externalizing, sharing, and developing knowledge artifacts that embody their ideas (Scardamalia & Bereiter, 2006). We consider the three metaphors as heuristic tools that assist in examining various aspects of learning. If the knowledge acquisition metaphor is *monological* in nature in terms of within-mind processing of knowledge, and the participation metaphor highlights *dialogical* interaction, the knowledge creation metaphor is said to emphasize *trialogical* processes because it focuses on activities organized around systematic and deliberate pursuit of advancing shared "objects" (Paavola et al., 2004), with the understanding that the latter may be epistemic, not having tangible or material form.

A CASE EXAMPLE: LEARNING THROUGH COLLABORATIVE DESIGNING (LCD)

In this chapter our discussion of the knowledge creation approach to collaborative learning is organized around an empirical case regarding the learning by collaborative design (LCD) model. Collaborative designing appears by definition to be a knowledge creation process that involves joint efforts in creating design artifacts. Such a process involves students actively communicating and working together to create a shared view of their design ideas, make joint design decisions, construct and modify their design solutions, and evaluate their outcomes through discourse (Hennessy & Murphy, 1999). Fostering learning through collaboration requires teachers or tutors to design, enact, and evaluate a specific kind of teaching and learning setting, paying attention to the nature of the design task, its context, and supportive pedagogy (Viilo, Seitamaa-Hakkarainen, & Hakkarainen, 2011). Successful collaboration is based on open-ended and authentic design tasks that allow students to confront the multidisciplinary or user-centered characteristics of design practice. The present investigators have investigated design processes from elementary-level education (e.g., design of lamps) and higher education (e.g., design of clothing for premature babies) to the professional level (design of various industrial products).

Seitamaa-Hakkarainen and her colleagues (Kangas, Seitamaa-Hakkarainen, & Hakkarainen, 2007; Seitamaa-Hakkarainen, Viilo, & Hakkarainen, 2010) have developed the learning by collaborative designing model, which highlights collaborative interaction among teams of students and between students and teachers or external domain experts in the design field. It examines the design process as a cyclical and iterative process in which workable solutions arise from a complex interaction between conceptualization, sketching, construction of materially embodied artifacts, explorations in which design constraints and ideas are revised and elaborated. The model illustrates relations between the following elements of the design process: (a) creation of the design context; (b) definition of the design task and related design constraints; (c) creation of conceptual and visual (physical) design ideas; (d) evaluation of design ideas and constraints, (e) experimentation with and testing of design ideas by sketching, modeling, and prototyping; (f) evaluation of prototype functions; and (g) elaboration of design ideas and redesigning. However, these phases should not be understood as a prescription for a rigidly specified sequence of design stages. The model merely illustrates the relations between elements of the collaborative design process (see Figure 3.1).

In settings where collaborative design learning takes place, the design context and the design task are defined through joint analysis; all participants have to learn to understand the external and internal constraints related to the problem or solution. In this phase, the teacher or external domain experts have the important task of helping students to define the diverse cultural, social, psychological, functional, and emotional aspects essential to the design of the product. There may well be conflicting issues that have an effect on the design process and its requirements that will need to be taken into consideration during the outlining of the design constraints. The design process moves forward cyclically by means of the acquisition of deepening knowledge, the sharing of that knowledge in a social context, production of varying design ideas, and evaluation of those ideas. Thus, constant cycles of idea generation, and testing of design ideas by visual modeling or prototyping, characterize the LCD process. Moreover, the critical role of the teacher or the external domain experts underscores the value of the physical context (i.e., diversity of concrete objects or material artifacts, interaction with tools) and social interaction in order to make design tasks shareable.

In what follows we will introduce an elementary level students' collaborative design project: the Artifact project. The project was designed together with the classroom teacher and took place in her classroom in Laajasalo Elementary School, Helsinki, Finland. It was based on the following ideas: (a) intensive collaboration between the teacher and researchers; (b) engagement of teams of students in design practices by collaborating with a professional design expert; (c) integration of many school subjects, such as

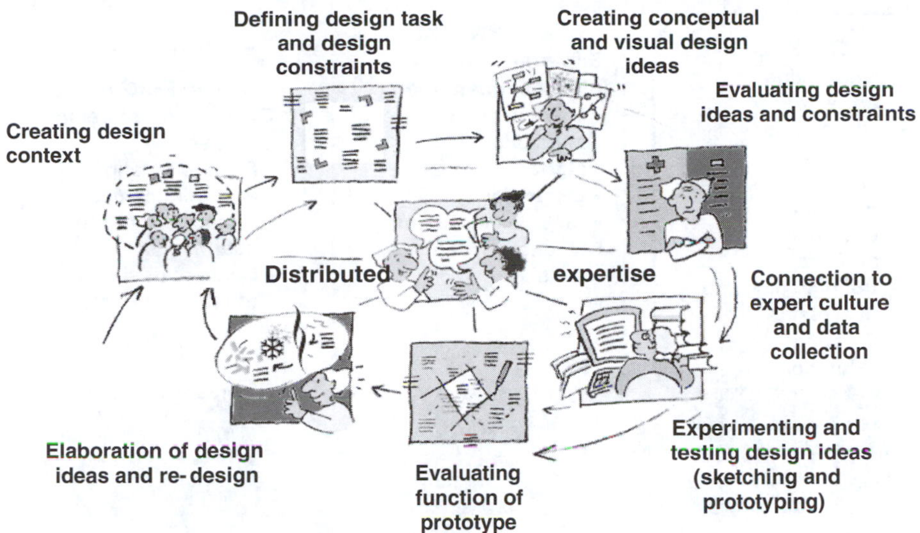

Figure 3.1 Learning by collaborative designing (LCD) model.

history, mother tongue, physics, chemistry, biology and geography, visual arts, technology, and craft education, for solving complex real-world problems; and (d) pursuit of collaborative design across an extended period of time. The Artifact project started with 31 elementary school students at the beginning of their second term of fourth grade and continued across 13 months until the end of fifth grade. Altogether, the Artifact project took 139 lessons (in Finland one lesson lasts 45 minutes) across three terms. The project highlighted the authentic design problems and the variety of conceptual and material aspects involved in design. The technical infrastructure of the project was provided by Knowledge Forum (KF; Scardamalia & Bereiter, 2006) and was designed to facilitate collaborative knowledge building. The phases of the project, their duration and main content, as well as the number of KF notes produced are presented in Figure 3.2. During the project, the students analyzed artifacts within their historical context, studied physical phenomena related to artifacts, examined designs of present-day artifacts, and finally designed artifacts for the future.

In the first phase of the Artifact project, The Past, an exploration of historical artifacts was conducted by looking into the evolution of artifacts as cultural entities. The item had to (a) be used daily, (b) have a long history, (c) originally be made by hand, and (d) be used by hand. Students chose items which most of them had used and which they found interesting: a clock, a spoon, money, a lock and a key, a jewel, a ball, and a flashlight. The students decided to research the historical aspects of the artifacts by visiting the Finnish National Museum, gathering offline and online reading materials, and interviewing grandparents.

- In the second phase of the project, The Present, the physical subject domains from the curriculum were integrated to the project. The teacher guided the students to investigate and ask research questions regarding the phenomena related to the chosen artifacts. The students planned, conducted, and reported their own experiments, or used ready-made tool kits to conduct expert-designed science experi-

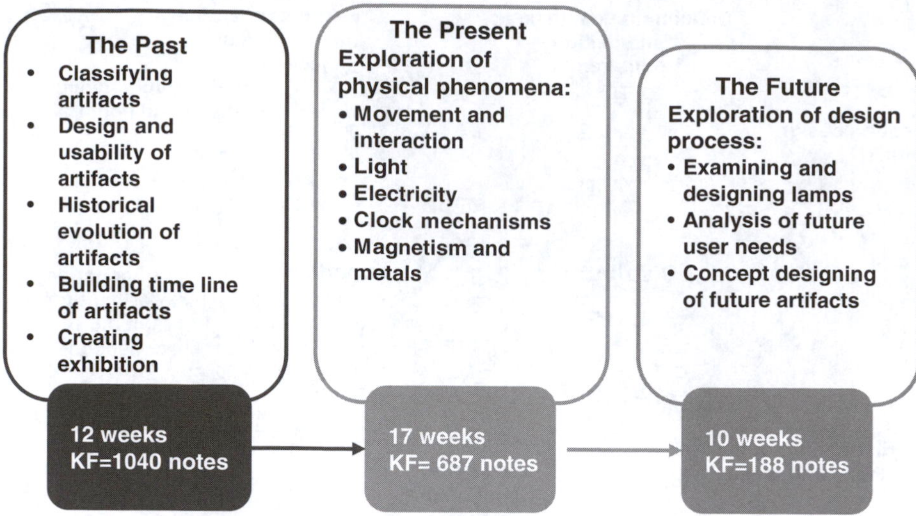

Figure 3.2 The phases of the Artifact project.

ments. In addition, the teacher arranged visits to a blacksmith's shop and the Clock Museum.

- The third phase of the project, The Future, addressed the designing of artifacts. First, the design process was rehearsed by designing a lamp. The leadership for this phase was provided by a professional designer together with the teacher. Beyond conceptual design relying on writing, the students supported their design through sketching and prototyping. The investigation of the present-day lamps design led the students toward the last stage of the project which was focused on projecting, in terms of design, how their chosen artifacts would look in the year 2020 (for a detailed description of the project, see Kangas et al., 2007; Seitamaa-Hakkarainen et al., 2010).

We now outline four aspects that we see as being central to the knowledge creation approach to collaborative learning: (a) CL is an object oriented process taking place across long periods of time, (b) the subject of CL is an inquiry community, (c) CL is mediated by collaborative technologies, (d) CL is a matter of expansive transformation of shared knowledge practices.

OBJECT-CENTERED APPROACH TO COLLABORATIVE LEARNING

According to the knowledge creation perspective, collaborative learning, particularly where innovation is involved, cannot be properly understood without addressing knowledge objects (i.e., symbolic-material artifacts, such as questions and theories, or practices) that are created, elaborated, advanced, built on, and which arise during the process. Instead of focusing on narrow textbook problems and transmission of predetermined rules and procedures, successful CL projects engage a learning community in a challenging series of inquiry objectives, such as building knowledge of natural or societal phenomena and designing artifacts, and induce students to commit to sustained efforts in attaining them. Independently finding solutions to complex problems is the only known way of preparing students to solve unanticipated problems encountered in the future (Marton & Trigwell, 2000). From the activity-theoretical perspective, such an approach may bring about spatial and temporal expansion of the object of educational activity in terms of working with objects across multiple lessons, diverse contexts, and extended periods of time (Engeström, Puonti, & Seppänen, 2003).

The knowledge creation approaches guide educators to engage students in collaborative pursuit of varying complex and multifaceted problems that often come from outside of educational institutions and, thereby, break the epistemic boundaries of school learning. In the case of the Artifact project, these objectives were related to understanding the historical evolution of cultural artifacts, scientific principles of designing these kinds of artifacts, and the actual design process of novel artifacts. Common awareness about the shared assignment of the learning community can be promoted with the help of classroom discussions. In collaborative classes, the students regularly work in groups, and joint inquiry can be supported by a shared screen that is projected on the wall (a blackboard, posters, or a smart board could be used as well), in which shared works can be presented and pondered and which assists in sharing the research results of all student teams; this was, indeed, a central aspect of the pedagogical practices of the class teacher who organized the Artifact project (Viilo et al., 2011). Joint discussions in front of the shared screen may be supported by a networked learning (software-based) environment, such as Knowledge Forum (Scardamalia & Bereiter, 2006). Such environments provide a shared database for which the participants may produce knowledge.

Although the nature of knowledge objects cannot be fully determined before inquiry, and emerge from the collaborative process (Sawyer, 2005), their basic size and shape is usually known. As we see it, the objects of CL can be concrete (yet nonmaterial) artifacts that can be manipulated, shared, extended, and transformed. Such objects may come in multiple forms. Such objects involve *conceptual artifacts* or ideas (Bereiter, 2002), such as questions, hypotheses, and working theories as well as plans and conceptual designs. The processes of creating epistemic artifacts by writing, visualization, or prototyping may be called *epistemic mediation*. Such processes allow remediating one's activity by externalization and materialization of inquiry processes to shareable knowledge artifacts. Remediation even involves ideas and conceptions that have to be externalized and materialized so as to be shared and jointly developed. In design activity, students are concerned with the usefulness, adequacy, improvability, and developmental potential of ideas (Scardamalia & Bereiter, 2006). It is essential to provide students with experiences of solving complex design tasks that engage them in iterative improvement of their ideas and the artifacts embodying them.

In the context of the Artifact project, the objects that the participants were working with were shared problems and design tasks. Students' sketches, from the first drafts of ideas and general visualizations to construction details, played an essential role in the design process. Through this externalization, ideas became visible and improvable, enabling their collaborative advancement. With Knowledge Forum, students developed knowledge and skills to model, design, and construct ideas into physical artifacts through interactive process. For example, the professional designer described his own design process and drew students' attention to the essential points of flashlight design. The students were given the task of picking a well or badly designed flashlight from their own environment and presenting an analysis of that particular flashlight to the whole class. The analyses were also saved in the Knowledge Forum database (Figure 3.3):

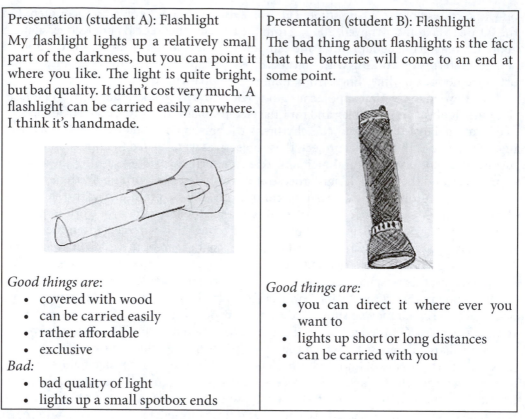

<table>
<tr>
<td>Presentation (student A): Flashlight
My flashlight lights up a relatively small part of the darkness, but you can point it where you like. The light is quite bright, but bad quality. It didn't cost very much. A flashlight can be carried easily anywhere. I think it's handmade.
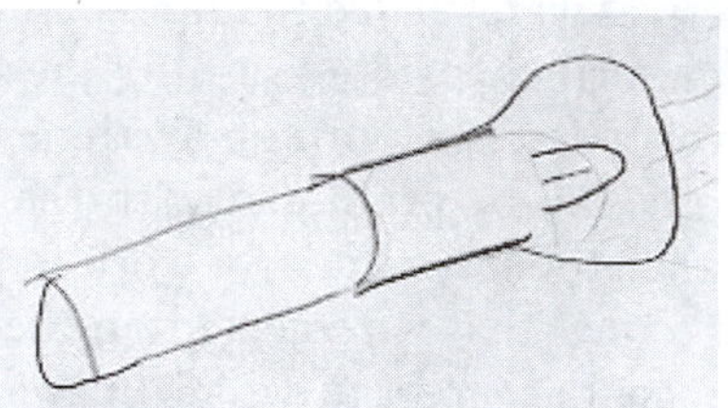
Good things are:
• covered with wood
• can be carried easily
• rather affordable
• exclusive
Bad:
• bad quality of light
• lights up a small spotbox ends</td>
<td>Presentation (student B): Flashlight
The bad thing about flashlights is the fact that the batteries will come to an end at some point.
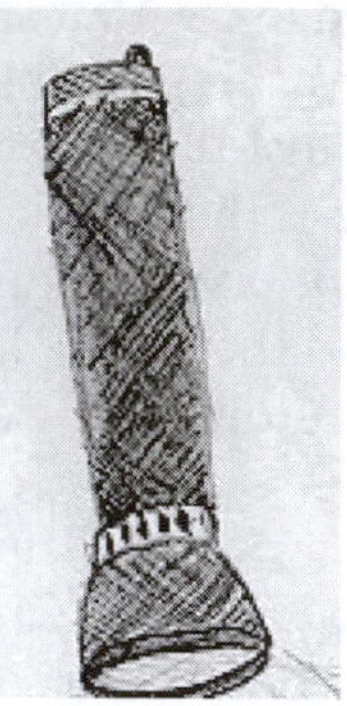
Good things are:
• you can direct it where ever you want to
• lights up short or long distances
• can be carried with you</td>
</tr>
</table>

Figure 3.3

After the analysis of existing flashlights, these two students started to design collaboratively and stated their aim to improve the flashlight in the following way:

> *New flashlight*: The flashlight could be improved by adding 2 batteries, so the power would last longer. It would still be easy to carry. It would be easy to point it anywhere. Main measurements: 16 cm × 3 cm. Carrying tape at one end (#1833).

The designer commented on the students' notes by writing annotations:

> Are there any other options than adding batteries, to prevent the power from ending? What shape of flashlight would be the easiest to use? Do we need other than focused light from a flashlight? (#1903)

It was crucial for the students to understand the important constraints and specific features of a flashlight, such as the functional nature of the particular type of flashlight, in order to improve their preliminary design. They produced a variety of conceptual and visual design ideas (for example, replacing the batteries with an accumulator, and adding folding legs in order to keep the flashlight standing in a vertical position) leading to a final presentation and evaluation of the new flashlight (Figure 3.4).

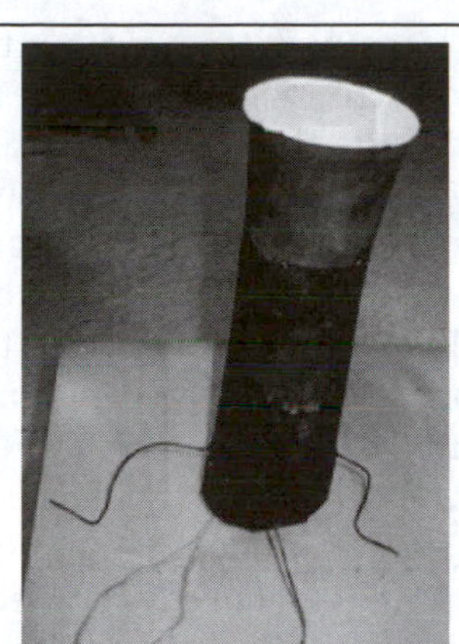

Conclusions: We designed "The Calamar" on the basis of the flashlight. We wanted the flashlight to have soles. The goals were attained. There were no problems. The flashlight is a bit too large, but still it fits in a backpack, for instance. The carrying tape is not needed, otherwise it's all right. "The Calamar" is a good flashlight for expeditions or use at home. Basic measurements: 16 × 3 cm.

Figure 3.4 Conclusions on the design process of a flashlight (student team's KF note #2047).

Rather than seeing objects only as conceptual ideas, those undertaking a knowledge creation approach examine them as *hybrids* (Latour, 1999), being both knowledge-laden and physically embodied as digital or other types of artifacts. The role of materials and artifacts in the design process is crucial. Designers are "working with things"; they express their ideas in "things themselves" rather than merely words (Baird, 2004, pp. 148–149); in a literal sense, designed artifacts carry and embody knowledge. In order to understand and improve the ideas being developed, they have to be given a material form by means of practical exploration, prototyping, and making. Learning to work with *thing knowledge* involved, for instance, in modeling and prototyping, is an essential aspect of appropriating design practices (Baird, 2004). The Artifact project was explicitly oriented toward parallel working with conceptual and materially embodied artifacts. Concrete materials and tools, as well as testing with models and prototypes, supported the development of ideas by adding the material aspect to the conceptual ideas. Students thought with different materials during the design activity; they formulated ideas with the help of tools and machines mediating the meaning making process. Consequently, in design settings, material artifacts and tools have a central role in mediating the learning processes.

CREATING KNOWLEDGE COMMUNITIES FOR SUPPORTING COLLABORATIVE LEARNING

In order to elicit knowledge creation processes, it is essential to build an inquiry community that structures and directs the participants' collaborative epistemic activities. Collaborative inquiry learning appears to represent a special kind of cultural practice that can be appropriated by learners through organizing classrooms as inquiry communities (Brown, Ash, et al., 1993; Scardamalia & Bereiter, 2006). Ann L. Brown's distributed expertise and Scardamalia and Bereiter's knowledge building community focus on transforming classrooms into collaborative learning communities through facilitating the same types of social processes, such as public construction of knowledge, that characterize progressive research communities. The community of practice approach (Lave

& Wenger, 1991) and Engeström's (1987) expansive learning framework, in turn, focus on integrating school learning with authentic cultural activities taking place in the surrounding society. All of these approaches are relevant from the knowledge creation perspective, because each of them underscores the importance of community building.

Brown and her colleagues' (1993) distributed expertise approach relies on an assumption that collaborative learning requires the creation of a shared object for working and the setting of distributed tasks which support it. This approach highlights the importance of organizing students to work in heterogeneous teams so as to capitalize on their complementary knowledge and expertise and jointly achieve higher level collaborative objectives. Such pedagogy was utilized in the Artifact project. In the first phase of the project, the students worked in "home teams" (about 4 students per group), which investigated chosen artifacts specific to each group and produced knowledge to the team views of KF. In order to capitalize on complementary knowledge and expertise, the teams were heterogeneous, consisting of boys and girls, as well as less and more advanced students. Distributed regulation of inquiry involves the teacher, students, or specifically nominated team members following and assessing advancement of CL and providing encouragement and guidance when necessary; CL does not produce good results without such metalevel activity. Distributing expertise does not always produce the best results; consequently there is reason, once in a while, for the whole CL community to study some particular problem or subject domain (Hakkarainen et al., 2004). In this case, the thematic groups temporarily suspend their activities and everyone focuses on solving a single group's problem or challenge. Accordingly, the composition of the home teams of the Artifact project was changed when the investigations concerning artifacts of the present time, began. During this phase, all students were asked to work with the same topics and created Knowledge Forum views collectively shared by the whole class. This method allowed everyone to be brought up to the same level of knowledge required by the distribution of expertise; this way helps the whole learning community work at the same pace. In the last phase, the student teams were formed on the basis of their presentations of existing lighting solutions: Teams that presented table lamps, formed table lamp teams; teams that presented pendant lamp, formed pendant teams, and so on. For the designing of future artifacts, the students returned to their original home teams that had been formed at the beginning of the project (Kangas et al., 2007; Seitamaa-Hakkarainen et al., 2010).

Socioemotional processes also play an important role in CL focused on collective creation of knowledge. The participants (students and the teacher) have to be willing to take the risk of jumping into the unknown and engaging in improvisational efforts in the pursuit of new ideas. Students may be afraid of unavoidable mistakes and fear failure in front of their peers if a very competitive culture prevails within a classroom; this is likely to hinder and constrain their participation in CL. The teacher and researchers put a great deal of effort into creating an encouraging atmosphere in the classroom community that is carrying out the Artifact project and developed practices of constructive feedback. This effort is important because there are big differences between students' cognitive capacities due to the heterogeneous cultural, social, linguistic, and financial resources of their families in which cognitive growth and intellectual socialization take place. Constant assessment and competitive relative grading are likely to empower high achieving students and make other students feel inferior and perform less than optimally. The knowledge of students coming from socioeconomically advantaged homes is often recognized by prevailing educational practices, whereas the knowledge and competence of the others is disregarded or underestimated (Roth & Barton, 2004). During the Artifact project, a number of students with special educational needs were successfully integrated into knowledge creating learning. It is beneficial to work in heterogeneous groups consisting of participants representing various levels of educational achievement and providing multiple zones of proximal development. Collaborative inquiry provides social structures that channel educational activity in a way that also engages disadvantaged students in more intensive meaningful learning efforts than otherwise would be the case. When working as a team, pursuit of challenging epistemic objects becomes attainable. Comprehensive supporting structures for eliciting focused inquiry, and the construction of a presentation or research reports are likely to assist in focusing on meaningful epistemic activities. A crucial role in classroom learning communities in general, and supporting disadvantaged students' learning in particular, is played by the teacher who, together with students, sets up higher-level inquiry objectives and shared milestones in negotiation with students, closely follows students' advancement, and directly instructs students when necessary. Overall, it is essential to allow students to build on their strengths, provide many paths to common educational objectives, and tailor pedagogical and rehabilitation efforts according to specific student characteristics; that is, what he or she knows and does not know, understands and does not understand (Clay, 1998; Olson, 2003).

Breaking boundaries between educational institutions and the surrounding society and providing experiences of taking part in genuine communities, networks, and social movements outside of school may provide experiences of CL and assist students in overcoming learning difficulties. The rationale of engaging students in collaborative designing in the context of the Artifact project was to cross-fertilize educational practices with those of professional designers. For example, the students were repeatedly asked to present their ongoing lamp design processes to the whole class, as professional designers present their ideas to clients. Situating the emerging ideas subject to collective evaluation, using expert practices and language, encouraged the students to reflect on and justify their ideas and make their reasoning clear. In addition, listening to other students' presentations helped in developing collaboration skills, such as turn-taking, listening, and respect for others' opinions. Roth and Barton (2004) have developed a novel approach to science education that involves engaging school children in actual collaboration with various external communities rather than merely simulating such activities. They argued that we need to rethink scientific literacy as involving the capacity to take a productive part in solving the strategic challenges of our time, such as protection of the environment and survival of the Earth. Roth and his colleagues have pursued a project during which students take part in protecting local waterways in collaboration with First Nation communities of British Colombia, Canada. Accordingly, students take part in collecting and analyzing samples, improving river banks, and reporting results in meetings of local environmental activists. Many students who do not show any visible promise within a school class, start to shine and produce sparkling ideas when engaged in a completely different type of educational activity that is involved in social movements (Roth & Barton, 2004); this observation also characterizes our experiences of the Artifact project. Expanding focus from classroom learning to authentic cultural activities appears essential for deepening CL approaches. Educational researchers have used the concept of "community" in a very shallow way, frequently without any deeper theoretical foundations whatsoever; for example, they have assumed that classrooms as such constitute learning communities; whatever group of agents (e.g., students) that was brought together for a short time was considered to represent a community (Roth & Lee, 2006). In order to be considered a community of learning, a group of students needs to have a shared object of activity. While this is likely to be the case in the most innovative pedagogical experiments involving iterative cultivation of classroom practices across extended periods, it is something that has to be shown, case by case.

TECHNOLOGY-MEDIATION OF COLLABORATIVE LEARNING

What is the specific role of computer technology in knowledge-creating approaches to collaborative learning? As indicated by the very term, *information and communication technologies* (ICTs) have for a long time emphasized either the information genre or communication genre with monologues and dialogues as respective social activities (Enyedy & Hoadley, 2006). The main uses have been either to deliver knowledge and provide access to learning materials or open up networking and communication possibilities, instead of deliberately facilitating collaborative advancement of epistemic artifacts. It appears that knowledge creating practices have become available for educational institutions because of new technologies specifically designed to facilitate shared knowledge advancement. Bereiter's (2002) theory of knowledge building emerged from efforts to conceptualize computer-supported collaborative learning practices, mediated by Knowledge Forum, a specially designed environment for knowledge building that could not be understood in terms of mere individual learning. The success stories of Wikipedia and open-source development communities give reason to believe that new technologies play a crucial role in facilitating collaborative knowledge creation. Knowledge creation typically relies on support provided by collaborative technologies involved in transforming participants' ideas to shareable digital and yet material artifacts with which participants can interact. This makes it feasible for elementary school students to collectively work with objects that extend across space and time and heterogeneous networks of people and artifacts. These tools also allow the participants to record and capture many aspects of their inquiry processes for subsequent reflection. Rather than relying only on here-and-now oral discourse, a technology-enhanced shared space mediates the participants' activity and assists in externalizing, recording, and visually organizing all aspects and stages of their inquiry process (question generation, theory formation, prototype designing, and so on).

Accordingly, knowledge creating learning is supported by flexible technology mediation designed to scaffold long-standing collaborative efforts of creating and sharing as well as elaborating and transforming knowledge artifacts (Muukkonen, Lakkala, & Hakkarainen, 2005). In the Artifact project, we used Knowledge Forum for sharing the collaborative design process. Toward that end, the participants documented, visually (drawings and photos in the background of views and within the notes) and conceptually (text notes), (a) encounters with experts, (b) results of field studies, (c) student-designed exhibitions, and (d) design of concrete artifacts created by the students (Kangas et al., 2007; Seitamaa-Hakkarainen at al., 2010). Our experiences indicate that KF can be productively used to facilitate a materially embodied ("hybrid") design process in addition to conceptual design.

It appears that the technology as such does not determine the nature of its implementation but coevolves with gradually transforming institutional practices. Only when ICT-based tools in general and collaborative technologies in particular have been fully merged or fused with social practices of teachers and students are the participants' intellectual resources genuinely augmented and learning achievements correspondingly facilitated. Appropriating technology as an instrument of personal and collective activity is a developmental process of its own (Beguin & Rabardel, 2000; Jaakko Virkkunen, personal communication). For the success of the Artifact project, it was crucial that the teacher had sophisticated ICT competences, had cultivated practices and methods of using collaborative technology, and as well guided her students to use ICTs and KF. This is our evidence that technology enhances learning only through transformed social practices (Hakkarainen, 2009). Meaningful technology-enhanced learning presupposes expansive learning processes (Engeström, 1987) in which novel technology-mediated practices of learning and instruction are iteratively developed. In the context of CL, profound transformation of social practices is called for that reorganizes classroom activities along the lines of those followed by scholarly communities. Advancement of the field requires a more comprehensive understanding of the complex and dynamic relations between technologies and social practices involved in educational transformation processes.

COLLABORATIVE LEARNING RELIES ON DELIBERATELY CULTIVATED KNOWLEDGE PRACTICES

Establishing an educational learning community is essential because it carries or bears social structures and practices critical for knowledge creating approaches to collaborative learning. In order to make CL to work, it is essential to create and cultivate shared knowledge practices that guide participants' activities in a way that elicits a pursuit of shared inquiry. The term *knowledge practices* is used by the present investigators to refer to personal and social practices related to epistemic activities that include creating, sharing, and elaborating epistemic artifacts, such as written texts (Hakkarainen, 2009). Such practices refer to relatively stable but dynamically evolving shared routines and established procedures, such as question generation, explication of working theories, search for information, and contributing notes to KF, which have deliberately been cultivated within a learning community. Knowledge practices show a range from rigid routines and habitual procedures to deliberate and constant pursuit of novelties.

One basic tenet of the knowledge creation approach to collaborative learning is that innovation and pursuit of novelty are special kinds of social practices cultivated in epistemic communities and their networks (Hakkarainen et al., 2004; Knorr Cetina, 2001). A successful learning community deliberately aims at "reinventing" prevailing practices so as to elicit knowledge-creating inquiry (Knorr Cetina, 2001, p. 178). Innovative CL cultures cannot be created from scratch; this requires sustained iterative efforts in transforming social practices prevailing within classrooms toward more innovative ones. This transformation is something that advanced teachers have spontaneously engaged in; all successful cultures of collaborative learning capitalize on long-standing efforts to elicit directed evolution of prevailing knowledge practices in a way that advances inquiry. It appears to the present investigators that CL cultures necessarily rely on *expansive learning* cultures (Engeström, 1987); that is, the creation of a local community by teachers, researchers, and students' efforts that deliberately reflects on and problematizes its prevailing practices, envisions and undergoes hands-on exploration of novel practices, and gradually consolidates those aspects of practices that appear productive. By using practical methods to explore various possibilities, getting rid of weaknesses, resolving tensions and disturbances, and promoting the desired characteristics, the teachers are able to promote directed evolution of classroom practices.

Consequently, directing of a CL does not only take place in a top-down fashion from teachers' guidance to redirection of students' activity, but involves reciprocal and improvisational efforts of making sense of the situation and finding productive lines of further inquiry. This process may be facilitated by engaging the students themselves in reflecting on and redesigning their practices. One of the teachers we are collaborating with has established a practice of, once in a while, bringing all activities in a classroom to a halt, and then asking all students to reflect on advancement of the overall project and jointly decide how to continue (Viilo et al., 2011). In the context of the Artifact project, the students were accustomed to design language in their interaction with the professional designer. He used authentic design terminology that was in many cases naturally adopted by the students in the course of their design work. Then again, the designer also appropriated some of the discursive practices of classrooms. He adopted epistemic practices of investigative learning by requesting students to explicate their design ideas and pushing them to undertake an in-depth inquiry. This process shows how successful CL cultures rely on gradual cultivation of knowledge practices that channel the participants' epistemic efforts toward knowledge advancement (Hakkarainen, 2009).

A new teacher should not become discouraged if collaborative learning does not immediately provide expected results. While it may be difficult to change an already established community's study practices, it is possible to intellectually socialize new student cohorts to advanced collaborative inquiry practices from the very beginning of their classroom studies (Hakkarainen, 2009; Hewitt, 1996). Through directed evolution of practices, a very advanced inquiry culture can be cultivated to which new cohorts of students can be socialized without repeating the initiators of the culture's developmental processes. It is advisable to engage in multiprofessional work with other teachers to create networks of classroom learning communities as well as promote corresponding transformation at the level of the whole school. This project implies overcoming spatial and temporary constraints on prevailing activities by multiprofessional collaboration between teachers, integration of instructional efforts initially fragmented according to disciplines, and boundary crossing between the school and the surrounding community (Engeström, Engeström, & Suntio, 2002); these means are crucially facilitated by the technology and learning environments. When integrated with iterative efforts to improve and develop the community by overcoming challenges and tensions encountered in classroom practices, it is possible to get into an expansive developmental trajectory of prevailing knowledge practices.

DISCUSSION

In the present chapter, we have briefly reviewed knowledge creation approaches to collaborative learning. We used terms such as *trialogue* and *trialogical learning* for those processes where people are organizing activities for developing concrete artifacts and practices (Paavola et al., 2004). While studying collaborative learning, it is, however, important to see a continuum from "participation" approaches to "knowledge creation" approaches, and from dialogical meaning making to trialogues in terms of collaborative work with shared objects (Paavola & Hakkarainen, 2009). Dialogic theories typically emphasize such things as communication skills, expression of different perspectives, multiple voices, shared meaning, and shared understanding (Stahl, 2006). Artifacts such as reports are mentioned, of course, but primarily as a *means* of dialogue. Trialogical inquiry appears to require extended efforts on the part of the participants, going beyond mere dialogues, for developing shared objects across relatively long periods of time. We emphasize that the objects themselves have a causative role. Trialogues necessarily require dialogue in the process of making and taking perspectives and negotiating their meaning by means of comment and discussion. Yet the defining feature of trialogical inquiry is creative work with externalized ideas and objectification and materialization of ideas to lead to the creation of epistemic artifacts in which subsequent inquiry takes place. Human beings are cognitive overachievers because they use various cognitive extensions for piggy-backing complex cognitions that could not be implemented without external aids (Donald, 2001). By being an intensive part of CL practices, even very young learners may learn to systematically augment their intellectual resources by crystallizing reasoning processes and inquiries to become shareable artifacts; this affects the learners in their joint cognitive processes. The Artifact project involved students learning to systematically capitalize on material-symbolic epistemic artifacts, created by themselves and their fellow learners, in their subsequent epistemic processes.

There is evidence of the educational value of CL in facilitating the development of participating students' agency and a transformation of their identity (Engeström, 1999; Hakkarainen et al., 2004). Productive CL takes place in mediated *interaction between personal and collective activities.* In many cases, individual agents have a key role in knowledge creation processes but are not, in fact, acting individually; their activities rely on a fertile ground provided by collective activities and upon the artifacts jointly created. Becoming a collaborative inquirer is a developmental process in itself. Participation in pursuit of complex collective projects is likely to elicit students' sociocognitive growth. Breaking boundaries between school and cultural communities often provides opportunities for appropriating novel roles and developing one's agency. Novel and more demanding roles become available to students when engaging in extracurricular activities taking place outside of the classroom. It often happens that new groups of students start excelling when engaged in activities across multiple contexts (Roth & Barton, 2004). Epistemic agency in the form of assuming collective cognitive responsibility for collective inquiry efforts appears to be especially important (Scardamalia, 2002). From a sociocultural perspective, learning is not, however, a mere epistemic improvement, but also an ontological transformation (Packer & Goicoechea, 2000) elicited by cultivating CL cultures that allow utilization of errors and mistakes in a safe context as collective learning experiences. Collaborative learning is always multivoiced and heterogeneous in nature. In interactions between teachers and the fresh and unique knowledge and experience of new cohorts of students there emerge practices that neither belong to official school discourse, nor to students' informal discourse; rather they are genuinely collaboratively emergent in nature (Sawyer, 2005), forming a third space (Gutierrez, Rymes, & Larson, 1995). Many aspects of the Artifact project were not anticipated by the investigators and appear to represent just such an emergent phenomenon that is following its own logic (trialogic!). Participants' activities had deeper meaning and cultural significance that went beyond regular concerns of individual school achievements or a separate school project.

REFERENCES

Baird, D. (2004). *Thing knowledge: A philosophy of scientific instruments.* Berkeley, CA: University of California Press.

Béguin, P., & Rabardel, P. (2000). Designing for instrument-mediated activity. *Scandinavian Journal of Information Systems, 12,* 173–190.

Bereiter, C. (2002). *Education and mind in the knowledge age.* Mahwah, NJ: Erlbaum.

Brown, A. L., Ash, D., Rutherford, M., Nakagawa, K., Gordon, A., & Campione, J. C. (1993). Distributed expertise in the classroom. In G. Salomon (Ed.), *Distributed cognition* (pp. 188–228). New York: Cambridge University Press.

Brown, J. S., Collins, A., & Duguid, P. (1989). Situated cognition and culture of learning. *Educational Researcher 18,* 32–42.

Clay, M. (1998). *By different path to common outcomes.* York, ME: Stenhouse.

Cole, M. (1996). *Cultural psychology: A once and future discipline.* Cambridge, MA: Harvard University Press.

Donald, M. (2001). *A mind so rare: The evolution of human consciousness.* New York: Norton.

Engeström, Y. (1987). *Learning by expanding.* Helsinki, Finland: Orienta-Konsultit.

Engeström, Y. (1999). Activity theory and individual and social transformation. In Y. Engeström, R. Miettinen, & R.-L. Punamäki (Eds.), *Perspectives on activity theory* (pp. 19–38). Cambridge, England: Cambridge University Press.

Engeström, Y, Engeström, R., & Suntio, A. (2002). Can a school community learn to master its own future? An activity theoretical study of expansive learning among middle school teachers. In G. Wells & G. Claxton (Eds.), *Learning for life in the 21st century: Sociocultural perspectives on the future of education* (pp. 211–224). Cambridge, MA: Blackwell.

Engeström, Y., Puonti, L., & Seppänen, L. (2003). Spatial and temporal expansion of the object as a challenge for reorganizing work. In D. Nicolini, S. Gherardi, & D. Yanow (Eds.), *Knowing in organizations: A practice-based approach* (pp. 151–186). London: Sharpe.

Enyedy, N., & Hoadley, C. M. (2006). From dialogue to monologue and back: Middle spaces in computer-mediated learning. *Computer-Supported Collaborative Learning, 1*(4), 413–439.

Gutierrez, K., Rymes, B., & Larson, J. (1995). Script, counterscript, and underlife in the classroom. *Harvard Educational Review, 65,* 445–472.

Hakkarainen, K. (2009). A knowledge-practice perspective on technology-mediated learning. *International Journal of Computer Supported Collaborative Learning, 4,* 213–231.

Hakkarainen, K., Palonen, T., Paavola, S., & Lehtinen, E. (2004). *Communities of networked expertise: Professional and educational perspectives* (Advances in Learning and Instruction Series). Amsterdam, Netherlands: Elsevier.

Hennessy, S., & Murphy, P. (1999). The potential for collaborative problem solving in design and technology. *International Journal of Technology and Design Education, 9*(1), 1–36.

Hewitt, J. (1996). *Progress toward a knowledge building community* (Unpublished doctoral dissertation). Department of Education, University of Toronto.

Kangas, K., Seitamaa-Hakkarainen, P., & Hakkarainen, K. (2007). The Artifact project: History, science and design inquiry in technology enhanced learning at elementary level. *Research and Practice in Technology Enhanced Learning, 2*(3), 213–237.

Knorr Cetina, K. (2001). Objectual practice. In T. Schatzki, K. Knorr Cetina, & E. von Savigny (Eds.), *The practice turn in contemporary theory* (pp. 175–188). London: Routledge.

Latour, B. (1999). *Pandora's hope.* Cambridge, MA: Harvard University Press

Lave, J., & Wenger, E. (1991). *Situated learning: Legitimate peripheral participation.* Cambridge, England: Cambridge University Press.

Marton, F., & Trigwell, K. (2000). Variatio est mater studiorum. *Higher Education Research, 19,* 380–395.

Mugny, G., & Doise, W. (1978). Socio-cognitive conflict and structure of individual and collective performances. *European Journal of Social Psychology, 8,* 181–192.

Muukkonen, H., Lakkala, M., & Hakkarainen, K. (2005) Technology-mediation and tutoring: How do they shape progressive inquiry discourse? *Journal of the Learning Sciences, 14*(4), 527–565.

Nonaka, I., & Takeuchi, H. (1995). *The knowledge-creating company: How Japanese companies create the dynamics of innovation.* New York: Oxford University Press.

Olson, D. R. (2003). *Psychological theory and educational reform: How school remakes mind and society.* Cambridge, England: Cambridge University Press.

Paavola, S., & Hakkarainen, K. (2009). From meaning making to joint construction of knowledge practices and artefacts—A trialogical approach to CSCL. In C. O'Malley, D. Suthers, P. Reimann, & A. Dimitracopoulou (Eds.), *Computer supported collaborative learning practices: CSCL2009 Conference Proceedings* (pp. 83–92). Rhodes, Greece: International Society of the Learning Sciences (ISLS).

Paavola, S., Lipponen, L., & Hakkarainen, K. (2004). Modeling innovative knowledge communities: A knowledge-creation approach to learning. *Review of Educational Research, 74,* 557–576.

Packer, M., & Goicoechea, J. (2000). Sociocultural and constructivist theories of learning: Ontology, not just epistemology. *Educational Psychologist, 35,* 227–241.

Roth, W.-M., & Barton, A. C. (2004). *Rethinking scientific literacy.* New York: Routledge.

Roth, W.-M., & Lee, Y.-J. (2006). Contradictions in theorizing and implementing communities in education. *Educational Research Review, 1,* 27–40.

Sawyer, R. K. (2005). *Emergence: Societies as complex systems.* Cambridge, MA: Cambridge University Press.

Scardamalia, M. (2002). Collective cognitive responsibility for the advancement of knowledge. In B. Smith (Ed.), *Liberal education in a knowledge society* (pp. 67–98). Chicago, IL: Open Court.

Scardamalia, M., & Bereiter, C. (2006). Knowledge building: Theory, pedagogy, and technology. In K. Sawyer (Ed.), *The Cambridge handbook of the learning sciences* (pp. 97–115). Cambridge, MA: Cambridge University Press.

Schatzki, T. (2000). Introduction: Practice theory. In T. Schatzki, K. Knorr Cetina, & E. von Savigny (Eds.), *The practice turn in contemporary theory* (pp. 1–14). London: Routledge.

Scribner, S., & Cole, M (1981). *The psychology of literacy.* Cambridge, MA: Harvard University Press.

Seitamaa-Hakkarainen, P., Viilo, M., & Hakkarainen, K. (2010). Learning by collaborative designing: Technology-enhanced knowledge practices. *International Journal of Technology and Design Education, 20*(2), 109–136,

Sfard, A. (1998). On two metaphors for learning and the dangers of choosing just one. *Educational Researcher, 27,* 4–13.

Stahl, G. (2006). *Group cognition: Computer support for building collaborative knowledge.* Cambridge, MA: MIT Press.

Viilo, M., Seitamaa-Hakkarainen, P., & Hakkarainen, K. (2011). Supporting the technology-enhanced collaborative inquiry and design project–A teacher's reflections on practices. *Teachers and Teaching Theory and Practice, 17,* 51–72.

Vygotsky, L. S. (1978). *Mind in society: The development of higher psychological processes.* Cambridge, MA: Harvard University Press.

4

THEORIES OF COGNITION IN COLLABORATIVE LEARNING

GERRY STAHL

Drexel University

There is no one theory of collaborative learning. Research in collaborative learning is guided by and contributes to a diverse collection of theories. Even the word *theory* means different things to different researchers and plays various distinct roles within collaborative learning work. The reading of the history of theory presented here is itself reflective of one theoretical stance among many held, implicitly or explicitly, by collaborative learning researchers.

The nature and uses of theory have changed over history and continue to evolve. The theories most relevant to collaborative learning—in the view developed in this paper—concern the nature of cognition, specifically cognition in collaborating groups. Through history, the analysis of cognition has broadened, from a focus on single concepts (Platonic ideas) or isolated responses to stimulae (behaviorism), to a concern with mental models (cognitivism) and representational artifacts (postcognitivism). Theories that are more recent encompass cognition distributed across people and tools, situated in contexts, spanning small groups, involved in larger activities and across communities of practice. For collaborative-learning research, theory must take into account interaction in online environments, knowledge building in small groups, and cognition at multiple units of analysis.

A BRIEF HISTORY OF THEORY

An important approach to collaborative learning research is the relatively recent field of computer-supported collaborative learning (CSCL). This chapter will focus on that field. CSCL is multidisciplinary by its nature and because of its origins (see Stahl, Koschmann, & Suthers, 2006, for a history of CSCL from a perspective similar to the one here). Consider the name, *Computer-supported Collaborative Learning*: it combines concerns with *computer* technology, *collaborative* social interaction, and *learning* or education—very different sorts of scientific domains. CSCL grew out of work in fields like informatics and artificial intelligence, cognitive science and social psychology, the learning sciences and educational practice—domains that are themselves each fundamentally multidisciplinary. Theory in these fields may take the form of predictive mathematical *laws*, like Shannon's (Shannon & Weaver, 1949) mathematical theory of information, or Turing's (1937) theory of computation; of *models* of memory and cognition; or of *conceptions* of group interaction and social practice. They may have very different implications for research, favoring either laboratory experiments that establish statistical regularities or engaged case studies that contribute to an understanding of situated behaviors.

In the European tradition, theory begins with the ancient Greeks—especially Socrates, Plato, and Aristotle—and continues through the 2,500-year-long discourse of philosophy. In recent times, theory has veered in unexpected directions as it has morphed into sciences based more on empirical research than on intellectual reflection. For instance, the work of Freud, Darwin, and Marx replaced traditional philosophic assumptions about fixed natures of minds, organisms, and societies with much more dynamic views. Theory always transcended the opinions of common sense—so-called *folk theories* based on the everyday experience of individuals—to synthesize broader views. But folk theories have also changed over time as they adopt popularized pieces of past theories; thus, a trained ear can hear echoes of previous theories in the assumptions of commonsense perspectives, including in current CSCL research literature.

After the dogmatic centuries of the medieval period, philosophy took some significant turns: the rationalism of Descartes, the empiricism of Hume, the Copernican revolution of Kant, the dialectical development of Hegel, the social situating of Marx, the existential grounding of Heidegger, and the linguistic turn of Wittgenstein. These all eventually led to important influences on theory in CSCL.

In particular, the field of educational research followed this sequence of philosophic perspectives. Empiricism and positivism in philosophy of science culminated in behaviorism in biology and the human sciences. The central metaphor was that of *stimulus* provoking *response*, all objectively observable and unambiguously measurable (as critiqued in Chomsky, 1959). The major theoretical move of the generation before ours was to assert the necessity of taking into account cognitive processes in studying human behavior, from Chomsky's (1969) theories of language based on deep grammar and brain mechanisms to the mental models and internal representations modeled by artificial intelligence programs. Human–computer interaction, the part of computer science dealing with designing for usage, has gone through a similar sequence of behaviorist and cognitivist theories (see Carroll, 2003, for numerous examples). More recently, post-cognitive theories have been influential in CSCL, as will be discussed later.

THE UNIT OF ANALYSIS

The history of theory can be tracked in terms of the following issue: At what unit of analysis should one study thought (*cognition*)? For Plato (340 BC/1941), in addition to the physical objects in the world, there are concepts that characterize those objects; philosophy is the analysis of such concepts, like goodness, truth, beauty, or justice. Descartes (1633/1999) argued that if there is thought, then there must be a mind that thinks it, and that philosophy should analyze both the mental objects of the mind and the material objects to which they refer, as well as the relation between them. Following Descartes, rationalism focused on the logical nature of mental reasoning, while empiricism focused on the analysis of observable physical objects. Kant (1787/1999) recentered this discussion by arguing that the mechanisms of human understanding provided the source of the apparent spatiotemporal nature of observed objects and that critical theory's task was to analyze the mind's structuring categorization efforts. Up to this point in the history of theory, cognition was assumed to be an innate function of the individual human mind.

Hegel (1807/1967) changed that. He traced the logical/historical development of mind from the most primary instinct of a living organism through stages of consciousness, self-consciousness, and historical consciousness to the most developed transnational spirit of the times (Zeitgeist). To analyze cognition henceforth, it is necessary to follow its biological unfolding through to the ultimate cultural understanding of a society. Figure 4.1 identifies Hegel's approach to theory as forming the dividing line between philosophies or theories oriented on the individual and those oriented to a larger unit of analysis.

Philosophy after Hegel can be viewed as forming three mainstreams of thought, following the seminal approaches of Marx (critical social theory), Heidegger (existential phenomenology), and Wittgenstein (linguistic analysis). As taken up within CSCL, one can trace how these approaches established expanded units of analysis.

Marx (1867) applauded Hegel's recognition of the historical self-generation of mankind and analyzed this historical process in terms of the dialectical codevelopment of the social relations of production and the forces of production. His analysis took the form of historical, political, and economic studies of the world-historical processes by which human labor produces and reproduces social institutions. Here, the study of the human mind and its understanding of its objects becomes focused at the epochal unit of analysis of social movements, class conflicts, and transformations of economic systems.

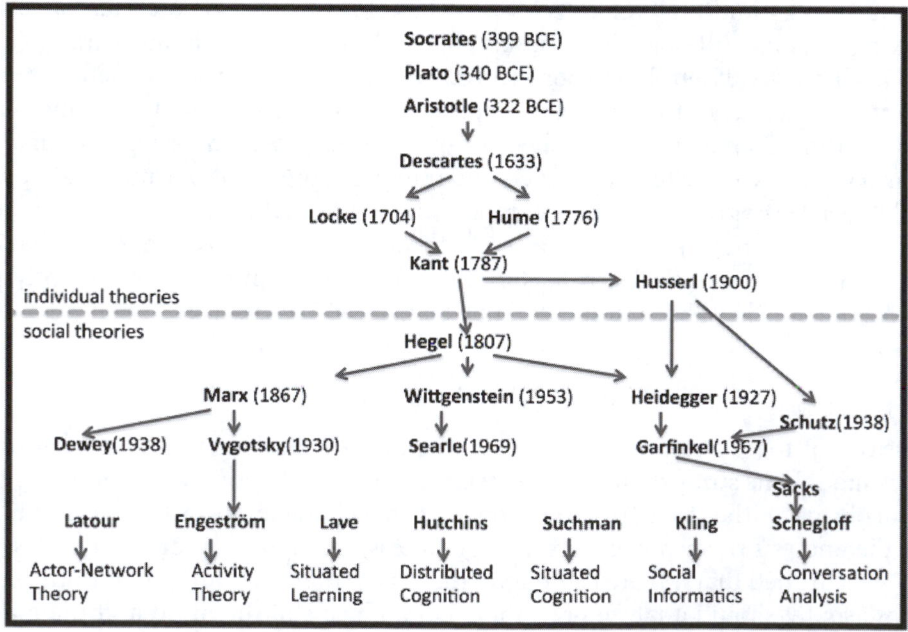

Figure 4.1 Adapted from Stahl, 2006, p. 289, Fig 14.1.

Heidegger (1927/1996) radicalized the Hegelian dialectic between man and nature by starting the analysis of man from the unified experience of *being-in-the-world*. The Cartesian problem of a distinction between an observing mind and an objective world was thereby reversed. Heidegger, instead, had to show how the appearance of isolated minds and an external world could arise through abstraction from the primary experience of being-there, human existence inseparable from the worldly objects that one cares for and that define one's activity. The primordial unit of analysis of cognition is the involvement of people in their world.

Wittgenstein (1953) focused increasingly on language as it is used to accomplish things in the world through interpersonal communication. He rejected his own early view (Wittgenstein, 1921/1974), which reduced a rationalist conception of propositional, logical language to a self-contradictory position. Now, linguistic meaning no longer dwelt in the heads of users or the definitions of the words, but in communicational usage. Echoing the *lived world* of phenomenology, Wittgenstein acknowledged the role of the human *form of life*. He also conceptualized language as the playing of *language games*, socially established forms of interaction. The unit of analysis shifted from mental meanings to interpersonal communications in the context of getting something done together.

Marx, Heidegger, and Wittgenstein initiated the main forms of post-Kantian, post-Hegelian philosophy and scientific theory (Stahl, 2010c). Kant represents the culmination of the philosophy of mind, in which the human mind is seen as the active constructor of reality out of its confrontation with the objects of nature, which are unknowable except through this imposition of human structuring categories. With Kant—over 200 years ago—the human mind is still a fixed unit consisting of innate abilities of the individual person, despite how much his philosophy differs from naïve realist folk theories, which accept the world as fundamentally identical with its appearance to the human observer. Hegel overthrows the Kantian view of a fixed nature of mind by showing how the mind has itself been constructed through long sequences of processes. The Hegelian construction of mind can be understood in multiple senses: as the biological development of the brain's abilities as it grows from newborn to mature adult; as the logical development from simple contrast of *being* and *nonbeing* to the proliferation of all the distinctions of the most sophisticated understanding; or as the historical development from primitive homo sapiens to modern, civilized, technological, and cultured person. After Hegel, theory shifted from philosophy to science, to explore the biological, logical, and historical processes in more detail and to verify them empirically. Followers of Marx, Heidegger, and Wittgenstein adopted approaches to this that can be characterized as *social, situated,* and *linguistic*. They are all constructivist, following Kant's insight that the structure of known objects is constructed by the knowing mind. However, they all focus on a unit of analysis broader than the isolated individual mind of Descartes.

SEMINAL THEORIES FOR CSCL

The social, situated, and linguistic theories of Marx, Heidegger, and Wittgenstein entered the discourse of CSCL literature with researchers coming from the various scientific traditions that went into forming CSCL as a research domain, including psychology, education, social science, design studies, computer science, and artificial intelligence (e.g., Dourish, 2001; Ehn, 1988; Floyd, 1992; Schön, 1983). Although these fields each introduced various theoretical perspectives, we can see the major philosophic influences largely through several seminal texts: *Mind in Society* (Vygotsky, 1930/1978), *Situated Learning* (Lave & Wenger, 1991), *Lectures on Conversation* (Sacks, 1962/1995), and *Understanding Computers and Cognition* (Winograd & Flores, 1986).

Mind in Society is an edited compilation of Vygotsky's writings from the early 1930s in postrevolutionary Russia, which has been influential in the West since it appeared in English in 1978. Critiquing the prevailing psychology as practiced by behaviorists, Gestaltists, and Piaget, Vygotsky did not try to fit psychology superficially into the dogmatic principles of Soviet Marxism, but rather radically rethought the nature of human psychological capabilities from the developmental approach proposed by Hegel and Marx. He showed how human perception, attention, memory, thought, play, and learning (the so-called mental faculties) were products of developmental processes—in terms of both maturation of individuals and the social history of cultures. He proposed a dynamic vision of the human mind in society, as opposed to a fixed and isolated function. The Hegelian term, *mediation*, was important for Vygotsky, as it is for CSCL. Even in his early years still talking about stimulus and response, he asked how one stimulus could mediate the memory of, attention toward, or word retrieval about another stimulus (p. iii). In Hegelian terms, this is a matter of mediating (with the first stimulus) the relation (memory, attention, retrieval) of a subject to an object (the second stimulus). This is central to CSCL because there the learning of students is mediated by technological networking as well as by collaborative interaction. Another popular term from Vygotsky is the *zone of proximal development* (pp. 84–91). This is the learning distinction and developmental gap between what individuals can do by themselves (e.g., on pre- and posttests) and what they can do in collaboration (e.g., situated in a small group). A group of children may be able to achieve cognitive results together that they will not be able to achieve as individuals for a couple more years. This is consistent with Vygotsky's principle that people develop cognitive abilities first in a social context—supported or mediated by peers, mentors, or cognitive aids like representational artifacts—and only later are able to exercise these cognitive abilities as individuals. Vygotsky's theory, if carried beyond where he had time to develop it, implies that collaborative learning provides the foundation upon which all learning is built. Methodologically, it argues against judging the outcomes of collaborative learning by testing individuals outside of their collaborative settings.

Situated Learning went beyond Vygotsky in expanding the unit of analysis for learning. For Vygotsky and his followers, analysis must include the mediating artifact (tool or word) and the mentor or group. For Lave and Wenger, the unit of analysis is a larger community of practice. Adopting the theoretical and analytical centrality of social practices in Marx, they focused on learning as the development of processes and relationships within the community in which individuals participated. Learning was viewed on the model of apprenticeship, in which an individual gradually—and primarily tacitly—adopts the practices that are established within the community in which the individual is becoming a member. Within CSCL, this approach can be seen in the idea that one learns mathematics by adopting the practices of mathematicians, such as using mathematical symbolisms, making conjectures about mathematical objects, and articulating deductive arguments (Sfard, 2008). The CSILE project (Scardamalia & Bereiter, 1996), a pioneering CSCL effort, tried to support the communicative practices seen in professional research communities within the learning communities of school classrooms; the unit of analysis for knowledge building mediated by the CSILE discussion software was the discourse of the classroom as a whole.

Lectures on Conversation laid the cornerstone of Conversation Analysis (CA), which studies the linguistic practices of communities. It was based on the ethnomethodological perspective (Garfinkel, 1967), grounded in both Wittgenstein's linguistic analysis and Heidegger's (1927/1996) and Husserl's (1936/1989) phenomenological approach. Like Wittgenstein, CA analyzed language at a unit larger than the isolated word or speech act. CA focuses on *adjacency pairs* used in conversation—see Schegloff (2007) for a systematic presentation based on 40 years of research by the CA community on adjacency pair structure. An adjacency pair is a sequence of two or three utterances that elicit or respond to each other, such as a question and answer. The significance of the adjacency pair as a unit of analysis is that it includes contributions by both people involved in an interaction, and thereby avoids treating speech as an expression of an individual mind. This is analogous to Marx's (1867) focus on the act of commodity exchange between two people as a unit of interaction in contrast to theories that dwell on rational decisions of an individual (Stahl, 2010c). What is important in CA is the mode of interaction carried out by the adjacency pair situated in its ongoing, sequential discourse context. This should be contrasted with approaches that code isolated utterances based on assumptions about mental models inside the individual mind of the speaker. A CA analysis explicates how a dyad or small group builds upon and solicits each other's contributions, thus providing insight into patterns of collaboration. In a sense, the CA unit of analysis is not simply the adjacency pair, which includes multiple speakers, but the linguistic community, which establishes the member methods underlying adjacency pair practices.

Understanding Computers and Cognition presented a Heideggerian critique of the rationalist foundations of artificial intelligence by a leading AI researcher. The book reviews three theories that endorse contextual analysis: Heidegger's (1927/1996) situated being-in-the-world, Gadamer's (1960/1988) historically grounded conception of interpretation, and Maturana and Varela's (1987) ecological version of cognition. These theories emphasize the inseparability of the mind from its larger context: human being engaged in the world, interpretation oriented within the horizon of history and the organism bound in a structural coupling with its environment. In contrast, AI software represents mental functions as isolatable units of rational computation, which in principle cannot capture the richness and complexity of situated human cognition and collaboration. The larger, primarily *tacit* (Polanyi, 1966) unit of context cannot be adequately represented in a computer system (Stahl, 2010d). Accordingly, the role of computer software should be to support human interaction and collaboration, rather than to replace or fully model human cognition.

The writings of Vygotsky, Lave and Wenger, and Sacks further develop the perspectives of Marx, Heidegger, and Wittgenstein that cognition is social, situated, and linguistic. Winograd—like others, including Ehn and Dourish—reviews the foundational postcognitive theories and considers the implications for computer-supported collaboration. But these theories can be—and have been—taken in different directions by CSCL researchers when it comes time to follow their implications for research conceptualizations and methods. These directions can perhaps best be seen in terms of alternative theories of individual, small-group and community cognition in CSCL research.

THEORIES OF INDIVIDUAL COGNITION IN CSCL

Many research questions within CSCL involve individual cognition. CSCL research is often treated as a subdiscipline of educational or social-psychological research, oriented to the mind of the individual student, within group contexts. Such research can follow traditional scientific research paradigms based on pre-Kantian empiricism (Hume) or rationalism (Locke). CSCL research often adopts a constructivist approach, based on the Kantian principle that the student constructs his or her own understanding of reality. Such constructivist theory is cognitivist in that it involves assumptions about cognitive processes in the mind of the student underlying the student's observed behaviors. For instance, a student's responses in a test situation are assumed to be reflective of the student's mental models of some knowledge content, as construed by the student.

Work within CSCL certainly acknowledges the importance of the larger social, historical, and cultural context. However, it often treats this context as a set of environmental variables that may influence the outcomes of individual student cognition, but are separable from that cognition. In this way, cognition is still treated as a function of an individual mind. This approach may be called *sociocognitive*. It acknowledges social influences but tries to isolate the individual mind as a cognitive unit of analysis by controlling for these external influences.

Followers of Vygotsky, by contrast, are considered *sociocultural*. They recognize that cognition is mediated by cultural factors. Yet, they still generally focus on the individual as the unit of analysis. They investigate how individual cognition is affected by cultural mediations, such as representational artifacts or even by collaborative interactions. Vygotsky himself—who was after all a psychologist—generally discussed the individual subject. For instance, his concept of the zone of proximal development measured an individual's ability when working in a group, not the group's ability as such. Vygotsky was trying to demonstrate that individual cognition was derivative of social or intersubjective experiences of the individual, and so his focus was on the individual rather than explicitly on the social or intersubjective processes in which the individual was involved.

In this sense, much CSCL research investigates individual cognition in settings of collaboration. In fact, if the research is based on testing of the individual before and after a collaborative interaction and does not actually analyze the intervening interaction itself, then it is purely an analysis at the individual unit of analysis, where the collaboration is merely an external intervention measured by presumably independent variables.

If one looks closely at most studies that claim to be about small-group collaboration, one finds that they adopt this kind of focus on the individual within a group setting and treat the group interaction as an external influence on the individual. This is particularly clear in the writings of *cooperative learning* that preceded CSCL (e.g., Johnson & Johnson, 1989). As defined within CSCL (Dillenbourg, 1999), in cooperative learning students divide up group work and then put the individual contributions together, whereas in collaborative learning students do the work together. Similarly on the methodological level, in cooperative learning the analyst distinguishes the contributions to the work and focuses on the learning by the individuals as a result of the cooperative experience, whereas in collaborative learning the analyst may chose to focus on the group processes. The same is true for small-group studies of sociology and social psychology: they usually treat the group process as a context and analyze the effects on the individual.

A final example of a theory of individual cognition is psycholinguistic contribution theory (Clark & Brennan, 1991). This particular paper is often cited in CSCL literature. Although the paper claims to be in the CA tradition, it translates the adjacency pair structure of grounding shared understanding into the contributions of the individuals. It analyzes the individual contributions as expressions of their mental representations or personal beliefs, and treats the resultant *shared understanding* as a matter of similar mental contents or acceptance of preconceived beliefs rather than as a negotiated group product of collaboratively coconstructed meaning making. In a later paper, Clark (1996) tries to unite cognitivism with CA, but he analyzes the situated, engaged interaction as an exchange of signals between rationally calculating minds, who identify deliberate actions based on "knowledge, beliefs and suppositions they believe they share" (p. 12). Interestingly, Clark (1996) concludes in favor of recognizing two independent theories with different units of analysis (the individual or the community, but ironically not the small group): "The study of language use must be both a cognitive and a social science" (p. 25).

THEORIES OF COMMUNITY COGNITION IN CSCL

In striking contrast to the steadfast focus on the individual as the unit of analysis is the social science perspective on social processes. Marx provided a good example of this. Where economists of his day analyzed economic phenomena in terms of rational choices of individual producers and consumers, Marx critiqued the ideology of individualism and analyzed sweeping societal transformations such as urbanization, the formation of the proletariat, the rise of the factory system, and the drive of technological innovation. Lave and Wenger (1991) brought this approach to educational theory, showing for instance how an apprenticeship training system reproduces itself as novices are transformed into experts, mentors, and masters. Learning is seen as situated or embedded in this process of the production and reproduction of structures of socially defined knowledge and power.

The theoretical importance of the *situation* in which learning takes place is widely acknowledged in CSCL. Suchman (1987) demonstrated its centrality for human–computer interaction from an anthropological perspective heavily influenced by both Heidegger (via Dreyfus) and Garfinkel, leading to conclusions similar to Winograd's. Suchman and Nardi have helped to establish ethnographic methods—oriented to community phenomena—as relevant to CSCL research. Unfortunately, even perspectives like situated cognition can take a reductive turn: Recent commentaries have framed the issues at the individual level on both situated cognition (Robbins & Aydede, 2009) and distributed cognition (Adams & Aizawa, 2008), even going to the extreme of reducing all cognitive phenomena to neural functions. Building on Vygotsky and his Russian colleagues, proponents of activity theory (Engeström, 1987; Engeström, 1999; Kaptelinin & Nardi, 2006) insist on taking an entire activity system as the unit of analysis. In his triangular analysis rubric, Engeström extends Vygotsky's mediation triple of subject, mediator, and object to include mediating dimensions from Marx's theory: the division of labor, the rules of social relations, and the community of productive forces. Activity theory, is repeatedly looking at small-group interactions, but only seeing the larger, societal issues; and in this it is like discourse analysis (Gee, 1992). For instance, when activity theory addresses the study of teams in the most detail in chapter 6 of Engeström (2008), it is mostly concerned with the group's situation in the larger industrial and historic context; rather than analyzing how the analyzed group interactionally builds knowledge, it paraphrases how the group deals politically with organizational management issues.

There is something of this avoidance of the small group as the scientific focus in other theories popular in CSCL as well; for instance even in distributed cognition. In defining statements of postcognitivist theory, Hutchins has indeed explicitly pointed to group-cognitive phenomena:

- "Cognitive processes may be distributed across the members of a social group" (Hollan, Hutchins, & Kirsh, 2000, p. 176).
- "The cognitive properties of groups are produced by interaction between structures internal to individuals and structures external to individuals" (Hutchins, 1996, p. 262).
- "The group performing the cognitive task may have cognitive properties that differ from the cognitive properties of any individual" (Hutchins, 1996, p. 176).

However, rather than focusing on these group phenomena in detail, he prefers to analyze sociotechnical systems and the cognitive role of highly developed artifacts (e.g., airplane cockpits or ship navigation tools). Certainly, these artifacts have encapsulated past cultural knowledge (community cognition), and Hutchins's discussions of this are insightful. But in focusing on what is really the community level—characteristically for a cultural anthropologist—he does not generally analyze the cognitive meaning making of the group itself (but see his analysis of group or organizational learning in chapter 8 of Hutchins, 1996, for an exception).

Even proponents of ethnomethodology (Garfinkel, 1967, 2006) and conversation analysis (Sacks, 1962/1995; Sacks, Schegloff, & Jefferson, 1974; Schegloff, 2007) consider them as social sciences, versions of sociology or communication studies, but not sciences of the small-group unit of analysis. They aim to analyze social practices, defined across a whole society or linguistic community. This may be a quibble over words, for they do in fact define many important processes at the group unit, although they call them *social*. Vygotsky, too, used the term *social* in an ambiguous way when he said that learning takes place socially first and then later individually: *Socially* can refer to two people talking as well as to transformations of whole societies. But for the sake of distinguishing levels of description or units of analysis in CSCL, it seems important to make clear distinctions. Table 4.1 suggests sets of different terms for referring to phenomena at the individual, small-group, and societal levels. The distinction of these three levels is argued for by Rogoff (1995), Dillenbourg, Baker, Blaye, and O'Malley (1996), Stahl (2006), and others in CSCL. We start with these three levels, which seem particularly central to much of CSCL work, although other levels might also usefully be distinguished, such as "collective intelligence" at the classroom level or "collective practices" at the school level (Guribye, 2005; Jones, Dirckinck-Holmfeld, & Lindström, 2006; Looi, So, Toh, & Chen, 2011). Perhaps consistent usage of such terminological distinctions would lend clarity to the discussion of theories in CSCL.

Table 4.1 Terminology for Phenomena at the Individual, Small-Group, and Community Levels of Description

Level of description	Individual	Small group	Community
Role	Person / student	Group participant	Community member
Adjective	Personal	Collaborative	Social
Object of analysis	Mind	Discourse	Culture
Unit of analysis	Mental representation	Utterance response pair	Socio-technical activity system, mediating artifacts
Form of knowledge	Subjective	Intersubjective	Cultural
Form of meaning	Interpretation	Shared understanding, joint meaning making, common ground	Domain vocabulary, artifacts, institutions, norms, rules
Learning activity	Learn	Build knowledge	Science
Ways to accomplish cognitive tasks	Skill, behavior	Discourse, group methods, long sequences	Member methods, social practices
Communication	Thought	Interaction	Membership
Mode of construction	Constructed	Co-constructed	Socially constructed
Context of cognitive task	Personal problem	Joint problem space	Problem domain
Context of activity	Environment	Shared space	Society
Mode of Presence	Embodiment	Co-presence	Contemporary
Referential system	Associations	Indexical field	Cultural world
Form of existence (Heidegger)	Being-there (*Dasein*)	Being-with (*Mitsein*), Being-there-together at the shared object	Participation in communities of practice (*Volk*)
Temporal structure	Subjective experiential internal time	Co-constructed shared temporality	Measurable objective time
Theory of cognition	Constructivist	Post-cognitive	Socio-cultural
Science	Cognitive and educational psychology	Group cognition theory	Sociology, anthropology, linguistics
Tacit knowledge	Background knowledge	Common ground	Culture
Thought	Cognition	Group cognition	Practices
Action	Action	Inter-action	Social praxis

Adapted from Stahl, 2010a, p. 27, Table 2.1.

THEORIES OF SMALL-GROUP COGNITION IN CSCL

As suggested above, the CSCL-related literature on small groups and on postcognitive phenomena provide some nice studies of the pivotal role of small groups, but they rarely account for this level of description theoretically. They are almost always in the final analysis based on either a psychological view of mental processes at the individual level or a sociological view of rules at the community level. They lack a foundational conception of small groups as a distinct level of analysis and description. They often confuse analysis at the small-group level and at the societal level, and they lack a developed account of the relationships among the individual, small group, and community of practice. Yet there are distinct phenomena and processes at each of these levels, and analyses at different levels of description reveal different insights.

It seems obvious that the small-group level should be considered particularly central to CSCL theory, because CSCL is explicitly concerned with supporting collaborative learning, knowledge building, or group cognition. There are few other domains in which collaborative learning, knowledge building, or group cognition by small groups is in principle such a central concern. Even computer-supported cooperative work (CSCW) is less concerned with small-group phenomena because the work is often divided up among individuals and is usually more directly affected by societal issues like economic competition—so CSCW is more concerned with communicating and coordinating ideas than with building them together. We have seen this, for instance, in the case of activity theory—which could profitably be used to investigate group processes—where Engeström (2008) argued against a focus on small groups because workplace teams tend to come and go quickly, forming changing *knots* of coworkers around ephemeral tasks.

Engeström's argument echoes the attitude of Schmidt and Bannon (1992) in their programmatic opening article of the inaugural issue of the CSCW journal. In rejecting the use of the term *group* as a defining concept for CSCW, they reduced the theoretical perspective to one focused on individuals "articulating" (i.e., coordinating) their "distributed individual activities" (p. 15). They made this move despite claiming that their concept of "cooperative work" was congruent with Marx's (1867) definition of cooperative work as "multiple individuals working together in a conscious way in the same production process." Marx was analyzing in detail the historic shift of the unit of production from the individual to the group, but Schmidt and Bannon insist on still focusing on the individual. They complain that the units of cooperative workers are not well-formed, clearly defined, persisting groups. But that is beside the point. The theoretical point is that interacting people accomplish work tasks and associated cognitive tasks (including articulation tasks and power struggles) through group interaction processes and that these should be analyzed as such, not simply as sums of individual actions and reactions or as effects of societal forces. In particular, as cooperative work shifts from the manual factory production of Marx's time to knowledge building and other forms of intellectual production in the information age, group-cognition phenomena call for analysis at the small-group unit.

There are distinct phenomena and processes at the individual, small-group and community-of-practice levels, and analyses at these different levels of description can reveal different insights. As Grudin (1994) put it,

> Computer support has focused on organizations and individuals. Groups are different. Repeated, expensive groupware failures result from not meeting the challenges in design and evaluation that arise from these differences. (p. 93)

There are theoretical, methodological, and practical reasons for both CSCL and CSCW to focus on the small-group unit of analysis.

If group phenomena are treated seriously as first-class objects of theory, then one can study how small groups engage in cognitive activities such as: interpersonal trains of thought, shared understandings of diagrams, joint problem conceptualizations, common references, coordination of problem-solving efforts, planning, deducing, designing, describing, problem solving, explaining, defining, generalizing, representing, remembering, and reflecting as a group. In CSCL studies of text chat or discussion forums, for instance, analysis can show group-cognitive accomplishments emerging from the network of meaningful references built up by postings, demonstrating how the group's self-formation and its cognitive accomplishments are enacted in situated interaction. An analytic focus on the group unit of analysis need not imply that groups exist as ontological entities whenever people are observed in proximity or in communication with one another. Of course, effective groups have to constitute themselves as such and they can change dramatically over time. It is not the physical group that is important, but the group processes, which may extend over seconds, days, or years. A single momentary exchange of greetings may be a group process of interest, as shown by the early conversation analyses of telephone answering on a help phone line (Hopper, 1992).

A theoretical approach that focuses on small-group interaction is that of dialogicality (Linell, 2001; 2009; Mercer, 2000; Wegerif, 2007). Dialogical theory goes back to Bakhtin (1986), a contemporary of Vygotsky. It stresses the linguistic nature of interaction. It also reiterates the idea that a person's identity as an individual arises through the confrontation with one's partners in dialogue—a view that goes back beyond Mead (1934/1962) to Hegel's (1807/1967) master–slave dialectic (Stahl, 2006, p. 333f). The notion of dialogue partners coming from different perspectives and negotiating from these is an important contribution of dialogic inquiry (Wells, 1999). Another key concept is that of a *shared dynamic dialogic space* within which knowledge building can take place (Kershner, Mercer, Warwick, & Staarman, 2010). This is similar to the *joint problem space* of Teasley and Roschelle (1993), but now developed in an unambiguously post-cognitive manner.

The idea of an interactional *space* for interaction within a small group is central to group cognition theory as well (Stahl, 2006). The term *group cognition* was coined to stress the goal of developing a postcognitive view of cognition as the possible achievement of a small group collaborating so tightly that the process of building knowledge in the group discourse cannot be attributed to any individual or even reduced to a sequence of contributions from individual minds. For instance, the knowledge might emerge through the interaction of linguistic elements, situated within a sequentially unfolding set of constraints defined by the group task, the membership of the group, and other local or cultural influences, as well as due to the mediation of representational artifacts and media used by the group.

The theory of group cognition absorbs many ideas from the theories discussed above, including that of a shared dynamic dialogical space. Despite some scattered case studies by the authors already mentioned and their colleagues, there is yet not much documentation and analysis of empirical instances of effective group cognition. The analysis of group cognition needs not only specially focused methods to track its occurrence, but even prior to that it needs appropriate CSCL technologies, group methods, pedagogy, and guidance to structure and support groups to effectively build knowledge that can be shown to be a group product not reducible to individual mental representations. The Virtual Math Teams Project was launched to generate a data corpus that would allow for the analysis of group cognition. This project and some analyses by a number of researchers are documented in Stahl (2009). Group cognition theory focuses on the sequential team interaction within case studies of small-group collaboration. This takes place within an interaction space or a *world* in the Heideggerian sense, which opens up to allow the production of group-cognitive accomplishments. The interaction that takes place within such a world—whether face-to-face or online—is subject to a variety of constraints, as pictured in Figure 4.2.

Note that Figure 4.2 is not intended to be a model of objects and processes. Rather it tries to present some of the complex constraints on the discourse through which group cognition might be achieved. Neither the physical individuals nor their group are represented here as such; the dialogical (Bakhtinian) voices of the individuals enter into the sequential small-group interaction and respond to it. Over time, the sequential small-group interaction forms the central shared dynamic dialogic space within which the group-cognitive constraints interact. Behind the individual voices that enter into this interaction space are not so much minds containing mental representations, as a fluid background of past experiences and developed resources for action, which surface based on relevance to the interaction. The team discourse is situated in the shared dialogical context generated by the ongoing interaction itself; the culture and history associated with the group's community of practice; and the sociotechnical environment including the media of communication. The interaction is goal-oriented toward the task—as given externally but as enacted by the group—and mediated by a variety of kinds of artifacts, including codifications of knowledge products previously generated by the group. These artifacts might end up among the team outcomes, in relation to the guiding task. Of course, other constraints and influences are possible as well, coming for instance from the guidance of a teacher or the motivations of a reward system. The point is that one can picture the whole system producing cognitive accomplishments without having to

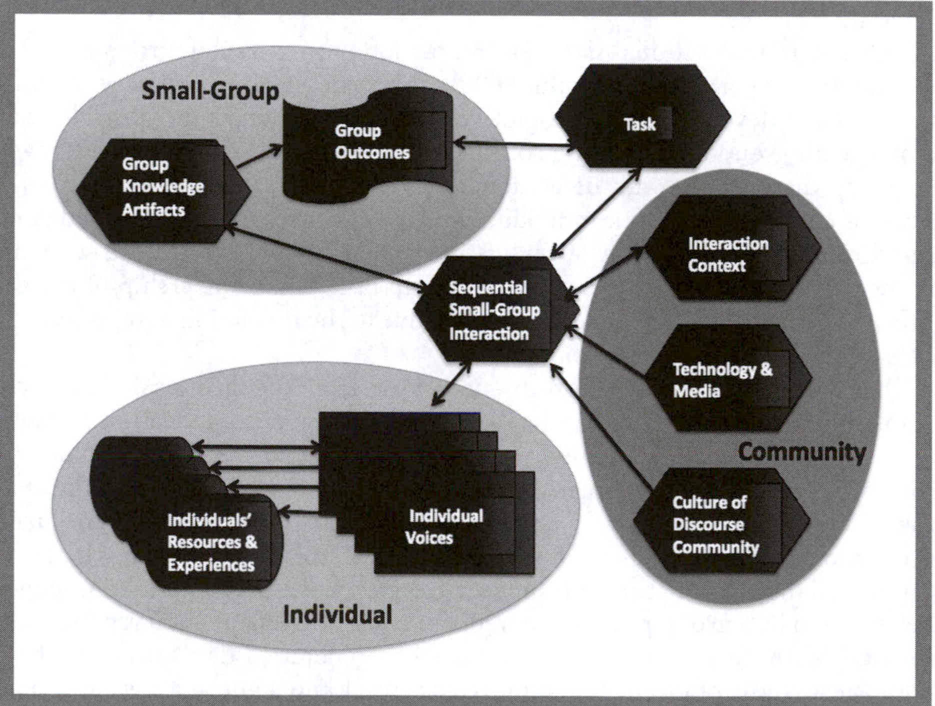

Figure 4.2 A diagram of constraints on sequential team interaction. Adapted from Stahl, 2010b, p. 256, Figure 1.

postulate mental representations in individual minds, let alone to reduce the whole system either to rational mental decisions or to regulation by social institutions.

The term *constraint* in Figure 4.2 is chosen to be a neutral term, not implicating a notion of mechanistic causality. While it is clear that the traditional conception of causality is inadequate—stemming back to Aristotle and metaphors of physical mechanics from the everyday world—it is less obvious how to think about the working of the constraints upon group cognition. Folk theory adopts a mechanistic worldview, or even an anthropomorphic view of nature combined with a mechanistic view of causality. Observable behavior of people is taken to be the result of rational decision making in the heads of individuals causing the people to behave as a result of the minds acting as the agency for causing words to be produced and limbs to be moved. But the *linguistic turn* of Wittgenstein (1953) and even more so the recent *practice turn* (Schatzki, Knorr Cetina, & Savigny, 2001) have veered radically away from such a view.

Latour (1992) seems to be working toward a postcognitive notion of causality, perhaps relying heavily on Hegel's notion of mediation. Interestingly, he not only argues against the hegemony of individual minds as agents in the social world, but he also argues against the adequacy of our notion of the *social* (Latour, 2007). History is made neither by rational decisions of individual minds nor by the workings of *society*. Rather, it is the result of a complex network of mediating actors, including all kinds of artifacts as well as human actors. Thus, Latour seems to be advocating an analytic approach that steers clear of both cognitive minds and social institutions to focus on a middle ground. Figure 4.2 may illustrate the kind of network that he would endorse for picking apart and then reassembling instances of group cognition.

A MULTIPLICITY OF THEORIES IN CSCL

In general, CSCL raises many fundamental questions for traditional theories, oriented as CSCL is to small groups and to online interaction. The accustomed characteristics of the physical world, in which colleagues and interlocutors are embodied and visible to each other, are often missing in CSCL settings, and that brings into question numerous assumptions of folk theories and traditional approaches. The group itself has no identity as a physical body and has no brain to possess its knowledge; it relies on external memories, which differ essentially from personal memories (Donald, 1991). The online world—shared dialogical space—has no location or extension. Group members can come from around the world and do not necessarily share local connections and culture. CSCL involves students in qualitatively different social relations of production, modes of being in the world or forms of life; even Marx, Heidegger, and Wittgenstein's foundational philosophies of postcognitive theory need to be rethought for virtual groups. Concepts of causality, world, knowledge, cognition, intersubjectivity, interaction, and presence need to be reconceptualized for theories in CSCL.

There are many avenues for developing theories in CSCL, as reviewed in this chapter. Although there are some similarities among these alternatives—often in terms of their critiques of earlier theories—there are strong differences of position and perspective. This is not necessarily a problem. There is a huge assortment of processes taking place in successful CSCL events: at multiple time scales and involving different aspects of interaction. It is possible to raise innumerable research questions, each requiring possibly different methods of investigation at various levels of analysis. It is likely that CSCL requires multiple theories, which are not reducible to one grand unifying theory and that even seem incommensurate with each other. This goes essentially beyond the common notion of *mixed methods*, in which two or more methods of analysis are used to triangulate a single phenomenon from different angles. There are distinct phenomena at different levels of description—and they interact with each other in complex ways in CSCL settings.

CSCL is the study of collaborative learning, from a design perspective. Collaborative learning often involves whole classrooms or schools and widespread educational practices. At the opposite end of the spectrum, much of the actual work comes down to tasks done by individuals. But much of the coordination, decision making, articulation, brainstorming, discovery, and knowledge building is accomplished by small groups. Community accomplishments are thereby mediated by small groups, which carry out the necessary activities and involve the individuals. Collaborative learning involves a tight and complex integration of processes at the individual, small-group, and community levels. Computer support for collaborative learning must provide supports at each level while also supporting the integration of the activities at all levels. To provide insight for this, CSCL research must recognize the levels as distinct and conduct analyses at all levels.

In CSCL, there are many phenomena of interest and they are largely defined by the theories that conceptualize them. Different theories in CSCL can be talking about quite different phenomena (although they may unfortunately be calling them by the same name). In order to avoid confusion and arguments about pseudo-problems, we need to be clear about the theories behind research questions, assumptions, methodologies, analysis tools, findings, and claims in the field of CSCL.

This chapter has sketched some of the theoretical landscape underlying CSCL research. Progress in further developing theories of CSCL will require careful analysis of case studies and experimental results guided by theoretical perspectives that are clearly enunciated.

REFERENCES

Adams, F., & Aizawa, K. (2008). *The bounds of cognition*. Malden, MA: Blackwell.

Bakhtin, M. (1986). *Speech genres and other late essays* (V. McGee, Trans.). Austin, TX: University of Texas Press.

Carroll, J. (Ed.). (2003). *HCI models, theories and frameworks: Toward a multidisciplinary science*. San Francisco, CA: Morgan Kaufmann.

Chomsky, N. (1959). Review of *Verbal Behavior*, by B. F. Skinner. *Language, 35*(1), 26–57.

Chomsky, N. (1969). *Aspects of a theory of syntax*. Cambridge, MA: MIT Press.

Clark, H. (1996). *Using language*. Cambridge, England: Cambridge University Press.

Clark, H., & Brennan, S. (1991). Grounding in communication. In L. Resnick, J. Levine, & S. Teasley (Eds.), *Perspectives on socially-shared cognition* (pp. 127–149). Washington, DC: American Psychological Association.

Descartes, R. (1999). *Discourse on method and meditations on first philosophy*. New York: Hackett. (Original work published 1633)

Dillenbourg, P. (1999). What do you mean by "collaborative learning"? In P. Dillenbourg (Ed.), *Collaborative learning: Cognitive and computational approaches* (pp. 1–16). Amsterdam, Netherlands: Pergamon, Elsevier Science.

Dillenbourg, P., Baker, M., Blaye, A., & O'Malley, C. (1996). The evolution of research on collaborative learning. In P. Reimann & H. Spada (Eds.), *Learning in humans and machines: Towards an interdisciplinary learning science* (pp. 189–211). Oxford, England: Elsevier.

Donald, M. (1991). *Origins of the modern mind: Three stages in the evolution of culture and cognition*. Cambridge, MA: Harvard University Press.

Dourish, P. (2001). *Where the action is: The foundations of embodied interaction*. Cambridge, MA: MIT Press.

Ehn, P. (1988). *Work-oriented design of computer artifacts*. Stockholm, Sweden: Arbetslivscentrum.

Engeström, Y. (1987). *Learning by expanding: An activity-theoretical approach to developmental research*. Helsinki, Finland: Orienta-Kosultit Oy.

Engeström, Y. (1999). Activity theory and individual and social transformation. In Y. Engeström, R. Miettinen, & R.-L. Punamäki (Eds.), *Perspectives on activity theory* (pp. 19–38). Cambridge, England: Cambridge University Press.

Engeström, Y. (2008). *From teams to knots*. Cambridge, England: Cambridge University Press.

Floyd, C. (1992). Software development and reality construction. In C. Floyd, H. Zuellinghoven, R. Budde, & R. Keil-Slawik (Eds.), *Software development and reality construction* (pp. 86–100). Berlin, Germany: Springer Verlag.

Gadamer, H.-G. (1988). *Truth and method*. New York: Crossroads. (Original work published 1960)

Garfinkel, H. (1967). *Studies in ethnomethodology*. Englewood Cliffs, NJ: Prentice-Hall.

Garfinkel, H. (2006). *Seeing sociologically: The routine grounds of social action*. Boulder, CO: Paradigm.

Gee, J. P. (1992). *The social mind: Language, ideology, and social practice*. New York: Bergin & Garvey.

Grudin, J. (1994). Eight challenges for developers. *Communications of the ACM, 37*(1), 93–105.

Guribye, F. (2005). *Infrastructures for learning: Ethnographic inquiries into the social and technical conditions of education and training* (Unpublished doctoral dissertation). Department of Information Science and Media Studies, University of Bergen, Bergen, Norway.

Hegel, G. W. F. (1967). *Phenomenology of spirit* (J. B. Baillie, Trans.). New York: Harper & Row. (Original work published 1807)

Heidegger, M. (1996). *Being and time: A translation of Sein und Zeit* (J. Stambaugh, Trans.). Albany, NY: SUNY Press. (Original work published 1927)

Hollan, J., Hutchins, E., & Kirsh, D. (2000). Distributed cognition: Toward a new foundation of human-computer interaction research. *ACM Transactions on Computer-Human Interaction, 7*(2), 174–196.

Hopper, R. (1992). *Telephone conversation*. Bloomington, IN: Indiana University Press.

Husserl, E. (1989). The origin of geometry (D. Carr, Trans.). In J. Derrida (Ed.), *Edmund Husserl's origin of geometry: An introduction* (pp. 157–180). Lincoln, NE: University of Nebraska Press. (Original work published 1936)

Hutchins, E. (1996). *Cognition in the wild*. Cambridge, MA: MIT Press.

Johnson, D. W., & Johnson, R. T. (1989). *Cooperation and competition: Theory and research*. Edina, MN: Interaction.

Jones, C., Dirckinck-Holmfeld, L., & Lindström, B. (2006). A relational, indirect, meso-level approach to CSCL design in the next decade. *International Journal of Computer-Supported Collaborative Learning, 1*(1), 35–56.

Kant, I. (1999). *Critique of pure reason*. Cambridge, UK: Cambridge University Press. (Original work published 1787)

Kaptelinin, V., & Nardi, B. A. (2006). *Acting with technology: Activity theory and interaction design*. Cambridge, MA: MIT Press.

Kershner, R., Mercer, N., Warwick, P., & Staarman, J. K. (2010). Can the interactive whiteboard support young children's collaborative communication and thinking in classroom science activities? *International Journal of Computer-Supported Collaborative Learning, 5*(4), 359–383.

Latour, B. (1992). Where are the missing masses? The sociology of a few mundane artifacts. In W. E. Bijker & J. Law (Eds.), *Shaping technology/building society* (pp. 225–227). Cambridge, MA: MIT Press.

Latour, B. (2007). *Reassembling the social: An introduction to actor-network-theory*. Cambridge, England: Cambridge University Press.

Lave, J., & Wenger, E. (1991). *Situated learning: Legitimate peripheral participation*. Cambridge, England: Cambridge University Press.

Linell, P. (2001). *Approaching dialogue: Talk, interaction and contexts in dialogical perspectives*. New York: Benjamins.

Linell, P. (2009). *Rethinking language, mind, and world dialogically: Interactional and contextual theories of human sense-making*. Charlotte, NC: Information Age.

Looi, C.-K., So, H.-j., Toh, Y., & Chen, W. (2011). CSCL in classrooms: The Singapore experience of synergizing policy, practice and research. *International Journal of Computer-Supported Collaborative Learning, 6*(1), 1–29.

Marx , K. (1867). *Das Kapital: Kritik der politischen Oekonomie* (Vol. 1) [Capital: Critique of political economy]. Hamburg, Germany: Otto Meisner.

Maturana, H. R., & Varela, F. J. (1987). *The tree of knowledge: The biological roots of human understanding*. Boston, MA: Shambhala.

Mead, G. H. (1962). *Mind, self and society*. Chicago, IL: University of Chicago Press. (Original work published 1934)

Mercer, N. (2000). *Words and minds. How we use language to think together*. New York: Routledge.

Plato. (1941). *The republic* (F. Cornford, Trans.). London: Oxford University Press. (Original work published 340 BC)

Polanyi, M. (1966). *The tacit dimension*. Garden City, NY: Doubleday.

Robbins, P., & Aydede, M. (Eds.). (2009). *The Cambridge handbook of situated cognition*. Cambridge, England: Cambridge University Press.

Rogoff, B. (1995). Sociocultural activity on three planes. In B. Rogoff, J. Wertsch, P. del Rio, & A. Alvarez (Eds.), *Sociocultural studies of mind* (pp. 139–164). Cambridge, England: Cambridge University Press

Sacks, H. (1995). *Lectures on conversation*. Oxford, England: Blackwell. (Original work published 1962)

Sacks, H., Schegloff, E. A., & Jefferson, G. (1974). A simplest systematics for the organization of turn-taking for conversation. *Language, 50*(4), 696–735.

Scardamalia, M., & Bereiter, C. (1996). Computer support for knowledge-building communities. In T. Koschmann (Ed.), *CSCL: Theory and practice of an emerging paradigm* (pp. 249–268). Hillsdale, NJ: Erlbaum.

Schatzki, T. R., Knorr Cetina, K., & Savigny, E. v. (Eds.). (2001). *The practice turn in contemporary theory*. New York: Routledge.

Schegloff, E. A. (2007). *Sequence organization in interaction: A primer in conversation analysis*. Cambridge, England: Cambridge University Press.

Schmidt, K., & Bannon, L. (1992). Taking CSCW seriously: Supporting articulation work. *CSCW, 1*(1), 7–40.

Schön, D. A. (1983). *The reflective practitioner: How professionals think in action*. New York: Basic Books.

Sfard, A. (2008). *Thinking as communicating: Human development, the growth of discourses and mathematizing*. Cambridge, England: Cambridge University Press.

Shannon, C., & Weaver, W. (1949). *The mathematical theory of communication*. Chicago, IL: University of Illinois Press.

Stahl, G. (2006). *Group cognition: Computer support for building collaborative knowledge*. Cambridge, MA: MIT Press.

Stahl, G. (2009). *Studying virtual math teams*. New York: Springer.

Stahl, G. (2010a). Group cognition as a foundation for the new science of learning. In M. S. Khine & I. M. Saleh (Eds.), *New science of learning: Cognition, computers and collaboration in education* (pp. 23–44). New York: Springer.

Stahl, G. (2010b). Guiding group cognition in CSCL. *International Journal of Computer-Supported Collaborative Learning, 5*(3), 255–258.

Stahl, G. (2010c). *Marx and Heidegger*. Philadelphia. PA: Gerry Stahl at Lulu. Retrieved from http://GerryStahl.net/elibrary/marx.

Stahl, G. (2010d). *Tacit and explicit understanding*. Philadelphia, PA: Gerry Stahl at Lulu. Retrieved from http://GerryStahl.net/elibrary/tacit.

Stahl, G., Koschmann, T., & Suthers, D. (2006). Computer-supported collaborative learning: An historical perspective. In R. K. Sawyer (Ed.), *Cambridge handbook of the learning sciences* (pp. 409–426). Cambridge, England: Cambridge University Press. Retrieved from http://GerryStahl.net/elibrary/global.

Suchman, L. (1987). *Plans and situated actions: The problem of human-machine communication*. Cambridge, England: Cambridge University Press.

Teasley, S. D., & Roschelle, J. (1993). Constructing a joint problem space: The computer as a tool for sharing knowledge. In S. P. Lajoie & S. J. Derry (Eds.), *Computers as cognitive tools* (pp. 229–258). Hillsdale, NJ: Erlbaum.

Turing, A. (1937). On computable numbers, with an application to the entscheidungsproblem. *Proceedings of the London Mathematical Society, 2*(1), 230.

Vygotsky, L. (1978). *Mind in society*. Cambridge, MA: Harvard University Press. (Original work published 1930)

Wegerif, R. (2007). *Dialogic, education and technology: Expanding the space of learning*. New York: Kluwer-Springer.

Wells, G. (1999). *Dialogic inquiry: Towards a socio-cultural practice and theory of education*. Cambridge, England: Cambridge University Press.

Winograd, T., & Flores, F. (1986). *Understanding computers and cognition: A new foundation of design*. Reading, MA: Addison-Wesley.

Wittgenstein, L. (1953). *Philosophical investigations*. New York: Macmillan.

Wittgenstein, L. (1974). *Tractatus logico philosophicus*. London: Routledge. (Original work published 1921)

II
Studying Collaborative Learning

5

QUANTITATIVE METHODS FOR STUDYING SMALL GROUPS

ULRIKE CRESS AND FRIEDRICH WILHELM HESSE

Knowledge Media Research Center, Tübingen, Germany

Quantitative methodology includes various different methods of gathering and analyzing empirical data. What these methods have in common is that they do not just categorize phenomena but measure them and express their relationships in terms of quantity. If applied to collaborative learning, these methods allow researchers to analyze both learning processes and learning outcomes of individuals, interaction processes among group members, and learning outcomes of groups. The aim of quantitative research is to go beyond simply describing processes and outcomes, but to make and test predictions about the interrelation of these processes and about factors that trigger them. For understanding the quantitative research approach, we will first describe some fundamental concepts of quantitative methodology: its hypothetico-deductive approach, its experimental logic, operationalization, measurement, and use of inferential statistics. On this basis, we will present some quantitative methods which are suited for collaborative learning (CL) studies. But quantitative research is a wide field, and this chapter will not be able to give an exhaustive overview of its methods. Here we would refer readers to standard literature like Everitt and Howell (2005), or Keeves (1997). The focus of this chapter is on showing quantitative approaches for analyzing data of collaborative learning. These consist of different types: data that describe interactional processes, data that describe individuals within groups, and data that describe groups. Considering this specific structure of data, we will introduce the concept of *units of analysis* and describe *events*, *interactions*, *persons*, and *groups* as relevant units in the context of analyzing collaborative learning. For each of these levels of analysis, we will explain some typical quantitative methods and provide examples from CL-relevant studies. In addition, one specific example will be cited throughout the whole chapter. This will make it easier to concentrate on relevant aspects of all the methods which are presented here.

FUNDAMENTAL CONCEPTS OF QUANTITATIVE RESEARCH

Theory-Based Approach

Quantitative research describes phenomena in the world and their interrelations in terms of quantity. In many cases it takes a *theory-based approach*: It starts with some theory about interrelations between constructs, and deduces from that a prediction about what will happen in the observable world. Such predictions, which serve as hypotheses, are then tested by observing empirical phenomena. With the help of statistical analyses, the researcher then decides whether or not the observed empirical phenomena are congruent with these predictions. This leads to the acceptance or rejection of the hypotheses and allows maintaining or falsifying the proposed theory (Popper, 1963). Figure 5.1 shows this hypothetico-deductive approach.

Theories mostly focus on causal relationships and try to explain phenomena as effects of well-defined causes. The fewest assumptions a theory needs to explain a phenomenon (principle of parsimony) the better it is. Based on this approach, quantitative research often aims at explaining as much as possible of occurring variation with as few predictors as possible.

The hypothetico-deductive model leads to the distinction between independent and dependent variables. The first describes causes, the second effects. The causal interrelation between both can best be tested with experiments, where different experimental conditions are established by experimental manipulation, which only differ with regard to the value of the independent variable. The subjects are assigned randomly to different experimental conditions. This ensures that differences between subjects in different conditions will not result from any other feature than the value of the independent variable. Only experiments can test causal relationships, because only randomization guarantees that variation in the dependent variable can be attributed—in a logically correct way—to variation in the independent variable.

Let us clarify these fundamental concepts of the quantitative approach by referring to a fictitious empirical study (which will serve as an example throughout this chapter). The example is simplified, but describes a prototypical research question in CL (as, for example, in Haake & Pfister, 2010; Rummel, Spada, & Hauser, 2008; Fischer et al. this volume; O'Donnell this volume): A researcher would like to know (the research question) if scripts are an effective way of instructing learners. Her research interest results from a theory—it may be an implicit underlying theory—that scripting has some influence on

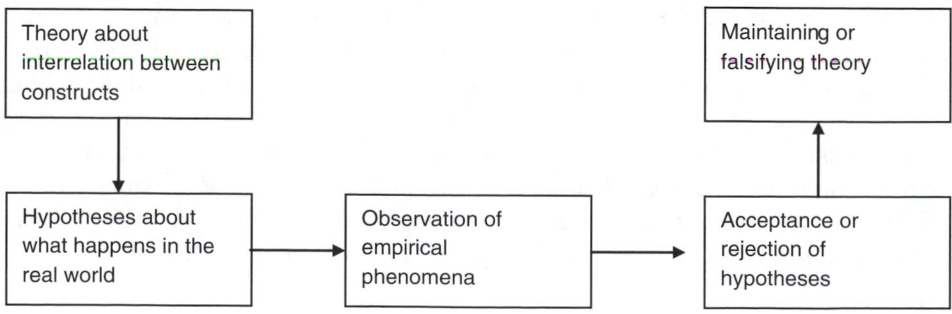

Figure 5.1 Hypothetico-deductive approach of quantitative research.

cooperative learning. So she has a theoretical assumption about some causal relationship. This assumption includes, at least, an idea of what makes cooperative learning effective, and how an interaction script might support such effective learning. As a first step, our researcher makes this theoretical consideration explicit, and finds an adequate operationalization of the script (independent variable) and a way of measuring effective cooperative learning (dependent variable). She then develops a prototypical script, with all relevant features, and plans an experiment with two conditions. In the experimental condition, groups of three learners (triads) have to work with this script, in the other condition (control condition), the triads do not use a script.

Operationalization and Measurement

As quantitative research typically starts with some theoretical assumption, the issue of adequate *operationalization* is crucial. What needs to be determined is the way in which theoretical constructs and their interrelations are made observable. Which variables serve as independent or dependent variables, how are they defined and measured? In the example about effects of scripting, the researcher first has to define what a script is, what its relevant features are, and how its effect on cooperative learning can be measured. The operationalization of the script (as independent variable) is good if the script which is used in the experiment is a prototypical realization of the underlying theoretical idea what scripts are. The goodness of the operationalization of the dependent variable can be described with its *reliability* and *validity* (Carmines & Zeller, 1979). A measurement is reliable if it is exact and if, for example, a retest turns out similar results, and it is valid if it really measures what it claims to measure. Testing the validity of a measurement may be difficult. A valid measure should show high correlations with other measures of the same concept, and low correlations with measurements of other concepts (construct validity). In our example, the researcher also has to decide how to measure the dependent variable. She may decide to test "effective cooperative learning" in three different ways: (a) by categorizing the learners' contributions during their interaction into the four categories questions, answers, statements, and off-task; (b) by measuring each learner's performance in an individual postexperimental knowledge test; (c) by measuring performance of the triads by checking the time they need for solving a following collaborative transfer task. Each of these measurements covers a different aspect of the idea of "effective collaborative learning," and each of these operationalizations leads to a different dependent variable. Taken as a whole, this may be a valid operationalization of the researcher's idea of collaborative learning.

Internal, External, and Statistical Validity

Not only single measurements should be valid. The study as a whole should be valid as well. The term *external validity* describes whether the results of a study can be generalized. In order to allow generalizations about other people, the participants of a study have to be a random sample of all learners covered by the theory. The participants of the study have to be *stochastically independent*, which means that each person of a population has the same chance of being part of the sample (this may be a problem in CL studies as we will describe in the next sections). External validity also requires that the results of the study can be generalized to other situations. This may be a problem with experimental studies. Experimental situations are sometimes very constructed and artificial, and generalizing their results to real-life situations may be critical. In our example, a study may show that a script leads to effective cooperative learning in the experiment. But it will still remain an open question whether this effect would also occur in a real school setting. It may be possible that in real life, where learning is affected by many different circumstances, scripts have no strong effect, or that the effect of a script is quite different from the experimental situation, in which all other influences were kept under control. Because experimental research works according to the principle of parsimony, and only focuses on the effect of a few independent variables on a few dependent variables, it does not take into account the complexity of all possible influencing factors. So it may lack external validity. But this tight focus is necessary for ensuring high *internal* validity. This kind of validity describes that an observed effect in the dependent variable can be attributed in a logically correct way to the independent variable. So, if we try to prove some causality, we need a high degree of internal validity. And this can only be taken for granted if the experimental conditions differ systematically *only* in the dependent variable, and in no other feature. And this is exactly what experiments with their randomized research designs ensure. But, of course, the results of an experiment can only then be generalized if its conclusions are statically valid. This means that *inferential statistics* must be used. Only then will data provided by a random sample allow valid statements about the respective population.

What would these fundamental concepts of quantitative research mean if applied to our example, a prototypical study about scripts? The researcher would have to select a representative sample of students as participants in her experiment. She would then have to assign them randomly to both conditions (with and without scripts). After conducting the experiment, she would compare the number of task-relevant statements, the learner's performance in the knowledge test, and problem solving time between both conditions. Using inferential statistics, she would decide if differences between the two conditions are statistically significant, that is to say, that they are unlikely to have occurred just by chance, and can be generalized to the population. On the basis of these results, she would maintain her theory that scripts are effective tools for cooperative learning, or consider it falsified.

EXPERIMENTAL AND NONEXPERIMENTAL RESEARCH

Most quantitative research is theory-based research, but it is not necessarily experimental. Quantitative research also plays a role in real settings, with people who act in their real everyday environment. In so-called *quasi-experimental* studies, people belong to naturally given conditions. Here, no randomization is possible, and people who belong to different conditions will not just differ in the value of one independent variable, but also in many other characteristics. Such studies raise the question of internal validity, because differences in the dependent variable have not necessarily been affected by differences of the independent variable. In our example about the effects of scripting, a quasi-experimental study would deal with naturally occurring groups who are working with or without scripts. Such groups might, for example, consist of different school classes. But these classes would not only differ in their use of scripts. There may be other differences as well: teachers who are using scripts might be more experienced in instructing pupils for cooperative work than teachers who have never used such scripts. So the use of scripts and the teachers' experience may be confounded. But when such data have been obtained, quantitative researchers try in many cases to find evidence for causality by statistically controlling for covariates. For example, Dewiyanti, Brand-Gruwel, Jochems, and Broers (2007) predicted students' satisfaction of CSCL courses by referring to characteristics of the individuals and to courses in which they had participated. Campbell and Stanley (1963) describe experimental and nonexperimental designs, their threads for internal and external validity, and ways to handle them.

However, finding causal effects is not always the aim of quantitative research. Some studies just examine relationships between variables. This is done by using correlations or regression models. They describe relationships between variables, without differentiating between cause and effect. For example, Hijzen, Boekaerts, and Vedder (2006) predicted the quality of cooperative learning by referring to different student goals. This type of studies also requires operationalization, but they do not distinguish between independent and dependent variables. They just show a covariation between variables. Such an exploratory approach may be necessary if a theory is not developed well enough to make a prediction. Quantitative research may even sometimes take an *inductive* approach and take phenomena into account that emerge from empirical data. This would apply, for example, when a researcher conducts a post hoc search for factors, which could explain a pattern found in the data. For example Dehler, Bodemer, Buder, and Hesse (2009) and Hmelo-Silver, Chernobilsky, and Jordan (2008) contrasted effective and noneffective groups in order to identify relevant processes. But in the logic of quantitative research, such exploratory analyses are not an end in itself, they provide just a starting point for generating hypotheses, which would then need to be tested in a hypothetico-deductive approach. Only then will it be possible to generalize results and make predictions about relationships.

METHODS ACCORDING TO DIFFERENT LEVELS OF ANALYSIS

CL research deals with different levels and granularities:

- the level of single events (which are the elements of interaction)
- the level of interactions (which are the sequences of such events)
- the level of learners
- the level of the group

It will always depend on the focus of a study and the underlying theory which of these units of analysis has to be considered. In turn, the choice of the unit of analysis will determine which statistical method is appropriate. For each of the four units of analysis, we provide some typical methods and refer to our example about the effects of scripts. In addition, we provide prototypical examples from previously published CL studies. A handbook chapter like this one cannot, of course, provide an exhaustive survey; what is intended here is an overview of a variety of different research questions according to the different levels.

Methods for Describing and Quantifying Single Events

The lowest level of analysis of CL deals with single activities of individual learners. These are the elements of the collaborative processes. *Quantitative content analysis* (Berelson, 1952; Rourke & Anderson, 2004) identifies important events that occur during the learners' interaction, and analyzes the frequencies of these events. In CL, such important events may consist of communicative acts, like utterances, questions, answers, or written messages, as well as nonverbal behavior, like gestures and other cue actions. It depends on the focus of study and underlying theory regarding which events are seen as important, and how these events are made observable and measurable. In order to produce reliable and valid measurements, several conditions must be fulfilled: (a) The procedure which creates the learning and interacting situation must be described in such a way that other researchers are able to replicate the study. In order to be able to categorize the content of communication, people's communication and interaction have to be segmented into units. For such segmentation, *manifest units* may be used (e.g., words or messages), but underlying *latent units* (e.g. meaning units, see Rourke, Anderson, Garrison, & Archer, 2000) may also be suitable. (b) The categorization should be based on a well-defined coding schema which guarantees a high degree of reliability. (c) The codes which are used should be derived from the research question, in the sense that these codes are valid operationalizations of the underlying theoretical concepts and constructs.

The coding schema itself provides categorical codes, which are in most cases (but not necessarily) mutually exclusive and exhaustive. This means that the use of a coding schema produces nominal data. The reliability of coding should be measured with the interrater reliability; this describes to what extent different people, who have coded the same content independently from each other, achieve similar results. The easiest way of measuring interrater reliability is the relative amount of agreement (Holsti, 1969), but this will not take into account the fact that different raters may also have agreed by chance. Measurements which correct this random agreement are *Cohen's kappa* (Cohen, 1960) and *Krippendorff's alpha* (Krippendorff, 2004). Cohen's kappa calculates the chance-corrected agreement between two raters, while Krippendorff's alpha deals with any number of raters and also takes into account the magnitude of misses. *Intraclass correlation* may also be used for calculating interrater correlation for more than two raters (Shrout & Fleiss, 1979).

If codes are assigned to latent units, not only the classification of content, but also its segmentation might jeopardize reliability (Strijbos, Martens, Prins, & Jochems, 2006). When referring to "meaning units," segmentation and coding are intertwined. Different raters may segment differently, which leads to overlapping units with different codes. This causes serious problems. Strijbos and Fischer (2007) state that finding the adequate unit of analysis is one of the big methodological challenges of CL research, and Strijbos et al. (2006) propose a segmentation procedure which is systematic and independent of the coding categories.

The *validity of a coding schema results* from adequate operationalization of the underlying theory (Rourke & Anderson, 2004). At the conceptual level, the coding schema should capture all relevant aspects of the theoretical construct. But at the empirical level, it will often be difficult to check validity. One possible way of estimating the validity of a coding schema is by comparing classification results of different coding schemas. A valid coding schema will lead to measurements that are consistent with those obtained through other methods. Another indicator for high validity is measurement that is sensitive to group differences or experimental interventions (e.g., Boxtel, van der Linden, & Kanselaar, 2000; Hron, Cress, Hammer, & Friedrich, 2007).

Strijbos and Stahl (2007) have drawn attention to the following paradox of reliable and valid coding in exploratory CL research: If research attempts to focus on unique interactions, it cannot use preexisting categories, because these will not be able to capture new, context-specific phenomena. For capturing these phenomena, new categories have to be defined in an inductive way. But these new categories lack reliability and validity. From a methodological point of view, this paradox cannot be solved by a single study. Coding schemas can only be tested for reliability and validity if the critical events occur frequently. So the paradox can only be solved in a deductive way: It requires, first of all, an assumption about the occurrence of the relevant critical events, and on the basis of this assumption a researcher can then create a situation in which these events are expected to occur frequently. A predefined coding schema will then be able to capture these critical events, and the reliability and validity of this schema can be measured. This means that, from the point of view of quantitative research, new and surprising events cannot be treated adequately in one study. When new phenomena have been observed, further studies are needed in order to be able to measure them reliably.

Because of this need to obtain many data and carry out multiple studies in order to test reliability and validity of a coding schema, we recommend reuse or adaptation of an existing coding schema where possible. In the last years, several suitable schemas have been introduced. De Wever, Schellens, Valcke, and Van Keer (2006) give an overview of 15 instruments which were used for analyzing online asynchronous discussion groups. The authors provide information about their theoretical foundation, reliability, and validity. Apart from that, there exist many other well-established coding schemas; for example, the multidimensional coding schema for individual actions in interactive group processes by Chiu (2001), or the functional category system by Poole and Homes (1995).

How can the data which result from coding schemas be analyzed? As described above, categorizing single events leads to nominal data. Such data can just be analyzed by counting the occurrence of the single categories, or by depicting the percentage of categories (e.g., Kanuka, Rourke, & Laflamme, 2007). This may be done for each learner or for the learning group. If we want to use inductive statistics and compare different situations, we should be aware that the single events are not stochastically independent. If we code, for example, learners' utterances by categorizing questions, answers, and statements, we might find that the learning partners show a symmetric interaction: If one learner asks many questions, this may induce many answers by the other learning partners. This means that different learners will not behave independently from each other. So the frequency of single events describes interaction within the group, not the behavior of independent learners. What we can do is to compare frequencies of events between different groups. But then the level of analysis is that of the group, not of the event. In our example about scripting, we might, for example, compare triads working with and without scripts with regard to the frequency of off-task talk. In such an analysis, the data will be based on a categorization of single events, but these will then be pooled within groups, and different groups will be compared. Many CL studies have taken this approach (e.g. Hron et al., 2007; Meier, Spada, & Rummel, 2007; Wolfe, 2007).

Methods that Focus on Interactions

In collaborative learning, it is often the interaction between learners that is of interest. Analysis of interaction processes is, in most cases, based on a categorization of single events, as described in the previous section. But it is mainly the sequence of these events that is meaningful for considering interaction. One way of analyzing interaction quantitatively is sequence analysis for categorical data (Bakeman & Gottman, 1997). It includes different methods; for example, lag-sequential analysis or log-linear methods. Even if these have been not used very often in CL research so far, they will be presented here briefly, because of their great potential for dealing with sequential processes.

Lag-sequential analysis describes sequences of events as Markov chains, in which current events determine the probability of events in the next period (Bakeman, Adamson, & Strisik, 1995; Bakeman & Gottman, 1997; Faraone & Dorfman, 1987; Gottman & Roy, 1990). So lag-sequence analysis focuses on transitional probabilities (probability of one event following the other), which describe typical patterns of event sequences. A typical research question is presented in Hou, Chang, and Sung's (2008) study, which searched for typical sequences of problem-solving events like "proposing a problem," "proposing a solution," "comparing," and "forming a conclusion." Jeong (2005) illustrates the use of lag-sequential analysis nicely. As a first step, events must be classified, using a coding schema. Then frequency with which each type of event category is followed by other event categories has to be analyzed. We might describe this process using prototypical data from our example about scripting. Here a coding schema could classify the events into (a) questions, (b) answers, and (c) statements. A prototypical sequence could be as follows:

a b c a b b c a b c b a b b c

Out of such a sequence, a frequency matrix may be constructed which shows how often each one of the event types succeeds the others. For constructing it, a moving two-unit window may be used which slides across the sequence.

(a b) c a b b c a b c b a b b c
a (b c) a b b c a b c b a b b c
a b (c a) b b c a b c b a b b c

The window moves across the stream of codes and we can tally the frequency of each event pair. This leads to the frequency matrix shown in Table 5.1. It shows, for example, that a question has never been succeeded by another question, but four times by an answer.

As a second step, these absolute frequencies are converted into relative frequencies. These describe the transitional probability that a question, answer or statement is succeeded by a question, answer or other statement (see Table 5.2).

Table 5.1 Frequency Matrix

	Succeeded by			
	Question (a)	**Answer (b)**	**Statement (c)**	**Total**
Question (a)	0	4	0	4
Answer (b)	1	2	4	7
Statement (c)	2	1	0	3
Total	3	7	4	14

Table 5.2 Transitional Probability Matrix

	Succeeded by		
	Question (a)	**Answer (b)**	**Statement (c)**
Question (a)	.00	1.00	.00
Answer (b)	.14	.29	.57
Statement (c)	.67	.33	.00

These probabilities are *conditional* probabilities. They describe the probability that an event category occurs if a preceding event has taken place. This transition matrix is the base of the transitional state diagram shown in Figure 5.2. Here the thickness of a pointed arrow represents transition probability.

In the last few years, the use of such transition state diagrams has become quite common in CL research, as a way of detecting and visualizing patterns of event sequences (e.g. Erkens, Kanselaar, Prangsma, & Jaspers, 2003; Hou, Sung, & Chang, 2009; Jeong, 2003; Jeong & Joung, 2007; Kanselaar et al., 2002).

Lag-sequential analysis may not only be applied to two-event sequences, but also to sequences containing more than two events. With three events, the window that slides over the event sequences will have three positions, and all possible chains of three events have to be tallied. This leads to a three-dimensional frequency matrix.

The longer the sequence of events, the (exponentially) larger the matrix of possible transitions will be. So with three-event sequences and a code of five categories, we would get a matrix of 125 cells (5^3). This means that with many codes, and longer sequences, the expected frequencies and probabilities will be very small. According to Bakeman and Quera (1995) and Tabachnick and Fidell (1989), the sample size of events should exceed five times the number of cells, and 80% of the cells should have an expected probability of greater than 5. This means that for longer sequences enormously large amounts of data are required to achieve valid results.

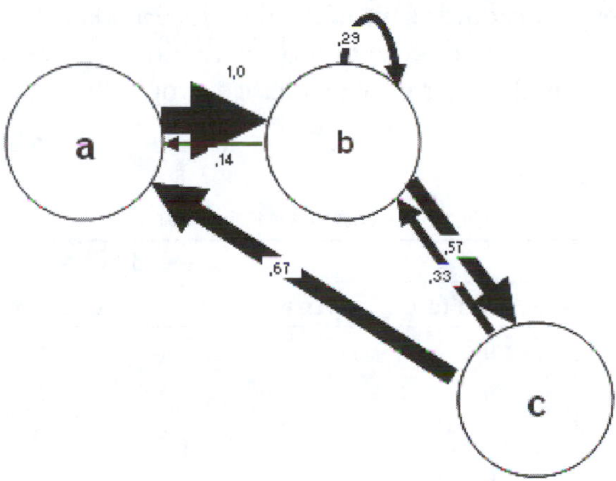

Figure 5.2 Transition state diagram for event sequences in (1).

Lag-sequential analysis is easy to use and flexible. It may be used for different types of sequences. The example shown above used overlapping sequences, in which the window slides in such a way that each event is observed twice: first as a prior event, and then as a succeeding event. But nonoverlapping chains are also possible. If, in our example, the script provided different roles, and one student acted as a mentor (X) and the other as a mentee (Y), we could analyze how the mentor reacts to the mentee. In order to tally the appropriate chains, we would have to use nonoverlapping windows.

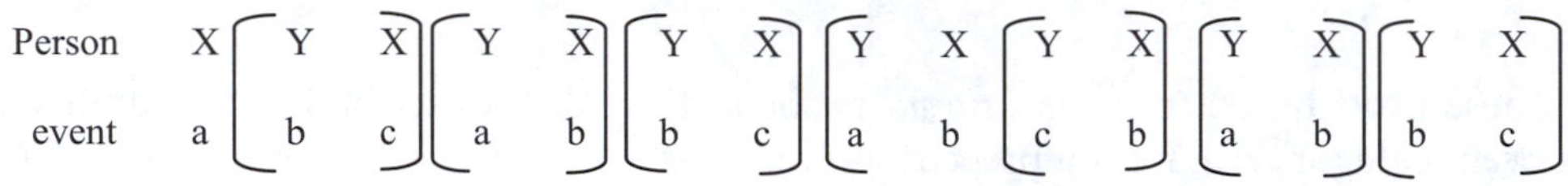

Person X [Y X] [Y X] [Y X] [Y X] [Y X] [Y X] [Y X]
event a [b c] [a b] [b c] [a b] [c b] [a b] [b c]

This would lead to a frequency matrix which is different from the one shown in Table 5.1.

Furthermore, not just a lag of 1 may be of interest, but also events that follow later. We can assume, for example, that with a larger group, a mentor will not be able to answer all questions immediately. The mentor's answers may follow after two, three, or even more events. This would require lags of 2, 3, or more in our analysis. For this purpose, a moving window with varying sizes of lags might be considered, and it could be tallied how often the tutor (mentor) answers within the next 2 or 3 events after a question.

These different examples show that a specific research question defines the way of tallying the relevant chains of a sequence, in order to obtain the adequate frequency matrix. It strongly depends on the research question and the underlying theory which type of sequence chain is of interest. For this reason, lag-sequential analysis is a very typical statistical procedure for the hypothetico-deductive model, where first a theoretical model is stated and, accordingly, the appropriate operationalization is found.

With lag-sequential analysis the use of inferential statistical may be problematic. Early articles have pointed out that binomial *z scores* can be used to test individual pairs of events for significance (Bakeman, 1978; Sackett, 1979). In this sense, in Table 5.2 and Figure 5.2, *z-values* could be calculated for all nine transition probabilities. This would make it possible to detect if some of them occur more frequently than would have been expected by chance. Several more recent articles have expressed some concern about such an exploratory procedure (Allison & Liker, 1982; Bakeman & Quera, 1995; Faraone & Dorfman, 1987), because the use of too many binomial tests may lead to too many significant results, which occur only by chance simply because of the large number of significance tests.

Table 5.3 Frequency Matrix for the Mentor's Teaction on the Mentee's Actions

Y	Succeeded by X's			
	Question (a)	**Answer (b)**	**Statement (c)**	**Total**
Question (a)	0	3	0	3
Answer (b)	0	0	2	2
Statement (c)	0	2	0	2
Total	0	5	2	7

Bearing in mind this problem, the use of *log-linear models* has become common for some types of research. These provide a whole-table view and allow the use of omnibus tests instead of many binomial tests (Bakeman & Quera, 1995). Log-linear models are the standard procedure for analyzing multidimensional contingency tables. As the frequency matrixes of lag-sequential methods are, in fact, such contingency tables, log-linear models are well suited to analyze event sequences. Log-linear models are rarely used in CL research, but we will present their basic principles here.

Log-linear models are ANOVA-like procedures, which interpret the rows and columns of a contingency table as factors. Log-linear models define the observed cell frequencies as a function of these factors. In a two-way table, we can model cell frequencies in terms of the average count (grand mean), a column effect, a row effect, and row-by-column interactions. In a first step, we have to specify a model, which means we have to specify if the observed cell frequencies are explained by just the grand mean, additionally by a row-and-column effect, or additionally by an interaction between both. Then the cell frequencies, which are expected under this model, are calculated. A statistical test (Pearsons chi-square or likelihood-ratio chi-square) then analyzes how well this model fits the observed data. The log-linear procedure compares different models and their goodness-of-fit value, in order to find the least complex model that, nonetheless, achieves a good fit to the data.

Let us explain this with the data from Table 5.1 (even if the very low cell frequencies make these data not very suited for the use of log-linear modelling). Let us name the *observed* cell frequencies f_{ij}, with i describing the rows and j describing the columns. Different models provide *expected* cell frequencies m_{ij}, which are then compared with the observed f_{ij} (which are the cell frequencies given in Table 5.1). For each model, the following Pearson chi-square evaluates how well the model fits the observed data.

$$X^2 = \sum_i \sum_j \frac{(f_j - m_j)^2}{m_j} \qquad \text{Eq. 1}$$

The least complex model is the *null model*. It states that all cell f_{ij} frequencies differ only randomly from the grand mean. So under the null model, we would expect that questions, answers and statements are equiprobable and that all cells will just randomly differ from 14/9 = 1.56 (overall-total through number of cells). With Eq. 1 this leads to a chi-square of $X^2 = 20.45$ with df = 8. The high value shows that the model does not fit the data very well.

A more complex model would be one that states that the event types (questions, answers, statements) have different probabilities, but that succeeding events are independent from the preceding ones. This would allow two main effects (varying row totals and varying column totals), but no interaction. The expected cell frequencies of such an independency model can be calculated by the formula:

$m_j = \dfrac{f_{i+}f_{+j}}{f_{++}}$ with f_{i+} being the total of the regarding row i and f_{+j} the total of the regarding column j, and f_{++} the overall total. Table 5.4 shows the frequencies which would be expected under this model.

With Equation (1) this model give a chi-square of $X^2 = 10.7$ with df = 4. Even if this chi-square is lower than the one of the null model, also this chi-square is significant.

Table 5.4 Expected Frequencies under the Main Effects Model

	Succeeded by		
	Question (a)	**Answer (b)**	**Statement (c)**
Question (a)	0.9	2	1.1
Answer (b)	0.6	1.5	0.9
Statement (c)	0.6	1.5	0.9

This shows that this model does not fit the data very well either. This means that a model must be accepted here which assumes that rows and columns are associated. In our example, this would be true of the *saturated model.* Saturated models take into account all possible effects: row effects, column effects and interaction effects. In our example, the saturated log-linear model allows that the three rows have different totals (row effect), that also the three columns have different totals (column effect), and that all cells have different means (interaction). In a saturated model, the expected frequencies are identical with the observed frequencies, so it cannot be tested for significance. But because of the large chi-square of the independency model, we must assume that columns and rows are associated and that preceding events determine succeeding ones. In order be more precise and to determine if some type of events occur quite frequently after other types, the *adjusted residuals* may be used. This statistical method gauges the extent to which a specific f_{ij} differs from its expected value m_{ij}. So it is a kind of post hoc test after a model has turned out a significant result in a preliminary omnibus test (for a further discussion see Bakeman & Quera, 1995).

For tables of higher dimension we can specify more main factors and interactions. Then the log-linear models will become more complex, and it is the task of the researcher to specify in detail which sequence patterns are expected. As in the example, significance tests estimate the probability of the observed data under each specified model. The larger this probability is, the better will the model fit the data. An example of the use of log-linear models is the study of Marttunen (1997). He studied e-mails with counterarguments and examined the associations between four different features: *level of counterargumentation* (good, moderate, or poor), *time of sending the message* (first/second half of the study), and *mode* (discussion vs. seminar). He started from a saturated model in which all the possible main and interaction effects of the four variables were included. Then all those parameters that were not statistically significant were dropped from the model step by step by starting from higher-order terms, ending at a minimal acceptable model. This final model had a main effect of *mode* (more counterarguments in discussion mode than in seminar mode), and an interaction between *mode* and *level of counterargumentation*, showing that there is more good or moderate counterargumentation in discussion mode than in seminar mode.

Log-linear modeling can be done with standard procedures in SPSS or SAS. Lag-sequential methods may not be applied so easily, but Bakeman, Adamson, and Strisik (1995) and O'Connor (1999) describe relevant SPSS and SAS procedures, and specific software tools were developed by Bakeman and Quera (http://www2.gsu.edu/~psyrab/gseq/index.html). For lag-sequential analysis and the construction of a transition state diagram, Jeong provides the easy-to-use Discussion Analysis Tool (http://myweb.fsu.edu/ajeong/dat/).

All described methods for analyzing interaction depend on frequency tables, which aggregate the relevant event chains across the whole sequence. So the models assume that event sequences are homogeneous across time and will not systematically differ between periods of time. But homogeneity is not always what occurs during collaboration. Group work often will be carried out in different phases, in which people interact differently. An analysis of event sequences with lag-sequential methods or log-linear models requires data from a stationary process. If nonstationary processes with phases of different interaction patterns are considered, an inductive approach for defining the breakpoints that divide the stationary sequences is described by Chiu (2008).

Methods that Focus on Individuals

The unit of analysis which most psychological or educational studies address is that of individual learners. Whenever the (potential) influence of a tool, an instruction, or a feature of a learning environment on learners' behavior, beliefs, or performance is the topic of a study, it will have to focus on the individual learner as the relevant unit of analysis. But in CL research this may be a pitfall. CL has to do with learners who collaborate, so these learners are generally nested within groups. We have to be aware that individual learners within a group are not stochastically independent. They do interact and this will influence their behavior and learning results.

In our example (triads work with and without scripts) we may be interested in finding out if a learner who works with a script shows less off-task talk and achieves higher scores in the knowledge post-test than a learner without a script. But it would not be permissible to compare the means of all learners working with and without scripts by using a standard method like t-test or ANOVA. This is not possible because all learners worked in groups, so the group mates have influenced each other. The resulting stochastical interdependency can be measured by intraclass correlation. It describes the higher (or lower) similarity of individuals within a group, compared to the similarity of people who belong to different groups. This is identical with the proportion of variance in the outcome variable which is caused by group membership. If the intraclass correlation in a given data set is significant (for the use of different test see McGraw & Wong, 1996), it will be necessary to deal explicitly with the hierarchical data structure and use multilevel methods (see Janssen et al., this volume). It would not be possible in this case just to pool individual learners across all groups and compare their means. Standard methods, such as OLS Regression or standard Analysis of Variance, rely heavily on the assumption of independent observation. If these standard methods are used and individuals pooled across different groups, then the standard error is systematically underestimated, and this will lead to an alpha-error inflation with an overestimation of significant results (Bonito, 2002; Kenny & Judd, 1986).

That means that a study which has its focus at the individual level and aims at predicting individual behavior or individual learning outcome *must* consider group effects. One approach, which is common in social psychology but little used in CL, is to deal with the group effect in an experimental way and to hold group behavior constant for each individual in the experiment. This may be achieved by using confederates (stooges), who simulate group mates and act in exactly the same way vis-à-vis each subject. In virtual settings, in which the group members do not interact face-to-face, the behavior of the group mates can be staged easily: A person is then told to be part of a group, but all online activities of the other "group" members are simulated on the basis of a standardized protocol. Then the individual subject behaves like being in a group, responds to the "group," but all the participants are statistically independent, because they do not influence each other. Simulating other group members eliminates group effects. In addition, the researcher can systematically vary the "group's" behavior as an independent variable and measure its influence on the behavior of individual learners. Using this method, Cress (2005) analyzed whether a group's sharing behavior influenced the individuals' behavior in a knowledge-sharing task, and Kimmerle and Cress (2008) showed that a group awareness tool was differentially effective with people in a group with a high and low degree of interpersonal trust. By simulating groups, it is possible to study aptitude treatment interactions, in which the aptitude variable is an individual-level variable and the treatment is a group-level one. Buder and Bodemer (2008) worked with simulated ratings of group members. Learners with a correct view of a Physics controversy, but in the role of a minority in a fictitious group, were confronted with a majority who presented a plausible but incorrect view of the matter. The experiment then compared learners working with and without a group awareness tool. In an analogous experiment, Dehler, Bodemer, Buder, and Hesse (2011) manipulated the knowledge distribution among dyads and measured the quality of a learner's explanation to questions of their learning partners. These questions were also faked.

But there are only few factors and short-term processes of social interaction that can be analyzed by experimentally controlling group effects. By faking activities of group members, group interaction is reduced to unidirectional effects from (simulated) teammates to target persons. *Real* interactions, however, will not only consist of unidirectional effects; people's behavior may be influenced by the group, but they also influence the group itself. This complex interaction cannot be considered by faking group interaction.

Another way of dealing with group effects is the actor-partner-interaction model (APIM), as proposed by Kenny and colleagues (Kashy & Kenny, 2000; Kenny, Mannetti, Pierro, Livi, & Kashy, 2002), but it has to our knowledge not been used in CL research so far.

Methods that Focus on Groups

CL is based on the assumption that learning in groups will not only influence the way in which learners interact, but also their learning results. We may even go as far as stating that CL research will naturally have to focus on groups as its unit of analysis. It assumes synergistic processes, which describe that what is going on in the group is not simply determined by individual characteristics of the group members; instead it proposes that the group situation introduces new processes and shapes the individuals' behavior and learning in specific ways. The interesting point in many cases is not the behavior of the different group members, but what happens with the group as a whole. Does the group construct new knowledge? Does collaborative meaning making happen?

For analyzing these processes at the level of the group, we can use all standard methods of inferential statistics, because different groups are stochastically independent. With t-tests or ANOVAs, we can test if groups from different experimental conditions differ significantly. As dependent variables we can use measures of the whole group, but also aggregated measures from group members, or events which have taken place within the group. In our example about scripting, possible dependent variables could be the learning time that dyads spent on a transfer group task (group measure), the mean of the learners' performance in the posttest (aggregated measure), or the number of different events which occurred during interaction (pooled measure of event frequencies). At the level of the group, all aggregated lower-level measures can serve as dependent variables: frequencies, means, sums, standards deviations, or any other transformed measures about events or individual scores. We could, for example, describe the heterogeneity of a group (group level variable) by the standard deviation of the prior-knowledge test scores of the group members (aggregated individual level variable). If we do not have an experimental design, we may use correlations to describe unidirectional relations, and we can use structural equation models to model causal relationships in nonrandomized settings. So once the group is used as the unit of analysis, all statistical methods are open. But it should be mentioned that the number of units which define our degree of freedom here is the number of *groups*, not the number of individual learners or distinct events. This leads to the practical problem that we need many more participants than we would need for analyses which consider the individual learner as their unit of analysis. With dyads, we need twice as many learners, with groups of n, we need the n-fold number of learners to perform tests with adequate power. Looking at results of any group-level analysis, we have to be aware that they describe groups, not individuals. Such results cannot simply be applied to the individual level. If a study has determined, for example, that groups who are more active achieve higher learning outcomes, we may *not* conclude likewise that the same correlation exists at the level of individuals and that a learner's activity predicts his or her individual learning outcome. This failure of transferring group-level effects to individual-level effects is known as the Robinson effect (Robinson, 1950), and was one of the reasons for developing specific methods for handling nested data. We will briefly describe multilevel analysis in the next section.

An additional, and also more practical, problem may be that we are really wasting data if we have obtained many data from group members during experiments, but just analyzed them at the level of the group. So, if possible, we will prefer *multilevel methods*, which are able to consider more than one level (see chapter 6 of this volume).

Apart from classical methods of inferential statistics, which can be used for all levels of analysis (if the units are stochastically independent), one method is particularly useful for describing groups and becoming more and more common in both CL and CSCL research: *social network analysis* (SNA). This method is based on analyzing interactions between group members, and it visualizes and measures these relations. For example, the e-mail traffic within a group constitutes a network, in which people may be represented as nodes, and the number of messages exchanged between them may be represented by weighted links. Each group member can be described by his or her location within the network. SNA provides a variety of measures to describe the centrality of individuals: *degree centrality* describes how many connections one individual has; *betweenness centrality* describes the extent to which a person connects different parts of the network; and *closeness centrality* describes the mean shortest distances to other persons. *Network centrality* describes centralization of the network as a whole. De Laat, Lally, Lipponen, and Simon (2007) use SNA to describe the interaction pattern between learners in a learning task during three different phases. Kimmerle, Moskaliuk, Harrer, and Cress (2010) use a two-mode SNA to describe the coevolution of a wiki artifact and its authors (Cress & Kimmerle, 2008). This two-mode SNA is based on links between webpages as well as links between authors and webpages. The dynamic SNA depicts the dynamic process of the growing network of webpages and the activities of its authors. SNA is an exploratory method, which allows looking at a network as a whole. It has frequently been used for purposes of evaluation (Martinez et al., 2006; Nurmela, Lehtinen, & Palonen, 1999), but, so far, not for testing hypotheses.

INTEGRATION OF DIFFERENT LEVELS

Statistical analyses may be conducted at each of four level of analysis (events, interactions, persons, groups), and the previous sections of this chapter have cited studies which focused on one of these levels in different ways. When we use data from individuals who interact in groups, we have to deal with a hierarchical structure of data. Events and interactions take place within groups, and the learners belong to groups. Learners will influence each other, shape each other's behavior, and influence each other's learning outcomes. Statistically speaking, learners are nested within their learning groups, and events are nested within learners. As we have emphasized before, data which describe events, interactions, or individuals are not statistically independent. With intraclass correlation, this independence can be measured, and if it is significant (see McGraw & Wong, 1996 for the respective tests), multilevel analysis will have to be applied. This method will be described in the following chapter of this handbook.

CONCLUSIONS

This chapter has shown that quantitative methods in CL vary according to the level of analysis. Different statistical methods are available to analyze events, event sequences, individual measures, or group measures. When we analyze events, it is clear that these are not independent. Lag-sequential analysis and log-linear approaches take this into account explicitly in the search for patterns between events. These patterns capture the independency of events. If we are interested in individuals, we can deal with the multilevel structure by eliminating group effects (for example, by faking a group) or by using multilevel analysis. Analyses at group level are much easier to perform because the groups are stochastically independent and we can use standard methods here—as long as the groups themselves are not nested within larger units (which may be the case in quasi-experimental designs, where we may, for example, work with learner groups from different schools).

In all cases, quantitative methodology works best, if the underlying assumption of the study provides a clear prediction of where the focus should be. The aim of considering all processes at all levels will only at first glance appear to be a good choice. If we try to take into account the full complexity of processes that take place in CL, then everything seems to be related to everything. For such a complex situation, there is no "good" method which would allow to separate systematic effects from all types of random effects. Only if we can work with clear predictions, will we be able to find an adequate method which allow for testing them. The clearer our predictions are, the better we can operationalize the theoretical constructs, and the easier it is to test them adequately.

REFERENCES

Allison, P. D., & Liker, J. K. (1982). Analyzing sequential categorical data on dyadic interaction. *Psychological Bulletin, 91*, 393–403.

Bakeman, R. (1978). Untangling streams of behavior: Sequential analyses of observational data. In G. P. Sackett (Ed.), *Observing behavior* (Vol. 2). Baltimore, MD: University Park Press.

Bakeman, R., Adamson, L. B., & Strisik, P. (1995). Lags and logs: Statistical approaches to interaction (SPSS version). In J. M. Gottman (Ed.), *The analysis of change* (pp. 279–308). Mahwah, NJ: Erlbaum.

Bakeman, R., & Gottman, J. M. (1997). *Observing interaction: An introduction to sequential analysis* (2nd ed.). Cambridge, England: Cambridge University Press.

Bakeman, R., & Quera, V. (1995). Log-linear approaches to lag-sequential analysis when consecutive codes may and cannot repeat. *Psychological Bulletin, 118*(2), 272–284.

Berelson, B. (1952). *Content analysis in communication research*. Glencoe, IL: Free Press.

Bonito, J. A. (2002). The analysis of participation in small groups: Methodological and conceptual issues related to interdependence. *Small Group Research, 33,* 412–438.

Boxtel van, C., van der Linden, J., & Kanselaar, G. (2000). Collaborative learning tasks and the elaboration of conceptual knowledge. *Learning and Instruction, 10*, 311–330.

Buder, J., & Bodemer, D. (2008). Supporting controversial CSCL discussions with augmented group awareness tools. *International Journal of Computer-Supported Collaborative Learning, 3*(2), 123–139.

Campbell, D. T., & Stanley, J. C. (1963). *Experimental and quasi-experimental designs for research.* Boston: Houghton Mifflin.

Carmines E. G., & & Zeller, A. R. (1979). *Reliability and validity assessment* (Qualitative Applications in Social Sciences, Vol. 17). Beverly Hills, CA: Sage.

Chiu, M. M. (2001). Analyzing group work processes: Towards a conceptual framework and systematic statistical analysis. In F. Columbus (Ed.), *Advances in psychology research* (Vol. 6, pp. 1–29). Huntington, NY: Nova Science.

Chiu, M. M. (2008). Flowing toward correct contributions during group problem solving: A statistical discourse analysis. *Journal of the Learning Sciences, 17*(3), 415–463.

Cohen, J. (1960). A coefficient of agreement for nominal scales. *Educational and Psychological Measurement, 20*(1), 37–46.

Cress, U. (2005). Ambivalent effect of member portraits in virtual groups. *Journal of Computer-Assisted Learning, 21,* 281–291.

Cress, U., & Kimmerle, J. (2008). A systemic and cognitive view on collaborative knowledge building with wikis. *International Journal of Computer-Supported Collaborative Learning, 3*(2), 105–122.

Dehler, J., Bodemer, D., Buder, J., & Hesse, F. W. (2009). Providing group knowledge awareness in computer-supported collaborative learning: Insights into learning mechanisms. *Research and Practice in Technology Enhanced Learning, 4*(2), 111–132.

Dehler, J., Bodemer, D., Buder, J., & Hesse, F. W. (2011). Guiding knowledge communication in CSCL via group knowledge awareness. *Computers in Human Behavior, 27*(3), 1068–1078.

De Laat, M., Lally, V., Lipponen, L., & Simons, R. J. (2007). Investigating patterns of interaction in networked learning and computer-supported collaborative learning: A role for social network analysis. International *Journal of Computer-Supported Collaborative Learning, 2*(1), 87–103.

De Wever, B., Schellens, T., Valcke, M., & van Keer, H., (2006). Content analysis schemes to analyze transcripts of online asynchronous discussion groups: A review. *Computers and Education, 46,* 6–28.

Dewiyanti, S., Brand-Gruwel, S., Jochems, W., & Broers, N. J. (2007). *Computers in Human Behavior, 23*(1), 496–514.

Erkens, G., Kanselaar, G., Prangsma, M. E., & Jaspers, J. G. M. (2003). Computer support for collaborative and argumentative writing. In E. De Corte, L. Verschaffel, N. Entwistle, & J. van Merriënboer (Eds.), *Powerful learning environments: Unraveling basic components and dimensions* (pp. 157–176). Amsterdam, Netherlands: Pergamon/Elsevier Science.

Everitt, B. S., & Howell, D. C. (Eds.). (2005). *Encyclopedia of statistics in behavioral science.* Chichester, England: Wiley.

Faraone, S. V., & Dorfman, D. D. (1987). Lag sequential analysis: Robust statistical methods. *Psychological Bulletin, 101*(2), 312–323.

Gottman, J. M., & Roy, A. K. (1990). *Sequential analysis—A guide for behavioral researchers.* Cambridge, England: Cambridge University Press.

Haake, J., & Pfister, H.-R. (2010). Scripting in distance-learning university course: Do students benefit from net-based scripted collaboration? *International Journal of Computer-Supported Collaborative Learning 1*(6), 155–175.

Hijzen, D., Boekaerts, M., & Vedder, P. (2006). The relationship between the quality of cooperative learning, students' goal preferences, and perceptions of contextual factors in the classroom. *Scandinavian Journal of Psychology 4* (1), 9–21.

Hmelo-Silver, C. E., Chernobilsky, E., & Jordan, R. (2008). Understanding collaborative learning processes in new learning environments. *Instructional Science, 36*(5–6), 409–430.

Holsti, O. (1969). *Content analysis for the social sciences and humanities.* Don Mills, ON: Addison-Wesley.

Hou, H.-T., Chang, K.-E., & Sung, Y.-T. (2008). Analysis of problem-solving-based online asynchronous discussion pattern. *Educational Technology & Society, 11*(1), 17–28.

Hou, H., Sung, Y.-T., & Chang, K.-E. (2009). Exploring the behavioral patterns of an online knowledge sharing discussion activity among teachers with problem-solving strategy. *Teaching and Teacher Education, 25,* 101–108.

Hron, A., Cress, U., Hammer, K., & Friedrich, H. F. (2007). Fostering collaborative knowledge construction in a video-based learning setting: Effects of a shared workspace and a content-specific graphical representation. *British Journal of Educational Technology, 38,* 236–248.

Jeong, A. C. (2003). The sequential analysis of group interaction and critical thinking in online threaded discussions. *The American Journal of Distance Education, 17*(1), 25–43.

Jeong, A. C. (2005). A guide to analyzing message-response sequences and group interaction patterns in computer-mediated communication. *Distance Education 26*(3), 367–383.

Jeong, A. C., & Joung, S. (2007). Scaffolding collaborative argumentation in asynchronous discussions with message constraints and message labels. *Computers and Education, 48*(3), 427–445.

Kanselaar, G., Erkens, G., Andriessen, J., Prangsma, M., Veerman, A., & Jaspers, J. (2002). Designing argumentation tools for collaborative learning. In P. A. Kirschner, S. J. B. Shum, & C. S. Carr (Eds.), *Visualization argumentation: Software tools for collaborative and educational sense-making* (pp. 51–74). London: Springer-Verlag.

Kanuka, H., Rourke, L., & Laflamme, E. (2007). The influence of instructional methods on the quality of online discussion. *British Journal of Educational Technology, 38*(2), 260–271.

Kashy, D. A., & Kenny, D. A. (2000). The analysis of data from dyads and groups. In H. T. Reis & C. M. Judd (Eds.), *Handbook of research methods in social and personality psychology* (pp. 451–477). Cambridge, England: Cambridge University Press.

Keeves, J. P. (1997). *Educational research, methodology and measurement: An international handbook* (2nd ed.). New York: Pergamon.

Kenny, D. A., & Judd, C. M. (1986). Consequences of violating the independence assumption in analysis of variance. *Psychological Bulletin, 99,* 422–431.

Kenny, D. A., Mannetti, L., Pierro, A., Livi, S., & Kashy, D. A. (2002). The statistical analysis of data from small groups. *Journal of Personality and Social Psychology, 83,* 126–137.

Kimmerle, J., & Cress, U. (2008). Group awareness and self-presentation in computer-supported information exchange. *International Journal of Computer-Supported Collaborative Learning, 3*(1), 85–97.

Kimmerle, J., Moskaliuk, J., Harrer, A., & Cress, U. (2010). Visualizing co-evolution of individual and collective knowledge. *Information, Communication and Society, 13*(8), 1099–1121.

Krippendorff, K. (2004). *Content analysis: An introduction to its methodology* (2nd ed.). Thousand Oaks, CA: Sage.

Martínez, A., Dimitriadis, Y., Gómez-Sánchez, E., Rubia-Avi, B., Jorrín-Abellán, I., & Marcos, J. A. (2006). Studying participation networks in collaboration using mixed methods in three case studies. *International Journal of Computer-Supported Collaborative Learning, 1*(3), 383–408.

Marttunen, M. (1997). Electronic mail as a pedagogical delivery system: An analysis of the learning of argumentation. *Research in Higher Education, 38*(3), 345–363.

McGraw, K. O., & Wong, S. P. (1996). Forming inferences about some intraclass correlation coefficients. *Psychological Methods, 1,* 30–46.

Meier, A., Spada, H., & Rummel, N. (2007). A rating scheme for assessing the quality of computer-supported collaboration processes. *International Journal of Computer-Supported Collaborative Learning, 2,* 63–86.

Nurmela, K., Lehtinen, E., & Palonen, T. (1999). Evaluating CSCL log files by social network analysis. In C. Hoadley & J. Roschelle (Eds.), *Proceedings of the Third International Conference on Computer Support for Collaborative Learning (CSCL'99)* (pp. 434–444). Mahwah, NJ: Erlbaum.

O'Connor, B. P. (1999). Simple and flexible SAS and SPSS programs for analyzing lag-sequential categorical data. *Behavior Research Methods, Instrumentation, and Computers, 31,* 718–726.

Poole, M. S., & Holmes, M. E. (1995). Decision development in computer-assisted group decision making. *Human Communication Research, 22*(1), 90–127.

Popper, K. R. (1963). *Conjectures and refutations.* London: Routledge & Kegan Paul.

Robinson, W. S. (1950). Ecological correlations and the behavior of individuals. *American Sociological Review, 15,* 351–357.

Rourke, L., & Anderson, T. (2004). Validity in quantitative content analysis. *Educational Technology Research and Development, 52*(1), 5–18.

Rourke, L., Anderson, T., Garrison, D. R., & Archer, W. (2000). Methodological issues in the content analysis of computer conference transcripts. *Journal of Artificial Intelligence in Education, 12,* 8–22.

Rummel, N., Spada, H., & Hauser, S. (2008) Learning to collaborate while being scripted or by observing a model. *International Journal of Computer-Supported Collaborative Learning, 4*(1), 69–92.

Sackett, G. P. (1979). The lag sequential analysis of contingency and cyclicity in behavioral interaction research. In J. Osofsky (Ed.), *Handbook of infant development* (pp. 623–649). New York: Wiley.

Shrout, P., & Fleiss, J. L., (1979) Intraclass correlation: Uses in assessing rater reliability. *Psychological Bulletin, 86*(2), 420–428.

Strijbos, J. W., & Fischer, F. (2007). Methodological challenges in collaborative learning research. *Learning and Instruction, 17,* 389–393.

Strijbos, J. W., Martens, R. L., Prins, F. J., & Jochems, W. M. G. (2006). Content analysis: What are they talking about? *Computers and Education, 46,* 29–48.

Strijbos, J. W., & Stahl, G. (2007). Methodological issues in developing a multi-dimensional coding procedure for small-group chat communication. *Learning and Instruction, 17*(4), 394–404.

Tabachnick, B. G., & Fidell, L. S. (1989). *Using multivariate statistics* (2nd ed.). New York: Harper & Row.

Wolfe, J. (2007). Annotations and the collaborative digital library: Effects of an aligned annotation interface on student argumentation and reading strategies. *International Journal of Computer-supported Collaborative Learning, 3*(2), 141–164.

6

MULTILEVEL ANALYSIS FOR THE ANALYSIS OF COLLABORATIVE LEARNING

JEROEN JANSSEN

Utrecht University, The Netherlands

ULRIKE CRESS

Knowledge Media Research Center, Tübingen, Germany

GIJSBERT ERKENS

Utrecht University, The Netherlands

PAUL A. KIRSCHNER

Open University, The Netherlands

INTRODUCTION

In a recent article "the widespread and increasing use" of collaborative learning (CL) has been called a "success story" (Cress & Hesse, chapter 5 this volume; Johnson & Johnson, 2009, p. 365). The study of CL has a long tradition, which has led to the publication of many studies which have examined the effects of CL on a range of dependent variables, such as student achievement (e.g., Nichols, 1996), time on task (e.g., Klein & Pridemore, 1992), motivation (e.g., Saleh, Lazonder, & De Jong, 2005), and use of metacognitive strategies (e.g., Mevarech & Kramarski, 2003). Johnson and Johnson (2009) identified over 1,200 studies comparing the relative effects of CL on, for example, individual learning. This line of research has become known as *effect-oriented research* because of its focus on the effects of CL (Dillenbourg, Baker, Blaye, & O'Malley, 1996; Van der Linden, Erkens, Schmidt, & Renshaw, 2000).

Traditionally, CL research has used well-known methods such as ANOVAs or (multiple) linear regression analysis to investigate how instructional interventions, student characteristics, and group characteristics affect the collaborative process and student learning. As we will show in this chapter, the datasets CL researchers collect often contain information about individual students (e.g., their motivation or their prior knowledge), about features of the groups (e.g., the type of task they work on or their composition), and sometimes even about features of the classroom (e.g., the teacher's CL teaching experience) or the school (e.g., school size or assignment to a treatment or control condition). These complex datasets create interdependencies between the different levels of analysis (i.e., student, group, classroom, or school). One way to deal with these interdependencies is to use multilevel analysis (MLA), also referred to as hierarchical linear modeling (HLM). The aim of this chapter is to demonstrate why and how MLA is an important technique for researchers who wish to investigate CL.

COMMON PROBLEMS ENCOUNTERED DURING COLLABORATIVE LEARNING RESEARCH

Consider a researcher who wants to conduct the following experiment. She wants to investigate how group member familiarity (i.e., how well do group members know each other before the start of the collaboration?) and group size (i.e., how many students constitute a group?) affect the communication and coordination process between group members and individual performance on a knowledge posttest. She therefore asks each group member to rate his or her familiarity with the other group members. Furthermore, she assigns group members to three-, four-, and five-person groups. She expects that as group member familiarity increases, the need for extensive coordination decreases. On the other hand, she also anticipates that when group size increases, the need for coordination increases. She suspects that in collaborative situations during which the need for coordination becomes very high, students' learning process may be hindered (cf., Kirschner, Paas, & Kirschner, 2009). She therefore hypothesizes that in familiar three-person groups, students will perform best on the posttest, while in unfamiliar five-person groups, students will perform worst on the posttest.

This example contains three features which require the researcher to use MLA if she wants to analyze her data appropriately: (a) Students work in groups and this creates a hierarchically nested dataset; (b) due to the mutual influence between group members, observations of the dependent variables are nonindependent; and (c) the research design contains variables measured at different levels (e.g., the dependent measures and group member familiarity are measured at the level of the student, while one of the independent variables, group size, is measured at the level of the group). Each of these problems will be discussed below.

Problem 1: Hierarchically Nested Datasets

During CL, students work in groups on an assigned group task. Often researchers are interested in the question how a certain instructional intervention (e.g., a training developed to promote helping behavior) affects the collaborative process and students' learning process. Other researchers might be interested in how contextual factors, such as the composition of the group, prior knowledge of group members, or features of the group task, affect the collaborative process. These situations lead to hierarchically nested datasets. Because groups consist of two or more students, individuals are nested within groups.

In many cases, researchers will encounter at least two levels. The lowest level is the individual, and the highest level is the group. The group is then the macro- or level-2 unit and the individual the micro- or level-1 unit (Hox, 2003; Snijders & Bosker, 1999). Researchers may encounter even more levels of analysis. A researcher might for example be interested in the effects of the teacher's experience with CL on the way his or her students cooperate. This researcher will have a dataset with three levels: students are nested within groups, while groups are nested within teachers' classrooms. Another researcher might be interested in the development of students' collaboration over time. This researcher would therefore collect data about students' collaboration on different occasions. This would also lead to a dataset with three levels: measurement occasions are nested within students and students are nested within groups (Kenny, Kashy, & Cook, 2006; Snijders & Bosker, 1999). In the example described at the beginning of this section, the researcher encounters two levels, because in her study students collaborate in small groups (students are nested in groups).

Whenever researchers encounter datasets with hierarchically nested data, MLA is needed to appropriately model this data structure because it can disentangle the effects of the different levels on the dependent variable(s) of interest (Snijders & Bosker, 1999; Strijbos & Fischer, 2007).

Problem 2: Nonindependence of Dependent Variables

Because students work in groups, the dependent variables CL researchers study are often nonindependent (Cress, 2008). This means that students within a group are likely more similar to each other than are persons from different groups (Kenny, Mannetti, Pierro, Livi, & Kashy, 2002). This nonindependence is caused by the mutual influence group members have on each other while they are interacting (Bonito, 2002; Kenny et al., 2006).

In the example described above, nonindependence may also occur. Group members have to discuss their strategies, formulate explanations, and coordinate their activities. In some groups this process will be more smooth and effective than in other groups. In the former case, it is likely that all group members will perform reasonably well on the posttest because they experienced a fruitful and effective collaborative experience. In the latter case however, it is likely that all group members will not perform well on the posttest because they experienced collaboration and coordination problems. In this example too, the observations of the dependent variable, posttest performance, may be nonindependent.

It should be noted that the mutual influence group members have on each other can not only cause students to behave more similarly, but may also cause students to behave differently from their group members. This is called the *boomerang effect* (Kenny et al., 2006). This may, for example, occur when roles are assigned to group members (cf., Schellens, Van Keer, & Valcke, 2005; Strijbos, Martens, Jochems, & Broers, 2004, 2007). If one group member, for example, is given the task of asking critical questions, while the other group member has to monitor task progress, this may lead to different behavior (e.g., the first student will ask many questions, but will display less metacognitive behavior, while the second student may display high levels of metacognitive behavior but may ask fewer questions).

Kenny et al. (2006) therefore make a distinction between *positive nonindependence* where group members influence each other in such a way that they behave more similarly and *negative nonindependence* where group members influence each other to behave differently. Thus, since group members influence each other, this will likely lead to either positive or negative nonindependence of the dependent variables that are being investigated. This nonindependence has to be dealt with during data analysis.

The degree of nonindependence can be estimated using the *intraclass correlation coefficient* (ICC, cf., Kashy & Kenny, 2000; Kenny et al., 2002). The ICC is computed by dividing the difference between the mean square between groups and the mean square within groups by the sum of the two mentioned mean squares. Values of the ICC can range from –1 to +1, and give an indication of how strongly members in a group resemble each other. A large positive value of the ICC indicates that within a group, group members tend to score similarly on the variable of interest. Conversely, a large negative value of the ICC indicates large differences between group members on the variable of interest. The ICC can also be thought of as the average correlation among all possible pairs within the groups (Kenny et al., 2006).

An alternative interpretation of the ICC is in terms of the *amount of variance that is accounted for by the group* (Kenny et al., 2006). When the ICC for satisfaction with the collaborative process is found to be .40, for example, this means that 40% of the variance in this measure is accounted for by the group and thus that 60% is accounted for by other (e.g., individual) factors.

High values of the ICC indicate a strong influence of the group on the individual. It is not uncommon for CL researchers to find ICC values of .30, .40, or higher (e.g., Janssen, Erkens, & Kanselaar, 2007; Janssen, Erkens, Kanselaar, & Jaspers, 2007; Paletz, Peng, Erez, & Maslach, 2004; Schepers, de Jong, Wetzels, & de Ruyter, 2008; Strijbos et al., 2004). Such a strong nonindependence needs to be addressed when conducting statistical analyses, because it distorts estimates of error variances, thus making standard errors, *p*-values, and confidence intervals invalid (Kenny, 1995; Kenny et al., 2006). MLA, unlike traditional statistical techniques such as *t*-tests and analysis of variance, is able to handle this distortion (Hox, 2003).

Problem 3: Different Units of Analysis

Some variables that are used during CL research are measured at the level of the student (e.g., gender, familiarity with other group members, prior knowledge), whereas other variables are measured at the level of the group (e.g., group size, group composition with respect to ability or gender). Strijbos et al. (2004), for example, studied the effects of roles on students' perceptions of the collaborative process. Their design contained two conditions. In the first condition groups were given different roles to fulfill during the collaboration, while in the second condition no roles were assigned to group members. In this case, Strijbos et al. used a dependent variable—perception of the collaborative process—that was observed at the individual level, and an independent variable—role or no role—that was observed at the group level. Such a dataset therefore contains variables with different units of analysis. Because traditional statistical techniques cannot properly take these different units of analysis into account, MLA is needed (Hox, 2003; Snijders & Bosker, 1999).

The researcher described at the beginning of this section also uses variables measured at different levels. The two independent variables she wants to investigate are measured at different levels. Group member familiarity is measured at the level of the student (i.e., each student rates his or her familiarity with the other group members). In contrast, group size is measured at the level of the group. The number of unique observations for group member familiarity will therefore be higher than for group size. Again, to cope with this problem MLA is needed.

COMMON STRATEGIES FOR ANALYZING COLLABORATIVE LEARNING DATA

In this section we will describe two strategies that researchers employ when they are confronted with datasets such as the ones described previously. We will also highlight the dangers of these strategies.

Ignoring Nonindependence

A common strategy is to ignore the hierarchical structure of the dataset, the nonindependence, and the different units of analysis (Cress, 2008; Kenny, Kashy, & Cook, 2006; Kenny, Mannetti, et al., 2002). When CL researchers ignore the nonindependence in their dataset, they use statistical analyses such as *t*-tests, (M)ANOVA's, or (multiple) regression analysis. When this is the case, they run an increased risk of committing Type I or Type II errors (Kashy & Kenny, 2000). Nonindependence needs to be addressed when conducting statistical analyses, because it distorts estimates of error variances. This distortion makes standard errors, *p*-values, and confidence intervals invalid, when it is not taken into account (Kenny, 1995; Kenny & Judd, 1986; Kenny, Kashy, & Cook, 2006). Whether the chance to falsely reject (Type I error) or falsely accept (Type II error) the null hypothesis is increased, depends on the sign of the ICC (either positive or negative), and the type of dependent variable for which the ICC was calculated (see Kashy & Kenny, 2000 for a detailed discussion).

Using data from a study on the effects of an awareness tool on students' online collaboration, Janssen, Erkens, Kirschner, and Kanselaar (2011) highlighted the dangers of ignoring the nonindependence in their dataset. In this study half of the groups were given access to an awareness tool (treatment condition), whereas the other half were not given access to this tool (control condition). Janssen et al. found an ICC of .41 for the dependent variable, online collaboration, indicating a considerable influence of the group on the dependent variable and the presence of nonindependence in their data. When Janssen et al. analyzed the data using multiple regression analysis they found no effect of condition on the collaborative process. In contrast, when MLA was used, a different conclusion was drawn. In this case, a significant effect of condition on the collaborative process was found.

This example highlights the dangers of ignoring nonindependence. It should be noted however, that not in all cases will the differences between using analyses such as regression analysis or ANOVA and MLA will be this dramatic (i.e., drawing different conclusions when MLA is used). On the other hand, running an increased chance of committing Type I or Type II errors is something researchers should avoid.

Aggregating or Disaggregating Data

Another common strategy is to *aggregate* individual data to the level of the group (Kenny, Kashy, & Cook, 2006; Snijders & Bosker, 1999). In this case, a researcher who for example wishes to investigate the effect of prior knowledge on levels of participation during group discussion, would compute the average prior knowledge for the group members and use this group level measure as an independent variable instead of the prior knowledge measured at the level of the student. A drawback of this strategy is that it ignores the fact that prior knowledge is in essence an individual level variable (although it may be affected by group level variables). Another drawback is that by aggregating data, a researcher uses fewer observations for prior knowledge than are actually available (Cress, 2008). This means the power to detect a significant effect of the independent variable on the dependent variable is lowered, which in turn increases the risk of committing a Type II error (Snijders & Bosker, 1999).

The opposite strategy—*disaggregation* of group level data to the individual level—is also used in CL research. This means a researcher treats data measured at the level of the group as if they were measured at the level of the individual. Consider, for example, the study by Savicki, Kelley, and Lingenfelter (1996) about the effects of gender group composition on students' satisfaction with the collaborative process. Group composition was measured at the group level (all male, all female, or mixed groups), while satisfaction was measured at the individual level (students completed a questionnaire individually). In total, their sample consisted of six unique groups and 36 students. Savicki et al. conducted an analysis of variance to examine whether group composition affected satisfaction. However, this analysis does not take into account that group composition was measured at the group level. Thus, Savicki et al.'s analysis uses 36 observations for the group composition variable, while in fact there are only six observations for this variable. This led to an exaggeration of the actual sample size for this variable and increased the chance of committing a Type I error (Snijders & Bosker, 1999).

Using data from a study on the effects of representational guidance on student performance on a knowledge posttest, Janssen et al. (2011) showed the dangers of aggregating data to the level of the group. The dataset they used contained two conditions: in one condition students used a graphical version of a tool to construct an external representation, while in the other condition students used a textual version of this tool. In this dataset the assumption of nonindependence was violated, because the ICC of the dependent variable, posttest performance, was .32. Furthermore, this dataset contained different units of analysis: condition was measured at the level of the group (some groups used the graphical tool, others the textual tool) and posttest performance was measured at the level of the individual student. When Janssen et al. aggregated their data to the level of the group by calculating, for each group, the average posttest score of the individual group members, and then analyzed the differences between the two conditions using analysis of covariance, they found no significant differences between the graphical and textual tool. In contrast, when they used MLA, a significant difference between the graphical and textual tool for posttest performance was found.

This example highlights the dangers of aggregating data to the level of the group to deal with the problems described in the previous section. In the next section we will describe MLA in more detail by explaining its foundations and assumptions.

MULTILEVEL ANALYSIS

Foundations and Assumptions of Multilevel Analysis

Multilevel analysis is based on linear regression analysis, but extends this technique by allowing researchers to model the data at the level of the individual and the group simultaneously (Hox, 2003; Snijders & Bosker, 1999). Unlike regression analysis, which can only incorporate fixed coefficients (e.g., intercept or slopes), ML models can incorporate random coefficients as well. This means that in ML models the intercepts or slopes of the regression lines can vary for different groups of students. Such a model with varying

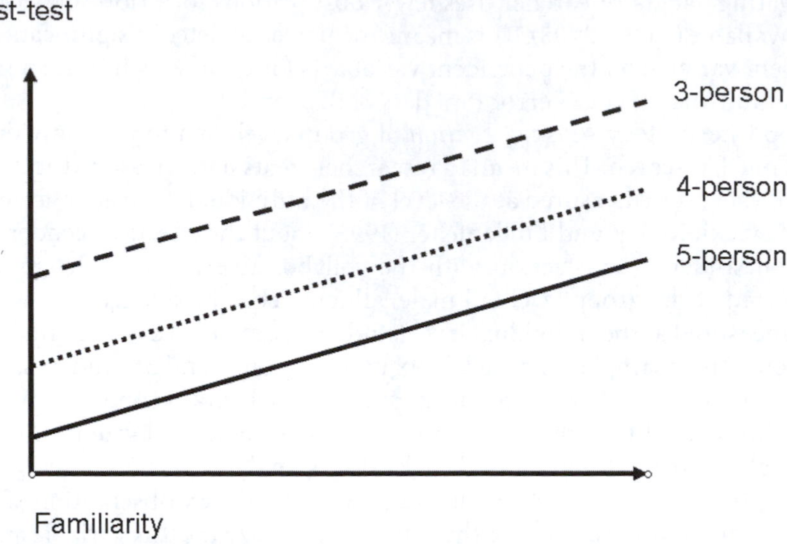

Figure 6.1 Depiction of a random intercept model.

intercepts is called a "random intercept model" (Hox, 2003; Snijders & Bosker, 1999). Figure 6.1 shows an example for a random intercept model for the fictional example introduced at the beginning of this chapter. Figure 6.1 shows not one regression line, but three different regression lines: one for each group in the sample. As can be seen, the intercepts of the three-person group and the four- and five-person groups differ.

The ML model can be extended by also allowing the slopes of the regression lines to vary. This is called a "random intercept, random slope model" (Hox, 2003; Snijders & Bosker, 1999). A graphical depiction of such a model for our fictional example is shown in Figure 6.2. In this case not only the intercept varies for the different groups in the

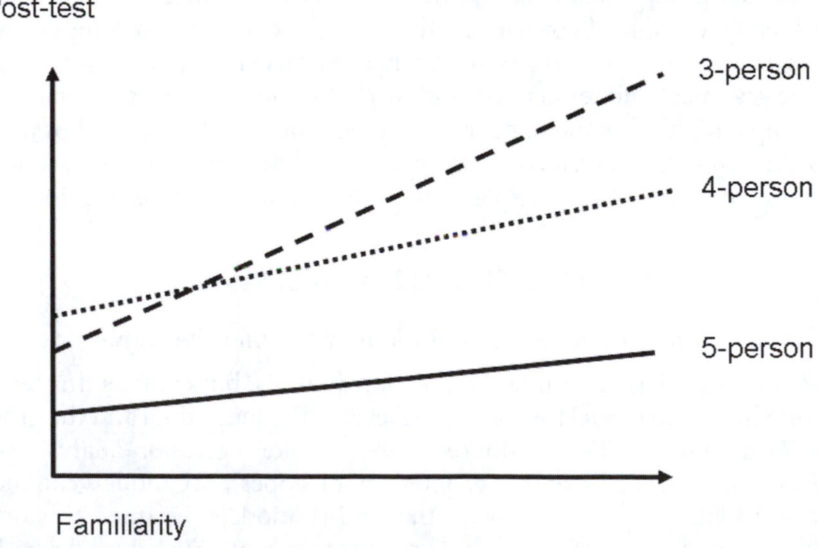

Figure 6.2 Depiction of a random intercept, random slope model.

dataset, but the slopes of the groups vary as well. Figure 6.2 shows that familiarity has a different effect on posttest performance for a three-person group than for four- and five-person groups (i.e., the slope is steeper for the three-person group).

ML models are estimated in two steps (Cress, 2008; Dedrick et al., 2009; Kenny, Kashy, & Cook, 2006; Snijders & Bosker, 1999). In the first step, the dependent variable (posttest performance in our example) is predicted by one or more *X* variables. *X* variables are measured at the lowest level, usually the individual. In our example group member familiarity is a level-1 variable and is thus used as an *X* variable. It is important to note that a *separate regression equation is computed for each level-2 unit.* In our example, groups are the level-2 unit. The first-step regression equation for group member j in group i is then

$$Y_{ij} = b_{0i} + b_{1i}X_{ij} + e_{ij} \tag{1}$$

In equation 1, b_{0i} represents the average post-test performance for group members in group i, and b_{1i} is the coefficient for the effect of *X*—group member familiarity—on posttest performance for group i.

During the second step of the MLA, the slopes and intercepts from the first-step analysis are treated as outcome variables in two separate regression models (Kenny et al., 2006). In these regression analyses, the regression coefficients b_{0i} and b_{1i} from equation 1 are assumed to be a function of a group-level predictor variable *Z* (group size, the level-2 variable in our example).

$$b_{0i} = a_0 + a_1Z_i + d_i \tag{2}$$

$$b_{1i} = c_0 + c_1Z_i + f_i \tag{3}$$

In equation 2, the intercepts from the first step are treated as a function of the *Z* variable, group size. This means that in equation 2 the average post-test performance, b_{0i}, in group i is predicted by group size. Parameter a_0 can be thought of as the grand mean of post-test performance across all students and groups, while parameter a_1 represents the effect of group size on post-test performance.

Equation 3 treats the effect of *X*—group member familiarity—as a function of the *Z* variable, group size. Thus, the effect of group member familiarity on posttest performance for group i, b_{1i}, is predicted by group size, Z_i. Parameter c_0 represents the overall effect of group member familiarity on post-test performance. Parameter c_1 represents the cross-level interaction between group member familiarity and group size. In other words, this parameter indicates the degree to which the effect of group size varies for students who know their group members well versus students who do not know their group members well.

In sum, the parameters a_0, a_1 and c_0 and c_1 describe *fixed effects*. The *random effects* are represented by the three parameters e_{ij}, d_i, and f_i. First, e_{ij} is the error component in the first regression equation (see equation 1). In our example, e_{ij} represents how post-test performance varies from student to student within groups, controlling for both group member familiarity and group size. Second, d_i represents the variance in the intercepts which cannot be explained by *Z* (see equation 2). In our example, this is the group variance in posttest performance that cannot be explained by group size. Finally, f_i is the group variance in the effects of *X* on *Y* (see equation 3). Thus, in our example f_i

represents how the effect of group member familiarity on posttest performance varies from group to group.

MLA usually involves estimating at least two models: an empty model, which includes no predictor, and just reveals the individual- and the group-level variances, and a model including one or more predictor variables. For both models, the deviance (a measure of the goodness of fit of the model) can be computed. By comparing the deviance of the latter model with the empty model, a decrease in deviance can be calculated. When this decrease in deviance is significant (tested with a χ^2-test), it can be concluded the latter model is a better model. Furthermore, the estimated parameters of the predictors can be tested for significance by dividing the regression coefficient by its standard error. This so-called *t*-ratio has approximately a standard normal distribution (Snijders & Bosker, 1999).

Table 6.1 shows a fictitious example of a MLA of the effects of group member familiarity (level-1 student predictor) and group size (level-2 group predictor) on posttest performance. This example was described at the beginning of this chapter and used earlier. Model 0 represents the empty model without level-1 or level-2 predictors. As can be seen, a large part of the variance in posttest performance is determined by the group (1.33 of a total of 1.33 + 2.83). The empty model also provides the ICC (.32). Model 1 contains group member familiarity as a level-1 predictor (*X*) and group size as a level-2 predictor (*Z*), as well as the cross-level interaction between these variables. It can be concluded from Table 6.1 that both group member familiarity and group size significantly affect posttest performance. As group member familiarity increases, posttest performance increases also. In contrast, when group size increases, post-test performance decreases. Finally, in this example no significant interaction effect is found between group member familiarity and posttest performance. This means that the effect of group member familiarity does not depend on the size of the group (i.e., the effect of group member familiarity on posttest performance is similar for small and large groups). Table 6.1 also shows the deviance of Model 1 is significantly lower than the deviance of the empty model, indicating the new model fits the data better than does the empty model.

Table 6.1 Fictitious Example of Multilevel Analysis of the Effect of Group Member Familiarity and Group Size on Post-Test Performance

	Parameter	Model 0		Model 1	
		β	SE	β	SE
Fixed effect					
Intercept	a_0	6.70	0.27	5.60	1.07
Group member familiarity (X)	a_1			0.28**	0.10
Group size (Z)	c_0			−0.42*	0.22
X * Z	c_1			0.28	0.26
Random effect					
Group level	σ_d^2	1.33	0.65	0.44	0.45
Individual level	σ_e^2	2.83	0.56	2.98	0.58
Deviance		355.70		344.63	
Decrease in deviance				11.07**	

$^*p < .05.$ $^{**}p < .01.$

It is important to note that MLA makes assumptions about the errors at each level in the ML model (Dedrick et al., 2009). The first-level errors, e_{ij} in equation 1, are assumed to be independently and normally distributed. Furthermore, it is also assumed that the second-level errors, d_i in equation 2 and f_i in equation 3, are also normally distributed. In most cases their covariance is not assumed to be equal to zero. Finally, all the assumptions that are made for linear regression analysis, such as linearity and no multicollinearity also apply to MLA (Field, 2009).

Applications of Multilevel Analysis to Collaborative Learning Data

Although MLA is a relatively new statistical technique in the field of CL research, several researchers have used MLA to answer their research questions. In this subsection we will shortly describe several studies that employed MLA to highlight its potential to answer meaningful research questions in the field of CL.

Paletz et al. (2004) examined how ethnic composition of groups affected satisfaction with the collaborative process using MLA. Their study contrasted groups that were composed of mostly Caucasians with groups that were composed of mostly ethnic minorities (e.g., Hispanic or African American). Students worked in groups of three. In total, their sample consisted of 108 students working in 36 groups. They found that 40% of the variance in satisfaction with the collaborative process was due to group-level factors. Furthermore, Paletz et al. were able to show that ethnic composition affected satisfaction: groups composed of mostly ethnic minorities reported higher satisfaction with the collaborative process than did groups composed of mostly Caucasian students.

Strijbos et al. (2004) investigated how role assignment affected online collaborative learning. Their sample consisted of 33 students collaborating in 10 groups. Strijbos et al. compared the perceived group efficiency (PGE) of groups with role assignments to the PGE of groups without role assignments. In Strijbos et al.'s study, a considerable part of the variance in PGE was due to group-level factors (ICC was found to be .47). MLA showed that in the role condition, groups reported higher PGE than in the nonrole condition.

Whereas the studies by Paletz et al. (2004) and Strijbos et al. (2004) used ML models with two levels (individual and group), Schellens et al. (2005) used a three-level model. Schellens et al. measured students' level of knowledge construction in asynchronous discussion groups at four different measurement occasions. Their study is therefore a good example of how MLA can also be used on repeated measure data and to investigate trends or developmental patterns in the data. In Schellens et al.'s study, measurement occasions were nested within students, and students were in turn nested within groups. In total their sample consisted of 286 students, collaborating in 23 groups. In contrast to the two previously described studies, the study conducted by Schellens et al. found only a small effect of group-level variables: 0.54% of the variance in knowledge construction could be attributed to differences between the groups.

In sum, the examples provided in this section highlight the usefulness of MLA for CL research. Although not all studies report large and significant ICCs, it seems that a moderate part of the variance in the dependent variables CL researchers investigate can be explained by group-level factors. This justifies the use of MLA for CL research. Moreover, due to the relatively small sample sizes in CL researcher (especially at the level of the group) the ICC may not be significant, while it is actually large enough to bias standard errors, *p*-values, and so on. Kenny et al. (2002) therefore propose assuming group data are nonindependent and use MLA even though the ICC is not significant.

Limitations of Multilevel Analysis

Of course not all data-analytic problems that CL researchers encounter are solved by using MLA. Furthermore, MLA has its own limitations. First, MLA is mostly used when the dependent variable is measured at the interval level of measurement. Sometimes however, researchers may be interested in dichotomous (e.g., success or failure of group work) or categorical dependent variables (e.g., levels of knowledge construction). Although MLA techniques have been developed to incorporate these kinds of dependent variables (multilevel logistic regression; see Snijders & Bosker, 1999), they are rarely adapted to CL data.

Second, for an adequate analysis of collaborative learning using MLA, it is often suggested that large sample sizes at all levels (individual as well as group) are necessary (Cress, 2008; Maas & Hox, 2005). Maas and Hox, using a simulation study, demonstrated that only a small sample size at the group level (less than 50 groups) is problematic and leads to biased estimates. A small sample size at the individual level (groups consisting of five group members or less), does not appear to be problematic. This means that, in order to use MLA confidently for CL data, researchers should collect data about at least 50 groups. CL researchers, however, often employ less than 50 groups in their studies (see, for example, the sample studies cited above). Given the complexity of CL research and how time-consuming data collection and analysis often are, a sample size of at least 50 groups places a heavy burden on researchers. We agree with Cress (2008) that as a minimum standard in CL research, the ICC should be calculated and tested for significance. This will give the researcher and his/her audience insight into the effect of group-level variables on the dependent variable and of the existence of nonindependence in the dataset. When this is the case, researchers can take other precautions when application of MLA seems problematic due to a small sample size at the highest level (less than 50 groups). One such precaution might be to use a more stringent alpha level (i.e., .01 instead of .05) or to aggregate all individual variables to the group level (cf., Kenny, Kashy, & Cook, 2006).

Software Applications for Multilevel Analysis

For the researcher who wants to conduct MLA on his/her dataset, several software applications are available (see Robert & McLeod, 2008 for an excellent overview). A commonly used application is MLwiN (http://www.cmm.bristol.ac.uk/MLwiN/index.shtml) developed by the team at the Centre for Multilevel Modelling at the University of Bristol. Another commonly used application for MLA is HLM (Raudenbush, Bryk, Cheong, Congdon, & Du Toit, 2004; see also http://www.ssicentral.com/hlm/index.html).

Conventional statistical software such as SPSS and SAS also incorporate procedures for carrying out MLA. For researchers who want to perform advanced MLA, using, for example, binary or binomial distributions, especially SPSS may be less suited than specialized applications such as MLwiN or HLM. On the other hand, SPSS and SAS are more user friendly with respect to data manipulation than MLwiN and HLM. For SAS, Campbell and Kashy (2002) illustrate how the MIXED procedure can be used to perform MLA on CL data. For SPSS, Field (2009) describes how the Mixed Models option can be used to perform MLA. In addition, the book written by Kenny, Kashy, and Cook (2006) and the text by Robert and McLeod (2008) contain detailed examples, including syntax, of how both SPSS and SAS can be used to perform MLA.

CONCLUSION

In this chapter we discussed the data analytical problems CL researchers frequently encounter, namely hierarchically nested datasets, nonindependence of dependent variables, and different units of analysis. We argued that, in order to take these problems into account, MLA should be used. We also demonstrated that alternative analysis strategies such as ignoring nonindependence or aggregating data can lead to different results and possibly to mistakes regarding the significance or non-significance of these results. We therefore strongly advocate the use of MLA in CL research. Fortunately, more and more CL researchers are beginning to use this technique to answer their research questions.

As noted before, not all data-analytic problems that CL researchers encounter are solved by using MLA because it is mostly suited for analyses of interval-level dependent variables. Sometimes, however, researchers may be interested in dependent variables measured at other levels (e.g., dichotomous or categorical). MLA can be adapted to those situations as well, but they are seldom applied in CL research. One of the key challenges for CL research is to develop and incorporate these more advanced applications of MLA as well.

Second, the issue of sample size and power addressed earlier can pose a problem for CL researchers who wish to use MLA to answer their research questions. Often, time and budget considerations do not allow researchers to collect data for large numbers of groups. An option to deal with this problem may be to focus on smaller groups, such as dyads or triads. Because the sample size at the group level seems to be the bottleneck with respect to sample size and power, using dyads or triads instead of larger groups limits the number of students needed to reach an adequate sample size (e.g., 100 students when dyads are used, 150 students when triads are used). Field (2009) however, concludes that many factors affect the power of MLA. It is therefore advisable that CL researchers use sample size and power calculators to determine the optimal sample size for their model. HLM will for example allow power calculations for a ML model. Additionally, Tom Snijders' homepage (http://stat.gamma.rug.nl/multilevel.htm) contains a program that performs power analysis for two-level models.

CL researchers are sometimes interested in data over time. An example might be how familiarity with group members affects trust development in groups over time. To investigate this question, a researcher would collect data about trust levels on different occasions. This adds even more problems to the data analysis. The effects of familiarity on trust may not be the same at every measurement occasion (e.g., its effects may be greater at the beginning of the collaboration). Furthermore, the level of trust at measurement occasion 1 may also have an effect on the level of trust at occasion 2 (if trust was high at occasion 1, this may affect trust at occasion 2). This creates a new type of nonindependence: autocorrelation (Kenny, Kashy, & Cook, 2006). Again, MLA techniques have been developed to analyze time-series data (cf., Chiu & Khoo, 2003, 2005; Kenny, Kashy, & Cook, 2006), but they are not often used in CL research. CL researchers should therefore begin to investigate the possibilities of using MLA for time-series data.

Finally, MLA will not be a suitable technique to answer all research questions. As was stated at the beginning of this chapter, quite a lot of CL research focuses on capturing the interactive processes that unfold between group members (i.e., process-oriented research). In some cases researchers are interested in providing "thick" or "rich" descriptions of the collaborative process (Baker, 2003; Hmelo-Silver & Bromme, 2007). In such cases, it is not necessary to apply MLA. Furthermore, it has been argued that studying intersubjective meaning making or group cognition should be the focus of CL research (Stahl, 2006; Suthers, 2006). This involves studying "how people make sense of situations and of each other" (Suthers, p. 321). Researchers with such a perspective on CL research could object to disentangling group and individual aspects of CL. They would argue that in order to understand the collaborative process, the group should be the unit of analysis, not the individual. Again, if one has such an approach to studying CL, using MLA will not be a sensible strategy.

CL research can still make progress by incorporating MLA in its repertoire of analysis techniques. It is an encouraging development that CL researchers are increasingly turning toward MLA. It is our hope and expectation that this development will continue and that CL researchers are going to find new ways to deal with the complex data analytical problems they are faced with. Ultimately, this will lead to a better understanding of how group-level factors (e.g., group composition), student-level factors (e.g., prior knowledge, motivation), and their interaction, affect the collaborative process and student learning. Furthermore, when researchers combine MLA with qualitative analyses in a mixed methods design (cf., Leech & Onwuegbuzie, 2009) an even more complete picture of the CL process is possible.

REFERENCES

Baker, M. (2003). Computer-mediated argumentative interactions for the co-elaboration of scientific notions. In J. Andriessen, M. Baker, & D. Suthers (Eds.), *Arguing to learn: Confronting cognitions in computer-supported collaborative learning environments* (pp. 47–78). Dordrecht, Netherlands: Kluwer Academic.

Bonito, J. A. (2002). The analysis of participation in small groups: Methodological and conceptual issues related to interdependence. *Small Group Research, 33*, 412–438.

Campbell, L., & Kashy, D. A. (2002). Estimating actor, partner, and interaction effects for dyadic data using PROC MIXED and HLM: A user-friendly guide. *Personal Relationships, 9*, 327–342.

Chiu, M. M., & Khoo, L. (2003). Rudeness and status effects during group problem solving: Do they bias evaluations and reduce the likelihood of correct solutions? *Journal of Educational Psychology, 95*, 506–523.

Chiu, M. M., & Khoo, L. (2005). A new method for analyzing sequential processes: Dynamic multilevel analysis. *Small Group Research, 36*(5), 600–631.

Cress, U. (2008). The need for considering multilevel analysis in CSCL research: An appeal for the use of more advanced statistical methods. *International Journal of Computer-Supported Collaborative Learning, 3*, 69–84.

Dedrick, R. F., Ferron, J. M., Hess, M. R., Hogarty, K. Y., Kromrey, J. D., Lang, T. R., … Lee, R. S. (2009). Multilevel modeling: A review of methodological issues and applications. *Review of Educational Research, 79*, 69–102.

Dillenbourg, P., Baker, M., Blaye, A., & O'Malley, C. (1996). The evolution of research on collaborative learning. In H. Spada & P. Reimann (Eds.), *Learning in humans and machine: Towards an interdisciplinary learning science* (pp. 189–211). Oxford, England: Elsevier.

Field, A. (2009). *Discovering statistics using SPSS* (3rd ed.). London: Sage.

Hmelo-Silver, C. E., & Bromme, R. (2007). Coding discussions and discussing coding: Research on collaborative learning in computer-supported environments. *Learning and Instruction, 17*, 460–464.

Hox, J. (2003). *Multilevel analysis: Techniques and applications*. Mahwah, NJ: Erlbaum.

Janssen, J., Erkens, G., & Kanselaar, G. (2007). Visualization of agreement and discussion processes during computer-supported collaborative learning. *Computers in Human Behavior, 23*, 1105–1125.

Janssen, J., Erkens, G., Kanselaar, G., & Jaspers, J. (2007). Visualization of participation: Does it contribute to successful computer-supported collaborative learning? *Computers & Education, 49*, 1037–1065.

Janssen, J., Erkens, G., Kirschner, P. A., & Kanselaar, G. (2011). Multilevel analysis in CSCL research. In S. Puntambekar, G. Erkens, & C. Hmelo-Silver (Eds.), *Analyzing interactions in CSCL: Methodologies, approaches and issues* (pp. 187-205). New York: Springer.

Johnson, D. W., & Johnson, R. T. (2009). An educational psychology success story: Social interdependence theory and cooperative learning. *Educational Researcher, 38*, 365–379.

Kashy, D. A., & Kenny, D. A. (2000). The analysis of data from dyads and groups. In H. T. Reis & C. M. Judd (Eds.), *Handbook of research methods in social and personality psychology* (pp. 451–477). Cambridge, England: Cambridge University Press.

Kenny, D. A. (1995). The effect of nonindependence on significance testing in dyadic research. *Personal Relationships, 2*, 67–75.

Kenny, D. A., & Judd, C. M. (1986). Consequences of violating the independence assumption in analysis of variance. *Psychological Bulletin, 99*, 422.

Kenny, D. A., Kashy, D. A., & Cook, W. L. (2006). *Dyadic data analysis*. New York: Guilford.

Kenny, D. A., Mannetti, L., Pierro, A., Livi, S., & Kashy, D. A. (2002). The statistical analysis of data from small groups. *Journal of Personality and Social Psychology, 83*, 126–137.

Kirschner, F., Paas, F., & Kirschner, P. A. (2009). A cognitive load approach to collaborative learning: United brains from complex learning. *Educational Psychology Review, 21*, 31–42.

Klein, J. D., & Pridemore, D. R. (1992). Effects of cooperative learning and need for affiliation on performance, time on task, and satisfaction. *Educational Technology Research and Development, 40*, 39–47.

Leech, N. L., & Onwuegbuzie, A. J. (2009). A typology of mixed methods research designs. *Quality & Quantity, 43*, 265–275.

Maas, C. J. M., & Hox, J. J. (2005). Sufficient sample sizes for multilevel modelling. *European Journal of Research Methods for the Behavioral and Social Sciences, 1*, 85–91.

Mevarech, Z. R., & Kramarski, B. (2003). The effects of metacognitive training versus worked-out examples on students' mathematical reasoning. *British Journal of Educational Psychology, 73*, 449–471.

Nichols, J. D. (1996). The effects of cooperative learning on student achievement and motivation in a high school geometry class. *Contemporary Educational Psychology, 21*, 467–476.

Paletz, S. B. R., Peng, K. P., Erez, M., & Maslach, C. (2004). Ethnic composition and its differential impact on group processes in diverse teams. *Small Group Research, 35*, 128–157.

Raudenbush, S., Bryk, A., Cheong, Y. F., Congdon, R., & Du Toit, M. (2004). *HLM6: Hierarchical linear and nonlinear modeling*. Lincolnwood, IL: Scientific Software International.

Robert, J. K., & McLeod, P. (2008). Software options for multilevel models. In A. A. O'Connell & D. B. McCoach (Eds.), *Multilevel modeling of educational data* (pp. 427–467). Greenwich, CT: Information Age.

Saleh, M., Lazonder, A. W., & De Jong, T. (2005). Effects of within-class ability grouping on social interaction, achievement, and motivation. *Instructional Science, 33*, 105–119.

Savicki, V., Kelley, M., & Lingenfelter, D. (1996). Gender and group composition in small task groups using computer-mediated communication. *Computers in Human Behavior, 12*, 209–224.

Schellens, T., Van Keer, H., & Valcke, M. (2005). The impact of role assignment on knowledge construction in asynchronous discussion groups: A multilevel analysis. *Small Group Research, 36*, 704–745.

Schepers, J., de Jong, A., Wetzels, M., & de Ruyter, K. (2008). Psychological safety and social support in groupware adoption: A multi-level assessment in education. *Computers & Education, 51*, 757–775.

Snijders, T. A. B., & Bosker, R. J. (1999). *Multilevel analysis: An introduction to basic and advanced multilevel modeling*. London: Sage.

Stahl, G. (2006). *Group cognition: Computer support for building collaborative knowledge*. Cambridge, MA: MIT Press.

Strijbos, J.-W., & Fischer, F. (2007). Methodological challenges for collaborative learning research. *Learning and Instruction, 17*, 389–393.

Strijbos, J.-W., Martens, R. L., Jochems, W. M. G., & Broers, N. J. (2004). The effect of functional roles on group efficiency: Using multilevel modeling and content analysis to investigate computer-supported collaboration in small groups. *Small Group Research, 35*, 195–229.

Strijbos, J.-W., Martens, R. L., Jochems, W. M. G., & Broers, N. J. (2007). The effect of functional roles on perceived group efficiency during computer-supported collaborative learning: A matter of triangulation. *Computers in Human Behavior, 23*, 353–380.

Suthers, D. D. (2006). Technology affordances for intersubjective meaning making. *International Journal of Computer Supported Collaborative Learning 1*, 315–337.

Van der Linden, J. L., Erkens, G., Schmidt, H., & Renshaw, P. (2000). Collaborative learning. In P. R. J. Simons, J. L. Van der Linden, & T. Duffy (Eds.), *New learning* (pp. 1–19). Dordrecht: Kluwer Academic.

7

QUALITATIVE METHODOLOGIES FOR STUDYING SMALL GROUPS

R. KEITH SAWYER

Washington University, St. Louis

INTRODUCTION

In a collaborative learning environment, students often talk to each other as they construct knowledge together. Collaborative learning environments often go by names such as project-based learning (Krajcik & Blumenfeld, 2006), problem-based learning (Hmelo-Silver & DeSimone, chapter 21 this volume), or inquiry-based learning (e.g., Slotta & Linn, 2009; Wells & Arauz, 2006). The teacher works closely with student groups to provide appropriate support and necessary information about relevant facts and procedures as they work to solve problems or to pursue project goals. The teacher often facilitates or channels the discussion, but if students are collaborating effectively an experienced teacher may realize that the best thing to do is to stay silent.

In contrast to the transmission and acquisition style of learning associated with lecture and explicit instruction, collaborative learning is more *improvisational*; the flow of the class is unpredictable and emerges from the actions of all participants, both teachers and students. Improvisational collaboration is difficult to achieve, and it requires substantial teacher expertise. The most effective uses of collaboration are what I have called *disciplined* improvisation (Sawyer, 2004, 2011); collaborative discourse among learners is more effective at achieving learning outcomes when it is improvised within broad structures and frameworks.

I use the term *collaborative emergence* to refer to improvisational and emergent group processes (Sawyer, 2003). Collaborative emergence is more likely to be found as a group becomes more aligned with the following four characteristics:

1. The activity has an unpredictable outcome, rather than a scripted, known endpoint.
2. There is moment-to-moment contingency: each person's action depends on the one just before.
3. The interactional effect of any given action can be changed by the subsequent actions of other participants.

4. The process is collaborative, with each participant contributing equally.

Collaborative emergence is a defining characteristic of social encounters that are improvisational, because only when the outcome is not scripted can there be unpredictability and contingency. Because collaborative emergence results from interactions among participants, it must be analyzed as a discursive, distributed process. My focus on collaborative emergence is closely related to studies of *distributed cognition* (Hutchins, 1995; Salomon, 1993) and *situated cognition* (Greeno & Sawyer, 2008; Lave & Wenger, 1991). Suchman and others (e.g., Winograd & Flores, 1986) argued for a perspective in which "the organization of situated action is an emergent property of moment-by-moment interactions between actors, and between actors and the environments of their action" (Suchman, 1987, p. 179). All of these perspectives argue that knowledge and intelligence reside not only in people's heads, but are distributed across situated social practices that involve multiple participants in complex social systems.

Collaborative emergence is characterized by improvisation, unpredictability, and responses that are contingent on each other. The meaning of a turn is not always clear at the moment it is spoken; meaning is often ascribed retroactively through a collective, discursive process (Cazden, 2001). During successful collaborations, the group constantly constructs and maintains *intersubjectivity* or shared meaning (Forman, 1992; Forman & McCormick, 1995, p. 151).

WHEN QUALITATIVE METHODS ARE DESIRABLE

Qualitative methods are particularly valuable in collaborations that are characterized by collaborative emergence. For example, in collaborations with a high degree of *contingency* (the second characteristic in the above list), one person's action at a given moment is highly influenced by the actions of their partners immediately before—such that prediction of a person's action cannot be made successfully, independent of the sequence of preceding actions of others. In such encounters, knowledge and action are often better viewed as social, rather than as located in the heads of individuals. When collaborative discourse is improvisational and emergent, its analysis requires a methodology that details the social interactions of the participants, in addition to the internal cognitive structures and mental models of those participants. In collaborative emergence, learning is an ongoing social process, and a full explanation of the processes of collaboration requires an empirical study of the moment-to-moment processes whereby individual actions result in the emergence of a collective outcome.

Qualitative methodologies are intended to reveal the improvisational mechanisms whereby groups learn through collaboration; they focus on the dynamics of collaborative dialogue, as it emerges over time. A focus on social interaction and on emergence over time is shared by many collaboration researchers; researchers from a wide range of theoretical perspectives have hypothesized that social interaction mediates between the group and individual learning (Fisher, 1993; Johnson & Johnson, 1992; Kumpulainen & Mutanen, 1999, 2000; Mercer, 1996; Vygotsky, 1978; Webb, 1991, 1995; Webb & Palincsar, 1996). Researchers that study collaborative learning have focused on three aspects of interaction that could contribute to learning. First, providing and receiving explanations are both thought to contribute to children's learning (Bargh & Schul, 1980; Fuchs et al., 1997; Swing & Peterson, 1982; Vedder, 1985; Webb, 1984,

1991, 1992; chapter 1 this volume). Second, researchers working within a Piagetian sociocognitive framework have emphasized the mediating role played by conflict and controversy (Bearison, Magzamen, & Filardo, 1986; Doise & Mugny, 1984; Miller, 1987; Perret-Clermont, 1980; Piaget, 1932/1948, 1950). Third, researchers working within a Vygotskian or sociocultural framework have emphasized how participants build on each other's ideas to jointly construct a new understanding that none of the participants had prior to the encounter (Forman, 1992; Forman & Cazden, 1985; Palincsar, 1998).

All of these aspects of collaboration are conversational phenomena; explanations are provided in the context of the ongoing collaborative discourse of the group, and argumentation and elaboration are fundamentally discursive notions. In the sociocultural tradition emerging from Vygotskian and related theory, studies of collaboration have focused more specifically on discursive interaction (Durán & Szymanski, 1995; Forman, 1992; Gee & Green, 1998; Hicks, 1995, 1996; Palincsar, 1998; Richmond & Striley, 1996; Wells & Chang-Wells, 1992). Much of this research has combined Piaget's emphasis on cognitive conflict with Vygotsky's emphasis on social interaction, to develop a view that knowledge is coconstructed in social settings (Kelly, Crawford, & Green, 2001; Musatti, 1993; Rogoff, 1990, 1998; Tudge & Rogoff, 1989; Verba, 1994), and that meanings are socially constructed through discursive interaction (Lemke, 1990; Wells & Chang-Wells, 1992). An emphasis on the processes of group interaction, rather than educational outcomes, has been a defining feature of the sociocultural tradition.

These three distinct traditions—cooperative learning, Piagetian sociocognitivism, and Vygotskian socioculturalism—have reached a consensus that the processes of social interaction are the mediating mechanism whereby collaboration contributes to learning. In the late 1990s, the idea that conversational interaction is responsible for the benefits of collaborative learning inspired a burst of research in how discourse contributes to learning. Studies have examined the discourse processes of collaboration in science (Boxtel, van der Linden, & Kanselaar, 2000; Finkel, 1996; Green & Kelly, 1997; Kelly & Crawford, 1997; Kelly, Crawford, & Green, 2001; Klaasen & Lijnse, 1996; Richmond & Striley, 1996); math (Chiu, 2000; Cobb, 1995; Cobb, Gravemeijer, Yackel, McClain, & Whitenack, 1997; Saxe, 2002; Saxe & Bermudez, 1996; Sfard & Kieran, 2001; Sfard & McClain, 2002); and literacy education (Durán & Szymanski, 1995; Gumperz & Field, 1995; Nystrand, Gamoran, Kachur, & Prendergast, 1997; Tuyay, Jennings, & Dixon, 1995). Many educational researchers have noted that collaborative discourse results in the emergence of new insights and representations, and that once they have emerged, these interactive social constructions both constrain and enable the ongoing collaboration (Cobb et al., 1997; Sawyer, 2003; Saxe, 2002). In this "emergent perspective" (Cobb et al., 1997; Saxe & Bermudez, 1996), a complete understanding of educational collaboration requires a focus on both individual development and on social change over time (Saxe & Bermudez, 1996). In group discussion, both the overall group dynamic and each individual's learning collaboratively emerge from the group's conversation.

INDIVIDUAL AND GROUP LEARNING

Within traditional individualist cognitive science, the study of learning focuses on how mental structures change within the mind of the learner. Traditionally, cognitive scientists focus on the activities of individuals as they answer questions, solve problems, study texts, or respond to stimuli. Cognitive explanations are models of the processes that individuals use to construct, store, retrieve, and modify patterns of information. Concepts and methods for analyzing these knowledge structures are the main focus of traditional individualist cognitive science.

Qualitative methods are particularly useful when the researcher is interested in studying both group learning and individual learning, and how they interrelate. In the *situative view* (Greeno & Sawyer, 2008), learning at an individual level involves transformation of the individual's participation in an activity system and occurs as part of a transformation of that activity system. Focusing only on individual learning, as traditional cognitive scientists do, requires an assumption that the cognitive processes involved in collaboration can be decomposed in such a way that specific elements can be associated with specific individual participants. But situative researchers have shown that collaborative groups differ in whether they are organized in ways that support such decomposition. The interactions of extremely improvisational groups, such as jazz or improvisational theater groups (Sawyer, 2003), are not decomposable in this way with our current methods of analysis, and for these collaborations, isolating the learning of any one individual would require more powerful analytical concepts and methods.

Learning scientists are interested in the learning associated with individual participants, as well as the learning that corresponds to transformations of group processes. Studying both forms of learning simultaneously is difficult, and this is an example of a general difficulty facing scientists who study complex systems: whether to proceed by reduction to study of the components, or by holistic study of the entire system (Sawyer, 2005). Qualitative methods are particularly useful in analyzing three levels simultaneously: starting with the symbolic interaction among members of the group, working up towards an analysis of the emergent group properties that result, and working down toward an analysis of the thinking processes and knowledge structures perceived and constructed by one or more of the individuals participating in the group.

A BRIEF HISTORY OF QUALITATIVE METHODS

Perhaps the first scientific studies of interaction were conducted by Bales (1950). Researchers watched people interacting, and, using a specially prepared coding sheet, checked off behaviors of interest as they occurred. However, this method was limited because even a trained observer cannot keep track of the overlapping activities of several different people; and the interpretations of the observer can never be subjected to later disconfirmation in any rigorous way. (For similar reasons, interviewing participants after the fact to discern what they remember about an encounter does not provide sufficient data to understand an encounter.)

In the 1960s, researchers first gained access to audio recording equipment, which allowed them to listen repeatedly to the same sequence of interactions and to produce accurate and detailed transcripts of verbal utterances. This resulted in a methodology known as *conversation analysis* (Psathas, 1995; Koschmann, chapter 8 this volume). Conversation analysts focused extremely closely on the microsecond dynamics of conversation that most people remain unaware of, and they created new methods of transcription to capture what words on the page cannot—pauses in speech, sighs, interruptions, and overlapping speech—as in this transcript of the beginning of a phone conversation, prepared by Emanuel Schegloff:

Example 1. Initial dialogue of a phone conversation (from Schegloff, 1986, p. 114).[1]

1		(phone rings)	
2	Nancy	H'llo:?	
3	Hyla	Hi:,	
4	Nancy	^Hi::.	
5	Hyla	Hwaryuhh =	
6	Nancy	= Fi:ne how'r you,	
7	Hyla	Okay:	[y
8	Nancy		[Goo:d,
9		(4 second pause)	
10	Hyla	'mkhhh	[hhh
11	Nancy		[What's doin,

We can all recognize this as an extremely ordinary conversation, but even though it's familiar, the transcript reveals many aspects that we all take for granted. For example, in line (3), Hyla does not introduce herself but simply says "Hi." The colon after the "i" indicates an elongated vowel—she draws out the "i" sound. Nancy's line (4) indicates that she recognizes Hyla's voice: she starts with a sharply higher pitch, indicated by the caret "^"; her volume is louder, indicated by the underlining, and she elongates her "i" vowel even longer than Hyla did. These subtle speech cues send several messages: In line (3) Hyla signals that she is a close friend and expects to be recognized simply by her voice; in line (4) Nancy signals that she has recognized her, and signals her pleasure at receiving the call.

In the remainder of the segment, the overlapping speech (indicated by the square brackets), the long pause at line (9), and the elongated vowels all symbolize a high degree of intimacy between these speakers. If we heard the tape of the conversation we would all "know" this at some subconscious level, but only with a detailed conversation analysis can we delve into the microsecond interactional features through which these understandings are possible.

Almost from the beginning of conversation analysis, researchers have applied these analytic methods to classrooms. The first study to tape and transcribe classroom discourse was reported in the 1966 book *The Language of the Classroom* (Bellack, Kliebard, Hyman, & Smith, 1966). They established a methodology that is still used today: they began by segmenting classroom discourse into interactional turns, or what they called "moves" by analogy with a board game. They then identified the speaker of each turn. And in the most important methodological step, they developed a system to categorize the interactional function of each move. After doing this, they looked for *teaching cycles*: routine sequences of moves that occurred frequently. They discovered that the most common teaching cycle, 48% of all cycles identified, was:

1. Soliciting move by teacher in the form of a question;
2. Responding move by the student addressed;
3. An optional evaluative reaction by teacher.

Interaction analysts usually refer to this kind of repeating sequence as an *interactional routine*. Interactional routines have a loose structure that is understood by participants who share a culture, and they all know how to participate in the routine to bring it off smoothly. For example, the first few turns of a phone conversation (Example 1) are a routine. Interaction analysts have also discovered that almost all routines allow for variation; although they specify the basic flow of interaction, there are often branching possibilities and flexible spaces for improvisational action. There are many different ways that the beginning of a phone conversation could play out, depending on the relationship between the speakers and the goal of the phone call; these all represent variations on the same basic routine.

The methodology used by Bellack et al. in 1966—segmenting conversation into turns, and then applying analytic codes to each turn—is subtly but importantly different from conversation analysis, because it does not involve detailed microsecond transcriptions, and overlapping speech is typically ignored. As a result of these differences, most scholars reserve the term *conversation analysis* for studies that use detailed transcription methods, and close qualitative analysis of single episodes of conversation (see Sawyer & Berson, 2004, summarized below). I use the term *interaction analysis* to refer broadly to all methodologies used to study verbal and nonverbal interaction, including the detailed methods of conversation analysis, the coding techniques of Bellack et al., and many others.

Interaction analysis was pursued at two U.S. institutions in the 1970s and 1980s: Michigan State University's Interaction Analysis Laboratory (1975–1988), which focused on medical settings, and Xerox Palo Alto Research Center and the Institute for Research on Learning, which studied a broader range of settings including mealtime conversation, mother–infant communication, children at play, human–machine interaction, and various forms of technology-mediated communication in the workplace (Jordan & Henderson, 1995). Interaction analytic methods were used in a series of important studies of classroom discourse in the 1970s. Sinclair and Coulthard (1975) studied the same routines as Bellack et al., but they extended the analysis by developing a more complex system of move types. Mehan (1979), who called this routine Initiation, Response, Evaluation (IRE), analyzed the ways that teachers and students improvise variations on the basic format of the routine, and the ways that these routines connect together to form an overall one-hour lesson.

By the 1980s, conversation researchers had a good understanding of traditional classroom discourse. They had ample documentation of exactly how the transmission-and-acquisition style of teaching was realized in the classroom. Just at this time, the learning sciences were demonstrating that transmission-and-acquisition styles of teaching like the IRE routine were not the most effective style for learning (Sawyer, 2006). As a result of findings emerging from the learning sciences, classrooms began to change their structure away from the transmission and acquisition model in which the teacher lectured or controlled the flow of discussion through IRE sequences. Studies of situativity and collaborative knowledge building convinced many teachers to have their students work together in groups, jointly engaged in a project, actively constructing their knowledge together (Greeno, 2006; Krajcik & Blumenfeld, 2006; Scardamalia & Bereiter, 2006). The collaborative learning conversations that occur in these classrooms are very different from traditional discourse patterns like IRE.

THE SIX STEPS OF INTERACTION ANALYSIS

Many education researchers believe that it is important to study collaborative interaction as it occurs in real-world settings: this is referred to as *naturally occurring conversation*. A group of students in a laboratory, working on an artificial task, may talk very differently than they would in a classroom. As a result of these concerns, the learning sciences have developed nonexperimental methodologies to study collaboration. These qualitative methodologies, which I refer to collectively as *interaction analysis* (following Jordan & Henderson, 1995), are designed to analyze naturally occurring conversation; in classrooms, naturally occurring conversation is the talk of students as they engage in their normal classroom activities. These methodologies have been central in the learning sciences since the early 1990s; several articles describing methodologies to analyze learning interactions have been widely influential among learning scientists, including (Chi, 1997; Jordan & Henderson, 1995; Lemke, 1998).

Standard interaction analysis procedures generally involve six steps (also see Jordan & Henderson, 1995).

1. *Videotape naturally occurring encounters as part of a broader ethnographic study, often using participant observation—when the researcher is an active participant in the interactions.* Interaction analyses often begin with an ethnographic phase, an essentially anthropological approach where the researcher is embedded in the learning environment for an extended period of time. The goal of this extended "participant observation" is to gain insights into the implicit cultural beliefs and practices of the community—those unstated assumptions that participants are often not consciously aware of, and thus not able to describe in interviews.

Conversation analysts, in contrast, rarely conduct full-fledged ethnographies, instead capturing single episodes on videotape. They argue that a broader ethnographic study is unnecessary, because any contextual or cultural factors that are relevant to the participants will become obvious by how participants behave during the interaction: the external context is only important to the extent that it is "demonstrably relevant to participants" (Schegloff, 1992a, p. 215; also see Schegloff, 1991). Thus, "if some 'external' context can be shown to be proximately (or intrainteractionally) relevant to the participants, then its external status is rendered beside the point; and if it cannot be so shown, then its external status is rendered equivocal" (1992a, p. 197).

2. *Once videotapes are made, the first analytic step is to watch through the videos and prepare a content log—each identifiably distinct episode is given a heading and a rough summary of events.* Content logs enable a quick overview of the dataset, allowing quick identification of episodes related to specific research questions, and guiding the decision about which portions of the data to transcribe in detail.

3. *Perhaps the most critical stage is the identification of general patterns—sequences of interaction that occur repeatedly and that provide insight into the nature of distributed creativity.* In practice, interaction analysts often index digital video data so that instances of similar events can be observed together. (Video analysis software like Transana supports such indexing.) The process proceeds inductively—attempting to develop statements about general patterns from multiple sets of empirical data.

4. *Depending on the researcher's interest, some portion of the video dataset is selected for transcription.* Transcription methods vary in detail depending on the researcher's interest; in some cases, only talk is transcribed; in other cases, nonverbal details such

as eye gaze and body position may also be important and recorded along with talk. In some cases, details of pauses, breathing, and overlapping speech are transcribed (following conversation analytic methodology); in other cases, only the words are transcribed.

5. *For many research questions, it can be valuable to quantify video data by coding the data.* Coding involves several steps (following Chi, 1997; Lampert & Ervin-Tripp, 1993): (a) delimit the stream of data into distinct episodes (these could be as large as "conversational encounters" or as small as "utterances," depending on the research question); (b) develop categories, or codes, within which the episodes can be grouped; (c) use two or more researchers to assign codes to each episode, and then calculate intercoder reliability of the coding scheme. The coding process is typically iterative, because often the initial coding scheme makes it impossible to attain reliability across coders and must be revised repeatedly. Once a reliable coding scheme is developed, and the many episodes found in the video data have been coded, then quantitative methods can be used to identify generalizable patterns.

6. *Some interaction analysts ask the original participants to watch the videotapes with the research team, with the goal of eliciting the participants' perspectives on what was happening* (Calderhead, 1981). This is sometimes referred to as "stimulated recall." Either the researcher or the participant can pause the videotape, to discuss how the previous dialogue emerged, and to explore the participant's own understanding of what is happening.

Interaction analysis is difficult and time consuming. A relatively small study might involve 6 months of participant observation, followed by another 6 months of transcription, coding, and interviews. But this sort of analysis has the potential to expand our understandings of the step-by-step processes whereby learning emerges from collaboration, and of the relationship between the distributed learning of the group, and the individual learning of each member of the group.

TWO KEY TENSIONS IN STUDIES OF COLLABORATION

In choosing a methodological approach, studies of collaborative learning always must balance two key tensions: how to blend inductive and deductive approaches, and to what degree to quantify naturally occurring data.

Inductive vs. Deductive Approaches

Bales's (1950) approach was a deductive approach: he derived his coding categories from Parsons's (1951) structural-functional theory, and then applied them to his observations. In contrast, most later qualitative methods took a more inductive approach, allowing their analytic categories to emerge from their observations. A particularly influential approach in qualitative methodology is grounded theory (Glaser, 1992; Glaser & Strauss, 1967). Grounded theory involves both inductive and deductive approaches in a process known as *constant comparison*: tentative coding categories are developed initially by reading field notes or transcripts, and then an iterative cycle continues, of comparing categories and merging and renaming them. The end result is a relatively stable set of coding categories that can then be applied to the data.

All studies of collaboration begin by making a choice about how to balance induction and deduction. The more quantitative methods associated with experimental designs tend to rely more on deduction; they begin with a theoretically motivated hypothesis, a set of variables and categories derived from the theory, and then they gather data to evaluate that hypothesis. More qualitative methods tend to incorporate a higher degree of induction, providing a greater range of possibilities to emerge from the data. As a result, more inductive methods are more likely to result in the development, construction, and modification of theory.

Quantification

In Step 5 above, I noted that many qualitative researchers choose to code their data, resulting in an abstracted representation of the data that is then amenable to quantitative analysis—such as descriptive statistics that show the percentage of occurrence of one action or another, and how those might differ in different collaborative contexts or with different speakers.

Some collaboration researchers are opposed to such quantification. For example, Schegloff (1993), drawing on an ethnomethodological paradigm, argued that coding and quantification were unnecessary in the study of collaborative discourse. Ethnomethodology represents an "explicit preoccupation with the procedures by which commonsense knowledge is acquired, confirmed, revised, and so on" (Schegloff, 1992b, p. 1298). Schegloff argued that analysts should focus on the interpretations that participants apply to discursive acts; and that coding schemes do not accurately reflect the understandings of participants. He further argued that discursive acts always only carry meaning in a particular sequential context of ongoing talk, and cannot be coded independently from their sequential position. As an example, he referred to instances of *back channeling*—when listeners say things like *uh huh*, *yeah*, or *mm hmm*. These are generally not intended to interrupt the speaker—but sometimes they do serve that function; Schegloff and other ethnomethodologists argued that the meaning of any conversational action is always determined by the interpretive response it receives from the other participants.

All collaboration researchers have to make a decision about how to balance the more in-depth understanding that results from a qualitative analysis, versus sacrificing some depth of understanding in exchange for the more generalizable and quantifiable data that results from coding.

THREE EXAMPLES

In the rest of this chapter, I provide summaries of three different approaches to interaction analysis. These three examples demonstrate how the six basic steps outlined above can be applied differently depending on the context of the collaboration and the research goals.

These three examples demonstrate how each researcher chooses a different level of detail for its analysis. The first two examples are taken from projects in which the researchers analyzed many hours of classroom discourse. When researchers gather a large amount of interactional data, they cannot analyze each episode in as much detail, simply due to time constraints—because interaction analysis is labor-intensive and time-consuming. The third example takes the smallest level of detail, using a conversation analytic methodology—with detailed microsecond transcription of interruptions, pauses, and overlapping speech. This example is taken from a study that analyzed only 12 minutes of conversation. I chose these examples to demonstrate the important methodological choice facing all interaction analysts: choosing an appropriate level of detail, one that corresponds to the research questions of the study.

Example 1: Computer Scaffolding for Scientific Collaboration

The learning sciences have found that the best way for students to learn science is to have them engage with science content in the same ways that professional scientists do. Kelly and Crawford (1996) argued that for students to participate authentically in a scientific community, they need to learn to use the language of science. They designed a computer-based lab for 12th grade science students with the intention of engaging the students in conversations about physical phenomena and giving them a chance to learn how to talk scientifically.

They studied groups of three and four 12th graders, and transcribed their conversation as they analyzed oscilloscope graphs that recorded the students' motion as they walked near a motion detector. The motion detector was attached to the floor, and when students walked by it or hopped up and down next to it, the oscilloscope would display a sine wave that represented the vibration of the floor. Kelly and Crawford analyzed each 45-minute group session by (a) breaking down the episodes into turns of dialogue; (b) identifying the ways that small episodes were put together to form larger participant structures; (c) using these larger units to identify patterns of interaction. Example 2 shows a sample transcript, and Figure 7.1 shows how the researchers represented these multiple levels of structure. They then identified *action units*, which were composed of one or more message units and defined as having a semantic relationship with each other, and which represent a single intended action by a group member. Action units represent the thinking that students chose to display publicly. In Figure 1, action units appear as vertically elongated rectangles in the "Map" column. Third, they identified *interaction units* composed of one or more action units. Interaction units include an action and a response. In Figure 7.1, interaction units are separated by arrows between action unit blocks in the "Map" column. The longest interaction unit starts with Nancy's question in line 236, and ends with Steve's response in line 244.

Example 2. Transcript analyzed in Figure 7.1.

Laura	That is really neat	looking at computer screen
Nancy	Do big circles Jump up and down	to Laura
Computer	the representation appears	
Nancy	So why does it go lower? Distance versus time so when you get closer, it goes further this way?	Nancy moves the mouse others look at the screen
Steve	[No, that's probably] just how far	Steve points to screen
Nancy	[No, that's time]	Nancy points with mouse.
Laura	That's time	
Steve	How far it is away	
Nancy	Time is that, and, and, distance is this when you're that close you go crazy Go crazy far away	Points with mouse Looks at Laura Shakes the mouse

line #	Nancy	Steve	Laura	computer	map	non-verbals	codes
232			that is really neat		r+	to computer screen	responding
233	do big circles				r+	to Laura	
234	jump up and down				r+	intiates an experimental run	
235				*produces representation*	r+	laughter (Nancy, Steve, Laura)	responding
236	so why does it go lower?				q+	Nancy moves mouse, others	looking for clarification
237	distance versus time				r+	look to the computer screen	demonstrating
238	so when you get closer				r+	"	claiming
239	it goes				r+	"	"
240	further this way?				q+	"	"
241	~no that's time~	~no that's probably~just how far			r+ r+	Nancy pointing with mouse. Steve points to screen	demonstrating (Nancy), claiming (Steve)
242			that's time		r+		
243		how far			r+		
244		it is away			r+		
245	time is that				r+	Nancy pointing with mouse while	claiming (Nancy)
246	and				r+	nodding her head	
247	and				r+	"	
248	distance is				r+	"	
249	this				r+		
250	when you're that close				r+	Nancy looks to Laura	
251	you go crazy				r+		
252	go crazy far away				r+	Nancy shakes the mouse	

Figure 7.1 A transcript of three students working together at a computer. From left to right, the columns represent the line numbers, the three speakers, the computer's actions, the discourse analysis map, the nonverbal actions, and the researcher-assigned codes. Source: Figure 3 (p. 699): Kelly, G. J., & Crawford, T. (1996). Students' interaction with computer representations: Analysis of discourse in laboratory groups. *Journal of Research in Science Teaching, 33*(7), 693–707. Copyright 1996 by the National Association for Research in Science Teaching.

Kelly and Crawford focused on how the students' conversations made use of the computer display's representation of motion. At the level of the turn, the transcript reveals what information students choose to make public. At the level of the action unit, the transcript reveals how turns are tied together to accomplish purposeful activity. The researchers used this level to understand the many different ways that the computer was used by students. In Figure 7.1, both verbal and nonverbal activity show how the computer is drawn into the conversation. Kelly and Crawford identified five ways that computer representations enter student conversations. In these five types of interaction, the computer is treated as a member of the group, participating almost as another entity in the conversation:

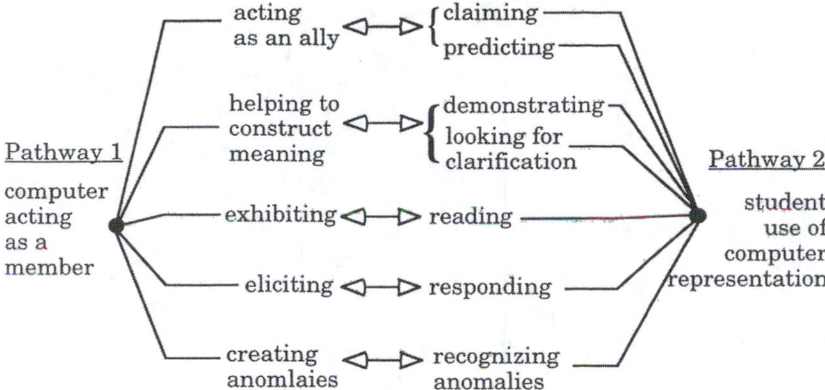

Figure 7.2 A list of the ways that computer representations are used in a conversation among three students. In Pathway 1, the computer functions as a fourth member in the conversation; in Pathway 2, the computer is used by a student in conversation. Each function in Pathway 1 is linked to its related function in Pathway 2. Source: Figure 5 (p. 703): Kelly, G. J., & Crawford, T. (1996). Students' interaction with computer representations: Analysis of discourse in laboratory groups. *Journal of Research in Science Teaching, 33*(7), 693–707. Copyright 1996 by the National Association for Research in Science Teaching.

- The computer is used by a student to support his or her efforts to make a case.
- The computer helps the group to construct meaning, for example by clarifying conceptual differences in the group.
- The computer is an external representation of important data.
- The computer elicits student responses (an example is line 235 in Figure 7.1).
- The computer presents students with unexpected information that sometimes is difficult for them to explain within their existing conceptual framework.

On other occasions, the computer representations are used by each student participant; instead of treating the computer as another participant, they are treating it as a source of support for their own position (see Figure 7.2). As a result, the computer has a special dual status in the group that makes it uniquely effective at supporting learning.

Example 2: Potential Pitfalls of Collaboration

Sfard and Kieran (2001) studied collaborative conversations in math classes, to evaluate the common claim that many school subjects are best learned through collaboration. They collected 2 months of videotape data from a pair of 13-year-old boys learning algebra (Sfard & Kieran, 2001). After the 2 months of collaborative work, both boys' math scores had increased above the class average, seeming to demonstrate the value of collaboration. But the researchers believed that the collaboration had not been as effective as it could have been; for example, although both boys' scores increased, one of the boys increased much more than the other. They conducted an interaction analysis to better understand what happened.

They analyzed two brief episodes extracted from their total of 30 hours of videotape. One of these was a discussion of how to understand a graph of the number of hours of daylight by the day of the year near the North Pole (showing 24 hours in the summer and 0 hours in the winter). They were asked to "Describe what happened to the number of hours of daylight over the year" and then given a series of five scaffolding questions such as "During which period of time did the number of hours of daylight increase most rapidly?" The transcript of one episode of this discussion appears in Figure 7.3.

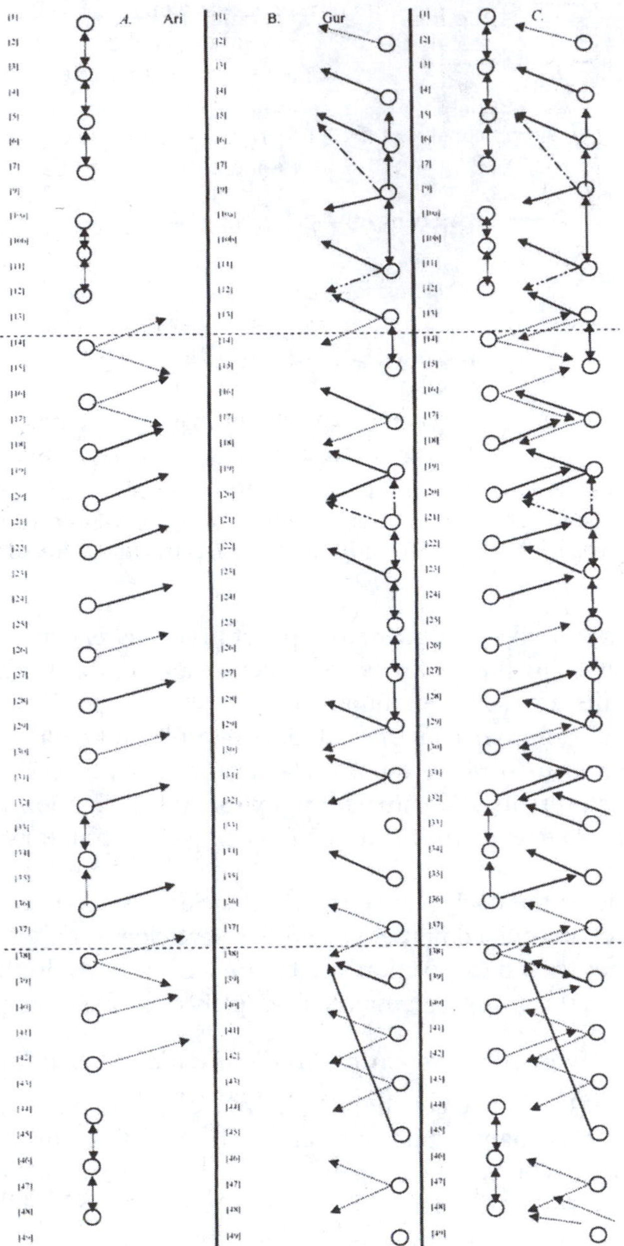

Figure 7.3 A transcript of two students analyzing a graph of the number of hours of daylight, throughout the year, at a point near the North Pole. Source: Figure 2 (p. 45): Sfard, A., & Kieran, C. (2001). Cognition as communication: Rethinking learning-by-talking through multi-faceted analysis of students' mathematical interactions. *Mind, Culture, and Activity, 8*(1), 42–76. Copyright 2001, Regents of the University of California on behalf of the Laboratory of Comparative Human Cognition.

Sfard and Kieran developed a new method of coding the transcript, one that resulted in an *interaction flowchart* (Figure 7.4). Ari is shown in the left column, Gur in the center column, and their combined actions in the right column. Each circle represents a single utterance that corresponds to the transcript in Figure 7.3. A *reactive* arrow points

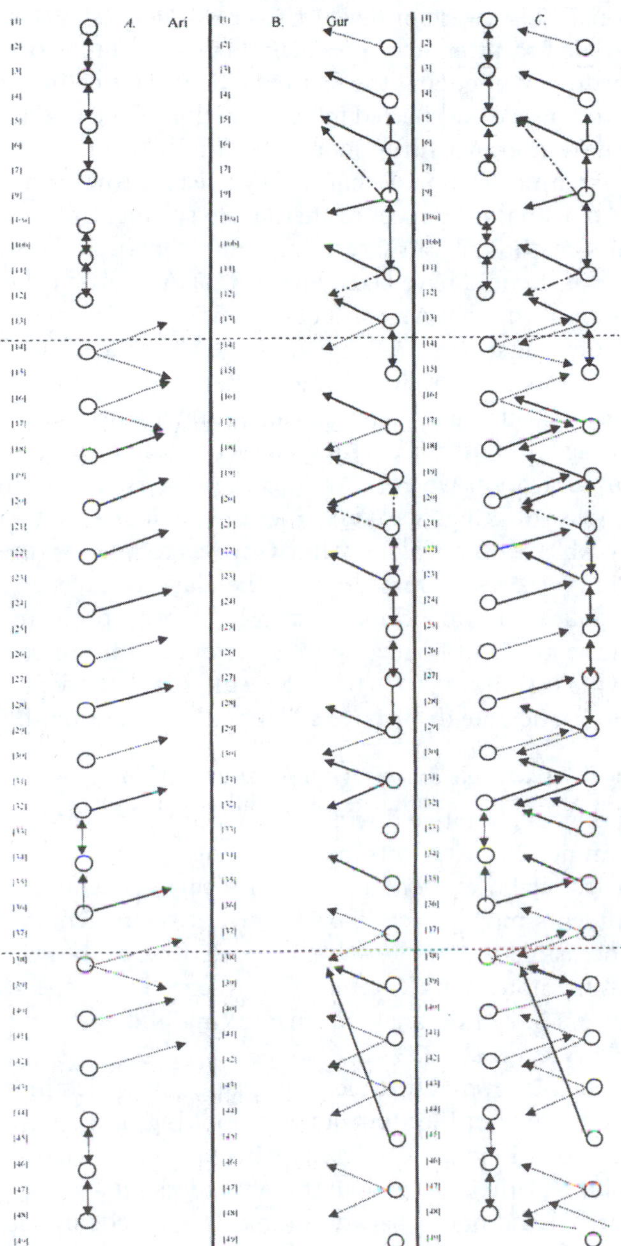

Figure 7.4 An interaction flowchart of the transcript in Figure 7.3. Ari's actions appear in the left column, Gur's in the center column, and a combination of both is shown in the right column. Up diagonal arrows are responses to previous utterances; down diagonal arrows invite responses from the other student. Source: Figure 6 (p. 59): Sfard, A., & Kieran, C. (2001). Cognition as communication: Rethinking learning-by-talking through multi-faceted analysis of students' mathematical interactions. *Mind, Culture, and Activity, 8*(1), 42–76. Copyright 2001, Regents of the University of California on behalf of the Laboratory of Comparative Human Cognition.

vertically or diagonally backward or upward, expressing the fact that the utterance is a reaction to the pointed-to utterance; a *proactive* arrow points vertically or diagonally forward or downward, symbolizing the fact that the utterance invites a response, and that the following utterance is expected to be a reaction. Note that a proactive arrow is drawn even if the next utterance turns out not to actually be a response; this would happen in cases of miscommunication or ignoring. Vertical arrows relate utterances by the same speaker, and diagonal utterances relate the two speakers.

This visual coding method reveals several important facts that show why this discourse was not as effective as it could have been. First is that Ari's first column has almost no proactive arrows—meaning that Ari was not directing his comments to Gur—he made very few response-inviting utterances. And although he made some reactive utterances, these were not very responsive—they were more often than not simple statements of disagreement. In contrast, Gur made many proactive statements; he attempted to sustain contact and encourage response. The visual coding method shows that Gur was interested in true communication whereas Ari was not. Interpersonal interaction seemed to interfere with Ari's thinking. Sfard and Kieran concluded that Ari was focused on solving the math problem, even if alone, while Gur was focused on the interaction itself. And while both boys' scores increased above the class average, Ari's final score was much higher than Gur's. They concluded that collaborative problem solving involves a trade-off between the needs of managing interpersonal communication, and the need to engage in individual thinking (p. 64). As a result, many students may need explicit coaching in how to participate in effective collaboration (Azmitia, 1996).

Example 3: Emergent Moments of Insight

In an analysis of the collaborative discourse of a university study group, Sawyer and Berson (2004) examined how students in a psychology class used their lecture notes to help structure their collaboration and their joint learning. During their study group discussion, the students mostly each looked down at their own notebooks while they were talking; but occasionally, they looked up at each other and engaged in conversation without looking at the notebooks. Conversation research has repeatedly demonstrated the importance of eye gaze in managing turn-taking and speaking rights (Goodwin, 1981; Kendon, 1990; Viechnicki, 1997).

Sawyer and Berson discovered that the conversation unfolded in very different ways, depending on whether or not the students were looking up at each other, or down at their notebooks. We identified three differences in conversational dynamics. First, when students were looking at their notebooks there was less *back channeling.* "Back channeling" refers to verbal and nonverbal communications made by the listener while the speaker continues talking. Second, when students were looking at their notebooks there was less overlapping speech, whereas overlapping speech frequently occurred while they were looking up. Third, while looking at the notebooks the participants left longer pauses between turns and within turns. For example, in the first turn of the transcript, Mary reads from her notes, and during this utterance, no back channeling occurs. Contrast Beth's turn, of comparable length and content, in (4). Susan and Mary each nod twice during this turn and Mary back channels with the word *yeah* once:

(1) M: *And, so Healy comes up with the U-Unitization Hypotheses that says that eventually, complex patterns are processed as whole units. The stimulus doesn't require any ((4))*

(2) S: *So that's just a hypothesis, it's not necessarily…?*

(3) M: I- I guess it's just like a (2) conclusion almost, um ((4))

Sa: *(nods)*

(4) B: Probably because related to the thing above- umm- we probably see the words like "of" like, a lot, so then it's auto[matic,] so that's probably why. (3)

Sa, M: (nod) M: [Yeah.] (nod)
Sa: (nod)

The use of the notebooks provided students with two different ways to engage in collaborative discourse. They could talk while each attending to an external representation, or they could talk directly to each other. The latter style had more of the characteristics of everyday conversation: verbal and nonverbal back channeling, overlapping speech, and shorter pauses.

Learning through Collaborative Discourse

Discursive phenomena like overlaps and back channeling are fundamentally interactional and collaborative, and would be difficult to identify if one did not transcribe the discourse in detail, or if one coded only individual turns of speakers, in isolation from the unfolding stream of discourse. Those three contrasts were revealed by applying the detailed transcription notation of conversation analysis, and this has demonstrated the potential value of conversation analytic methods for studies of educational collaboration. However, it is not yet clear how these contrasts affect individual and group learning.

Occasionally a speaker shifted eye gaze within a turn; there were eight instances of shifts from looking up to down, and 15 instances of shifts from looking down to up. These shifts served several distinct pedagogical functions. Perhaps the most interesting was that a shift from looking down to up allowed the speaker to revoice lecture material in her or his own words. When students read from their lecture notes, they are generally speaking in a scientific style of discourse, invoking the authoritative voice of the professor. The change in eye gaze corresponds to a change in voice—from the instructor's voice as encoded in the lecture material, to the student's own voice commenting on that material. Turn (11) demonstrates this revoicing pattern. Beth summarizes the LaBerge and Samuels model, and at the point where she looks up, she begins to revoice what she has already said. She originally uses the technical term *recognize*, and after looking up, changes her wording to the more colloquial "you're gonna pay more attention." Beth's mode shift occurs at the same time that she revoices her lecture notes.

(11) B: *So like the younger you are, the (1) more you're gonna recognize,* you're gonna pay more attention to each, each step.

These shifts in eye gaze serve an important educational function: they provide students with a technique to help them construct their own understanding. Within the sociocultural perspective, learning is a creative appropriation of material (Rogoff, 1998).

Many researchers have focused on the differences between authoritative scientific discourse and everyday discourse, examining how teachers help students to appropriate scientific or mathematical forms of speech (Forman, 1992, 1996; O'Connor & Michaels, 1993). The use of the notebooks as mediating artifacts scaffolds students in the use of two discursive styles—a scientific style and an everyday style—and these are used as collective tools by students to help them appropriate the material. By revoicing the lecture material in their own words, the students appropriate it and thus enhance their own comprehension of the material. These analyses of students' shifts in eye gaze show how collaborative discourse with external representations helps participants to advance from simply memorizing lecture material to making it their own.

Group Learning through Collaborative Discourse

A focus on discourse allows the researcher to examine patterns of collaboration that emerge from the successive actions of speakers. Sawyer and Berson (2004) found that discussion of a topic began primarily with all students examining their notebooks; the group began their discussion of each topic by reading from their notebooks. Throughout the discussion, discourse gradually began to incorporate more and more face-to-face conversation, as the group members looked up and conversed about the topic, revoicing the lecture material, and making connections to personal experience or to other lecture material. Finally, the topic unit concluded with all students looking up before moving to the next topic unit. This overall pattern is evidence of a collective group learning process. The pattern is not planned in advance, but emerges from the improvisational flow of the group's collaboration (cf. Cobb, 2002). The group's collective shift to a conversational style supports a learning process in which the group members gradually absorb the material and become less reliant on the notes. The external representations function as a scaffold for a collective appropriation of the material; as the group discussion proceeds, the scaffold is needed less and less—the typical pattern of guided participation emphasized by learning scientists.

Note that this emergent group pattern is parallel to the within-turn pattern identified above: individual speakers shift from looking down to looking up to revoice notebook material. The shift in eye gaze serves a similar function both at the individual level and at the group level; the external representations of the notebooks scaffold both individual learning and collective learning. This is one of the benefits of external representation that have been documented by studies of CSCL (Stahl, 2006). The detailed transcription methods of conversation analysis resulted in the identification of an emergent group-level process of guided participation—where the external representation is gradually used less and less, as students increasingly revoice and appropriate the information.

LIMITATIONS

Qualitative methods can be used to study several aspects of collaborative learning: argumentation, communication, and critique; externalizing and articulating knowledge; how group patterns and communities of learners scaffold individuals in authentic practices. This kind of study requires an extended analysis over a longer period of time, and results in a large amount of data. For example, one paper that combined interaction analysis and cognitive content required 80 published pages (Cobb et al., 1997), and that length is not unusual.

The transcripts in Sawyer and Berson (2004) contain a large amount of detailed, microsecond notation. Generating this type of transcript is incredibly time consuming; if research goes into this much detail, it is only practical to study a rather small amount of discourse. Researchers who use the detailed transcription notation developed by the conversation analysts typically focus on only a few isolated cases at a time. The advantages of this method are that it can reveal implicit understandings and cognitive competencies that could not be discovered any other way. Transcribing a lot of detail, including overlapping speech, interruptions, and backchanneling, can provide many insights into the distributed, collaborative nature of group activities that are otherwise missed. Transcribing eye gaze, for example, can reveal a lot about how joint focus and intersubjectivity is established and maintained in groups. This is particularly important when two or more students are working together at a computer (or more generally, in the presence of shared external representations); without detailed transcriptions of where the students are looking, it will be difficult to fully explain the role of external representations in mediating collaborative learning.

The disadvantage of this method is that it can only focus on one small segment of the complex flow of a classroom. A 30-second segment of conversation can easily take 10 hours to transcribe. Consequently, the studies by Sfard and Kieran and by Kelly and Crawford did not use this level of detail. Their transcriptions were more in the style of a screenplay: just the words spoken, leaving out volume and pitch marks, elongated vowels, and overlapping speech. The disadvantage of transcribing this way is that a lot of information is lost; and often, the importance and relevance of that detailed information doesn't become apparent until the transcript analysis stage. But the advantage is that it becomes feasible to study a much larger volume of discourse. An entire 1-hour class can often be transcribed in 10 hours.

Researchers who take a more narrow approach typically use the more qualitative methods of conversation analysis. With this approach, it can take an entire journal article to identify everything educationally relevant that is going on in a 30-second segment of discourse. The advantage is that this level of detail can often provide highly nuanced insights into what each participant must have known at each moment, and can identify the exact moment when a group of learners is constructing a new understanding. It is difficult to analyze emerging understandings in authentic, situated contexts any other way; stopping the interaction to administer a test of each student, for example, would destroy the situated nature of the activity.

Researchers who take a more broad approach typically categorize each of the turns of conversation using a *coding manual* that specifies what type of conversational turn qualifies as an example of each category. Because a large number of hours can be studied simultaneously, it becomes possible to apply quantitative and statistical methods to the database of turn codes. For example, classrooms at two different schools can be studied, and their broad conversational patterns can be contrasted statistically. And like the very first study of classroom discourse in 1966, descriptive statistics can indicate how often a given sequence of turns occurs, and what contexts are most likely to result in a particular sequence. Another advantage with the broad approach is that it becomes possible to group turns into higher-level organizing units, as Kelly and Crawford did.

CONCLUSION

Qualitative research methodologies can contribute to our knowledge of collaborative learning in several ways. First, they provide the researcher with a method to study how peer groups learn both with and without a teacher present. In many learning environments based in learning sciences research, teachers act as facilitators, providing guidance that fosters collaborative emergence in student dialogue (Sawyer, 2011). And several decades of research into cooperative groups has proven that peer groups contribute to learning. However, this tradition has not examined the conversational dynamics of these groups; studies of cooperative learning primarily focus on individual outcomes, task structures, and incentive structures (e.g. Slavin, 1990). The studies I have reviewed here demonstrate how qualitative methods can allow us to look inside the "black box" of collaboration (Bossert, 1988–1989) to identify specific discourse processes that make collaboration a uniquely effective learning environment.

Second, qualitative methods can reveal the interactional mechanics whereby external representations affect discourse processes and learning. Learning scientists have explored the important educational role played by articulation and externalization. Qualitative methods can extend this work by examining how the discourse processes of the group are mediated by these representations. As in the three examples given here, external representations act as scaffolds that guide the group's activity, and this guided participation seems to allow a group to attain a higher level of shared focus and intersubjectivity.

The learning sciences have increasingly examined the conversational dynamics of educational classroom talk. Many of these studies have focused on short, isolated episodes of discourse. Qualitative methods can also be used to examine the longer-term emergent patterning of educational talk (Cobb & McClain, 2006). For example, Sawyer and Berson (2004) found that students always engaged in a period of talk on a given topic by looking down at their notebooks, and only later did they begin to engage in face-to-face conversation on that same topic. This pattern collaboratively emerged from the group's conversation, and it became an important element contributing to the educational value of collaboration.

Qualitative methods have the potential to reveal how these emergent patterns can contribute to individual learning. Very few studies have examined how collective group phenomena emerge from extended sequences of discourse, and how these unintended emergent effects might then contribute to learning; rather, most studies of classroom discourse have examined the knowledge that students are meant to learn, often by focusing on individual students in the classroom. For example, Sawyer and Berson (2004) found that a speaker sometimes begins talking while reading from the notebook, invoking the instructor's voice, and then looks up to revoice the material in his or her own words. This shift served as an interactional technique that scaffolded students in their appropriation of the lecture material. The fact that this sequential pattern is reproduced on both the individual and the group level suggests that external representations guide not only individual learning but also group learning. These analyses suggest that a full explanation of collaborative learning requires a simultaneous examination of both individual and group processes.

NOTE

1. Transcript conventions can be found in (Atkinson & Heritage, 1999) and are summarized as follows:
   [] overlapping speech
   ((*x*)) unintelligible speech of *x* seconds
   (*x*) a pause of *x* seconds
   = indicates two turns were spoken together without any pause, or "latched"
   : elongated vowel each colon indicates one second of elongation
   __ (underlining) emphasis
   ˆ Pitch rise
   , a comma indicates a pause of less than one second
   - an en dash at the end of an utterance indicates flat pitch

REFERENCES

Atkinson, J. M., & Heritage, J. (1999). Jefferson's transcript notation. In A. Jaworkski & N. Coupland (Eds.), *The discourse reader* (pp. 158-166). New York: Routledge.

Azmitia, M. (1996). Peer interactive minds: Developmental, theoretical, and methodological issues. In P. B. Baltes & U. M. Staudinger (Eds.), *Interactive minds: Life-span perspectives on the social foundation of cognition* (pp. 133–162). New York: Cambridge University Press.

Bales, R. F. (1950). *Interaction process analysis: A method for the study of small groups*. Cambridge, MA: Addison-Wesley.

Bargh, J. A., & Schul, Y. (1980). On the cognitive benefits of teaching. *Journal of Educational Psychology, 72*(5), 593–604.

Bearison, D. J., Magzamen, S., & Filardo, E. K. (1986). Socio-cognitive conflict and cognitive growth in young children. *Merrill-Palmer Quarterly, 32*(1), 51–72.

Bellack, A. A., Kliebard, H. M., Hyman, R. T., & Frank L. Smith, J. (1966). *The language of the classroom*. New York: Teacher's College Press.

Bossert, S. T. (1988–1989). Cooperative activities in the classroom. *Review of Research in Education, 15*, 225–252.

Boxtel, C. v., van der Linden, J., & Kanselaar, G. (2000). Deep processing in a collaborative learning environment. In H. Cowie & G. van der Aalsvoort (Eds.), *Social interaction in learning and instruction: The meaning of discourse for the construction of knowledge* (pp. 161–178). New York: Elsevier Science.

Calderhead, J. (1981). Stimulated recall: A method for research on teaching. *British Journal of Educational Psychology, 51*(2), 211–217.

Cazden, C. B. (2001). *Classroom discourse: The language of teaching and learning* (2nd ed.). Portsmouth, NH: Heinemann.

Chi, M. T. H. (1997). Quantifying qualitative analyses of verbal data: A practical guide. *Journal of the Learning Sciences, 6*(3), 271–315.

Chiu, M. M. (2000). Group problem-solving processes: Social interactions and individual actions. *Journal for the Theory of Social Behaviour, 30*(1), 27–49.

Cobb, P. (1995). Mathematical learning and small-group interaction: Four case studies. In P. Cobb & H. Bauersfeld (Eds.), *The emergence of mathematical meaning: Interaction in classroom cultures* (pp. 25–129). Hillsdale, NJ: Erlbaum.

Cobb, P., Gravemeijer, K., Yackel, E., McClain, K., & Whitenack, J. (1997). Mathematizing and symbolizing: The emergence of chains of signification in one first-grade classroom. In D. Kirshner & J. A. Whitson (Eds.), *Situated cognition: Social, semiotic, and psychological perspectives* (pp. 151–233). Mahwah, NJ: Erlbaum.

Cobb, P., & McClain, K. (2006). Guiding inquiry-based math learning. In R. K. Sawyer (Ed.), *Cambridge handbook of the learning sciences* (pp. 171–185). New York: Cambridge.

Doise, W., & Mugny, G. (1984). *The social development of the intellect*. New York: Pergamon Press.

Durán, R. P., & Szymanski, M. H. (1995). Cooperative learning interaction and construction of activity. *Discourse Processes, 19*, 149–164.

Finkel, E. A. (1996). Making sense of genetics: Students' knowledge use during problem solving in a high school genetics class. *Journal of Research in Science Teaching, 33*(4), 345–368.

Fisher, E. (1993). Distinctive features of pupil-pupil classroom talk and their relationship to learning: How discursive exploration might be encouraged. *Language and Education, 7*(4), 239–257.

Forman, E. A. (1992). Discourse, intersubjectivity, and the development of peer collaboration: A Vygotskian approach. In L. T. Winegar & J. Valsiner (Eds.), *Children's development within social context, Volume 1: Metatheory and theory* (pp. 143–159). Mahwah, NJ: Erlbaum.

Forman, E. A. (1996). Learning mathematics as participation in classroom practice: Implications of sociocultural theory for educational reform. In L. P. Steffe, P. Nesher, P. Cobb, G. A. Goldin, & B. Greer (Eds.), *Theories of mathematical learning* (pp. 115–130). Mahwah, NJ: Erlbaum.

Forman, E. A., & Cazden, C. B. (1985). Exploring Vygotskian perspectives in education: The cognitive value of peer interaction. In J. V. Wertsch (Ed.), *Culture, communication, and cognition: Vygotskian perspectives* (pp. 323–347). New York: Cambridge University Press.

Forman, E. A., & McCormick, D. E. (1995). Discourse analysis: A sociocultural perspective. *Remedial and Special Education, 16*(3), 150–158.

Fuchs, L. S., Fuchs, D., Hamlett, C. L., Phillips, N. B., Karns, K., & Dutka, S. (1997). Enhancing students' helping behavior during peer-mediated instruction with conceptual mathematical explanations. *The Elementary School Journal, 97*(3), 223–249.

Gee, J. P., & Green, J. L. (1998). Discourse analysis, learning, and social practice: A methodological study. *Review of Educational Research, 23*, 119–169.

Glaser, B. G. (1992). *Basics of grounded theory analysis: Emergence vs. forcing.* Mill Valley, CA: Sociology Press.

Glaser, B. G., & Strauss, A. L. (1967). *A discovery of grounded theory: Strategies for qualitative research.* Chicago, IL: Aldine.

Goodwin, C. (1981). *Conversational organization: Interaction between speakers and hearers.* New York: Academic Press.

Green, J., & Kelly, G. (Eds.). (1997). Discourse in science classrooms [Special issue]. *Journal of Classroom Interaction, 32* (2). University of Houston.

Greeno, J. G. (2006). Learning in activity. In R. K. Sawyer (Ed.), *Cambridge handbook of the learning sciences* (pp. 79-96). New York: Cambridge University Press.

Greeno, J. G., & Sawyer, R. K. (2008). Situativity and learning. In P. Robbins & M. Aydede (Eds.), *The Cambridge handbook of situated cognition* (pp. 347–367). New York: Cambridge University Press.

Gumperz, J. J., & Field, M. (1995). Children's discourse and inferential practices in cooperative learning. *Discourse Processes, 19*, 133–147.

Hicks, D. (1995). Discourse, learning, and teaching. *Review of Research in Education, 21*, 49–95.

Hicks, D. (Ed.). (1996). *Discourse, learning, and schooling.* New York: Cambridge University Press.

Hutchins, E. (1995). *Cognition in the wild.* Cambridge, MA: MIT Press.

Johnson, D. W., & Johnson, R. T. (1992). Positive interdependence: Key to effective cooperation. In R. Hertz-Lazarowitz & N. Miller (Eds.), *Interaction in cooperative groups: The theoretical anatomy of group learning* (pp. 174–199). New York: Cambridge University Press.

Jordan, B., & Henderson, A. (1995). Interaction analysis: Foundations and practice. *Journal of the Learning Sciences, 4*(1), 39–103.

Kelly, G. J., & Crawford, T. (1996). Students' interaction with computer representations: Analysis of discourse in laboratory groups. *Journal of Research in Science Teaching, 33*(7), 693–707.

Kelly, G. J., & Crawford, T. (1997). An ethnographic investigation of the discourse processes of school science. *Science Education, 81*, 533–559.

Kelly, G. J., Crawford, T., & Green, J. (2001). Common task and uncommon knowledge: Dissenting voices in the discursive construction of physics across small laboratory groups. *Linguistics & Education, 12*(2), 135–174.

Kendon, A. (1990). *Conducting interaction: Patterns of behavior in focused encounters.* New York: Cambridge University Press.

Klaasen, C. W. J. M., & Lijnse, P. L. (1996). Interpreting students' and teachers' discourse in science classes: An underestimated problem? *Journal of Research in Science Teaching, 33*(2), 115–134.

Krajcik, J. S., & Blumenfeld, P. (2006). Project based learning. In R. K. Sawyer (Ed.), *Cambridge handbook of the learning sciences* (pp. 317–333). New York: Cambridge University Press.

Kumpulainen, K., & Mutanen, M. (1999). The situated dynamics of peer group interaction: An introduction to an analytic framework. *Learning and Instruction, 9*, 448–474.

Kumpulainen, K., & Mutanen, M. (2000). Mapping the dynamics of peer group interaction: A method of analysis of socially shared learning processes. In H. Cowie & G. v. d. Aalsvoort (Eds.), *Social interaction in learning and instruction: The meaning of discourse for the construction of knowledge* (pp. 144–160). New York: Elsevier Science.

Lampert, M. D., & Ervin-Tripp, S. M. (1993). Structured coding for the study of language and social interaction. In J. A. Edwards & M. D. Lampert (Eds.), *Talking data: Transcription and coding in discourse research* (pp. 169–206). Mahwah, NJ: Erlbaum.

Lave, J., & Wenger, E. (1991). *Situated learning: Legitimate peripheral participation.* New York: Cambridge University Press.

Lemke, J. L. (1990). *Talking science: Language, learning, and values.* Norwood, NJ: Ablex.

Lemke, J. L. (1998). Analyzing verbal data: Principles, methods, and problems. In B. J. Fraser & K. G. Tobin (Eds.), *International handbook of science education, Part Two* (pp. 1175–1189). Dordrecht: Kluwer Academic.
Mehan, H. (1979). *Learning lessons*. Cambridge, MA: Harvard University Press.
Mercer, N. (1996). The quality of talk in children's collaborative activity in the classroom. *Learning and Instruction, 6*, 359–377.
Miller, M. (1987). Argumentation and cognition. In M. Hickmann (Ed.), *Social and functional approaches to language and thought* (pp. 225–249). San Diego, CA: Academic Press.
Musatti, T. (1993). Meaning between peers: The meaning of the peer. *Cognition and Instruction, 11*(3/4), 241–250.
Nystrand, M., Gamoran, A., Kachur, R., & Prendergast, C. (1997). *Opening dialogue: Understanding the dynamics of language and learning in the English classroom*. New York: Teacher's College Press.
O'Connor, M. C., & Michaels, S. (1993). Aligning academic task and participation status through revoicing: Analysis of a classroom discourse strategy. *Anthropology and Education Quarterly, 24*(4), 318–335.
Palincsar, A. S. (1998). Social constructivist perspectives on teaching and learning. In J. T. Spence, J. M. Darley, & D. J. Foss (Eds.), *Annual Review of Psychology* (Vol. 49, pp. 345–375). Palo Alto, CA: Annual Reviews.
Parsons, T. (1951). *The social system*. Glencoe, IL: Free Press.
Perret-Clermont, A. N. (1980). *Social interaction and cognitive development in children*. New York: Academic Press.
Piaget, J. (1948). *The moral judgment of the child* (M. Gabain, Trans.). Glencoe, IL: Free Press. (Original work published 1932)
Piaget, J. (1950). *The psychology of intelligence*. London: Routledge & Kegan Paul.
Psathas, G. (1995). *Conversation analysis: The study of talk-in-interaction*. Thousand Oaks, CA: Sage.
Richmond, G., & Striley, J. (1996). Making meaning in classrooms: Social processes in small-group discourse and scientific knowledge building. *Journal of Research in Science Teaching, 33*(8), 839–858.
Rogoff, B. (1990). *Apprenticeship in thinking: Cognitive development in social context*. New York: Oxford University Press.
Rogoff, B. (1998). Cognition as a collaborative process. In D. Kuhn & R. S. Siegler (Eds.), *Handbook of child psychology: Vol. 2, Cognition, perception, and language* (5th ed., pp. 679–744). New York: Wiley.
Salomon, G. (Ed.). (1993). *Distributed cognitions: Psychological and educational considerations*. New York: Cambridge.
Sawyer, R. K. (2003). *Group creativity: Music, theater, collaboration*. Mahwah, NJ: Erlbaum.
Sawyer, R. K. (2004). Creative teaching: Collaborative discussion as disciplined improvisation. *Educational Researcher, 33*(2), 12–20.
Sawyer, R. K. (2005). *Social emergence: Societies as complex systems*. New York: Cambridge University Press.
Sawyer, R. K. (2006). The new science of learning. In R. K. Sawyer (Ed.), *Cambridge handbook of the learning sciences* (pp. 1–16). New York: Cambridge University Press.
Sawyer, R. K. (2011). What makes good teachers great? The artful balance of structure and improvisation In R. K. Sawyer (Ed.), *Structure and improvisation in creative teaching* (pp. 1–24). New York: Cambridge University Press.
Sawyer, R. K., & Berson, S. (2004). Study group discourse: How external representations affect collaborative conversation. *Linguistics and Education, 15*(4), 387–412.
Saxe, G. B. (2002, April). *Form and function in children's mathematical representations: A cultural-developmental framework*. Paper presented at the American Educational Research Association Annual Meeting, New Orleans, LA.
Saxe, G. B., & Bermudez, T. (1996). Emergent mathematical environments in children's games. In L. P. Steffe, P. Nesher, P. Cobb, G. A. Goldin, & B. Greer (Eds.), *Theories of mathematical learning* (pp. 51–68). Mahwah, NJ: Erlbaum.
Scardamalia, M., & Bereiter, C. (2006). Knowledge building. In R. K. Sawyer (Ed.), *Cambridge handbook of the learning sciences* (pp. 97–115). New York: Cambridge University Press.
Schegloff, E. A. (1986). The routine as achievement. *Human Studies, 9*, 111–151.
Schegloff, E. A. (1991). Reflections on talk and social structure. In D. Boden & D. H. Zimmerman (Eds.), *Talk and social structure: Studies in ethnomethodology and conversation analysis* (pp. 44–70). Berkeley, CA: University of California Press.
Schegloff, E. A. (1992a). In another context. In A. Duranti & C. Goodwin (Eds.), *Rethinking context: Language as an interactive phenomenon* (pp. 191–227). New York: Cambridge.
Schegloff, E. A. (1992b). Repair after next turn: The last structurally provided defense of intersubjectivity in conversation. *American Journal of Sociology, 97*(5), 1295–1345.
Schegloff, E. A. (1993). Reflections on quantification in the study of conversation. *Research on Language and Social Interaction, 26*(1), 99–128.

Sfard, A., & Kieran, C. (2001). Cognition as communication: Rethinking learning-by-talking through multi-faceted analysis of students' mathematical interactions. *Mind, Culture, and Activity, 8*(1), 42–76.
Sfard, A., & McClain, K. (Eds.). (2002). Analyzing tools: Perspectives on the role of designed artifacts in mathematics learning [Special issue]. *Journal of the Learning Sciences, 11*(2 & 3).
Sinclair, J. M., & Coulthard, R. M. (1975). *Towards an analysis of discourse: The English used by teachers and pupils.* London: Oxford University Press.
Slavin, R. E. (1990). *Cooperative learning: Theory, research, and practice.* Boston, MA: Allyn & Bacon.
Slotta, J. D., & Linn, M. C. (2009). *WISE science: Web-based inquiry in the classroom.* New York: Teachers College Press.
Stahl, G. (2006). *Group cognition: Computer support for building collaborative knowledge.* Cambridge, MA: MIT Press.
Suchman, L. A. (1987). *Plans and situated actions: The problem of human-machine communication.* New York: Cambridge University Press.
Swing, S. R., & Peterson, P. L. (1982). The relationship of student ability and small-group interaction to student achievement. *American Educational Research Journal, 19*(2), 259–274.
Tudge, J., & Rogoff, B. (1989). Peer influences on cognitive development: Piagetian and Vygotskian perspectives. In M. Bornstein & J. Bruner (Eds.), *Interaction in cognitive development* (pp. 17–40). Hillsdale, NJ: Erlbaum.
Tuyay, S., Jennings, L., & Dixon, C. (1995). Classroom discourse and opportunities to learn: An ethnographic study of knowledge construction in a bilingual third-grade classroom. *Discourse Processes, 19,* 75–110.
Vedder, P. (1985). *Cooperative learning: A study on processes and effects of cooperation between primary school children.* Groningen, Netherlands: Rijksuniversiteit Groningen.
Verba, M. (1994). The beginnings of collaboration in peer interaction. *Human Development, 37,* 125–139.
Viechnicki, G. B. (1997). An empirical analysis of participant intentions: Discourse in a graduate seminar. *Language & Communication, 17*(2), 103–131.
Vygotsky, L. S. (1978). *Mind in society* (A. Kozulin, Trans.). Cambridge, MA: Harvard University Press.
Webb, N. M. (1984). Stability of small group interaction and achievement over time. *Journal of Educational Psychology, 76*(2), 211–224.
Webb, N. M. (1991). Task-related verbal interaction and mathematics learning in small groups. *Journal for Research in Mathematics Education, 22*(5), 366–389.
Webb, N. M. (1992). Testing a theoretical model of student interaction and learning in small groups. In R. Hertz-Lazarowitz & N. Miller (Eds.), *Interaction in cooperative groups: The theoretical anatomy of group learning* (pp. 102–119). New York: Cambridge University Press.
Webb, N. M. (1995). Group collaboration in assessment: Multiple objectives, processes, and outcomes. *Educational Evaluation and Policy Analysis, 17*(2), 239–261.
Webb, N. M., & Palincsar, A. S. (1996). Group processes in the classroom. In D. C. Berliner & R. C. Calfee (Eds.), *Handbook of educational psychology* (pp. 841–873). New York: Simon & Schuster.
Wells, G., & Arauz, R. M. (2006). Dialogue in the classroom. *Journal of the Learning Sciences, 15*(3), 379–428.
Wells, G., & Chang-Wells, G. L. (1992). *Constructing knowledge together: Classrooms as centers of inquiry and literacy.* Portsmouth, NH: Heinemann.
Winograd, T., & Flores, F. (1986). *Understanding computers and cognition.* Norwood, NJ: Ablex.

8

CONVERSATION ANALYSIS AND COLLABORATIVE LEARNING

TIMOTHY KOSCHMANN

Southern Illinois University

The current volume is dedicated to gathering and summarizing research extant on collaborative learning (CL). For the purposes of the discussion that follows, we shall take CL to represent a broad class of pedagogical methods that involve engaging learners in a variety of instructional activities (e.g., small-group discussions, team projects, etc.) carried out collaboratively. It is often presented as an alternative to more traditional methods of didactic instruction (see, for example, Koschmann, Kelson, Feltovich, & Barrows, 1996). Conversation analysis (CA) involves research into the organization of talk-in-interaction. Since talk-in-interaction plays a crucial and indisputable role in the enactment of all kinds of instruction it might seem reasonable to expect that the large literature on CA might in some way be able to inform understandings of how interaction is organized in instructional settings, including those in which CL-based methods are being employed. The purpose of this chapter, therefore, is to work out these fruitful points of contact between CA and research on CL.

As will be argued, CA offers a new way of studying understanding as it is produced in interaction. Indeed, it offers a new way of understanding understanding itself (Koschmann, 2011). To see how this is so we need to characterize what distinguishes CA research from other ways of studying interaction and review some of its important findings. The list of studies comprising the CA literature is a long one, however, and numbers in the thousands. To help make this discussion manageable, we will focus on three articles published early on in the development of the field, articles that came to serve as cornerstones for that literature. I will provide a brief synopsis of each of these articles and illustrate how the constructs they introduced can be applied to the task of describing a fragment of recorded interaction. I will then explain how these constructs relate to research on the organization of instruction generally and, more specifically to research on instruction in settings of collaboration. The essay concludes by explaining how research on interactional organizations relates to understanding. Before launching into this exposition, however, let us begin by examining some of the essential features of CA research.

CA METHODOLOGY

The sociologist Harvey Sacks is generally credited with establishing CA as an area of inquiry (Silverman, 1998). He did so in a series of lectures delivered in the late '60s and early '70s (Sacks, 1992a,b). Sacks's approach to studying talk-in-interaction found its roots in ethnomethodology, a school within sociology that focuses on the ways in which members of society produce their everyday world as sensible. As a program of study, ethnomethodology assigns "exclusive priority to the study of the methods of concerted actions and methods of common understanding" (Garfinkel, 1967, p. 31). As Garfinkel clarifies, it is a plurality of such methods: "Not *a* method of understanding, but immensely various methods of understanding are the professional sociologist's proper and hitherto unstudied and critical phenomena" (p. 31). CA focuses on the methods whereby speakers and hearers collaboratively produce sense within talk-in-interaction.

Sacks' procedure for studying conversation was a designedly austere one. He began working with recorded telephone conversations. As he described:

> I started to play around with tape-recorded conversations for the single virtue that I could replay them; that I could type them out somewhat, and study them extendedly, who knew how long it might take. And that was a good record of what happened, to some extent. Other things, to be sure, happened, but at least that [what was on the tape] had happened. (1992a, p. 622)

In addition to being convenient to work with, recordings make it possible for others to evaluate the adequacy of an analysis. Sacks recounted, "others could look at what I had studied, and make of it what they could, if they wanted to be able to disagree with me" (1992a, p. 622). Nowadays, video recordings are the analytic materials of choice. Because of this, research on conversation is no longer restricted to simple vocal productions, but has been expanded to include a broader repertoire of communicative behaviors, including gesture, gaze, posture, and other elements (Streeck, Goodwin, & LeBaron, 2011).

Recordings are cataloged and transcriptions are prepared for selected fragments. Our understanding of how an utterance is to be construed is often shaped by various aspects of its delivery. CA transcripts capture not only what is said, but also details of delivery (intonation, volume, pace, and timing). By including these features in the transcript, they are made available to the analysis and, later, serve as a means whereby others can reconstruct the practices upon which the analysis was based. Gail Jefferson developed a conventionalized notation system for representing these details.[1] Transcripts utilizing Jefferson's conventions have become emblematic of conversation analytic work.

Sacks advocated a form of "unmotivated examination" of one's data. He (1984) suggested, "Treating some actual conversation in an unmotivated way, that is, giving some consideration to whatever can be found in any particular conversation we happen to have our hands on, subjecting it to investigation in any direction that can be produced from it, can have strong payoffs" (p. 27). Rather than approaching a set of materials with particular questions in mind (e.g., Is this good teaching? Are these students learning?), Sacks favored an approach that set such concerns aside and instead asked, what are they doing and exactly how are they doing it?[2]

Schegloff and Sacks (1973) observed, "A pervasively relevant issue (for participants) about utterances in conversation is 'why that now'?" (p. 299). It turns out to be an important question for conversation analysts as well. The goal of CA is "to explicate the ways in which the materials are produced by members in orderly ways that exhibit their orderliness, have their orderliness appreciated and used, and have that appreciation displayed and treated as the basis for subsequent action" (Schegloff & Sacks, 1973, p. 290). Through this organization, participants' understandings are made available to the conversation analyst for detailed study:

But while understandings of other turns' talk are displayed to co-participants, they are available as well to professional analysts, who are thereby afforded a proof criterion (and a search procedure) for the analysis of what a turn's talk is occupied with. Since it is parties' understandings of prior turns' talk that is relevant to their construction of next turns, it is THEIR understandings that are wanted for analysis. The display of those understandings in the talk of subsequent turns affords both a resource for the analysis of prior turns and a proof procedure for professional analyses of prior turns—resources intrinsic to the data themselves (Sacks, Schegloff, & Jefferson, 1974, p. 729).

The method of CA, therefore, is to conduct an analysis into participants' everyday analyses—the witnessible procedures whereby they produce their interaction as sensible. The goal of the technical analysis is to produce an account of how understanding is achieved within the participants' talk, not through speculation about causes and effects, but rather by simply describing just how it was done based on what is available to be seen and heard in the recording. This insistence that all claims must be grounded in the recorded materials is a hallmark of CA research and a source of its rigor. The participants' joint production of understanding is fundamental to how instructional and collaborative interaction is organized. This is an important point to which we will return a bit later.

THREE KEY CA FINDINGS

We will now turn to some basic findings in the CA literature. The matters to be taken up here—turn and sequence construction and repair organization—were first introduced in Sacks's lectures, but were more thoroughly described in three later papers. Our exploration of these topics, therefore, will entail revisiting these classic reports. As we shall see, the three constructs speak to participant understanding in different ways. They will provide us with a vocabulary for discussing the organization of instructional and collaborative interaction.

The Turn-Taking System

Sacks (n.d.) noted, "In a single conversation at least one and not more than one party talks at a time." This stunningly simple observation raises a host of puzzling questions, however. How is it, for example, that there are rarely long unfilled gaps in conversation and that speakers just as rarely speak in overlap? The speaker's audience analyzes a turn-in-progress listening for the place where a transition to a new speaker *might* be relevant. Sacks et al. (1974) proposed a model which they termed the "simplest systematics" to explain how this is done. The model had two parts: the Turn-Constructional Component and the Turn-Allocation Component. The first is definitional and describes how a turn at talk is put together. In their terms, a turn at talk is built up from one or more Turn Constructional Units (TCUs). A TCU might consist of a grammatically correct sentence, but could also be a clause, phrase, or even a single term. To determine the boundaries of a TCU involves detecting the places in a developing turn where a transfer of speakership might be appropriate. Sacks et al. refer to such positions as

Rule 1: On arriving at a "transition-relevance place" (TRP),

(a) if the next speaker has been designated by the current speaker or another speaker self-selects to speak,

(b) then the current turn ends and a new turn is initiated,

(c) otherwise, the current speaker continues with a another "turn constructional unit" (TCU).

Rule 2: Reapply Rule 1.

Figure 8.1 The Turn-Allocation Component of Sacks et al.'s (1974) "simplest systematics" model.

a "Transition-Relevance Place" (TRP). The listener's (and the analyst's) task is one of projecting when the next TRP might arrive. Grammar may play some role in this, but timing and intonation (and probably other factors) are also important (Ford, Fox, & Thompson, 1996).

The Turn-Allocation Component is algorithmic and describes the analysis that occurs when a TRP is reached as summarized in Figure 8.1. Note that the rules are applied in serial fashion. If the conditions specified in 1(a) or 1(b) are not met, the current turn continues and Rule 1 is reapplied recursively. As Sacks et al. make clear, the operation of the model is locally managed, contingent, and interactional: "the turn is a unit whose constitution and boundaries involve such a distribution of tasks as we have noted: that a speaker can talk in such a way as to permit projection of possible completion to be made from his talk, from its start, allowing others to use its transition places to start talk, to pass up talk, to affect directions of talk etc.; and that their starting to talk, if properly placed, can determine where he ought to stop talk" (p. 727).[3]

The simplest systematics model has important implications for participant understanding. Sacks et al. (1974) observe that (a) it obliges a special form of listening, (b) that entailed in this listening is a recognition of the type of action that the preceding turn performs, and (c) that the enactment of this model serves as a demonstration of understanding or "proof procedure" (p. 728). They note further that turns at talk are constructed in ways that mark their connection to the turns that immediately proceed and follow. This leads naturally, to the next important development, sequence construction.

Adjacency Pairs and Sequence Construction

Pairs of adjacently positioned turns were taken up by Sacks as the central topic of his last set of published lectures, those of the spring semester of 1972 (1992b, pp. 521–575). The analysis of sequences has assumed central importance in contemporary CA studies and adjacency pairs are both the simplest possible sequence and an organizing unit in longer sequences. As Schegloff (2007) described, "the adjacency pair is the prime resource in conversation for getting something to happen, because it provides a determinate *place* for it to happen—next" (p. 264). Adjacency pairs were taken up in an early paper that became another CA classic.

In "Opening Up Closings," Schegloff and Sacks (1973) introduced adjacency pairs as a means of explaining how conversations are brought to an end. The "simplest systematics" paper (Sacks et al., 1974) described an algorithm for speakership transition that was nonterminating. One of many uses of adjacency pairs in conversation is to produce a "terminal exchange" (e.g., "Bye."; "Good bye."). Adjacency pairs consist of two coupled utterances, commonly termed the first pair-part (FPP) and the second pair-part (SPP). The occurrence of an FPP makes relevant an appropriately fitted SPP.

The adjacency pair represents the smallest possible sequence. Simple base pairs can be elaborated through various forms of pre-, insert-, and postexpansion (Schegloff, 2007). In addition to elaborated adjacency pairs there are other kinds of sequences with a basic architecture involving 3 or more turns. We will see some examples of these shortly.

Like the turn-taking model described earlier, sequences are implicated in understanding:

> What two utterances produced by different speakers can do that one utterance cannot do is: by an adjacently positioned second, a speaker can show that he understood what a prior aimed at, and that he is willing to go along with that. Also, by virtue of the occurrence of an adjacently produced second, the doer of a first can see that what he intended was indeed understood, and that it was or was not accepted. Also, of course, a second can assert his failure to understand, or disagreement, and inspection of a second by a first can allow the first speaker to see that while the second thought he understood, indeed he misunderstood. It is then through the use of adjacent positioning that appreciations, failures, corrections, etcetera can be themselves understandably attempted. (Schegloff & Sacks, 1973, p. 298)

These potential misunderstandings and corrections bring us to a third foundational area of inquiry in CA, namely the organization of conversational repair.

The Organization of Conversational Repair

Sacks et al. (1974) noted that "the various organizations operative in conversation are susceptible to errors, violations, and troubles" (p. 723). Repair sequences serve as "a self-righting mechanism built in as an integral part of the organization of talk-in-interaction" (Schegloff, 1992, p. 1299). In a third paper, Schegloff, Jefferson, and Sacks (1977) summarized how these sequences are organized. The authors label the matter that stands in need of repair as the *repair target* or the *repairable*. A distinction is made between repair initiation, how the repair process is begun, and the repair itself. Repair sequences can take a variety of forms. In the simplest case, the repair target and its repair are located within the same turn. An example would be what we might colloquially term a "mis-speaking" in which the speaker interrupts a turn in progress to restate or repair some portion of that turn. Schegloff et al. described two two-turn repair sequence types—repairs produced by the original speaker ("self-repair" in the TRP) and repairs produced by the listener ("other-repair" in the next turn). Subsequent research has predominately focused on the latter. Three-turn sequences are seen when the listener initiates repair ("next turn repair initiation") and the original speaker then addresses the problem in the subsequent turn.[4] In all cases we can see that the work of repair is generally done in close proximity to the trouble source.

The authors observe that there is a marked "preference" for self-repair in a three-turn repair sequence over other-repair in a two-turn repair sequence. The notion of preference in CA is frequently misunderstood. It does not denote someone's partiality for one practice over another, but rather is an organizing feature of how talk is produced.[5] With regard to repair, we might say our methods of overcoming misunderstandings are built to favor correction by the first speaker. Schegloff et al. (1977) cite the following lines of evidence: when repairs are self-initiated, they are always self-repaired; when repairs are other-initiated, they are still "overwhelmingly" self-repaired; "other-initiations occur after a slight gap, the gap evidencing a withhold beyond the completion of the trouble-source turn—providing an 'extra' opportunity, in an expanded transition space, for speaker of trouble source to self-initiate repair" (p. 374); when other-repair does occur it is done in a "modulated" fashion (e.g., delivered with uncertainty markers, produced as a question, presented ironically); finally, when other-repairs appear, it is often preliminary to a disagreement.

It should be noted that the organization of repair is tightly integrated with the previously described mechanisms for turn construction and sequence design. In the "simplest systematics" paper, Sacks et al. wrote about the relation between turn-taking and repair:

> The compatibility of the model of turn-taking with the facts of repair is thus of a dual character: the turn-taking system lends itself to, and incorporates devices for, repair of its troubles; and the turn-taking system is a basic organizational device for the repair of any other troubles in conversation. The turn-taking system and the organization of repair are thus 'made for each other' in a double sense. (p. 724)

Not surprisingly, repair plays an important role in the ways that understanding is negotiated and maintained in talk. In most situations where it is clear to speakers and listeners what would count as an appropriate next turn, they carry on by simply producing that turn. As Schegloff (1992) observed, "[U]nderstandings are displayed en passant for the most part ... as by-products of bits of talk designed in the first instance to do some action such as agreeing, answering, assessing, responding, requesting, and so on" (p. 1300). It is only when it is not clear how to go on that the need for conversational repair arises.

ANALYZING A SEQUENCE OF TALK-IN-INTERACTION

Let us now look at how the constructs introduced in the three described articles (Sacks et al., 1974; Schegloff & Sacks, 1973; and Schegloff et al., 1977) can be employed to reveal the structure of a fragment of talk. The data presented in Exhibit 1 were previously published in Roschelle (1992). Roschelle's study is a classic example of a practice-based investigation of a CL-based activity. He described how two students, Carol and Dana, worked together at a computer conducting experiments in basic mechanics using a computer program.[6]

The transcript employs the notational conventions developed by Jefferson (2004). The excerpt begins with an utterance produced by Dana (lines 1–3). Features of her delivery and timing are captured in the transcript. Note, for example, the word *how* (line 1) includes two colons indicating that the vowel sound was prolonged. The period enclosed in parentheses following *how* indicates that a micropause (<.2 s.) was heard there. The text at the beginning of the next line is enclosed in parentheses indicating that the transcriber was unsure how to transcribe the talk. Two possible hearings are suggested. The letters O and W in *arrow* in line 3 are underscored indicating that that syllable was stressed. At the end of line 3 we find a number enclosed in parentheses. This represents a timed pause, expressed to the nearest tenth of a second.

Dana prefaces her turn with "What I don't understand is." She continues with "ho::w the length thing" (or possibly "the lengthening"), but pauses and restarts. Restarting

Excerpt 1

3:30:17 Dana: **What I don't understand is ho::w (.) the**
(length thing/lengthening) (0.2) **the:-**
(.) **the positioning of that** **arr<u>ow</u>:** (1.5)
3:30:23 Dana: ((*traces the initial position of the velocity*
vector on the screen using the cursor))
3:30:24 Carol: **(.hh) Oh y'know what I think it is¿=It's**
like the ⌈l<u>i</u>:ne (.) (that/fat) arrow is the
l<u>i</u>:ne, of where it ⌈pulls that down. Like see
how that makes ⌈this dotted li:ne?
(.hhh)/(0.2) **<u>T</u>hat was the black arrow:.**
(.) **It ⌈pu:lls it.**
3:30:26 Carol: ⌊((*traces the acceleration vector*
with forefinger of her right hand))
3:30:28 Carol: ⌊((*using thumb and*
forefinger gesturally pinches the tip of the
velocity vector and pulls it down))
3:30:30 Carol: ⌊((*retraces the acceleration*
vector twice with her forefinger))
3:30:33 Carol: ⌊((*repeats pulling gesture*))
(0.2)
3:30:34 Dana: **mn.hhh (Nw)you're saying ⌈this is the black**
arrow?=
3:30:35 Dana: ⌊((*traces the*
acceleration arrow with the cursor))
3:30:36 Carol: **=Yeah.=**
3:30:36 Dana: **=And it ⌈pull:s the other arrow ⌈on its**
hinge.
3:30:37 Dana: ⌊((*traces the resultant vector with*
the cursor))
3:30:38 Carol: ⌊**on its**
hinge.
(0.8)
3:30:40 Carol: **It pulls the other arrow on its hinge**
down to the tip of the black arrow, (1.0)
3:30:45 Dana: **making the line that you s'⌈<u>he</u>:re.**
3:30:46 Dana: ⌊((*traces the*
trajectory of the black ball with the
cursor))
(0.8)
3:30:47 Carol: (°**Right.**°)
(0.2)
3:30:48 Dana: **So if you were to ha:ve like** (0.4) **this**
3:30:51 Dana: ⌈**Who:a.**
3:30:51 Carol: ⌊**Who:a. Put that back.**
3:30:53 Dana: **I, can't move that or, like, am I**
not allowed?=
3:30:55 Carol: =((*coughs*)) **I wouldn't mess with it**

with "the," she thereby retains the rest of the beginning of the utterance as spoken. In this way, she corrects herself to produce something that could be heard as "What I don't understand is how—the positioning of that arrow." "Arrow" is not produced with the falling intonation of a completed sentence, nor is it given the rising intonation of a question. This might project something more to come, but instead a long pause follows.[7] Lindwall and Lymer (2011) report that declarations of a failure to understand are often treated as requests for explanation. It operates as a first pair-part, making relevant some sort of response related to the matter raised.

After Dana's prolonged pause, Carol self-selects to produce the next turn. Her extended turn (lines 6–11) is heard as a second-pair part to Dana's request for an explanation. The 'H's preceded by a period and enclosed in parentheses indicate a possible audible in-breath at the beginning of line 4. The inverted question mark after *is* indicates a partial upward shift in intonation with the delivery of that word. "Y'know what I think it is" takes the grammatical form of a question. The equal sign preceding *it's,* however, indicates that there was no hearable pause between the two words leaving no place for Dana to respond. Carol produces a gesture described in lines 12–13 and concurrent with the enunciation of "line" in line 7. Note how this coordination of talk and gesture is represented in the transcript. She produces three additional gestures (lines 14–19) over the course of her turn.

Koshik (2005) has argued that so-called 'rhetorical' questions, rather than seeking information, often serve to inform. As Schegloff (2007) explained, the making of an announcement is often preceded by a "pre-telling" or a "pre-announcement." He notes that such actions "serve as an alert to recipients that what is to follow is built to be an informing" and also "may give evidence of the recency of what is to be reported" (p. 3). This is how we hear Carol's question in line 6. Carol's long turn is a complex one involving stops, restarts, and repeats. She begins her account with "It's like the lines," but then stops, produces a micropause, and then restarts with a word we find hard to hear, saying either "that arrow" or "fat arrow."

The pronoun *it* appears recurrently in her developing account ending with the marvelously succinct, "It pulls it." Sacks described various "tying rules" for linking utterances together. One had to do with the use of proterms like *it*. He wrote, "To decide what it is that the tied turn term—for example, 'it'—refers to, requires finding somewhere in the conversation that the term it ties to occurs" (1992a, p. 163). Here we find a succession of statements tied using the mechanism described by Sacks. We hear the first two ("y'know what *it* is"; "*it*'s like the line") as referring back to the problem enunciated by Dana ("the positioning of that arrow"). The use of the pronoun in this way does the work of tying Carol's offered account back to Dana's request for an explanation. The latter two instances ("*it* pulls that down"; "*It* pulls it"), on the other hand, constitute the account itself. Both employ the transitive verb *pulls*. The challenge for the listener (and analysts) is to determine what is serving as the verb's subject and object. Roschelle (1992) describes how some of this ambiguity is resolved through Carol's embodied actions. They are examples of what Goodwin (2007) described as "environmentally-coupled" gestures. They are precisely coordinated with her talk (see Hindmarsh & Heath, 2000) and with events unfolding on the computer screen. Despite the availability of these visual resources, however, additional work was needed to unpack Carol's account.

Treating Carol's just delivered account as a potential source of trouble, Dana produces a query (line 21) that initiates a repair of understanding. It seeks confirmation of the referent of "black arrow" and makes relevant some sort of agreement from Carol. It is an example of what we have been describing as self-repair in a three-turn repair sequence or what Schegloff (1992) discusses as a "Next Turn Repair Initiation (NTRI)." Relative to the sequence still in progress, Dana's repair initiation is a "post-second expansion" (Schegloff, 2006) on the base adjacency pair.

Following Carol's response (line 25), Dana advances a candidate understanding of Carol's explanation (line 26), thereby making relevant another sign of agreement from Carol. The candidate understanding is tied to the previous repair sequence, both by its use of the pronoun *it*, referring to the black arrow, and its "*and*-prefacing" (Heritage & Sorjonen, 1994). It is another postexpansion of the base adjacency pair. Instead of waiting for Dana to complete her formulation and then ratifying it, however, Carol does something else. She starts a turn in overlap with Dana (line 30), coproducing the tail of Dana's as yet uncompleted utterance. Completing someone else's utterance, either for them or with them, is a very persuasive way of showing that you understand what they are saying.[8]

By tying the phrase "on its hinge" to their jointly produced formulation, Carol and Dana, have moved beyond just clarifying what "It pulls it" might mean to extending it in certain ways. The appended phrase speaks to how the pulling is enacted. Having initiated a repair in line 21 and receiving ratification, one might expect to hear a "sequence-closing-third" (Schegloff, 2006, p. 118) at line 32. Instead we find silence. In lieu of any sort of uptake, Carol, therefore, restates the collaboratively constructed explanation (lines 33–34), adding an additional descriptive phrase ("down to the tip of the black arrow"). "Arrow," however, is not produced with the falling intonation usually found at the completion of a sentence. This suggests that there might be more of her turn to come, but instead a long pause follows. Dana completes the account-in-progress with the clause, "making the line that you s'here" (line 35). Where Carol (line 30) previously completed Dana's proposal by joining in overlap, Dana now completes Carol's proposed explanation by supplying a clause that ties the explanation to what they see on the screen. Carol ratifies their joint construction with a quietly spoken "right" (line 401). Dana's next turn (line 42) is so-prefaced, marking its dependency on the understandings just established while at the same time moving out of that sequence to new matters. By using their newly developed understanding to plan their next step, Dana displays what Waring (2002) has described as "substantive recipiency" (p. 464).

ORGANIZATIONS OF INSTRUCTION AND COLLABORATION

To build a robust program of research related to CL, we need to begin from a basic understanding of how instruction and collaboration are organized. Though they are distinct phenomena, they can be considered to be "cooperating" organizations in that they can be simultaneously drawn upon to accomplish certain sorts of things.[9] To better understand what they are and how they operate together, we need to define them in terms of observable practices.

When I refer to interaction as instructional, it is so not because it occurs in a classroom or because it was interaction managed by a teacher. It is instructional because it does a certain kind of work. It is a way of organizing interaction such that one member is produced as the more knowledgeable with regard to some matter. It also establishes what will count as knowledge for current purposes. Instruction, therefore, is a type of understanding and what it achieves is *knowledgeability* (Macbeth, 2004). The important point here is that interaction becomes instructional in the very ways that it is done, in the ways that it is witnessably organized. Since much of what transpires between teachers and students in classrooms does precisely this kind of work, teacher–student talk often (but not always) qualifies as instructional interaction. A considerable amount of CA-based work has been done studying the organization of interaction in educational settings (e.g., Koschmann, Glenn, & Conlee, 2000; Koshik, 2002; Lee, 2007; Lerner, 1996; Macbeth, 1991, 2004, 2011; McHoul, 1979; Payne, 1976; Payne & Hustler, 1989; Zemel & Koschmann, 2011).[10] But instruction is by no means restricted to classrooms and formal pedagogical settings. If someone asks me for directions, their question and my response serve to establish me as a local authority with regard to the matter in question. Exchanges like this, therefore, also qualify as instructional and they are ubiquitous.

A second sort of organization with natural relevance to CL-based activities is collaboration. Collaboration (literally "laboring" + "with") is another kind of understanding. It is a way of organizing an activity as if the participants share a goal or task orientation. Note that I say *as if*, because we have no way of truly determining (either as participants or as analysts) whether or not observed participants are actually pursuing the same goal except what we can infer from their embodied actions. "Intersubjectivity," "mutual understanding," "common ground," and the like speak to the same issue: how do we know what others know? We have no direct knowledge of what participants hold in common, our knowledge is only of what they *do* to organize their interaction as if at least some things were mutually understood.[11] Despite this, we regularly and routinely carry out all manner of concerted activities. The work of organizing our interaction with others as if mutual understanding was secured is the interactional work of collaboration of which we have been speaking. It is based in the myriad ways in which we display an orientation to a shared task or goal. Our ability to fluidly coordinate our actions with those of others, then, is collaboration's achievement. Like instructional interaction, collaborative interaction is not only found in classrooms, but is seen everywhere and everywhen. There is an extensive literature consisting of CA-based studies of collaboration in the workplace (Goodwin & Goodwin, 1996; Heath, Sanchez-Svensson, Hindmarsh, Luff, & vom Lehn, 2002; Koschmann, LeBaron, Goodwin, Zemel, & Dunnington, 2007; Murphy, 2005; Nevile, 2004, to name just a few).[12]

However, when we turn to collaboration in educational settings a puzzle arises. As mentioned at the beginning of this chapter, we are treating CL as a class of teaching methods in which learners are engaged in a variety of instructional activities carried out in collaboration with their peers. How can such an approach be instructive, however, if it doesn't produce one member as the more knowledgeable? One of the distinguishing features of this kind of teaching, in fact, is that it doesn't employ rigid roles of instructor and instructee. In the Roschelle materials, neither Dana nor Carol was *the* expert. Carol's presentation of a candidate explanation and Dana's uptake of that proposal, however, served to produce Carol as a local authority, if not with regard to what was happening on the computer screen, at least with regard to *her theory* of what was happening on the screen. In this way, they can be seen to instruct each other in turns and as their advancing work requires. The *it* in Carol's preannouncement, "Y'know what I think it is¿" (Excerpt 1, line 6), is left "evidently vague" (Garfinkel, Lynch, & Livingston, 1981, p. 135). Positioned as it is after Dana's previous report of a failure to understand, it might be heard as referring to the un-understood matter. It could also refer, however, to the goal of their overall project, the assigned task of elucidating the mechanism of the observed simulations (Koschmann & Zemel, 2009). In it we see some of the possible ways in which participants work to display an orientation to a common task. Evidence of both instructional and collaborative interaction can be seen, therefore, in the fragment discussed previously.

Understanding just how collaboration and instruction are carried out together is one of the places in which CA can make important contributions to scholarship on collaborative learning. There is a small but growing literature that examines how CL-based activities are organized interactionally (e.g., Ford, 1999; Koschmann & Zemel, 2009; Lindwall & Lymer, 2008; Roschelle, 1992), and it is to be hoped that there will be more work in this area in the future. We will now look at how the three CA constructs introduced earlier—turn design, sequence construction, repair organization—are relevant to the work of instruction and collaboration.

Turn Design in Instructional Interaction

In the classroom students are generally not free to self-select for next turn at talk. The common refrain, "Raise your hand and wait for me to call upon you" alters the functioning of the turn allocation component of the Sacks et al. (1974) simplest systematics model. McHoul (1979), in one of the earliest CA papers to focus on classroom interaction, proposed a modified version of the simplest systematics model designed to reflect the institutional arrangements relevant to talk in the classroom. It seeks to accommodate the fact that teachers play a special role in turn allocation. This is part of what makes classroom talk recognizably "institutional" (Heritage, 2005). When teachers engage in classroom management activities they do so through instructional interaction as defined earlier, but they do so in a special sense. They establish themselves as local authorities on classroom decorum, while simultaneously providing instruction into what such proper decorum might be.

This is not the only way in which classroom talk departs from the simple model of turn construction described by Sacks et al. (1974). The notion of conversational participation also needs to be a little better elaborated. Schegloff (1995) clarified that a "party" to talk need not be an individual speaker. Participants may speak for themselves, but in some situations, they speak on behalf of some sort of situationally relevant group and, under these circumstances, it is the group that becomes the party to the conversation. This has particular relevance to classrooms. Lerner (1996) observed, "when a teacher presents a lesson to the whole class, the students participate in part as co-incumbents of a single association—'the class'" (p. 218). In addition to the teacher's active role in allocating turns, therefore, the way in which the body of students is addressed and responds as a "collectivity" (Lerner, 1996, p. 228) also alters the systematics of turn construction in classrooms.

A clear example of collaboration in the design of a turn can be seen in teachers' use of "designedly-incomplete utterances" (Koshik, 2002). This is a commonly used device for structuring student responses in the classroom. Here a TRP is created, but the TCU that preceded it is produced as hearably incomplete, often ending with a prolongation of the final syllable and a rising intonation. This makes relevant the provision of a candidate completion by one or more volunteers from the class. Lerner (1995) has described how this same device is sometimes used in peer-to-peer interaction as well. In this we not only see turns being constructed collaboratively, but also a way in which the design of a turn supports the work of doing collaboration.

Before leaving the topic of turn design, it is worth noting the important role that gestures can play in the production of instruction and collaboration. We saw, for example, how the gestures produced by Carol in Excerpt 1 were instrumental in the development of her explanation (Roschelle, 1992). The production of a gesture is carefully choreographed with its accompanying talk. Hindmarsh and Heath (2000) described how the enunciation of particular terms within an unfolding turn punctuate the affiliated gestural performance, "displaying just the moment at which it is sequentially relevant" (p. 1864).[13] They wrote, "Whereas we might normally think of gestures as working to support the talk, here we see how the talk reflexively works on behalf of the gesture" (p. 1864). Gestures are formulated in particular ways and not others to produce particular forms of understanding and this has been documented in instructional settings (e.g., Koschmann et al., 2007). For teachers and students alike, gestures contribute in important ways to the design of turns, in some cases playing a role in the selection of the next speaker and often revealing just how the turn is to be understood (Koschmann & LeBaron, 2002).

Sequence Construction in Instruction and Collaboration

It is a commonplace observation that classroom talk is dominated by teacher question asking. McHoul (1979) noted, "In the classroom situation [the adjacency pair] becomes an 'utterance-triad', question-answer-comment on the sufficiency of that answer (A-A-C)" (p. 191). Such sequences, in fact, are the distinctive signature of classroom recitation. In the literature on classroom discourse these are often described as IRE sequences (Inquiry, Response, Evaluation).

How does the production of evaluative triads in classrooms align with the previously made proposal to study sequences in terms of adjacency pairs? Schegloff (2007) offered the following thoughts:

> Some students of talk-in-interaction take the basic minimal size of a sequence to be *three* turns.... From this point of view, two-turn sequences are elliptical; they are missing something, ordinarily their third turn—a view which may reflect its origin in the study of classroom interaction. [We take the position] that the basic, minimal form of a sequence is *two* turns, and that sequences composed of more are expansions. On the former view, it is the absence of a third turn in a two-turn sequence which requires explanation. On the latter view, it is the presence of additional turns in sequences longer than two turns which requires analytic accounting. (footnote 1, p. 22)

Schegloff made a distinction between a basic dyadic sequence with a third-turn expansion and *true* triadic sequential structures (p. 224). IRE sequences belong to the latter category. They are recognizable as such by virtue of the fact that withholding the third turn in such sequences is treated by participants as an accountable matter. Given that we are now working with a triadic structure, a new system of designation is required. Where previously we had just first and second pair-parts, we now have first, second, and third *triple*-parts.

McHoul (1979) reported, "there is a mutual orientation on the part of teacher and selected-student to have that student produce sufficient answers, where the decidability of that sufficiency is a matter for teachers and teachers only" (p. 190). That sufficiency is established in the third triple-part. It is helpful to note that the queries constituting the first triple-part generally pertain to matters already known to the teacher and the fact that it is a "known-answer" question is displayed in the third turn (see Mehan's [1979] "What time is it, Denise?" example). As Macbeth (2004) describes, "What these direct instructional sequences yield, and what they are posed to yield, is something like accountably correct answers, and, by implication, knowledge and competence" (p. 704). They are, in short, a method for doing instruction as described earlier. However, it can sometimes get complicated as to how this gets worked out in the moment,. There are a variety of trajectories that the sequence can assume (Lee, 2007). The teacher, for example, might produce a positive assessment in the third turn thereby ending the sequence, but there are other possibilities—the teacher, for example, might repair the student's answer, restate the question, possibly in a different way (Zemel & Koschmann, 2011), or negatively assess the student's response and solicit an alternative. How the third turn in the sequence is designed may reflect differences in pedagogical strategy (Koschmann et al., 2000).

Moving from teacher-directed, instructional interaction to collaboration, we can see how sequence organization is employed by students to order their actions within an assigned task. There is a need to coordinate just where they are in the unfolding activity and, for each step in the activity there is the problem of translating an abstract instruction into an embodied action. Collaboration is achieved through the sequential organization of their talk. Ford (1999), for example, reported how the utterance "Two" (pp. 378–380), produced by a student working on an exercise with a lab partner, served to initiate a new course of action while simultaneously bringing the prior course of action to its close. She described the various ways in which the students used their worksheet as a resource for ordering their activity. The worksheet, in this instance, provided a means of specifying the next step in the procedure without having to actually describe it. The one-word utterance "Two," therefore, represents a directive to undertake the next step listed on the worksheet. The directive serves as a FPP making relevant not a vocal response, but an embodied action. Directive-action pairs can be elaborated through all the mechanisms described by Schegloff, as is the case with all adjacency pairs (2007).

The Role of Repair in Instruction and Collaboration

Schegloff et al. (1977) speculated that adult–child or parent–child interaction might be one place in which the preference for self-repair might not hold. They wrote:

> There, other-correction seems to be not as infrequent and appears to be one vehicle for socialization. If that is so, then it appears that other-correction is not so much an alternative to self-correction in conversation in general, but rather a device for dealing with those who are still learning or being taught to operate with a system which requires, for its routine operation, that they be adequate self-monitors and self-correctors as a condition of competence. (p. 381)

This would suggest that repair trajectories in the classroom might show a higher incidence of other-correction. McHoul (1990) undertook a study to see if correction in the classroom differed from the types of repair trajectories described by Schegloff et al. (1977). He focused his attention on cases of teacher correction in the third triple-part or student correction in the turn following it. The first would correspond to a two-turn repair sequence with other-repair and the latter to a three-turn repair sequence with self-repair. He reported that teacher correction in the third turn is infrequent but does arise in certain situations: "(a) where redirections and reformulations of questions (and/or cluings) have failed to generate self-corrections or (b) where a single (often procedural) question criterion is corrected so as to allow some other (often substantive) criterion to proceed to completion" (p. 375). He concluded, two-turn repair sequences with teacher correction "are formulated as last resorts or as completion facilitators" (p. 375). As Macbeth (2004) notes, however, classroom correction and the kinds of repair trajectories described by Schegloff et al. may not be strictly comparable phenomena.

Conversational repair pertains to intervals of talk in which "the ongoing trajectory of the interaction has been stopped to deal with possible trouble" (Schegloff, 2000, p. 209). Schegloff (1992) elaborated: "particular aspects of particular bits of conduct that compose the warp and weft of ordinary social life provide occasions and resources for understanding, which can also issue in problematic understandings" (Schegloff, 1992, p. 1299). Repair after next turn, he suggested, might be thought of as "the last structurally-provided defense of intersubjectivity in conversation" (p. 1295). Schegloff et al. (1977) made a distinction between *repair* and *correction*. They observed: "The term 'correction' is commonly understood to refer to the replacement of an 'error' or 'mistake' by what is 'correct'" (p. 363). But what they chose to treat as repair was "neither contingent upon error, nor limited to replacement" (p. 363). Thus, correction, as they used the term, is a subdomain of repair.

Correction and repair take on a different significance in classrooms:

> In such settings, explaining and understanding are very likely to constitute the main line of activity occupying the talk, and problems of understanding and dealing with such problems are endogenous to the core activities of the setting.... Discriminating the main trajectory of the interaction from temporary suspension of it for repair can be far less clear than in other, nonpedagogical settings. Yet this is crucial for the application of this domain of CA's resources to be warranted. Not every correction is *repair*; not every problem in understanding implicates the operations of *repair* for its solution. (Schegloff, Koshik, Jacoby, & Olsher, 2002, pp. 7–8)

Macbeth (2004) suggests that McHoul (1990) conflated two different treatments of correction. Correction, as defined by Schegloff et al. (1977), is a general mechanism oriented to negotiating and maintaining intersubjectivity, whereas classroom correction addresses a more specific institutional purpose. Macbeth argued that the two analytic constructs are not independent, but are instead "concurrent" (p. 719) or "co-operating" (p. 729) organizational domains. As he summarizes:

> Repair is implicated in the very organizational possibilities of [classroom] correction, as in the production of what a correct or correctable utterance, reply or response, could be. My point is that without the sense of difference and co-operation, we would not only lose the work and relevance of repair in classroom lessons; we would be left with an understanding of correction—irrespective of

> setting and occasion—that is uncoupled from the first work of common understanding and the organizations that ensure its recurrent achievement. (p. 730)

This "first work" of ensuring common understanding stands logically anterior to classroom correction (Macbeth, 2011). It is a precursor as well to what we have been discussing here as the twin organizations of instruction and collaboration. Let us consider now how they are related to understanding.

RESPECIFYING UNDERSTANDING IN (AND AS) PRACTICE

In one of his later lectures, Sacks described an exchange between two speakers, Al and Roger (Lecture 3, Winter Quarter 1969). Though the analyzed exchange consisted of only four turns, Sacks used it to illuminate how understanding is done as a practical matter. In Sacks's terms, "the way Al has of showing that he sees what Roger is doing is to do something that *fits* [emphasis added] there" (1992b, p. 112). Sacks was proposing what might be described as a praxeological respecification of understanding, that is a way of reconceptualizing understanding in terms of socially organized and publicly produced practices.[14] As he explained, speakers display understanding in the ways in which they organize their actions:

> Not to say, e.g., "I understand," or to say "What you said was…" but to produce an action that fits there, and that sets up another which can fit with it. That is to say, probably from the kind of academic training one gets, one has acquired the idea that what "understanding" means is to be able to paraphrase, or to be able to say what somebody means that they didn't say. Now, I think that the natural place for the notion "understanding" is in something like this. In terms of sequencing in conversation and many other things, you do "*showing that you understand* something" when what you do is, not talk about it, repeat it, paraphrase it, etc.—*that* would normally mean that you're puzzled or doubtful. The way that you go about exhibiting your understanding is just to produce another that you intend belongs, given what just has been done. You can put another item in that is consistent with the sort of thing you figure they're doing. (1992b, pp. 112–113)

Rather than treating understanding as a mental predicate, Sacks sought to locate it in the organization of the talk, in the very ways that each turn is "fitted" to the kind of action that is being produced. Recognizing just what that action might be requires an analysis on the part of speaker and listener alike. And it is here that the notion of an analysis of an analysis becomes relevant. As Heritage and Atkinson (1984) described:

> [I]n examining talk the analyst is immediately confronted with an organization which is implemented on a turn-by-turn basis, and through which a context of publicly displayed and continuously updated intersubjective understandings is systematically sustained. It is through this turn-by-turn character of talk that the participants display their understandings of the state of the talk for one another, and because these understandings are publicly produced, they are available for analytic treatment by social scientists. Analysts may thus proceed to study with some assurance the factual exhibits of understandings that are displayed and ratified at the conversational surface. (p. 11)

This could be clearly seen, for example, in the exchange between Dana and Carol discussed earlier. Examining the details of turn design, sequence construction, and repair serves to orient our attention to the specifics of how understanding is produced in any particular situation. It helps us to understand understanding as an organizational matter.

This then represents the most fruitful point of convergence between CA and CL. CL, by its nature, involves a mix of instructional and collaborative interaction. For the conversation analyst, therefore, CL offers a natural laboratory for studying how understanding is produced in settings of collaboration. The findings that accrue from such investigations would, of course, be invaluable to future research in CL, but CA has something of even greater value to contribute. The Sacksian treatment of understanding points in the direction of an entirely new way of studying CL, locating understanding as it does in (and as) observable interactional practices. In dealing with understanding, not as a curricular matter abstracted and decontextualized, but rather as a contingent, interactional accomplishment, CA lays the foundation for a new sort of inquiry. Instead of asking whether or not some curricular matter has been acquired, it seeks to discover what the participants themselves have produced as understood within their own conduct. The difference, though subtle, is a crucial one.

NOTES

1. A summary of these conventions can be found in Jefferson (2004). Examples of how a Jeffersonian transcript is produced can be found on Schegloff's excellent website: http://www.sscnet.ucla.edu/soc/faculty/schegloff/.
2. For a more elaborate development of this point, see Livingston's (1987) discussion of "bracketing" (pp. 55–58). Bracketing is a methodological requirement of all ethnomethodologically-informed inquiry and ties back to its philosophical roots in phenomenology (Langsdorf, 1995). The notion of "ethnomethodological indifference" is closely related to this notion of bracketing.
3. Ford et al. (1996) describe some of the details of how this is done. Garcia and Jacobs (1999) raise the question of how the Turn Allocation Component might operate within CHAT interaction. This is of special interest here, since it is becoming more and more common to utilize CHAT-based communication within CL activities (see, for example, Stahl, 2009).
4. Schegloff (1992, pp. 1320–1324) also describes a four-turn repair sequence. If a single-turn repair represents a mis-speaking, a four-turn repair sequence would occur when the original speaker treats the listener's response as presenting evidence of a mis-hearing. These are the least common type of repair sequence, and we won't deal with them here.
5. The notion of preference in CA is not limited to repair. Sacks (1992b, pp. 414–415) talked about the difference between "'Yes' –period" and "'No' – plus" responses. Negative responses require elaboration, while positive responses do not. He offered this as evidence of a preference organization in question-answer pairs. Other kinds of adjacency pairs may display other forms of preference (see Schegloff, 2007, chap. 5).
6. Further details can be found in Roschelle's dissertation (1991) and Koschmann and Zemel (2009). The fragment presented here corresponds to Episode 1 in Roschelle's (1992) report, but continues a bit beyond it. It is picked up in Excerpts 6 and 5 in Koschmann and Zemel (2009). I thank Alan Zemel and Manny Schegloff for their helpful suggestions with regard to the transcription of this fragment and how it might be described.
7. It is considered a pause and not a gap. Sacks et al. (1974) made a distinction between pauses, gaps, and lapses. They defined the terms in these ways: "intra-turn silence (not at a transition-relevance place) is a 'pause', and initially not to be talked in by others; silence after a possible completion point is, initially a gap, and to be minimized; extended silences at transition-relevance places may become lapses" (p. 715, note 26). Dana's pause comes before a TRP, so it is considered to be "owned" by her.
8. This harks back to a distinction made by Sacks (1992b) between proved demonstrations of an understanding and claimed understanding. He wrote:

Things like, e.g., at the end of some first story a recipient says "I know just what you mean." Period. We can say that that's a claimed understanding as compared to having some way to produce some materials that exhibit an understanding. (1992b, p. 252)

9. I borrow the term from Macbeth (2004) who was discussing a different pair of "cooperating" organizations. As we will see in short order, he was describing the organizations of classroom correction and conversational repair.
10. See Watson (1992) and Heap (1997) for earlier reviews of this literature.
11. See Koschmann and LeBaron (2003) for further development of this point.
12. While most CA-informed work examining interaction in the workplace has focused on collaboration, there have been notable exceptions. Goodwin and Goodwin's (1997) account of one witness's sworn testimony in the Rodney King trial is as good a description of instructional organization as you could hope to find.
13. See, for example, Maria's lifting gesture in Exhibit 1 in Koschmann and LeBaron (2002).
14. Sacks was not alone in seeking a shift from the ascription of mental predicates to the study of practice. Similar proposals were made by ordinary language philosophers and in early writings in ethnomethodology (Koschmann, 2011).

REFERENCES

Ford, C. (1999). Collaborative construction of task activity: Coordinating multiple resources in a high school physics lab. *Research on Language and Social Interaction, 32*, 369–408.

Ford, C., Fox, B., & Thompson, S. (1996). Practices in the construction of turns: The "TCU" revisited. *Pragmatics, 6*, 427–454.

Garcia, A., & Jacobs, J. (1999). The eyes of the beholder: Understanding the turn-taking system in quasi-synchronous computer-mediated communication. *Research on Language and Social Interaction, 32*, 337–368.

Garfinkel, H. (1967). *Studies in ethnomethodology.* Englewood Cliffs, NJ: Prentice-Hall.

Garfinkel, H., Lynch, M., & Livingston, E. (1981). The work of discovering science construed with materials from the optically discovered pulsar. *Philosophy of Social Science, 11*, 131–158.

Goodwin, C. (2007). Environmentally-coupled gestures. In S. Duncan, J. Cassell, & E. Levy (Eds.), *Gesture and the dynamic aspect of language* (pp. 195–212). Philadelphia, PA: John Benjamins.

Goodwin, C., & Goodwin, M. H. (1996). Seeing as situated activity: Formulating planes. In Y. Engestrom & D. Middleton (Eds.), *Cognition and communication at work* (pp. 61–95). New York: Cambridge University Press.

Goodwin, C., & Goodwin, M. H. (1997). Contested vision: The discursive constitution of Rodney King. In B.-L. Gunnarsson, P. Linell, & B. Nordberg (Eds.), *The construction of professional discourse* (pp. 292–316). New York: Longman.

Goodwin, C., Streeck, J., & LeBaron, C. (Eds.). (forthcoming). *Embodied interaction.* New York: Cambridge University Press.

Heap, J. (1997). Conversation analysis methods in researching language and education. In N. H. Hornberger & D. Corson (Eds.), *Research methods in language and education* (Vol. 8, pp. 217–226). Dordrecht, Netherlands: Kluwer Academic.

Heath, C., Sanchez Svensson, M., Hindmarsh, J., Luff, P., & vom Lehn, D. (2002). Configuring awareness. *Computer Supported Cooperative Work, 11*, 317–347.

Heritage, J. (2005). Conversation analysis and institutional talk. In K. L. Fitch & R. E. Sanders (Eds.), *Handbook of language and social interaction* (pp. 103–147). Mahwah, NJ: Erlbaum.

Heritage, J., & Atkinson, J. M. (1984). Introduction. In J. M. Atkinson & J. Heritage (Eds.), *Structures of social action* (pp. 1–15). Cambridge, England: Cambridge University Press.

Heritage, J., & Sorjonen, M. L. (1994). Constituting and maintaining activities across sequences: And-prefacing as a feature of question design. *Language in Society, 23*, 1–29.

Hindmarsh, J., & Heath, C. (2000). Embodied reference: A study of deixis in workplace interaction. *Journal of Pragmatics, 32*, 1855–1878.

Jefferson, G. (2004). Glossary of transcript symbols with an introduction. In G. Lerner (Ed.), *Conversation analysis: Studies from the first generation* (pp. 13–31). Amsterdam, Netherlands: John Benjamins Publishing.

Koschmann, T. (2011). Understanding understanding in action. *Journal of Pragmatics, 43*, 435–437.

Koschmann, T., Glenn, P. J., & Conlee, M. (2000). When is a problem-based tutorial not a tutorial? Analyzing the tutor's role in the emergence of a learning issue. In D. Evensen & C. Hmelo (Eds.), *Problem-based learning: A research perspective on learning interaction* (pp. 53–74). Mahwah, NJ: Erlbaum.

Koschmann, T., Kelson, A. C., Feltovich, P., & Barrows, H. S. (1996). Computer-supported problem-based learning: A principled approach to the use of computers in collaborative learning. In T. Koschmann (Ed.), *CSCL: Theory and practice of an emerging paradigm* (pp. 83–124). Mahwah, NJ: Erlbaum.

Koschmann, T., & LeBaron, C. (2002). Learner articulation as interactional achievement: Studying the conversation of gesture. *Cognition & Instruction, 20*, 249–282.

Koschmann, T., & LeBaron, C. (2003). Reconsidering common ground: Examining Clark's contribution theory in the OR. In K. Kuutti, G. Karsten, P. Fitzpatrick, P. Dourish, & K. Schmidt (Eds.), *ECSCW 2003: Proceedings of the Eighth European Conference on Computer-Supported Cooperative Work* (pp. 81–98). Amsterdam, Netherlands: Kluwer Academic Publishing.

Koschmann, T., LeBaron, C., Goodwin, C., Zemel, A., & Dunnington, G. (2007). Formulating the triangle of doom. *Gesture, 7*, 97–118.

Koschmann, T., & Zemel, A. (2009). Optical pulsars and black arrows: Discoveries as occasioned productions. *Journal of the Learning Sciences, 18*, 200–246.

Koshik, I. (2002). Designedly incomplete utterances: A pedagogical practice for eliciting knowledge displays in error correction sequences. *Research on Language and Social Interaction, 35*, 277–309.

Koshik, I. (2005). *Beyond rhetorical questions: Assertive questions in everyday interaction*. Amsterdam, Netherlands: John Benjamins.

Langsdorf, L. (1995). Treating method and form as phenomena: An appreciation of Garfinkel's phenomenology of social action. *Human Studies, 18*, 177–188.

Lee, Y.-A. (2007). Third turn position in teacher talk: Contingency and the work of teaching. *Journal of Pragmatics, 39*, 1204–1230.

Lerner, G. (1995). Turn design and the organization of participation in instructional activities. *Discourse Processes, 19*, 111–131.

Lerner, G. (1996). Collectivities in action: Establishing the relevance of conjoined participation in conversation. *Text, 13*, 213–245.

Lindwall, O., & Lymer, G. (2008). The dark matter of lab work: Illuminating the negotiation of disciplined perception in mechanics. *Journal of the Learning Sciences, 17*, 180–224.

Lindwall, O., & Lymer, G. (2011). Uses of "understand" in science education. *Journal of Pragmatics, 43*, 452–474.

Livingston, E. (1987). *Making sense of ethnomethodology*. London: Routledge & Kegan Paul.

Macbeth, D. (1991). Teacher authority as practical action. *Linguistics and Education, 3*, 281–313.

Macbeth, D. (2004). The relevance of repair for classroom correction. *Language and Society, 33*, 703–736.

Macbeth, D. (2011). Understanding understanding as an instructional matter. *Journal of Pragmatics, 43*, 438–451.

McHoul, A. (1979). The organization of turns at formal talk in the classroom. *Language and Society, 7*, 183–213.

McHoul, A. (1990). The organization of repair in classroom talk. *Language and Society, 19*, 349–377.

Mehan, H. (1979). "What time is it, Denise? Asking known information questions in classroom discourse. *Theory into Practice, 18*, 285–294.

Murphy, K. M. (2005). Collaborative imagining: The interactive use of gestures, talk and graphic representation in architectural practice. *Semiotica, 156*, 113–145.

Nevile, M. (2004). *Beyond the black box: Talk-in-interaction in the airline cockpit*. Burlington, VT: Ashgate.

Payne, G. C. F. (1976). Making a lesson happen: An ethnomethodological analysis. In M. Hammersley & P. Woods (Eds.), *The process of schooling: A sociological reader* (pp. 33–40). London: Routledge & Kegan Paul.

Payne, G., & Hustler, D. (1989). Teaching the class: The practical management of a cohort. *British Journal of Sociology of Education, 1*, 49–66.

Roschelle, J. (1991). *Students' construction of qualitative physics knowledge: Learning about velocity and acceleration in a computer microworld* (Unpublished dissertation). University of California, Berkeley, CA.

Roschelle, J. (1992). Learning by collaboration: Convergent conceptual change. *Journal of the Learning Sciences, 2*, 235–276.

Sacks, H. (1984). Notes on methodology. In J. M. Atkinson & J. Heritage (Eds.), *Structures of social action* (pp. 21–27). Cambridge, U.K.: Cambridge University Press.

Sacks, H. (1992a). *Lectures on conversation* (Vol. 1). Oxford, England: Blackwell.

Sacks, H. (1992b). *Lectures on conversation* (Vol. 2). Oxford, England: Blackwell.

Sacks, H. (n.d.). *Aspects of the sequential organization of conversation*. (Unpublished manuscript?

Sacks, H., Schegloff, E., & Jefferson, G. (1974). The simplest systematics for the organization of turn-taking for conversation. *Language, 50*, 696–735.

Schegloff, E. (1992). Repair after next turn: The last structurally provided defense of intersubjectivity in conversation. *American Journal of Sociology, 97*, 1295–1345.

Schegloff, E. (1995). Parties and joint talk: Two ways in which numbers are significant for talk-in-interaction. In P. ten Have & G. Psathas (Eds.), *Situated order: Studies in the social organization of talk and embodied activities* (pp. 31–42). Washington, D.C.: University Press of America.

Schegloff, E. (2000). When 'others' initiate repair. *Applied Linguistics, 21*, 205–243.

Schegloff, E. (2007). *Sequence organization in interaction: A primer in Conversation Analysis*. New York: Cambridge University Press.

Schegloff, E., Koshik, I., Jacoby, S., & Olsher, D. (2002). Conversation analysis and applied linguistics. *Annual Review of Applied Linguistics, 22*, 3–31.

Schegloff, E., Jefferson, G., & Sacks, H. (1977). The preference for self-correction in the organization of repair in conversation. *Language, 53*, 361–382.

Schegloff, E., & Sacks, H. (1973). Opening up closings. *Semiotica, 8*, 289–327.

Silverman, D. (1998). *Harvey Sacks: Social science and Conversation Analysis*. NY: Oxford University Press.

Stahl, G. (Ed.). (2009). *Studying virtual math teams*. New York: Springer.

Streeck, J., Goodwin, C., & LeBaron, C. (Eds.). (2011). *Embodied interaction: Language and body in the material world*. New York: Cambridge University Press.

Waring, H. Z. (2002). Displaying substantive recipiency in seminar discussion. *Research on Language and Social Interaction, 35*, 453–480.

Watson, D. R. (1992). Ethnomethodology, conversation analysis and education: An overview. *International Review of Education, 38*, 257–274.

Zemel, A., & Koschmann, T. (2011). Pursuing a question: Reinitiating IRE sequences as a method of instruction. *Journal of Pragmatics, 43*, 475–488.

9

VERBAL DATA ANALYSIS FOR UNDERSTANDING INTERACTIONS

HEISAWN JEONG

Hallym University, Korea

WHAT IS VERBAL DATA ANALYSIS?

Background

From the beginning of scientific investigation of the mind, researchers have used verbal data. When the first psychological laboratory was established in Germany, introspection was the dominant research method. In introspection, researchers asked participants to report their conscious experiences during exposure to various sensory stimuli, such as colors or tones. The researchers believed that introspection could reveal the elements of basic consciousness, which could then be combined to describe all human experiences. It soon became clear, however, that the verbal data produced by introspection was too subjective and unreliable, which led to its abandonment as a scientific method. Psychologists started using verbal data again with the cognitive revolution. The prevailing data collected for psychological research, especially in human memory studies, were response time and error data. However, as researchers began to examine more complex processes such as problem solving, they needed a method that could provide more direct access to the contents and processes of problem solving and reasoning. Newell and Simon (1972) established the use of "think-aloud" protocol, in which participants speak their thoughts while engaging in various problem-solving tasks. This process differed from the earlier introspection method in that it did not force participants to reflect and comment on their thinking. Still, questions were raised about the method's validity, since verbalization can influence the very cognitive process that it aims to investigate (Nisbett & Wilson, 1977; Schooler & Engstler-Schooler, 1990). Distinctions were made between concurrent and retrospective verbalizations. It was argued that while retrospective verbalization influences cognitive performance, the concurrent verbalization of the think-aloud method does not, since it only gives voice to already-ongoing inner speech (Ericsson & Simon, 1993). As the field began studying complex forms of knowledge development, researchers were again in need of a method that allows the examination of complex representational changes accompanying learning and development. Verbal data analysis, often abbreviated to "verbal analysis," was initially developed in the process of meeting these challenges (Chi, 1997, 2006). As the field expands its research focus to collaborative interactions, verbal analysis is being used widely to address research questions that arise in the studies of collaborative learning. This chapter will examine verbal analysis and its use in addressing various questions about human learning and cognition.

Key Features and Underlying Assumptions

According to Chi (1997), "verbal analysis is a methodology for quantifying the subjective or qualitative coding of contents of verbal utterances. In verbal analysis, one tabulates, counts, and draws relations between the occurrences of different kinds of utterances to reduce the subjectiveness of qualitative coding" (p. 273). Verbal analysis is predicated on the belief that verbal data can be treated as a form of objective data to examine the state of participants' knowledge and thought processes. Verbal analysis tries to remove the subjective and qualitative nature of the raw verbal data so that it can produce objective results verifiable by other analysts. To achieve this goal, verbal analysis emphasizes operational definitions and systematic applications of coding that can lead to quantifiable outcomes. Statistics are used to ensure that the obtained results are generalizable beyond the specific sample.

Verbal analysis developed in the cognitive tradition. Its analysis strategies are closely related to the development and application of cognitive theories about problem solving, cognitive development, and expertise. In this respect, it would be fair to say that the method is closely aligned to research questions aimed at understanding human cognition. Note, however, that cognition is no longer equated with individual cognition. Theories of cognition may have started out explaining individual cognition, but this is no longer the case. A comprehensive understanding of how cognition works requires not only an understanding of how individuals perceive, remember, and solve problems, but also how they interact with their social and physical environments and participate in the collective processes of problem solving and knowledge building (Galantucci & Sebanz, 2009; Hutchins, 1995; Resnick, Levine, & Teasley, 1991; Scardamalia & Bereiter, 2006; Stahl, 2006). Although verbal analysis has proven useful in addressing research questions that arise in the studies of individual and collaborative learning, this does not preclude the application of the method to noncognitive questions. Verbal data reveal not only one's cognitive processes, but also affective and social processes as well. The method can also be expanded to analyze nonverbal data such as gestures and activities. The essence of the analysis is to systemize and objectify the process of analyzing qualitative data. Whether to analyze verbal or nonverbal data, or to examine cognitive or noncognitive processes is up to the researchers and questions they aim to address.

Relationship to Other Methodologies

There are many ways to analyze verbal data. Analysis methodologies such as protocol analysis, content analysis, conversation analysis, and discourse analysis all analyze some form of verbal data. These methodologies developed in different research traditions with different analytical objectives, but they share some commonalities. This section briefly compares their similarities and differences. The goal of the comparisons, however, is only to highlight key features of the verbal analysis rather than to make definitive comparisons of different methods.

Protocol Analysis. Protocol analysis is both a method of eliciting verbal reports from participants and a method of analysis. Protocol analysis was initially developed to study the cognitive processes involved in problem solving (Ericsson & Simon, 1993; Newell & Simon, 1972). Researchers typically elicit think-aloud protocols from participants by instructing them to verbalize their thoughts concurrently while they solve problems or carry out other tasks. Protocol analysis and verbal analysis share many similarities, but also have some differences. One key difference is that protocol analysis has a strong restriction on how verbal data should be collected. Because certain types of verbalization (e.g., giving explanations or retrospectively thinking about past events) can influence the thought processes, participants are asked to engage in concurrent verbalizations, that is, to merely give expression to their inner thought processes. Verbal analysis, however, does not require that verbal data be collected in such a way. Verbal analysis was developed more to capture representational changes occurring as a result of learning and the development of expertise. In this research, the influences produced by reflective verbalizations, such as self-explanations, do not need to be avoided, but rather welcomed as mechanisms of learning (see Chi, 1997 for more extended discussions about the differences between verbal analysis and protocol analysis). In spite of the differences, protocol and verbal analyses share much in common. Both use verbal data as windows into cognition and are committed to objective and systematic analysis, which is in sharp contrast to other methods that are rooted more in the qualitative analysis traditions (e.g., Sawyer, chapter 7 this volume; Koschmann, chapter 8 this volume).

Content Analysis. The content analysis methodology analyzes the contents of recorded human communication. It analyzes specific characteristics of the messages and is considered a technique for documentary research (Holsti, 1969). Unlike verbal analysis, content analysis typically deals with existing textual data that were generated as byproducts of various communicative activities, such as newspapers, books, and speeches. The two methods also differ in the kind of research questions they address. Verbal analysis focuses on examining cognitive phenomena, whereas content analysis addresses a wider range of topics, such as cultural differences in communication, detection of propaganda, and the communication trends in political discourse. Although content analysis is often included under the general category of qualitative analysis, content analysis can also be quantitative (Neuendorf, 2002). Quantitative content analysis focuses on quantifying textual data by using methods such as counting the frequencies of certain words present within texts or sets of texts (e.g., how many times the word "science" appeared in the 19th century literature). In addition, it analyzes the relationships of such words and concepts, within the texts, the writer(s), the audience, and the culture. Although analysis techniques are different, as in verbal analysis, quantitative content analysis often emphasizes the need for explicit coding categories and rules in order to produce reliable analyses. The boundaries between verbal analysis and quantitative content analysis are becoming less clear-cut, especially in studies of computer-mediated communications (de Wever, Schellens, Valcke, & van Keer, 2006). These online environments produce a large amount of written texts, which researchers then use to answer questions regarding students' learning and knowledge construction processes. The application of quantitative content analysis to these written communications is quite similar to the application of verbal analysis.

Conversation Analysis. Conversation or conversational analysis is the study of speech in interactions. It analyzes conversations produced in naturally occurring settings and attempts to describe its orderliness, structure, and sequential patterns of interaction within various contexts. It examines recurring patterns of interaction, turn-taking and repair mechanisms, and the social organization of conversation (Goodwin & Heritage, 1990; Sacks, Schegloff, & Jefferson, 1974). Although verbal analysis does not discriminate between verbalizations collected in experimental and natural settings, conversation analysis tends to limit data collection to naturally occurring interactions. Conversation analysis considers that verbal data collected in research settings, such as recordings of interview data or conversations in laboratories, are unnatural, because such data are subject to researchers' manipulations and biases. Another major difference is in the analysis itself. In general, conversation analysis is not guided by theories or hypotheses. In analyzing and interpreting the data, it hardly considers the research situations, genders, or ages of the conversation participants. Conversation analysis views such information as a potential source of bias. It is more focused on studying each conversation as it is and seldom carries out quantitative analyses.

Discourse Analysis. Discourse analysis is used to refer to analyses of discourse whose objective is to understand either the linguistic and psycholinguistic properties of discourses (Brown & Yule, 1983) or the processes that are mediated by the discourses (Gee, 2005). What is of relevance and interest to the readers of this book is mostly the latter kind. In this version of discourse analysis, discourse is considered not just as a medium of communication but a tool to support social activities, identities, and affiliations within social groups, institutions, and cultures (Gee, 2005). Discourse analysis is socioculturally sensitive in that it sees individual actions and institutional dimensions as inseparable, and the realm of its analysis extends beyond the text or dialogue itself. It focuses on larger scale events such as the impact of political and educational policy, economic and cultural influences, or group dynamics that are revealed in the discourse, whereas verbal analysis often focuses on small-scale events such as step-by-step changes in learner's mental models and structural features of individual cognition. Unlike verbal analysis, discourse analysis, with its focus on language-in-use, restricts its analysis to spoken and written data generated in the contexts of natural language use, such as conversations, news reports, books, political debates, media's portrayals, and literary works. In addition to differences in analytical aims and the types of verbal data it analyzes, discourse analysis also differs from verbal analysis in the kinds of analysis it performs. Unlike the more-or-less systematic approach to coding in verbal analysis, discourse analysis adopts qualitative approach to analysis. Discourse analysis is meant to be a "thinking device" with which researchers explore different aspects of the discourse under given questions, rather than as a step-by-step set of rules or procedures.

Although distinctions exist, it is not always possible or useful to draw firm boundaries between different analysis methods. Verbal analysis has much in common with protocol analysis. They share similar theoretical commitments and analysis procedures. There is also quite an overlap between verbal analysis and some versions of the content analysis, with their mutual focus on learning-related issues and the use of systematic coding procedures. Perhaps not surprisingly, researchers typically carry out analyses without explicit references to the methodological traditions with which they are aligned. In addition, researchers often use analysis method that is at the boundaries of different traditions or combine different analytical traditions, a trend increasing with the popularity of multimethod or mixed method research (Hmelo-Silver, 2003). The term *verbal analysis* is used loosely in the rest of this chapter, to refer to analyses that examine verbal data in a manner consistent with the verbal analysis method.

VERBAL ANALYSIS IN THE STUDY OF INDIVIDUAL LEARNING

Verbal analysis has become a standard methodology in areas involving complex forms of learning and problem solving. Two areas of research have been particularly fruitful with respect to verbal analysis. One is with identifying steps and strategies involved in learning and problem solving. This typically involves collecting verbal protocols during problem solving, although the analytic focus varies depending on the research objectives. For example, Simon and Simon (1989) analyzed the problem solving steps students took in physics problem solving and found that participants first read the problem, then evoked relevant equations, completed the equations using quantities given in the problem statement, and solved for the unknown. Chi, Bassok, Lewis, Reimann, and Glaser (1989) similarly studied physics problem solving. They analyzed the kinds of verbalization generated while students studied worked-out physics problems and found that the kinds of verbalization mattered. Students profited from the study of examples to the extent that they explained the solutions to themselves, suggesting the importance of self-explanations.

Verbal analysis has also been used to identify and capture the nature and development of complex representations. In a classic study of children's understanding of the Earth, Vosniadou and Brewer (1992) investigated children's intuitive knowledge about the shape of the Earth. In individual interviews, they asked the children to answer a set of questions (e.g., "What is the shape of the Earth?"; "What is above the Earth?") and to draw (e.g., "Make a drawing of the Earth"). The researchers used the children's verbal answers to identify their mental models of the Earth, which showed that children's models of the Earth were not always the culturally accepted spherical model and the process of assimilating the culturally accepted model was not a straightforward process. Chi, de Leeuw, Chiu, and LaVancher (1994) similarly captured students' mental models of the circulatory system. Based on students' drawing, verbalizations, and answers to a set of questions, they constructed a set of mental models about the circulatory system that students constructed in the process of developing their understanding.

Verbal analysis has provided ways to reveal the content and structure of knowledge representations and helped researchers to understand key differences between experts and novices. In a classic study, Chi, Feltovich, and Glaser (1981) asked physics experts and novices to sort a set of physics problems and to discuss everything they knew regarding a set of physics terms (e.g., Newton's Second Law, block on incline). Participants also read problem statements and thought aloud about the approaches they would take to solve these problems. Results from the sorting task showed that physics experts and novices begin their problem representations using different categories. Experts abstracted physics principles from the problems and included potential solution methods in their representations. Novices, on the other hand, based their representation on the problem's literal features.

As can be seen in these studies, verbal analysis helped to reveal structures and processes that could not be easily captured in more traditional methodologies such as reaction time or questionnaire methods and provided a basis to build theories about how complex forms of learning and problem solving might occur. As the focus of the field shifts toward understanding collaborative learning processes, the basics of verbal analysis are extended and adapted to address questions related to collaboration and collective knowledge building. The next section will examine how verbal analysis is applied to understand collaborative interaction.

VERBAL ANALYSIS IN THE STUDY OF COLLABORATIVE INTERACTION

Understanding the Product of Collaborative Interaction

One of the research questions that occupied researchers at the beginning was the outcome of collaboration. Researchers initially investigated the effectiveness of the collaborative learning condition against individual learning condition and later the efficacy of different collaborative conditions with different scripts or task arrangements (Berkowitz & Gibbs, 1983; Coleman, Brown, & Rivikin, 1997; Okada & Simon, 1997; Rummel & Spada, 2005). In these studies, students' performances or learning outcomes were often assessed based on their verbalizations to individually administered tests (e.g., answers to posttest questions or probes) (Azmitia, 1988; Coleman, Brown, & Rivikin, 1997). This means that analysis methods developed and honed in the studies of individual learning can be used without much change. For example, Azevado, Moos, Greene, Winters, and Cromley (2008) compared self-regulated learning conditions where students regulated their own learning and externally regulated learning conditions where students had access to a tutor who facilitated their regulation. They used the learning materials and tests used in Chi et al. (1994) and carried out more or less the same analyses such as mental model analysis to determine the effectiveness of the two conditions.

Analyses become more challenging when researchers examine the outcome of collaboration at the group level. The need to determine the extent of the group's knowledge arises when researchers ask questions such as whether the group or the individual is the more effective unit (Barron, 2000), whether and how the group produces qualitatively different outcomes than the individual (Shirouzu, Miyake, & Masukawa, 2002), and how to characterize and differentiate group outcomes that may result from different collaborative interactions (Rummel & Spada, 2005). To answer these questions, group outcomes need to be compared against either individual outcomes or group outcomes obtained in different group conditions. Such analysis requires that groups be used as a unit of analysis. Treating the group as a unit of analysis has implications beyond using it as a unit of coding and statistical analysis. It means viewing it as an agent that processes information; that is, as an agent that can learn, solve problems, and carry out complex cognitive tasks. Understanding how this group level cognition works requires addressing conceptual as well as methodological challenges. Different conceptualizations of what it means for groups or communities to understand something as a group leads to different strategies and methodologies. The field is still working out different solutions to these questions (Akkerman et al., 2007), but so far roughly three kinds of analytic strategy have been tried to assess and capture group knowledge.

The first strategy is assessing what a group does or produces as a unit (e.g., group answers, group proposals, artifacts produced by the group). Researchers often assess individual knowledge representations based on individuals' answers to posttest questions or performances on various tasks. In a similar manner, group knowledge and understanding can be assessed based on answers or performances the group produces as a whole (Jeong, Chen, & Looi, 2011), and verbal analysis can be used if the group outcome contains verbalizations in some forms. Barron (2000) adopted this strategy when she compared the problem-solving performances of triads and individuals. In her study, children were asked to solve a series of problems and to complete a workbook alone or collaboratively. Barron compared the workbooks groups produced to the workbooks individual students produced in order to determine the effect of collaboration on problem solving performance. Suthers and Hundhausen (2003) compared the effectiveness of three collaborative groups supported by different representations (e.g., text, matrix, or graph) and used collaborative essays as one of the measures to compare the outcomes of different conditions. Methodologically speaking, this strategy of using group answers or artifacts as a basis to gauge groups' collective understanding is again a straightforward process. It does not require any new analytic approaches and is quite useful for comparing the quality and outcomes of different units. One limitation of this strategy, however, is that the group product may not accurately reflect what the group knows. Depending on how the group members pool their individual resources and interact in the process of generating their group solutions, the group product may be biased toward contributions from certain members but not others.

The second strategy is to assess group knowledge or understanding based on aggregate measures of individual outcomes. The method of aggregation can vary a great deal. The simplest method is probably to sum or average individual members' performance, as was often done in social psychology and organizational research. For example, Austin (2003) assessed the amount of knowledge different industry teams possessed by summing up the knowledge scores of its members. More complex aggregation methods have been tried using verbal analysis. In a study to examine the amount of common knowledge constructed during collaborative learning (Jeong & Chi, 2007), we first assessed individual students' understanding before and after collaborative learning. By comparing the answers that each member of the student pairs gave, we then came up with a set of measures such as "unique total knowledge," which reflects group knowledge as a whole, "common knowledge," which refers to what both members know in common, and "unique knowledge," which refers to unshared knowledge that is only known by one person. For example, if Student A knew 20 knowledge pieces and Student B knew 15 knowledge pieces, of which they held 10 in common, then, as a group, they knew 25 knowledge pieces (unique total), of which 10 were in common (common knowledge) and 15 were unique to the individual, that is, possessed by only one member (unique knowledge). Note that these measures focused on specific aspects of group knowledge and did not assess notions such as intersubjectivity. However, this was one of the first attempts to operationalize group level cognition based on relationships in individual knowledge.

The third strategy is to use group discourse. According to sociocultural theorists, discourse activity itself as an understanding since cognition and learning, including conceptual understanding and conceptual growth, are functions that are accomplished by activity systems and communities of practice (Greeno & van de Sande, 2007; Stahl, 2006). Unlike sociocultural perspectives, verbal analysis, coming from cognitive traditions, distinguishes process and product. Discourse or dialogues are typically analyzed to understand interactive processes, not the contents of group understanding. Still, process and product are not independent, and the contents of group understanding can be captured from the discourse. The application of this strategy can be seen in the analysis of common ground in psycholinguistic research. Common ground, a form of joint understanding, is inferred from dialogue moves, such as acknowledgments or continuations of previous contributions (Clark & Schaefer, 1989). Another example is Jeong et al. (2011) which attempted to capture group understanding based on the artifact-mediated discourse. In this study, students collaborated both face-to-face and online using a tool that allowed them to share individual notes. Analyses captured group understanding by identifying the major contributions to the group space and how each contribution arose from the artifact-mediated discourse. In this study, the discourse consisted of both verbal and nonverbal forms as students often interacted by carrying out certain actions in the environments (e.g., posting a note), thereby extending verbal analysis to include nonverbal actions and activities.

Understanding the Processes of Collaborative Interaction

As the facilitative effect of social interaction became evident, researchers' attentions were directed at understanding the critical mechanisms of collaborative interaction that are responsible for learning gains. Collaboration dialogues were examined in detail, at first in comparison to individuals' talking aloud. Analyses were guided by research hypotheses about the key differences between individual and collaborative learning processes in a given learning or problem solving task. For example, Teasley (1995) analyzed the amount and types of talks produced while fourth graders engaged in computer-based scientific reasoning task (i.e., discover the functions of a mystery task) and reported that *talk dyads* produced a greater amount of talk overall and a greater amount of interpretive types of talk than *talk alones*. Okada and Simon (1997) examined the scientific discovery process by individuals and pairs. Using students' verbalizations and talks produced while they performed a laboratory simulation task, they examined various aspects of the discovery process such as amount of time spent, number of hypotheses and alternative hypotheses entertained. Their results showed that pairs were more active than individuals in entertaining hypotheses and considering alternative ideas and justifications. Shirouzu et al. (2002) analyzed verbal and nonverbal actions as students carried out mathematical tasks (e.g., shading parts of the materials such as origami or cardboard paper). Although both individuals and dyads heavily relied on nonmathematical strategies, dyads tended to shift to a mathematical strategy in their second trials. In order to find the potential reasons for such divergence, they analyzed verbal references, solution paths, and role changes and found that frequent changes between the task-doing and monitoring roles enabled pairs to abstract rules as they worked on solving mathematical problems. These studies all relied on the analysis of verbal data collected during problem solving and learning, but what they examined in their analyses varied depending on their hypotheses.

Although the benefits of social interaction are undeniable, unstructured collaboration does not systematically produce learning. Researchers actively searched for the characteristics of critical dialogue moves and interaction events that strongly predict learning outcomes. Researchers were also interested in how collaborative processes were affected by various factors such as technologies or collaboration scripts. These studies required detailed examinations of how collaboration proceeds. Researchers adopted a number of strategies to identify critical collaboration events or moves. One strategy was to carry out detailed analyses of dialogues and then relate them (e.g., asking questions, monitoring, receiving explanations) to learning outcomes (Chi, Siler, Jeong, Yamauchi, & Hausmann, 2001; Webb, 1989). Another related strategy is to compare how groups differ with respect to various interactive moves either by studying different collaboration conditions (e.g., scripted versus unscripted arguments) (Stegmann, Weinberger, & Fischer, 2007) or creating post hoc groups of successful versus less successful groups based on some outcome measures (e.g., learning gains). A vast array of dialogue features was examined in these studies such as the grounding moves in a multimodal collaborative problem-solving environment (Dillenbourg & Traum, 2006), giving and receiving explanations (Webb, 1989), generation of arguments and counterarguments (Chinn, O'Donnell, & Jinks, 2000), and monitoring and regulation of the learning processes (Azevedo et al., 2008).

Partly due to the sociocultural view's influence, numerous research efforts have been directed toward understanding the overall characteristics of discourse itself that span beyond specific statements, turns, or sequences of moves. Due to confluences of theory and method, it is difficult to identify studies using verbal analysis in this area. However, unlike analyses rooted in the qualitative analysis tradition, analyses more closely aligned with verbal analysis attempt to analyze discourse systematically, often relying on explicit coding schemes and quantitative analyses. In addition, although analyses place less emphasis on individuals, individual level moves are still considered in the context of the larger discourse events. Hogan, Nastasi, and Pressley (2000) examined discourse patterns in peer- and teacher-guided discussions occurring in an eighth grade classroom. They transcribed and analyzed interactions within peer- and teacher-guided small-group discussions in a number of ways. For example, they analyzed discourse at both the macro- (conversational turns) and microlevels (statement units ranging from words and phrases to sentences) and differentiated discourse activities directed to the self (e.g., elaborating oneself) from discourse activities directed to others (e.g., elaborating another's idea). Through a detailed examination of how peer- and teacher-guided discourses proceeded, Hogan et al. showed that, in both peer and teacher-guided small-group discussions, the key feature was working with weak or incomplete ideas until they improved, but how this was accomplished differed somewhat depending on the presence or absence of a teacher in the discussion. In another example, van Aalst (2009) attempted to differentiate three modes of discourse—knowledge-sharing, knowledge-construction, and knowledge-creation discourses—within an asynchronous, computer-mediated discourse. He proposed seven discourse dimensions that can differentiate the three modes of discourse and further subdivided the seven dimensions into 33 subordinate codes. By coding individual students' note postings in the online discourse using the framework, he was able to identify critical discourse dimensions for differentiating the three modes of discourse and to determine the kind of discourses specific student groups engaged in.

ISSUES IN USING VERBAL ANALYSIS

This section examines some of the key issues that analysts need to consider in carrying out verbal analysis. Due to space limitations, this section focuses on general research and analytic strategies associated with verbal analysis. For a practical and step-by-step guide to verbal analysis, including issues of coding units and segmentation, please refer to Chi (1997).

Research Questions and Design

The method was developed to answer research questions about cognition. However, the mechanics of the method can be applied to the studies of noncognitive questions as long as the target constructs or processes are reflected in verbal data. Verbal analysis is a tool. It is up to the researchers to decide which questions to use the analysis for. It would be fair to say, however, that verbal analysis has so far shown its greatest strength in examining questions related to individual and collaborative cognition. Its analyses tend to be microgenetic and suited for examining detailed progression of knowledge development and strategy changes. Verbal analysis is especially suited for the studies of collaborative learning because collaborative interaction typically generates a large amount of verbal data, in both spoken (as in face-to-face interactions) and textual forms (as in distributed interactions through e-mail or chats). With its unique ability to analyze these data and emphasis on systematic and quantitative analysis, verbal analysis is suitable for addressing various issues related to collaborative interactions.

Although some aspects of verbal data are readily quantifiable (e.g., word frequency), interpreting verbal data requires qualitative meaning-making processes. Because of this, some researchers, especially those coming from strictly quantitative research traditions, often view verbal analysis as a branch of qualitative analysis and incompatible with experimental studies. However, although verbal analysis may use qualitative data, its analyses are not qualitative. The essence of verbal analysis is to reduce potential subjectivity inherent in meaning-making processes by systematizing the analyses. In addition, unlike conversation or discourse analyses which restrict themselves to naturally generated conversations or discourses, verbal analysis has been, and can be, used in combination with a variety of research designs, including experimental or quasi-experimental design. An example of experimental studies with verbal analysis is Chan (2001), which compared learning in four different experimental conditions. She collected students' answers to questions (e.g., explain how ducks evolved webbed feet) and recorded students' discussions with peers. Verbal data were used as a basis for comparing the four learning conditions. When collecting verbal data in experimental studies, it is a good strategy to keep the experimental design simple since analysis of verbal data can become quite complex. Verbal analysis has also been used successfully with quasi-experimental studies examining conceptual development and differences between experts and novices (Chi & Koeske, 1983; Chi et al., 1981; Vosniadou & Brewer, 1992) and with descriptive studies that collected verbal data in more-or-less naturalistic settings such as classrooms (Hogan et al., 2000).

Collection of Verbal Data

The elicitation of verbal responses is an important issue when verbal data are used to study individual problem solving processes. Because not everyone is accustomed to think aloud when they work alone, researchers often provide practice or prompting in order to ensure that the process of verbalization does not interfere with the ongoing process of problem solving or discovery process being studied (see Ericsson & Simon, 1993; Chi, 1997 for details on these issues). Such issues and concerns are mostly non-existent when verbal data are collected during collaboration. People tend to talk when they interact. No special instructions or trainings are needed in order to get students to talk. Researchers can just record the verbalizations that occur as part of the naturally occurring interactive processes. Still, there are a few issues researchers need to be aware of when collecting data in collaborative settings. First, the act of recording can make students become conscious of what and how they talk and this might make them behave and interact differently. Researchers thus need to ensure that the act of recording does not interfere with their routine interactive behaviors. Second, even though people do talk when they interact, being in a group does not always make them talk or interact. This is especially the case when collaboration is studied in laboratory settings with randomly assigned group membership. The generic instruction to "collaborate" does not always lead to active interaction among these students. In such cases, care needs to be taken so that students feel comfortable with each other and can engage in the kinds of interaction that the researchers want to examine. The same problem can also occur when collaboration is studied in naturalistic settings. The group might be newly formed, there might be some hidden tensions or conflicts that make members reluctant to talk, or they might not have anything to talk about. In addition, even when group members talk, students might talk about off-topic issues or get into squabbles. In such cases, researchers may prompt students to talk, collaborate, or stay on-task, but need to be aware of the possibility that such prompting or suggestion can influence the group process and dynamics. In general, such prompting should be used only when it does not influence the process that the study aims to investigate. If one's research question concerns examining how collaboration ebbs and flows, for example, then researchers must study the collaboration as is. Prompting group members to talk or collaborate would render the data useless.

By tradition, verbal analysis has typically relied on transcripts of spoken verbalizations. Spoken verbalizations, either in the form of think-aloud or verbal interactions, can provide a more detailed picture of what is happening both inside and between individuals. However, not only have written verbal responses been successfully used in various studies (Coleman et al., 1997), but they are also becoming increasingly popular due to the proliferation of computer-mediated learning environments (de Wever et al., 2006). In online environments, much interaction occurs through written communication. Even in the offline environment, having students write their answers reduces the burden and cost associated with transcribing. However, it should be noted that talking usually takes place much faster than writing and is more likely to match the speed of thought. In addition, participants are more likely to edit and censor their written responses than their speech. If research questions are not about a detailed, ongoing collaborative process of learning and group work, it would probably be acceptable to collect written verbalizations. When research questions require a detailed analysis of ongoing collaborative processes or representational changes, however, it is appropriate to avoid written transcripts unless it is unavoidable (e.g., computer-mediated interaction).

Although coding can be and is carried out directly from audio- or videotapes (Meier, Spada, & Rummel, 2007), recordings of verbal interaction are typically transcribed before coding. When transcriptions are made, they typically include not only the words spoken, but other linguistic and nonlinguistic information available on the tapes (e.g., pauses, sighs, facial expressions, change in intonations, etc.). One cannot transcribe all aspects of the interaction unless such details are useful for answering the research questions. Nonetheless, transcribing contextual information can be very helpful in interpreting the data. As researchers examine collaboration in online environments, student actions with respect to the technological tools often play an important role in interpreting student interaction and learning process. Such actions can also be transcribed and analyzed in the same fashion as verbal data (Jeong et al., 2011).

Analytic strategies

Verbal analysis codes raw verbal utterances into analyzable and inferentially productive code. Deciding what to code and devising coding schemes are both theoretically and data-driven processes (see Chi, 1997, for more details on these two approaches for developing coding schemes). The exact decision regarding what and how to code depends on the research questions, but the following three analytic strategies can be considered. First, verbal utterances can be coded into categories that represent meaningful learning events or outcomes. Examples of coding categories are: whether students give or receive explanations (Webb, 1989); whether students requested information, evaluated task difficulty, or elaborated what their partner said earlier (Hogan et al., 2000); whether an idea is repeated and if so, whether it was repeated by the speaker or a peer (Barron, 2003); or whether a given online post qualifies for any of the features that distinguish three different discourse modes (van Aalst, 2009). Coding utterances into categories allows the researcher to determine whether or not the target events or activity occurred and if so, how often. Once utterances are coded into categories, researchers can examine the relationships among different codes and also apply appropriate statistical procedures.

The second strategy is coding utterances into a scale. This is to assign a numerical value to segments of verbal utterances to indicate the degree or strength of the concepts being coded. For example, van Aalst (2009) analyzed collaborative summary notes created by students and rated each note on a 4-point scale in terms of knowledge quality and significance of findings. Suthers and Hundhausen (2003) also used rating in combination of category coding in their examination of collaborative scientific reasoning. After first coding the learning transcripts using eight categories such as "evidential relations" or "epistemic classifications," they further rated a subset of them using a 3-point scale in order to capture the fact that a certain evidential relation is more important than others and difficult to infer. When rating scales are used in verbal analysis, they are often used with the same kind of detailed coding schemes used for category coding. Coders do not merely rate the utterances in an intuitive manner, but specific coding guidelines are used for each value of the scale. After verbal utterances are coded into such a scale, they can then be subjected to statistical analysis.

In the third strategy, verbal data can be coded into event sequences or structural representations that capture students' understanding or learning processes. This was carried out both to represent the learning processes and the contents of understanding. For example, Chi and Koeske (1983) asked children to name dinosaurs they knew and link them to various properties (e.g., eating plants). Verbal protocols were used to capture children's knowledge about dinosaurs. If children mentioned two different dinosaurs in succession, those two were assumed to be linked in their minds. Dinosaurs' properties were also similarly linked to dinosaurs. The frequency of mention was assumed to reflect the strength of that linkage in their minds. Note that some initial coding is necessary before it can be combined into structural representations. In the above example, researchers first coded the references to dinosaurs and whether they were mentioned together, but instead of tallying the frequency of utterances (e.g., how frequently tyrannosaurs are mentioned), the researchers constructed them into a networked representation. This analysis strategy was initially used to capture the structural properties of an individual's representation (see also the mental model analysis by Chi et al., 1994; Vosniadou & Brewer, 1992), but can also be used to capture the group processes. For example, Chinn et al. (2000) attempted to code argument structures into similar networked representations. Their analysis coded argument events such as claims, explicit warrants, and challenges into a structured network. Once verbal utterances are coded into structured representations such as argument networks, the representations can be compared quantitatively as well as qualitatively, by using measurements such as the numbers of nodes and links contained in the networks, the breadth and depth of the networks, or the extent to which arguments are supported by explicit warrants. Statistics can be applied as well.

Although most researchers develop coding schemes tailored for specific hypotheses, it is possible to use schemes developed in other studies (Azevedo et al., 2008) as well as coding schemes developed for general use. Meier et al. (2007) developed a rating scheme to assess the "quality" of collaborative interaction. It was developed partly in the context of medical problem solving in a video-conferencing environment, but aims to assess general collaboration quality along nine dimensions. Another example is the *Rainbow* scheme developed by Baker, Andriessen, Lund, van Amelsvoort, and Quignard (2007). The goal of this scheme is to determine the extent to which students actually engage in argumentative activities in online learning environments and consists of seven categories that represent key aspects of knowledge-based argumentative interaction. In using coding schemes developed in other studies, whether they are specific or general, researchers need to examine carefully what the scheme was designed for and whether it is appropriate to use it for the current study. A scheme developed to study asynchronous online collaboration, for example, may not be suitable for studying offline collaboration or collaboration mediated by different technologies. It might also be the case that the existing scheme is not detailed enough to address more fine-tuned nuances of collaboration that the current study aims to examine. In such cases, researchers need to adapt existing schemes or develop a new one from scratch so as to appropriately address the hypotheses of the current investigations.

CONCLUSIONS

Whenever there is a theoretical shift, there is a need to develop a method that can capture the newly proposed concepts and processes. Verbal analysis was initially developed when theories of problem-solving and knowledge representation developed. There was a strong need for a method that could capture various problem-solving steps, strategies, and representational changes. Verbal data analysis successfully met these demands. It captured the representational changes accompanying cognitive development and expertise and identified learning mechanisms such as self-explanation. As the theoretical focus shifts again, this time to accommodate the social constructivist nature of learning, researchers are again in need of methods that can accurately examine group cognitive processes and outcomes. Verbal analysis is particularly well suited to address these challenges, due in part to the abundance of verbal data collected during collaborative interaction. So far, verbal analysis has been useful in helping researchers to understand the precise effects of social interactions and some of the mechanisms responsible for the outcomes. With further conceptual advances in how to conceptualize group cognition, verbal analysis is expected to make greater contributions to the field.

Although the strengths and weaknesses of any single analysis method can be discussed at length, verbal analysis is not the only methodology that can contribute to our understanding of collaborative learning. In addition, researchers are increasingly becoming eclectic with regard to data collection and analysis methods. Mixed- or multimethod studies are becoming more common (Hmelo-Silver, 2003). The field is undergoing, not just a theoretical shift, but also a methodological shift. In this new research environment, one of the challenges researchers often face is how to align different methodologies. Reconciling differences in the mechanics of different analytic traditions is relatively easy. A more difficult challenge is reconciling the different epistemologies associated with different methodologies. Verbal analysis, with its firm roots in positivist tradition, systematizes and quantifies analyses in order to achieve objectivity and generality. On the other hand, in many of the qualitative analysis traditions, the goal is more to reveal meaningful patterns or demonstrate the strength of a metaphor, rather than to unearth objective and general reality. Reconciling such different views will not be easy, and yet the field needs to find ways for these different analytical traditions to coexist in meaningful ways. With significant progress both on the conceptual and the methodological fronts, it is expected that meaningful progress in our understanding will soon be possible.

ACKNOWLEDGMENTS

The writing of this chapter was supported by the National Research Foundation of Korea (NRF) (Grant No. 2009-0068919). Any opinions, findings, and conclusions or recommendations expressed in this chapter are those of the author and do not necessarily reflect the views of the funding agency.

REFERENCES

Akkerman, S., van den Bossche, P., Admiraal, W., Gijselaers, W., Segers, M., Simons, R.-J., & Kirschner, P. (2007). Reconsidering group cognition: From conceptual confusion to a boundary area between cognitive and socio-cultural perspectives? *Educational Research Review, 2*, 39–63.

Austin, J. R. (2003). Transactive memory in organizational groups: The effects of content, consensus, specialization, and accuracy on group performance. *Journal of Applied Psychology, 88*(5), 866–878.

Azevedo, R., Moos, D. C., Green, J. A., Winters, F. I., & Cromley, J. G. (2008). Why is externally-facilitated regulated learning more effective than self-regulated learning with hypermedia? *Education Technology Research Development, 56*, 45–72.

Azmitia, M. (1988). Peer interaction and problem solving: When are two heads better than one? *Child Development, 59*, 87–96.

Baker, M., Andriessen, J., Lund, K., van Amelsvoort, M., & Quignard, M. (2007). Rainbow: A framework for analyzing computer-mediated pedagogical debates. *International Journal of Computer-Supported Collaborative Learning, 2*, 315–357.

Barron, B. (2000). Problem solving in video-based microworlds: Collaborative and individual outcomes of high-achieving sixth-grade students. *Journal of Educational Psychology, 92*(2), 391–398.

Barron, B. (2003). When smart groups fail. *The Journal of the Learning Sciences, 12*(3), 307–359.
Berkowitz, M., & Gibbs, J. (1983). Measuring the developmental features of moral discussion. *Merrill-Palmer Quarterly, 29*, 399–410.
Brown, G., & Yule, G. (1983). *Discourse analysis*. Cambridge, England: Cambridge University Press.
Chan, C. (2001). Peer collaboration and discourse patterns in learning from incompatible information. *Instructional Science, 29*, 443–479.
Chi, M. T. H. (1997). Quantifying qualitative analyses of verbal data: A practical guide. *Journal of the Learning Science, 6*(3), 271–315.
Chi, M. T. H. (2006). Two approaches to the study of experts' characteristics. In K. A. Ericsson, N. Charness, P. Feltovich, & R. Hoffman (Eds.), *Cambridge handbook of expertise and expert performance* (pp. 21–30). Cambridge, England: Cambridge University Press.
Chi, M. T. H., Bassok, M., Lewis, M. T., Reimann, P., & Glaser, R. (1989). Self-explanations: How students study and use examples in learning to solve problems. *Cognitive Science, 13*, 145–182.
Chi, M. T. H., de Leeuw, N., Chiu, M., & LaVancher, C. (1994). Eliciting self-explanations improves understanding. *Cognitive Science, 18*, 439–477.
Chi, M. T. H., Feltovich, P. J., & Glaser, R. (1981). Categorizing and representation of physics problems by experts and novices. *Cognitive Science, 5*, 121–152.
Chi, M. T. H., & Koeske, R. D. (1983). Network representation of a child's dinosaur knowledge. *Developmental Psychology, 19*(1), 29–39.
Chi, M. T. H., Siler, S. A., Jeong, A., Yamauchi, T., & Hausmann, R. G. (2001). Learning from human tutoring. *Cognitive Science, 25*, 471–533.
Chinn, C. A., O'Donnell, A. M., & Jinks, T. S. (2000). The structure of discourse in collaborative learning. *The Journal of Experimental Education, 69*(1), 77–97.
Clark, H. H., & Schaefer, E. F. (1989). Contributing to discourse. *Cognitive Science, 13*, 259–294.
Coleman, E. B., Brown, A. L., & Rivikin, I. D. (1997). The effect of instructional explanations on learning from scientific texts. *The Journal of the Learning Science, 6*(4), 347–365.
de Wever, B., Schellens, T., Valcke, M., & van Keer, H. (2006). Content analysis schemes to analyze transcripts of online asynchronous discussion groups: A review. *Computers and Education, 46*, 6–28.
Dillenbourg, P., & Traum, D. (2006). Sharing solutions: Persistence and grounding in multimodal collaborative problem solving. *The Journal of the Learning Sciences, 15*(1), 121–151.
Ericsson, K. A., & Simon, H. A. (1993). *Protocol analysis: Verbal report as data*. Cambridge, MA: MIT Press.
Galantucci, B., & Sebanz, N. (2009). Joint action: Current perspectives. *Topics in Cognitive Science, 1*, 255–259.
Gee, J. P. (2005). *An introduction to discourse analysis: Theory and method* (2nd ed.). New York: Routledge.
Goodwin, C., & Heritage, J. (1990). Conversation analysis. *Annual Review of Anthropology, 19*, 283–307.
Greeno, J. G., & van de Sande, C. (2007). Perspectival understanding of conceptions and conceptual growth in interaction. *Educational Psychologist, 42*(1), 9–23.
Hmelo-Silver, C. E. (2003). Analyzing collaborative knowledge construction: Multiple methods for integrated understanding. *Computers and Education, 41*, 397–420.
Hogan, K., Nastasi, B. K., & Pressley, M. (2000). Discourse patterns and collaborative scientific reasoning in peer and teacher-guided discussions. *Cognition and Instruction, 17*, 379–432.
Holsti, O. R. (1969). *Content analysis for the social sciences and humanities*. Menlo Park, CA: Addison-Wesley.
Hutchins, E. (1995). *Cognition in the wild*. Cambridge, MA: MIT Press.
Jeong, H., Chen, W., & Looi, C. K. (2011). Analysis of group understanding in artifact-mediated discourse. In G. Stahl, H. Spada, & N. Myake (Eds.), *Proceedings of the 9th International Conference on Computer-Supported Collaborative Learning*. Hong Kong: International Society of the Learning Sciences.
Jeong, H., & Chi, M. H. (2007). Knowledge convergence and collaborative learning. *Instructional Science, 35*, 287–315.
Meier, A., Spada, H., & Rummel, N. (2007). A rating scheme for assessing the quality of computer-supported collaboration processes. *International Journal of Computer-Supported Collaborative Learning, 2*, 63–86.
Neuendorf, K. A. (2002). *The content analysis guidebook*. Thousand Oaks, CA: Sage.
Newell, A., & Simon, H. A. (1972). *Human problem solving*. Englewood Cliffs, NJ: Prentice Hall.
Nisbett, R. E., & Wilson, T. D. (1977). Telling more than we can know: Verbal reports on mental processes. *Psychological Review, 84*(3), 231–259.
Okada, T., & Simon, H. A. (1997). Collaborative discovery in a scientific domain. *Cognitive Sciences, 21*(2), 109–146.
Resnick, L. B., Levine, J. M., & Teasley, S. D. (Eds.). (1991). *Perspectives on socially shared cognition*. Washington, DC: American Psychological Association.

Rummel, N., & Spada, H. (2005). Learning to collaborate: An instructional approach to promoting collaborative problem solving in computer-mediated settings. *The Journal of the Learning Sciences, 14*(2), 201–241.

Sacks, H., Schegloff, E., & Jefferson, G. (1974). A simplest systematics for the organization of turn-taking in conversation. *Language, 50*(4), 696–735.

Scardamalia, M., & Bereiter, C. (2006). Knowledge building: Theory, pedagogy, and technology. In R. K. Sawyers (Ed.), *Cambridge Handbook of the Learning Sciences* (pp. 97–115). New York: Cambridge University Press.

Schooler, J. W., & Engstler-Schooler, T. Y. (1990). Verbal overshadowing of visual memories: Some things are better left unsaid. *Cognitive Psychology, 22*(1), 36–71.

Shirouzu, H., Miyake, N., & Masukawa, H. (2002). Cognitively active externalization for situated reflection. *Cognitive Science, 26*, 469–501.

Simon, D. P., & Simon, H. A. (1989). Individual differences in problem solving physics problem. In H. A. Simon (Ed.). *Models of thought. Volume II* (pp. 215–231). New Haven, CT: Yale University Press. (Original worked published 1978)

Stahl, G. (2006). *Group cognition: Computer support for building collaborative knowledge*. Cambridge, MA: MIT Press.

Stegmann, K., Weinberger, A., & Fischer, F. (2007). Facilitating argumentative knowledge construction with computer-supported collaboration script. *International Journal of Computer-Supported Collaborative Learning, 2*, 421–447.

Suthers, D. D., & Hundhausen, C. D. (2003). An experimental study of the effects of representational guidance on collaborative learning processes. *The Journal of the Leaning Sciences, 12*(2), 183–218.

Teasley, S. D. (1995). The role of talk in children's peer collaborations. *Developmental Psychology, 31*(2), 207–220.

van Aalst, J. (2009). Distinguishing knowledge-sharing, knowledge-construction, and knowledge-creation discourse. *International Journal of Computer-Supported Collaborative Learning, 4*, 259–287.

Vosniadou, S., & Brewer, W. F. (1992). Mental models of the earth: A study of conceptual change in childhood. *Cognitive Psychology, 24*, 535–585.

Webb, N. M. (1989). Peer interaction and learning in small groups. *International Journal of Educational Research, 13*, 21–40.

10

LINGUISTIC ANALYSIS METHODS FOR STUDYING SMALL GROUPS

IRIS HOWLEY, ELIJAH MAYFIELD, AND CAROLYN PENSTEIN ROSÉ

Carnegie Mellon University

INTRODUCTION

Linguistic analysis of collaboration is a research area with stakeholders from multiple fields, including learning sciences, organizational behavior, sociolinguistics, other areas of linguistics, language technologies and machine learning, social psychology, and sociology. Each field brings its own valuable store of wisdom as well as its own sets of research questions and methodologies. While we view collaboration from a multidisciplinary perspective, we adopt a technical definition of linguistic analysis as an analysis that employs constructs from the field of linguistics that are designed to study language as a primary focus of inquiry. While a wide variety of valuable frameworks for studying the language of collaboration have been developed within the learning sciences community, instead of considering these as linguistic analyses of collaboration, we consider them as applications of theory from the learning sciences to language interaction. The focus of these existing frameworks is on learning processes viewed through language rather than the language processes themselves. The advantage of a linguistic framework is that it allows us to avoid making a commitment to one specific theoretical perspective within the learning sciences.

Within the broad field of linguistics, we focus on a specific subcommunity referred to as Systemic Functional Linguistics (SFL). The field of systemic functional linguistics is a largely descriptive linguistic tradition that provides a firm foundation in analyses of genres of writing and text-based interaction (Martin & Rose, 2007; Martin & White, 2005), as well as face-to-face interaction (Veel, 1999), characterized in terms of the choices authors and speakers make about how to present themselves through language (Halliday, 1994). The choices that authors and speakers make are mapped out in decision tree representations referred to as systems, which is where the subcommunity gets its name. The constructs coming from the field of systemic functional linguistics provide us with a common foundation for exploring stylistic norms of conversational behavior across genres of dialogic interactions. What makes SFL an ideal choice for our efforts is that it grew up side-by-side with one of the few sociological theories informed by linguistic data. As such, in contrast to other existing linguistic theories, it was fashioned specifically for the purpose of explaining sociological processes at multiple levels and within a wide range of contexts. Beyond these social phenomena, mechanisms such as grammatical metaphor (Halliday, 1994) endow it with the ability to represent how reasoning processes and conceptual development are displayed through language as well. Thus, it holds the potential to bridge between more cognitively oriented theoretical perspectives from the learning sciences as well as more socially oriented ones. We will introduce three constructs from systemic functional linguistics that we believe are valuable for analysis of collaboration.

In the remainder of the chapter we will first discuss the role of conversation in collaborative learning. We will then discuss how conversational processes can be operationalized using constructs from the learning sciences as well as linguistics, with an emphasis on systemic functional linguistics. We will then integrate these perspectives and discuss work toward automation of these constructs using machine learning and text mining technology. Finally, we will discuss limitations of this work as well as future work.

THE ROLE OF CONVERSATION IN COLLABORATIVE LEARNING

The importance of linguistic analysis of collaborative learning is directly related to the importance placed on conversational interactions in collaborative learning encounters. Beyond that attribution, we must also understand how we come to know and evaluate the role of those interactions, which are insights we draw from research methodology and the philosophy of science. Here we summarize our conceptualization of the lay of the land, which draws from previously published comparisons across research methodologies (Morrow & Brown, 1994). We will describe the role that linguistic analysis has played along this continuum, showing how it may play a bridge-building role between alternative methodological and theoretical camps within the learning sciences.

Before we can begin to ask what the role of linguistic communication is in group learning we must consider what we mean by learning. At one end of the spectrum, within the cognitivist tradition, the most common view is that learning is cognitive restructuring, which is typically studied with the individual student as the unit of analysis. At the extreme end within this paradigm, the role of discussion is mainly viewed as a stimulus for triggering cognitive processes, which are seen as the more direct causes of learning. At this endpoint, research questions related to collaborative discussion tend to focus on evaluating conversational patterns with respect to which cognitive processes they trigger and why, as well as how they rank in terms of their ability to trigger those processes. Secondary questions focus on how to increase the concentration of these valuable processes so that more opportunities to learn will be provided. In order to understand conversation in this light, conversational patterns must be categorized and defined in a reproducible way so that they can be counted. Otherwise it is not possible to determine whether there is a statistical relationship between those occurrences and learning. It is not surprising that within this cognitive sphere, typical approaches to analyzing collaborative discussions have fallen into what is known as "coding and counting." Within the cognitivist tradition, although the main purpose of conversational interactions may be as a stimulus for learning, the social function of language is still acknowledged. For example, the motivational benefits of social interaction in learning contexts are often considered as benefits of collaborative learning even within that paradigm. Sometimes socially oriented constructs, such as motivation, identification, or positive regard for peers are operationalized as outcome variables and related to conversational constructs through inferential statistics within that tradition.

Moving further along the continuum away from the cognitivist paradigm, the idea of cognitive apprenticeship is one in which learning occurs through interaction in an apprenticeshiplike fashion (Collins, Brown, & Newman, 1989). In this case, as in the cognitivist tradition, learning is located in the mind of the individual, and may still be measured with tests, but because it begins through interaction, conversational or otherwise, it is considered that learning is inherently social. Within this sphere, because the learning is a joint activity involving multiple actors, its conceptualization is subtly more complex than that of the cognitivist tradition. It thus becomes less natural to justify a postpositivistic experimental approach, although not impossible. Losing postpositivism as a convenient methodology would render the researcher unable to make causal claims about what types of interactions improve learning. Thus, within this sphere we see two camps of researchers, sometimes at odds with one another; namely, those who hold to postpositivist practices for causal explanations that can serve as the foundation for interventions improving learning, and those who adopt a qualitative stance in order to preserve the complexity of the relationships between the participants within the joint action. Within the postpositivist camp, the need for "coding and counting" approaches to enable statistical inference pushes for the codification of the conversational processes, such as scaffolding and help exchange, which are used within the apprenticeship process. On the other side, within the qualitative camp, more of an emphasis is placed on thick description for explaining socialization processes. Categories of behaviors may or may not be identified and labeled, and when they are, they may or may not be counted, since counting plays less of a role where the identification of causal connections is not the goal. Within the qualitative methodological sphere, systemic functional linguistics style analyses have sometimes played a role in the process of developing thick descriptions (e.g., Iedema, Degeling, Braithwaite, & White, 2003).

Taking a further step away from the cognitivist tradition, in the sociocultural tradition, learning is apprenticeship into deeper participation (Lave, 1993). The focus may still be on the individual, but the target is the individual's role within the community. Students learn through participation, first in a peripheral role, and then in more and more integral roles. As they participate, they observe the contributions of central community members in their more integral participation firsthand. The conversation between the student and community members through the apprenticeship process is key.

As we move still further along the methodological spectrum, the focus becomes more generally on socialization into community practices through conversation, and broadens from the individual within a community to the community's common practices. In this perspective, the focus is on cultural practices, or mediations (Morrow & Brown, 1994), and how they are appropriated in interactions within a community. Within this sphere, conversation is not simply viewed as a means of scaffolding as it is within the Vygotskian apprenticeship model. But the cultural practices themselves become an object of study as well as how they are transmitted, mutated, and transferred from one context into the next. For example, Christie (1999) explains the connection between the field of systemic functional linguistics and Bernstein's sociological theory, where analyses of linguistic style are used as markers of socialization processes within the home, the school, and other spheres, in order to investigate why students of working class families are more prone to fail in school. It is important to note that where the transfer of cultural practices from one community to the next is an important target of investigation, the object of study is an open system, and thus the research questions lend themselves to a qualitative approach much more readily. While systemic functional linguistics provides detailed codifications of cultural practices through systems of choices speakers make in how they present themselves and their ideas within a social context, these cultural practices are viewed as resources that may be used creatively, viewed subjectively, and negotiated in the moment of interaction between the parties present (Bucholtz & Hall, 2003; Iedema at el., 2003), thus again we see a move away from "coding and counting" as the primary approach to analysis of verbal data. Investigation of conversation from a linguistic perspective is the topic for the next section.

DESIDERATA FOR A LINGUISTIC ANALYSIS FRAMEWORK

Here we will begin with a construct that has arisen within the cognitive learning tradition, but when we look more closely, we see how it has both cognitive and social associations. Earlier we discussed the idea that one function conversation plays in collaborative learning interactions is knowledge sharing, knowledge integration, and even knowledge creation. A property of collaborative discussions that is associated with productive group knowledge construction that has its roots within a Piagetian theoretical framework is Transactivity (Berkowitz & Gibbs, 1997; de Lisi & Golbeck, 1999). In order for a contribution to count as transactive, it must include a display of reasoning, and must in some way reference a previously articulated idea from the conversation. Sionti, Ai, Rosé, and Resnick (2012) describe a simple two-dimensional operationalization of this construct in which one dimension signifies displays of reasoning processes, and a second dimension distinguishes reasoning displays that express a connection with a prior reasoning display from those that are merely externalizations. We include an overview of this operationalization in the appendix. In our own prior work (Joshi & Rosé, 2007) as well as that of others (Azimitia & Montgomery, 1993; Weinberger & Fischer, 2006), we see evidence that prevalence of Transactivity in collaborative discussions correlates with learning.

Results from other synergistic work also raise questions about how social processes affect properties of conversation that lead to a cognitive effect. In the Azmitia and Montgomery (1993) study, fifth-grade students worked in pairs on math problems. Half of the pairs (i.e., the experimental condition) were students who self-reported themselves as friends prior to the study. The other half (i.e., the control condition) were not friends prior to the study. Students who worked with a friend were found to be more successful in problem solving, at least on the most difficult problems, than students in the control condition. What explained this difference was the occurrence of transactive contributions in the discussion, which were more frequent in the experimental condition, and mediated the effect of friendship on learning. Here we see two important considerations. First, the status of the relationship between students appears to have an effect on the level of Transactivity. It could then be seen as a reflection of that relationship, and it would therefore be a mistake to relegate Transactivity as being strictly within the purview of a cognitivist theoretical framework. Second, the level of difficulty of the problem was also a factor in whether the relationship between friendship or Transactivity was significant or not. Therefore, we have more evidence that properties of conversational style, such as Transactivity, should be considered in connection with the content of what is being discussed. So, we are left with questions about the process through which friendship increases Transactivity in interactions, which is beyond the scope of what can be addressed within a purely cognitivist framework, and yet is a question that should be important to that community based on this result. Furthermore, we can ask about the social processes related to friendship that affect the navigation within the discussion of the conceptual space and problem solving space of the problem being solved.

Other constructs associated with a cognitivist perspective on learning also have social connections. We mentioned that in our earlier work (Joshi & Rosé, 2007) we observed a significant correlation between the occurrence of Transactivity in collaborative design discussions in the thermodynamics domain and learning gains as measured by a test related to concepts in thermodynamics and Rankine cycles (Kumar, Rosé, Wang, Joshi, & Robinson, 2007). However, from an earlier study of individual learning supported by human tutors using the same design task (Rosé, Kumar, Aleven, Robinson, & Wu, 2006), the predictive value of a measure of topic coverage within a conversation is also significant and even more substantial. Thus, we must consider that it is both the content and how the content is discussed that explains how beneficial an interaction is for learning. Both of these can be considered within the purview of a purely cognitivist framework. However, we are left wondering what factors were discussed, possibly social, affected which concepts, , and how?

In another example, Wang and colleagues (Wang, Rosé, Cui, et al., 2007) present a study that argues for considering a connection between cognitive factors and social factors, even when characterizing learning within a cognitivist framework. This study presents a 2X2 factorial design where students worked either individually or in pairs, either with feedback or without feedback, in an idea generation task. Consistent with earlier work on process losses in group idea generation (Dugosh et al., 2000; Nijstad & Stroebe, 2006), students who worked in pairs produced significantly fewer ideas than those in the condition where students worked individually. A post hoc analysis of the conversational interactions supported the interpretation that the process losses were an effect of cognitive interference between students (Wang & Rosé, 2007a). While this is not surprising, what is surprising is that students in the pairs condition also learned significantly less, and that the learning was mediated by success at the idea generation task. The feedback was designed to mitigate the process loss effect without offering any domain level instruction, using a type of idea generation support discussed in earlier work (Dugosh, Paulus, Roland, & Yang, 2000). Pairs with feedback produced significantly more ideas and learned significantly more than pairs without feedback. In additional post hoc analyses of the conversational data, pairs with feedback stayed on topic longer and talked more similarly to one another than pairs without feedback (Wang & Rosé, 2007b). Thus, the feedback, designed to achieve a cognitive effect, also had a social effect, as displayed through linguistic properties of the conversation. While these characteristics of conversation are not formally the same as Transactivity, what we see here is related. Students were informally observed to refer to each other's ideas and build off of each other's ideas frequently in the feedback condition. The overall picture is that the content of the discussion was what was demonstrated to have a strong predictive relationship with learning gains. And yet, social factors influenced the extent to which those cognitive factors were present. The introduction of feedback did not completely mitigate the process loss effect; however, it led both to significantly higher learning gains and a richer interaction. Shallow indicators of conversational richness (i.e., staying on the same topic longer and demonstrating higher lexical cohesion between speakers) also significantly predicted learning separately from content oriented concerns. However, just as the predictive value of Transactivity alone was low in the Joshi and Rosé (2007) study, the predictive value was substantially lower than that of the number of ideas discussed within the conversation. Nevertheless, a deeper look at the social interaction might allow us to understand how the feedback affected the dynamic between students and thereby influenced the direction the conversation took, which then influenced the learning.

INTEGRATING COGNITIVE AND SOCIAL PERSPECTIVES THROUGH SYSTEMIC FUNCTIONAL LINGUISTICS

Now that we have introduced a variety of views on why conversation is believed to be important for collaborative learning, and important for what, we can now dig deeper into what conversation is and what makes it work, especially with respect to integrating theoretical perspectives.

The field of systemic functional linguistics provides a wealth of constructs that can be used as lenses through which to view the stylistic choices of conversational participants. However, in order to bound our work for the purpose of this chapter, we limit ourselves to three, namely Martin and Rose's (2007) Negotiation system, Martin and White's (2005) conceptualization of Bakhtin's theory of heteroglossia (Bakhtin, 1986), and the more elaborate Engagement system, which is part of the larger system of appraisal.

We illustrate the operationalization of our chosen constructs using example interactions that come from the thermodynamics domain where sophomore mechanical engineering undergrads are working together in pairs to design a power plant using a paradigm known in mechanical engineering as the Rankine cycle. We have run a series of studies investigating learning in this design task over the past several years, both in connection with individual learning (Rosé et al., 2006), collaborative learning (Ai, Kumar, Nguyen, Nagasunder, & Rosé, 2010; Chaudhuri, Gupta, Smith, & Rosé, 2009), and the comparison between the two (Kumar et al., 2007). In recent years (Ai et al., 2010; Chaudhuri et al., 2009), we have assigned the two students in each pair to opposing goal conditions. Specifically, one student was assigned the goal of achieving the highest power output as possible (Power condition), and the other student was assigned the goal of achieving the lowest level of negative environmental impact (Green condition). The students were told that they had to work together to agree on a single design, but that they would be evaluated individually with respect to how well their group design met their personal design objective. Nevertheless, the instructional objective of the activity is not to produce a good design but for students to explore the design space and understand the implications of design choices in light of the theory. Thus, the apparently opposing goal orientations are simply to provide a motivation for the exploration of the design space.

NEGOTIATION

The Negotiation system is concerned with the codification of how information, goods, and services are exchanged within a conversation. In a collaborative learning setting, relevant goods and services frequently include helping actions. However, the Negotiation system is more general than this, and can be applied to the exchange of all types of goods and services through conversation. For example, something as different from help exchange as a clerk requesting a customer to pay a certain amount of money can be analyzed within the same framework. What makes this system particularly valuable is the way it serves to provide a natural segmentation of an ongoing interaction into episodes where some transaction between parties within the conversation has been accomplished; that is, either some piece of information has been exchanged, or some service has been rendered. These small accomplishments then become the building blocks for larger and more complex accomplishments that might require a more concerted, long term effort, such as building an integrated understanding of a phenomenon, developing a plan, or solving a problem. Some of these exchanges may occur with minimal representation in terms of conversational moves. For example, a speaker could simply express an unsolicited piece of information, and it could be tacitly accepted without comment by the other members of the conversation. In this case, the exchange may require only one conversational move. However, it may not be that simple. The full exchange system allows for exchanges to transpire over multiple moves, which can all be seen as connected. The provision of the information or goods and services, and possibly the preceding request if there was one, are treated as being in a prominent position within the exchange. Other kinds of moves play a supporting role in the exchange.

Within the Negotiation framework, speakers take up transitory speech roles within an exchange structure, in which one speaker takes up the primary role, thereby placing the other speaker into the secondary role. It can also happen that a speaker places himself into a secondary role, which then casts the other speaker into a primary role. In group discussions, overhearers who are present but are neither cast in the primary or secondary role are by default cast into a tertiary role. Where information is exchanged, the roles are termed *primary knower* and *secondary knower.* Where goods and services are exchanged, the roles are termed *primary actor* and *secondary actor.* For example, when a clerk requests a customer to pay, that clerk is placing himself within the secondary actor role, and thus casting the customer in the primary actor role, the one who is

		Negotiation
Student 1	I don't know what to do.	Secondary Knower
Student 2	What does it say on the sheet?	setup move
Student 1	Oh, I see, now I know what the task is.	Secondary Knower
Student 2	Right.	Primary Knower
Student1	any idea what we open to start?	Secondary Knower
Student2	I just opened the reheat cycle. It's blank, and it's already a system. We can substitute values in as we go.	Primary Knower
Student1	hm okay, do you understand how to maximize the efficiency of a reheat cycle?	Secondary Knower

Figure 10.1 Chat examples coded for Martin and Rose's (2007) Negotiation Framework.

the source of the payment. Our Negotiation framework codes are further described in the Appendix.

While implications with respect to status relationships can be drawn from speech roles where they are treated as sanctioned, such as the teacher's role as primary knower within an initiation-response-evaluation (IRE) classroom (Veel, 1999), we will see that this need not be the case. Typically the roles of primary and secondary speakers are highly volatile and do not appear to carry any particular lasting significance with respect to status distribution within the conversation. Frequent shifting in speech roles may even serve to underscore the equal footing between the two students, possibly despite their difference in ability level. Furthermore, speech roles are meaningful even where transitory in that they signify which speakers are treated as the source and recipient respectively of what is being exchanged. Thus, it allows us to ask not only which speakers are cast as authoritative within an interaction, but authoritative with respect to what.

Applying Negotiation

In Figure 10.1 we offer an example where we can see the value of examining collaboration from a systemic functional linguistics perspective. This is a reanalysis of a dataset from a previously published study (Kumar, Gweon, Joshi, Cui, & Rosé, 2007). Thirty sixth-grade students worked in pairs on fractions word problems in two conditions: a personalization condition, and a control condition. The pairs of students communicated through a computer interface that was part chat window (like an instant messenger) and part intelligent tutoring system. The first day had a lab session, then a pretest and the second day had another lab session and a posttest quiz as well as a collaboration questionnaire. From the previously published analysis of the data there was a significant increase in perception of amount of help given and received, and there were also marginally higher learning gains for the personalization condition ($p = .06$, effect size .55σ). There was also a significant increase in amount of help given per problem ($F(1,15) = 16.8$, $p < .001$, effect size 1σ), as well as students being marginally more likely to complete a step on their own after receiving help ($p = .07$) (Cui et al., 2009). An informal analysis of the discussion data also noted that there were many more insults exchanged between students in the control condition. So we see strong trends that indicate both more learning and more of a tendency to complete a step on their own after experiencing difficulty. This would make considerable sense as a connection within a cognitivist perspective. However, what that perspective does not tell us is why there was more of a tendency to complete a step after having difficulty in the personalization condition, and what the connection was with the negative affective behavior, if any. Our reanalysis suggests an answer.

In the reanalysis we recoded for authoritative behavior using the Negotiation framework, giving each student an authoritativeness score for each lab day based upon the proportion of primary knower statements to total number of primary and secondary knower statements. Each student also received a shift score, which was computed from the residual after doing a simple linear regression predicting day 2 authoritativeness from day 1 authoritativeness. We also used a naïve coding of "aggressiveness" to identify insults and exhibits of pushy behavior. The student in each pair who was observed to engage in more instances of aggressive behavior was labeled with a binary indicator as the Aggressor, whereas the other student was labeled as the de facto Victim.

We would expect instances of aggressiveness and changes in authoritativeness to have an effect on learning, as hostile learning environments are not conducive to positive learning gains. However, looking at the learning analysis, we do not see a main effect of aggressiveness on learning, but with a post hoc analysis we see that victimized students in the control condition learned significantly less than the aggressors as well as less than all students in the personalization condition ($F(1, 18) = 9.26$, $p<.01$). This is possibly due to how help was received differently in the control condition. Shifting to a less authoritative stance than predicted reduced learning in the control condition, and there was a significant correlation between shift and learning only within that condition ($F(1,20) = 7.91$, $p = .01$). In the personalization condition there was barely any variance in shift, which might explain the lack of correlation.

In each of the dimensions analyzed, the results favor the personalization condition. We see that the control condition in this study appears to have created a social environment in which the students who portrayed more aggressive behavior on the first day, shifted to a more authoritative stance than predicted while the targets of the aggression shifted to a less authoritative stance than their first day scores predicted. We also see that students in that condition, when they experienced trouble with a step, tended to drop out of the picture and let their partner finish the step for them. Meanwhile, both aggressors and victims in the personalization condition barely shifted more/less in authoritativeness. And, consistent with this, students had more of a tendency to continue trying in the face of difficulty. We see here then, through this linguistic analysis, a potential social explanation for a behavior that led to a cognitive effect.

HETEROGLOSSIA AND ENGAGEMENT

As a second construct that we consider, the Martin and White (2005) theory of heteroglossia yields further insights into the status relationship between the two speakers. A closely related construct, the Engagement system, begins with the distinction between heteroglossia and monoglossia, but expands this notion with a system of progressively finer grained distinctions. Heteroglossic statements encode the contributor's anticipation of other voices and opinions on the topic, as well as seat the contribution in an already existing discourse. This view of statements positioning a speaker within both current and future discourses ensures its place as a relevant member of the systemic functional linguistics community.

Defining Heteroglossia and Engagement

Note that Bakhtin's approach to monoglossia versus heteroglossia seems to be much broader than the interpretation in Martin and White. Heteroglossia always refers to multiple voices in a text or in a discourse community, but it can mean, for example, different registers in which someone speaks depending upon what context they are in. In Martin and White (2005), heteroglossia refers to ways in which speakers directly encode in their expression of a clause their awareness of other stakeholders in the interaction.

In Martin and White's specification of what counts as heteroglossic as a precursor to analysis using the Engagement system, which we will discuss next, three requirements must be met: first, some propositional content must be asserted in some form, although it may be done in such a way as to communicate extreme uncertainty. Thus, questions that are framed where the speaker was asking an honest question, and not

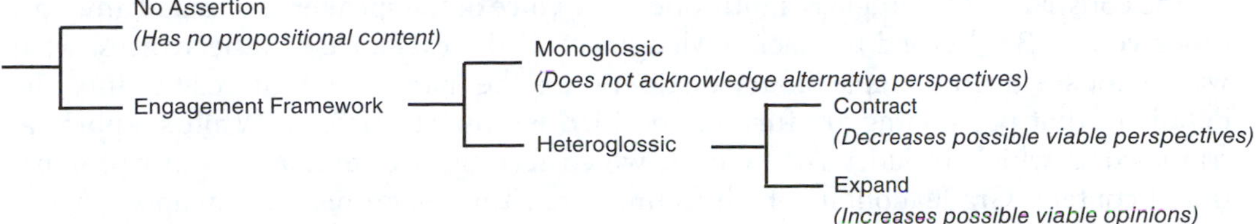

Figure 10.2 A simplified decision tree representation of the Engagement System Framework.

expecting a specific answer do not count as heteroglossic. Interjections, like *Yay*, that cannot be interpreted as ellipsis, and thus have no propositional content are not considered heteroglossic; however, fixed expressions like *no*, and *yes* that implicitly assert the propositional content of the yes/no question they are a response to do count as expressing propositional content. Other forms of ellipsis (e.g., "coal" in response to "Which type of fuel would you choose?") and do-anaphora (i.e., "I did." In response to "Did you select a fuel type?") also count as having propositional content. Second, an awareness must be made visible to the presence of alternative perspectives than that represented by the propositional content of an utterance. Thus, bald claims, even if they are biased, do not acknowledge alternative perspectives. For example, "Natural gas is the superior choice" is undoubtedly subjective, but it is not heteroglossic. It does not show any awareness that someone else might disagree. A third requirement is that in order to count as heteroglossic, the acknowledgement of other perspectives must be expressed grammatically (e.g., through a model auxiliary like "might") or paraphrastically (e.g., "I think") within the articulation of that propositional content rather than signaled only through the discourse structure. Figure 10.2 shows our operationalization of the tree structure used to determine the heteroglossic label of a contribution, while Figure 10.3 presents an illustrative example.

		Engagement
Student1	hm okay, do you understand how to maximize the efficiency of a reheat cycle?	No Assertion
Student2	I think I do, but since we have opposing goals i'll be helping you along to a point. =)	Heteroglossic-Expand
	Anyway, we have constants that we have to deal with such as the material being SS and the fluid being water.	Monoglossic
Student1	woah woah woah, what's your goal? Efficiency?	Heteroglossic-Expand
Student2	No, no, I'm going for green. Yay team.	Monoglossic
	Anyway, did you want to do reheat or simple? You seemed to have reservations before.	Heteroglossic-Expand
Student1	i think reheat. I'll explore the simple one quickly.	Heteroglossic-Expand
Student2	By the way, I take it your goal is power?	Heteroglossic-Expand
Student1	yup	Monoglossic
Student2	Great... Well, the biggest variable is fuel then, not so much reheat or simple.	Heteroglossic-Contract
	Well, I would like to do solar, what about you?	Heteroglossic-Expand

Figure 10.3 Examples of Martin and White's Heteroglossia Construct.

The construct of heteroglossia introduces the voice of the speaker as situated amongst other voices. But beyond that acknowledgment of the existence of other voices, what we do not see in this simple binary distinction is the manner of that positioning. The details of that positioning are further specified within Martin and White's Appraisal framework, which includes Attitude, in which feelings are revealed toward propositional content, Graduation, in which feelings are either magnified or downplayed, and Engagement, in which a speaker positions herself in relation to the propositional content of the utterance, positions the audience in relation to the propositional content, and positions herself in relation to the audience (Martin & White, 2005). Thus, it gives us the ability to identify how the choices speakers and writers make position that person within their speech context in relation to the other conversational participants as well as with the content of the discussion.

Once we have determined that an utterance counts as heteroglossic, we can then subdivide it into utterances that contract the positions or perspectives treated as viable within a conversation, or conversely, ones that expand the scope of what is treated as viable. Either way, an acknowledgment is made that more than one way of looking at the world is at play. Utterances that contract that scope, such as making an absolute assertion that leaves no room for questioning, or outright rejecting a position, are typically seen as taking a more authoritative stance than ones that expand the options, such as making a suggestion. This notion of levels of authoritativeness is one important component of expressing the positioning of the speaker in relation to the propositional content. However, it also says something about where the speaker positions himself in relation to the audience. Taking an authoritative stance casts the other speaker into a less authoritative stance. However, when this system is further subdivided, we see other options for positioning. For example, a Distancing move, in which the source of authority is ascribed to a third party, allows an authoritative statement to be made, which may contract options, but does not interfere with the positioning between the speaker and the audience. The speaker remains committed to the authoritative proposition, but not responsible for it. For example, if a student says, "The book says solar power is a good choice," then the student may be presenting information that he knows the other student will be opposed to, but he positions the book as the party standing in opposition, rather than himself.

Applying Heteroglossia and Engagement

Now we will discuss the connection between Transactivity from the collaborative learning community and the related constructs of heteroglossia and Engagement from the systemic functional linguistics community. As earlier, we illustrate this with an example interaction from the thermodynamics domain.

In the collaborative discussion presented in Figure 10.4, Student 1 has been assigned to the Power condition, and Student 2 has been assigned to the Green condition. They discuss their opposing goal orientations in the first nine contributions, and in the remainder of this excerpt, they discuss which type of fuel they should use in their Rankine cycle, examining their choices based on implications for these two opposing goals. In the end, they settle on solar-thermal, which is a good choice for Green, but not Power. Thus, one could consider that on this aspect of the design, Student 2 has achieved an advantage in terms of how the design will be evaluated in light of the two opposing goal orientations.

		Transactive	Engagement
Student1	any idea what we open to start?	Not Reasoning	No Assertion
Student2	I just opened the reheat cycle. It's blank, and it's already a system. We can substitute values in as we go.	Not Reasoning	Monoglossic
Student1	hm okay, do you understand how to maximize the efficiency of a reheat cycle?	Not Reasoning	No Assertion
Student2	I think I do, but since we have opposing goals I'll be helping you along to a point. =)	Externalization	Heteroglossic-Expand
	Anyway, we have constants that we have to deal with such as the material being SS and the fluid being water.	Not Reasoning	Monoglossic
Student1	woah woah woah, what's your goal? Efficiency?	Not Reasoning	Heteroglossic-Expand
Student2	No, no, I'm going for green. Yay team.	Not Reasoning	Monoglossic
	Anyway, did you want to do reheat or simple? You seemed to have reservations before.	Not Reasoning	Heteroglossic-Expand
Student1	i think reheat. I'll explore the simple one quickly.	Not Reasoning	Heteroglossic-Expand
Student2	By the way, I take it your goal is power?	Not Reasoning	Heteroglossic-Expand
Student1	yup	Not Reasoning	Monoglossic
Student2	Great... Well, the biggest variable is fuel then, not so much reheat or simple.	Transactive	Heteroglossic-Contract
	Well, I would like to do solar, what about you?	Not Reasoning	Heteroglossic-Expand
Student1	ha i'd try natural gas for power. but i dont understand this very well.	Externalization	Heteroglossic-Expand
	do we need to come up with the same system? if so, we'll have to do something in-between	Transactive	Heteroglossic-Expand
Student2	Yes, we need to agree on a system that fits both of our goals.	Not Reasoning	Monoglossic
	Well, single cycle is more friendly to the environment, so if we do that I'll conced to nuclear as the fuel.	Transactive	Heteroglossic-Expand
Student1	ok let's do single cycle and go with.... coal? nuclear isnt allowed :(natural gas is 2560, coal is 2400, oil is 800, etc	Transactive	Heteroglossic-Expand
Student2	Nuclear isn't allowed in the program, but it still can be used by manually entering the Q value.	Transactive	Monoglossic
Student1	True. eh lets just go with coal. so lets do 2400	Externalization	Heteroglossic-Expand
Student2	Coal, the worst of the fuels for green.	Transactive	Monoglossic
Student1	kk want to do solar-thermal? 240? Your end goal is just "green"?	Transactive	Heteroglossic-Expand
Student2	I'd love to, do you want to use it? Yep, green at any cost.	Not Reasoning	Heteroglossic-Expand
Student1	ya lets go with it	Not Reasoning	Heteroglossic-Expand

Figure 10.4 A collaborative design exercise coded for Transactivity and Heteroglossia.

Transactive conversational contributions are viewed as important steps in a knowledge building or consensus building process (Weinberger & Fischer, 2006). In making connections between newly articulated ideas and material contributed earlier in a conversation, ideas build upon one another, and differing understandings are elaborated, integrated, and possibly transformed. In the example presented in Figure 10.4, we see the decision making process about the selection of fuel unfold. Key moves from a decision making standpoint include where they agree to find a decision that would be a compromise between their two opposing goal orientations, where the idea of encoding the fuel choice as a number is articulated, and which then becomes a theme carried throughout the remainder of the conversation, and where the final choice is introduced. All three of these would be coded as transactive.

In this interaction, we see both students articulating their reasoning in a transactive manner throughout the discussion, which might suggest an equal status relationship between the speakers, based on Piaget's theory. However, more of those were contributed by Student 2, which might suggest an imbalance. At least Speaker 2 exhibits a greater ability to articulate reasoning and to relate those reasoning displays to previously articulated material. A heteroglossic contribution need not be counted as an explicit display of reasoning. Thus, it would not serve the function of assessing the ability to articulate reasoning the way Transactivity may, although there are other constructs like grammatical metaphor in systemic functional linguistics that have been used to assess level of sophistication of thought displayed through writing (Halliday, 1994).

Because of being applicable to contributions where reasoning is not explicitly displayed, what heteroglossia gives us beyond what is marked in transactive utterances is a more exhaustive accounting of how the power balance is maintained through a conversation. Throughout the conversation, we see both speakers doing work to maintain their solidarity, often through heteroglossic contributions that express deference to the other student's perspective. For example, "We have constraints that we have to deal with" casts the obligations toward the task at hand and their opposing goal orientations as coming from outside the interaction, and thus reduces the importance of internal pressures. "Did you want to do reheat or simple?" offers two alternatives without expressing preference, and thus leaves both options open, rather than restricting the issue to a personal preference. The other speaker's response "I think reheat" expresses a preference, but not in a way that limits options. We know from prior work that heterogeneous learning groups can be problematic, and inequalities within the status balance can easily ensue, which interfere with the productive functioning of the group. Heteroglossia allows us to see students working to avoid falling into this behavior. It may eventually shed light on what influences which topics students spend time considering within an interaction.

TECHNOLOGY FOR AUTOMATIC CONVERSATION ANALYSIS

Earlier in the chapter, we highlighted different aspects of collaborative discussions that are relevant depending upon the theoretical and methodological framework that is used as a lens through which collaboration is studied. In particular, we have highlighted the potential value that linguistic analysis, such as those related to constructs we have discussed from systemic functional linguistics, may be of value to the CSCL community. In this section we focus on how we can develop computational models that can assist in automating such analyses. We will begin this discussion with a description of work which has been done on problems similar to those we would like to study, introducing concepts from machine learning as they are necessary. Then, we conclude with a preliminary view of how to build computational models of systemic functional linguistics constructs using machine learning technology.

Looking Back: A Historical Perspective on Text Mining

In recent years, the computer supported collaborative learning community has shown interest in automatic analysis of data from collaborative learning settings, building on and extending work in text mining from the language technologies community. Application of such technology can be very direct, particularly where interests are very similar, such as detecting where attitudes are encoded in the expression of ideas, which is currently a very active area of research in the language technologies community. In other cases, the specific types of analysis, for example, the operationalizations of knowledge building and social positioning are less directly related to what is most centrally of concern to the language technologies community. There is a body of work in collaborative learning—for instance, studying automatic analysis of Transactivity (Ai et al., 2010; Joshi & Rosé, 2007; Rosé et al., 2008) and other collaborative learning constructs (McLaren et al, 2007; Wang & Rosé, 2007a)—these are the exception.

Automatic analysis approaches as we know them today are only capable of identifying patterns that occur in a stable and recognizable way. Although those patterns can be arbitrarily complex, there are limitations to contexts in which an approach of this nature is appropriate. These approaches are most naturally usable within research traditions that value abstraction and quantification. The most natural application of such technology is within traditions that employ coding and counting approaches to analysis of verbal data. Nevertheless, recent work pushes beyond these strict boundaries. For example, Ai and colleagues (2010) have demonstrated how a structured topic modeling approach can be used to measure influence within a conversation between one conversational participant and another in a graded way, which was validated through questionnaire data. Nevertheless, the very idea of operationalizing collaboration practices in a rule-based way, even if those rules can be arbitrarily complex functions, requires some abstraction and simplification of reality. Thus, research traditions that value preservation of complexity and avoid abstraction and generalization will find it uncomfortable to consider using such an approach in their research. By nature, empirical modeling approaches involving statistics and machine learning are mainly useful for capturing what is typical. In contrast, within many qualitative research traditions, it is the unusual occurrences and practices that are worthy of study. Thus, it is unlikely that such technology would be directly usable for producing the kind of findings that are valued within those traditions. However, what it may be able to assist with is finding the unusual occurrences within a mass of data, which might then be worthy of study in a more traditional way.

The wide range of conversational constructs that have been explored within this chapter provide new opportunities for exploration of automatic analysis technology and ways in which that technology can be improved. Machine learning algorithms are designed with the goal of finding mappings between input features and output categories. They do this by collecting hand-coded "training examples" for each output category, then using statistical techniques to find characteristics that exemplify each category. The goal of such an algorithm is to learn general rules from these examples, which can then be applied effectively to new data. In order for this to work well, the set of input features must be sufficiently expressive, and the training examples must be representative. Machine learning researchers are tasked with designing input features expressive enough to capture the subtleties of the categories they are trying to learn. At the shallowest level, these input features are simply the words in a document. Many other features, such as word collocations, part of speech tags, and low-level lexical features are routinely used.

In the past decade, a variety of approaches to text categorization have been developed and refined. Major advances have been made due to the development of powerful machine learning algorithms, the increase in speed of computers, and the availability of very large relevant corpora. The biggest limitation, perhaps, is the shallow nature of the representations of text that are typically used in this computational work, which treat text as though it were an unstructured collection of words, or pairs of words, or pairs of grammatical categories. We have made this argument in earlier publications related to analysis of attitudes displayed in text (Joshi & Rosé, 2009). These two problems—the features used to represent the text to be analyzed, and the annotation of the text in a way that suitably operationalizes the construct of interest—are two sides of the same coin. The operationalization determines which instances should be grouped and distinguished from instances in other groups. And the features used to represent the text allow the definition of the conditions under which instances are assigned to groups to be expressed. Unless these two are in alignment, the model building will not be successful no matter how powerful is a machine learning algorithm and how much training data is available. Thus, both of these issues are vital to future progress in computational linguistics.

Even in much earlier work, limitations of feature spaces have been noted in connection with topic and content oriented classification tasks such as home page classification (Furnkrantz, Mitchell, Mitchell, & Riloff, 1998), and knowledge component classification for an essay grading task (Rosé & VanLehn, 2005). Closer to the topic at hand, text representation was the key to improving performance of classification of segments of a newsgroup style discussion with a 5-category operationalization of Transactivity (Rosé et al., 2008). In that work, the key additional features that improved performance were ones that represented how similar a segment was to others contributed earlier by other participants in the discussion as well as features that represented the position of the segment within a message, and the position of the message on a thread.

What is important here from the standpoint of a CSCL research considering using such technology as part of his or her research methodology is to understand what kind of thinking and preparation is necessary in order to use machine learning to the best of its potential.

COMPUTATIONAL MODEL OF NEGOTIATION

Currently, results on computationalization of systemic functional linguistics are somewhat limited. So far, to the best of our knowledge, there has not been any published work on the Engagement system or even the simpler notion of heteroglossia. Argamon and colleagues have worked on a computationalization of a different construct referred to as Attitude (Argamon et. al, 2007; Whitelaw & Argamon, 2004), which is one of three constructs under the broader construct of appraisal, of which Engagement is another one. The primary computational approach pursued in that work has been to build lists of cue words which are likely to occur only in certain contexts, such as *worst, awful,* and *terrible* with a negative attitude. Such a list of words is termed a "sentiment lexicon." The initial approaches to machine learning for appraisal theory used lexicons like these. Initially, the lists contained only adjectives (Taboada & Grieves, 2004), but later work expanded this format to a complex taxonomy of words and cue phrases (Whitelaw & Argamon, 2004). This approach is popular because it requires no hand annotating of training examples (words in the lexicon can be found automatically); it can be expanded to larger lists because the level of detail in the list can be adapted to individual problems and because such lexicons can be built automatically in some cases.

Our work has so far focused on the Negotiation system. We found, however, that a key phrase matching approach such as taken by Argamon and colleagues in connection with attitude would not work for Negotiation. The same contribution uttered in different contexts can take on a totally different status within the Negotiation framework. Thus, we needed a framework that would allow us to leverage these contextual constraints in the interpretation process. In order to accomplish this, we have used a paradigm called *integer linear programming* (ILP). This allows us to define a set of contextual rules for our machine learning algorithm to follow. For instance, we can state the order in which Negotiation codes usually appear together. Then, if the output category assigned to a line of a conversation does not follow these rules, the algorithm knows to "back off" to a less likely category that fits better in context. If we take a simpler approach where we make predictions about the codes just from the content of the contributions themselves, our machine generated authoritativeness measures explained only 35% of the variance in those computed based on human annotations, where interannotator agreement on the human codes has been evaluated at .71 Kappa. In contrast, the ILP formulation that leverages context with rules is able to explain 95% of the variance in scores computed based on human annotations. Thus we see how important it is for the considerations that are built into the computational framework to reflect the conceptual essence of the definitions of those constructs.

LIMITATIONS AND CHALLENGES

We conclude this chapter by outlining the limitations of this review and discussion of the biggest challenges we seek to address moving forward. We started out the chapter outlining the major subcommunities within the learning sciences, how they view learning differently, and how those differences change the role they see discussion as playing in the learning. We have introduced some subcommunity-specific frameworks for investigating issues that are of concern within the associated communities. We raised questions that fall at the frontiers between communities and have argued how we think systemic functional linguistics may have the potential to serve as an aid to communication between communities, as an extensive descriptive linguistic framework encompassing aspects of linguistic expression that are interesting when viewed by the full gamut of perspectives, and may serve as a useful boundary object. Much work is left to do to flesh out and formalize what has been provided by the systemic functional linguistics community so that it can be applied broadly. Ultimately, our hope is to be able to develop automatic analysis technology, and we have outlined the state-of-the-art in language technologies related to Negotiation and some constructs within the appraisal system.

ACKNOWLEDGMENTS

This work was funded by NSF grants SBE 0836012 and DRL 0835426 and ONR grant N00014-10-1-0277.

REFERENCES

Ai, H., Kumar, R., Nguyen, D., Nagasunder, A., & Rosé, C. P. (2010). Exploring the effectiveness of social capabilities and goal alignment in computer supported collaborative learning. In *Proceedings of Intelligent Tutoring Systems* (pp. 134–143). New York: Springer.

Argamon, S., Whitelaw, C., Chase, P., Hota, S., Garg, N., & Levitan, S. (2007). Stylistic text classification using functional lexical features. *Journal of the American Society for Information Science and Technology, 58*(6), 802–822.

Azmitia, M., & Montgomery, R. (1993). Friendship, transactive dialogues, and the development of scientific reasoning. *Social Development*, 2(3 202–221.

Bakhtin, M. (1986). *Speech genres and other late essays* (V. W. McGee, Trans.; C. Emerson & M. Holquist, Eds.). Austin: University of Texas Press.

Berkowitz, M., & Gibbs, J. (1979). *Manual for coding transactivity.* Unpublished manuscript.

Bucholtz, M., & Hall, K. (2005). Identity and interaction: a sociocultural linguistic approach. *Discourse Studies, 7*(4–5), 585–614.

Chaudhuri, S., Gupta, N., Smith, N. A., & Rosé, C. P. (2009). Leveraging structural relations for fluent compressions at multiple compression rates. In *Proceedings of the Association for Computational Linguistics* (pp. 101–104). Stroudsburg, PA: Association for Computational Linguistics.

Christie, F. (1999). *Pedagogy and the shaping of consciousness: Linguistic and social processes.* London: Cassell.

Collins, A., Brown, J. S., & Newman, S. E. (1989). Cognitive apprenticeship: Teaching the craft of reading, writing and mathematics. In L. B. Resnick (Ed.), *Knowing, learning, and instruction: Essays in honor of Robert Glaser* (pp. 453-494). Hillsdale, NJ: Erlbaum.

Cui, Y., Chaudhuri, S., Kumar, R., Gweon, G., & Rosé, C. P. (2009). Helping agents in VMT. In G. Stahl (Ed.), *Studying virtual math teams: Computer supported collaborative learning* (Vol. 11 [4], pp. 335–354). New York: Springer.

de Lisi, R., & Golbeck, S. L. (1999). Implications of the Piagetian theory for peer learning. In *Cognitive perspectives on peer learning* (pp. 3–37). Mahwah, NJ: Erlbaum.

Dugosh, K. L., Paulus, P. B., Roland, E. J., & Yang, H. (2000). Cognitive stimulation in brainstorming. *Journal of Personality and Social Psychology, 79*(5), 722–735.

Furnkranz, J., Mitchell, T., Mitchell, M., & Riloff, E. (1998). A case study in using linguistic phrases for text categorization on the WWW. In *Proceedings from the AAAI/ICML Workshop on Learning for Text Categorization* (pp. 5–12). Palo Alto, CA: AAAI Press.

Halliday, M. (1994). *An introduction to functional grammar.* London: Edward Arnold.

Iedema, R., Degeling, P., Braithwaite, J., & White, L. (2003). "It's an interesting conversation I'm hearing": The doctor as manager. *Organizational Studies, 25*(1), 15–33.

Joshi, M., & Rosé, C. P. (2007). Using transactivity in conversation summarization in educational dialog. In *Proceedings of the SLaTE Workshop on Speech and Language Technology in Education,* IEEE Signal Processing Society. Suntec, Singapore: Association for Computational Linguistics.

Joshi, M., & Rosé, C. P. (2009). Generalizing dependency features for opinion mining. In *Proceedings of the ACL-IJCNLP 2009 Conference Short Papers* (pp. 313–317).

Kumar, R., Gweon, G., Joshi, M., Cui, Y., & Rosé, C. P. (2007). Supporting students working together on math with social dialogue. In *Proceedings of the SLaTE Workshop on Speech and Language Technology in Education,* IEEE Signal Processing Society.

Kumar, R., Rosé, C. P., Wang, Y. C., Joshi, M., & Robinson, A. (2007). Tutorial dialogue as adaptive collaborative learning support. In *Proceedings of Artificial Intelligence in Education* (pp. 383–393). Lansdale, PA: IOS Press.

Lave J. (1993). The practice of learning. In S. Chaiklin & J. Lave (Eds.), *Understanding practice: Perspectives on activity and context* (pp. 200-208). Cambridge, England: Cambridge University Press.

Martin, J. R., & Rose, D. (2007). *Working with discourse: Meaning beyond the clause.* New York: Continuum.

Martin, J. R., & White, P. R. (2005). *The language of evaluation: Appraisal in English.* New York: Palgrave.

McLaren, B., Scheuer, O., De Laat, M., Hever, R., de Groot, R., & Rosé, C. P. (2007). Using machine learning techniques to analyze and support mediation of student e-discussions. In *Proceedings of Artificial Intelligence in Education* (pp 331–338). Lansdale, PA: IOS Press.

Morrow, R. A., & Brown, D. D. (1994). *Critical theory and methodology.* Thousand Oaks, CA: Sage.

Nijstad, B. A., & Stroebe, W. (2006). How the group affects the mind: a cognitive model of idea generation in groups. *Personality and Social Psychology Review, 10*(3), 186–213.

Rosé, C. P., Kumar, R., Aleven, V., Robinson, A., & Wu, C. (2006). CycleTalk: Data driven design of support for simulation based learning [Special issue]. *International Journal of Artificial Intelligence in Education, 16,* 195–223.

Rosé C. P., & VanLehn, K. (2005). An evaluation of a hybrid language understanding approach for robust selection of tutoring goals. *International Journal of AI in Education, 15(4),* 325–355.

Rosé, C. P., Wang, Y.C., Cui, Y., Arguello, J., Stegmann, K., Weinberger, A., & Fischer, F. (2008). Analyzing collaborative learning processes automatically: Exploiting the advances of computational linguistics in computer-supported collaborative learning, *International Journal of Computer Supported Collaborative Learning* 3(3), 237–271.

Sionti, M., Ai, H., Rosé, C. P., & Resnick, L. (2012). A framework for analyzing development of argumentation through classroom discussions. In N. Pinkwart & B. McClaren (Eds.), *Educational technologies for teaching argumentation skills.* Oak Park, IL: Bentham Science.

Taboada, M., & Grieve, J. (2004). Analyzing appraisal automatically. In *Proceedings of AAAI Spring Symposium on Exploring Attitude and Affect in Text.* Palo Alto, CA: AAAI Press.

Veel, R. (1999). Language, knowledge and authority in school mathematics. In F. Christie (Ed.), *Pedagogy and the shaping of consciousness: Linguistic and social processes.* New York: Continuum.

Wang, H. C., Rosé, C.P., Cui, Y., Chang, C. Y, Huang, C. C., & Li, T. Y. (2007). Thinking hard together: The long and short of collaborative idea generation for scientific inquiry. In *Proceedings of Computer Supported Collaborative Learning* (pp. 754–763). New York: Springer.

Wang, H., & Rosé, C. P. (2007a). A process analysis of idea generation and failure. In *Proceedings of the Annual Meeting of the Cognitive Science Society* (pp. 1629–1634).

Wang, H. C., & Rosé, C. P. (2007b). Supporting collaborative idea generation: A closer look using statistical process analysis techniques. In *Proceedings of Artificial Intelligence in Education* (pp. 659–661). Lansdale, PA: IOS Press.

Weinberger A., & Fischer F. (2006). A framework to analyze argumentative knowledge construction in computer supported collaborative learning. *Computers & Education, 46,* 71–95.

Whitelaw, C., & Argamon, S. (2004). Systemic functional features in stylistic text classification. In *Proceedings of AAAI Fall Symposium on Style and Meaning in Language*. Palo Alto, CA: AAAI Press.

APPENDIX

Negotiation Framework Coding Manual

An organized view of the Negotiation Framework codes is provided below in Figure 10.5.

Label	Example
Primary Knower	"This is the end."
Secondary Knower	"Is this the end?" (not all questions)
Primary Actor	"I'm going to the end."
Secondary Actor	"Go to the end."
Challenge	"I don't have an end marked."
Other	"So…"
Setup Move	"Where do you think the end is?" (with ability to judge correctness)

Figure 10.5 An overview of the Negotiation Framework codes.

Engagement Framework Coding Manual

Below, in Figure 10.6, is a simplified view of our Engagement Framework codes and definitions.

Label	Definition
No Assertion	No propositional content is asserted (honest questions, "yay", etc).
Monoglossic	Does not acknowledge alternate perspectives (bald claims, no hedging, etc).
Heteroglossic	
Expand	Increases possibility of other viewpoints (making a suggestion, "might", etc).
Contract	Decreases viable opinions (outright rejection, absolute assertions, etc).

Figure 10.6 An overview of the Engagement Framework codes and definitions.

Transactivity Coding Manual

An overview of the guide for labeling Transactive contributions is provided below in Figure 10.7. Further information on details of the coding scheme can be found in Sionti et al. (2012).

Label	Definition
Not Reasoning	
Off-task	Blatantly off-topic contributions.
Social	Socially-oriented off-task contributions.
Tangent	Not related directly to the task at hand.
Assertion	Plain answers or procedures, or off-task reasoning.
Repetition	Purely repetitive contributions.
Reasoning	
Externalization	No reference to another's explicit reasoning.
Transactive	Connection to another's explicit reasoning.

Figure 10.7 An overview of the Transactivity codes and definitions.

11

ADVANCING UNDERSTANDING OF COLLABORATIVE LEARNING WITH DATA DERIVED FROM VIDEO RECORDS

BRIGID J. S. BARRON AND ROY PEA

Stanford University

RANDI A. ENGLE

University of California, Berkeley

The study of collaborative learning is a multimethod and multidisciplinary affair (Strijbos & Fischer, 2007). As the chapters in this volume attest, controlled experiments, ethnographic portraits, surveys, and qualitative or quantitative analysis of talk and interaction all have their roles to play in advancing our understanding of this vital form of human interaction. Hybrid or mixed methods approaches are increasingly used to integrate studies of interactional processes and learning outcomes in collaborative learning and education more generally (Creswell & Plano Clark, 2007; Maxwell & Loomis, 2003; Tashakkori & Teddlie, 2003). Our field seeks to better understand how technological tools and artifacts amplify or hinder productive collaborative interactions. What may be involved in planning and completing a study using video records? In this chapter, we consider the importance of theory inquiry cycles, the development of viewing practices, and the usefulness of intermediate representations of video records, and we summarize how researchers use video records to create datasets and make claims about collaborative learning phenomena.

How exactly one approaches or should approach an analysis of collaborative learning using video recordings depends crucially on one's theoretical commitments, on the specific research questions being pursued, and on practical constraints of time, money, and personnel. A video analysis is high quality to the extent that the researcher can make a convincing case that one's analytic choices and argumentation connecting claims to data were sufficiently responsive to these considerations. Issues of reliability and validity of all kinds (internal, convergent, external, and descriptive) apply to video-based data as they do to any other kind of quantitative or qualitative data analysis. Concerns about generalizability of findings can be countered by explicit attention to the logic of one's inquiry, one's approach to collecting records, and an articulation of the processes used to create explanations and generate claims. As a result, performing analyses with video recordings is frequently an iterative process that involves cycling between the video records themselves, one's evolving hypotheses and data interpretations, and a variety of intermediate representations for discovering, evaluating, and representing them for oneself and others.

Our chapter is organized into four sections:

Rationale: In this section we summarize aspects of collaborative interaction that make video records useful for investigations of this form of learning, and outline some of the research questions animating recent work with video.

Research: Here we organize our discussion around several types of research designs productively using video records as a core data source.

Strategies for representing and analyzing video records: In this section we share documented approaches to representing video data.

Approaches to reporting video-based analyses and making arguments: Here we present examples from the literature showcasing alternative ways that researchers share data and warrant claims connecting data to theory.

WHY USE VIDEO RECORDS TO UNDERSTAND COLLABORATIVE LEARNING?

Collaborative accomplishments are increasingly understood as involving the intertwining of cultural, cognitive, relational, and embodied phenomena. Hutchins (1995) argues that human intelligent action is productively conceived as an accomplishment arising from *properties of interactions* between people or between people and artifacts in the world. How a particular interaction unfolds depends on the efforts of the individuals involved, their understanding of the activity, the material and symbolic resources they have available, implicit or explicit conventions for proceeding with joint work, and the nature of the interpersonal relationships among partners.

A core implication of this view is that to understand the nature of productive collaboration, we need to articulate how social goals and discourse practices interact with knowledge building processes that lead to coconstruction of understanding. Clark (1996) uses the term *ensembles* to capture the interdependencies of partners in conversation. By focusing on the group or "ensemble," researchers can describe interactions that capture the dynamic interplay in meaning-making over time in discourse between participants, what they understand, the material and symbolic resources they use, the types of contributions that they make, and how they are taken up or not in a given discourse. Video records of interactions make possible the incorporation of multiple kinds of data into the analyses beyond talk. Silence, repetition of ideas, eye gaze, gestures, physical synchrony, laughter, pauses, interruptions, intonation, and overlaps in turn taking do not have single meanings but have a productive ambiguity so that depending on the context they can serve to signal different things to participants at different times (Kendon, 1982, 1997). Such behavioral displays become available through video interaction analysis for making sense of how interaction unfolds over time and for drawing out the relational and social aspects of collaborative problem solving (Barron, 2003). In addition, video allows researchers to replay the recording of collaborative interaction in order to gradually enrich their perceptions and understanding of its moment-by-moment processes reflected through intonation, facial expressions, and body language in addition to conversation.

Attending to between-person processes has surfaced emergent properties of collaborative interactions. For example, the key notion of a "joint problem solving space" was generated from a video-based case study (Roschelle, 1992; Teasley & Roschelle, 1993). Phenomena such as coordinated mutual engagement (Bakeman & Adamson, 1984), as revealed through reciprocity, coregulation, and the degree of intent to collaborate are dimensions of collaborative activity that can be operationalized, measured, and analyzed from high quality video records. The intention to collaborate, or what has been called an "intersubjective attitude" (Crook, 1996), is expressed behaviorally and can be assessed by studying how a participant orients to others and by how willing they are to engage in coregulation of the interaction (Fogel, 1993), their attention to partner's contributions through acknowledgment or elaboration, and sharing of ownership over the work.

RESEARCH DESIGNS THAT USE VIDEO TO STUDY COLLABORATIVE LEARNING

Given the time-consuming nature of analyzing and collecting video records, one must plan carefully to make best use of one's resources. Although situations arise in which video already collected becomes the object of analysis (e.g., Goodwin, 1994; Leonard & Derry, 2006), ideally research video is guided by a research design and a set of research questions based on familiarity with the phenomena being studied. Such planning is particularly helpful when the researcher is new to video analysis. The amount of information captured in video recordings makes them a powerful resource when compared to what a human observer can record in real time, but provides corresponding challenges. Erickson (2006) argues that video records are not data but are resources for developing data. Turning records into data is enormously time consuming. Accordingly, it is sensible to develop a project with theoretically motivated questions that originate from the research literature and observations. Good orienting questions help maintain a perspective that prevents one from getting lost in the prolific bounties of information that video records open up to scrutiny.

Reflecting on which theoretically motivated questions to pursue can and should fundamentally influence strategies for data collection. For example, many investigators have found it fruitful to combine video records with other forms of data, such as interviews, performance data or surveys. Field notes, photographs of the surrounding field of action, copies of documents used, or artifacts created by groups can enrich the data derived from video records and offer opportunities for triangulation across multiple sources of evidence. We now describe several types of research designs that use video records, sometimes in combination with other data sources, and we provide examples of published studies, summarizing the questions that drove their design.

Ethnographic Studies

Several researchers have carried out video-based studies for examining how collaborative phenomena change over time in classrooms or workplaces. For example, Hall, Wieckert, and Wright (2010) used analyses of videotaped interactions to understand how a group of entomologists collaborated with statisticians to find better ways to classify termites.

The more general questions driving the work included how people collaboratively make concepts general and shared and how work environments function as learning environments. Video was used to record typical periods of work, and it was combined with biographical interviews, interviews focused on work activity, collection of working and published documents, and participant observations. These multiple forms of data collection reflected phenomena occurring at different time scales. Coordinating these data sources longitudinally allowed these researchers to articulate a number of processes that take place over substantial periods of time including describing how future work is assembled through narrative in conversation, how parables were used to position coworkers in alternative ways of working, and how infrastructure was established through analogical reasoning that built upon the prior work of other scientists.

Another example that fits into this category is a study of game play among children at home (Stevens, Satwicz, & McCarthy, 2008). This work also builds on a tradition of everyday cognition and had as a goal to describe how "in-game" activity is also tangled up with activity that is occurring "in-room." To capture both strands of co-occurring activity the team captures the game play directly from the computer or game console and a separate camera captures the "in-room" activity where the players are sitting, lounging, crouching, or reclining. Resources such as game manuals and interactions with family and friends are captured. The two video streams are then synchronized into a single image so that the analysts can view them simultaneously.

Experimental Designs Coupled with Video Capture

Several studies have combined experimental designs that vary some aspect of the collaborative situation with video capture of the interactions. These kinds of enhanced experimental designs can be productive for both theory building and for testing hypotheses (Maxwell, 2004; Shadish, Cook, & Campbell, 2002); in this case, about how an experimental manipulation might be influencing collaborative interactions. For example, Zahn, Pea, Hesse, and Rosen (2010) assigned dyads to one of two conditions that involved collaboratively designing a video-based web presentation for a virtual museum. The researchers combined and synchronized video recordings of the interaction between the dyads with digital screen recordings of the dyads' collaborative development of the multimedia website. In their experiment they compared the design processes and learning outcomes of 24 collaborating dyads that used two contrasting types of video tools for history learning. The advanced video tool WebDiver supported segmenting, editing, and annotating capabilities. In the contrasting condition, students used a simple video playback tool with a word processor to perform the design task. Results indicated that the advanced video editing tool was more effective in relation to (a) the students' understanding of the topic and cognitive skills acquisition; (b) the quality of the students' design products; and (c) the efficiency of dyad interactions. For the two experimental groups, in addition to quantitative comparisons of content knowledge, cognitive skills acquisition, measurable properties of the joint design products, and the distribution of talk content categories during their dyadic interactions, the researchers developed case analyses of some of the dyads' collaborative processes to examine possible tool effects on microprocesses such as achieving common ground in dyadic interaction.

In an experiment that randomly assigned students to an individual or a group problem solving condition, video records made of the triadic sessions were used to explain differences in outcomes for different collaborative groups (Barron, 2000, 2003). The video-based analysis was motivated by the observation of significant variability in quantitative group problem solving scores within the collaborative condition, despite random assignment of students to triads and equal levels of prior mathematical knowledge. The tapes were first viewed to assess whether or not correct answers were generated in discourse by all teams. It became apparent that in all groups the correct solutions were generated, but in about a third of the cases they were never fully documented. Accounting for the differences between the teams led to a number of insights about the role of joint attention and to the proposal that collaboration might be productively thought about in terms of a dual problem space. In particular, Barron (2000, 2003) found that all groups faced coordination problems that could have prevented correct ideas from being recognized and used by the group. However, it was only the more successful groups that used verbal and nonverbal strategies for addressing these problems. They could be seen to maintain joint attention and ownership through mutual gaze and by "huddling" around workbooks. When documenting solutions, the writer might "broadcast" his or her writing and thus make it available for monitoring. In addition, some groups evolved more explicit expressions of metacommunicative awareness as indicated by their monitoring of joint attention and possible disruptions to it. Thus, as the detailed video analyses showed, successful coordination was accomplished through a variety of strategies that included the use of external representations, conversational devices, and physical moves; also see Mercier (2010) for another example.

Arranged Collaborations in Natural Settings

Another research design that productively allows for the study of collaboration involves arranging for intact groups, such as families or friendship pairs, to visit learning environments and then following their conversations with video. An example of this kind of design can be found in a study of the conversations of bilingual families during visits to an aquarium (Ash, 2007). The researchers recruited families who participated in a Head Start program and invited them to visit a particular set of exhibits on multiple occasions. The goal of the research was to describe the kinds of informal learning conversations that families produced, and how the content and form of their conversations changed over time. The research challenge in this kind of study is to figure out how to capture ideas that "emerge, submerge, and reappear in morphed forms, traceable over time but often only in hindsight" (Ash, 2007, p. 211), and how to capture family members' conversations or interactions with exhibits when they split off from the main group, as often happens. The solution for this team involved having separate microphones for each family member with one videographer following the groups, but also having audio recorders on hand for the times that members split up. They also used some of the video in interviews to gather data on what family members had been thinking about when they were looking at exhibits but not speaking (see Cherry, Fournier, & Stevens, 2003; Stevens & Toro-Martell, 2003 for another example of a video-based stimulated recall approach).

Hybrid Designs

Some video-based collaborative learning studies move between two or more of these approaches. For example, in a classroom study by Engle, Conant, and Greeno (2007), the research team began with a pre/post design. They used video to follow group and whole class discussions during an inquiry-based curriculum unit taking place in a fifth grade classroom, and included pre- and postassessments to measure changes in individual and group conceptual understanding. This strategy allowed the team to make an explicit connection between the disciplinary discourse practices that were being used in whole class discussions and the small-group interactions that took place when students worked independently. However, like in ethnographic studies, the authors also reported findings that emerged during analysis and that were totally unanticipated. For example, at the prompting of a colleague they decided to look more closely at an instance of a conversation taking off. Though they had not anticipated this as a focus before they began the study, the video records allowed them to pursue it fully in the context of one group, which allowed them to propose general principles for fostering this and similar cases of productive disciplinary engagement (Engle & Conant, 2002). A second unanticipated focus was the important role that the teacher played in students' learning and transfer when she repeatedly attributed authorship of ideas and information to students (Engle & Conant, 2002; see also Engle, 2006; Greeno, 2006). Although the good questions the researchers started with were addressed, the novel phenomena were especially fruitful theoretically. Thus, formulating questions at a general level does not preclude more discovery-oriented work with video records; in fact, this is one of their valuable properties—they can be revisited at different times with different viewpoints and by different researchers for continued learning and analysis.

STRATEGIES FOR REPRESENTING AND ANALYZING RECORDS: DATA CREATION, ORGANIZATION, AND ANALYSIS

Video records are often rich with interactional phenomena, including eye gaze, body posture, content of talk, tone of voice, facial expressions, physical artifacts, as well as between-person processes such as the alignment and maintenance of joint attention (Barron, 2003). It is easy to become lost in detail and so explicit strategies for focusing the attention of the analysts are needed. Strategies are also needed for establishing the content of the tapes and making decisions about how to represent the phenomena included within them. Erickson (2006) provides three sets of guidelines, each reflecting different approaches to inquiry along the inductive–deductive orientation. He provides suggestions about stages of viewing, types of summaries to make at each stage, the importance of time code, and ways to enhance perception by slowing down or speeding up the tape or watching without sound. These suggestions are very helpful for the beginning or experienced researcher. Yet as we will summarize below, there are numerous ways to go about understanding video records of interaction and building up an analysis.

Practices for Analytically Viewing Video Data

One advantage of video recordings as a source of data is that they can be viewed multiple times in different ways, with different people, at different times in the history of a research project, and even across research groups. Investigators can strengthen their research findings by coordinating what they learn from multiple viewing opportunities. In early stages of a video analysis, before interpretations of events become fixed, it can be quite helpful to share a key video segment with a group of other researchers in order to gather multiple interpretations of the events and to brainstorm potential issues to investigate more deeply (Jordan & Henderson, 1995). The video segment can be viewed and reviewed to look for data consistent or inconsistent with initial hunches about what's going on for those involved in the interaction. Watching the video at speeds slower or faster than normal or simply listening to the audio or watching the video can also be used to focus analysts' attention on particular aspects of interest (Erickson, 1982). Group viewing can be used in later stages of work to see whether multiple researchers notice similar phenomena (e.g., Engle et al., 2007). Finally, it can sometimes be helpful to have participants from the events that have been recorded watch the video in the presence of the researcher in order to provide their own interpretations of what was going on. It is preferable to obtain participant reflections as soon as possible after recording and without imposing leading questions (Ericsson & Simon, 1980, 1993; Jordan & Henderson, 1995). It is also important to recognize that such participant interpretations do not provide researchers with access to "what really happened" or what the participant was "really thinking," but instead represent whatever interpretation of the interaction the participant now has that he or she considers acceptable to present to the researcher. Thus these accounts needed to be treated as one data source among many that can be used to understand the collaborative interaction.

Intermediate Representations for Data Selection and Pattern Finding

Various kinds of what we refer to as "intermediate representations" of the video records are important for identifying which segments of collaborative interactions to analyze and for beginning to see patterns within and across segments. Transcripts of talk and nonverbal information are common, and we will mention a variety of approaches to this method of representing the content of video records. Often researchers construct other kinds of intermediate representations to better understand their video datasets and start the process of pattern finding. Such representations can help the researcher decide what should be transcribed and at what level of detail as well as the focus of later analyses. Below we describe several approaches to intermediate representations and the variety of decisions that are involved in using them.

Indexing. Indexes to events in a given videotape are one kind of intermediate representation. The first opportunity to interpret the phenomena of interaction recorded by the video is while it is being collected. If a researcher can be present during recording, then he or she can make time-indexed field notes that provide a basic outline of the events or possible examples of phenomena of interest that occur (Hall, 2000). This also provides an opportunity for filling in relevant complementary information that may be difficult to discern later from the video. Absent this stage, it is still very helpful if a researcher can quickly watch the video soon after its capture to create a content log, which like the field notes provides a time-indexed outline of the video events. Content log notes can be extremely detailed, taking a brief standard unit of time (e.g., 1 minute) and describing the major events that took place, or they can consist of a several sentence description of the content of a whole hour of instruction. Field notes and content logs allow the research team to develop a sense of what is in the corpus of data and facilitate the selection of episodes for subsequent detailed analysis (Jordan & Henderson, 1995). This kind of indexing should be distinguished from systematic coding, which, as we will discuss, is best done after extensive work has been completed to establish the meaning of codes and the central units that should be coded.

Transcription. Although there are exceptions (e.g., see Angelillo, Rogoff, & Chavajay, 2007), during the process of video analysis most researchers produce transcripts that re-represent the events recorded in their video. Initial transcripts may help researchers flesh out from their field notes or content logs what occurred in a particular segment of video in order to decide whether and how to pursue an analysis (Jordan & Henderson, 1995). In later stages of research, transcripts are iteratively revised while analyses of the video recordings proceed until they gradually provide a reliable record of what the researchers view as the most relevant aspects of the video for providing evidence relevant to their research questions (e.g., Engle et al., 2007; Mischler, 1991). *Accuracy* is a relative term for transcripts, and minute aspects of speech timing, intonation, body posture, etc., are relevant to some but not other research questions. Like a map, a transcript's features are integrally tied to the purposes it is designed to serve, and it is thus theory-laden. Whether explicitly intended or not, transcripts end up embodying theoretical commitments about the events that were recorded (Lapadat & Lindsay, 1999; Ochs, 1979). Through this process, transcripts become key data that can be used directly for additional coding, interpretation, or creation of other analytical representations. However, when research is written up, transcripts must be edited for public consumption in order to illustrate a study's analyses or findings (e.g., Du Bois et al., 1993).

There are many existing—and in many cases competing—conventions for how one might transcribe different aspects of the social interactions captured on video (Atkinson & Heritage, 1984; Dressler & Kreuz, 2000; Du Bois et al., 1993; Edwards & Lampert, 1993; Lapadat & Lindsay, 1999; Ochs, 1979). Typically, researchers adapt existing conventions in ways that make sense given their research questions, their theoretical commitments, and practical constraints like available time and personnel, the audiences for their work, and the systematic availability and accessibility of information in the video record and other data sources. The important thing is to explain how one's own choices of conventions for use make sense given these various considerations. We provide a synopsis in Table 11.1 of common choices made in producing transcriptions.

Macrolevel Coding. Because transcription is costly and time consuming and not always suited for pattern finding, video researchers often invent ways to summarize video records more synoptically. For example, Ash (2007), who studied family conversations in museums, begins with a representation she calls the "Flow Chart," which catalogs a family's museum visit from start to finish, including any pre/post interviews that were conducted. The goal is to mark major events and the occurrence of conversations about biological themes. Topics and themes can be coded from this representation in order to compare families across visits or visits across families. The flow chart representation is also instrumental for selecting the data used in her second level of analysis—the *significant event*. Significant events are selected based on four criteria: (a) they have recognizable beginnings and endings (usually they take place in one exhibit); (b) they have sustained conversational segments; (c) they integrate different sources of knowledge; and (d) they involve inquiry strategies such as questioning, inferring, and predicting. The third level of analysis involves more microlevel examinations of the interactions occurring within selected significant events. For example, Ash and her team use discourse analytic frameworks to study how an idea develops over time.

Table 11.1 Common Transcription Choices (expanded from Edwards, 1993, p. 19)

Aspect of Transcript	Common Options	Considerations
Spatial arrangement (Edwards, 1993; Jordan & Henderson, 1995; Ochs, 1979)	• Playscript • Organize into columns • Musical score (e.g., Erickson, 2003)	• Common playscript format is most accessible to a wide audience, but awkward for showing overlaps and multimodality • Columns good for distinguishing relative contributions of different speakers and/or types of actions • Musical score helpful for showing precise timing of actions with respect to each other as well as even rhythm and pitch
Notation of words (Du Bois et al., 1993)	• Orthography (dictionary spellings) • Using the International Phonetic Alphabet (IPA, 1996) • Noting other word features –variants: "gonna" –unfinished words: "mis-" –disfluencies: "uh," "um" –vowel lengthening: "we:::ll" –emphasis: ALL caps, bold, or underlining –voice quality: "[excitedly]"	• Standard orthography is easiest to read • Phonetic alphabet useful when exact pronunciation is important for research questions; if so, also consider waveform software • Similarly, record those other word features that are relevant for your research questions
Signaling uncertainty (Atkinson & Heritage, 1994)	• Unclear words in ( )'s: "(yeah)" • Unheard words: [inaudible] or (xxx-xxx), with # of xxx's indicating number of inaudible syllables	• Very important to note when something is missing or unclear • Indicate number of missing syllables when word length crucial • Descriptions of actions can signal uncertainty directly with hedges: "appears to," "maybe," etc.
Units for segmenting discourse (Chafe, 1980; Dressler & Kreuz, 2000; Gee, 1999; Gumperz & Berenz, 1993)	• Intonation or idea units: –"," to mark fall-rise intonation –"?" to mark rising intonation –"." to mark falling intonation • Spoken turns-at-talk • Stanzas or narrative sentences • Events or episodes	• Does the grain size of your units correspond with those of your coding schemes and other analytical methods? • Some recommend dividing speech into units one level lower than the lowest level of coding and/or analysis you will do • Each unit reflects a different theory about discourse structure: are the units you are using consistent with your own view?
Pauses (Atkinson & Heritage, 1994; Du Bois et al., 1993)	• Record only especially salient ones by annotating them: "[pause]" • Record pauses as shorter or longer relative to the speaker's speech rate: "(.)", "(..)", and "(…)" for increasingly longer pauses • Time all pauses over a particular length: "[1.2 sec pause]" or "(1.2s)"	• How important are speakers' pauses for understanding the phenomenon you are studying? • For purposes of your study, is it more informative to relativize pauses or objectively time them? • What theory of discourse does this decision reflect?

(continued)

Table 11.1 Continued

Aspect of Transcript	Common Options	Considerations
Overlapping speech and other actions (Dressler & Kreuz, 2000; Du Bois et al., 1993)	• Record beginnings of overlaps using paired /'s or large ['s • Record beginnings and endings of overlaps using paired sets of [ ]'s • Record timings of overlap by spatially aligning them on a musical score transcript or on adjacent lines in a playscript transcript	• Is it important for your study to know about when overlaps end as well as when they begin? • What level of precision (nearest word, syllable, or phoneme) do you need? If the latter, then consider looking at waveforms. • Musical transcript best for precisely depicting timing of overlaps
Visible actions (Bavelas, 1994; Goodwin & Goodwin, 1996; Leander 2002a; McNeill, 1992)	• Insert screenshots • Create line drawings • Physically describe actions: "[*shakes head up and down*]," "[*touches board with index finger at equation*]" • Characterize likely meaning: "[*nods yes*]," "[*indicates equation*]"	• Which is the quickest method that provides the information you need given your research questions? • Degree of interpretation increases from screenshots to physical descriptions and drawings to meaning characterizations • To what degree do you need raw data vs. interpreted data? If differing interpretations of a visible action would significantly affect the findings, then may need both.
Other things to consider recording in transcripts (Edwards & Lampert, 1993)	• Specific people addressed by an utterance, especially if not all who are present: "[*to Nathan*]" • Gaze or body direction: "[*looking at Marcia*]" "[*facing board*]" • Laughter (see Du Bois et al., 1993) • Anything else potentially relevant to research questions	• As with everything, include only what matters for addressing your research questions, but there is no need to do it all at once. Instead you can systematically refine transcripts as needed. • Descriptions can be set off in brackets in the examples to the left • But they can also be put into separate columns devoted to particular kinds of information as in a columnar transcript

Narrative Summaries. Other researchers employ narrative accounts to analytically capture events on a tape. For example, Angellio et al. (2007) conducted a video study that compared mother–child interactions in four distinct cultural communities. Their first step was to generate descriptive, narrative accounts of each 90 minute-long video recorded home visit during which mothers helped their toddlers learn about the novel objects. These were not event logs but comprised descriptions of events as long as 30 pages. These descriptive accounts were used to help the rest of the research team visualize the sequence of interactions and to capture the purposes and functions of action and dialogue. Engle, Langer-Osuna, and McKinney de Royston (2008) extended this approach by creating explanatory narratives that were focused specifically on explaining a particular phenomenon by coordinating within the narrative the particular theoretical concepts that were being investigated.

Diagrams. Other researchers summarize aspects of video records using still frames or diagrams that show spatial or other coordinations. For example, in a study that investigated patterns of joint activity between Guatemalan Mayan mothers and children completing puzzles, the goal was to categorize patterns of joint attention, mutual orientation, and ways of distributing work (Angelillo et al., 2007). A representational innovation that turned out to be important for the team was the creation of a diagramming method that allowed the researchers to characterize types of coordination around shared tasks that involved multiple people. The diagrams were then used to help code 1-minute intervals of video. Similarly, Leander (2002b) and Engle, McKinney de Royston, Langer-Osuna, Bergan, and Mazzei (2007) used synoptic bird's-eye diagrams to characterize students' relative spatial configurations and the social relationships they embodied; Barron (2003) complemented narratives with still images in an analysis of variability in small-group interaction. For additional inspirational uses of diagrams captured from still frames and annotated for analytical purposes, see Chuck Goodwin's papers (e.g., Goodwin, 2003, 2007).

APPROACHES TO REPORTING AND MAKING A CASE

In this section we discuss several major approaches to analysis and refer the reader to additional examples in the literature.

Play by Play

One common way of reporting a video analysis in a publication is providing a "play-by-play" description in which interpretations of episodes that follow each other in time are presented sequentially. Play-by-play analyses are particularly effective at showing how the sequential context that has been created so far in an interaction informs what happens next. With rich transcripts to support them, these kinds of analyses also are particularly good at demonstrating how multiple actions and people collectively produce collaborative and other social phenomena. Finally, in an extension of play-by-play analyses, a researcher might analyze selected episodes that all focus on a particular topic or other issue over the course of days, weeks, or even months to show how that issue was transformed over time. In one well-known longitudinal study, Ninio and Bruner (1978) followed one mother–infant dyad engaged in joint picture-book reading, using video recordings of their free play in a period between 0;8 and 1;6. They found this activity very early on had the ritualized structure of a dialogue in which learning is by participation rather than imitation. The child's early communicative forms of babbling, smiling, reaching, and pointing were richly interpreted by the mother as expressing the child's intention of requesting or providing a label, and later the child uses lexical labels in these same dialogical slots. Other examples of this approach in the published literature include Engle (2006), Koschmann, Glenn, and Conlee (1999), Ochs and Taylor (1996), and Wortham (2004).

Coding, Counting, and Statistical Analysis

Methods of analysis that code videos are rooted in practices of *disciplined observation*, a core feature of scientific methodology. Independent of the advent of video technologies, social scientists developed approaches that allowed them to document, analyze, and report human behavior to their colleagues. For example, scientists interested in child development created formal approaches for observing, recording, and describing the natural world in ways that were convincing to others who followed positivist empirical traditions. Systematic observational approaches relied on preestablished coding schemes and were designed to yield reliable judgments by independent observers of behavior taking place in natural contexts. Techniques for narrowing the foci of observation through methods such as time sampling, event sampling, or focal person approaches were articulated and used in many early studies of child development, and later, human and animal behavior more generally (see Altmann, 1974 for a highly influential paper on sampling methods for observational study of behavior).

For example, early studies of children's play often relied on what was called repeated short samples (Goodenough, 1928) where a child would be observed for one minute a day and their play coded into one of six mutually exclusive categories (Parten, 1932). After a substantial number of observations were made, proportions could be computed so as to draw conclusions about how a particular child or category of children spends their playtime. Statistical approaches for determining interrater reliability were key innovations that allowed researchers to determine whether their coding approaches led to similar observations across human coders. Before video, these methods required that the focus of inquiry and coding systems were well worked out before the collection of data and were simple enough for two or more observers to achieve interrater reliability after only a single viewing. Video relieves this constraint such that coding systems can be developed over time after the analysts decide what to code.

Despite the number of studies that use coding approaches for video (and the many tools used to support them: Derry et al., 2010; Pea & Hoffert, 2007), it is by no means universally agreed upon that data derived from video records should be primarily coded in a way that can yield quantitative data to yield theoretical and empirical insights. Many researchers prefer to focus on examples (such as in the play-by-play approach) and do not care for counting types of events within or across cases. However, others find coding and quantification a useful aspect of their project. Erickson (1977, 1982, 1986) has written extensively about possible roles of quantification in qualitative research and has a useful discussion of the synergies between approaches. He argues that determining what to count is more challenging than doing the actual counting. Schegloff (1993) adds to this discussion with a set of criteria he believes are necessary to satisfy for the quantification of interactional data to be meaningful. Other excellent discussions of the development and use of observational coding schemes and associated statistical techniques include a primer on the topic of sequential analysis by Bakeman and Gottman (1997) and a paper by Chi (1997).

In video-based research, coding and other systems of analysis often develop over the course of multiple research projects. For example, Ash et al. (2007) articulate the changes that have occurred in her coding system and the evolution that resulted in a system they call Tools for Observing Biological Talk Over Time (TOBTOT). Through the careful analysis of the talk of families, consultation with biologists, psychologists, and educators, and through the work of the research team, they have developed a system that can be used across projects and by teams outside their research group. Ash et al. note that more than a dozen iterations have occurred to get to what they consider to be a stable yet generative analytical system. Another example is provided by Meier, Spada, and Rummel (2007), who developed coding systems for capturing the quality of collaboration using video and extended the system to study online collaborating learners.

Like the processes of generating questions or creating representations, the development of a coding approach benefits from iterative cycles and distributed expertise. For example, Angelillo et al. (2007) describe one approach to investigating patterns of shared engagement that combines qualitative and quantitative methods. The core of the process involves close ethnographic analysis of a few cases in order to build up a coding scheme based on the observed phenomena that can then be applied to multiple cases. They illustrate this approach in their study focused on cultural variation in mothers' and toddlers' contributions to understanding novel objects across four culturally distinct communities. The research team approached their analyses having in mind the kinds of interactions that might differ across the four cultural groups. For example, they expected some differences in the relative reliance on words vs. nonverbal demonstration. However, as is the case with many video studies, the video-based data of interactions led to the discovery of new phenomena such as differences in ways the mothers from different cultures motivated engagement. Once these phenomena were identified, the team worked to refine the definitions of the categories so that they could be reliably coded.

Analytic Induction and Progressive Refinement of Hypotheses

In a recent volume on video research in the learning sciences, many research groups contributed chapters including rationales and detailed accounts concerning their video practices (Goldman, Pea, Barron, & Derry, 2007). This volume provides examples of studies that interweave both top-down planned analyses while also reporting unanticipated phenomena. Some authors describe processes that share a family resemblance with an approach to qualitative research, more generally called analytic induction, developed by Znaniecki (1934). In analytic induction a few cases are explored in depth and explanations are developed. New cases are examined for their consistency with the explanations, and when they are not consistent, the explanation is revised.

A similar approach offered by Engle et al. (2007) is "progressive refinement of hypotheses." In this approach a general question is framed, and video and related records are collected in an appropriate setting. Once records are collected, more specific hypotheses are formed after preliminary viewing of the records. These hypotheses are then examined in relation to other aspects of the dataset leading to more encompassing explanatory hypotheses until both data and theoretical ideas have been exhausted. They argue that multiple iterations through hypothesis generation and evaluation leads to greater robustness and increased likelihood that the findings will be replicated in other contexts. A similar approach was proposed earlier by Cobb and Whitenack (1996).

Reporting Results

Although there have been some attempts to create multimedia journals that could include video as part of the publication (e.g., Beardsley, Cogan-Drew, & Olivero, 2007; Sfard & McClain, 2002) and fully multimedia video-based papers (e.g., DiMattia, 2002), in most cases the video records will be left behind in the reporting phase of the project, and what was observed must be re-represented in written form. Coding and subsequent quantification is a common approach to reporting results. However, while our ability to code behaviors can rest on the well-worked-out techniques and methods described earlier, there is still the limitation of losing the context of an interaction. Narrative description is another method of representation; although there are well-warranted accounts of the distinctive values brought by narrative accounts to understanding human interaction, they may also be considered less credible to many experimentally minded social scientists (for National Science Foundation workshop reports on the scientific foundations of qualitative research, see Lamont & White, 2009; Ragin, Nagel, & White, 2004). Others revise and then share their intermediate representations, though such representations can easily be opaque to readers who are not provided with careful preparation for what to look for within the records.

One solution to the reporting problem is to use multiple methods of representation in reporting video research. For example, Barron (2000, 2003) used quantitative methods to find response patterns that reliably differentiated more and less successful collaborative groups. However, the ways these sequences unfolded for individual groups differed in some important ways that were masked by the quantification. Thus she combined what Bruner (1986) described as a paradigmatic approach (coding and statistical analysis) with a narrative approach (that preserved the sequence of interactions). Her narrative approach employed three types of representations to convey the complexity of interaction: transcripts to illustrate key aspects of dialogue; behavioral descriptions that conveyed aspects of the interaction such as facial expression, tone, and gesture; and still frames to further illustrate the body positioning of the interacting students at key points.

The problems of re-representing the complexity in video are not trivial, and we are in the beginning stages of figuring out as a field creative ways to do this. We can learn a great deal from one another's attempts to do this well within and across disciplines. Erickson (2006) provides a particularly strong argument that readers of analyses should not only come away "tree-wise" but "forest-wise" (p. 185). That is, it is not enough to provide rich examples, the analysts must also provide a sense of the broader sample and how typical or atypical the instances presented are relative to some larger corpus of data. In addition, as Lemke (2007) has emphasized, it is also important that we draw on video to represent processes that develop over different timescales and how they interact with each other. Our discussion therefore has suggested ways of communicating multiple levels of analysis and their interrelationships.

CONCLUDING COMMENTS

There is an increasing desire to better understand the transactional processes involved in the coordinated unfolding of collaborative interaction over time, and for this effort video records are needed. In this chapter we have described the kinds of video-based research designs that have been used to enhance collaborative learning research, and shared some especially helpful strategies for the analysis of video records and the subsequent reporting of findings. For those starting to plan a project that will use video records, it is wise to focus first on theory-driven questions and develop concrete plans for a first pass at using the video records. Having good questions will help maintain perspective and prevent one from getting buried in the cornucopia of human interactional phenomena at play. At the same time, one should anticipate new discoveries and be ready to articulate questions that can be followed, refined, and tested through multiple passes in analyzing the video records. These passes can be made most fruitful by using intermediate representations. Multiple cycles are to be expected and an explicit approach to this objective can strengthen the likelihood of generating strong findings that are both reliable and valid.

REFERENCES

Altmann, J. (1974). Observational study of behavior: Sampling methods. *Behaviour, 49*, 227–267.

Angelillo, C., Rogoff, B., & Chavajay, P. (2007). Examining shared endeavors by abstracting video coding schemes with fidelity to cases. In R. Goldman, R. Pea, B. Barron, & S. J. Derry (Eds.), *Video research in the learning sciences* (pp. 189–206). Mahwah, NJ: Erlbaum.

Ash, D. (2007). Using video data to capture discontinuous science meaning making in non-school settings. In R. Goldman, R. Pea, B. Barron, & S. J. Derry (Eds.), *Video research in the learning sciences* (pp. 207–226). Mahwah, NJ: Erlbaum.

Ash, D., Crain, R., Brandt, C., Loomis, M., Wheaton, M., Bennett, C. (2007). Talk, tools, and tensions: Observing biological talk over time. *International Journal for Science Education, 29*, 1581–1602.

Atkinson, J. M., & Heritage, J. (Eds.). (1984). *Structures of social action: Studies in conversation analysis*. Cambridge, England: Cambridge University Press.

Bakeman. R., & Adamson, L. B. (1984). Coordinating attention to people and objects in mother-infant and peer-infant interaction. *Child Development*, 55, 1278–1289.

Bakeman, R., & Gottman, J. M. (1997). *Observing interaction: An introduction to sequential analysis*. New York: Cambridge University Press.

Barron, B. (2000). Achieving coordination in collaborative problem-solving groups. *Journal of the Learning Sciences, 8*, 403–436.

Barron, B. (2003). When smart groups fail. *Journal of the Learning Sciences, 12*, 307–359.

Bavelas, J. B. (1994). Gestures as part of speech: Methodological implications. *Research on Language and Social Interaction, 27*, 201–221.

Beardsley, L., Cogan-Drew, D., & Olivero, F. (2007). VideoPaper: Bridging research and practice for pre-service and experienced teachers. In R. Goldman, R. Pea, B. Barron, & S. Derry, (Eds.), *Video research in the learning sciences* (pp. 479–494). Mahwah, NJ: Erlbaum.

Bruner, J. (1986). *Actual minds, possible worlds*. Cambridge, MA: Harvard University Press.

Chafe, W. L. (1980). *The pear stories: Cognitive, cultural, and linguistic aspects of narrative production*. Norwood, NJ: Ablex.

Cherry, G., Fournier, J., & Stevens, R. (2003). Using a digital video annotation tool to teach dance composition. *Interactive Multimedia Electronic Journal of Computer-Enhanced Learning*. Retrieved from http://imej.wfu.edu/articles/2003/1/01/

Chi, M. T. H. (1997). Quantifying qualitative analyses of verbal data: A practical guide. *Journal of the Learning Sciences, 6*, 271–315

Clark, H. H. (1996). *Using language*. Cambridge, England: Cambridge University Press.

Cobb, P., & Whitenack, J. W. (1996). A method for conducting longitudinal analyses of classroom videorecordings and transcripts. *Educational Studies in Mathematics, 30*, 213–228.

Creswell, J. L., & Plano Clark, V. L. (2007). *Designing and conducting mixed methods research*. Thousand Oaks, CA: Sage.

Crook, C. (1996). *Computers and the collaborative experience of learning*. East Sussex, England: Taylor & Francis/ Routledge.

Derry, S., Pea, R. D., Barron, B., Engle, R. A., Erickson, F., Goldman, R., … Sherin, B. L. (2010). Conducting video research in the learning sciences: Guidance on selection, analysis, technology, and ethics. *Journal of the Learning Sciences, 19*, 3–53.

DiMattia, C. (2002). VideoPapers. *Hands On! 25*, 12–15.

Dressler, R. A., & Kreuz, R. J. (2000). Transcribing oral discourse: A survey and model system. *Discourse Processes, 29*, 25–36.

Du Bois, J. W., Schuetze-Coburn, S., Cumming, S., & Paolino, D. (1993). Outline of discourse transcription. In J. A. Edwards & M. D. Lampert (Eds.), *Talking data: Transcription and coding in discourse research* (pp. 45–89). Hillsdale, NJ: Erlbaum.

Edwards, J. A. (1993). Principles and contrasting systems of discourse transcription. In J. A. Edwards & M. D. Lampert, (Eds.), *Talking data: Transcription and coding in discourse research* (pp. 3–31). Hillsdale, NJ: Erlbaum.

Edwards, J. A., & Lampert, M. D. (Eds.). (1993). *Talking data: Transcription and coding in discourse research*. Hillsdale, NJ: Erlbaum.

Engle, R. A. (2006). Framing interactions to foster generative learning: A situative explanation of transfer in a community of learners' classroom. *The Journal of the Learning Sciences, 15*, 451–498.

Engle, R. A., & Conant, F. C. (2002). Guiding principles for fostering productive disciplinary engagement: Explaining an emergent argument in a community of learners classroom. *Cognition and Instruction, 20*, 399–483.

Engle, R. A., Conant, F. R., & Greeno, J. G. (2007). Progressive refinement of hypotheses in video-supported research. In R. Goldman, R. Pea, B. Barron, & S. J. Derry (Eds.), *Video research in the learning sciences* (pp. 239–254). Mahwah, NJ: Erlbaum.

Engle, R. A., Langer-Osuna, J., & McKinney de Royston, M. (2008). Toward a model of differential influence in discussions: Negotiating quality, authority, and access within a heated classroom argument. In B. C. Love, K. McRae, & V. M. Sloutsky (Eds.), *Proceedings of the 30th annual conference of the Cognitive Science Society* (pp. 2010–2015). Austin, TX: Cognitive Science Society.

Engle, R. A., McKinney de Royston, M., Langer-Osuna, J., Bergan, J., & Mazzei, P. (2007). *From positioning to differential influence in a student-led argument: Students' negotiating authority, the conversational floor, and interactional space.* Paper presented at AERA, Chicago, IL.

Erickson, F. (1977). Some approaches to inquiry in school-community ethnography. *Anthropology & Education Quarterly, 8*, 58–69.

Erickson, F. (1982). Audiovisual records as a primary data source. *Sociological Methods & Research, 11*, 213–232.

Erickson, F. (2006). Definition and analysis of data from videotape: Some research procedures and their rationales. In J. L. Green, G. Camilli, & P. B. Elmore (Eds.), *Handbook of complementary methods in education research* (pp. 177–205). Mahwah, NJ: Erlbaum.

Ericsson, K. A., & Simon, H. A. (1980). Verbal reports as data. *Psychological Review, 87*, 215–251.

Ericsson, K. A., & Simon, H. A. (1993). *Protocol analysis: verbal reports as data* (2nd ed.). Cambridge, MA: MIT Press.

Fogel, A. (1993). *Developing through relationships: Origins of communication, self, and culture.* Chicago IL: University of Chicago Press.

Gee, J. P. (1999). *An introduction to discourse analysis: Theory and method.* New York: Routledge.

Goldman, R., Pea, R., Barron, B., & Derry, S. (2007). (Eds.). *Video research in the learning sciences.* Mahwah, NJ: Erlbaum.

Goodenough, F.L. (1928). Measuring behavior traits by means of repeated short samples. *Journal of Juvenile Research*, 12, 230–235.

Goodwin, C. (1994). Professional vision. *American Anthropologist, 96*, 606–633.

Goodwin, C. (2003). Pointing as situated practice. In S. Kita (Ed.), *Pointing: Where language, culture and cognition meet* (pp. 217–241). Mahwah, NJ: Erlbaum,

Goodwin, C. (2007). Participation, stance, and affect in the organization of activities. *Discourse and Society, 18*, 53–73.

Goodwin, C., & Goodwin, M. H. (1996). Formulating planes: Seeing as a situated activity. In D. Middleton & Y. Engestrom (Eds.), *Cognition and communication at work* (pp. 61–95). Cambridge, England: Cambridge University Press.

Greeno, J. G. (2006). Authoritative, accountable positioning and connected, general knowing: progressive themes in understanding transfer. *Journal of the Learning Sciences, 15*, 537–547.

Gumperz, J. J., & Berenz, N. (1993). Transcribing conversational exchanges. In J. A. Edwards & M. D. Lampert (Eds.), *Talking data: Transcription and coding in discourse research* (pp. 91–122). Hillsdale, NJ: Erlbaum.

Hall, R. (2000). Video recording as theory. In D. Lesh & A. Kelley (Eds.), *Handbook of research design in mathematics and science education* (pp. 647–664). Mahwah, NJ: Erlbaum.

Hall, R., Wieckert, K., & Wright, K. (2010). How does cognition get distributed? Case studies of making concepts general in technical and scientific work. In M. Banich & D. Caccamise (Eds.), *Generalization of knowledge: Multidisciplinary perspectives* (pp. 225–246). East Sussex, England: Psychology Press.

Hutchins, E. (1995). *Cognition in the wild.* Cambridge, MA: MIT Press.

Jordan, B., & Henderson, A. (1995). Interaction analysis: foundations and practice. *Journal of the Learning Sciences, 4*, 39–103.

Kendon, A. (1982). The study of gesture: Some observations on its history. *Recherches S´emiotiques/Semiotic Inquiry, 2*, 45–62.

Kendon, A. (1997). Gesture. *Annual Review of Anthropology, 26*, 109–128.

Koschmann, T., Glenn, P., & Conlee, M. (1999). Theory presentation and assessment in a problem-based learning group. *Discourse Processes*, 27, 119–133.

Lamont, M., & White, P. (2009). *Workshop on interdisciplinary standards for systematic qualitative research.* Arlington, VA: National Science Foundation. Retrieved from http://www.nsf.gov/sbe/ses/soc/ISSQR_workshop_rpt.pdf.

Lapadat, J. C., & Lindsay, A. C. (1999). Transcription in research and practice: From standardization of technique to interpretive positionings. *Qualitative Inquiry, 5*, 64–86.

Leander, K. M. (2002a). Locating Latanya: The situated production of identity artifacts in classroom interaction. *Research in the Teaching of English, 37*, 198–250.

Leander, K. M. (2002b). Silencing in classroom interaction: Producing and relating social spaces. *Discourse Processes, 34*, 193–235.
Lemke, J. (2007). Video epistemology in- and outside the box: traversing attentional spaces. In R. Goldman, R. Pea, B. Barron, & S. J. Derry (Eds.), *Video research in the learning sciences* (pp. 39–51). Mahwah, NJ: Erlbaum.
Leonard, M. J., & Derry, S. J. (2006). Tensions and tradeoffs in a "design for science" classroom: The "forces in balloon lecture." In S. A. Barab, K. E. Hay, & D. T. Hickey (Eds.), *Proceedings of the Seventh International Conference of the Learning Sciences* (pp. 411–417). Bloomington, IN: International Society of the Learning Sciences.
Maxwell, J. A. (2004b). Using qualitative methods for causal explanation. *Field Methods, 16*, 243–264.
Maxwell, J. A., & Loomis, D. (2003). Mixed methods design: An alternative approach. In A. Tashakkori & C. Teddlie (Eds.), *Handbook of mixed methods in social and behavioral research* (pp. 241–271). Thousand Oaks, CA: Sage.
McNeill, D. (1992) *Hand and mind: What gestures reveal about thought.* Chicago, IL: University of Chicago Press.
Meier, A., Spada, H., & Rummel, N. (2007). A rating scheme for assessing the quality of computer-supported collaboration processes. *International Journal of Computer-Supported Collaborative Learning, 2*, 63–86.
Mercier, E. (2010). *The influence of achievement goals on dyadic interactions and outcomes* (Unpublished doctoral dissertation). Stanford University, Stanford, CA.
Mischler, E. G. (1991). Representing discourse: The rhetoric of transcription. *Journal of Narrative and Life History, 1*, 255–280.
Ninio, A., & Bruner, J. S. (1978). The achievement and antecedents of labelling. *Journal of Child Language, 5*, 1-15.
Ochs, E. (1979). Transcription as theory. In B. Schieffelin (Ed.), *Developmental pragmatics* (pp. 43–72). New York: Academic Press.
Ochs, E., & Taylor, C. (1996). "The father knows best" dynamic in family dinner narratives. In K. Hall (Ed.), *Gender articulated: Language and the socially constructed self* (pp. 99–122). London: Routledge.
Parten, M. B. (1932). Social participation among preschool children. *Journal of Abnormal and Social Psychology, 27*, 243–269.
Pea, R., & Hoffert, E. (2007). Video workflow in the learning sciences: Prospects of emerging technologies for augmenting work practices. In R. Goldman, R. Pea, B. Barron, & S. Derry (Eds.), *Video research in the learning sciences* (pp. 427–460). Mahwah, NJ: Erlbaum Associates.
Ragin, C. C., Nagel, J., & White, P. (2004). *Workshop on scientific foundations of qualitative research.* Arlington, VA: National Science Foundation. Retrieved from http://www.nsf.gov/pubs/2004/nsf04219/nsf04219.pdf
Roschelle, J. (1992). Learning by collaborating: Convergent conceptual change. *The Journal of the Learning Sciences, 2*, 235–276.
Schegloff, E. A. (1993). Reflections on quantification in the study of conversation. *Journal of Language and Social Interaction, 26*, 99–128.
Sfard, A., & McClain, K. (Eds.). (2002). Analyzing tools: Perspectives on the role of designed artifacts in mathematics learning [Special issue]. *The Journal of the Learning Sciences*, 11.
Shadish, W. R., Cook, T. D., & Campbell, D. T. (2002). *Experimental and quasi-experimental designs for generalized causal inference.* Boston, MA: Houghton-Mifflin
Stevens, R., Satwicz, T., & McCarthy, L. (2008). In-game, in-room, in-world: Reconnecting video game play to the rest of kids' lives. In K. Salen (Ed.), *The ecology of games: Connecting youth, games and learning* (pp. 41–66). Cambridge, MA: MIT Press.
Stevens, R., & Toro-Martell, S. (2003). Leaving a trace: Supporting museum visitor interpretation and interaction with digital media annotation systems. *Journal of Museum Education, 28*, 25–31.
Strijbos, J-W, & Fischer, F. (2007). Methodological challenges for collaborative learning research. *Learning and Instruction, 17*, 389–393.
Tashakkori, A., & Teddlie, C. (Eds.). (2003). *Handbook of mixed methods in social and behavioral research.* Thousand Oaks, CA: Sage.
Teasley, S. D., & Roschelle, J. (1993). Constructing a joint problem space: The computer as a tool for sharing knowledge. In S. P. Lajoie & S. J. Derry (Eds.), *Computers as cognitive tools* (pp. 229–258). Hillsdale, NJ: Erlbaum.
Wortham, S. (2004). From good student to outcast: The emergence of a classroom identity. *Ethos, 32,* 164–187.
Zahn. C., Pea, R., Hesse, F. W., & Rosen, J. (2010). Comparing simple and advanced video tools as supports for collaborative design processes. *Journal Learning Sciences, 19*, 1–38.
Znaniecki, F. (1934). *The method of sociology.* New York: Holt, Rinehart & Winston.

12

MIXED METHODS FOR ANALYZING COLLABORATIVE LEARNING

SADHANA PUNTAMBEKAR

University of Wisconsin-Madison

Collaborative learning is a complex interplay of the individual, the group, and the context in which learning occurs. This presents a complex methodological challenge because of its dual focus on understanding how a group as a whole constructs knowledge through joint activity, while at the same time examining individual contribution and learning. This is a distinct shift from the traditional lens of viewing learning and knowledge as a highly individualistic process and product. As Reimann (2007) described, learning in Computer-Supported Collaborative Learning (CSCL) environments occurs "in individuals in the form of learning and in groups in the form of participation and knowledge building" (p. 611). Because both the process and learning outcomes are important in collaborative learning, mixed methods that draw from the strengths of both qualitative and quantitative paradigms provide researchers with a way to address the unique methodological challenges.

Mixed methods research can be defined "as the class of research where the researcher mixes or combines quantitative and qualitative research techniques, methods and approaches, concepts or language into a single study" (Johnson & Onwuegbuzie, 2004, p. 17), often in either a parallel or sequential manner. The qualitative versus quantitative debate is as old as the two paradigms themselves, with advocates for each tradition. But both these paradigms have strengths that can complement each other, while at the same time minimizing their weaknesses (Johnson & Onwuegbuzie, 2004). The rich descriptions of events in qualitative research can provide insights into how learning occurred in a particular context, while quantitative analyses of student contributions, activity logs, and learning outcomes can help us understand the learning processes and outcomes. By combining methods that can address both the breadth and depth of learning, mixed methods can help researchers draw stronger inferences by examining divergent findings from qualitative and quantitative methods (Teddlie & Tashakkori, 2003).

Johnson and Onwuegbuzie (2004) pointed out that a key issue in decisions with regard to using mixed methods is to carefully consider the major characteristics as well as the strengths and weaknesses of the qualitative and quantitative methods. According to them, quantitative methods focus on deduction and hypothesis testing, while qualitative methods are inductive and allow for discovery. Citing Turner's fundamental principle of mixed research, they state "researchers should collect multiple data using different strategies, approaches, and methods in such a way that the resulting mixture or combination is likely to result in complementary strengths and nonoverlapping weaknesses" (Turner 2003, cited in Johnson & Onwuegbuzie, 2004, p. 18). Collaborative learning is a multidisciplinary field so the methods used reflect a range of theoretical and methodological traditions (Hmelo-Silver & Bromme, 2007; Strijbos & Fischer, 2007). A wide variety of quantitative and qualitative methods are used for data collection and analysis in this field, ranging from content analysis of discourse (e.g., De Wever, Schellens, Valcke, & Van Keer, 2006), to social network analysis (e.g., Wasserman & Faust, 1994) to multilevel modeling (Cress, 2008; Janssen, Erkens, Kirschner, & Kanselaar, 2011; Stylianou-Georgiou, Papanastasiou, & Puntambekar, 2011), to name a few. Methods may be mixed at the time of data collection, data analysis, or both. However, the selection of mixed methods in collaborative learning needs to take into account the unique challenges posed by a dual focus on individual learning and group processes, as will be discussed in the next section.

The rest of this chapter is organized as follows. First, I will discuss the key variables that are important in documenting and analyzing collaborative interactions. Next, I will discuss the principles of mixed methods studies. Finally, I will discuss three examples that illustrate how the principles can be applied to the variables in collaborative learning.

USING MIXED METHODS IN COLLABORATIVE LEARNING

Variables of Interest in Collaborative Learning

At least four variables are considered important by researchers in collaborative learning: (a) individual learning; (b) group processes; (c) sequence or temporality of interactions; and (d) context in which learning takes place.

As found in research on learning in general, a key variable of interest in collaborative learning is *individual* learning outcomes, mostly measured by some form of pre- and posttests or other outcome measures. Teasley et al. (2008), pointed out that collaborative learning may not always facilitate individual learning, resulting in differing levels of learning gains. This necessitates understanding the processes of individual learning within a group in some detail. Tracing an individual's contribution in a group is therefore important to understand how an individual member contributes to the emerging discourse, and how the members build on their own as well as other members' contribution (e.g., Schwartz, 1999; Angelillo, Rogoff, & Chavajay, 2007). Early research in collaborative learning, especially in CSCL, mainly focused on the extent of participation (De Wever et al., 2006), in that researchers examined the frequency of individual contributions and the number of follow-up posts in the form of thread-lengths in asynchronous learning environments (Hewitt & Teplovs, 1999). Currently, content and discourse analyses of contributions, based on transcripts of audio and video recordings, are the most often used methods of analyzing an individual's contributions to collaborative discourse, which might be analyzed both qualitatively and quantitatively. Analyzing discourse helps us understand both the extent and quality of the individual's participation, as well as enabling researchers to use parametric and nonparametric statistical methods based on the frequencies of the specific codes. However, the reductionist nature of this analysis largely neglects the context and its effect on learning. Further, focusing on the individual as the unit of analysis does very little to reveal how ideas were accepted, refuted, or changed as a result of group interactions, and how the group changed over time.

Therefore, the second variable of importance is *the group* as a whole. Although group interactions are influenced by what the individual participants bring to the group, group processes are more than the sum of its parts, and need to be understood as an entity within themselves (Reimann, 2007; Stahl, Koschmann, & Suthers, 2006). According to De Wever et al. (2007), "individual learners are influenced by the social group and larger context (e.g., class, university) to which they belong, and the properties of this group are in turn influenced by the individuals who make up that group" (p. 3). This implies nested data structures and interdependencies in the data; that is, the individual members are nested within groups and groups might be nested within classrooms. This creates interdependencies in the data (dependent variables) because the individuals are dependent on the group and groups are dependent on the classroom (Janssen, Erkens, Kirschner, & Kanselaar, 2011). Advanced statistical techniques such as multilevel modeling that enable us to model dependencies in data can help us understand the interdependencies and are now being used in collaborative learning (Cress, 2008). Stylianou-Georgiou et al. (2011) have used multilevel modeling to analyze nested data by modeling the dependencies in their data to understand relationships between the variables of interest. In their study, they used both individual and group measures and applied a two-level model to understand the role of group membership in individual students' learning outcomes. Their analysis allowed them to understand how attributes of the learning environment interacted with group measures to affect individual learning outcomes. In this study, both individual and groups as units of analysis were used to understand how dependent variables at the individual level were impacted by membership in a group.

Data regarding several aspects of group functioning are important in collaborative learning. Typically, researchers are interested in at least two aspects of a group's functioning. First is the subject matter of the discourse; that is, how group members build content knowledge (e.g., math or science). Second, is the study of interpersonal dynamics of the group, which enables researchers to understand what factors related to the workings of the group might have affected the learning of members. For example, Meier, Spada, and Rummel (2007), studied nine dimensions of quality of collaborative processes: sustaining mutual understanding, dialogue management, information pooling, reaching consensus, task division, time management, technical coordination, reciprocal interaction, and individual task management. Van der Aalst (2009) makes a distinction between knowledge sharing, knowledge building, and knowledge construction: "knowledge-sharing practices involve the introduction of information and ideas without paying extensive attention to their interpretation, evaluation, and development" (p. 261). Knowledge construction refers to a deeper level of discourse in which students explain, review, and critique ideas to generate novel understanding of concepts or phenomena. Weinberger, Stegmann, and Fischer (2007) make a distinction between two types of shared knowledge: attaining similar knowledge levels by members in a group, and a transactive form of sharing, which is similar to Van der Aalst's knowledge construction.

Another variable of importance is the *temporality* or *sequence* of interactions. In collaborative situations, learning occurs and changes over time and cannot be accounted for fully by analyzing a set of discrete events. Collaborative experiences need to be understood beyond the single sessions that the activity occurs in, because any particular session is influenced by the group members' prior experiences and history (Mercer, Littleton, & Wegerif, 2004). As Mercer (2008) described, "the coherence of educational experience is dependent on talk among participants, and so analyses of the ways that their continuing shared experience is represented and the ways that talk itself develops and coheres over an extended period are required" (Mercer, 2008, p. 55). Sequential analysis (Bakeman & Gottman, 1997) can be applied to analyze links or relationships between events, thereby helping researchers understand how group interactions progressed over a period of time. Reimann, Yacef, and Kay (2011) analyzed event sequences using data mining techniques to identify patterns in-group interactions in data collected in log files. Chronological representations of the discussions have also been used to understand temporal sequences by Luckin (2003) and Hmelo-Silver (2003) in their use of the CORDFU and CORDTRA methodologies respectively. These methodologies enable a graphical representation of the chronology of discourse allowing an understanding of how it changes over time.

The final variable of importance is the *context* in which learning occurs. Mercer et al. (2004) note that when a group of learners is "working together, the interaction observed is located within a particular historical, institutional and cultural context" (p. 199). Collaborative learning is influenced by several contextual variables, such as the immediate physical context of learning, group members' beliefs about themselves and other members, prior knowledge of members, the teacher/facilitator, as well as the tool in cases where technology is used for collaborative learning (Arvaja, 2011).

These variables require that researchers in collaborative learning need to determine the appropriate unit of analysis, to account for both individual and group learning. Further, within each level, the grain size of the unit needs to be determined based on the research questions that drive the analysis in a particular study (Chi, 1997). Grain sizes can vary from analyzing a set of single utterances, chunks of discourse segmented along topics or themes, or both (e.g., Ash, 2007; De Wever, Schellens, Valcke, & Van Keer, 2006). The examples discussed later in this chapter illustrate how individual and group learning, temporality and context are addressed using mixed methods.

USING MIXED METHODS: EXAMPLES

In this section, I will discuss several examples that applied mixed methods to analyze collaborative interactions. I will start with discussing the principles of mixed methods designs and studies that address these principles. Then, I will discuss two examples from my research that used mixed methods of data collection and analysis. A key point to note about the examples is that each of them addresses the variables of interest discussed earlier, by using qualitative and quantitative methods.

Five Principles of Mixed Methods Designs

To address the four key variables mentioned above, researchers in collaborative learning use multiple qualitative and quantitative methods of data collections and analysis. Greene, Caracelli, and Graham (1989), in their discussion of mixed methods designs in evaluation studies, report five purposes for using mixed methods: (a) *triangulation*—the use of multiple sources of data and methods of analysis to increase the validity of their claims and to reduce bias; (b) *complementarity*—the use of one method as a way to further explain the results from using another method; (c) *development*—the use of one method is followed by another in a sequence of methods, so that findings from one method help inform the next method in a single study or a set of studies conducted sequentially; (d) *initiation*—use of different methods to uncover contradictions; and (e) *expansion*—the use of different methods to analyze components of a study to broaden the scope of the study. According to Teddlie and Tashakkori, (2003), triangulation and complementarity often result in inferences that "confirm or complement each other" (p. 16). On the other hand, development, initiation, and expansion often refer to multiple methods being used sequentially so that questions that arise after using one set of methods are answered using a second set. While the boundaries of these five techniques are somewhat fuzzy at times as the examples below illustrate, they nonetheless provide researchers with ways to design their studies and research questions, and a framework for collecting and analyzing data.

The most often used methods by researchers in collaborative learning are triangulation and complementarity, both during data collection and analysis. For example, researchers might collect observation and audio data from classrooms, as well as data regarding students' learning outcomes (e.g., Arvaja, Salovaara, Häkkinen, & Järvelä, 2007; Barron, 2003). Arvaja et al. (2007) collected two types of data in a web-based environment—students' online discussions and their responses to a self-report questionnaire that asked students about their collaborative experiences. The self-report measure provided triangulation and helped explain the results from the content analysis of discussions, especially the issue of uneven participation during collaboration. Barron (2003) used multiple methods such as coding of solutions to problems, coding of conversations, and case analyses of groups to better understand successful and unsuccessful groups. While the coding helped quantitatively analyze group members' responses, the narrative descriptions helped preserve the context and sequential nature of the discourse. Further, Barron also used behavioral descriptions of the gestures and tones, and still frames, thus providing triangulation, an important purpose of using mixed methods. Using both quantitative and qualitative approaches in this study also addressed the issue of complementarity.

Jeong, Clark, Sampson, and Menekse (2011) used two levels of analysis in their study aimed at understanding the development of scientific argumentation. First, they coded the nature of individual contributions to group discourse. The discourse was coded for the following: (a) individual contributions such as claims, counterclaims, and rebuttals; (b) grounds for comments, based on whether evidence or explanations were included; (c) conceptual quality of the discourse. Further, they conducted a sequential analysis of the discourse moves to understand better how students responded to one another, by using probabilities between the observed discourse moves. In their study, the two methods, coding of the discourse and the sequential analysis helped gain insights into findings that emerged from coding of the discourse.

In collaborative learning, triangulation is also achieved by mixing many levels of analysis, such as using different units of analysis and segmentation within qualitative or quantitative methods. Ash (2007) used three levels of segmentation in analyzing video data of informal science learning. The first level is a holistic examination of an entire

Table 12.1 Examples of Mixed Methods Studies

Study	Variables addressed	Measures	Analyses	Mixed methods principle
Puntambekar et al.	*Context and Temporality* Individual learning outcomes Classroom implementations, teacher facilitation	Pre and posttests, multiple choice and open ended questions Concept maps Classroom observations Videos	t-tests Analysis of covariance Narrative descriptions of classroom implementations Descriptions of discourse Coding of discourse Chronological visualization and narrative descriptions of classroom dialogue	Complementarity and triangulation Development and Extension
Gnesdilow et al.	*Unit of analysis: individual and group* Individual learning (outcomes and process) Group learning outcome Group processes	Concept maps Individual contribution to discourse Group learning outcomes (concept maps) Concept maps Group learning processes (discourse)	Qualitative (structure and layout of maps) quantitative (scores on maps) Coding of individual contributions Qualitative (structure and layout of maps) quantitative (scores on maps) Coding of discourse	Triangulation and Complementarity

event—a "flow chart"—for example, a family's visit to a museum exhibit. The second level is an analysis in greater detail, of a significant event, a section of the flow chart that might be of interest. Finally, the third level is a microgenetic analysis of a specific significant event, which involves a dialogic analysis using multiple data sources. Each of these three levels is a different grain size, moving from a holistic coarse-grained analysis to a finer grained analysis of dialogue. While these levels are crucial for a complete understanding of group events, a major issue that needs to be considered is that of segmenting the discourse data into appropriate sections.

In the next section, I will discuss the issues of triangulation and complementarity, as well as extension and development, as they apply to addressing individual and group learning processes. Table 12.1 summarizes the two examples.

Example 1: Understanding Individual Learning in Context

An example of using a mixed methods approach is a study by Puntambekar, Stylianou, and Goldstein (2007). In this study, two teachers implemented a sixth grade curriculum unit on simple machines. The curriculum consisted of a hypertext system CoMPASS, and design challenges to support students' understanding of key science ideas in mechanics. The main premise underlying the design of both the hypertext system and the design challenges was to enable students to understand connections between science concepts and principles. The CoMPASS system is designed using dynamic concept maps, such that students can visually see the science concepts related to the one they are reading about. The focus concept in the maps is always on the concepts that students select to read (e.g., force or work), and this concept is shown with related concepts in the form of a concept map. The design challenges reinforced these connections through concrete experiences. Our aim in this study was twofold: first, we wanted to understand students' learning outcomes, especially whether they understood relations between science ideas. Second, we were also interested in how the classroom context, most notably teacher facilitation strategies, helped students gain a richer understanding of physics. The role of the teacher as a facilitator of small groups as well as the whole-class discussions is critical to successful learning in complex environments. A teacher leading a whole-class discussion has to take into consideration "a whole group of students who are at varying places in their learning" (Hogan & Pressley, 1997). Very often, the kinds of experiences that students have in small groups are very different for each group, depending on their investigation paths and the specific stage at which the teacher interacts with them (Tabak & Reiser, 1997). The teacher therefore plays a crucial role in making students' private learning opportunities public and in moving them from "local" to "global" understanding (Tabak & Reiser, 1997). We were interested in understanding the classroom context by examining teacher facilitation strategies, and the classroom culture prevalent in classes taught by two teachers.

Mixing Methods of Data Collection

In this study, we used both qualitative and quantitative sources of data. We used two data sources for measuring students' learning outcomes: a pre- and posttest of physics that included multiple choice and open-ended items, and a concept mapping test. We used a coding scheme for the open-ended questions, to enable us to get a quantitative measure of learning outcomes. Similarly, we scored the concept maps by examining the number of concepts and the number of connections. We scored each connection on a scale ranging from 0 to 3. We then changed the scores into two ratios: *richness* and *depth ratio*, each of us helped understand the extent to which students made connections between the science concepts and principles they were learning. These data sources provided complementarity and triangulation, because each had strengths that complemented each other. The multiple choice items in the pre- and posttests helped us get an idea of students' overall understanding of physics, and the open-ended questions and concept maps enabled us to see the extent of students' understanding in terms of the connections they were able to make.

We also collected qualitative data in the form of observations and video data from classrooms, to help us understand the context of our implementations, especially teacher strategies.

Mixing Methods of Data Analysis: Development and Expansion

We analyzed data using both quantitative and qualitative methods. First, we examined students' learning using quantitative methods such as t-test and analysis of covariance.

We conducted t-tests on the multiple choices and open-ended scores separately to examine pre- and posttests gains in students taught by the two teachers. Then, we conducted analysis of covariance on the pre- and posttest as well as the concept mapping scores to compare the two groups. Our quantitative data showed that there were significant differences in the learning outcomes of students in classes taught by the two teachers. We found that students in the two teachers' classes did not differ in their scores on the multiple choice test, but differed significantly in scores on open-ended items and concept mapping test, indicating that they had a better understanding of the connections between science concepts and principles.

To further explain these results, we qualitatively examined classroom enactments by the two teachers, to understand the differences in the learning outcomes. We specifically focused on how teacher led discussions helped (a) connect the activities within a curriculum unit and (b) deeper conceptual understanding by enabling students make connections between science concepts and principles. Our qualitative analyses consisted of rich descriptions of the classroom context, and narratives of teacher facilitation during small group collaboration and whole class discussions. We also coded the discourse and used visual representations to chronologically represent the discourse. The chronological representation helped us understand how teacher facilitation strategies changed over time during the 10-week unit. Our qualitative analyses showed dramatic differences in the ways in which the two teachers facilitated whole class and small group discussions.

The quantitative analysis of students' learning and qualitative analysis videos was conducted *sequentially*. Quantitative analysis lead to a new set of questions about classroom enactments, and these were then taken up in the qualitative analysis. Our qualitative analyses showed us the differences in classroom enactments, allowing us to explain the differences in students' learning outcomes, by extension and development of new questions and better understanding of factors that might have affected students' learning. Our results pointed to important differences in the classroom contexts of the two enactments, helping us understand better what strategies might enable a deeper conceptual understanding of the science content.

Example 2: Understanding Individual and Group Learning

This study was conducted in my research group to understand how small groups of students constructed a shared understanding of science concepts while creating concept maps, and the effect of collaborative mapping on individual learning (Gnesdilow, Bopardikar, Sullivan, & Puntambekar, 2010). The study was conducted in a sixth grade science class where students engaged in a design-based science curriculum to learn about simple machines using the CoMPASS hypertext system to complete a set of design challenges (Puntambekar et al., 2007). As a part of this inquiry unit, students engaged in several individual and collaborative concept mapping activities intended to help them understand the relationships between the science ideas they were learning. The main aim of this study was to understand: (a) if convergence of science concepts occurs during collaborative concept mapping and (b) how convergence or divergence during collaboration influences individual map construction.

We collected three types of data in this study. First, we collected students' concept maps that they drew individually as pre- and posttest measures. Next, we also collected a collaborative concept map that students drew together with their group members. Finally, we also collected audio files of students' discourse as they drew the collaborative concept maps. This study thus used both the individual and group as a unit of analysis, addressing an important challenge in analyzing collaborative learning.

We used both qualitative and quantitative methods to analyze students' concept maps. To start with, we qualitatively examined map sophistication by looking at the structure of the maps in terms of layout and root word choices. This analysis was another way to attempt to understand how students' postindividual concept maps may have changed as a result of participating in the collaborative mapping activity. Then, we used a coding scheme to quantitatively score the maps. For this analysis, we scored the propositions in each map. A proposition is two concepts connected by a linking word to form a semantic unit. We scored all concept maps based on (a) the number of accurately described concept propositions and (b) the sophistication of science ideas expressed in the propositions. We assigned proposition scores according to a 5-point scale. This scale ranged from: -1 to 3. We then calculated a *depth ratio* for each concept map. The depth ratio was calculated by dividing the sum of the scores for each of the propositions on a map by the total number of propositions on the map. A higher depth ratio value meant more sophisticated understanding of the relationships between concepts. Together these two methods complemented each other, each giving us an understanding of students' science knowledge. The qualitative analysis that examined the overall structure of the map was useful in giving us an idea, at a holistic level, of students' science reasoning. The quantitative scores (depth ratios) on the maps enabled us to get a more in-depth understanding of students' science conceptions.

In this study, we also analyzed students' dialogue that was recorded as they drew their group maps. We inductively developed a set of nine codes after a preliminary examination of transcripts to capture the convergent and divergent exchanges between group members as they talked about science to construct their group map. We examined percentages of group dialogue to understand both the patterns of overall interactions in each group and the contributions offered by individual students. Thus once again we used the group and the individual as our unit of analysis. Analysis of the dialogue that happened during the collaborative concept mapping activity further developed our understanding of how the group concept mapping activity might have affected students' individual concept maps.

In this study, using a mixed methods approach provided a far richer picture of the students' collaboration and individual learning than a quantitative or qualitative approach alone. The quantitative concept mapping scores and qualitative look at the map structure provided converging evidence for the level of sophistication of the map products. Further, the qualitative analysis of the group dialogue gave an insight into the kinds of interactions that might have led to more sophisticated map products and better individual learning outcomes. The multiple perspectives provided by these complementary data sources offered greater support for making claims and suggesting implications.

CONCLUSION

Collaborative learning presents a unique set of challenges because of the focus on individual and group learning. There are many qualitative and quantitative methods that can be used to analyze both, and mixed methods provide researchers with opportunities to understand the multifaceted nature of learning in collaborative situations. As described in the examples above and in Table 12.1, mixed methods provide opportunities to address the methodological challenges that collaborative learning poses. The examples discussed in the previous section demonstrate how the issues of unit of analysis, temporality, and context of learning were addressed by using a range of quantitative and qualitative methods. In example 1, qualitative and quantitative analyses were conducted sequentially, so that the qualitative analyses helped us better understand results obtained from our quantitative methods. In both examples, the multiple data sources helped with triangulation enabling a far richer picture of students' learning and collaboration. Further, in example 2, we also addressed the issue of unit of analysis by combining individual and group measures of student learning.

Rummel and Spada (2004) propose a "methodological toolbox" to "support an informed choice of appropriate methods of analysis" (p. 23), so that the multiple facets of collaborative learning can be understood. However, the selection of the appropriate methods is ultimately determined by the research question and the context of a particular study (Angelillo et al., 2007). The particular issues that a researcher is interested in should determine the selection of methods in a particular study; such as a focus on relationships between group members' participation, individual learning based on group interactions, group processes, and analysis across events.

REFERENCES

Angelillo, C., Rogoff, B., & Chavajay, P. (2007). Examining shared endeavors by abstracting video coding schemes with fidelity to cases. In R. Goldman, R. Pea, B. Barron, & S. J. Derry (Eds.), *Video research in the learning sciences* (pp. 189–206). Mahwah, NJ: Erlbaum.

Arvaja, M. (2011). Contextual perspective in analyzing students' collaborative activity in CSCL contexts. In S. Puntambekar, G. Erkens, & C. E. Hmelo-Silver (Eds.), *Analyzing interactions in CSCL: Methods, approaches and issues* (pp. 25–46). New York: Springer.

Arvaja, M., Salovaara, H., Häkkinen, P., & Järvelä, S (2007). Combining individual and group-level perspectives for studying collaborative learning in context. *Learning and Instruction, 17*, 448–459.

Ash, D. (2007). Using video data to capture discontinuous science meaning making in non-school settings. In R. Goldman, R. Pea, B. Barron, & S. J. Derry (Eds.), *Video research in the learning sciences* (pp. 207–226). Mahwah, NJ: Erlbaum.

Bakeman, R., & Gottman, J. M. (1997). *Observing interaction: An introduction to sequential analysis*. New York: Cambridge University Press.

Barron, B. (2003). When smart groups fail. *Journal of the Learning Sciences, 12*(3), 307–359.

Chi, M. T. H. (1997). Quantifying qualitative analysis of verbal data: A practical guide. *The Journal of the Learning Sciences, 6*(3), 271–315.

Cress, U. (2008). The need for considering multilevel analysis in CSCL research: An appeal for more advanced statistical methods. *International Journal of Computer-Supported Collaborative Learning, 3*, 69–84.

De Wever, B., Schellens T., Valcke, M., & Van Keer H. (2006). Content analysis schemes to analyze transcripts of online asynchronous discussion groups: A review. *Computers & Education, 46*, 6–28.

De Wever, B., Van Keer, H., Schellens, T., & Valcke, M. (2007). Applying multilevel modelling to content analysis data: Methodological issues in the study of role assignment in asynchronous discussion groups. *Learning & Instruction, 17*(4), 436–447.

Gnesdilow, D., Bopardikar, A., Sullivan, S. A., & Puntambekar, S. (2010). Exploring convergence of science ideas through collaborative concept mapping. *Proceedings of the* 9th International Conference of the Learning Sciences, Chicago, IL.

Greene, J. C., Caracelli, V. J., & Graham, W. F. (1989). Toward a conceptual framework for mixed-method evaluation design. *Educational Evaluation and Policy Analysis, 11*, 255–274.

Hewitt, J., & Teplovs, C. (1999). An analysis of growth patterns in computer conferencing threads. In C. Hoadley & J. Roschelle (Eds.), *Proceedings of the Computer Supported Collaborative Learning Conference 1999* (pp. 232–241). Palo Alto, CA: Erlbaum.

Hmelo-Silver, C. E. (2003). Analyzing collaborative knowledge construction: Multiple methods for integrated understanding. *Computers & Education, 41*(4), 397–420.

Hmelo-Silver, C., & Bromme, R. (2007). Coding discussions and discussing coding: Research on collaborative learning in computer-supported environments. *Learning and Instruction, 17,* 460–464.

Hogan, K., & Pressley, M. (1997). Becoming a scaffolder of student learning. In K. Hogan & M. Pressley (Eds.), *Scaffolding student learning: Instructional approaches and issues* (pp. 185–191). Cambridge, MA: Brookline Books.

Janssen, J., Erkens, G., Kirschner, P. A., & Kanselaar, G. (2011). Multilevel analysis in CSCL research. In S. Puntambekar, G. Erkens, & C. E. Hmelo-Silver (Eds.), *Analyzing interactions in CSCL: Methods, approaches and issues* (pp. 187–205). New York: Springer.

Jeong, A., Clark, D., Sampson, V. D., & Menekse, M. (2011). Sequential analysis of scientific argumentation. In S. Puntambekar, G. Erkens, & C. E. Hmelo-Silver (Eds.), *Analyzing interactions in CSCL: Methods, approaches and issues* (pp. 207–233). Springer: New York.

Johnson, R. B., & Onwuegbuzie, A. J. (2004). Mixed methods research: A research paradigm whose time has come. *Educational Researcher, 33,* 14–26.

Luckin, R. (2003). Between the lines: Documenting the multiple dimensions of computer-supported collaborations. *Computers & Education, 41*(4), 379–396.

Meier, A., Spada, H., & Rummel, N. (2007). A rating scheme for assessing the quality of computer-supported collaboration processes. *International Journal of Computer-Supported Collaborative Learning, 2,* 63–86.

Mercer, N. (2008). The seeds of time: Why classroom dialogue needs a temporal analysis. *Journal of the Learning Sciences, 17*(1), 33–59.

Mercer, N., Littleton, K., & Wegerif, R. (2004). Methods for studying the processes of interaction and collaborative activity in computer-based educational activities. *Technology, Pedagogy and Education, 13,* 2, 193–209.

Puntambekar, S., Stylianou, A., & Goldstein, J. (2007). Comparing classroom enactments of an inquiry curriculum: Lessons learned from two teachers. *Journal of the Learning Sciences, 16*(1), 81–130.

Reimann, P. (2007). Time is precious: Why process analysis is essential for CSCL (and also can help to bridge between experimental and descriptive methods). In C. Chinn, G. Erkens, & S. Puntambekar (Eds.), *Mice, minds, and society: Proceedings of the Computer-Supported Collaborative Learning Conference* (*CSCL 2007*) (pp. 598–607). New Brunswick, NJ: International Society of the Learning Sciences.

Reimann, P., Yacef, K., & Kay, J. (2011). Analyzing collaborative interactions with data mining methods for the benefit of learning. In S. Puntambekar, G. Erkens, & C. E. Hmelo-Silver (Eds.), *Analyzing interactions in CSCL: Methods, approaches and issues* (pp. 161–185). New York: Springer.

Rummel, N., & Spada, H. (2004). Cracking the nut—but which nutcracker to use? Diversity in approaches to analyzing collaborative processes in technology-supported settings. In Y. B. Kafai, W. A. Sandoval, N. Enyedy, A. S. Nixon, & F. Herrera (Eds.), *Proceedings of the 6th International Conference of the Learning Sciences* (pp. 23–26). Mahwah, NJ: Erlbaum.

Schwartz, D. L. (1999). The productive agency that drives collaborative learning. In P. Dillenbourg (Ed.), *Collaborative learning: Cognitive and computational approaches* (pp. 197–219). Amsterdam, Netherlands: Pergamon.

Stahl, G., Koschmann, T., & Suthers, D. D. (2006). Computer-supported collaborative learning: An historical perspective. In R. K. Sawyer (Ed.), *Cambridge handbook of the learning sciences* (pp. 409–426). Cambridge, England: Cambridge University Press.

Strijbos, J., & Fischer, F. (2007). Methodological challenges for collaborative learning research, *Learning and Instruction, 17*(4), 389–393.

Stylianou-Georgiou, S., Papanastasiou, E., & Puntambekar, S. (2011). Analyzing collaborative processes and learning from hypertext through hierarchical linear modelling. In S. Puntambekar, G. Erkens, & C. E. Hmelo-Silver (Eds.), *Analyzing interactions in CSCL: Methods, approaches and issues.* New York: Springer.

Tabak, I., & Reiser, B. J. (1997). Complementary roles of software-based scaffolding and teacher-student interactions in inquiry learning. In R. Hall, N. Miyake, & N. Enyedy (Eds.), *Proceedings of Computer Supported Collaborative Learning Conference* (*CSCL '97*) (pp. 289–298). Mahwah, NJ: Erlbaum.

Teasley, S. D., Fischer, F., Weinberger, A., Stegmann, K., Dillenbourg, P., Kapur, M., & Chi, M. 2008. Cognitive convergence in collaborative learning. In G. Kanselaar, J. van Merriënboer, P. Kirschner, & T. de Jong (Eds.), *Proceedings of the 8th International Conference for the Learning Sciences* (Vol. 3, pp. 360–367). Utrecht, The Netherlands: ICLS.

Teddlie, C., & Tashakkori, A. (2003). Major issues and controversies in the use of mixed methods in the social and behavioral sciences. In A. Tashakkori & C. Teddlie (Eds.), *Handbook of mixed methods in social and behavioral research* (pp. 3–50). Thousand Oaks, CA: Sage.

Van der Aalst, J. (2009). Distinguishing knowledge-sharing, knowledge-construction, and knowledge-creation discourses. *International Journal of Computer-Supported Collaborative Learning, 4*(3), 259–287.

Wasserman, S., & Faust, K. (1994). *Social network analysis.* Cambridge, England: Cambridge University Press.

Weinberger, A., Stegmann, K. & Fischer, F. (2007). Knowledge convergence in collaborative learning: Concepts and assessment. *Learning and instruction, 17,* 416–426.

III

Instructional Issues and Approaches to Collaborative Learning

13

CULTIVATING A COMMUNITY OF LEARNERS IN K–12 CLASSROOMS

KATERINE BIELACZYC

Clark University

MANU KAPUR

National Institute of Education, Singapore

ALLAN COLLINS

Northwestern University

The goal of communities of learners (CoL) models is to foster deep disciplinary understanding—an understanding of both subject matter and the ways the disciplinary community works with knowledge in a domain. Through working collectively to carry out investigations, learners develop the agency and social capacities necessary for creatively working with knowledge. Such models require teachers and students to engage in new modes of inquiry that tend to be very different from the ways in which learning and teaching occur in more traditional classrooms. In fact, we have previously described this type of educational model as a "radical reconceptualization of educational practice" (Bielaczyc & Collins, 1999). Similarly, Bereiter (2002) claims "Students need to be socialized into the world of work with knowledge, and that is an even more radical cultural change than becoming 'digital'" (p. 220). Thus, we believe that one of the greatest challenges facing the implementation of CoL models concerns how to support the change processes that teachers and their students must move through.

The intention of this chapter is to collect together what has been learned in the educational community and in our own work with teachers concerning how to cultivate a community of learners. We discuss both key theoretical underpinnings (design principles, epistemology, and an understanding of how students learn) along with five key changes in the classroom that we believe provide the most transformational leverage in bringing CoLs to life in K–12 classrooms.

WHAT IS MEANT BY A COMMUNITIES OF LEARNERS MODEL

We describe what is meant by a CoL model by highlighting a particular family of models from the K–12 educational literature, followed by a description of what we see as the defining characteristics. We have chosen three specific lines of research to discuss in the present paper: Brown and Campione's fostering communities of learners (FCL) model, Scardamalia and Bereiter's knowledge building communities (KBC) model, and Lampert's model of mathematics classrooms. We also point interested readers to the work of Barbara Rogoff, who worked for years in the creation of a school based on a learning communities approach (Rogoff, 1994; Rogoff, Turkanis, & Bartlett, 2001). We do not include Rogoff's work here because we wanted to choose models that have focused on classroom-specific implementations within more traditional school settings, since we felt that this captured the circumstances that a majority of teachers interested in these types of models might themselves be faced with. Clearly, though, if an entire school community adopts a CoL approach, the overall environment better supports CoL classrooms.

Fostering a Communities of Learners Model

The FCL model was developed by Ann Brown and Joseph Campione and their colleagues in the early 1990s (Brown, 1992, 1994; Brown & Campione, 1996). According to Brown and Campione (1996), "FCL is designed to promote the critical thinking and reflection skills underlying multiple forms of higher literacy: readings, writing, argumentation, technological sophistication, and so forth" (p. 290). The FCL approach promotes a diversity of interests and talents in order to enrich the knowledge base of the classroom community as a whole. The overall structure of the FCL model involves students (a) carrying out research in a particular area of inquiry where individuals or small groups specialize in a particular subtopic area, (b) sharing what they learn with other students in their research group and in other groups, and (c) preparing for and participating in a consequential event that requires students to combine their individual learning, so that all members in the class come to a deeper understanding of the central topic and subtopics. Brown and Campione (1996) describe how the basic FCL structure of carrying out research *in order* to share information *in order* to perform a consequential task "should be viewed as a system of interacting activities that results in a self-consciously active and reflective learning environment" (p. 292).

Knowledge Building Community Model

The KBC model was created by Marlene Scardamalia, Carl Bereiter, and their colleagues in the early 1990s, and has been developing as one of the "longest running design experiments in education" (Bereiter, 2005–2006). The vision of classrooms as knowledge building communities is for students to build collective knowledge with "fidelity to the ways work with ideas is carried out in the real world" (Scardamalia, 2002, p. 6). "Advancing the frontiers of knowledge" is the central aim of the community. Students are meant to develop the "epistemic agency" to identify problems of understanding, create theories, carry out research and investigations in order to refine their theories over time, revise their problems and strategies, and share and monitor the progress of the community toward its goals. The KBC model is embodied in Knowledge Forum, a computer-based environment that allows learners to construct a communal multimedia knowledge base (Scardamalia, 2004). Ideas in the database are viewed as objects of inquiry that can be tinkered with, combined with other knowledge objects, and improved upon (Scardamalia, 2002).

Lampert's Mathematics Classrooms

Magdelene Lampert taught mathematics in a Michigan fifth-grade classroom in the 1980s and 1990s, where she developed an approach to teaching that reflected her view of an idealized mathematics community (Lampert, 2001; Lampert, Rittenhouse, & Crumbaugh, 1996). The class usually starts with a problem posed to the students, which they work on alone or in groups, developing their solutions in notebooks that retain all their work during the year. Lampert encourages students to discuss different ideas and solutions, so that they develop a deep understanding of the mathematical principles underlying their work. Participating in the mathematical discussions, learning how to make mathematical arguments, and learning the language of mathematics (terms such as *conjectures* and *commutativity*) are the central activities in the classroom.

Although the three models each have distinct features (e.g., FCL is well-known for its system of activity structures based upon Vygotskian theory, KBC for its Knowledge Forum environment, and Lampert's work for its detailed examination of teacher actions), there are several characteristics that they share in common. These include: (a) a diversity of expertise among its members, who are valued for their contributions and given support to develop, (b) a shared objective of continually advancing the collective knowledge and skills, (c) an emphasis on learning how to learn, and (d) mechanisms for sharing. It is these features that we take together as the essential elements of the CoL model.

The overall goal of a CoL classroom is to foster a culture of learning, where both individuals and the community as a whole are learning how to learn. Further, members of the community share their individual efforts toward a deeper understanding of the subject matter under study. This includes understanding how to pose disciplinary problems, explore problem spaces within a domain, and create and critique possible problem solutions. Students learn to synthesize multiple perspectives, solve problems in a variety of ways, and use each other's diverse knowledge and skills as resources to collaboratively advance their understanding. The intent is to develop deep disciplinary understanding of both subject matter and ways of working with knowledge, and for members to come to respect and value differences within the community.

BRINGING A COMMUNITY OF LEARNERS TO LIFE IN K–12 CLASSROOMS

The CoL model provides the specification of a desired goal state for K–12 classrooms. However, one of the key design challenges that teachers face is that the creation of CoL classrooms is not enacted on a blank slate. Bringing a CoL to life in K–12 classrooms involves fostering a very different culture from those found in industrial-era classrooms, and even most reform classrooms. We are interested in how to support the necessary shifts that teachers and their students must move through.

In order to support these change processes, teachers need a means for understanding how to cultivate a community of learners in their own classrooms. Describing CoL models in terms of activities or methods (e.g., reciprocal teaching) has led to problems, as developers point out that these elements of the model often become routinized to the point of "lethal mutations" (Brown, 1992). Such routinization is problematic because the key theoretical underpinnings tend to be replaced with only a superficial understanding of their relevance. Further, the necessary flexibility to respond to the particular accomplishments and needs of participants is hindered. In order to keep visible the theoretical underpinnings and to promote flexibility, the models have tended to be specified in terms of design principles (Bielaczyc & Collins, 1999; Brown, 1994; Brown & Campione, 1996; Scardamalia, 2002).

The principles are themselves grounded in an epistemology and a theory of learning that need to be understood if the principles are to be enacted appropriately in classroom designs. The CoL model is founded on theoretical perspectives emphasizing learning as a process of enculturation, with a focus on *learning to be* rather than simply *learning about* (Sawyer, 2006; Thomas & Brown, 2007). Rogoff's work underscores how it can be quite challenging for adults who have grown up with models of learning based on transmission and acquisition of knowledge to come to understand a sociocultural perspective: "it is difficult for people unfamiliar with the concept to avoid assimilating it to the adult-run/children-run dichotomy" (Rogoff, 1994, p. 210).

The design principles, underlying epistemology, and perspectives on learning provide the theoretical grounding for the CoL approach. This grounding provides a strong foundation from which to work in that these elements help teachers to navigate the myriad implementation decisions and provide parameters that constrain the implementation design space. In turn, enacting the theory results in what we term "epistemological perturbations"[1] that disturb the regular functioning of the classroom. Given that school cultures tend to be "deeply rooted in the past" (Fullan, 2007, p. 35; see also Tharp & Gallimore, 1988, chapter 7), many of these perturbations are resolved in ways that return the classroom to familiar ways of functioning, rather than resulting in the necessary shifts (Cohen, 1988; Tyack & Cuban, 1995). Here we examine five aspects of classroom life where we feel change is crucial. We focus on these five points of change because we believe that they provide the most transformational leverage in bringing a CoL to life in the classroom:

- The curricular content (using student work as the driver)
- What students do (playing epistemic games as a collective)
- What teachers do (engaging in pedagogical moves at both the individual and collective level)
- The identity of students and teachers ("I am part of a community that is making progress on important problems")
- The contextual landscape (employing the social infrastructure as a mutually reinforcing system)

In addition to considering how these particular aspects of the classroom must change, we feel it is important to highlight a cross-cutting idea that provides support to such shifts. Implementing a CoL classroom involves bringing a specific classroom culture into being. If the community that students are being enculturated into is thought of as existing only in the classroom, then this culture must be created from scratch if implementation is to take place. This poses an enormous undertaking and raises issues of how to bootstrap a rich culture of inquiry. However, we feel that further transformational leverage is gained by instead viewing the CoL as engaging students in *peripheral participation* in authentic disciplinary communities (Lave & Wenger, 1991). The disciplinary culture can thus guide the workings of the classroom, and students are socialized into working with knowledge in ways consistent with disciplinary norms and practices. Facilitating participation in existing communities that extend beyond the boundaries of the classroom provides a grounded and generative starting point. The perspective of enculturating students into disciplinary communities is a thread that runs throughout each of the shifts that we discuss below.

SHIFTING THE CURRICULAR CONTENT: USING STUDENT WORK AS THE DRIVER

It is common for teachers to create classroom activities that are meant to encourage students to think deeply about certain ideas. In CoL classrooms, the process works in reverse: students engage with their own ideas and those of others in the community in ways that determine the activities that get carried out. Even in Lampert's classroom where the teacher decides a specific mathematical problem to initially frame the community inquiry, the subsequent investigations and class discussions are driven by the students' own strategies, questions, and arguments. Scardamalia (2002) characterizes moving student ideas to the center with activities becoming subordinate as a dramatic change akin to the Copernican shift, and how "everything is understood differently and it becomes possible to move into new levels of work with ideas that could not even have been imagined before" (p. 76).

Putting students' ideas at the center of the community work communicates to students that their ideas matter to others and that they have a position of responsibility in contributing to the community's advancement. Further, centering on the students' own work is intended to support students in learning how to take control of the learning process. In this way, students not only learn about the subject matter, but also come to understand the means for working with and creating knowledge (e.g., finding problems, locating resources, testing ideas through experimentation, developing skills in argumentation, and the critique of various perspectives, etc.). Many teachers have observed an increase in student engagement when students' ideas drive the inquiry. For example, Richard Messina (2001) describes, "Rather than limit the students to passive 'clients' to a curriculum I had designed, I observed the incredible energy and interests of the students that sustained the knowledge building when they were encouraged to express their ideas and become more involved in the design of the curriculum" (p. 10).

Diversity in student work is valued. Brown and Campione (1996) point out that "diversity of interest and talents within the context of inquiry should enrich the knowledge base of the community as a whole" (p. 319). Not all student investigations need to resolve "successfully" for the community to advance its understanding. One strength of the community is participants' ability to compare among and learn from the diverse investigation paths. The key notion is that these different paths are not abstract entities, but rather the students' own paths. Students have opportunities to reflect on their personal efforts and the interrelationships their efforts have with the work of others in their community. The intent is that students come to "feel comfortable with the knowledge that their own ideas, no matter how satisfactory they may seem at present, are improvable" (Scardamalia & Bereiter, 2003, p. 6) and realize that they have the agency and are building the capacity for improving them.

Creating classrooms that are driven by student work can be challenging. Just because students are provided with opportunities to generate questions and ideas that drive inquiry does not mean that they are at ease doing so. For example, the Whitman Team, a team of sixth- and seventh-grade teachers who worked to create a KBC classroom (Bielaczyc & Collins, 2006), described how transferring control of question generation to the learners can be challenging because (a) students who enter sixth grade have already been schooled to respond to questions, not to generate them, and (b) over time teachers have become used to asking the questions. For teachers, it can be difficult to prepare ahead of time, as each cohort of students can generate a completely different set of questions and investigations to pursue (Caswell & Bielaczyc, 2002). Further, Messina (2001) points out how teachers might not realize how they retain control, even when it feels like they have made significant changes in the classroom:

> Initially I felt comfortable thinking that knowledge building was occurring because students were not only reading but were doing experiments—"hands-on learning." I slowly realized that they were trying to solve my knowledge problems rather than their own. Experiments, on their own, do not guarantee that children are knowledge building. Authentic knowledge building takes place when students are making sense of information about a problem that is of interest to them. (Scardamalia & Bereiter, 1994, p. 279)

In order for student work to serve as a resource to the community, it is critical that this work be kept public. This is often accomplished through producing artifacts or performances that can be used by the community to further their understanding. In our work with teachers, it is very common to hear "I didn't know that my students could do that." We find that teachers' confidence (and students' confidence) in putting student ideas at the center tends to increase as they become more acquainted with all that is possible for students to accomplish. Teachers play an important role in bringing the community's attention to different aspects of the work, using the students' work as a resource for modeling, making connections to big disciplinary ideas, and other critical perspectives on learning. For example, the Whitman Team describes how:

> See, I think we're continually evaluating what's going on and setting models for performance, and showing kids examples from the database[2] of where somebody was thinking about something and as they were writing here, they said "oh, you know" and then came to some kind of a conclusion. So that they can, as they're doing it themselves or reading other people's notes, they can see ideas develop. And we do that a lot. I think we're continually pushing them forward. But not so that they can get a better grade. It's so that they can be a better learner.

An important issue raised in having student work as a driver involves concerns with curriculum coverage. Often there is a worry that if student work is driving the path of inquiry then the specific curricular objectives may not be met. One aspect that needs to be considered is *what is meant by "curriculum coverage"*? That is, coverage tends to be thought of as a linear sequence of topic-by-topic alignment to curriculum guidelines. However, a topic-by-topic approach may miss opportunities to develop a deep, interconnected understanding of the subject matter under study. In contrast, inquiry in a CoL involves engaging students with various facets of the discipline, approaching subject matter from multiple angles, and drawing connections across different aspects.

For example, Lampert (2001) describes how "Multiple situations are required for the mathematics to emerge; it is not in the situations but across them" (p. 255). She examines the fifth-grade mathematics curriculum through the lens of "conceptual fields." Such fields extend across topics and contexts in order to highlight key mathematical ideas. She points out that:

> The purposeful long-term work of making connections among the topics... remains largely invisible to many classroom observers. The work involved in raising mathematical structures to a level where they can be studied would be hard for someone to see if they were only looking for coverage in terms of getting through a linear series of topics one after the other.... In contrast to the familiar topic-by-topic approach, I worked on constructing lessons that were occasions for my students to investigate a number of different but related topics, and to investigate them repeatedly in different problem contexts. (pp. 259–260)

Lampert (2001) further elaborates upon the idea that what gets "covered" is not just about the mathematics subject matter. In addition, she works with the students from where they are and the issues that come up for them in thinking through how to cover the curriculum.

Clearly, even with breaking away from a topic-by-topic approach, if a curriculum favors breadth over depth, it can be difficult to achieve "coverage" with students pursuing investigations in depth. However, we share here Richard Messina's experience as a provocative consideration. Messina (2001) tells about the first time he taught using a KBC approach:

> When I presented to the class the fact that we were not covering the material other grade four students would have learned in a public school, the response I received was quite "illuminating." One child reported that they probably know more about light than any other grade four students because of how much time was spent in the study and the way they had built the knowledge by sharing it on the database. They also added that if they ever wanted to learn about sound, for example, they now knew how to conduct an inquiry: state a question, then offer a conjecture/personal theories, research through reading and experimentation, share your knowledge advances on Knowledge Forum and build the knowledge together. (p. 9)

In a fourth-grade class Messina had several years later, when the class specifically compared their work on light in the Knowledge Forum database with the expectations for understanding light in the Ministry of Education guidelines, the students determined that they had surpassed the expectations set for a grade 4 class.

SHIFTING WHAT STUDENTS DO: PLAYING EPISTEMIC GAMES AS A COLLECTIVE

One of the central aims of the CoL model is to help students become "socialized into the world of work with knowledge" (Bereiter, 2002, p. 220). The community engages with ideas as objects of inquiry that can be tinkered with, combined with other knowledge objects, and improved, similar to the corresponding disciplinary community of practice. The intent is for students to develop a repertoire of disciplinary knowledge moves, and be able to engage in metadiscourse concerning the nature of these moves, along with the forms, goals, and rules of the knowledge work. To capture such goals, we use the framing of learning to play *"epistemic games"* (Collins & Ferguson, 1993; Morrison & Collins, 1995; Perkins, 1997).

Epistemic games are directed toward building knowledge and understanding (Perkins, 1997). Learning to play such games involves developing an understanding of the moves, constraints, and strategies for working with various types of *epistemic forms*, the representations used by disciplines to communicate knowledge work (e.g., classification trees, stage models). The overall goal is to support learners in developing *epistemic fluency*, "the ability to recognize and practice a culture's epistemic games, to understand their different forms of expression and evaluation, and to take the perspective of interlocutors who are operating within different epistemic forms" (Morrison & Collins, 1995, p. 44). Engaging students in the epistemic game play of a discipline is meant to provide insight into the workings of the disciplinary community. Lampert (2001) says: "Studying mathematics in this way involves my students in finding out what kind of activity mathematics is; it provides them an opportunity to learn and use the concepts, tools, and procedures that the field has developed" (p. 6).

As an example, one way that we might represent explanation-seeking inquiry within CoL classrooms is the "Progressive Investigation Game" (Figure 13.1). Students work together on a common problem (*Our Problem*) by proposing *Initial Ideas*. They also generate *Questions* that identify areas in need of further investigations in order to refine their initial ideas. The students then work to gather further information through *Investigative Work* or the *Exchange of Ideas*. This, in turn, leads to a refinement of the current ideas of the classroom community and further questions to pursue (*Improved Ideas and Questions*).

When students are first learning how to work collectively to play the Progressive Investigation Game it can be difficult to understand critical events and features, thus making it difficult to develop the necessary epistemological perspectives on community practices and an understanding of the moves, constraints, and strategies for working

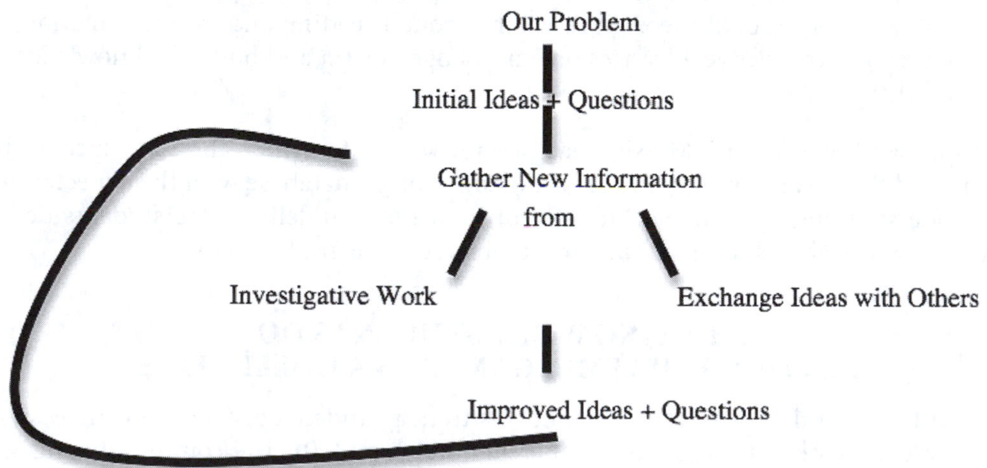

Figure 13.1 The basic flow of the Progressive Investigation Game.

with various forms of knowledge (i.e., epistemic fluency). In working with teachers to create KBC classrooms in grade 3 and 4 classrooms in Singapore, we have created specific tools that isolate parts of the full Progressive Investigation Game for practice and reflection (Bielaczyc & Kapur, 2010; Bielaczyc & Ow, 2010). For example, the Think Cards (Figure 13.2) are intended to physically reify students' knowledge building moves. They capture a sequence of explanations (*My Idea is …*), the new information that they bring to their inquiry (*New information …*), questions that drive their inquiry (*INTU* stands for "I need to understand"), and improvements that they make to their explanations (*A better idea is …*). The small, mobile nature of the Think Cards make it easy for children to work with their ideas—jotting down notes in the library or during discussions, spreading their cards out to examine the collection of ideas, literally "exchanging ideas" with others. We believe that it is important that a child can physically accompany the written form of his or her idea into a group discussion, thereby disrupting the conception that a written idea is a static response to a question when the child holding the Think Card is asked by peers to further elaborate the idea or the child defends the idea when it is challenged. The Think Cards also make visible the diversity of ideas that students generate for a particular problem of understanding and that can be collected from various resources, and the multiple pathways possible in moving from initial ideas to construct new knowledge. In this manner, students are scaffolded toward more complex knowledge building moves in Knowledge Forum.

One of the distinctions between the epistemic game play of the CoL classroom and that of most classrooms, including many reform classrooms, is that the play takes place in the form of *multiplayer games*. In other words, it is not the case that each player needs to make the full range of moves in a given game by him- or herself, but rather it is in interaction with each other's contributions[3] that the knowledge advances are made. In the Progressive Investigation Game this is accomplished by ensuring that the ideas, questions, and results of investigative work and exchanges are made available to all members of the community. In this way, one student can propose an initial idea, a different student may independently carry out investigative work related to this idea, and yet another student may contribute an insight that comes from synthesizing the

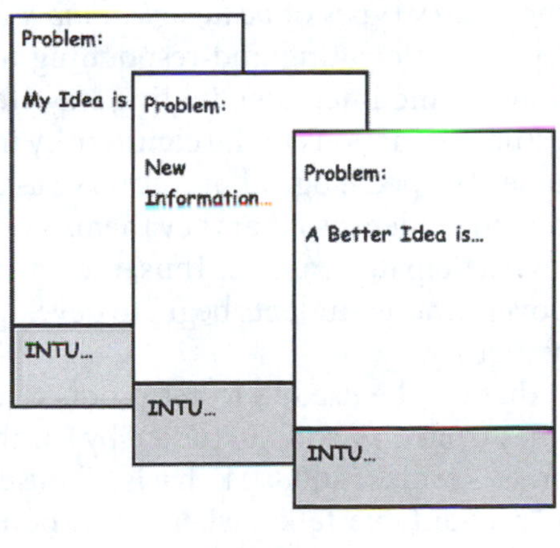

(front view)

Our Ideas

Scientists keep working to better understand the world.

(back view)

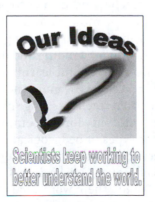

To support the concept of game play and break from the practice of filling in worksheets, each Think Card is a bright color and the backside of the cards are printed to resemble a deck of playing cards.

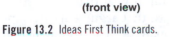

Figure 13.2 Ideas First Think cards.

investigative work with the contributions made by others. Playing epistemic games as a collective permits a community to advance further than might be possible by individual epistemic game play alone. The classroom community thus mirrors disciplinary communities where individual members make contributions, others act upon such contributions (improve upon, synthesize, argue against, etc.), and knowledge is created and refuted through the collective workings of the whole. Scardamalia and Bereiter (1994) comment on this approach: "More significant implications follow when the question is reformulated at the level of the group rather than the individual. Can a classroom function as a knowledge building community similar to the knowledge building communities that make up the learned disciplines?" (p. 270). In CoL classrooms, students engage in epistemic game play in ways that contribute to the collective, distributed construction of knowledge.

An important issue raised in playing epistemic games as a collective is that engaging students in shared, public efforts involving argumentation and explanation construction can lead to social discomfort. Lampert and her colleagues (1996) documented how students in her classroom found the emphasis on argumentation at odds with their desire to get along with other students and not to criticize them. They described the "difficulties that arise from mixing social interaction with the refinement of ideas" (p. 757), such as the feeling of "personal assault" (p. 744) or worries of being ostracized by others in the community.[4] Cultivating a CoL in the classroom involves working over time to develop a culture of trust. Scardamalia (2002) points out that: "For such work to prosper, the culture must be one of psychological safety, so that people feel safe in taking risks—revealing ignorance, voicing half-baked notions, giving and receiving criticism" (p. 78). There is a need for sensitivity to student comfort levels and the ways in which students' previous experiences have prepared them.

SHIFTING WHAT TEACHERS DO: ENGAGING IN PEDAGOGICAL MOVES AT BOTH THE INDIVIDUAL AND COLLECTIVE LEVEL

Describing teachers as "facilitators" or "a guide on the side," while accurate, does not address the necessary level of detail for helping teachers to shift the ways in which they support students in their learning. What are the necessary types of *pedagogical moves*? In CoL classrooms, teachers need to become adept at anticipating and responding to student needs (both in the moment and across longer time intervals), finding ways to scaffold student participation, and reflecting back students' actions to the community in ways that foster shared understanding and discourse. The pedagogical moves serve as a means of transferring control of the learning process to students so that they themselves come to understand and enact the moves needed to participate in a CoL. Thus, the types of pedagogical moves that teachers engage in shift over time as students begin to develop agency and take responsibility for the community inquiry.

An example of the types of pedagogical moves that can be used to foster productive discourse to advance the community's inquiry comes from classrooms studied by Sarah Michaels and her colleagues (Michaels, O'Connor, & Resnick, 2008; Michaels, Shouse, & Schweingruber, 2008). Their work focuses on "accountable talk," where classroom talk is held accountable to three elements: (a) to the community so that everyone is supported to learn and contribute, (b) to logical reasoning so that arguments are supported with evidence, and (c) to knowledge so that students base their arguments on established facts and concepts. In regard to the community, they suggest a number of conversational moves that teachers can use to open or extend a discussion, such as: "Who can put into their own words what Keisha just said?" or "Does anyone else want to add on?" (Michaels, O'Connor, & Resnick, 2008, p. 286). They find that "teachers who have implemented these discourse strategies have shifted away from simple questions and one-word answers and opened up the conversation to problems that support multiple positions or solution paths" (p. 287).

Pedagogical moves go beyond discourse moves. They may involve highlighting the actions or information from a particular group to the entire class, bringing in specific resources for student investigations, and modeling of various inquiry strategies. For example, Lampert writes multiple conjectures on the board to make visible students' ideas in order to foster both agreement or disagreement, and elaboration or modification (Lampert, 2001).

One key aspect of pedagogical moves in CoL classrooms is that they are directed toward responsiveness and guidance at both the individual and collective levels. Because the goal is to cultivate a community that mirrors the types of knowledge work carried out by disciplinary communities in the world, there is a need for attention to the progression of the community itself, and thus for pedagogical moves that address the community as a whole. Understanding how well the collective is progressing is aided by keeping student work public and coming at the developing understanding from multiple perspectives. Pedagogical moves that provide opportunities to interact with persons, ideas, and problems from outside of the classroom community may help the collective to realize: "What do we know?"; "What are we capable of?"; and "Where do we need to improve and grow?"

An important issue raised in engaging in the needed types of pedagogical moves is that doing so may lead to social discomfort for teachers. The nature of this discomfort tends to revolve around issues of authority and respect (e.g., feeling comfortable enough to say "I don't know" to students), as well as worries in seeing students struggle in their learning (e.g., allowing students to explore and fail to find solutions without intervening with "the answer"). The power of working as a collective to advance understanding is that the classroom community often goes deeply into disciplinary content and engages more fully with the complexities of the learning process. This can be both exciting and challenging for teachers. Similar to the discussion earlier about building a culture of trust for students, it is critical that the school environments in which the teachers work support them in learning and taking risks (Darling-Hammond & Sykes, 1999; Evans, 1996; Fullan, 2007).

SHIFTING THE IDENTITY OF STUDENTS AND TEACHERS: "I AM PART OF A COMMUNITY THAT IS MAKING PROGRESS ON IMPORTANT PROBLEMS"

In shifting toward CoL classrooms, we pointed out that social discomfort may arise for both students and teachers. This discomfort stems in part from changes to one's *identity* in the classroom; that is, how one views oneself and how one is perceived by the community. Who one is expected to be in a CoL classroom may be quite different from who one is expected to be in one's existing educational context, resulting in uncertainty and discomfort as one moves away from familiar roles.

Who are students and teachers meant to be in a CoL classroom? We feel that the positioning of students and teachers is nicely captured in the phrase: "I am part of a community that is making progress on important problems."[5] This statement captures both an *individual* identity of contributing in a variety ways to helping to advance the work of the collective and a *community* identity of a group that is working together on important problems. Members of the community take on different roles and develop individual areas of expertise and talents. In turn, by working toward common goals and developing a collective awareness of the expertise available among the members of the community, a sense of "who we are" is fostered.

The development of student identity within a CoL involves students assuming positions of responsibility, where they serve as resources for each other and they have a say in the overall workings of the community. For example, Brown (1994) describes how students in FCL classrooms take on multiple roles—for example, "students as researchers and teachers" (p. 8) and "everyone in the community is at some stage an actor and an audience" (p. 10)—and the community itself functions as a community of researchers. Further, both the FCL and KBC models position students as codesigners of the intervention itself with a role in improving the principles (Brown 1992; Scardamalia & Bereiter, 2006). The variety of roles provides ways for students to participate in shaping both their own paths and the ways in which their community functions.

Teachers are meant to see themselves not as lone change agents, but rather as joining others as part of a larger effort to understand how to cultivate CoLs in K–12 classrooms. It is important that teachers view their role not as an implementer of a *given* approach, but rather as a participant in a community inquiring into ways of bringing a CoL to life in a classroom. Because a CoL involves a way of being, if teachers participate in a CoL among professional colleagues, then not only does it allow them to engage with a supportive community working together to advance understanding of the model, it also deepens their understanding of "what it means to be part of a CoL." As an example, teachers working to create a KBC classroom can participate in the existing international community among teachers, researchers, and other educational stakeholders who are working to implement the model in their local contexts.[6] The international community itself employs Knowledge Forum as a means of supporting knowledge creation among participants. Participants also meet face-to-face at professional conferences, in visits to each other's schools, and at the yearly Knowledge Building Communities Summer Institute.

The intention of the CoL approach is to legitimize and value differences among participants. Brown (1994) describes the richness of such an approach as follows:

> It is very much our intention to increase diversity in these classrooms.... In our program, although we assuredly aim at conformity on the basics (everyone must read, write, think, reason, etc.), we also aim at nonconformity in the distribution of expertise and interests so everyone can benefit from the subsequent richness of knowledge. The essence of teamwork is pooling expertise. Teams composed of members with homogenous ideas and skills are denied access to such richness. (p. 10)

Valuing diversity provides space for exploring and developing one's own varieties of talents, rather than calling for conformity to a fixed norm. An individual can be working on something that no one else in the community is working on, yet the work can be of interest to others in contributing to the collective goals. In addition, the community may come to depend on the expertise developed by various individuals. Thus, students and teachers can feel empowered at being part of a collective enterprise that works together toward shared goals, impacting motivation and engagement.

An important issue raised in developing identity within a CoL classroom concerns the time that may be required to shift the culture of the classroom. The shift depends on the current state of the classroom and the nature of the immersion into a CoL approach. That is, if the participants are already acculturated quite differently from a CoL, then making a shift in individual and collective identities may take several months or years.

SHIFTING THE CONTEXTUAL LANDSCAPE: EMPLOYING THE SOCIAL INFRASTRUCTURE AS A MUTUALLY REINFORCING SYSTEM

Creating a CoL classroom also involves attending to the contextual landscape of the entire classroom environment. The contextual landscape involves a broad spectrum of social structures, including the classroom norms and practices, the means for participating in shared activities, and ways of accessing various technical elements. It is critical that the various social structures of the classroom are seen as forming a systemic whole, rather than being experienced as separate parts. That is, there is a need to not only understand the importance of individual elements, but to also attend to the interconnections among the elements and the emergent properties of these interactions. Brown and Campione (1996) wrote about this point in a colorful manner in describing the importance of viewing the design of FCL as an integrated system, rather than a set of individual components that could be chosen like items from a Chinese menu. They emphasize the power of a system of elements that mutually influences and reinforces each other:

> There are by now many procedures available that were designed to foster thinking. These procedures are part of the teacher's toolbox. But the procedures are understood as unrelated tools, not as systems of interdependent activities.... Teachers may, for example, decide to include forms of cooperative learning, the use of long-term projects, a writer's workbench approach, etc. The problem we see is that such an approach ignores the potential power of creating a classroom system of activities that mutually influence and reinforce each other.... There is a purpose for every activity, and nothing exists without a purpose. All members of the community—students, teachers, parents, and researchers alike— should be aware of this. (p. 314)

Based on the perspective of a mutually reinforcing system, Bielaczyc developed the Social Infrastructure Framework in order to make explicit the various elements of classroom social structures impacting the design of classroom learning environments (Bielaczyc, 2006). The Social Infrastructure Framework highlights four dimensions of classroom social structures:

- The *Cultural Beliefs Dimension* refers to the mind-set that shapes the way of life of the classroom. The design considerations include the ways in which knowledge and learning are conceptualized, students' and teachers' social identities, and how technology-based tools are perceived.

- The *Practices Dimension* concerns the ways in which teachers and students engage in both online and offline learning activities relating to the technology-based tool. This includes issues such as whether students work individually, in groups, or both; and how such groupings are organized. It also includes the various roles a teacher assumes in using a technology-based tool with his or her students
- The *Socio-Techno-Spatial Relations Dimension* refers to the organization of physical space and cyberspace as they relate to the teacher and student interactions with technology-based tools.
- The *Interaction with the "Outside World" Dimension* refers to the ways in which students interact, online and offline, with people outside of their immediate classroom context.

Although listed separately, these dimensions of social infrastructure are interdependent, with the cultural beliefs posited as a substrate for the interactions (Figure 13.3).

In our current work with teachers, we have been using the Social Infrastructure Framework as an explicit tool for designing and analyzing teacher implementations of CoL classrooms. We find that it not only serves as a useful shared language among teachers, but that it also helps to create awareness of the interconnectedness of classroom social structures. The idea is to move beyond consideration of individual classroom components to look for systemic relationships among the various social and technical support structures.

In creating a system of mutually reinforcing social structures, one consideration involves the "embodied epistemology" found in the practices, tools and classroom arrangements of learning environments. For example, there is a story about John Dewey buying desks for his Chicago school. A sales clerk showed him desks typical of the time—wooden desks with seats attached directly to the desk and legs that bolted to the floor. Dewey was reputed to have said that the desks were inappropriate because they were built for listening not learning. Because the desks would be fixed in position, they would have a bias against more participatory ways of learning. The idea is that elements of a classroom-learning environment, whether they are physical artifacts or cultural practices, embody a particular epistemology that biases different ways of knowing (Ow & Bielaczyc, 2008; Scardamalia & Bereiter, 2008). Thus, changing the contextual

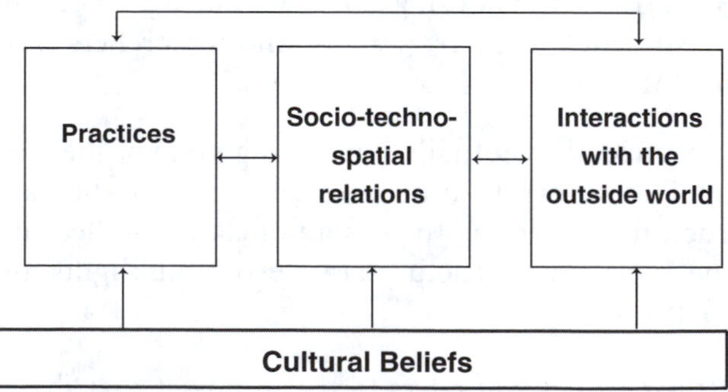

Figure 13.3 The social infrastructure framework as a system of interactions.

landscape so that the biases across the social infrastructure of the classroom mutually reinforce the epistemologies of the CoL approach constitute an important means of supporting the shift to the new model.

CONCLUSION

In considering how to cultivate a CoL in K–12 classrooms, we have discussed both key theoretical underpinnings along with five key changes in classroom life that we believe provide the most transformational leverage in bringing a CoL to life. These key changes comprise: (a) the curricular content (using student work as the driver); (b) what students do (playing epistemic games as a collective); (c) what teachers do (engaging in pedagogical moves at both the individual and collective level); (d) the identity of students and teachers (becoming part of a community that is making progress on important problems), and (e) the contextual landscape (employing the social infrastructure as a mutually reinforcing system). In discussing these areas, we have emphasized that each involves both an individual and collective aspect (reflecting both participant- and community-level considerations), along with the associated challenges and implementation considerations.

Although the CoL model may require a "radical reconceptualization in practice" (Bielaczyc & Collins, 1999), we believe that there are many benefits to making such a change. The model is intended to foster deep disciplinary understanding of both subject matter and the ways in which the disciplinary community works with knowledge in a domain. In this way, the model supports moving beyond "learning about" content knowledge to "learning to be" active in community practices and to develop a more robust epistemology. Students develop the agency and tools for engaging in complex disciplinary investigations. They also begin to understand the value of multiple perspectives, reflection, and the time and processes involved in knowledge work. In addition, student motivation and engagement may be impacted, as students' talents and the work that they are doing matters to others in the community.

ACKNOWLEDGMENTS

We would like to thank Myrna Cooney, Bill Peters, Joel Rainbow, Karen Wesack, Alinda Hakinson, Richard Messina, Bev Caswell, John Ow, Marlene Scardamalia, Carl Bereiter, Joe Campione, Magdelene Lampert, Sarah Michaels, and the wonderful teachers and students of Townsville Primary School for their contributions at various stages of this research.

NOTES

1. Elsewhere we have described how we use the purposeful creation of "epistemological perturbations" as a design strategy in design research (Bielaczyc & Ow, 2007; Ow & Bielaczyc, 2007, 2008).
2. The teacher is referring to the Knowledge Forum database, which allows the contributions of each student to be visible to all members of the classroom community.
3. Note that we did not speak of "interactions among the players themselves," but instead of "interactions among the players' contributions." In CoL classrooms, just as in disciplinary communities, the players need not specifically engage each other for their contributions to indeed interact and lead to advances in the community's knowledge. Of course, as in disciplinary communities, actual interactions and collaborations among players can also play a valuable role within the community.

4. Interestingly, their work underscored that such difficulties occur not only with children in CoL classrooms, but also with adults in the professions and other scholarly communities that involve critiquing ideas as well.
5. This quote is drawn from Bereiter's (2002) descriptions of participation in knowledge creating communities.
6. Refer to http://ikit.org

REFERENCES

Bereiter, C. (2002). *Education and mind in the knowledge age*. Mahwah, NJ: Erlbaum.

Bereiter, C. (2005–2006). Design research: The way forward. *Education Canada, 46*(1), 16–19.

Bielaczyc, K. (2006). Designing social infrastructure: Critical issues in creating learning environments with technology. *Journal of the Learning Sciences, 15*, 301–329.

Bielaczyc, K., & Collins, A. (1999). Learning communities in classrooms: A reconceptualization of educational practice. In C. M. Reigeluth (Ed.), *Instructional design theories and models* (Vol. 2). Mahwah, NJ: Erlbaum.

Bielaczyc, K., & Collins, A. (2006). Fostering knowledge-creating communities. In A. M. O'Donnell, C. E. Hmelo-Silver, & G. Erkens (Eds.), *Collaborative learning, reasoning, and technology* (pp. 37–60). Mahwah NJ: Erlbaum.

Bielaczyc, K., & Kapur, M. (2010) Playing epistemic games in science and mathematics classrooms. *Journal of Educational Technology, 50*(5), 19–25.

,Bielaczyc, K., & Ow, J. (2007). Shifting the social infrastructure: Investigating transition mechanisms for creating knowledge building communities in classrooms. In *Proceedings of the International Conference for Computers in Education 2007 workshop for knowledge building research in Asia-Pacific*. Hiroshima, Japan.

Bielaczyc, K., & Ow, J. (2010). Making knowledge building moves: Toward cultivating knowledge building communities in classrooms. In *Proceedings of the International Society of the Learning Sciences* (pp. 865–872), Chicago, IL.

Brown, A. L. (1992). Design experiments: Theoretical and methodological challenges in creating complex interventions. *Journal of the Learning Sciences, 2*(2), 141–178.

Brown, A. L. (1994). The advancement of learning. *Educational Researcher, 23*(8), 4–12.

Brown, A. L., & Campione, J. C. (1996). Psychological theory and the design of innovative learning environments: On procedures, principles, and systems. In L. Schauble & R. Glaser (Eds.), *Innovations in learning: New environments for education* (pp. 289–325). Hillsdale, NJ: Erlbaum.

Caswell, B., & Bielaczyc, K. (2002). Knowledge Forum: Altering the relationship between students and scientific knowledge. *Education, Communication and Information, 3*, 281–305.

Cohen, D. (1988). "Teaching practice: Plus ça change…." In P. Jackson (Ed.), *Contributing to educational change: Perspectives on research and practice* (pp. 27–84). Berkeley, CA: McCutchan.

Collins, A., & Ferguson, W. (1993). Epistemic forms and epistemic games: Structures and strategies for guiding inquiry. *Educational Psychologist, 28*(1), 25–42.

Darling-Hammond, L., & Sykes, G. (Eds.). (1999). *Teaching as the learning profession: A handbook of policy and practice*. San Francisco, CA: Jossey-Bass.

Evans, R. (1996). *The human side of school change*. San Francisco, CA: Jossey-Bass.

Fullan, M. (2007). *The new meaning of educational change* (4th ed.). New York: Teachers College Press.

Lampert, M. (2001). *Teaching problems and the problems of teaching*. New Haven, CT: Yale University Press.

Lampert, M., Rittenhouse, P., & Crumbaugh, C. (1996). Agreeing to disagree: Developing sociable mathematical discourse. In D. Olson & N. Torrance (Eds.), *Handbook of education and human development* (pp. 731–764). Oxford, England: Blackwell.

Lave, J., & Wenger, E. (1991). *Situated learning: Legitimate peripheral participation*. New York: Cambridge University Press.

Messina, R. (2001, April). *Interactive learners, cooperative knowledge building, and classroom inventions*. Paper presented at the annual Conference of the American Educational Research Association. Seattle WA.

Michaels, S., O'Connor, C., & Resnick, L. (2008). Reasoned participation: Accountable talk in the classroom and in civic life. *Studies in Philosophy and Education*, 27(4), 283–297.

Michaels, S., Shouse, A., & Schweingruber, H. (2008). *Ready, set, SCIENCE!: Putting research to work in the K-8 science classroom*. Washington, DC: National Academies Press.

Morrison, D., & Collins, A. (1996). Epistemic fluency and constructivist learning environments. In B. G. Wilson (Ed.), *Constructivist learning environments: Case studies in instructional design* (pp. 107–119). Englewood Cliffs NJ: Educational Technology. (Original work published 1995)

National Research Council. (2007). *Taking science to school: Learning and teaching science in grades K-8* (Committee on Science Learning, Kindergarten through Eighth Grade). Washington, DC: National Academies Press.

Ow, J., & Bielaczyc, K. (2007). Epistemic perturbations: Using material artifacts to cultivate a knowledge building culture in classrooms. In *Proceedings of the 8th International Conference for Computer-Supported Collaborative Learning* (pp. 583–585). New Brunswick, NJ.

Ow, J., & Bielaczyc, K. (2008). *Designing artifacts for "epistemological perturbations"—Changing the bias of learning environments for Knowledge Building.* Paper presented at the Eleventh Annual Knowledge Forum Summer Institute, Toronto, CA.

Perkins, D. (1997). Epistemic games. *International Journal of Educational Research, 27*(1), 49–61.

Rogoff, B. (1994). Developing understanding of the idea of communities of learners. *Mind, Culture, and Activity, 1*(4), 209–229.

Rogoff, B., Turkanis, C. G., & Bartlett, L. (2001). *Learning together: Children and adults in a school community.* New York: Oxford University Press.

Sawyer, K. (2006). *The Cambridge handbook of the learning sciences.* New York: Cambridge University Press.

Scardamalia, M. (2002). Collective cognitive responsibility for the advancement of knowledge. In B. Smith (Ed.), *Liberal education in the knowledge society* (pp. 67–98). Chicago, IL: Open Court.

Scardamalia, M. (2004). CSILE/Knowledge Forum®. In *Education and technology: An encyclopedia* (pp. 183–192). Santa Barbara, CA: ABC-CLIO.

Scardamalia, M., & Bereiter, C. (1994). Computer support for knowledge-building communities. *Journal of the Learning Sciences, 3*(3), 265–283.

Scardamalia, M., & Bereiter, C. (2003). Beyond brainstorming: Sustained creative work with ideas. *Education Canada, 43*(4), 4–7.

Scardamalia, M., & Bereiter, C. (2006). Knowledge building: Theory, pedagogy and technology. In R. K. Sawyer (Ed.), *Cambridge handbook of the learning sciences* (pp. 97–115). New York: Cambridge University Press.

Scardamalia, M., & Bereiter, C. (2008). Pedagogical biases in educational technologies. *Educational Technology, 3*, 3–10.

Tharp, R., & Gallimore, R. (1988). *Rousing minds to life.* New York: Cambridge University Press.

Thomas, D., & Brown, J. S. (2007). The play of imagination: Extending the literary mind. *Games and Culture, 2*(2), 149–172.

Tyack, D., & Cuban, L. (1995). *Tinkering toward utopia: A century of public school reform.* Cambridge, MA: Harvard University Press.

14

MOTIVATION IN COLLABORATIVE GROUPS

TONI KEMPLER ROGAT

Rutgers University

LISA LINNENBRINK-GARCIA

Duke University

NICOLE DiDONATO

Montclair State University

While small groups have often been conceptualized as a "hook" for initiating an individual's motivation for learning (Mitchell, 1993), there may be reason for reexamining this claim. Collaborative groups are increasingly prevalent, yet motivation researchers have predominantly studied individual motivation during independent learning, with few studies investigating students' motivational responses to learning in group contexts (Järvelä, Volet, & Järvenoja, 2010). Moreover, learning with peers in groups raises challenges that may undermine rather than support an individual's motivation. Within the small-group literature, most researchers focus on the benefits of groups for learning and achievement, but largely ignore motivational outcomes (Webb & Palincsar, 1996). Accordingly, the goal of this chapter is to synthesize extant research in order to examine the evidence for the motivational benefits and challenges of collaborative groups. This review also serves as the basis for suggesting new directions for future research.

WHY IS MOTIVATION IMPORTANT TO CONSIDER FOR SMALL-GROUP CONTEXTS?

It is critical to consider the potential of motivation to enhance students' learning and engagement during group work. Drawing from studies examining motivation when students learn independently (Wigfield, Eccles, Schiefele, Roeser, & Davis-Kean, 2006), it is clear that motivation supports learning by enhancing students' effort, persistence in the face of challenge, and use of self-regulated and deep-level learning strategies. Although motivation has primarily focused on independent learners, the underlying theoretical tenets are not specific to individuals. Thus, one can readily employ these theoretical frameworks for understanding motivation in group settings and developing hypotheses about the role that motivation plays.

Researchers studying collaborative and cooperative groups have developed a number of programs aimed at facilitating student interactions in ways that benefit learning (e.g., Palincsar & Brown, 1984). There is an assumption that these programs support engagement and learning by supporting motivation, but few studies consider the benefits of group work for motivation. Notably, many of these programs integrate features that have the potential for motivating learning. For example, the integration of interesting and challenging tasks (Complex Instruction; Cohen, 1994), individual accountability (Johnson & Johnson, 1991; Slavin, 1995), and interdependence (Learning Together; Johnson & Johnson, 1991) are features of established programs that may facilitate motivation. Moreover, working with peers can potentially foster students' social goals and feelings of relatedness, which can enhance motivation.

Unfortunately, these motivating features may not have the intended benefits given several challenges for motivation raised by group work. First, there are challenges raised by the group's composition, such as differences in ability and cultural background (Cohen, 1994; O'Donnell & Kelly, 1994). For example, high ability students may feel that working with less knowledgeable classmates slows down their progress. Status differences in the group may have implications for motivation, especially given the central role that social comparison plays within motivation theories (Ames, 1992), as we will discuss later. In addition, there are problems raised by interpersonal dynamics. Some students may diminish their level of contribution while relying on others to do the work (i.e., free rider effect or social loafing; Karau & Williams, 1995), leading to diminished motivation. Similarly, off-task behavior and pursuit of nonacademic goals by some members of the group may discourage the motivation of remaining group members. Finally, the necessity of working jointly with others on a task can create motivational challenges as students try to establish common goals, work in a shared problem space, and negotiate multiple perspectives (Barron, 2003). Students may experience declines in motivation when they recognize that group work requires more personal responsibility and ownership in comparison with independent learning. Ultimately, the enhanced effort, time, and social negotiation required by working with others may diminish the motivating potential of learning in groups.

A second issue concerning the motivational benefits of group work is that some program features directly conflict with recommendations for supporting student motivation. For example, some programs rely on intergroup competition and rewards (Slavin, 1996). However, motivation researchers contend that an emphasis on competition fosters performance goals aimed at besting others, rather than an orientation toward learning and understanding (Ames, 1992). The use of rewards is also problematic in that it may foster extrinsic motivation instead of facilitating task enjoyment for its own sake (i.e., intrinsic motivation; Ryan & Deci, 2000a).

In sum, there are unique motivational challenges to group work as well as potentially untapped benefits from applying a motivational lens for supporting group learning and engagement. Accordingly, the purpose of the current chapter is to synthesize the somewhat limited research on motivation in group contexts and highlight avenues for future research that may be particularly fruitful based on motivational theory. In conducting this review, we included studies that examined the role of motivation in both collaborative and cooperative groups (see Dillenbourg, 1999 for a review of the distinction). The included studies draw on three contemporary theories of motivation: achievement goal theory, self-determination theory, and social cognitive theory. Each of these theories accounts for the situation-specific nature of motivation and the facilitating role of peers, thus making them fruitful for considering how group contexts shape motivation. These theories also consider how individual motivation shapes learning and engagement, thus they are useful for considering how individual differences in motivation may alter students' interactions, learning, and engagement in the group context.

We excluded studies of dyads from this review because issues specific to tutoring and pair learning are different from learning among three to six group members. In addition, we excluded research on online and computer-supported collaborative learning, given that much of this work involves asynchronous learning. We sought to identify research that examined the role of group work in the context of reform-oriented learning environments (e.g., problem-based learning, project-based science, reformed-based mathematics). However, even though these programs include group work as a motivating feature (Blumenfeld, Kempler, & Krajcik, 2006), we identified few studies that examined motivation while isolating the impact of group work.

Our discussion of each theory is organized around two guiding questions:

How does engaging in group work shape students' motivation? Here, we consider whether small-group contexts lead to higher quality student motivation relative to direct or traditional instruction. In answering this question, we also identify features that may have facilitated these effects and consider potential benefits for both the motivation of the group as well as individual student motivation.

How does motivation shape learning and engagement in small groups? In this section, we account for both students' incoming personal motivation and situation-specific motivation for supporting engagement and learning during group work. We also investigate the role motivation plays in differentiating successful or productive groups.

ACHIEVEMENT GOAL THEORY

According to achievement goal theory, achievement goals provide a framework for interpreting and responding to events (Dweck & Leggett, 1988). There are thought to be two primary goals or reasons why students engage in achievement behavior. A mastery goal, also called a learning or task goal, refers to a focus on learning with the aim of developing understanding or skills. A performance goal, sometimes called an ego or ability-focused goal, reflects a focus on demonstrating one's ability or competence, often in comparison to others. These two primary goals have been further differentiated based on whether students adopt an approach or avoidance focus (Elliot, 1999; Pintrich, 2000). While the distinction between performance-approach (focus on demonstrating competence) and performance-avoidance (focus on avoiding appearing incompetent) is widely accepted, mastery-avoidance has received far less attention (Maehr & Zusho, 2009). As such, we focus our discussion here on mastery, performance-approach, and performance-avoidance goal orientations.

These three goals differentially predict students' behavior, affect, and strategy use. In general, mastery goals are beneficial and support interest, self-efficacy, emotional well-being, and cognitive engagement (Linnenbrink & Pintrich, 2000). The findings regarding achievement are somewhat mixed, but generally suggest that mastery goals are beneficial, at least to the same degree as performance-approach goals (Linnenbrink-Garcia, Tyson, & Patall, 2008). Performance-avoidance goals are consistently associated with less adaptive outcomes such as heightened anxiety, superficial strategy use, avoidance of help seeking, and decreased academic self-efficacy, intrinsic motivation, and achievement (e.g., Church, Elliot, & Gable, 2001; Elliot, McGregor, & Gable, 1999; Karabenick, 2004; Middleton & Midgley, 1997; Skaalvik, 1997). The relative benefits and detriments of performance-approach goals have received a great deal of attention within the literature (cf., Harackiewicz, Barron, & Elliot, 1998; Midgley, Kaplan, & Middleton, 2001). Performance-approach goals may be beneficial for supporting achievement, persistence, and effort (Elliot et al., 1999; Linnenbrink-Garcia et al., 2008); however, they are also linked to maladaptive learning outcomes such as avoidant help seeking (Karabenick, 2004), shallow cognitive processing (Graham & Golan, 1991), and test anxiety (Huang, 2011). The possibility that performance-approach goals may be adaptive has led some goal theorists to suggest that espousing both mastery and performance-approach goals may be most adaptive because students may benefit from both goals (Pintrich, 2000).

One of the strengths of applying achievement goal theory to small groups is that the classroom context shapes goal orientations (Ames, 1992). Specifically, variations in tasks, autonomy support (e.g., providing students with choices, reducing control), recognition and evaluation practices, flexibility of time, and grouping practices all shape students' tendency to endorse mastery versus performance (both approach and avoidance) goal orientations (Ames, 1992; Maehr & Midgley, 1996; Patrick, Anderman, Ryan, Edelin, & Midgley, 2001).

Specific to collaborative group settings, groups have the potential to foster mastery goals when pedagogical strategies encourage learners to see fellow group members as helpful and sources of information (Webb, Ing, Kersting, & Nemer, 2006). Group tasks can help sustain a mastery focus when they encompass interesting topics, authentic problems, and are moderately challenging. In contrast, students may adopt performance-approach goals when relative ability information is salient. Teachers who publicly comment on the smartest or top performing group make information about a group's relative class standing readily available. In response, students may endorse performance- approach or performance-avoidance goals. Students who endorse performance-approach goals could prioritize looking good in comparison to others within the group, without necessarily ensuring that everyone understands (Kempler & Linnenbrink, 2004). When students hold performance-avoidance goals, they may avoid asking questions within the group because they are reluctant to admit not understanding the task (Middleton & Midgley, 1997). It may be more advantageous for educators to provide private feedback that informs groups on their progress, so that students sustain a mastery focus. In addition, interventions where the focus is on the task and everyone's contributions are encouraged and valued, such as Complex Instruction (Cohen, 1994), may help to support mastery goal endorsement.

Influence of Group Programs and Features on Goal Orientations

A key controversy relevant to achievement goal theory is the use of between-group competition. Group researchers have advocated between-group competition to facilitate motivation and engagement (Slavin, 1996). This approach dates back to Deutsch's

(1949) suggestion that competition fosters group cohesion as a result of the group pulling together to beat other teams. Competition has also been advocated as a strategy for decreasing social loafing, because individuals and groups are less likely to loaf when they have access to information about themselves and their abilities. Achievement-goal theorists, in contrast, suggest that between-group competition may promote performance goal adoption. Performance goals may be promoted because relative ability information is available when groups are publicly recognized for besting others through public postings or announcing group rankings (Kempler & Linnenbrink, 2004; Linnenbrink, 2005).

Most studies that have contrasted the motivational benefits of competition-based cooperative learning programs indicate that, in comparison to traditional classrooms, students who work in cooperative groups are more likely to adopt mastery goals (Nicholls, 1996; Nicholls & Miller, 1994; Sharan & Shaulov, 1990). These findings may seem to conflict with achievement goal theorists' hypothesis that the competition structure of the STAD program (Slavin, 1995) provokes performance goal adoption. However, because these studies examined cooperative learning programs (STAD, TAI, Group Investigation) with a variety of motivating features, it is unclear which features explain mastery goal adoption. For instance, it may be that mastery goals were encouraged more than performance goals because points were awarded based on group improvement scores; a focus on improvement tends to promote mastery goals.

Linnenbrink (2005) investigated this issue by teasing apart the aspects of between-group competition and group improvement that are central features of STAD. Specifically, she created three types of group evaluation practices: a mastery condition (groups received improvement points, but no between-group comparison information); a performance condition (groups received feedback about their normative performance (rather than improvement) relative to other groups); and a combined mastery-performance condition (groups received improvement points and comparison information about how their improvement compared to other groups). The combined mastery-performance condition was most similar to Slavin's STAD (1995). Findings indicated that both the mastery condition and the performance condition facilitated achievement goal adoption in line with expectations. Students in the combined mastery-performance condition espoused similarly high mastery goals relative to the mastery condition, and somewhat higher, though not statistically significant, mastery goals than those in the performance-condition. A similar pattern was observed for performance-approach goals in the combined mastery-performance condition. These findings suggest that programs like STAD may be fostering both mastery and performance-approach goals; however, Linnenbrink also manipulated the overall classroom context, so it is not clear if the observed effects are due to the change in the group evaluation procedures or if they also reflected the broader changes to the classroom context.

While not specifically studying the impact of between-group competition, Nolen's (2007) research highlights the detriments of salient relative ability information during group learning and its potential for fostering an ego or performance focus. Her examination of K–12 reading and writing instruction indicated that some classroom practices resulted in the development and gradual coconstruction of performance goal (ego) concerns, by positioning some students as capable readers, while distinguishing others as struggling readers. Ego concerns were heightened when less fluent readers were provided with fewer opportunities to read aloud in groups and had limited access to coaching strategies (i.e., simply giving students the word). There were significant costs for the less fluent readers, whose behavior seemed to indicate a performance-avoidance focus. Struggling readers avoided reading aloud by physically withdrawing their chairs from the group, voicing a preference for reading alone, and by acting out. Ultimately, salient ability relevant information had costs because struggling readers had fewer opportunities for skill improvement (Nolen, 2007). In contrast, in classrooms where all students were viewed as contributing to understanding, students espoused a more positive view of less fluent readers. Student interviews indicated that struggling readers could improve during group reading, make significant group contributions, and no stigma was attached to being less fluent.

Overall, these findings suggest that relative ability information, which may be especially salient in some cooperative learning settings (e.g., Slavin, 1995) may be more likely to facilitate the endorsement of a performance-approach or performance-avoidance goal orientation. However, the emphasis on learning and supporting other group members, which is also prevalent during small-group instruction, has the potential to support mastery goal endorsement.

Role of Goal Orientations on Group Processes

Research has also considered how students' goal orientations influence the attitudes they develop toward group activity and the quality with which they participate. Kaplan (2004) proposed that how students approach group work depends on the match between their entering goal orientation and whether cooperative tasks are perceived as a match with their personal achievement goals. Mastery-oriented students may have positive attitudes toward group work when the task provides opportunities to enhance learning and when the group jointly focuses on task mastery (Minnaert, Boekaerts, & deBrander, 2007). In contrast, mastery-focused students would be less willing to cooperate if they perceived the task as interfering with an aim to improve and understand. In support of these hypotheses, Levy, Kaplan, and Patrick's (2004) research suggests that mastery-oriented students evaluated cooperative tasks based on how they contributed to their academic goals. Students who espoused mastery goals were more concerned with learning, relative to their focus on impression-management and social relationships. However, this contrasts with Linnenbrink's (2005) study in which she found no significant personal goal orientation x classroom goal condition interactions.

Hänze and Berger (2007) also examined the role of goal orientations on students' perceived support for their three basic needs (see "Intrinsic Motivation" section) during Jigsaw and traditional instruction. Their hypothesis was that mastery-oriented students would be more likely to perceive enhanced support for developing competence and autonomy during group work. While mastery-oriented students experienced themselves as increasingly competent, autonomous, and socially integrated relative to students with low mastery levels, this was true regardless of the method of instruction. That is, Jigsaw did not afford a heightened sense of achievement goal match or support than did traditional instruction.

Research has also explored the role of achievement goals in differentiating productive from less effective groups. Hijzen, Boekaerts, and Vedder (2007) identified effective and less effective groups in terms of the quality of cooperative learning and task-relevant engagement. Students attended secondary vocational schools where cooperative learning was a commonly employed instructional method. Interview results suggested that effective groups could be distinguished by their reported mastery and social responsibility goals. In contrast, groups who demonstrated more task irrelevant behaviors prioritized work avoidant and belongingness goals. Interestingly, members of the less effective groups also seemed to be less conscious of their goals, as indicated by fewer statements during interviews that referred to goal preferences.

Other studies have considered whether similar achievement goals within groups enhance motivation and learning; motivation may be facilitated when students share common achievement goals among group members, relative to groups with conflicting priorities. In addition, a shared mastery goal should have enhanced learning benefits relative to a shared performance focus. Kempler, Hruda, and Maehr (2003) explored how students' shared perceptions of their group's achievement goal focus related to social-behavioral engagement. Hierarchical Linear Modeling (HLM) analyses suggested that students who shared a perception of their group as mastery-focused were less likely to behaviorally disengage, while a shared performance-approach focus resulted in disengagement. In related research, Summers (2006) considered how shared academic and social goal endorsement shaped goal adoption. Here, academic goals referred to students wanting groups to work well together and to share their ideas and questions.[1] HLM findings indicated that sixth graders belonging to groups with shared academic goals were more likely to endorse performance-avoidance goals. Taken together, these studies suggest that when collaborating as a group, students may gradually come to hold common (achievement or academic) goals. However, questions remain as to when shared goals lead students to become overly concerned with their group's evaluation of their capabilities resulting in a focus on avoiding embarrassment in front of their peers.

Summary and Future Directions

An achievement goal theory perspective contributes a different lens from group research for interpreting the role of between-group competition within group settings. Rather than suggest a benefit via promoting group cohesion, research that has teased apart the influence of improvement points from the impact of between-group competition indicates that between-group competition may have a deleterious effect on student motivation (Linnenbrink, 2005). These results can be interpreted as evidence that between-group competition makes relative ability information salient, leading to a performance goal focus, with students aiming to avoid looking stupid during group work or working to look smart relative to other students (Nolen, 2007). Group performance goal adoption warrants concern, as a shared performance focus is associated with group members' tendency to disengage and be less productive (Hijzen et al., 2007; Kempler et al., 2003).

Future research should investigate *how* between-group competition influences group process and learning. Achievement goal theory suggests that encouraging competition may inadvertently transition from competition between groups, to fostering within-group competition. In particular, it is possible that as students draw comparisons to the capabilities of other groups, they may attempt to demonstrate competence to members of their own group. Kempler and Linnenbrink's (2004) qualitative analyses of two groups that were part of the combined mastery-performance condition in the larger Linnenbrink (2005) study suggested that between-group competition yielded conversations focused on team rank and points relative to other groups, and even a whole-group conversation about forming a "smart group." However, results also provided evidence that not all between-group competition fosters the same type of social comparison. The second group used social comparison as a source of information as they compared their progress and speed with that of other groups. This informative role of social comparison is consistent with suggestions that social comparison is useful in self-regulatory processes (Ruble & Frey, 1991).

Achievement goal theory research also suggests that students' entering goal orientations can alter their responses to group work. When students enter the group with a mastery goal focus, they may be more attuned to the learning aspects of cooperative tasks, which in turn may facilitate effective group work (Levy et al. 2004). In addition, an initial or jointly established focus on mastery may be especially beneficial (Kempler et al., 2003; Hijzen et al., 2007). However, there is very limited research examining how students' initial goal orientations alter responses to group settings as well as how goal orientations shift and change as a function of group work. This is an area where future research is needed.

SELF-DETERMINATION THEORY

Self-determination theory (SDT) differentiates between types of motivation (intrinsic v. extrinsic) that are based on the different goals that provoke action (Ryan & Deci, 2000a). Intrinsic motivation involves engaging in an activity for its own sake and because it is inherently enjoyable. Intrinsically motivated students benefit in terms of preference for challenge, use of deep-level learning strategies, creativity, and learning. In contrast, students who are extrinsically motivated engage to achieve a separable outcome. Extrinsic motivation falls along a continuum with extrinsic motivations including some self-endorsement falling closer to intrinsic motivation. For instance, extrinsically motivated students may engage in a group task because of a contingent reward, to earn a high grade, to impress the teacher, or because of perceived value of a future outcome.

Self-determination theory also posits that intrinsic motivation is facilitated in classroom and group contexts that support students' basic psychological needs for competence, autonomy, and relatedness (Ryan & Deci, 2000a). Autonomy needs are facilitated when students experience themselves as causal agents, which is conceptually similar to an internal perceived locus of causality (deCharms, 1968). Group work likely supports autonomy because students have enhanced responsibility for their learning in comparison to direct instruction, and group work provides opportunities for choosing topics and planning how to accomplish a task. Students' competence needs are supported when they experience success after investing effort, accomplish optimally challenging tasks, and receive positive informational feedback. Programs like Jigsaw may facilitate competence because students become "experts" as they develop familiarity during their investigation. More generally, students who take leadership roles, provide explanations to their peers, and have opportunities to contribute to the group's understanding, likely perceive competence support. Finally, students' needs for relatedness are supported by forming close relationships with peers and teachers, and by becoming a contributing member of the community. Students' relatedness needs are fostered through opportunities to work closely with and develop relationships with their peers during group work (Hänze & Berger, 2007).

A related theoretical approach is that of interest development (Hidi & Renninger, 2006; Schiefele, 2009). Although interest development and SDT represent separate theoretical perspectives, many of the features thought to facilitate interest are similar to those proposed by SDT (Krapp, 2005). Briefly, research on interest development differentiates between *individual interest*, which is relatively stable, resides within the individual, and includes a deep personal connection to and enjoyment of the domain, and *situational interest*, which emerges from and is supported by the context, is relatively brief, and based more on the situation than an enduring quality residing within the individual (Hidi & Renninger, 2006; Schiefele, 2009). When situational interest is supported, it has the potential to develop into individual interest (Hidi & Renninger, 2006; Linnenbrink-Garcia, Patall, & Messersmith, 2012).

With respect to small-group learning, the construct of situational interest is most relevant, as there are several components of the small-group context that may encourage situational interest. Specifically, class work that supports opportunities for students to be actively involved, including engaging in cooperative learning, may support situational interest (Bergin, 1999; Freeman, McPhail, & Berndt, 2002; Mitchell, 1993). Other indirect aspects of small-group instruction may also enhance situational interest. For example, as noted above, autonomy support is likely enhanced in small-group settings and initial research suggests that support for autonomy may help to support situational interest (Hijzen et al., 2007; Linnenbrink-Garcia et al., 2008, 2012). Additionally, many small-group learning tasks are more authentic than traditional tasks, helping to highlight the connections between course material and real life. An emphasis on real world connections helps to support situational interest (Durik & Harackiewicz, 2007; Linnenbrink-Garcia et al., 2012; Mitchell, 1993). Thus, while there is very little research that isolates the role of small-group learning in supporting situational interest, both theory and preliminary evidence suggest that several aspects of small-group instruction should facilitate situational interest, which may ultimately enhance individual interest.

Below we highlight the role of small groups in shaping intrinsic motivation and situational interest. We are not aware of research examining how existing levels of intrinsic motivation or interest alter group processes, thus our discussion of SDT and small-group functioning focuses solely on the first question of how group contexts support motivation.

Influence of Group Programs and Features on Intrinsic Motivation

Some research has studied motivation to explain *why* small group instruction is more advantageous than direction instruction for promoting achievement. Both Jigsaw (Aronson, 1978) and Group Investigation (Sharan & Shaulov, 1990) explored the benefits of these small-group programs for supporting intrinsic motivation. These two programs allow students to explore a topic or conduct an in-depth experiment without incorporating reward structures that are likely to undermine intrinsic motivation. Hänze & Berger (2007) found that Jigsaw supported intrinsic motivation. However, results for Group Investigation are mixed, with some indicating enhanced intrinsic motivation (Sharan & Shaulov, 1990), no benefit (Tan, Lee, & Sharan, 2007), or motivational declines (Shachar & Fischer, 2004) relative to a control group. However, Tan et al. (2007) and Shachar and Fischer (2004) both suggested that their unexpected findings should be interpreted cautiously given that the group work in these studies were temporally close to a national exam, and students found the grouping technique less appropriate when preparing for the national exam.

Studies have also explored how specific features of group work benefit motivational outcomes. Ciani, Summers, Easter, and Sheldon (2008) examined whether choice of group membership benefits intrinsic motivation. This question fits within a SDT framework because autonomy supportive teachers provide students with choice in ways that facilitate intrinsic motivation (Ryan & Deci, 2000a). Ciana et al.'s (2008) results were in line with SDT; students in university classes that were offered choices when selecting their groups reported significantly higher intrinsic motivation, even after accounting for students' perceptions of teachers' autonomy support and differences in class size.

In another approach for examining how group work supports intrinsic motivation, studies have investigated whether program features that support students' basic needs (autonomy, competence, relatedness) lead to intrinsic motivation. In line with these proposed relations, Hänze and Berger (2007) found that Jigsaw led to enhanced intrinsic motivation and deeper processing in high school physics due to Jigsaw's support for students' basic needs. Additionally, they found that physics students with low initial academic self-concept in physics benefited from group learning relative to direct instruction because Jigsaw supported their competence, suggesting an added benefit of Jigsaw for students with low academic self-concept.

Finally, studies of university and vocational students' coursework suggest that support for students' basic needs predicts situational interest (Boekaerts & Minnaert, 2006; Minnaert et al., 2007). Minnaert et al. (2007) explored how each basic need may play a varying role in explaining situational interest over the course of a long-term group project. Perceptions of relatedness support enhanced motivation across all phases of the project. In contrast, competence needs contributed most to explaining motivation during the orientation or initial planning phase of the project. Autonomy support afforded by group collaboration gained importance for situational interest later in the project, during the execution and closing phases.

Summary and Future Directions

Group research using self-determination theory has focused on how particular program features enhance intrinsic motivation and situational interest. Results indicate a benefit of pedagogical strategies that promote choice and facilitate students' needs for autonomy, competence, and relatedness. Boekaerts and her colleagues (Boekaerts & Minnaert, 2006; Minnaert et al., 2007) further extended this work by examining the uniquely facilitative role for each basic need during varying phases of a group project.

One program feature whose impact remains under considerable debate and warrants continued attention is the influence of reward structures. There has been significant debate in the motivation literature regarding the influence of rewards on intrinsic motivation (Ryan & Deci, 2000b), with a series of meta-analyses indicating that tangible rewards that are contingent on task performance undermine intrinsic motivation. The interpretation has been that rewards have an undermining effect on intrinsic motivation when they are perceived as trying to control behavior (i.e., low autonomy support). However, when the informational component of rewards is made salient, rewards do not have this same undermining effect due to support for competence and autonomy.

Although a number of group programs employ incentive structures to foster engagement and accountability, the evaluation studies of these programs have not examined motivational outcomes (Slavin, 1996). It is not clear whether the results from motivation research with individuals can be generalized to small-group learning. On the one hand, rewards may not have the same undermining effect if group rewards foster interdependence (Slavin, 1996) and consequently foster feelings of competence, relatedness, and cohesion. In addition, because students take on more responsibility for their learning during group tasks, it may be that autonomy support is more salient for students relative to the extrinsic, controlling aspect of rewards. Alternatively, if students perceive these group rewards as controlling, they may have a deleterious impact on intrinsic motivation. Thus, the influence of reward structures in groups on intrinsic motivation, engagement, and learning is a worthwhile extension for future research. In this work, it will also be important to differentiate competition from extrinsic rewards.

SOCIAL COGNITIVE THEORY

Social cognitive theory is grounded in the principle that learning new behavior is influenced by both social interactions and aspects of the individual (Bandura, 1997). The theoretical framework of triadic reciprocity describes the mutual interactions among (a) personal cognitive, affective, and biological factors, (b) behavior, and (c) environmental influences that jointly affect learning and engagement (Bandura, 1997). One of the most powerful personal factors in social cognitive theory is self-efficacy beliefs (Bandura, 1997). Self-efficacy refers to an individual's belief in his or her ability to succeed in a particular academic domain or on a given task. Self-efficacy beliefs are important because they affect students' choices, effort, persistence, and academic performance (Schunk & Pajares, 2005). It is not surprising then that students engage in tasks in which they feel a sense of efficacy and avoid tasks in which they do not. Self-efficacy is positively associated with effort, persistence, and deep levels of cognitive processing (Greene & Miller, 1996; Nolen, 1988; Pintrich, 2000) as well as achievement in a variety of domains (Linnenbrink & Pintrich, 2003; Multon, Brown, & Lent, 1991).When encountering obstacles, highly efficacious students are more likely to attribute difficulty to low effort or skills, both of which can be improved in the future.

Self-efficacy is shaped by four primary sources (Bandura, 1997). Mastery experiences, such as successful completion of challenging tasks, are the strongest predictors of self-efficacy (Usher & Pajares, 2008). Students also build efficacy beliefs through the vicarious experience of observing teachers and peers. When students observe other's successful behaviors, they can contrast their own capabilities in relation to observed behavior, and then form judgments about the likelihood of success, informing their self-efficacy beliefs. In addition, verbal and social persuasions, such as encouragement from teachers or peers, also support self-efficacy. Finally, self-efficacy can be influenced by emotional and physiological states such as experienced anxiety or mood. For instance, heightened anxiety may trigger a reduction in self-efficacy.

When considering these four sources of efficacy, it seems reasonable that small groups may promote efficacy beliefs. Perhaps most relevant is the role of vicarious learning. During group work, students may benefit from opportunities to observe and model behavior and strategies. In addition, group members may provide positive feedback (i.e., verbal persuasion) when they value an individual's task contributions. However, there are also potential challenges to self-efficacy beliefs. Students may not always model and learn the most productive behaviors. Also, it may be easier to undermine a group member's self-efficacy via negative feedback or discouragement (Bandura, 1997). And, as noted previously, vicarious learning may not universally enhance self-efficacy, as some students may use this information to infer that they are less able. Bandura's (1997) characterization of collective efficacy is also particularly relevant to the role of efficacy beliefs during collaboration. Collective efficacy refers to a group's shared belief in their team's capabilities to execute tasks and produce a specific level of attainment (Bandura, 1997). Thus, in addition to individual efficacy, group-level efficacy may be particularly important for supporting students' learning and engagement in small-group settings.

Influence of Group Programs and Features on Academic Self-Efficacy

Prior research suggests that collaborative learning promotes individuals' self-efficacy beliefs in introductory physics (Fencl & Scheel, 2004) and among nonphysics majors enrolled in science classes (Fencl & Scheel, 2005).Very little research, however, has identified specific program features that shape efficacy beliefs, although the findings from self-determination theory related to competence needs provide some insight (see earlier review).

More fine-grained qualitative investigations of group interactions suggest, however, that not all group interactions are likely to support self-efficacy, as some group members exhibit highly disrespectful and critical feedback toward other's task work (Linnenbrink-Garcia, Rogat, & Koskey, 2011; Rogat & Linnenbrink-Garcia, 2011). While not specifically examining repercussions for lowered self-efficacy, these observed negative group interactions may lower self-efficacy through negative verbal persuasion. Additionally, negative group interactions had consequences for discouraging participation, experienced negative affect (i.e., frustration), and the quality of socially shared regulation. These findings bring into question the extent to which students benefit from vicarious learning experiences in small-group settings, especially when a group member is openly criticized or discouraged from participating.

Finally, it is important to note the potential benefit of group settings for supporting collective efficacy. Specifically, tasks that require group members to work interdependently and in coordination may help to foster collective efficacy (Shamir, 1990; Weldon & Weingart, 1993). As noted below, the establishment of collective group efficacy may be especially important for shaping group learning outcomes (cf., Gully, Incalcaterra, Joshi, & Beaubien, 2002).

Role of Self-Efficacy in Group Learning and Engagement

Students' level of self-efficacy within the group can potentially increase the quality of students' collaborative interaction and group performance. Groups with higher self-efficacy were more likely to use deep-level strategies, engage in higher quality discussions, and demonstrate higher group performance (Wang & Lin, 2007). Additionally, collaboration may be strengthened when group members establish collective efficacy (Gully et al., 2002). And, collective efficacy may lead group members to use resources more effectively and exert greater effort on tasks, even when they encounter difficulties (Bandura, 2002). Although the level of individual self-efficacy for each group member is related to the overall collective efficacy of the group, it is still possible that groups can establish high collective efficacy beliefs even when all group members do not individually feel efficacious (Gibson, 1999). The potential benefits of collective efficacy for group performance may also vary as function of task demands. Katz-Navon and Erez (2005) found that when interdependence was low among group members there was a stronger relation between individual self-efficacy and group performance. However, when groups engaged in tasks that required high interdependence, collective efficacy was a better predictor of group effectiveness and performance.

Summary and Future Directions

Group researchers examining self-efficacy point to the reciprocal relation between self-efficacy beliefs and academic and social collaborative outcomes. These findings maintain that self-efficacy beliefs contribute to the quality of group performance and that high quality collaborative interactions support individual student's personal efficacy beliefs. More recently, researchers have examined whether group interactions lead to the development of collective efficacy. This research found that the quality of group members' interactions appeared to mediate the relation between collaborative learning, efficacy beliefs, and performance. That is, when group members function interdependently, collective efficacy beliefs had a greater impact on performance than when tasks were divided among group members.

The extant research provides initial steps toward understanding the role peers have in fostering feelings of efficacy. In considering possible avenues for research it may be interesting to consider how particular conditions influence efficacy beliefs. For instance, complex tasks may exceed students' perceptions of a moderate level of challenge, with consequences for efficacy. One future direction is to consider the role of task scaffolding for facilitating motivation and ensuring that group tasks build efficacy. Future research should also consider whether task elements can be adapted to foster both individual and collective self-efficacy based on the four primary sources of self-efficacy (mastery experiences, vicarious experiences, verbal persuasion, and physiological experiences). As noted earlier, small-group settings have the potential to enhance self-efficacy via the first three sources, but there are also potential pitfalls that may reduce self-efficacy via these same mechanisms. Furthermore, researchers may also benefit from examining the process by which collective efficacy develops within the group.

CONCLUSION

Through a synthesis of research on motivation in collaborative and cooperative groups, our review explored two questions: (a) how does group work shape students' motivation and (b) how does motivation shape learning and engagement within small groups? Our synthesis suggests that group research has primarily investigated particular program features that may promote motivation. However, this research does not often consider current motivational theory when establishing these programs, nor have researchers consistently evaluated the impact of small-group programs on motivational outcomes. Adding to this dearth of research, motivational researchers primarily investigate motivation for individual learners, examining the benefits of fostering motivation for supporting high quality engagement, strategy use, and learning.

Although we organized this chapter by examining how groups shape motivation and the role of motivation in small groups, much can be gained from considering how these processes work in combination. Bridging these areas may provide a richer understanding of how program features optimize both motivation and group functioning. From this perspective, motivation can be conceptualized as mediating the impact of group features on student outcomes. That is, we can identify particular motivating features of small-group instruction that promote high quality motivation during group work, which in turn supports students' engagement and learning.

Using the integration of motivation and group research as a starting point, we propose several recommendations for future research. From a group research perspective, it is important to consider how using a motivational lens informs the design of small-group instruction. Specifically, motivation theories help in identifying features that foster student motivation during group work. When programs foster mastery, enjoyment, and feelings of relatedness, autonomy, and competence, student engagement and learning is enhanced. These principles derived from current motivational theories and research conducted in group settings can work in coordination with the expertise of group researchers to formulate design principles for small-group programs.

Our synthesis proposes four initial recommendations for program design, grounded in motivation research. First, we can no longer assume that working with peers in groups is sufficient for motivating students in ways that benefit engagement and learning. Working in small groups raises significant challenges for motivation. Second, group research should design group programs that integrate some of the recommendations derived from motivational research in individual and group contexts. Third, programs should extend beyond a focus on interest and rewards as strategies for fostering motivation. Motivational research highlights the need for caution when relying on rewards and competition to facilitate high quality motivation in group settings and suggests that a broader range of motivation principles should be incorporated. For instance, introducing strategies for modeling effective behaviors and providing positive feedback before introducing criticism, and using authentic group tasks may help to support high quality motivation. Finally, to better assess the effectiveness of group instruction in supporting motivation, we recommend designing program evaluations to examine how features of small-group instruction impact several aspects of motivation including achievement goals, individual and collective academic self-efficacy, and intrinsic motivation or situational interest.

Bridging the areas of motivation and group research is not unidirectional, and motivation research has much to learn from research conducted in groups. There is richness to studying motivation in group contexts because of the dynamic nature of motivational processes during social interaction, which is not captured by relying on an individual difference perspective. Social constructivist and situative perspectives that consider how students jointly coconstruct meaning and negotiate multiple perspectives are central to research on groups, but is just beginning to inform motivation research (Nolen & Ward, 2008). Methodologically, it is not sufficient to aggregate the motivation of individual group members when drawing conclusions about the dynamics of motivation within a group (Hickey, 2003).

The initial research exploring the shared nature of motivation has considered the implications of group achievement goals and collective efficacy. These studies raise important questions for further understanding the shared nature of motivation and highlight some challenges to motivating group work. For instance, initial findings raise concerns for establishing group performance goals with consequences for fostering disengagement (Hijzen et al., 2007; Kempler et al., 2003). Similarly, negotiating academic goals (Summers, 2006) and engaging in social comparison within the group (Kempler & Linnenbrink, 2004) may significantly undermine the quality of group motivation.

A consideration of these issues suggests several new avenues for research, particularly regarding the conceptualization of motivation as co-constructed among group members. For example, how does establishing shared motivation benefit group and individual outcomes? It is possible that group collaboration may elevate the quality of motivation for those group members with less adaptive motivation (i.e., lower efficacy, extrinsic motivation, performance-avoidance goal orientations). Moreover, research should also examine how shared, group-level motivation relates to productive engagement and learning for the entire group. To date, only a few studies have considered these processes at the group level. The nature of coconstructed motivation also raises questions about how shared motivation develops across time. Finally, it is important to understand how individual and group processes work together to explain group outcomes.

Advancing motivation research will require new methodologies that examine the shared nature of group activity and how shared motivation changes over time. In addition, we should extend beyond a limited conceptualization that separates individual's entering orientations from the shared motivation among group members into two distinct programs of research (Järvelä et al., 2010). Instead, future research needs to consider how multiple individuals with entering orientations jointly construct their motivation for the group task. In addition, drawing on the rich research histories of both small-group research and motivational research will be critical for further advancing research in this area and for informing practice.

NOTE

1. Academic goals are distinct from achievement goals as specified in achievement goal theory.

REFERENCES

Ames, C. (1992). Classrooms: Goals, structures, and student motivation. *Journal of Educational Psychology, 84*, 261–271.

Aronson, E. (1978). *The jigsaw classroom*. Beverly Hills, CA: Sage.

Bandura, A. (1997). *Self-efficacy: The exercise of control*. New York: Freeman.

Bandura, A. (2002). Social cognitive theory in cultural context. *Applied Psychology: An International Review, 51*, 269–290.

Barron, B. (2003). When smart groups fail. *Journal of the Learning Sciences, 12*, 307–359.

Bergin, D. A. (1999). Influences on classroom interest. *Educational Psychologist, 34*, 87–98.

Blumenfeld, P. C., Kempler, T. M., & Krajcik, J. S. (2006). Motivation and cognitive engagement in learning environments. In K. Sawyer (Ed.), *The Cambridge handbook of the learning sciences* (pp. 475–488). New York: Cambridge University Press.

Boekaerts, M., & Minnaert, A. (2006).Affective and motivational outcomes of working in collaborative groups. *Educational Psychology, 26*, 187–208.

Church, M. A., Elliot, A. J., & Gable, S. L. (2001). Perceptions of classroom environment, achievement goals, and achievement outcomes. *Journal of Educational Psychology, 93*, 43–54.

Ciani, K. D., Summers, J. J., Easter, M. A., & Sheldon, K. M. (2008). Collaborative learning and positive experiences: Does letting students choose their own groups matter? *Educational Psychology, 28*, 627–641.

Cohen, E. G. (1994). *Designing group work: Strategies for the heterogeneous classroom* (2nd ed.). New York: Teachers College Press.

deCharms, R. (1968). *Personal causation*. New York: Academic Press.

Deutsch, M. (1949). An experimental study of the effects of co-operation and competition upon group process. *Human Relations, 2*, 197–292.

Dillenbourg P. (1999). What do you mean by collaborative learning? In P. Dillenbourg (Ed), *Collaborative-learning: Cognitive and computational approaches* (pp. 1–19). Oxford, England: Elsevier.

Durik, A. M., & Harackiewicz, J. M. (2007). Different strokes for different folks: How individual interest moderates the effects of situational factors on task interest. *Journal of Educational Psychology, 99*, 597–610.

Dweck, C., & Leggett, E. (1988).A social-cognitive approach to motivation and personality. *Psychological Review, 95,* 256–273.

Elliot, A. J. (1999). Approach and avoidance motivation and achievement goals. *Educational Psychologist, 34,* 169–189.

Elliot, A. J., McGregor, H. A., & Gable, S. (1999). Achievement goals, study strategies and exam performance: A mediational analysis. *Journal of Educational Psychology, 91,* 549–563.

Fencl, H., & Scheel, K. (2004). Pedagogical approaches, contextual variables, and the development of student self-efficacy in undergraduate physic courses. In J. Marx, S. Franklin, & K. Cummings (Eds.), *Physics Education Research Conference, AIP Conference Proceedings* (720), 173–176, Melville, NY: AIP.

Fencl, H., & Scheel, K. (2005).Engaging students. An examination of the effects of teaching strategies on self-efficacy and course climate in a non-majors' physics course. *Journal of College Science Teaching, 35,* 20–24.

Freeman, J. G., McPhail, J. C., & Berndt, J. A. (2002). Sixth graders' views of activities that do and do not help them learn. *The Elementary School Journal, 102,* 335–347.

Gibson, C. B. (1999). Do they do what they believe they can? Group efficacy beliefs and group performance across tasks and cultures. *Academy of Management Journal, 42,* 138–152.

Graham, S., & Golan, S. (1991). Motivational influences on cognition: Task involvement, ego involvement, and depth of information processing. *Journal of Educational Psychology, 83,* 187–194.

Greene, B. A. & Miller, R. B. (1996). Influences on course achievement: Goals, perceived ability, and cognitive engagement. *Contemporary Educational Psychology, 21,* 181–192.

Gully, S. M., Incalcaterra, K. A., Joshi, A., & Beaubien, J. M. (2002). A meta-analysis of team efficacy, potency, and performance: Interdependence and level of analysis as moderators of observed relationships. *Journal of Applied Psychology, 87,* 819–832.

Hänze, M., & Berger, R. (2007). Cooperative learning, motivational effects, and student characteristics: An experimental study comparing cooperative learning and direct instruction in 12th grade physics classes. *Learning and Instruction, 17,* 29–41.

Harackiewicz, J. M., Barron, K. E., & Elliot, A. J. (1998). Rethinking achievement goals: When are they adaptive for college students and why? *Educational Psychologist, 33,* 1–21.

Hickey, D. T. (2003). Engaged participation versus marginal nonparticipation: A stridently sociocultural approach to achievement motivation. *The Elementary School Journal, 103,* 401–429.

Hidi, S., & Renninger, K. A. (2006). The four-phase model of interest development. *Educational Psychologist, 41,* 111–127.

Hijzen, D., Boekaerts, M., & Vedder, P. H. (2007). Exploring the links between students' engagement in cooperative learning, their goal preferences and appraisals of instructional conditions in the classroom. *Learning & Instruction, 17,* 673–687.

Huang, C. (2011). Achievement goals and achievement emotions: A meta-analysis. *Educational Psychology Review, 23,* 359–388.

Järvelä, S., Volet, S., & Järvenoja, H. (2010). Research on motivation in collaborative learning: Moving beyond the cognitive-situative divide and combining individual and social processes. *Educational Psychologist, 45, 15–27.*

Johnson, D. W., & Johnson, R. T. (1991). *Learning together and alone: Cooperative, competitive, and individualistic learning* (3rd ed.). Englewood Cliffs, NJ: Prentice Hall.

Kaplan, A. (2004). Achievement goals and intergroup relations. In P. R. Pintrich & M. L. Maehr (Eds.), *Advances of motivation and achievement: Motivating students, improving schools; The legacy of Carol Midgley* (pp. 97–136). Stamford, CT: JAI Press.

Karabenick, S. A. (2004). Perceived achievement goal structure and college student help seeking. *Journal of Educational Psychology, 96,* 569–581.

Karau, S. J., & Williams, K. D. (1997). The effects of group cohesiveness on social loafing and social compensation. *Group Dynamics: Theory, Research and Practice, 1,* 156–168.

Katz-Navon, T., & Erez, M. (2005).When collective- and self-efficacy affect team performance: The role of task interdependence. *Small Group Research*, *36*, 437–465.

Kempler, T. M., Hruda, L. Z., & Maehr, M. L. (2003, April). *Engaging students in cooperative learning tasks: Individual and group-level factors.* Paper presented at the Annual Convention of the American Educational Research Association, Chicago, IL.

Kempler, T. M., & Linnenbrink, E. A. (2004, April). *Re-examining the influence of competition structures in group contexts: Implications for social and cognitive interactions in small groups.* Paper presented at the Annual Convention of the American Educational Research Association, San Diego.

Krapp, A. (2005). Basic needs and the development of interest and intrinsic motivational orientations. *Learning and Instruction, 15,* 381–395.

Levy, I., Kaplan, A., & Patrick, H. (2004). Early adolescents' achievement goals, social status, and attitudes towards cooperation with peers. *Social Psychology of Education, 7,* 127–159.
Linnenbrink., E. A. (2005). The dilemma of performance-approach goals: The use of multiple goal contexts to promote students' motivation and learning. *Journal of Educational Psychology, 97,* 197–213.
Linnenbrink, E. A., & Pintrich, P. R. (2000). Multiple pathways to learning and achievement: The role of goal orientation in fostering adaptive motivation, affect, and cognition. In C. Sansone & J. M. Harackiewicz (Eds.), *Intrinsic and extrinsic motivation: The search for optimal motivation and performance* (pp. 195–227). San Diego, CA: Academic Press.
Linnenbrink, E. A., & Pintrich, P. R. (2003). The role of self-efficacy beliefs in student engagement and learning in the classroom. *Reading & Writing Quarterly, 19,* 119–137.
Linnenbrink-Garcia, L., Patall, E. A., & Messersmith, E. E. (2012). Antecedents and consequences of situational interest. *British Journal of Educational Psychology.* Advance online prublcation: doi:10.111/j.2044-8279.2012.02080.X.
Linnenbrink-Garcia, E. A., Rogat, T. K., & Koskey, K. L. (2011). Affect and engagement during small group instruction. *Contemporary Educational Psychology, 36,* 13–24.
Linnenbrink-Garcia, L., Tyson, D. F., & Patall, E. A. (2008). When are achievement goal orientations beneficial for academic achievement? A closer look at moderating factors. *International Review of Social Psychology, 21,* 19–70.
Maehr, M. L. & Midgley, C. (1996). *Transforming school cultures.* Boulder, CO: Westview Press.
Maehr, M. L., & Zusho, A. (2009). Achievement goal theory: The past, present, and future. In K. R. Wenzel & A. Wigfield (Eds.), *Handbook of motivation at school* (pp. 77–104). New York: Routledge.
Middleton, M., & Midgley, C. (1997). Avoiding the demonstration of lack of ability: An under-explored aspect of goal theory. *Journal of Educational Psychology, 89,* 710–718.
Midgley, C., Kaplan, A., & Middleton, M. (2001). Performance-approach goals: Good for what, for whom, under what circumstances, and at what cost? *Journal of Educational Psychology, 93,* 77–86.
Minnaert, A., Boekaerts, M., & deBrabander, C. (2007). Autonomy, competence, and social relatedness in task interest within project-based education. *Psychological Reports, 101,* 574–586.
Mitchell, M. (1993). Situational interest: Its multifaceted structure in the secondary school mathematics classroom. *Journal of Educational Psychology, 85,* 424–436.
Multon, K. D., Brown, S. D., & Lent, R. W. (1991). Relation of self-efficacy beliefs to academic outcomes: A meta-analytic investigation. *Journal of Counseling Psychology, 38,* 30–38.
Nicholls, J. D. (1996). The effects of cooperative learning on achievement and motivation in a high school geometry class. *Contemporary Educational Psychology, 21,* 467–476.
Nicholls, J. D., & Miller, R. B. (1994).Cooperative learning and student motivation. *Contemporary Educational Psychology, 19,* 167–178.
Nolen, S. B. (1988). Reasons for studying: Motivational orientations and study strategies. *Cognition and Instruction, 5,* 269–287.
Nolen, S. B. (2007). Young children's motivation to read and write: Development in social contexts. *Cognition and Instruction, 25,* 219–270.
Nolen, S. B., & Ward, C. (2008).Sociocultural and situative approaches to studying motivation. In M. L. Maehr, S. A. Karabenick, & T. C. Urdan (Eds.), *Advances in motivation and achievement: Social psychological perspectives* (Vol. 15, pp. 425–460). Stamford, CT: JAI Press.
O'Donnell, A. M., & O'Kelly, J. (1994). Learning from peers: Beyond the rhetoric of positive results. *Educational Psychology Review, 4,* 321–349.
Palincsar, A. S., & Brown, A. L. (1984).Reciprocal teaching of comprehension-fostering and comprehension-monitoring activities. *Cognition and Instruction, 1,* 117–175.
Patrick, H., Anderman, L. H., Ryan, A. M., Edelin, K., & Midgley, C. (2001).Teachers' communication of goal orientations in four fifth-grade classrooms. *The Elementary School Journal, 102,* 35–58.
Pintrich, P. R. (2000). Multiple goals, multiple pathways: The role of goal orientation in learning and achievement. *Journal of Educational Psychology, 92,* 544–555.
Rogat, T. K., & Linnenbrink-Garcia, L. (2011). Socially shared regulation in collaborative groups: An analysis of the interplay between quality of social regulation and group process. *Cognition and Instruction, 29,* 375–415.
Ruble, D., & Frey, K. (1991). Changing patterns of comparative behavior as skills are acquired: A functional model of self-evaluation. In J. Suls & T. A. Wills (Eds.), *Social comparison: Contemporary theory and research* (pp. 79–113). Hillsdale, NJ: Erlbaum.
Ryan, R. M., & Deci, E. L. (2000a). Intrinsic and extrinsic motivations: Classic definitions and new directions. *Contemporary Educational Psychology, 25,* 54–67.

Ryan, R. M., & Deci, E. L. (2000b). When rewards compete with nature: The undermining of intrinsic motivation and self-regulation. In C. Sansone & J. M. Harackiewicz (Eds.), *Intrinsic and extrinsic motivation: The search for optimal motivation and performance* (pp. 13–54). San Diego, CA: Academic Press.

Schiefele, U. (2009). Situational and individual interest. In K. R. Wentzel & A. Wigfield (Eds.), *Handbook of motivation at school* (pp. 197–222). New York: Routledge.

Schunk, D. H., & Pajares, F. (2005). Self-efficacy and competency beliefs in academic function. In A. J. Elliot & C. Dweck (Eds.), *Handbook of competence and motivation* (pp. 281–303). New York: Guilford.

Shachar, H., & Fischer, S. (2004). Cooperative learning and the achievement of motivation and perceptions of students in 11th grade chemistry classes. *Learning and Instruction, 14*, 69–87.

Shamir, B. (1990). Calculations, values, and identities: The sources of collectivistic work motivation. *Human Relations, 43*, 313–332.

Sharan, S., & Shaulov, A. (1990). Cooperative learning, motivation to learn, and academic achievement. In S. Sharan (Ed.), *Cooperative learning: Theory and research* (pp. 173–202). New York: Praeger.

Skaalvik, E. M. (1997). Self-enhancing and self-defeating ego orientation: Relations with task and avoidance orientation, achievement, self-perceptions, and anxiety. *Journal of Educational Psychology, 89*, 71–81.

Slavin, R. E. (1995). *Cooperative learning: Theory, research, and practice* (2nd ed.). Boston, MA: Allyn & Bacon.

Slavin, R. E. (1996). Research for the future: Research on cooperative learning and achievement: What we know, what we need to know. *Contemporary Educational Psychology, 21*, 43–69.

Summers, J. S. (2006).Effects of collaborative learning in math on sixth graders' individual goal orientations from a socioconstructivist perspective. *The Elementary School Journal, 106*, 273–290.

Tan, I. G. C., Lee, C. K. E., & Sharan, S. (2007). Group investigation effects on achievement, motivation, and perceptions of students in Singapore. *Journal of Educational Research, 100*, 142–154.

Usher, E. L., & Pajares, F. (2008). Sources of self-efficacy in school: Critical review of the literature and future directions. *Review of Educational Research, 78*, 751–796.

Wang, S. L., & Lin, S. S. J. (2007).The application of social cognitive theory to web-based learning through NetPorts. *British Journal of Educational Technology, 38*, 600–612.

Webb, N. M., Ing, M., Kersting, N., & Nemer, K. M. (2006). Help seeking in cooperative learning groups. In S. A. Karabenick & R. S. Newman (Eds.), *Academic help seeking: Goals, groups and contexts* (pp. 45–88). Mahwah, NJ: Erlbaum.

Webb, N. M., & Palincsar, A. S. (1996). Group processes in the classroom. In D. Berliner & R. Calfee (Eds.), *Handbook of educational psychology* (pp. 841–873). New York: Macmillan.

Weldon, E., &Weingart, L.R. (1993). Group goals and group performance. *British Journal of Social Psychology, 32*, 307–334.

Wigfield, A., Eccles, J. S., Schiefele, U., Roeser, R. W., & Davis-Kean, P. (2006). Development of achievement motivation. In N. Eisenberg, W. Damon, & R. M. Lerner (Eds.), *Handbook of child psychology: Vol. 3. Social, emotional, and personality development* (6th ed., pp. 933–1002). Hoboken, NJ: Wiley.

15

CHILD LEADERS IN COLLABORATIVE GROUPS

BRIAN MILLER, JINGJING SUN, XIAOYING WU, AND RICHARD C. ANDERSON

University of Illinois at Urbana-Champaign

In the past, leadership has not been a commonly used construct in research on children's group work. Students who assist others are often called helpers or peer-tutors (Webb & Palincsar, 1996) or simply more advanced students. In this chapter we will make the argument that the leadership construct can be an important addition to the list of constructs for understanding the dynamics of cooperative groups. It describes a type of dynamic not addressed by other constructs and focuses on important issues not usually considered in research on classroom learning and instruction.

Furthermore, using the construct of leadership can help to integrate research involving groups within the classroom and research involving groups in business, industry, military, and civic settings. Leadership as a construct has a long research history and has spawned many theories (Chemers, 2000). It has been a major emphasis in conceptions of school reform (Spillane, Halverson, & Diamond, 2004) and teacher training (Harris, 2003). However, leadership has not been emphasized in scholarly research on how students work amongst themselves in groups. If this were to change, research on classroom learning could utilize and enrich a large research base. In addition, this integration of fields could lead to a school curriculum to better prepare students for the 21st century business world in which leadership ability is increasingly valued.

As a personal endorsement, our interest in children's leadership began only unintentionally as we discovered its explanatory power in describing the dynamics of student interactions during Collaborative Reasoning (CR) discussions (Anderson, Chinn, Waggoner, & Nguyen, 1998). CR is an approach to discussion in which small groups of children meet to discuss a dilemma raised by a story. When research on CR began, we did not believe that leadership was a salient issue, because in CR discussions leaders are not nominated by teachers or otherwise officially appointed. However, CR uses free participation, so while the teacher is present as a guide, students are in charge of their own turn taking and topic management. As we watched CR discussions unfold in many diverse classrooms, we watched again and again as one or more students spontaneously emerged to take the role of guiding the discussions while other students spontaneously followed their guidance (Li et al., 2007).

DEFINING LEADERSHIP

As with many popular constructs, leadership has a multitude of definitions in and out of the research community. Many of these definitions focus on the traits of leaders. Owen (2007) found that many young children equate leadership with being "bossy," whereas older children thought that leaders should be confident, kind, clever, and good listeners. Teachers views student leaders as confident, expressive, independent, good listeners, and helpful to others. These findings suggest that both teachers and older students identify leadership as a characteristic of individuals who are both extroverted and nice. The trait definition of leadership has also been used by researchers who conceptualize leadership as a set of characteristics that are possessed by individuals in positions of power.

The trait definition of leadership is useful and some findings in this tradition that are applicable to education will be reviewed in this chapter. However, in the context of collaborative learning, we need a definition of leadership that focuses on an interpersonal phenomenon that can help shape and improve group interactions. Therefore, we will primarily define leadership as the reciprocal social processes in which some individuals guide, coordinate, or enhance the behavior of other individuals. This definition has several key features. First, it is a broad set of processes rather than a trait or skill. Second, as a process, leader and follower roles can be performed by single persons or by multiple people, and the individuals performing these roles can change over time. Third, the process must be reciprocal, because it requires the coordinated action of leaders and followers. As a result of these three features, leadership can be seen as an emergent property of the interaction of a group of leaders and followers rather than as merely the summative actions of individuals (Spillane et al., 2004).

The following transcript from Brigid Barron's article "When Smart Groups Fail" (2003, pp. 242–243) illustrates the value of a process definition of leadership. Three boys are trying to solve a difficult math word problem about a person in a boat trying to get home:

Adam: Now, seven and a half.
Ben: No, eight.
Adam: Times twenty-four.
Ben: No times eight. That's eight miles an hour, times eight.
Carlos: Eight miles an hour, it goes eight miles an hour.
Adam: Listen.
Ben: Wait, what time is?
Adam: Shut up, I'm right.
Carlos: Wait a minute.
Ben: What?
Carlos: If it takes him eight miles an hour, it will take him 3 hours!
Ben: What are you talking about?

While all three boys attempt to be leaders of the group, successful leadership does not occur. The attempts at leadership do not lead to coordinated action because it seems none of the three is able or willing to follow. Leaders and followers need to coordinate their behavior for leadership to succeed, especially in collaborative groups in which people cannot just do their own thing.

The coordination of individuals needed for effective leadership is most likely to occur over time through group interaction. Furthermore, individuals need certain skills for this development to occur. As the leadership develops in groups, each individual has the opportunity to develop new leadership skills. For this reason, leadership as a process can be both a means to making group learning more effective as well as a valuable learning goal itself.

LEADERSHIP AND RELATED CONSTRUCTS

There are constructs well known in cooperative group research that share features with the construct of leadership. In order to better understand the construct of leadership and how it might benefit education, we will discuss the similarities and differences between leadership and the related constructs of helping behavior, peer-tutoring, cooperative learning skills, and scaffolding.

Helping Behavior and Peer Tutoring

Helping behavior is the giving and receiving of assistance during collaborative group work (Webb & Palincsar, 1996). Peer-tutoring can be seen as a formalization of helping behavior into an instructional design in which one child teaches another (Rohrbeck, Ginsburg-Block, Fantuzzo, & Miller, 2003). While this teaching technique can be enacted in a unidirectional or reciprocal fashion (Fantuzzo, King, & Heller, 1992; Palincsar & Brown, 1984) at any one moment the task is directional so that one student teaches another. Students' motivation and achievement have been shown to increase—both those being helped and those doing the helping—by means of helping behavior and peer-tutoring (Cohen, Kulik, & Kulik 1982; Webb & Palincsar, 1996).

However, not all "helping" is effective. Helping behavior is not successful unless both the giver and receiver of help seek a quality interaction. The student seeking help needs to ask for a thorough explanation, the student giving help needs to provide it, and they both need to persist in the activity until the student has reached a better understanding and has succeeded in applying it (Webb & Mastergeorge, 2003). For this reason, successful peer tutors need to learn certain skills such as asking explanatory questions, providing enough wait time, and giving feedback and encouragement. Leadership is very similar to helping and peer-tutoring in that all three constructs require high quality, coordinated interactions between individuals, coordination which develops over time.

What differentiates leadership from helping behavior and peer-tutoring is that leadership is a broader construct. If we place these constructs on a continuum of behavior ranging from purely procedural to purely inspirational, helping and peer-tutoring would cover a range including procedural knowledge about tasks, explanations of underlying concepts, and immediate motivation. Leadership covers a wider range on this continuum in both directions. On the mundane side, leadership also includes organizing, structuring, and managing group activities. On the more lofty side, leadership includes providing a vision of the group's ultimate mission. In this way, the concept of leadership is akin to the idea of being a classroom teacher. A teacher helps students by scaffolding their learning. However, a teacher also manages the classroom, motivates students, and provides a vision of what learning means. In this way, leadership is like teaching in its broadest sense.

Cooperative Learning

There are five widely accepted key elements to successful cooperative learning: positive interdependence, individual accountability, promotive interaction, social skills, and group processing (Gillies, 2007; Johnson, Johnson, & Holubec, 1998). Of these, promotive interaction and social skills are both constructs similar to leadership. Johnson and Johnson (1999, p. 71) describe promotive interaction as "helping, assisting, supporting, encouraging, and praising each other's efforts to achieve." This description covers a very similar breadth of behavior to our definition of leadership, which might be thought of as a perspective on how and why promotive interaction can occur.

Social skills are a broader construct than leadership and include all types of interactive skills including those that go beyond the context of leadership such as sharing, making friends, and having a sense of humor. According to many cooperative learning researchers, some key social skills must be explicitly taught if children are to benefit from small-group experiences (Gilles & Ashman, 1998). While social skills certainly are needed for leadership, in our perspective leadership is not a set of skills. Like promotive interactions, it is a process that requires coordination across individuals.

Scaffolding

We want to suggest that the constructs of leadership and scaffolding can complement each other. Leadership, helping, peer tutoring, and peer scaffolding are all processes that occur between two or more coordinated students. However, scaffolding is a construct that is embedded in a model of sociocultural learning. Wood, Bruner, and Ross (1976), explained that scaffolding is the "process that enables a child or novice to solve a problem, carry out a task, or achieve a goal which would be beyond his unassisted efforts" (p. 90). Cazden (1979) connected the idea of scaffolding with the Vygotskian concept of the zone of proximal development, which is the cognitive region between what a student can accomplish by themselves and what they can accomplish with the assistance of a more knowledgeable other. Scaffolding became the name for the type of assistance a more knowledgeable other performs to bridge the zone of proximal development (Rogoff, 1990).

Unlike scaffolding, leadership is not inherently connected to sociocultural theory, and it includes both teaching and learning tasks and the coordination, guidance, and motivation of individuals who may already be highly capable. One valuable theoretical goal of research into the leadership process in collaborative groups will likely be an attempt to create a synthesis between the sociocultural theory and the organizational perspective of leadership theories.

LEADERSHIP—AGGRESSION AND DOMINANCE

Unfortunately, leadership is not always a positive force. Leadership can be abused. Dominance is the dark side of leadership, and it is not unknown in children's groups (Pettit, Bakshi, Dodge, & Coie, 1990). Unlike prosocial forms of leadership, dominance hinders the successful operation of small collaborative groups and can lead to a decrease in performance and learning (Yamaguchi, 2001).

To avoid dominate-dominated relationships among group members, it is desirable to structure groups with a focus on learning and improving (mastery-orientation) instead of competition and comparison (goal-orientation) (Ames & Archer, 1988; Maehr & Midgley, 1996). Educational researchers have established that students will learn more if they have learning goals rather than performance goals (Dweck, 1986). Likewise, groups that have the goal of collective improvement rather than better performance tend to have better long term outcomes (Kozlowski & Bell, 2006). Teaching students ways to lead in which none dominate should be considered a curriculum goal for 21st-century education.

LEADERSHIP THEORIES

One of the advantages of using leadership as a construct in addition to helping, peer-tutoring, promotive interaction, or scaffolding, is that there is a vast literature on leadership. In this section, we will review some of the major leadership theories and how they might be useful in understanding and improving collaborative group work in classroom settings.

Trait Theories of Leadership

As was mentioned earlier, a lot of research has examined the dispositional predictors of leadership. Surprisingly little consensus has emerged in terms of what specific traits distinguish leaders from nonleaders. However, some traits have been shown to be important in multiple studies, such as intelligence, self-confidence, determination, integrity, and sociability (Northouse, 2010). Leadership has also been connected with the five-factor personality model. Extraversion has been shown to be the most important predictor of leadership emergence followed by conscientiousness, openness, low neuroticism, and agreeableness (Judge, Bono, Ilies, & Gerhardt, 2002). Among the very few studies of leadership in children's collaborative groups, similar personality traits were found to be important in the emergence of child leaders (e.g., Coie & Dodge, 1983; Li et al., 2007).

One striking dissimilarity between the characteristics of child and adult leaders is the role of gender. Contrary to the adult literature, which has indicated that women are less likely to be chosen as leaders, especially in domains perceived as masculine (Northouse, 2010), Petersen, Johnson, and Johnson (1991) reported that school aged girls in collaborative learning groups had similar perceived ratings of leadership. Similarly, Li et al. (2007) found that female fourth-grade students were far more likely than male students to emerge as leaders in collaborative discussion groups. This phenomenon held across male-majority, female-majority, and equal-sex groups

While trait theories of leadership do not directly correspond to our conception of leadership as a process in which everyone can participate, it is useful in understanding why some individuals might be considered by others or by themselves as the natural choice for the role of leader. For the teacher, this research might be useful in placing individuals in groups so that each group is likely to have several individuals who can perform leadership roles in different contexts.

Leadership as a Set of Skills

While trait approaches to leadership suggest that leadership abilities are stable features of certain individuals, the skills approach assumes that people can learn to be better leaders. Mumford, Zaccaro, Harding, Jacobs, and Fleishman (2000) identified three key competencies needed for leadership: problem-solving skills, social judgment skills, and knowledge (in particular schema formation).

The leadership skills approach shares many similarities with work on social skills training in cooperative and collaborative groups. However, it is important to note that even if there is a person in a group with exceptional social skills, leadership may still not occur if that person does not coordinate her or his behavior with other students who possess the skills and motivation to be followers. Therefore, leadership skill theory can be informative for educators in elucidating the kind of skills expected of successful leaders, but is likely not comprehensive enough to fully explain leadership in the educational setting.

Leadership Styles

What styles of leadership are there, and which styles are best? In general, leadership research has identified two major categories of leadership style: task- and relationship-oriented leadership (Stogdill, 1969). Task-oriented leadership is aimed at helping the group successfully accomplish a task. For example, one student in a collaborative math group might suggest that they need to first read the problem carefully and then decide what math operation to do. Relationship-oriented leadership is aimed at making sure that everyone in the group gets along. For example, in the collaborative math group another student might suggest that some people need help reading the problem so that they can feel like they are fully part of the group. The two styles are not mutually exclusive. Leadership can be both task and relationship focused. In fact, Blake and McCanse (1991) suggest that leadership which is both high task and high relationship is best; however, most researchers believe that no one leadership style can be effective in all situations.

The distinction between task- and relationship-oriented leadership appears to be a powerful categorization. Even children seem to define leadership in these terms (Yamaguchi & Maehr, 2003). While research does not provide evidence that one type is consistently best, it does provide a useful way to categorize leadership behavior and to organize leadership training.

Contingency Theories of Leadership

Prompted by the failure of the style approach to define a universally effective leadership style, researchers developed a number of theories that define under what circumstances certain leadership approaches will be more successful (Chemers, 2000). Among these theories are situational leadership (Blanchard, Zigarmi, & Nelson, 1993), contingency theory (Fiedler 1964), and path-goal theory (House & Mitchell, 1974). These theories suggest that people who are in need of structure because they feel they are not competent or because the situation is chaotic may need the focus of task-oriented leadership, whereas people who feel unmotivated, unchallenged, or devalued particularly need relationship-oriented leadership.

In the context of collaborative group work, the teacher can often control the conditions in which leadership will be needed by assigning groups and by varying the task difficulty and structure. For this reason, contingency theories might prove helpful to teachers when guiding student leadership to be most effective during a particular lesson.

Transformational Leadership

Downton (1973) created the term *transformational leadership* to contrast it with previous theories of leadership which he termed *transactional.* In transformational leadership both leader and follower are changed so that they exceed their former limitations. Bass and Avolio (1990) identified four key factors that characterize transformational leadership: idealized influence or charisma, motivation through inspiration, intellectual stimulation of followers, and individualized consideration of followers. Classic examples of transformative leaders are Mahatma Gandhi, Nelson Mandela, and George Washington. Through the process of leadership, all of these leaders were radically changed as well as changing the countries they led. Transformational leadership has been a major focus of leadership research in recent years (Lowe & Gardner, 2001), and it is associated with both worker motivation and performance (Yukl, 1999).

If we are to translate leadership theories developed to characterize CEOs, presidents, prophets, and conquering generals into the K–12 classroom, we need to start by looking at the modest beginning stages of transformative leadership. We might take as an example the following interchange in a fourth grade class between two student leaders named Anne and Jim and a quiet student named Luke [pseudonyms] (Miller & Anderson, 2007, p. 41). They are having a discussion, and Luke has not significantly contributed to the discussion.

Anne: Luke, what do you think?
Luke: [Shrugged his shoulders.]
Anne: Luke, that's not acceptable. Could you give us some of your ideas?
Luke: I'm still thinking. I don't know what I think.
Anne: [pause for 7 seconds] Becky, what do you think?
[Anne asks the remaining students what they think, and they give their position and reasons, and then she returns to Luke]
Anne: Luke, what do you think?
Luke: Um, [pause 5 seconds] I think he should win.
Jim: Why do you think that? Luke, why do you think that?
Anne: We've given you some of our ideas, could you please give us some of yours?
Luke: [pause 8 seconds]

Luke does eventually give his opinion and at the end of the discussion Anne said, "I think Luke did really good today. He talked a lot today and gave us reasons." By the end of the next session, Luke did not want the discussion to stop, and he even took the leadership role on one occasion and asked another student to speak. Anne, Jim, and Luke may show the beginnings of a transformative leadership relationship. Anne has a clear vision of what discussion participation should be, Jim is supporting her vision, and Luke is inspired to follow her vision.

Team Leadership

Perhaps the theory of leadership which is most applicable to collaborative group work in classrooms is team leadership theory. In this theory, teams can have assigned leaders or they can be self-managed. Self-managed teams often have one or more leaders emerge from the interaction of its members (Cohen, Chang, & Ledford, 1997). These processes are also evident in the classroom context. There is evidence that the method of assigning roles in cooperative groups in classrooms is effective (Saleh, Lazonder, & de Jong, 2007). These roles are often akin to leadership positions. For example, the student assigned to be the "time keeper" has influence over the pace of work of all the students in the group because of the authority of her role.

However, if an activity is well structured so that leadership development is facilitated, emergent leadership can also be successful. Research with adults has consistently shown that groups often can and do work effectively without any appointed or elected formal leader (Cohen, Chang, & Ledford, 1997). They do so as various members of the group enact leadership behavior, which contributes to effective group functioning.

Team leadership research has even found that teams with shared leadership can be more effective than groups with single leaders in certain respects (Solansky, 2008). This can be true for children as well. For example, McMahon and Goatley (1995) reported that in book club discussions without assigned leaders, more experienced students began as leaders, but as students became more familiar and comfortable with the discussion format, even the inexperienced group members exhibited leadership behavior.

In another example from Collaborative Reasoning discussions, Li et al. (2007) found that in 11 out of 12 discussion groups at least one child leader emerged, and in 5 groups leadership was shared among several children. Even in groups with a dominant leader, leadership functions were widely distributed among group members. In addition, the frequency of leadership moves increased significantly with the progression of the discussions, suggesting that emerging child leaders learned how to lead through experience.

Research in both education and business also converge on the idea of common schemas as one important element in the development of emergent and distributed group leadership. Schemas are large generalized forms of knowledge representation (Anderson & Pearson, 1984). Li et al. (2007) proposed that through group interaction students develop a generic representation of leadership. Mumford, Friedrich, Caughron, and Byrne (2007) have used a related version of schema theory to explain how leadership effectiveness in business and industry is related to the schemas that leaders have for the company, the products, people, and relationships. Better leaders are able to rely on a more complex schema. In the same way, groups can build a form of shared cognition (Resnick, 1991) in which a schema is shared knowledge among the members of a group.

Leadership in the collaborative context can be improved as the schema of the group becomes more rich and flexible over time, and as leaders and followers develop complimentary schemas of leadership and other group processes (Lord & Brown, 2001).

LEADERSHIP DEVELOPMENT

Can leadership be taught? With the exception of some extreme trait and contingency theorists, most leadership theories strongly support the idea that leadership can and should be taught. Skills-based approaches focus on the capabilities that individuals possess to effectively perform organizational leadership roles (Mumford, Zaccaro, Harding, Jacobs, & Fleishman, 2000). Situational leadership theory and path-goal theory would advocate for leaders to learn how to adjust their style to fulfill the needs of their followers. Transformational leadership would emphasize the development of a vision and the ability to inspire others. Team leadership requires the development of shared skills and knowledge distributed through the relationships in the team.

In transferring leadership training models from business settings to classroom settings, several existing educational models can be applied. The first is the social skills model. This model has been extensively applied to cooperative learning (Johnson, 2003). Social skills training usually uses a direct teacher-led instructional method. For example, Mize and Ladd (1990) developed a method of social skills training in which prosocial behaviors are modeled by the teacher, rehearsed by the student, and then the student is given feedback by the teacher.

Several studies have shown that explicit leadership skills training which includes deliberate practice and fairly long time frames is successful in increasing the leadership skills of college-aged participants. For example, Posner (2009) reported a longitudinal study that examined the effect of a leadership training program given in college. The study reported significant change for those leadership training participants in the frequency of engaging in leadership behavior from freshman to senior years. At the K–12 level, social skills training has also been widely implemented. Cooperative learning social skills training (Johnson & Johnson, 1999), peer-tutoring training (King, Staffieri, & Adelgais, 1998), and helping behavior training (Webb & Farivar, 1994) have all been shown to be successful. This suggests that a similar leadership skills training approach is also likely to be successful since it involves an overlapping although not identical set of skills.

However, an alternative to the direct instruction of social skills and one more congruent with the process view of leadership is the social propagation of leadership. Li et al. (2007) directly applied this principal to children's leadership in the context of CR discussions. She demonstrated that once a student pioneers a useful leadership move such as asking another student "Do you have something to share?" then other students acquire and utilize these moves in a process of social diffusion (Anderson et al., 2001). Jadallah et al. (2011) found that the same process happens between teachers and students during CR discussions. After teachers prompted and praised children's use of textual evidence, asked children for clarification, and challenged children to consider alternative points of view, children not only used more of the encouraged behaviors, but also began to use the same leadership moves to facilitate each other. This leadership development was unprompted by the teacher, and came as a result of students appropriating the moves of the teacher. Sun, Anderson, Perry, and Lin (2011) further examined if the leadership skills that developed through the process of social propagation during CR discussions would transfer to a different context. They found that, as compared to students who received no CR discussions, students who experienced five CR discussions initiated more effective leadership moves in a later group problem solving activity even though the groups had been shuffled.

Of course, for the social propagation of student and teacher leadership moves to occur, students need extensive high quality collaborative group activities. It can also be enhanced by teacher supported reflection on the quality of group interactions, instruction and modeling of leadership, and well-chosen groups (McMahon & Goatley, 1995). Through interviewing children, Owen (2007) found that over three-quarters of students said that leadership could be learned (p. 55) and the most common answer to when they could learn leadership was "group work in school" (p. 42).

CONCLUSION

Leadership research in children's collaborative groups is in its infancy, but it has the possibility of growing quickly in the following years. The leadership concept fits well with established lines of educational research including cooperative and collaborative group work as well as work on other related topics such as peer-tutoring, but also has the ability to expand the field of collaborative learning by allowing educational researchers to embrace a well-established and diverse theoretical tradition dating back well over a century.

This trend is also well timed as we move into a new century that will create many critical leadership challenges. If one of the goals of education is to prepare students to be successful and productive members of adult society, and leadership is one of the key elements of business, military, civic life, and school administration, then leadership development might be one of the most important additions we can make to a comprehensive curriculum for the 21st century.

REFERENCES

Ames, C., & Archer, J. (1988). Achievement goals in the classroom: Students' learning strategies and motivation processes. *Journal of Educational Psychology, 80*, 260–267.

Anderson, R. C., Chinn, C., Waggoner, M., & Nguyen, K. (1998). Intellectually stimulating story discussions. In J. Osborn & F. Lehr (Eds.), *Literacy for all* (pp. 170–186). New York: Guilford.

Anderson, R. C., Nguyen-Jahiel, K., McNurlen, B., Archodidou, A., Kim, S., Reznitskaya, A., ... Gilbert, L. (2001). The snowball phenomenon: Spread of ways of talking and ways of thinking across groups of children. *Cognition and Instruction, 19*, 1–46.

Anderson, R. C., & Pearson, P. D. (1984). A schema-theoretic view of basic processes in reading comprehension. In P. D. Pearson (Ed.), *Handbook of reading research* (pp. 255–291). New York: Longman.

Barron, B. (2003). When smart groups fail. *Journal of the Learning Sciences, 12*, 307–359.

Bass, B. M., & Avolio, B. J. (1990). The implications of transactional and transformational leadership for individual, team, and organizational development. *Research in Organizational Change and Development, 4*, 231–272.

Blanchard, K., Zigarimi, D., & Nelson, R. (1993). Situational leadership after 25 years: A retrospective. *Journal of Leadership Studies, 1*, 22–36.

Blake, R. R., & McCanse, A. A. (1991). *Leadership dilemmas: Grid solutions*. Houston, TX: Gulf.

Cazden, C. B. (1979). *Peekaboo as an instructional model: Discourse development at home and at school*. (Papers and Reports on Child Language Development No. 17). Palo Alto, CA: Stanford University, Department of Linguistics.

Chemers, M. M. (2000). Leadership research and theory: A functional integration. *Group Dynamics: Theory, Research and Practice, 4*, 27–43.

Cohen, S. G., Chang, L., & Ledford, G. E. (1997). A hierarchical construct of self-management leadership and its relationship to quality of work life and perceived work group effectiveness. *Personnel Psychology, 50*, 275–308.

Cohen, P. A., Kulik, J. A., & Kulik, C-L. C. (1982). Educational outcomes of tutoring: A meta-analysis of findings. *American Educational Research Journal, 19*, 237–248.

Coie, J. D., & Dodge, K. A. (1983). Continuities and changes in children's social status: A five-year longitudinal study. *Merrill-Palmer Quarterly, 29*, 261–281.

Downton, J. V. (1973). *Rebel leadership: Commitment and charisma in a revolutionary process*. New York: Free Press.

Dweck, C. S. (1986). Motivational processes affecting learning. *American Psychologist, 41*, 1040–1048.

Fantuzzo, J. W., King, J. A., & Heller, L. R. (1992). Effects of reciprocal peer tutoring on mathematics and school adjustment: A component analysis. *Journal of Educational Psychology, 84*, 33–339.

Fiedler, F. E. (1964). A contingency model of leadership effectiveness. In L. Berkowitz (Ed.), *Advances in experimental social psychology* (Vol. 1, pp. 149–190). New York: Academic Press.

Gillies, R. M. (2007). *Cooperative learning: Integrating theory and practice*. Thousand Oaks, CA: Sage.

Gillies, R., & Ashman, A. (1998). Behavior and interaction of children in cooperative groups in lower and middle elementary grades. *Journal of Educational Psychology, 90*, 746–757.

Harris, A. (2003). Teacher leadership as distributed leadership: Heresy, fantasy or possibility? *School Leadership & Management, 23*, 313–324.

House, R. J., & Mitchell, R. R. (1974). Path-goal theory of leadership. *Journal of Contemporary Business, 3*, 81–97.

Jadallah, M., Anderson, R. C., Nguyen-Jahiel, K., Miller, B. W., Kim, I., Kuo, L., ... Dong, T. (2011). Influence of a teacher's scaffolding moves during child-led small-group discussions. *American Educational Research Journal, 48*, 194–230.

Johnson, D. (2003). Social interdependence: Interrelationships among theory, research, and practice. *American Psychologist, 58*, 934–945.

Johnson, D., & Johnson, R. (1999). Making cooperative learning work. *Theory into Practice, 38*, 67–73.

Johnson, D. W., Johnson, R., & Holubec, E. (1998). *Cooperation in the classroom* (7th ed.). Edina, MN: Interaction.

Judge, T. A., Bono, J. E., Ilies, R., & Gerhardt, M. W. (2002). Personality and leadership: A qualitative and quantitative review. *Journal of Applied Psychology, 87*, 765–780.

King, A., Staffieri, A., & Adelgais, A. (1998). Mutual peer tutoring: Effects of structuring tutorial interaction to scaffold peer learning. *Journal of Educational Psychology, 90*, 134–152.

Kozlowski, S. W. J., & Bell, B. S. (2006). Disentangling achievement orientation and goal setting: Effects on self-regulatory processes. *Journal of Applied Psychology, 91*, 900–916.

Li, Y., Anderson, R. C., Nguyen-Jahiel, K., Dong, T., Archodidou, A., Kim, M., ... Miller, B. (2007). Emergent leadership in children's discussion groups. *Cognition and Instruction, 25*, 75–111.

Lord, R. G., & Brown, D. J. (2001). Leadership, values, and subordinate self-concepts. *Leadership Quarterly, 12*, 133–152.

Lowe, K. B., & Gardner, W. L. (2001). Ten years of the Leadership Quarterly: Contributions and challenges for the future. *Leadership Quarterly, 11*, 459–514.

Maehr, M. L., & Midgley, C. (1996). *Transforming school cultures.* Boulder, CO: Westview Press.

McMahon, S. I., & Goatley, V. J. (1995). Fifth graders helping peers discuss texts in student-led groups. *The Journal of Educational Research, 89*, 25–34.

Miller, B. W., & Anderson, R. C. (2007, April). *Quiet students in small group discussions.* Paper presented at the annual meeting of the American Educational Research Association, Chicago, IL.

Mize, J., & Ladd, G. (1990). Social learning approach to social skills training with low status preschool children. *Developmental Psychology, 26*, 388–397.

Mumford, M. D., Friedrich, T. L., Caughron, J. J., & Byrne C. L. (2007). Leader cognition in real-world settings: How do leaders think about crises? *Leadership Quarterly, 18*, 515–543

Mumford, M. D., Zaccaro, S. J., Harding, F. D., Jacobs, T. O., & Fleishman, E. A. (2000). Leadership skills for a changing world: Solving complex social problems. *Leadership Quarterly, 11*, 11–35.

Northouse, P. G. (2010). *Leadership: Theory and practice.* Los Angeles, CA: Sage.

Owen, H. (2007). *Creating leaders in the classroom: How teachers can develop a new generation of leaders.* New York: Routledge.

Palincsar, A. S., & Brown, A. L. (1984). Reciprocal teaching of comprehension monitoring activities. *Cognition and Instruction, 2*, 117–175.

Petersen, R., Johnson, D., & Johnson, R., (1991). Effects of co-operative learning on perceived status of male and female pupils. *Journal of Social Psychology, 131*, 717–735.

Pettit, G. S., Bakshi, A., Dodge, K. A., & Coie, J. D. (1990). The emergence of social dominance in young boys' play groups: Developmental differences and behavioral correlates. *Developmental Psychology, 26*, 1017–1025.

Posner, B. Z. (2009). A longitudinal study examining changes in students' leadership behavior. *Journal of College Student Development, 50*, 551–563.

Resnick, L. B. (1991). Shared cognition: Thinking as social practice. In L. B. Resnick, J. M. Levine, & S. D. Teasley (Eds.), *Perspectives on socially shared cognition* (pp. 1–20). Washington, DC: American Psychological Association.

Rogoff, B. (1990). *Apprenticeship in thinking: Cognitive development in social context.* New York: Oxford University Press.

Rohrbeck, C. A., Ginsburg-Block, M. D., Fantuzzo, J. W., & Miller, T. R. (2003). Peer-assisted learning interventions with elementary school students: A meta-analytic review. *Journal of Educational Psychology, 95*, 240–257.

Saleh, M., Lazonder, A.W., & de Jong, T. (2007). Structuring collaboration in mixed-ability groups to promote verbal interaction, learning, and motivation of average-ability students. *Contemporary Educational Psychology, 32*, 314–331.

Solansky, S. T. (2008). Leadership style and team processes in self-managed teams. *Journal of Leadership & Organizational Studies, 14*, 332–341.

Spillane, J. P., Halverson, R., & Diamond, J. P. (2004). Towards a theory of leadership practice: A distributed perspective. *Journal of Curriculum Studies, 36*, 3–34.

Stogdill, R. M. (1969). Validity of leader behavior descriptions. *Personnel Psychology, 22*, 153–158.

Sun, J., Anderson, R. C., Perry, M., & Lin, T. (2011, August). *Transfer of emergent leadership from collaborative reasoning discussions to collaborative problem solving.* Poster Presented at the Annual Convention of American Psychologist Association, Washington, DC.

Webb, N., & Farivar, S. (1994). Promoting helping behavior in cooperative small groups in middle school mathematics. *American Education Research Journal, 31*, 369–395.

Webb, N. M., & Mastergeorge, A. M. (2003). The development of students' learning in peer-directed small groups. *Cognition and Instruction, 21*, 361–428.

Webb, N. M., & Palincsar, A. S. (1996). Groups processes in the classroom. In D. C. Berliner & R. C. Calfee (Eds.), *Handbook of educational psychology* (pp. 841–873). New York: Macmillan.

Wood, D., Bruner, J. S., & Ross, G. (1976). The role of tutoring in problem solving. *Journal of Child Psychology and Psychiatry, 17*, 89–100.

Yamaguchi, R. (2001). Children's learning groups: A study of emergent leadership, dominance, and group effectiveness. *Small Group Research, 32*, 671–697.

Yamaguchi, R., & Maehr, M. L. (2003, April). *A multi-method study of children's emergent leadership in collaborative learning groups.* Paper presented at the annual meeting of the American Educational Research Association, Chicago, IL.

Yukl, G. (1999). An evaluation of conceptual weaknesses in transformational and charismatic leadership theories. *Leadership Quarterly, 10*, 285–305.

16

ASSESSMENT IN COLLABORATIVE LEARNING

JAN VAN AALST

University of Hong Kong

INTRODUCTION

Learning and assessment are mutually dependent because both students and teachers tend to pay greater attention to learning objectives that are assessed (Biggs, 1996; Shepard, 2000). This relationship has profound implications for the large-scale uptake of collaborative learning, which is defined for the purpose of this chapter as any educational approach in which students work toward a shared learning goal. Examples include learning in small groups, learning from online discussions, and learning in communities, which are discussed in other chapters in this handbook.

This chapter considers four issues with assessment in collaborative learning:

1. If assessment is based on a *group product*, then it is difficult, if not impossible, to ascertain what individual students have learned. Grades are often based on participation in the group process, but participation is also difficult to ascertain, and often confuses learning with effort. This kind of assessment is frequently regarded as unfair by students, parents, and other stakeholders.
2. If students are assessed *individually* after learning in a small group, then what they know is measured correctly, but is attributed incorrectly to their personal achievement; at least some of their learning is a shared accomplishment. A well-functioning collaborative group can solve more difficult problems than any single student in the group. Stahl's (2010) theory of group cognition refers to learning effects that are *irreducible* to individual learning effects.
3. Assessment practices treat collaboration as a *method* for accomplishing learning, but it can be argued that it should be seen as a *human capability* worth assessing in its own right. Collaboration distributes the learning process over students, and there is a potentially powerful role for assessment in the development of such practices. The development of this competence has been identified as an important 21st century skill (Assessment of 21st Century Skills [ACT21] Project, n.d.).

4. Situations in which collaborative learning is *most necessary*, in the sense that it would be impossible to achieve the learning goals without the cognitive benefits of collaboration referenced in Issue 2, all involve novelty, problem solving, and creativity. In these situations, there are qualitative differences in the outcomes generated by different teams, rendering objective and reliable assessment difficult.

Unless practical solutions to these issues are found, the widespread use of collaboration in formal education seems unlikely. This chapter presents a review of the research on assessment in collaborative learning, primarily of the cognitively oriented studies published between 1994 and 2009, to examine the foregoing issues. The next section places this review in the context of the historical trends in research on assessment in general, and the subsequent sections discuss the major themes that emerge from the literature review: formative assessment, assessment of learning in small groups, assessment of online learning, and peer- and self-assessment. These themes draw from research in K–12 education, nursing and medical education, engineering education, and teacher education. The final section returns to the four aforementioned assessment issues and outlines opportunities for further research.

HISTORICAL CONTEXT

In the first half of the 20th century, assessment was greatly influenced by intelligence testing and psychometric test theory. As Gipps (1994) explained, intelligence testing assumes that aptitude is a stable, universal, and one-dimensional construct. Glaser (1963; cited in Gipps, 1994) noted a corresponding preoccupation with aptitude, selection, and prediction, and proposed criterion-referenced testing as an alternative to norm-referenced testing. Criterion-referenced tests focus on whether a student reaches a given standard regardless of how many other students do so.

Subsequent decades saw a trend away from norm-referenced government examinations toward school- and criterion-based assessment. In the 1970s, many Canadian and U.S. jurisdictions abolished government examinations in favor of teacher-designed tests. In the Netherlands, a school examination was introduced in addition to the government examination, and a Teacher Assessment Scheme for science education was introduced in Hong Kong. Since the mid-1980s, there has been a major effort to develop national benchmarks and standards in a variety of school subjects (American Association for the Advancement of Science [AAAS], 1993; National Council of Teachers of Mathematics [NCTM], 2000; National Research Council [NRC], 1996). In recent assessment reforms in Hong Kong, the government has placed greater emphasis on school-based assessment to assess practical skills in science and conversational skills in English (Center for Curriculum Development [CDC]/Hong Kong Examinations and Assessment Authority [HKEAA], 2007), arguing that a student's own school and teacher provide a better context for eliciting his or her best performance. An important aspect of the school-based assessment movement is the introduction of formative assessment carried out while learning is still occurring and that is used to *improve* the learning process (Scriven, 1967). Such assessment utilizes formative feedback (Ramaprasad, 1983), which is based on the gap between a student's current performance and the desired standard.

Effort has also been devoted to providing a conceptual foundation for school-based assessment. Referring to the "one-dimensional" and "universal" nature of aptitude implied by norm-referenced testing, Gipps (1994) proposed a comprehensive framework for *educational* assessment that recognizes that domains of knowledge are complex, emphasizes standards, encourages students to think rather than regurgitate facts, elicits students' best performance, and involves grading by the teacher, possibly subject to moderation. Shepard (2000, p. 7) proposed a framework that aligns a contemporary view of curricula (e.g., addressing challenging content and higher-order thinking, establishing an authentic relationship between in-school and out-of-school learning, and fostering important habits of mind), cognitive and constructivist learning theories, and school-based assessment.

The foregoing developments, sketched in brief here, indicate progress toward a view of learning that acknowledges its complexity, attempts to specify the most important dimensions of learning via educational standards, and increases emphasis on school-based assessment. However, this general literature pays little attention to collective outcomes (Issue 2) or collaboration as a human competence (Issue 3); it is almost exclusively concerned with the learning outcomes of individual students.

THEMES IN RESEARCH ON ASSESSMENT

This section describes the main themes emerging from a review of the literature on assessment relevant to collaborative learning: formative assessment, assessment of learning in small groups, assessment of online discussions, and self- and peer-assessment. The main findings of the research on these themes is then connected to the four issues outlined above.

Formative Assessment

Formative assessment, students' use of feedback to improve learning while the learning process is ongoing, provides a potentially powerful resource for collaborative learning. For example, having received feedback from the teacher, students can help one another to understand that feedback and then devise and monitor a plan together for making use of it to improve their learning performance. Such collaborative interactions can lead to improvements in understanding of the nature and standard of performance desired. If a group of students receives feedback on a project from their teacher, then collaboration is necessary for developing a shared understanding of that feedback and making use of it to improve the project. Students can also peer-assess one another's performance rather than rely on the teacher to provide feedback, and can then help one another to understand how the performances can be improved. This kind of collaborative interaction can be a precursor to a more self-directed approach to learning that involves self-assessment. This section discusses the literature on formative assessment published since the well-known review by Black and Wiliam (1998), with the aims of determining the extent to which these practices are already occurring and identifying the theoretical and pedagogical development that is still needed.

Black and Wiliam (1998) discussed learning effects, existing practice, the role and nature of feedback, students' reception to feedback, and systemic considerations such as the influence of external and summative assessment systems. They reviewed 250 papers published between 1988 and 1998, including approximately 20 rigorous quantitative studies that involved comparisons of learning effects. Their major finding was that formative assessment has a consistently positive impact on student learning outcomes across educational settings ranging from the early elementary school years to undergraduate study at university. However, they also found classroom assessment practices to be generally underdeveloped, finding few examples of formative assessment initiated by students or approaches that involve collaboration; the role of the student was limited primarily to receiving feedback from the teacher and acting on it individually.

Since Black and Wiliam's (1998) review, significant effort has been invested in the development of classroom formative practices. For example, Black, Harrison, Lee, Marshall, and Wiliam (2003) collaborated with teachers of science and mathematics at six secondary schools to enhance teachers' questioning, feedback by marking, peer- and self-assessment, and formative uses of summative tests, and reported that questioning became more focused on student thinking over time, and feedback more specific. Ruiz-Primo and Furtak (2007) proposed a modification to the IRE model of classroom discourse (i.e., teacher *I*nitiates, student *R*esponds, and teacher *E*valuates) by adding a fourth step, in which the teacher uses students' responses to modify his or her teaching plan. However, in most approaches, classroom discourses appear to have remained dialectical, with the teacher controlling most of the talk. Yorke (2003) questioned whether, if a student employs feedback on a draft from the teacher to improve the final version of the assignment, then he or she can also perform adequately when such feedback is *not* available. Nevertheless, in a society in which collaboration is pervasive, it is usually possible to find someone who can provide feedback on a work-in-progress. From this perspective, one of the competencies that students should be developing is the ability to seek and make use of feedback from peers.

A number of theoretical points have also been raised about formative assessment. Taras (2009) argued that the dichotomy between formative and summative assessment that has emerged in the literature was not intended by Scriven (1967), and called for better integration of the two concepts. She explained that the concept of formative feedback proposed by Ramaprasad (1983) involves information about the gap between actual performance and a reference level, and therefore has a summative aspect. Assessment, whether its function is formative or summative, involves a judgment about quality relative to some criterion. Yorke (2003) pointed out the need for a theory of formative assessment that aligns it with a constructivist theory of learning, takes into account epistemological models that are relevant to the subject that students are studying, provides cognitive models for learning from feedback, and takes into account such factors as readiness to learn and the impact of feedback on student characteristics such as motivation and self-esteem. However, in the model he proposed (Yorke, 2003, p. 487), the assessor sets the assessment task and grading criteria, which are then modified on the basis of student performance. Students' interpretation of feedback from the assessor influences their long-term development (i.e., performance on the next task), but not their performance on the task at hand. In other words, Yorke's model does not make use of feedback to enhance learning while it is in progress, limits the role of students as the agents of their learning, and is not collaborative. Perrenoud (1998) pointed out that Black and Wiliam (1998) missed an important body of literature published in French, which develops the *regulation of learning* as a central concept integrating formative assessment, the didactic content of the disciplines in question, and differentiation in teaching. This French literature has strong foundations in a cognitive theory of learning that involves scaffolding; however, Perrenoud's (1998) concern was with regulation by the *teacher*, not by the students, and did not include collaboration.

More recently, Black and Wiliam (2009) proposed a theory of formative assessment that partly responds to the foregoing criticisms and developments, and attempts to incorporate self-regulated learning and limited collaboration. Here, they began from Ramaprasad's (1983) three key processes of teaching and learning (establishing where students are in their learning, where they need to be going, and what needs to be done to get them there), and pointed out that although the teacher has been primarily responsible for all three, students also have a role to play. Black and Wiliam's (2009) theory refers to five strategies for formative assessment: (a) clarifying and sharing learning intentions and criteria for success; (b) engineering effective classroom discussions and other learning tasks that elicit evidence of student understanding; (c) providing feedback that moves students forward; (d) activating students as instructional resources for one another (a collaborative strategy); and (e) activating students as the owners of their own learning. Following a suggestion by Hattie and Timperley (2007), Black and Wiliam conceptualized feedback at three levels: task, processes needed to understand the task, and self-regulation (self-monitoring, directing, and regulating actions).

In summary, formative assessment has received considerable attention in the review period, but most of this research focuses on a teacher-directed activity in which students make use of feedback from the teacher. Nevertheless, the theory recently proposed by Black and Wiliam (2009) pays more attention to empowering students as the agents of their own learning through self-regulated learning and includes collaboration among students in making use of the teacher's feedback.

Assessment of Learning in Small Groups

Learning in small groups is the most prevalent form of collaborative learning in formal education. It occurs in science learning laboratories, in which available resources such as equipment and physical space do not allow students to carry out experiments individually, and in project-based learning, in which it is infeasible for the teacher to guide and provide feedback on projects by individual students. In these situations, the use of small-group arrangements is often motivated by practical constraints rather than the potential cognitive benefits of collaboration, and, in the formation of these groups, teachers do not always pay adequate attention to findings from social psychology and the sociocognitive dynamics of learning in small groups. As a result, learning in small groups is often fraught with inequities (Issue 1). Individual learner variables such as prior knowledge, motivation, interest in the task, and social skills all influence group performance, and it is quite common for high-performing students to learn less individually in groups than they would have done solo, even though the group as a whole benefits from having such students as collaborators. This section discusses several important studies that have investigated these phenomena.

Webb, Nemer, Chizhik, and Sugrue (1998) investigated the impact of group composition on group performance, the quality of group discussions, and individual achievement in a study of 445 seventh and eighth grade students drawn from 21 classes studying 3-week instructional units on electricity and electric circuits. The students came from a range of socioeconomic backgrounds. Prior to teaching, students completed three pretests measuring vocabulary, verbal reasoning, and nonverbal reasoning. After teaching, they completed two tests individually: a practical test in which they were required to assemble simple electric circuits, draw diagrams of their circuits, and answer questions about them; and a paper-and-pencil test involving similar circuits. A month later, 80%

of the students repeated the practical test collaboratively in triads, and the remaining 20% completed them individually as a control; all of the students repeated the paper-and-pencil test. Group interactions were videotaped and coded for collaborative assessment. Multilevel covariate analysis was then used to analyze the results, with students nested within groups (or as individuals) and groups within types of group composition.

This study produced a number of important findings. Regression analysis of three group composition variables (the highest, lowest, and average ability levels in each group) on achievement showed that (a) the *highest ability level* in the group was the only significant predictor of achievement for students in the bottom three quarters of the sample, whereas (b) the *lowest ability level* in the group was the only significant predictor of achievement for those in the top quarter. Thus, most students would benefit from working in a group with a high-ability student. Further analysis showed this effect to be especially strong for students in the bottom two quarters: working with high-ability students enhanced the performance of these students on both the group test and the individual test, and the video analysis showed that they had learned from hearing more high-quality explanations than other students. In contrast, high-ability students performed better when they worked in homogeneous groups than in heterogeneous groups. However, their performance did not suffer when they worked with low-ability students, relative to their performance when they worked with students of medium to high ability (i.e., the third quarter). Webb et al. (1998) pointed out that their findings raised important questions about the *fairness* of group assessment: "If the purpose of collaboration on an assessment is to measure students' performance after they have an opportunity to learn from others, then, to give all students the same advantage, all groups must have a high-achieving student" (p. 643). However, the results for high-achieving students indicated that this would not be the optimal configuration for them.

To replicate this study and clarify the impact of group composition on the achievement of high-ability students, Webb, Nemer, and Zuniga (2002) employed similar methods to examine the coconstruction of task solutions, helping behavior such as responses to questions and corrections of one another's statements, and the socioemotional processes in operation when students work in groups. The authors drew three main conclusions: (a) high-ability students perform well in homogeneous groups, as well as in some, but not all, heterogeneous groups; (b) the types of group interaction that occur during group work strongly influence performance; and (c) *group interaction* predicts performance more strongly than either student ability or the overall ability composition of the group. The average level of help that the high-ability students both gave and received in this study (Webb, Nemer, & Zuniga, 2002) was significantly related to these students' delayed posttest scores, and how frequently high-ability students heard other students verbalize fully correct answers was positively correlated with their delayed posttest performance. Negative socioemotional behavior such as domineering, insulting, and off-task behavior predicted the frequency with which high-ability students handed in work less complete than their immediate posttest answers at the delayed posttest. The researchers called for strategies that *maximize group functioning* to activate the intellectual resources of all groups.

In another study focusing on high-ability students, Barron (2003) investigated collaborative problem solving in 12 triads of sixth graders. She controlled for ability by including only students who scored above the 75th percentile on a national standardized achievement test on mathematics. The participants viewed a 15-minute video adventure from the *Adventures of Jasper Woodbury* series as a class, and they then solved a challenge related to the adventure in triads. Next, they completed two tests individually: a repeat of the initial challenge and a second, structurally equivalent challenge. The triads were divided into less successful and more successful, using a score of 50% for the triad's solution as the dividing line. Barron (2003) found that the more successful triads accepted or discussed correct proposals more often and produced a higher proportion of proposals that were directly related to the challenge than the less successful groups. She presented four case studies designated as follows to illustrate archetypes of interaction that rendered the triads less or more successful in the coconstruction of solutions. In *Competing to know* (less successful), the participants were unable to coregulate problem solving; instead, they competed with one another to have their solutions heard. In *Two's company* and *Wait, listen, and watch*, the interactions primarily involved only two students; in the former case, the third student made three attempts to contribute to the solution construction, all of which were ignored by the other two, whereas, in the latter case, the third student was more assertive and insisted that his contribution be heard. Finally, the fourth (more successful) case, *Coordinated coconstruction*, illustrated effective collaborative problem solving. Barron's (2003) study shows that even heterogeneous groups with students of high ability can be inequitable in terms of assessment (Issue 1) because groups differ in their ability to coregulate the collaborative problem-solving process, a similar conclusion to that reached by Webb et al. (2002). Barron therefore called for a shift from an instrumental view of collaboration to one that treats it as an important human capability in its own right (Issue 3).

Learning in groups is widespread in higher education, particularly in professional fields such as health care and engineering, in which the ability to work in teams is an important professional area of competence. In these contexts, concerns about fairness and the uneven contributions of group members are well known. To mention just one study, Colbeck, Campbell, and Bjorklund (2000) interviewed 65 undergraduate students from seven college campuses who had just completed, or were completing, engineering courses that involved a group design project. Many of the students mentioned their concerns about "slackers" and "leaders." Slackers did not contribute their fair share of effort to the project, and leaders frequently took up the leadership role because other group members did not keep their commitments or make quality contributions, often ending up doing most of the work themselves. However, high-performing students were also found to assume leadership roles because other students in the group were not performing to their standards. Students were also found to complain if the leader did not accept their ideas or let them carry out part of the project.

There is relatively little research on assessment practices themselves in the literature reviewed here, but one exception is in medical education, where teams are widely used in problem-based learning (PBL). Willis et al. (2002) investigated the assessment preferences of medical students who used PBL at the University of Manchester, and developed a rubric for assessing group interaction and activity. Their rubric emphasizes efficiency and engagement with the task: task-oriented inputs, the posing of questions that are salient to the task, and task completion. On the basis of a 1998 survey of registered nurses who graduated from a PBL program at McMasters University in Canada, Ladouceur et al. (2004) reported that assessment was "among the three worst aspects of the program" (p. 447). These authors suggested that a common challenge is finding a way to standardize assessments when there is a common curriculum. In this respect, one problem with collaborative learning is that although the curriculum implemented in multiple versions of a course or tutorial group may differ considerably, the intended curriculum remains the same. In professional fields, in which it is often important to certify that students have attained certain outcomes, objective and consistent assessment is regarded as being of paramount importance. Pauli, Mohiyeddini, Bray, Michie, and Street (2008) developed a questionnaire designed to measure individual differences in negative experiences of learning in groups, which can be used to examine the extent to which students feel such problems exist in their group work. This questionnaire has four subscales: lack of group commitment, task disorganization, storming group, and fractional group. A storming group is characterized by arguments, rows, and gossip, whereas a fractional group is characterized by feelings of isolation, the development of factions, and difficulties in deciding roles.

In summary, the literature discussed in this section reveals substantial problems in the assessment of learning in small groups. The major problem is that collaborative learning is rarely developed to the point that the potential cognitive benefits of collaboration are realized in all groups (Issues 1 and 3). The reasons for this underdevelopment include variations in prior achievement, ability to coordinate contributions from multiple group members, interaction style, and motivation and interest in the task. There is also relatively little research on the quantitative measurement of group processes, and there are concerns about objectivity and reliability in courses with multiple tutorial sections, in which the nature of learning outcomes can vary substantially (Issue 4).

Assessment of Learning in Asynchronous Online Discussion Forums

The use of asynchronous discussion forums has become widespread, and provides an opportunity for collaborative learning. Online discussions are employed by students in secondary and postsecondary education to prepare for or extend in-class learning (e.g., Guzdial & Turns, 2000; Hsi & Hoadley, 1997), and it has been noted frequently that online discussions provide greater opportunities for students to share ideas and information than classroom discussions. Many instructors look to online discussions to promote critical thinking, argumentation, and knowledge construction. However, the majority of studies on online discussions reveal low levels of participation and interactivity (Guzdial & Turns, 2000; Hewitt, 2005), and there is little consensus on how such discussions should be assessed. This section reviews research on participation rates, portfolio assessments, and the emerging uses of server-log data.

Instructors often treat online discussions as an *addition* to classroom learning, something incidental to it, and they are therefore not generally assessed; deep integration between online discussions and classroom learning is rare. When online discussions *are* assessed, such assessment is often limited to measures of participation, such as the number of notes that are created and read by individual students. Furthermore, although some studies suggest a positive correlation between participation rates and measures of conceptual knowledge (e.g., Lee, Chan, & van Aalst, 2006), the research is mixed, and a model of how participation in online discussions contributes to learning is lacking. The research literature nevertheless suggests that the nature of the discourse (e.g., interaction and focus on concepts rather than facts) plays an important role in learning, in conjunction with quantitative indicators (Hakkarainen, 2003).

There also are conceptual difficulties with current uses of participation rates for assessment because they treat individual events such as note creation as independent of one another, but they clearly are related. For example, when a class is summarizing online what has been learned over a certain period of time, students who are late in submitting their contributions may find it unnecessary to contribute at all because the points they wished to make have already been made several times. As numerous authors have noted, a discursive act is always a response to an earlier act (Wells, 1999). Hence, treating note creations as independent events removes the *collaborative* aspect of learning in online discussions (Stahl, 2002). Although it is useful to examine whether all students in a class are, over time, creating and reading notes, posing questions, and generating ideas, it is important to assess online discourse at additional levels to understand what groups of students, and the class as a whole, are doing and accomplishing together.

A focus on individual learning outcomes dominates the research on the educational uses of online discussions, but there are more powerful models in which the students constitute a *community*. In these models, individual students work to achieve collective goals, and are appreciated for the unique contributions they make to this joint effort (Bielaczyc & Collins, 1999). A prominent example is the *knowledge-building community* model, in which the community's goals are focused on extending the frontier of knowledge, as the community understands it (see Chan, chapter 25 this volume; Scardamalia & Bereiter, 2006). In knowledge building, ideas are regarded as epistemic objects: after they are introduced into a public space, the community works to improve them. The discourse of knowledge building involves much more than sharing ideas; it requires substantial interaction to improve ideas and extensive synthesis and rise-above to reach new levels of conceptualization (Scardamalia & Bereiter, 2006; van Aalst, 2009). Whereas most examples of online discussions span from only a few days to weeks, knowledge-building discourse can last for many weeks or even months, making the need for rise above and synthesis particularly important. Thus, the technology generally used to support knowledge building, Knowledge Forum, is designed to support synthesis and rise-above (Chan, chapter 25 this volume). There is a particular need for assessment to scaffold the development of knowledge-building discourse. If assessment focuses on this kind of work, then it reduces the need for teachers to read and evaluate a large number of initial contributions and raises the standard of online work. Students not only need to contribute notes, but they must also demonstrate that their collective efforts lead to shared knowledge advances.

Along these lines, van Aalst and Chan (2007) employed electronic portfolio notes in Knowledge Forum®. Students were provided with principles that describe knowledge building, and were asked to assess the extent to which their class's work on Knowledge Forum fit these principles. Although students completed this task individually, the principles represented both individual and collective aspects of knowledge building. Interviews showed that the task helped 12th grade and university students to understand better how they should contribute to online discourse to enhance knowledge building. Lee et al. (2006) employed this approach with 9th grade students, and found that portfolio scores made a significant contribution to conceptual understanding scores after controlling for measures of participation, depth of inquiry, and depth of explanation obtained from analysis of the Knowledge Forum database content. However, although this approach can provide students and teachers with useful information about the efficacy of their discourse, the gathering of evidence by students is highly labor-intensive. Thus, tools to simplify this aspect of the assessment process are needed. Many researchers are therefore attempting to develop computer-based assessment tools that can provide semiautomatic analyses of online discussions.

In this respect, the information stored in online discussion forums, such as note content, keyword use, vocabulary, participation, and interactivity, provides a large database that can, in principle, be analyzed by a computer. If such analysis provides useful feedback to teachers and students, then it could become a valuable resource for formative assessment. One kind of analysis that has been employed widely is social network analysis (de Laat, Lally, & Lipponen, 2007; Haythornthwaite, 2002), a set of techniques for analyzing aspects of the social structure of discourse, such as the centrality of certain participants, the emergence of subgroups, and the extent to which all participants have coparticipants who follow or use their contributions. These techniques can provide useful information to teachers about *interactivity*, but they lack information on *content*, such as the concepts that participants are using. Nevertheless, in computer science, substantial progress has been made in data mining and text mining techniques that open up new possibilities for formative assessment. For example, latent semantic indexing, which was initially developed to improve a web search engine, is a set of techniques designed to discover the semantic structure of a large corpus of texts (Foltz, 1997). It has been successfully applied to such assessments as the machine grading of essays (Landauer, Laham, & Foltz, 2003). Chen and Chen (2009) provided an initial framework for the application of data mining techniques in general to formative assessment. They used five computational schemes—correlational analysis, gray relational analysis, k-means clustering, fuzzy clustering algorithms, and fuzzy association—and argued that the results obtained from such techniques can be used for precise formative assessments based on the learning portfolios of individual learners collected from a web-based learning system. The teacher-side formative assessment tool in their study is able to provide information on individual students, including their degree of concentration, question-and-answer responses, and comments.

In sum, both the educational uses and assessment of asynchronous online discussions require substantial development; online discussions often lack sustained participation and interaction and are dominated by sharing practices. Whereas equity issues are important in small-group learning, here the conceptual difficulties arising from an emphasis on learning by individual learners is more important (Issue 2). There is a mismatch between the learning models that underpin the use of online discussions and most assessments of these discussions (Chan & van Aalst, 2004). The formative use of assessments based on the content of online discussions can be an important resource for improving the nature and quality of these discussions, but work in this arena is still in an early stage of development (Issue 3).

Peer- and Self-Assessment

If collaboration is oriented toward improving learning outcomes, then it must involve the use of criteria for commenting on and raising questions about a collaborator's work. Peer-assessment is one structured approach to this kind of collaboration. Indeed, peer-assessment can be a method for learning how to collaborate. It can also serve as a first step toward self-assessment, as it is often more difficult to see the limitations in one's own work than those in that of others. This section briefly discusses peer- and self-assessment as the fourth theme in research on assessment.

The literature search, which emphasized cognitively oriented research, revealed relatively few studies in this arena, but it is clear that these studies are just the tip of the iceberg. Much of the impetus for peer- and self-assessment comes from the literature emphasizing critical thinking and authentic assessment tasks, in which students have a role in defining criteria and standards and then apply these criteria/standards to peer- and self-assessments of performance. Presumably, this kind of involvement leads to deeper student understanding of the expected learning outcomes. The literature reveals mixed evidence on whether students are capable of peer- and self-assessment, and raises a number of questions about the validity and reliability of such assessments (Issue 4).

White and Frederiksen (1998) found that reflective assessments carried out by middle-school students had a positive impact on their performance on a science inquiry test and physics test and that the process was particularly beneficial to low-achieving students. In a study by Ross and Starling (2008), secondary school students were involved in setting criteria, were taught to use those criteria, were given feedback on their self-assessments, and used assessment data to develop action plans. These researchers found self-assessment to be a valid and reliable method of assessing student performance, particularly when it is used for formative rather than summative purposes. In the medical education arena, Dannefer et al. (2005) also found peer assessment to be a reliable and valid method of assessing both cognitive and interpersonal aspects of medical students' performance. Tiwari and Tang (2003) examined portfolio assessment in healthcare education, and found that students enjoyed preparing their portfolios and that doing so improved their cognitive outcomes and affect toward their course of study. One of the things that these adult students appreciated was the ability to choose material for their portfolios to demonstrate their learning. However, in their study of peer assessment in a computer-supported collaborative learning (CSCL) environment, Prins, Sluijsmans, Kirschner, and Strijbos (2005) raised concerns about the completion rates of these assessments and the quality of the assessment performance. Davis, Kumtepe, and Aydeniz (2007) concluded from their review of numerous studies in this arena that although peer assessment is conducive to the improvement of learning, its validity and reliability are open to question, mainly because students lack sufficient subject knowledge.

These studies suggest that self- and peer-assessment may be more suitable for formative than summative assessment purposes, although further research is necessary to determine the impact of incorrect formative assessments on eventual performance. As mentioned earlier, Webb et al. (2002) found that the eventual performance (i.e., delayed posttest results) of high-ability students was negatively influenced by the earlier receipt of partially incorrect or incomplete explanations. Nevertheless, the "authenticity" of assessments that students have codeveloped with the teacher may make students more ready to learn from assessment results—an important key to formative assessment.

CONCLUSIONS AND IMPLICATIONS

This chapter has reviewed collaborative learning-related, cognitively oriented research on assessment published between 1994 and 2009. The beginning of this period coincides with the publication of Gipps's (1994) *Beyond Testing: Towards a Theory of Educational Assessment*, which argues for a shift from psychometric views of assessment to views that honor the multidimesnional and context-dependent nature of educational performance. All of the studies discussed herein are relevant to an understanding of the intersection of collaborative learning and assessment, although they do not all deal with both topics. The assessment strategies that have been discussed include formative assessment involving individual students; assessment of individual students' science knowledge and inquiry and problem-solving abilities after working in small groups; quantitative measures of individual students' participation in online discussions; assessment of class knowledge building using portfolios created by individual students; and a variety of self- and peer-assessments focusing on learning by individual students after they have worked in small groups. This section elaborates upon why collaborative learning is a necessity, despite the substantial difficulties in assessment, and then returns to the four issues highlighted in the Introduction to outline a research agenda.

The Necessity of Collaborative Learning

The author contends that in a 21st century educational worldview, collaborative learning is no longer an instructional *choice* but a necessity. Learning and working in teams is pervasive in the world of work; for example, software design teams, executive teams, and restaurant staff. In work situations, collective goals and achievements are the raison d'être for collaborative teams, but individual contributions and achievements are also important. The world of work requires that individuals are able to work with others in a variety of situations, and the need for workplace collaboration has increased substantially in recent decades. Technological developments throughout the 20th century led to phenomenal increases in access to travel, information, and communications, and rendered the world more globally competitive and faster-paced. The need for up-to-date knowledge that goes beyond the boundaries of what is known and "disruptive innovation" (Hagel & Seely Brown, 2005) has increased dramatically. Knowledge work is significantly more difficult than traditional learning, and relies on teamwork. Equally important, the new work-related conditions are mirrored by the experience of students, who also have unprecedented access to information and social networks (e.g., Google and other Internet search engines, Facebook, and Twitter) and now use them in their everyday lives. However, although students can make use of online communities for learning (Gee, 2007), their information and digital literacy and inquiry and collaboration skills still require substantial development. Thus, educational priorities must be altered to provide a better balance between domain knowledge and development of the capacity for new learning. Collaboration is necessary because it can lead to better results than individual efforts and because it can render development of the capacity for new learning more feasible.

Issues 1 and 2: Assessment of Learning in Small Groups

Collaborative learning strategies are frequently employed for practical reasons, for example, because they are effective, involve mutual engagement with learning goals, distribute effort, and lead to collective learning outcomes that surpass what students can accomplish solo. However, many difficulties arise from individual differences in prior knowledge, motivation, interest in the task, effort, and ability to coordinate the contributions of multiple students (e.g., Barron, 2003; Colbeck et al., 2000; Webb et al., 1998), rendering the assessment of collaborative learning in small groups inequitable. Some groups clearly learn more than others for reasons that have little to do with the degree of effort invested in the learning process. Webb and colleagues (Webb, Nemer, Chizhik, & Sugrue,1998; Webb, Nemer, & Zuniga, 2002) suggested that each group must have at least one high-achieving student.

Another strategy for addressing these problems is to have students work with many different collaborative partners over time, to ensure that they are not always part of an advantaged or disadvantaged team and that they have opportunities to learn to work with students who vary in such variables as prior knowledge and interaction style. Learning communities may provide a better configuration than fixed small groups because they place more emphasis on collective goals, articulated in part by the commnity members, and allow for expertise to be distributed to a greater extent than is possible in small groups (Bielaczyc & Collins, 1999). Thus, more students can benefit from the various competencies that different students bring to the community's learning. In a study of three successive knowledge-building communities in Grade 4 classes taught by the same teacher, Zhang, Scardamalia, Reeve, and Messina (2009) found that the diffusion of ideas was greatest in the "opportunistic group" configuration, in which students formed collaborative groups to deal with emerging inquiry questions and, over time, worked in many different groups, compared with the "fixed group" and "interacting group" configurations, in which they worked with the same students throughout the school year. Strategies for diffusing learning across small groups, such as gallery walks and presentations, can also be helpful (Kolodner et al., 2003). Another important variable is the *nature of the task*; a strong commitment to shared goals is more likely to occur when all collaborating students grasp the educational value of the task in question. Almost all of the studies examined in this review involved relatively short-term collaborations in small groups. More research that examines issues of equity and learning longitudinally and at different levels of analysis (individual, group, and community) would be useful.

There also are problems with the *validity* of assessments of collaborative learning, both in small groups and in general. Because, as Stahl (2010) argues, the major cognitive benefit of collaborative learning is that it leads to collective learning outcomes that are irreducible to individual learning outcomes, it seems important to report learning outcomes at both levels. Reporting a grade for the group-level outcome, such as the overall quality of the project, as well as that reflecting a particular student's own knowledge relative to that of other group members, would provide a more complete picture of learning performance. Doing so could show, for example, that the group had developed a high-quality project, but that the particular student in question had learned less from the project than his or her peers, that is, less than the group-level grade would suggest. This kind of assessment approach would allow us to learn more about whether individual students are benefiting cognitively from collaboration. Current practice neglects one or the other of the two levels of learning performance: it measures individual learning outcomes but neglects group-level outcomes or measures group-level outcomes and incorrectly infers individual learning, often confusing it with effort. The more widespread uptake of collaborative learning, it seems, requires assessments that provide clear evidence of the benefits of collaboration.

Issue 3: Developing Collaborative Learning as a Human Competence

Following Barron (2003), it is proposed that collaborative learning is not merely a method for learning but a *human competence* that is difficult to achieve and requires effort to develop. As indicated earlier, it is also an important 21st-century competence. It could be argued that the "collaborative" in collaborative learning should refer to an aspect of learning that, if well-developed, empowers students to achieve learning that would be impossible without collaboration. Learning how to learn collaboratively then becomes an aspect of learning how to learn, a skill emphasized in many recent curriculum reforms (e.g., CDC, 2000). Although collaboration is more difficult than solo learning in some respects (i.e., coordination, social skills), it can scaffold learning how to learn by distributing cognitively difficult processes such as regulation and reflection. Formative assessment and self- and peer-assessment have important roles to play in this arena.

However, although the current research on formative assessment is helpful in clarifying the possibility of using assessment as a learning resource, it falls short in demonstrating how students can be empowered as agents of their own learning; formative assessment is largely done to students by teachers. By comparison, self- and peer-assessments are performed by students and provide better opportunities for them to reflect and understand what constitutes quality performance, particularly on complex tasks. Further theoretical and empirical research is required to align formative assessment and self- and peer-assessment with a theory of agency in collaborative learning. Although agency is important in theories of self-regulated learning (Winne & Hadwin, 1998), these theories are primarily concerned with individual learning.

Issue 4: Objectivity and Reliability in Assessment

Objectivity and reliability are crucial to high-stakes assessments such as matriculation examinations and international evaluations of educational progress, which are beyond the scope of this chapter. However, as noted earlier, there has been substantial growth in the use of school-based assessments of complex performance, which sometimes involves collaboration (e.g., the ability to converse with others in a second language).

In some countries, teachers have considerable freedom in the conduct of school-based assessments, but, when external examinations also exist, these assessments often are designed to provide practice for the external examinations rather than an opportunity to assess more complex student performance than is amenable to large-scale testing. Substantial work is necessary to establish a school-based assessment method that is suitable for assessing those types of performance that are unsuitable for large-scale testing. In many situations that require collaboration, the learning products may vary substantially between groups (for example, one group may solve a mathematics problem geometrically and another algebraically), and requiring solutions to be more uniform (e.g., only geometric) would undermine the goal of stimulating creativity. Standards-based approaches can be useful, but the dimensions of performance should be generative of future learning rather than merely descriptive of the content knowledge that is of immediate concern. In their work on portfolio assessment in knowledge building, van Aalst and Chan (2007) provided such dimensions (e.g., collaborative effort and progressive problem solving) and asked students to analyze the extent to which there was evidence of these dimensions in their class's Knowledge Forum database.

Apart from these qualitative features of collaborative learning, research is also needed both to develop instruments that students and teachers can use to guide the improvement of collaborative practices and to determine *how* these instruments are used. As noted earlier, participation data such as the number of notes created by individual students are easily obtained, but they do not provide clear recommendations for improving online discussions. Advanced techniques such as social network analysis fail to address this problem. Of course, the way in which a class of students makes use of information depends on such contextual factors as students' previous experience and goals, but it would still be useful to know whether writing more notes is likely to lead to conceptual change or whether another strategy would be more beneficial. Willis et al. (2002) developed a rubric for assessing group interaction and activity among medical students engaged in PBL, but few studies developing such instruments for use in other education fields were found in the literature review carried out for this chapter. Such development would thus constitute a fruitful direction for future research.

ACKNOWLEDGMENTS

The preparation of this chapter was supported by a General Research Fund grant from the Research Grants Council of Hong Kong (Grant HKU 752508H). The author would also like to thank Li Sha for useful discussions.

REFERENCES

American Association for the Advancement of Science (AAAS). (1993). *Benchmarks for science literacy.* New York: Oxford University Press.

Assessment of 21st Century Skills (ACT21) Project. (n.d.). Retrieved from www.act21.org

Barron, B. (2003). When smart groups fail. *Journal of the Learning Sciences, 12*, 307–359.

Bielaczyc, K., & Collins, A. (1999). Learning communities in classrooms: A reconceptualization of educational practice. In C. M. Reigeluth (Ed.), *Instructional design theories and models* (Vol. 2, pp. 269–292). Mahwah, NJ: Erlbaum.

Biggs, J. (Ed.). (1996). *Testing: To educate or to select? Education in Hong Kong at the crossroads.* Hong Kong SAR, China: Hong Kong Educational.

Black, P., Harrison, C., Lee, C., Marshall, B., & Wiliam, D. (2003). *Assessment for learning: Putting it into practice.* New York: Open University Press.

Black, P., & Wiliam, D. (1998). Assessment and classroom learning. *Assessment in Education: Principles, Policy, and Practice, 5*, 7–74.

Black, P., & Wiliam, D. (2009). Developing the theory of formative assessment. *Educational Assessment, Evaluation and Accountability, 21*(1), 5–31.

Center for Curriculum Development (CDC). (2000). *Learning to learn: The way forward in curriculum development.* Hong Kong SAR, China: Author.

Center for Curriculum Development (CDC)/Hong Kong Examinations and Assessment Authority (HKEAA). (2007). *Liberal studies curriculum and assessment guide (secondary 4–6).* Hong Kong SAR, China: Author.

Chan, C. K. K., & van Aalst, J. (2004). Learning, assessment, and collaboration in computer-supported learning environments. In J. W. Strijbos, P. A. Kirschner, & R. L. Martens (Eds.), *What we know about CSCL: And implementing it in higher education* (pp. 87–112). Dordrecht, Netherlands: Kluwer.

Chen, C.-M., & Chen, M.-C. (2009). Mobile formative assessment tool based on data mining techniques for supporting web-based learning. *Computers & Education, 52*, 256–273.

Colbeck, C., Campbell, S., & Bjorklund, S. (2000). Grouping in the dark: What college students learn from group projects. *The Journal of Higher Education, 71*(1), 60–83.

Dannefer, E. F., Henson, L. C., Bierer, S. B., Grady-Weliky, T. A., Meldrum, S., Nofziger, A. C., & Epstein, R. M. (2005). Peer assessment of professional competence. *Medical Education, 39*, 713–722.

Davis, N. T., Kumtepe, E. G., & Aydeniz, M. (2007). Fostering continuous improvement and learning through peer assessment: Part of an integral model of assessment. *Educational Assessment, 12*, 113–135.

de Laat, M., Lally, V., & Lipponen, L. (2007). Investigating patterns of interaction in networked learning and computer-supported collaborative learning: A role for social network analysis. *International Journal of Computer-Supported Collaborative Learning, 2*, 87–103.

Foltz, P. (1997). Latent semantic analysis for text-based research. *Behavior Research Methods, Instruments and Computers, 28*, 197–202.

Gee, J. P. (2007). *What video games have to teach us about learning and literacy. Revised and updated edition.* New York: Palgrave Macmillan.

Gipps, C. V. (1994). *Beyond testing: Towards a theory of educational assessment.* Abingdon, England: RoutledgeFalmer.
Guzdial, M., & Turns, J. (2000). Effective discussion through a computer-mediated anchored forum. *Journal of the Learning Sciences, 9*, 437–469.
Hagel, J. III, & Seely Brown, J. (2005). *The only sustainable edge: Why business strategy depends on productive friction and dynamic specialization.* Boston, MA: Harvard Business School Press.
Hakkarainen, K. (2003). Emergence of progressive-inquiry culture in computer-supported collaborative learning. *Learning Environments Research, 6*, 199–220.
Hattie, J., & Timperley, H. (2007). The power of feedback. *Review of Educational Research, 77*, 81–112.
Haythornthwaite, C. (2002). Building social networks via computer networks: Creating and sustaining distributed learning communities. In K. A. Renniger & W. Shumar (Eds.), *Building virtual communities: Learning and change in cyberspace* (pp. 159–190). New York: Cambridge University Press.
Hewitt, J. (2005). Toward an understanding of how threads die in asynchronous computer conferences. *Journal of the Learning Sciences, 14*, 567–589.
Hsi, S., & Hoadley, C. M. (1997). Productive discussion in science: Gender equity through electronic discourse. *Journal of Science Education and Technology, 6*, 23–36.
Kolodner, J. L., Camp, P. J., Crismond, D., Fasse, B., Gray, J., Holbrook, J., … Ryan, M. (2003). Problem-based learning meets case-based reasoning in the middle-school science classroom: Putting Learning by Design into practice. *Journal of the Learning Sciences, 12*, 495–547.
Ladouceur, M. G., Rideout, E. M., Black, M. E. A., Crooks, D. L., O'Mara, L. M., & Schmuck, M. L. (2004). Development of an instrument to assess individual student performance in small group tutorials. *Journal of Nursing Education, 43*, 447–455.
Landauer, T. K., Laham, D., & Foltz, P. (2003). Automatic essay assessment. *Assessment in Education: Principles, Policy & Practice, 10*, 295–308.
Lee, E. Y. C., Chan, C. K. K., & van Aalst, J. (2006). Students assessing their own collaborative knowlegde building. *International Journal of Computer-Supported Collaborative Learning, 1*, 277–307.
National Council of Teachers of Mathematics (NCTM). (2000). *Principles and standards for school mathematics.* Reston, VA: Author..
National Research Council (NRC). (1996). *National science education standards.* Washington, DC: National Academic Press.
Pauli, R., Mohiyeddini, C., Bray, D., Michie, F., & Street, B. (2008). Individual differences in negative group work experiences in collaborative student learning. *Educational Psychology, 28*, 47–58.
Perrenoud, P. (1998). From formative evaluation to a controlled regulation of learning processes. Towards a wider conceptual field. *Assessment in Education: Principles, Policy & Practice, 5*, 85–102.
Prins, F. J., Sluijsmans, D. M. A., Kirschner, P. A., & Strijbos, J.-W. (2005). Formative peer assessment in a CSCL environment: A case study. *Assessment and Evaluation in Higher Education, 30*, 417–444.
Ramaprasad, A. (1983). On the definition of feedback. *Behavioral Science, 28*, 4–13.
Ross, J. A., & Starling, M. (2008). Self-assessment in a technology-supported environment: The case of grade 9 geography. *Assessment in Education: Principles, Policy & Practice, 15*, 183–199.
Ruiz-Primo, M. A., & Furtak, E. M. (2007). Exploring teachers' informal formative assessment practices and students' understanding in the context of scientific inquiry. *Journal of Research in Science Teaching, 44*, 57–84.
Scardamalia, M., & Bereiter, C. (2006). Knowledge building: Theory, pedagogy, and technology. In R. K. Sawyer (Ed.), *The Cambridge handbook of the learning sciences* (pp. 97–115). New York: Cambridge University Press.
Scriven, M. (1967). The methodology of evaluation. In R. Tyler, R. Gagne, & M. Scriven (Eds.), *Perspectives on curriculum evaluation* (pp. 121–132). Chicago, IL: Rand McNally.
Shepard, L. E. (2000). The role of assessment in a learning culture. *Educational Researcher, 29*(7), 1–14.
Stahl, G. (2002). Rediscovering CSCL. In T. Koschmann, R. Hall, & N. Miyake (Eds.), *CSCL 2: Carrying forward the conversation* (pp. 169–181). Mahwah, NJ: Erlbaum.
Stahl, G. (2010). Group cognition as a foundation for the new science of learning. In M. S. Khine & I. M. Saleh (Eds.), *The new science of learning: Cognition, computers and collaboration in education* (pp. 23–44). Dordrecht, Netherlands: Springer.
Taras, M. (2009). Summative assessment: The missing link for formative assessment. *Journal of Further and Higher Education, 33*, 57–69.
Tiwari, A., & Tang, C. (2003). From process to outcome: The effect of portfolio assessment on student learning. *Nurse Education Today, 23*(4), 269–277.
van Aalst, J. (2009). Distinguishing knowledge sharing, construction, and creation discourses. *International Journal of Computer-Supported Collaborative Learning, 4*, 259–288.

van Aalst, J., & Chan, C. K. K. (2007). Student-directed assessment of knowledge building using electronic portfolios. *Journal of the Learning Sciences, 16*, 175–220.
Webb, N. M., Nemer, K. M., Chizhik, A. W., & Sugrue, B. (1998). Equity issues in collaborative group assessment: Group composition and performance. *American Educational Research Journal, 35*, 607–651.
Webb, N. M., Nemer, K. M., & Zuniga, S. (2002). Short circuits or superconductors? Effects of group composition on high-achieving students' science assessment performance. *American Educational Research Journal, 39*, 943–989.
Wells, G. (1999). *Dialogic inquiry: Toward a sociocultural practice and theory of education*. New York: Cambridge University Press.
White, B. Y., & Frederiksen, J. (1998). Inquiry, modeling, and metacognition: Making science accessible to all students. *Cognition and Instruction, 16*, 1–118.
Willis, S. C., Jones, A., Bundy, C., Burdett, K., Whitehouse, C. R., & O'Neill, P. A. (2002). Small-group work and assessment in a PBL curriculum: A qualitative and quantitative evaluation of student perceptions of the process of working in small groups and its assessment. *Medical Teacher, 24*, 495–501.
Winne, P., & Hadwin, A. (1998). Studying as self-regulated learning. In D. J. Hacker, J. Dunlosky, & A. C. Graesser (Eds.), *Metacognition in educational theory and practice* (pp. 277–304). Mahwah, NJ: Erlbaum.
Yorke, M. (2003). Formative assessment in higher education: Moves towards theory and the enhancement of pedagogic practice. *Higher Education, 45*, 477–501.
Zhang, J., Scardamalia, M., Reeve, R., & Messina, R. (2009). Designs for collective cognitive responsibility in knowledge-building communities. *Journal of the Learning Sciences, 18*, 7–44.

17

COLLABORATIVE LEARNING FOR DIVERSE LEARNERS

ADRIAN F. ASHMAN AND ROBYN M. GILLIES

School of Education, University of Queensland

THE LEARNING CONTEXT

For over 40 years educators have advocated the inclusion of students with diverse learning needs in mainstream classes. The arguments in support of inclusion have various bases, from philosophical and social justice imperatives to claims about the academic and social benefits of including students with modest to very high special learning needs. While legislation, education policy, and rhetoric in support of inclusive education has become a global phenomenon, the claims of successful inclusion and positive outcomes for all those involved have fallen considerably short of the ideal (e.g., Curcic, 2009; Drudy & Kinsella, 2009; Melekoglu, Cakiroglu, & Malmgren, 2009).

The philosophical and moral arguments have not remained unchallenged (e.g., Cigman, 2007), and those claiming academic and social advantages as a result of inclusion have not been supported by unequivocal empirical data. Indeed, a comprehensive review of the literature would suggest that the assertions and claims of success made by advocates and disciples of inclusive education is far from a reality. In his encyclopedic review of 800 meta-analyses in education research, Hattie (2009) reported effect sizes for mainstreaming that ranged from 0.08 to 0.47 with a mean effect size of $d = 0.28$. To put this into perspective, Hattie found that the average effect size for educational interventions was 0.40 and has argued that effect sizes below that figure are more disadvantageous than advantageous in respect of student outcomes (Hattie, 2007).

If inclusive education has not been the success that one might have expected, why is this so? There have been many assertions, including persistent negative attitudes toward disability and difference among teachers and students, the lack of financial support for classroom adaptations, inadequate initial teacher education, and continuing professional development. One of the more important deficiencies that teachers assert is their lack of teaching-learning strategies needed to deal with the needs of students exhibiting learning and behavioral difficulties.

It is not within the scope of this contribution to argue for and against inclusive education. It is important, however, to address the last point raised in the preceding paragraph. Humphrey (2009) argued that the teaching and learning strategies that are effective in mainstream classes for students performing according to the age norms are exactly the same as those that are effective with students with a range of special learning needs. Florian (2008) put this point in a slightly different way. She stated that regular education teachers are already adequately equipped to teach students with a diversity of skills and abilities typically found in mainstream classes. Florian's assertion would, therefore, suggest that peer-mediation as applied in regular education classes should be effective in supporting students with diverse learning needs.

If this is the case, how effective is peer-mediated learning in improving the knowledge, skills, and performance of students with diverse learning needs? This is the question we address in this chapter. Throughout, we use the term *peer-mediated learning* to describe the collection of teaching-learning strategies in which student peers work with and support each other.

PEER SUPPORT: CONCEPTUAL FRAMEWORKS

Mediated learning derives from Vygotsky's writings (e.g., Vygotsky, 1962, 1978). He emphasized the importance of social interaction during which an expert guides a novice through a task to ensure that the novice acquires the higher-level skills desired. Vygotsky has had a major and continuing impact upon the theory and practice of cognitive psychology and its applications to education. One of his primary assertions was the need to accelerate children's cognitive development through education. In other words, schools should not only provide experiences at an individual's current level of cognitive maturity but also should provide a social construction in which learning and cognitive development occurs. This milieu will be affected by the interactions that individuals have with others who are more or less skilled or more or less knowledgeable.

Like the literature and the anecdotal reports that relate to many (if not most) education innovations and technologies, the literature on peer-mediated learning provides a revealing lesson in contradiction. When asked, many classroom teachers at the primary/elementary and secondary levels will claim to use one or a range of peer-mediated learning strategies in their classrooms although most will confess that they do not adhere to the set procedures for any of the well-researched and documented programs. This may be a crucial factor when dealing with students with diverse abilities in any classroom, many of whom need structured learning experiences that build slowly and purposefully on their existing knowledge bases (see Mastropieri & Scruggs, 2001).

We take a step backward here to consider the conceptual frameworks that have guided peer-mediated learning. As others in this compendium have outlined the theory more fully than it is our intention here, we focus specifically on peer-mediated approaches that have been used commonly in inclusive education settings, namely, peer tutoring, peer collaboration, and cooperative learning. While each deals with the way in which students mediate each other's learning, each is different in its conceptual roots and implementation.

Peer Tutoring

Peer tutoring has its roots in teacher-directed learning and the assumption that the most powerful influences on children's behavior at school are other children. This position is predicated on the assumption that peers can do what teachers do, that is, teach.

Interaction with others is seen as critical for the development of children's higher cognitive functions because capable adults and peers mediate children's environments by focusing attention on relevant information and providing the tools for problem solving, such as speech, learning artifacts (e.g., memory strategies), and ways of reasoning.

Children are introduced to new ways of reasoning and patterns of thought when they engage in dialogs with more competent others, so eventually, after repeated exposure to these experiences, a child's thinking and communication processes become internalized as part of his or her repertoire of cognitive skills. By interacting with others, children not only acquire new information but also new ways of thinking that are implicit in the interaction. Furthermore, learning supports (i.e., scaffolding) enable them to complete tasks that they could not do alone (Vygotsky, 1978).

Peer tutoring involves a more able peer (the tutor) working with a less-able peer (the tutee) to help the latter master specific information or tasks; an ideal situation in inclusive classrooms. The tutor is assumed to have greater competence and transmits this expertise to the tutee. The tutor is essentially a surrogate teacher who has control of the information to be imparted and the process(es) to be employed. The relationship between the tutor and the tutee is asymmetrical and the instruction process involves direct teaching, guided practice, feedback, and reteaching until mastery is obtained. This form of direct teaching has been shown to promote students' learning (see Rosenshine, 2009).

Peer Collaboration

Peer collaboration is a second form of peer-mediated learning. Collaboration facilitates the exploration of new ideas, the discovery of solutions, and creation of knowledge unrestrained by a knowledgeable expert who might impose a solution on the problem being addressed. This form of peer-based learning has its origin in Piaget's theory of cognitive growth (Piaget, 1950) with its emphasis on peer interaction. Piaget believed that interactions expose children to different points of view and give rise to a state of cognitive conflict as children are challenged to keep their own points of view in mind while taking account of others that are incompatible. This dilemma creates cognitive tension and disequilibrium, which if it is to be resolved, forces the child to decenter and consider what others have to say. Because individuals are strongly motivated to reconcile contradictions, they will reevaluate and restructure their own thinking on the basis of new the information. Interaction with others is a trigger to social and cognitive change.

Peer collaboration usually involves students of equal abilities actively exchanging ideas about a problem rather than one learning from the other. In this respect, peer collaboration involves symmetrical relationships that are high on equality and mutuality with each member working synchronously on the same part of the problem at the same time (Foot, Morgan, & Shute, 1990). Like peer tutoring, peer collaboration is based on the assumption that children can teach each other, albeit in a more informal manner and with no prescribed roles.

Early studies by Mugny and Doise (1978) and Doise and Mugny (1984) demonstrated the role of sociocognitive conflict in children's cognitive development. Specifically, children learn to coordinate their own actions with those of others to construct new cognitive understandings. Studies such as these have implications for how teachers might establish collaborative learning experiences in classrooms. Providing children with opportunities to explain their thinking processes, even when they are incorrect, enables them to reflect on different perspectives and to revise their cognitions in the light of new information and ideas. Peers are a particularly compelling source of cognitive conflict because they speak to each other in ways that can be understood easily, they take feedback from each other seriously, and they are strongly motivated to reconcile differences (Damon, 1984).

Cooperative Learning

Cooperative learning is a third form of peer-mediated learning. Cooperative learning involves students working in small groups (3 to 4 members) to accomplish shared goals. Cooperative learning has many characteristics in common with peer tutoring and peer collaboration but differs in its operation as group members have specific behaviors, roles, and tasks to fulfill. Like peer collaboration, cooperative learning is based on an essentially symmetrical relationship so that no member is dominant and all are required to contribute to completing the task and assisting others to do likewise.

While Piaget's (1950) and Vygotsky's (1978) theories explain how children challenge and scaffold each other's learning when they cooperate, social interdependence theory (Deutsch, 1949) offers an explanation for the underlying psychological processes that motivate members to cooperate. Social interdependence theory is based on the premise that the way in which interdependence is structured determines how individuals interact, and the interaction pattern determines the outcomes of the situation. Positive interdependence exists when members perceive that they cannot succeed unless others do and they must coordinate their actions to ensure that this occurs. As group members realize that their success is dependent on the success of others, cohesiveness develops as a direct result of goal interdependence and the perceived interdependence of group members. Once this occurs, group members understand that their efforts are indispensable to the success of the group and if they want to succeed they must work together. This realization motivates cooperation (Johnson & Johnson, 2003).

Numerous studies over the last four decades have attested to the benefits that students derive from working cooperatively together, as will be obvious from other contributions to this volume. Notable highlights within the literature are meta-analyses by Johnson, Maruyama, Johnson, Nelson, and Skon (1981), Johnson and Johnson (2003, Lou, Abrami, Spence et al. (1996), Lou, Abrami, and d'Apollonia (2001), and Slavin (1996).

FROM THEORY TO APPLICATION WITH SPECIAL STUDENT POPULATIONS

While peer tutoring, peer collaboration, and cooperative learning differ in the roles and the activities in which students are expected to engage, the extensive body of research on each approach draws attention to the benefits to students who are achieving according to grade expectations from the early years of school to college, and across different subject areas. And yet, despite the many positive reports of peer-mediated programs that one finds in the professional literature, including our own work (see e.g., Gillies, Ashman, & Terwell, 2008; Heron, Villareal, Yao, Christianson, & Heron, 2006; Maheady, Mallette, & Harper, 2006; Rohrbeck, Ginsburg-Block, Fantuzzo, & Miller, 2003; Topping, 2005; Webb, 2009), there are many mixed messages in terms of the success, or lack of it. Large-scale research is also difficult to find and there is an abundance of reports in which very small-group or small-sample studies predominate (e.g., Baker, Gersten, Dimino, & Griffiths, 2004; Mortweet et al., 1999; Wolford, Heward, & Alber, 2001).

While peer-mediated learning has received considerable attention in mainstream education contexts, there are still relatively few reports of effective use with students with diverse learning needs. Some writers have claimed that well-validated dyadic peer-mediated programs benefit students with and without learning disabilities (e.g., Fuchs, Fuchs, Yazdian, & Powell, 2002) but the evidence to support such claims is far from convincing (e.g., Fuchs, Fuchs, Mathes, & Simmons, 1997; Kuntz, McLaughlin, & Howard, 2001; Rohrbeck et al., 2003).

There are confounding issues in operation in special populations. For example, there are important prerequisite skills for effective and cooperative interactions between peers. So, a student who presents with severe challenging or aggressive behavior might benefit little from social interactions with students in the same classroom who are socially very adept. A student with a severe intellectual disability might not possess the skills needed to communicate with age-peers.

There are also methodological issues that have been raised in the literature. McMaster, Fuchs, and Fuchs (2002), for example, argued that inconsistencies in results might be (partly) attributable to the use of multicomponent interventions that might make it impossible to separate the influence of peer mediation from other aspects of the intervention. And drawing attention to their own program, McMaster, Fuchs, and Fuchs (2006) discussed limitations of the often-reported successful peer-assisted learning strategies (PALS) program. They stated that about 20% of low-achieving nondisabled students do not make expected achievement gains following PALS interventions and more than 50% of students with disabilities fail to show benefits when assessed on reading achievement tests. They drew attention to these students' low phonological competence, low socioeconomic background, low cognitive competence, and attention and behavior difficulties.

PEER MEDIATION AND DIVERSE LEARNING NEEDS

In this section we draw attention to the success (or otherwise) of peer-mediated learning approaches in classrooms that contain students who experience a range of learning challenges. We begin our discussion by focusing on students with learning difficulties where there are arguably more positive outcomes for peer-mediated interventions than in other special groups. We then consider students with emotional/behavior disorders, students with more serious learning difficulties, minority groups, and finally students with special gifts or talents.

Students with Learning Difficulties

Students with learning difficulties comprise a heterogeneous population. Commonly, members of this group experience difficulties with literacy and numeracy that are identified early in the individual's schooling and continue throughout their lives. These students often display difficulties with number and calculation or word recognition, and processing spoken and printed words.

Peer tutoring has a long history although it was not until the 1960s that empirical research began to emerge about the academic and social benefits that accrue to both tutor and tutees (e.g., Allen, 1976; Cloward, 1967; Damon, 1984; Shamir & Lazerovitz, 2007).

In a review of five meta-analyses of the effectiveness of peer tutoring, Lipsey and Wilson (1993) found that tutored students consistently showed improvements in achievement across primary/elementary, secondary, and special education contexts. Mean effect sizes ranged from 0.33 to 0.98 with effect sizes of 0.59 and 0.65 in two analyses using special education students as tutors and tutees. A recent large-scale study would seem to supports these findings (see Kamps, Greenwood, Arreaga-Mayer, Veerkamp, & Bannister, 2008).

Kamps et al. (2008) examined the efficacy of class-wide peer tutoring (CWPT) in 52 Grade 6 to 8 classrooms in six urban schools. All students participated in CWPT and three or four of the lowest performing students from each class were also targeted for observation during classroom sessions. Seventy-five such students were observed over the 3 years of the study. The results showed the effectiveness of CWPT and an improvement in the activity level of students in peer tutoring sessions when compared to teacher-led sessions. While the analyses of learning achievements were conducted at the classroom level, an examination of the single-subject results showed strong effects for lower ability students.

Researchers have also targeted specific curriculum areas. Kunsch, Jitendra, and Sood (2007), for example, synthesized the effects of peer-mediated interventions on the mathematics performance of students with disabilities and those at risk of mathematics disabilities. Meta-analytic techniques were used to calculate the effect sizes in 17 studies. Effect sizes ranged from 0.44 to 1.77 for 12 of the studies while the remaining five showed no, or very modest improvement (-0.02 to 0.39). Peer-mediated interventions in regular and special education classrooms achieved mean effect size of 0.56 and 0.32 respectively. The data showed that students at-risk of mathematics disabilities improved most following intervention (mean effect size = 0.66) compared with students with identified learning disabilities (mean effect size = 0.21). A more recent study by Menesses and Gresham (2009) on students at risk of academic failure in mathematics also found large effect sizes ranging from 0.83 to 1.58 postintervention and at the follow-up 3 weeks after the completion of the study.

In reading, Palinscar and Brown built on earlier collaborative learning research to develop their popular Reciprocal Reading program. In a 1984 study, they found that when children with reading difficulties were taught the strategies that successful readers use to comprehend text (i.e., reciprocal teaching strategies), they demonstrated significant improvement over comparison with peers in the quality of summaries and questions they were able to generate, and obtained significantly higher scores on a follow-up comprehension test. Of importance, these results were maintained over time and generalized to classroom comprehension tests, to novel tasks that tapped the reciprocal teaching skills they had been taught, and led to improvements in standardized comprehension scores.

Since then, there have been many studies based on reciprocal teaching. Kelly, Moore, and Tuck (1994) showed significant improvements in students' comprehension scores that were not evident in their comparison peers on a standardized reading test and in daily comprehension tests after 20 days of instruction. Later, Alfassi (1998) investigated differences between reciprocal teaching methods (strategy instruction) and traditional methods of remedial reading (skill acquisition) in students attending remedial reading classes. The results showed that the students who participated in the reciprocal teaching classes obtained significantly higher postintervention scores on experimenter-designed comprehension tests. Gajria, Jitendra, Sood, and Sacks (2007) found comparable results in a meta-analysis of 29 studies that focused on improving the comprehension of text by students with learning disabilities. Four studies used reciprocal teaching with effect sizes ranging from 0.39 to 1.21.

Positive outcomes have also been shown for collaborative strategic reading (CSR), also based on Palinscar and Brown's (1984) reciprocal teaching. Bryant et al. (2000), for example, used CSR as part of a multicomponent reading intervention with students with reading disabilities, low-achieving, and average-achieving students in Grade 6 classes. Only moderate effect sizes were found with a subgroup of students with severe reading difficulties showing no improvements as a result of the intervention. Klinger, Vaughn, Arguelles, Hughes, and Leftwich (2004) reported somewhat similar result in another CSR study. They found a low overall effect size of 0.19 although when compared by achievement level, low-achieving students and students with learning disability outperformed their peers in the control condition recording effect sizes of 0.51 and 0.38 respectively.

In summary, the effects of specific peer-mediated interventions on students with learning difficulties appears to be positive with many studies attesting to the benefits these students derive from such interventions. However, the results are less clear for students with severe or challenging behaviors who may not have the requisite social or intellectual skills needed to communicate with their peers to enable them to benefit from such interventions.

Students with Emotional and Behavioral Disorders

Students with these difficulties present with a range of characteristics, from what might be considered unacceptable behavior within a classroom (e.g., calling out, distracting others from their work) to those diagnosed with Asperger's syndrome, attention deficit hyperactivity disorder, and autism spectrum disorder (although we deal with this more explicitly below).

Social skills have often been a target of peer-mediated learning programs. At times, the affective outcomes have been considered as secondary consequences to academic skills. In other times, changes in social interactions have been the researchers' primary concern.

Peer-mediated learning, such as class-wide peer tutoring and cooperative learning, have been used to promote academic gains with students with emotional and behavior disorders in mainstream and special school settings (e.g., Bowman-Perrott, 2009; Bowman-Perrot, Greenwood, & Tapia, 2007). The results, however, have not been spectacular despite reviewers' optimistic conclusions. Ryan, Reid, and Epstein (2004), for example, examined 14 studies undertaken between 1982 and 2000. They found positive academic outcomes across all forms of peer-mediated interventions with overall high consumer satisfaction. They noted, however, that only eight studies were conducted in general education classrooms. While the reviewers were complimentary in their conclusions, an examination of their summary table prompts caution. The results for eight studies were uniformly positive. For three, there were mixed results showing gains and no gains, and in three studies there were marginal or no appreciable gains.

Sutherland, Wehby, and Gunter (2000) reported similar findings to those of Ryan et al. (2004) in a review of eight cooperative learning studies and Spencer (2006) reported comparable results. Spencer reviewed 38 peer-tutoring studies undertaken between

1972 and 2002 and examined data according to grade levels. Many of the studies undertaken in elementary classrooms showed positive outcomes for participants in reading, language, and mathematics. She reported mixed findings on attitude measures although there were increases in positive social interactions between students with and without a disability. In contrast, studies undertaken in the middle years and senior years of schooling were not as positive. Despite the variability of outcomes, Spencer concluded on a positive note, stating that there is an emerging body of evidence to suggest that students with emotional or behavior disorders may benefit from peer tutoring.

Comments that we made earlier about the importance of prerequisite social skills were also raised by Hodges, Riccomini, Buford, and Herbst (2006) in their report of peer-mediated interventions with students with emotional or behavior disorders. They stated that peer-mediated instruction might be beneficial for these students in social and academic areas but because of the difficulties that many of these students have in interpersonal relationships, it would seem imperative that researchers include specific training on interpersonal skills to enable them to work effectively in dyads or small groups. They cautioned that the lack of research related to academic achievement would suggest that replication and systematic collection of student performance data would be necessary to validate intervention outcomes.

Research by Cohen and her colleagues is relevant here (Cohen, Lotan, Abram, Scarloss, & Schultz, 2006; Cohen, Lotan, Scarloss, & Arellano, 1999). In a series of studies, these investigators documented the success of Complex Instruction in addressing issues of social and academic competence in diverse classrooms; that is, classrooms with students with a range of learning, linguistic, and social needs. Cohen et al. argued that low status is often assigned to students in classes because they are perceived as not having the social or academic competencies of their peers. To overcome this problem, she advocated two strategies: (a) the multiple-abilities treatment and (b) the assignment of competence to low-status peers. Both strategies require the teacher to publicly recognize the wealth of intellectual abilities that are valued in daily life in the classroom and the importance of positively evaluating the competencies of low-status students.

Results of their work indicate that the interventions increased participation by low-status students in peer group discussions and the quality of the group products produced. While these results provide teachers with an instructional approach to ensuring that students with low status are included in peer group work, Cohen, Lotan, Abram, et al. cautioned that groups need to be structured to ensure that students are able to participate and all "students must be trained in the skills for harmonious and helpful discourse" (2006, p. 1066) if small-group work is to succeed.

Students with Low Incidence Disabilities

This a heterogeneous group of individuals including those with moderate intellectual disability, acquired brain injury, physical, and sensory impairments. Young people with autism spectrum disorder (ASD) would also fall within this classification, recognizing that some display serious social and emotional disturbances. Consistent with comments in the previous section, not all attempts to improve academic and social outcomes via peer-mediated learning have been successful (e.g., Brinton, Fujiki, & Higbee, 1998; Brinton, Fujiki, Montague, & Hanton, 2000).

Many studies involving students with severe impairments or disabilities have focused on social and emotional outcomes rather than academic outcomes (e.g., Liberman,

Dunn, van der Mars, & McCubbin, 2000; Morgan, Whorton, & Turtle, 1999; McDonnell, Mathot-Buckner, Thorson, & Fister, 2001; Ryan & Paterna, 1997). Most studies of peer-mediated learning with students with intellectual disability have been conducted in special classes or other special education settings. Few have been undertaken in general education classrooms (see Mortweet et al., 1999). One such study by Jacques, Wilton, and Townsend (1998) examined the effects of interactions between 24 students with mild intellectual disability and their nondisabled peers in the context of cooperative learning. All of the students were in regular education settings although half had attended special education classes prior to the intervention. The nondisabled students in the experimental condition demonstrated significant increases in their social acceptance of the children with a disability immediately after the program using a sociometric procedure. There were no changes in social acceptance in the control setting. Jacques et al. noted that teacher ratings of the experimental group's social adjustment were not significantly different from those of the control group immediately after the intervention, or at the 5-week follow up.

In a later study, Piercy, Wilton, and Townsend (2002) again implemented a cooperative learning program to improve the social acceptance of children with moderate to severe intellectual disabilities. The children interacted over 10 weeks in three experimental conditions (cooperative learning, social-contact, and no classroom contact). At the completion of the program, the students without a disability in the cooperative learning groups rated the students with disability more positively on peer acceptance, popularity, and social-distance than children who participated in the two control group settings.

One infrequently addressed issue is students' perceptions of peer-mediated learning. Koh, Tan, Wang, Ee, and Liu (2007) interviewed 13- to 14-year old Singaporean students with low ability to gain an understanding of the students' views about the effectiveness of group project work. They found that while students appreciated some of the benefits of group work, they did not view group work as a high priority and tended to put less effort into those activities. Students also reported that they received little training in the skills required for group work and perceived the teacher, rather than themselves, as being in control of the process and outcomes.

A number of studies have also been conducted on the effectiveness of peer-mediated learning with students with ASD. The usual focus of attention has been either social acceptance by peers or the development of social, cooperative behavior in the student with ASD. Weiss and Harris (2001), for example, discussed the importance of the placement of socially competent students with peers displaying autistic behavior, the training of peers to manage autistic behavior, and the initiation of interactions with autistic students. Other social skills of importance to the success of cooperative learning activities include answering questions, turn-taking, and looking at others when they speak. Weiss and Harris argued that proximity alone does not bring about enduring social change or the generalization of social skills beyond the training context.

Other writers have expressed similar views to Weiss and Harris (e.g., Downs & Smith, 2004; Harrower & Dunlap, 2001). Harrower and Dunlap, for example, drew attention to investigations in which class-wide peer tutoring and cooperative learning models were used successfully. In these, they referred to improvement in targeted academic skills and engagement. There were also increased interactions between children with ASD and their classmates who learned to cue and prompt the students successfully to facilitate achievement in the target areas. While these approaches may seem to work effectively in inclusive classrooms, Harrower and Dunlap cautioned that increasing the rate of social interaction among children with disability through peer-mediation might not always lead to enduring changes outside of the program settings, echoing comments made by Cook and Semmel (1999).

Additional issues have been raised about peer-mediated interventions with students with ASD. Chan et al. (2009), for example, argued that there is potential for exaggerating target students' deficits when they are paired with typically developing peers, in particular the potential for adverse effects on students who might miss learning important academic skills while they were involved in peer-teaching. Chan et al. also drew attention to the lack of fidelity in classroom/teacher-managed interventions, and the need to evaluate the classroom environment carefully to support peer-mediated interventions.

The Chan et al. (2009) review highlights concerns that are common to peer-mediated intervention studies with special student populations. Of the 42 studies, 34 had no more than three participants, and only two studies had more than 15 participants. Many of the studies did not measure the fidelity of the intervention. It is perhaps of greatest concern that the reviewers concluded their paper with the comment, "This review and others…indicate that PMI is supported by a solid research base" (p. 887). From our point of view, this is a considerable exaggeration.

Students with Minority Group Background

Every country has its minority groups. These include the indigenous inhabitants, ethnic minorities that have resulted from immigration, and more recently through refugee programs. Most cultural knowledge is mediated by relationships that exist within a community. In indigenous societies, this often occurs between youths and elders. But in all cultural contexts, there is a need for someone to translate social and cultural knowledge so that it can be internalized by the learner. Children must learn cultural standards, mores, values, and traditions and integrate this knowledge into their own thinking and behavior. In other words, they must transform external stimuli into internal codes that are consistent with their own knowledge by changing and modifying the original ideas and applying their unique cognitive character to them.

The commitment to social connectedness and cooperative learning are often listed among the learning styles that are characteristic of indigenous cultures and in multicultural societies. Watkins (2002) focused on these issues in African American communities in the United States. Watkins found that 2- to 5-year-olds were able to distinguish between the relative utility of teachers and peers. Contrary to what one might expect, they commonly approached teachers for social help and peers for academic help. Older children and youths are often more successful in mediating learning for their peers than are adults. One important reason for this is their use of language that expresses commonly held values, attitudes, beliefs, and shared life experiences. Young people are also often observed to employ a form of apprenticeship with each other that involves coaching, modeling, and observational learning. This behavior can be seen readily at any skateboard park.

It is not surprising that peer-mediated learning is seen as a valuable teaching tool in schools where there is broad cultural diversity (e.g., McDuffie, Mastropieri, & Scruggs, 2009) as the outcomes might benefit students from the nondominant culture. In their meta-analysis, Rohrbeck et al. (2003) reported that these students benefited more in terms of academic outcomes from peer-assisted learning (PAL) interventions than students from the dominant culture. They suggested that PAL (conceptually similar to peer collaboration) might establish links between home and school, thereby providing continuity in the learning process. For vulnerable students, Rohrbeck et al. suggested that the messages about academic achievement might be communicated across family, school, and peer group boundaries. The one complication here is the degree to which the results of collaboration endure beyond any intervention. Samaha and De Lisi (2000) have provided a useful example of this.

Samaha and De Lisi (2000) worked with Hispanic and African American Grade 7 students (nearly 78% were Hispanic). One group worked independently while others worked in mixed- or same-sex small groups on nonverbal reasoning tasks that required the selection of correct answers and the generation of explanations for their solutions. The mixed-sex groups outperformed other groups although the quality of judgments declined significantly across all groups at the posttest when compared with their performance during the experimental phase. Samaha and De Lisi argued that peer interactions appeared to be beneficial at the time of the collaboration although there was little generalization of learning when the participants were later required to work on their own. Despite this, the quality of explanations made by the collaborating students did not decline as much as their peers. The authors cautioned, however, that their study involved only one class period and dealt with abstract problem solving rather than typical curriculum tasks.

Gifted and Talented Students

Giftedness refers to above average performance in one or more domains of human natural abilities, such as intellectual, creative, socioaffective, or sensorimotor. Talent is reflected in above-average performance on systematically developed skills in one or more areas of human endeavor, such as technical, artistic, interpersonal, or athletic capability.

Usually, we think of diverse learners as those with learning difficulties, forgetting that at least some gifted and talented students find school a very lonely, frustrating, and discouraging place (Ashman & Merrotsy, 2009). There has been debate in the professional literature over the advantages and disadvantages of peer-mediated learning activities for students who are gifted and talented. Some writers have argued that peer-mediated learning fails to take the needs of these students into consideration, especially their need for flexibility, variety, curiosity, and independent discovery learning (Gallagher & Gallagher, 1994; Robinson, 1991). There have been several studies that have produced mixed outcomes in terms of these students' achievements, attitudes toward the curriculum and learning, self-efficacy, and learning style (e.g., Coleman & Gallagher, 1995; Neber, Finsterwald, & Urban, 2001; Robinson, 2003). Robertson considered that the role often given to gifted students as the "explainer" and the teacher's helper constitutes exploitation of brighter students, echoing views expressed by Ross and Smyth (1995).

Understandably, supporters of peer-mediated learning do not believe that the interactions and experiences of the brighter students that occur in mixed ability groups are exploitive, and even those who are critical of mixed ability grouping, express at least some support for peer-mediated learning. Melser (1999), for example, found that Grade 4 and 5 gifted students gained in self-esteem in heterogeneous groups and lost self-esteem in homogeneous groups although, in both contexts they gained in the targeted academic area, reading. Contrary affective and academic results were reported by Sheppard and Kavevsky (1999) and Ramsay and Richards (1997) who claimed that gifted students were less positive about cooperative learning than their average-ability peers although it appeared as though their attitude toward school subjects was unaffected. More recently, Garduno (2001) found that Grade 7 and 8 gifted students made some limited academic gains in cooperative learning settings but lost motivation when they were required to explain content and processes to their peers. Overall, participants had a more positive attitude toward mathematics in whole-group, competitive settings than in cooperative settings.

Individual differences among students may account for equivocal results across peer-mediation studies that involve gifted and high-achieving students. In their cluster and factor analytic study, Feldhusen, Dai, and Clinkenbeard (2000) differentiated students into five relatively homogeneous groups. Some gifted students presented a desire to outperform their peers while others viewed competition as an energizing agent within the classroom learning context. Feldhusen et al. noted that gifted students generally were not negative about competitive or cooperative learning conditions. They were able to discriminate between situations in which each was an appropriate learning context and self-aware of their own preferred learning style.

In their meta-analysis of cooperative learning studies involving gifted students, Neber et al. (2001) concluded that cooperative learning approaches can result in small to medium learning gains for gifted and high-achieving students, notably in the low and middle grades. They claimed that there were few studies available that had the methodological precision to enable more robust conclusions to be made about peer-mediated learning, and cooperative learning in particular. Specifically, they stated that there are some studies in which gifted students have been advantaged in mixed ability settings while other researchers have reported gains for these students in homogeneous groups of gifted or high-achieving students only. One of the complications it seems, is the lack of detail in the description of research methods in terms of the accurate application of cooperative learning, and in particular the explicit requirement for goal-interdependency among work group members.

More recently, Patrick, Bangel, Jeon, and Townsend (2005) took a slightly different approach to the debate about the efficacy of peer-mediated learning for gifted and talented students. They claimed that the discussion about whether peer-mediation (cooperative learning in this case) is beneficial to high-achieving students should concentrate on the process of task-related interactions. Rather than viewing cooperative learning as a single approach, there should be a more substantive analysis of the similarities and differences in the nature and type of the dialogues that are promoted by different cooperative learning approaches. They concluded that the types of task and the cognitive and interactive processes are important. Formats that emphasize transmission of factual information seem most likely to engender concerns when gifted students' are placed in mixed ability groups because of differences in learning speed between average and gifted students. In contrast, there appear to be benefits for both average and gifted students when higher order thinking and comprehension is required, when students are expected to explain and justify their ideas and reasons.

At this point, it appears that there are situations in which the intellectual needs of gifted students can be accommodated in peer-mediated learning. Patrick et al. (2005), however, have warned that mixed ability grouping and collaborative learning approached do not inevitably benefit those students.

THE FUTURE OF PEER-MEDIATION AND INCLUSION

The evidence we have presented above suggests that we might have some distance to go to validate the claim that peer-mediated learning is successful in bringing about academic gains and social benefits to students with diverse learning needs. The lessons to be learned from the literature in regard to these students parallels those derived from the large body of literature on peer-mediated learning. Kavale (2007) and Hattie (2009) have not been overly enthusiastic about the outcomes of peer-mediated learning research. Kavale quoted mean effect sizes for peer mediation as 0.64, for peer tutoring as 0.62, and cooperative learning as 0.40. Hattie found mean effect sizes for cooperative learning as 0.41 and for peer tutoring as 0.55, both of these being in his zone of desirable effects. Notwithstanding this, the studies we have presented above show very large variations in effect sizes, from near zero to a very substantial 1.77.

There are many reasons for these outcome variations, not the least important is the lack of systematic application of well-researched interventions, to which Chan et al. (2009) referred as the lack of fidelity in teacher-managed interventions. Walker et al. (1998) had already made similar comments. They stated that many teachers seem to rely upon a somewhat unsystematic assortment of activities, unplanned curricula, and conceptually incompatible interventions in their teaching and classroom management.

Rohrbeck et al. (2003) appear to take Walker et al. (1998) to heart when they stated that at-risk students generally receive instruction marked by poor use of instructional time, lower expectations, and less opportunity for learning. However, they still went on to conclude that there is strong evidence for the effectiveness of PAL interventions with these vulnerable students. Comments by Antil, Jenkins, Wayne, and Vadsy (1998) add to this point. They conducted follow-up interviews with 21 teachers involved in their study who reported using some form of cooperative learning. Only one of those interviewed said that they used the five fundamental components (i.e., positive interdependence, individual accountability, promotive interaction, group processing, and development of small group social skills). Five others reported using positive interdependence and individual accountability. And while one might casually pass judgment on teacher adaptations of well-researched programs, the recommendations offered by researchers to guide the implementation of peer-mediated strategies are often vague and unhelpful. Mortweet et al. (1999), for example, suggested that successful inclusive environments for students with special learning needs should be designed to maximize academic achievement through teacher-directed group activities, high levels of student engagement, student–teacher interactions, appropriate pacing of lessons, questioning and feedback, and the structured use of peers. These are all sensible ideas, but lacking in practical application.

We conclude by referring to comments found at the conclusion of many journal contributions, that peer-mediated learning in any of its high profile forms has the potential to improve the learning outcomes and social skills of students with diverse learning needs. Patrick et al. (2005) take this point further. They stated that students with special learning needs might benefit from peer-mediating learning experiences but it is not inevitable that they will if placed in such a learning context, and it is certain that peer mediation is not necessarily the most efficient or effective learning strategy for all.

There are lessons to be learned from an analysis of the peer-mediated learning literature as it relates to students with special needs. First, peer-mediation approaches must be applied with fidelity. All of the well-known approaches have been tested persistently over the years and their success requires accurate and authentic application of the processes. Second, careful consideration must be given to the characteristics of the students involved. In a class of 25 students there are 25 personalities, 25 learning histories, and arguably 25 preferred approaches to learning. It is not unreasonable to suggest that peer-mediation will be appealing in every learning situation or with every student peer. Third, we echo the sentiments of several meta-analysts that a larger body of research is warranted to unravel the constellation of issues that contribute to successful outcomes for students with diverse learning needs.

Over many years, we have advocated strongly for the use of peer-mediated learning in primary/elementary through the secondary years of schooling. We recognize that teachers are skilled practitioners and, like Florian (2008) we believe that they are suitably prepared to teach students with a diversity of skills and abilities typically found in mainstream classes. It is also our view that some do not recognize the importance of preparing students for cooperative and collaborative learning activities. If students do not possess the necessary prerequisite skills, including social and interactive skills, then peer-mediated learning is bound to be less successful than desired.

REFERENCES

Alfassi, M. (1998). Reading for meaning: The efficacy of reciprocal teaching in high school students in remedial reading classes. *American Educational Research Journal, 35,* 309–332.

Allen, V. (1976). Children helping children: Psychological processes in tutoring. In J. Levin & V. Allan (Eds.), *Cognitive learning in children: Theories and strategies* (pp. 241–290). New York: Academic Press.

Antil, L. R., Jenkins, J. R., Wayne, S. K., & Vadsy P. F. (1998). Cooperative learning: Prevalence, conceptualizations, and the relation between research and practice. *American Education Research Journal, 35,* 419–454.

Ashman, A., & Merrotsy, P. (2009). Diversity and educational environments. In A. Ashman & J Elkins (Eds.), *Education for inclusion and diversity* (pp. 63-96). Frenchs Forrest, NSW: Pearson Education Australia.

Baker, S., Gersten, R., Dimino, J. A., & Griffiths, R. (2004). The sustained use of research-based instructional practice: A case study of peer-assisted learning strategies in mathematics [Special issue on Sustainability]. *Remedial and Special Education, 25,* 5–24.

Bowman-Perrott, L. (2009). Classwide peer tutoring: An effective strategy for students with emotional and behavioral disorders. *Intervention in School and Clinic, 44,* 259–267.

Bowman-Perrott, L., Greenwood, C. R., & Tapia, Y. (2007). The efficacy of CWPT used in secondary alternative school classrooms with small teacher/pupil ratios and students with emotional and behavioral disorders. *Education and Treatment of Children, 30,* 65–87

Brinton, B., Fujiki, M., & Higbee, L. M. (1998). Participation in cooperative learning activities by children with specific language impairments. *Journal of Speech, Language, and Hearing Research, 41,* 1193–1206.

Brinton, B., Fujiki, M., Montague, E. C., & Hanton, J. L. (2000). Children with language impairment in cooperative work groups: A pilot study [Special issue on Collaboration and inclusion: Multiple perspectives—one focus]. *Language, Speech, and Hearing Services in Schools, 31,* 252–264.

Bryant, D., Vaughn, S., Linan-Thompson, S., Ugel, N., Hamff, A., & Hougen, M. (2000). Reading outcomes for students with and without reading disabilities in general education middle-school content area classes. *Learning Disability Quarterly, 23*(4), 238–252.

Chan, J. M., Lang, R., Rispoli, M., O'Reilly, M., Sigafoos, J., & Cole, H. (2009). Use of peer-mediated interventions in the treatment of autism spectrum disorders: A systematic review. *Research in Autism Spectrum Disorders, 3,* 876–889.

Cigman, R. (2007). A question of universality: Inclusive education and the principle of respect. *Journal of Philosophy of Education, 41,* 775–793

Cloward, R. (1967). Studies in tutoring. *Journal of Experimental Education, 36,* 14–25.

Cohen, E., Lotan, R., Abram, P., Scarloss, B., & Schultz, S. (2006). Can groups learn? *Teachers College Record, 104,* 1045–1068.

Cohen, E., Lotan, R., Scarloss, B., & Arellano, A. (1999). Complex instruction: Equity in cooperative learning classrooms. *Theory into Practice, 38,* 80–86.

Coleman, M. R., & Gallagher, J. J. (1995). The successful blending of gifted education with middle school and cooperative learning: Two studies. *Journal for the Education of the Gifted, 18,* 362–384.

Cook, B., & Semmel, M. I. (1999). Peer acceptance of included students with disabilities as a function of severity of disability and classroom composition. *Journal of Special Education, 33,* 50–61.

Curcic, S. (2009). Inclusion in PK-12: An international perspective. *International Journal of Inclusive Education, 13,* 517–538.

Damon, W. (1984). Peer education: The untapped potential. *Journal of Applied Developmental Psychology, 5,* 331–343.

Deutsch, M. (1949). A theory of co-operation and competition. *Human Relations, 11,* 129–152.

Doise, W., & Mugny, G. (1984). *The social development of the intellect.* Oxford, England: Pergamon .

Downs, A., & Smith, T. (2004). Emotional understanding, cooperation, and social behavior in high-functioning children with autism. *Journal of Autism and Developmental Disorders, 34,* 625–635.

Drudy, S., & Kinsella, W. (2009). Developing an inclusive system in a rapidly changing European society. *International Journal of Inclusive Education, 13,* 647–663.

Feldhusen, J. F., Dai, D. Y., & Clinkenbeard, P. R. (2000). Dimensions of competitive and cooperative learning among gifted learners. *Journal for the Education of the Gifted, 23,* 328–342.

Florian, L. (2008). Special or inclusive education: Future trends. *British Journal of Special Education, 35,* 202–208.

Foot, H. Morgan, M., & Shute, R. (Eds.). (1990). *Children helping children.* Chichester, England: Wiley.

Fuchs, D., Fuchs, L. S., Mathes, P. G., & Simmons, D. C. (1997). Peer-assisted learning strategies: Making classrooms more responsive to diversity. *American Educational Research Journal, 34,* 176–206.

Fuchs, L. S, Fuchs, D., Yazdian, L., & Powell, S. R. (2002). Enhancing first-grade children's mathematical development with peer-assisted learning strategies. *School Psychology Review, 31,* 569–583.

Gajria, M., Jitendra, A., Sood, S., & Sacks, G. (2007). Improving comprehension of expository text in students with LD: A research synthesis. *Journal of Learning Disabilities, 40,* 210–225.

Gallagher, J. J., & Gallagher, S. A. (1994). *Teaching the gifted child* (4th ed.). Boston, MA: Allyn & Bacon.

Garduno, E. L. H. (2001). The influence of cooperative problem solving on gender differences in achievement, self-efficacy, and attitudes toward mathematics in gifted students. *Gifted Child Quarterly, 45,* 268–282.

Gillies, R. M., Ashman, A. F., & Terwel, J. (Eds.). (2008). *The teacher's role in implementing cooperative learning in the classroom.* New York: Springer.

Harrower, J. K., & Dunlap, G. (Eds.). (2001). [Special issue on Autism]. *Behavior Modification, 25*(Part 1), 762–784.

Hattie, J. (2007, April). *What works best and what evidence assists for narrowing the gap and addressing education disadvantage.* Keynote speech at Narrowing the Gap: Addressing Educational Disadvantage conference, University of New England, Armidale, NSW, Australia.

Hattie, J. A. (2009). *Visible learning: A synthesis of over 800 meta-analyses relating to achievement.* Abingdon, England: Routledge.

Heron, T. E., Villareal, D. M., Yao, M., Christianson, R. J., & Heron, K. M. (2006). Peer tutoring systems: Applications in classroom and specialized environments. *Reading & Writing Quarterly: Overcoming Learning Difficulties, 22,* 27–45.

Hodges, J., Riccomini, P. J., Buford, R., & Herbst, M. H. (2006). A review of instructional interventions in mathematics for students with emotional and behavioral disorders. *Behavioral Disorders, 31,* 297–311.

Humphrey, N. (2009). Including students with attention-deficit/hyperactivity disorder in mainstream schools. *British Journal of Special Education, 36,* 19–25.

Jacques, N., Wilton, K., & Townsend, M. (1998). Cooperative learning and social acceptance of children with mild intellectual disability. *Journal of Intellectual Disability Research, 42,* 29–36.

Johnson, D., & Johnson, R. (2002). Learning together and alone: Overview and meta-analysis. *Asia Pacific Journal of Education, 22,* 95–105.

Johnson, D., & Johnson, R. (2003). Student motivation in cooperative groups: Social interdependence theory. In R. Gillies & A. Ashman (Eds.), *Cooperative learning: The social and intellectual outcomes of learning in groups* (pp. 136–176). London: RoutledgeFalmer.

Johnson, D., Maruyama, G., Johnson, R., Nelson, D., & Skon, L. (1981). Effects of cooperative, competitive, and individualistic goal structures on achievement: A meta-analysis. *Psychological Bulletin, 98,* 47–62.

Kamps, D., Greenwood, C., Arreaga-Mayer, C., Veerkamp, M., & Bannister, H. (2008). The efficacy of class wide peer tutoring in middle schools. *Education and Treatment of Children, 31,* 119–152.

Kavale, K. A. (2007). Quantitative research synthesis: Meta-analysis of research on meeting special educational needs. In L. Florian (Ed.), *The Sage handbook of special education* (pp. 205–221). Los Angeles, CA: Sage.

Kelly, M., Moore, D. W., & Tuck, B. F. (1994). Reciprocal teaching in a regular primary classroom. *Journal of Educational Research, 88,* 53–61.

Klinger, J., Vaughn, S., Arguelles, M., Hughes, M., & Leftwich, S. (2004). Collaborative strategic reading: Real-world lessons from classroom teachers. *Remedial and Special Education, 25*(5), 291–302.

Koh, C., Tan, O. S., Wang, C. K. J., Ei, J., & Liu, W. C. (2007). Perceptions of low ability students on group project work and cooperative learning. *Asia Pacific Education Review, 8,* 89–99.

Kunsch, C., Jitendra, A., & Sood, S. (2007). The effects of peer-mediated instruction on mathematics for students with learning problems: A research synthesis. *Learning Disabilities Research & Practice, 22,* 1–11.

Kuntz, K. L., McLaughlin, T. F., & Howard, V. F. (2001). A comparison of cooperative learning and small group individualized instruction for math in a self contained classroom for elementary students with disabilities. *Educational Research Quarterly, 24,* 41–56.

Liberman, L. J., Dunn, J. M., van der Mars, H., & McCubbin, J. (2000). Peer tutors' effects on activity levels of deaf students in inclusive elementary physical education. *Adapted Physical Activity Quarterly, 17,* 20–39.

Lipsey, M., & Wilson, D. (1993). The efficacy of psychological, educational, and behavioral treatment: Confirmation from meta-analysis. *American Psychologist, 48,* 1181–1209.

Lou, Y., Abrami, P., & d'Apollonia, S. (2001). Small group and individual learning with technology: A meta-analysis. *Review of Educational Research, 71,* 449–521.

Lou, Y., Abrami, P., Spence, J., Poulsen, C., Chambers, B., & d'Apollonia, S. (1996). Within-class grouping: A meta-analysis. *Review of Educational Research, 66,* 423–458.

Maheady, L., Mallette, B., & Harper, G. F. (2006). Four classwide peer tutoring models: Similarities, differences, and implications for research and practice. *Reading & Writing Quarterly: Overcoming Learning Difficulties, 22,* 65–89.

Mastropieri, M. A., & Scruggs, T. E. (2001). Promoting inclusion in secondary classrooms. *Learning Disability Quarterly, 24,* 265–274.

McDonnell, J., Mathot-Buckner, C., Thorson, N., & Fister, S. (2001). Supporting the inclusion of students with moderate and severe disabilities in junior high school general education classes: The effects of classwide peer tutoring, multi-element curriculum. And accommodations. *Education and Treatment of Children, 24,* 141–160.

McDuffie, K. A., Mastropieri, M. A., & Scruggs, T. E. (2009). Differential effects of peer tutoring in co-taught and non-co-taught classes: Results for content learning and student-teacher interactions. *Exceptional Children, 75,* 493–510.

McMaster, K. L., Fuchs, D., & Fuchs, L. S. (2006). Research on peer-assisted learning strategies: The promise and limitations of peer-mediated instruction. *Reading and Writing Quarterly: Overcoming Learning Difficulties, 22,* 5–25.

McMaster, K. N., & Fuchs, D. (2002). Effects of cooperative learning on the academic achievement of students with learning disabilities: An update of Tateyama-Sniezek's review. *Learning Difficulties Research & Practice, 17,* 107–117.

McMaster, K. N., Fuchs, D., & Fuchs, L. S. (2002). Using peer tutoring to present early reading failure. In J. S. Thousand, F. A. Villa, & A. I. Nevin (Eds.), *Creativity and collaborative learning: The practical guide to empowering students, teachers, and families* (2nd ed., pp. 235–246). Baltimore, MD: Brookes.

Melekoglu, M. A., Cakiroglu, O., & Malmgren, K. W. (2009). Special education in Turkey. *International Journal of Inclusive Education, 13,* 287–298.

Melser, N. A. (1999). Gifted students and cooperative learning: A study of grouping strategies. *Roeper Review, 21,* 315.

Menesses, K., & Gresham, F. (2009). Relative efficacy of reciprocal and nonreciprocal peer tutoring for students at-risk for academic failure. *School Psychology Quarterly, 24,* 266–275.

Morgan, R. L., Whorton, J. E., & Turtle, L. B. (1999). Use of peer tutoring to improve speech skills in a preschooler with a severe hearing impairment. *Educational Research Quarterly, 23,* 44–55.

Mortweet, S. L., Utley, C. A., Walker, D., Dawson, H. L., Delquardri, J. C., Reddy, S. S., … Ledford, D. (1999). Classwide peer tutoring: Teaching students with mild mental retardation in inclusive classrooms. *Exceptional Children, 65,* 524–536.

Mugny, G., & Doise, W. (1978). Socio-cognitive conflict and structure of individual and collective performances. *European Journal of Social Psychology, 8,* 181–192.

Neber, H., Finsterwalk, M., & Urban, N. (2001). Cooperative learning with gifted and high-achieving students: A review and meta-analyses of 12 studies. *High Ability Studies, 12,* 199–214.

Palincsar, A., & Brown, A. (1984). Reciprocal teaching of comprehension-fostering and comprehension-monitoring activities. *Cognition and Instruction, 1,* 117–175.

Patrick, H., Bangel, N. J., Jeon, K-N., & Townsend, M. A. R. (2005). Reconsidering the issues of cooperative learning with gifted students. *Journal for the Education of the Gifted, 29,* 90–110.

Piaget, J. (1950). *The psychology of intelligence.* London: Routledge & Kegan.

Piercy, M., Wilton, K., & Townsend, M. (2002). Promoting the social acceptance of young children with moderate-severe intellectual disabilities using cooperative-learning techniques. *American Journal on Mental Retardation, 107,* 352–360.

Ramsay, S. G., & Richards H. C. (1997). Cooperative learning environments: Effects on academic attitudes of gifted students. *Gifted Child Quarterly, 41,* 160–168.

Robinson, A. (1991). Cooperation or exploitation? The argument against cooperative learning for talented students. *Journal for the Education of the Gifted, 14,* 9–27.

Robinson, A. (2003). Cooperative learning and high ability students. In N. Colangelo & G. Davis (Eds.), *Handbook of gifted education* (3rd ed., pp. 282–292). Boston, MA: Allyn & Bacon.

Rohrbeck, C. A., Ginsburg-Block, M. D., Fantuzzo, J. W., & Miller, T. R. (2003). Peer-assisted learning interventions with elementary school students: A meta-analytic review. *Journal of Educational Psychology, 95,* 240–257.

Rosenshine, B. (2009). The empirical support for direct instruction. In S. Tobias & T. Duffy (Eds.), *Constructivist instruction: Success for all* (pp. 201–220). London: Routledge.

Ross, J. A., & Smyth, E. (1995). Thinking skills for gifted students: The case for correlational reasoning. *Roeper Review, 17,* 239–243.

Ryan, S., & Paterna, L. (1997). Junior high can be inclusive: Using natural supports and cooperative learning. *Teaching Exceptional Children, 30,* 36–41.

Ryan, J. B., Reid, R., & Epstein, M. H. (2004). Peer-mediated intervention studies on academic achievement for students with EBD. *Remedial and Special Education, 25,* 330–341.

Samaha, N. V., & De Lisi, R. (2000). Peer collaboration on a nonverbal reasoning task by urban, minority students. *Journal of Experimental Education, 69,* 5–21.

Shamir, A., & Lazerovitz, T. (2007). Peer mediation interventions for scaffolding self-regulated learning amoung children with learning disabilities. *European Journal of Special Needs Education, 22,* 255–273.

Sheppard, S., & Kavevsky, L. S. (1999). Nurturing gifted students' metacognitive awareness: Effects of training in homogeneous and heterogeneous classes. *Roeper Review, 21,* 266–275.

Slavin, R. (1996). *Education for all.* Lisse, Netherlands: Swets & Zeitlinger.

Spencer, V. G. (2006). Peer tutoring and students with emotional or behavioral disorders: A review of the literature. *Behavior Disorders, 31,* 204–222.

Sutherland, K. S., Wehby, J. H., & Gunter, P. L. (2000). The effectiveness of cooperative learning with students with emotional and behavioural disorders: A literature review. *Behavior Disorders, 25,* 225–238.

Topping, K. J. (2005). Trends in peer learning [Special issue on Developments in educational psychology: How far have we come in 25 years?]. *Educational Psychology, 25,* 631–645.

Vygotsky, L. S. (1962). *Thought and language.* Cambridge, MA: MIT Press.

Vygotsky, L. S. (1978). *Mind in society: The development of higher psychological processes.* Cambridge, MA: Harvard University Press.

Walker, H. M., Forness, S. R. Kauffman, J. M., Epstein, M. H. Gresham, F. M., Nelson, C. M., & Strain, P. S. (1998). Macro-social validation: Referencing outcomes in behavioral disorders to societal issues and problems. *Behavior Disorders, 24,* 7–18.

Watkins, A. F. (2002). Learning styles of African American children: A developmental consideration. *Journal of Black Psychology, 28,* 3–17.

Webb, N. M. (2009). The teacher's role in promoting collaborative dialogue in the classroom. *British Journal of Educational Psychology, 79,* 1–28.

Weiss, M. J., & Harris, S. L. (2001). Teaching social skills to people with autism. *Behavior Modification, 25,* 785–802.

Wolford, P. L., Heward, W. L., & Alber, S. R. (2001). Teaching middle school students with learning disabilities to recruit peer assistance during cooperative learning group activities. *Learning Disabilities Research & Practice, 16,* 161–173.

18

LEARNING THROUGH COLLABORATIVE ARGUMENTATION

CLARK A. CHINN

Rutgers University

DOUGLAS B. CLARK

Vanderbilt University

When students are learning collaboratively, they may engage in a variety of different discourses. Students who are trying to understand a text may elaborate on each other's statements about what the text means. Students solving mathematics problems may give each other answers or state a series of steps to follow. Another prominent form of discourse is argumentation, which involves taking positions, making claims, and giving reasons and evidence for claims that are made. Often, although not always, argumentation will involve some disagreement and participants will take and defend different positions. In this chapter, we discuss learning through a specific form of this discourse, which we call collaborative argumentation.

Collaborative argumentation can occur in a variety of educational settings. Students discussing how to solve mathematics problems may find they disagree about a solution, and provide reasons for their different procedures, trying to determine which solution or solutions are correct (Cobb, McClain, & Gravemeijer, 2003). Students in a science class may engage in argumentation to discuss which of several alternative explanatory models proposed by different students in the class best explains the available evidence they have on photosynthesis (Buckland & Chinn, 2010). Preservice teachers may engage in a synchronous or asynchronous online threaded debate about how to respond to student errors (Jermann & Dillenbourg, 2003). Researchers interested in collaborative argumentation have sought to foster and investigate learning scenarios such as these.

In this chapter, we discuss a broad range of interconnected issues related to collaborative argumentation. We discuss the following, in turn: (a) general background issues, (b) major traditions of research on argumentation within education, (c) approaches to analyzing and evaluating collaborative argumentation, (d) empirical findings on cognitive and motivational benefits of collaborative argumentation, (e) specific instructional methods that have been developed to scaffold learning through collaborative argumentation, and (f) methods for orchestrating sustained argumentation in classrooms. We close with conclusions from our survey in light of the increasing centrality of collaborative argumentation in upcoming standards for learning.

WHAT IS COLLABORATIVE ARGUMENTATION?

Argumentation has been a subject of philosophical and rhetorical investigation since the age of Greece. Today argumentation is studied by scholars in fields ranging from philosophy and rhetoric to communications, psychology, and education. Much of the work from historical times until today has focused on written arguments or arguments constructed by a single speaker; scholars analyzed and evaluated the ways in which writers or speakers individually support claims with evidence and reasons (e.g.,Toulmin, 1958). In recent decades, intense interest has focused on collaborative argumentation (e.g.,van Eemeren & Grootendorst, 2004). This chapter focuses on learning through collaborative argumentation rather than through the construction of individual arguments, although both aspects of argumentation are important in educational settings.

Collaborative argumentation occurs in a dialogue, in an interchange of statements, questions, or replies involving two or more participants (van Eemeren & Grootendorst, 2004). Participants in the dialogue typically make claims and support them with reasons. The participants often disagree in the positions they take, and thus their argumentation may be directed at exploring and perhaps resolving this disagreement. However, by our definition of collaborative argumentation, people may engage in collaborative argumentation when they do not disagree. For example, people may jointly develop reasons to support a position that both agree with, or they may work together to use evidence to develop and refine a position (e.g., a scientific explanation), using evidence to support their developing ideas. In such cases, there is collaborative argumentation due to the joint participation in the activity of building arguments (reasons and evidence to support claims, entertaining other positions and evidence for those other positions, and so). Because of its dialectical nature, collaborative argumentation can also be labeled *dialectical argumentation.*

One reason why educators have advocated the use of argumentation in educational settings is that argumentation is believed to feature prominently in real-life practices. For instance, historians and philosophers of science have viewed argumentation as a critical discourse through which science and mathematics progress (Duschl & Osborne, 2002; Lakatos, 1976). Argumentative discourse can also be used in many other settings, from city council members discussing ethical and practical dimensions of a policy decision to family members deliberating about which of several available houses to purchase. Thus, educators promote collaborative argumentation as a practice that is useful outside of educational settings. The importance of argumentation is reflected in their greater emphasis recent in educational standards.

A second reason for promoting collaborative argumentation in education is that argumentation can help students learn core content. Later in the chapter, we will explore in more detail the different kinds of learning goals that can be promoted by collaborative argumentation.

Educators who advocate collaborative argumentation as an educational method distinguish between argumentation and personal quarrels (e.g., Walton, 1989), which are marked by heightened emotion and personal attacks rather than rational inquiry. Because students are likely to come to the classroom thinking that "arguing" means "quarreling," educational researchers have urged that teachers who employ argumentation in the classroom explicitly explain to students that the type of argumentation that they will engage is *not* a fight. In fact, it might prove productive in light of students' everyday experiences with arguments and argumentation initially to introduce argumentation in the classroom as "collaborative knowledge building" and "working together to make sense of data," rather than starting with the terms *argument* and *argumentation*.

Much educational research has viewed argumentation as *persuasion dialogues* (Walton, 1989), in which participants use arguments to try to persuade each other of their positions by using arguments, counterarguments, and rebuttals of others' counterarguments (e.g., Chinn, Anderson, & Waggoner, 2001; Clark, D'Angelo, & Menekse, 2009). But collaborative argumentation can also involve *inquiry dialogues* (Walton, 1989), with which participants attempt to construct knowledge using agreed-upon methods of inquiry. Often, these dialogues begin where there is a lack of knowledge, and discussion is used to try to elaborate what is known and to develop new knowledge claims (e.g., Sampson & Clark, 2009). Evidence is used to support these claims, but there is rarely a focus on resolving disagreement, as sharp disagreement may not arise. Yet, these may be called a form of collaborative argumentation because learners are engaged in using evidence and reasons to support knowledge claims. Some researchers have described such dialogues without necessarily labeling them as argumentation; in our view, however, they are a form of collaborative argumentation.

Many researchers advocate a form of argumentation that combines elements of persuasion dialogues and inquiry dialogues (e.g., Mercer, 2009). Even when students disagree, they take each other's ideas seriously, working in the spirit of collaborative inquiry to develop the best solutions. When they encounter new evidence and arguments, they are willing to adapt their ideas to new information and evidence rather than to simply dig in and keep trying to persuade others of their position. Persuasion may sometimes be a means to understanding the world, but the ultimate goal is to work together to develop understanding (e.g., Clark & Sampson, 2007, 2008); the ideal end and goals involve developing better ideas.

MAJOR AREAS OF EDUCATIONAL RESEARCH ON ARGUMENTATION

During the past three decades, there has been a rapidly growing body of educational research on argumentation. Although any attempt to define particular traditions will inevitably oversimplify, one can distinguish a number of relatively distinct areas of research.

One influential area of research has investigated strengths and weaknesses in students' evaluation of arguments and their ability to generate arguments. Among the conclusions from this research are that students tend to have trouble generating arguments on both sides of a question and to provide low-quality arguments even for their own position (e.g., Kuhn, 1991).

A second area of developmental research (e.g., Mirza, Perret-Clermont, Tartas, & Iannaccone, 2009) has found that the ability to argue emerges in the preschool years (Stein & Albro, 2001). This has raised questions about why very young children exhibit proficiency in arguing about everyday matters (e.g., arguing over use of a toy with a sibling), while exhibiting less sophistication later on. One reason may be the more challenging topics, which require more domain knowledge, that are used in research and educational settings with older students and with adults.

A third area has focused on analyzing the discourse of argumentation as students engage in collaborative argumentation in school and other educational settings. These studies have spurred the development of new methods for analyzing the discourse of argumentation; we discuss several prominent methods in the next section of this chapter.

Fourth, researchers have investigated what students gain from engaging in argumentation (e.g., what they learn about content and about how to argue). We will examine some of this research later in the chapter.

The fifth and perhaps largest current of research includes investigations into instructional methods for promoting argumentation and for helping students learn through argumentation. This research is diverse and will be discussed in the last two major sections of this paper.

EVALUATING ARGUMENTATION

Researchers have developed a range of methods for analyzing and evaluating argumentation (cf., Clark, Sampson, Weinberger, & Erkens, 2007; Sampson & Clark, 2008).

Analyzing Functions of Statements

One very frequently used method for evaluating argumentation is to trace the function or speech acts of statements made in the discussion. For example, Erduran, Simon, and Osborne (2004) characterized the argumentative operations of each conversational turn during episodes of oppositional dialogue into the following categories: (a) opposing a claim, (b) elaborating on a claim, (c) reinforcing a claim with additional data or warrants, (d) advancing claims, and (e) adding qualifications. Their approach then categorizes the structural quality of the dialogic argumentation based on the types and numbers of categories involved during the dialogic argumentation. Another approach by Felton and Kuhn (2001) codes for 25 distinct discourse moves that can be grouped into four broad categories: exposition (e.g., an extension of previous statement or a clarification of speaker's argument), challenge (e.g., disagreements and counterarguments), requests (questions), and other nonrequest discourse moves. As one other example, Janssen, Erkens, and Kanselaar's (2007) framework identifies the communicative function of each utterance (e.g., argumentative, responsive, informative, eliciting, and imperative) in terms of 29 more specific types of dialogue acts typed by the students during their online collaboration and communication. Analyses of statement functions highlight important aspects of the quality of collaborative argumentation (cf. Kuhn, Goh, Iordanou, & Shaenfield, 2008). Similarly, they can identify sequences of discourse acts that statistically prove more or less productive (e.g., Jeong, Clark, Sampson, & Menekse, 2010).

Analyzing Collaborative Argument Structure

A second, closely related approach to analyzing collaborative argumentation is to map the structure of arguments (see Chinn, 2006; Chinn & Anderson, 1998; Toulmin, 1958).

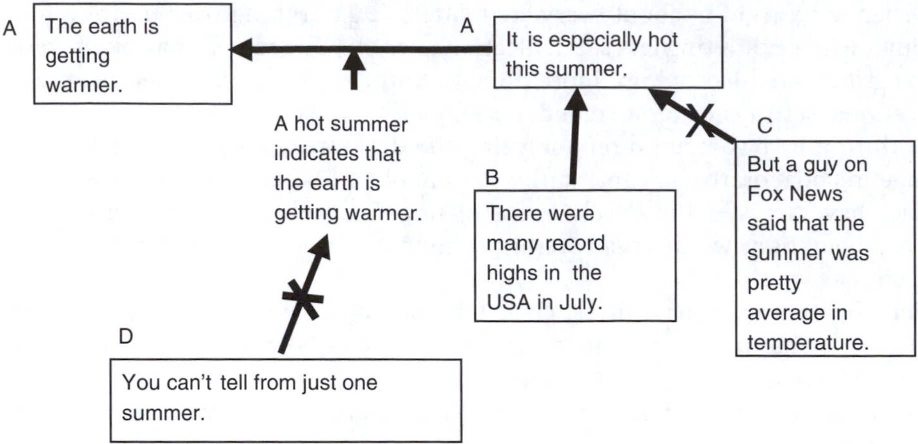

Figure 18.1 An example of a graphical representation of a collaborative argument structure.

Instead of just labeling utterances as "taking positions," "giving reasons," and so on, the analyst uses an argument structure graph to map out the structural interrelations among different positions and reasons. A simple example appears in Figure 18.1: plain arrows denote that one statement provides support for another, and an arrow with an X through it denotes that one statement militates against another. Different letters indicate different speakers.

Structurally, the argumentation exhibited in Figure 18.1 is sophisticated, even though it represents only a few turns of discourse. Student A argues that the earth is getting warmer, because it is especially hot this summer. Although Student A does not say so explicitly, she appears to be committed to believing something like: A hot summer indicates that the earth is getting warmer. Student B provides a reason ("There were many record highs in the USA in July") to believe Student A's reason (that it is especially hot this summer). Conversely, Student C gives a reason to disbelieve Student A's reason—this counts as a rebuttal of Student A's reason. Finally, Student D provides a reason to disbelieve the unstated commitment of Student A that "a hot summer indicates that the earth is getting warmer" by stating that "you can't tell from just one summer," which seems to indicate an understanding that one must look at longer term trends and greater sample sizes than just one year in order to draw conclusions about global warming. Chinn, O'Donnell, and Jinks (2000) show that collaborative argumentation with more complex structure correlated with greater learning than argumentation with simpler structure.

Another approach, known as *Rainbow* (Baker et al., 2007), focuses primarily on the epistemic nature of participants' contributions. Non-task-focused activity is categorized as either *social relation* or *interaction management.* Task-focused activity is categorized as *task management, opinions, argumentation,* and *explore and deepen.* Comments are coded for their primary nature in the context of the ongoing debate.

Evaluating the Quality of Reasoning

A serious limitation of both analytic methods discussed so far is that they provide only a very coarse measure of the extent to which certain argument components are being used (reasons, counterreasons, rebuttals, etc.). However, these methods do not distinguish between very good reasoning (e.g., a student gives a detailed explanation of why several studies collectively show that global warming is occurring) and very bad reasoning (e.g., a student living in Michigan says in February that global warming is not occurring because it snowed today). Similarly, these methods do not distinguish between students who are working with, for example, scientifically accepted ideas versus common alternative conceptions.

A number of researchers have attempted to develop ways of analyzing arguments that more properly evaluate the quality of arguments. For example, Kuhn and Udell (2003) analyzed the conceptual quality of argumentation by classifying the arguments contributed by participants in a discussion, including: *Nonjustificatory Arguments*, which have little or no argumentative force; *Nonfunctional Arguments*, which focus on tangential aspects of the problem rather than core issues; and *Functional Arguments* that address core aspects of the problem.

Similarly, Clark and Sampson (2008) developed analytic schemes designed to provide information about the quality of these arguments. One of these was the extent to which students used normative scientific ideas in their arguments (that is, the accepted scientific ideas about heat). The other was whether students' arguments incorporated empirical evidence and, if so, how thoroughly they linked this evidence to their explanation.

Nussbaum (2011) proposed that research on argumentation would profit by drawing on Walton's work in rhetoric and philosophy on argumentation schemas. Walton (1996) has discussed numerous argumentation schemas that people use, such as arguments from classification, arguments from analogy, arguments from expert opinion, and arguments from cause to effect. Associated with each are critical questions that can be asked about the appropriateness of that argument in a particular situation. For example, the argument from sign argues that because a sign is present, a cause can be inferred (e.g., because there are bear tracks in the snow, a bear must have passed this way). Critical questions for this argument are: (a) What is the strength of the correlation of the sign with the event signified? (b) Are there other events that would more reliably account for the sign? (Walton, 1996, pp. 47–48). Walton's schemes could be used to evaluate collaborative argumentation (Duschl, 2008; Nussbaum, 2011). For example, analysts can identify which specific argumentation schemes are used, and whether arguers exhibit sensitivity to the issues raised by the critical questions (e.g., do students use the argument from signs, and if so do they show awareness that they should consider how strong the relationship between the sign and the cause is?). Argumentation quality would be higher if students consider the critical questions and arrive at defensible answers (e.g., they consider other tracks that might look like bear tracks, but conclude that all other candidates would be too small).

There is a need for more research that investigates argumentation quality using these and other approaches. These approaches could also be used to help educators identify specific ways in which they would like to help students improve their argumentation (e.g., use a wider variety of argument schemes, and consider critical questions more extensively).

BENEFITS OF ARGUMENTATION

In this section, we discuss five educational benefits that can result from engagement in argumentation including improvements in: (a) motivation, (b) content learning, (c) general argumentation skills, (d) specific argumentation skills, and (e) knowledge building practices. As we will discuss below, there is evidence that argumentation can promote each of these benefits.

Broadly, there are two prominent theoretical accounts for the benefits of argumentation (Schwarz, 2009). The first is a cognitive account, which focuses on individual learning and accounts for learning in terms of improved individual representations. For example, Chinn (2006) explained improvement in students' ability to argue in terms of students developing better argument schemas—better internal representations of the conditions under which different argument forms are applicable, such as when it is appropriate to argue that a study is flawed because of small sample size. A second theoretical perspective, which includes sociocultural and other social approaches to learning (see Schwarz, 2009), treats learning through argumentation as the adoption of social practices of specific groups (i.e., a student who initially participates in few or none of these practices gradually comes to participate in more of them). Further, as an individual joins in more and more practices, the practices themselves are transformed through the actions of the new participant. In this theory, the locus at which learning occurs is the social level of group practices as well as the ability of the individual to productively participate in those practices.

Enhanced Motivation

One potential benefit of engagement of argumentation is enhanced motivation. There is some evidence for this benefit, although more research on this topic is needed. Chinn et al. (2001) compared the discourse of students who engaged in argumentation during small-group reading lessons with students who participated in traditional reading lessons. Students who engaged in argumentation talked more and showed greater eagerness to talk even to the point of interrupting others. Smith, Johnson, and Johnson (1981) reported that sixth graders who engaged in argumentation were more willing to spend some of their recess time learning more about the topic they had discussed than were students who had not learned through an argumentation method.

Several possible mechanisms could account for increased motivation through argumentation. First, argumentation may be enhanced because students have more autonomy over what they say in argumentation-based discussions than in traditional teacher-led recitations, in which teachers tightly limit students to answering their numerous questions. Motivation researchers have found autonomy to be a potent motivator (see Rogat et al., chapter 14 this volume). Second, argumentation may simply afford more interaction with peers, which can itself be motivating (see Rogat et al., chapter 14 this volume). Third, as students engage in argumentation, they discover that their peers have ideas that differ from their own, which may make them curious about finding out which ideas are more defensible. They may thus adopt mastery goals to understand the topic better; mastery goals are associated with intrinsic motivation, deeper learning strategies, and positive emotions about learning (Linnenbrink & Pintrich, 2002).

However, there is a danger that argumentation can devolve into quarrels or debates that focus on winning or losing the argument. Quarrels can lead to unpleasant interactions. Debates, with a focus on winners and losers, can promote performance goals to outperform peers—which are viewed by many motivation researchers as less conducive to deep learning in classroom settings. Indeed, there is evidence that some students are not comfortable engaging in argumentation, as they do not like the conflict of it (e.g., Nussbaum & Bendixen, 2003). Thus, when developing instructional methods with argumentation, there is a challenge to ensure that norms of collaborative knowledge construction replace norms of quarrels or winning and losing debates.

Content Learning

Another benefit of collaborative argumentation is content learning. A number of argumentation researchers have distinguished between *learning to argue* and *arguing to learn* (e.g., Andriessen, 2006; Schwarz, 2009). When students learn to argue through argumentation, they are learning the components of argumentation and how to engage effectively in the practice of argumentation. When students argue to learn, they engage in argumentation for the purpose of mastering the content about which they are arguing. For instance, students engaged in argumentation about how to explain the results of experiments with electric circuits may learn something general about how to construct arguments, counterarguments, and rebuttals (learning to argue), and they may also learn core ideas about electric circuits, such as Ohm's Law (arguing to learn). With arguing to learn, the focus is on content learning—learning the core concepts and principles of the domain of instruction.

Studies have demonstrated that collaborative argumentation can promote content learning (see Andriessen, 2006; Scheuer, Loll, Pinkwart, & McLaren, 2010; Schwarz, 2009). For example, developmental psychologists have found that episodes of argumentation among children promoted the ability to conserve in nonconservers (e.g., Perret-Clermont, 1980). MacArthur, Ferretti, and Okolo (2002) provided evidence from a sixth-grade project on the topic of American immigration that students with and without learning disabilities gained in knowledge about immigration from an instructional intervention that featured argumentation as part of the intervention. Similarly, Asterhan and Schwarz (2007) found that undergraduates who engaged in argumentation about evolutionary theory showed more gains in understanding evolutionary theory principles than did undergraduates who simply collaborated without specific encouragement to engage in argumentation. Sampson and Clark (2009) investigated high school students learning about melting through argumentation. Students who engaged in collaborative argumentation demonstrated greater mastery of ideas about heat and temperature than did students who wrote arguments individually but did not engage in collaborative argumentation. This result is interesting because previous research has demonstrated that asking students to write arguments is a very effective instructional technique (Wiley & Voss, 1999); collaborative argumentation appears to have benefits over and above individual argumentation.

Three processes that may explain why argumentation may promote content learning are:

- *Explicit elaborative processing, including modification of ideas.* When engaging in collaborative argumentation, students engage in a variety of explicit elaborative processes, such as explanation, that are known to promote learning (see Andriessen, 2006; Schwarz, 2009). For example, in defending their explanation for why melting occurs, students may need to articulate their explanation in much more detail than they would have if they had not needed to resolve a disagreement with a peer with a different explanation. Similarly, the process of considering connections between evidence and explanations may lead students to refine and improve their explanations.

- *Learning from others.* In the process of argumentation, students learn from their peers. They may learn from their peers of a better explanation, of a modification to an explanation that they had not thought of, or of a telling piece of evidence that they were unaware of.
- *Reason to believe.* The process of providing evidence for claims can also give learners not only a better *understanding* of the ideas they are learning but also greater reason to believe the claims they are developing (Chinn, 2006). A student who has strong reason to believe a claim (e.g., a science explanation) may be more likely to use that explanation outside of the learning context. Without such reasons, a student may not take the explanation seriously as one to use outside of school.

IMPROVED GENERAL ARGUMENTATION SKILLS

Collaborative argumentation can also improve general argumentation skills. This is the "learning to argue" goal that we discussed in the previous section. Students who develop improved general argumentation skills will demonstrate improved fluency in articulating arguments (e.g., positions, reasons, and a justification for why the reason supports their position) across various situations. They should also demonstrate greater skill at articulating counterarguments to others' positions, at anticipating others' counterarguments to their positions, and to rebutting others' counterarguments. Ideally, they also will greater skill at being able to consider and discuss reasons both for and against their own positions.

A great deal of research has documented that instructional methods that engage students in argumentation help them learn to argue and to evaluate arguments better (e.g., Dong, Anderson, Kim, & Li, 2008; Kuhn et al., 2008; Kuhn & Udell, 2003; Reznitskaya, Anderson, & Kuo, 2007; Reznitskaya et al., 2001). Some of these studies have documented that engagement in collaborative argumentation promotes greater individual skill at writing arguments (such as persuasive essays), even though the instruction in argumentation did not provide any instruction in how to write (e.g., Reznitskaya et al., 2001). Zohar and Nemet (2002) similarly demonstrated that engagement in collaborative argumentation in genetics promotes the ability to write written arguments on both similar and dissimilar topics.

Other studies have demonstrated that instruction centered on collaborative argumentation improves skill in collaborative argumentation. In a series of studies, Deanna Kuhn and her colleagues have developed methods for providing instruction in general argumentation components such as counterarguments and rebuttals; this instruction is paired with very extensive opportunities to engage in argumentation. The results of these studies show that, in comparison to control students, students who learn to argue and practice argumentation become better at arguing, including on new transfer topics (e.g., Kuhn et al., 2008).

A number of researchers have provided a Vygotskian explanation for these findings. Vygotsky (1981) proposed that when people learn to think, the functions of their thinking first appear in a social plane, and only later are internalized by the individual. This provides a compelling explanation for the finding that engagement in argumentation promotes better individual writing. For example, on the social plane of collaborative argumentation, students learn that their positions may be challenged with counterarguments and that they may need to revise their position in response to these counterarguments or else develop rebuttals for the counterarguments. After many such experiences, students internalize the previously externalized social process of considering and rebutting counterarguments. They gradually learn to anticipate these counterarguments individually, even in the absence social interaction. The social process of considering other viewpoints gets internalized to the point that individuals can engage in the process alone. Reznitskaya (in press) added to this Vygotskian explanation a schema-based explanation. She theorized that the internalization process involves developing internal schemas for engaging in argumentation that include slots for counterarguments, rebuttals, and the like.

Improved Specific Argumentation

In the previous section, we discussed effects of argumentation on general argumentation skills such as making arguments and counterarguments, anticipating counterarguments, and making rebuttals. These are very general skills because they can, in principle, be used in any situation that could involve argumentation, from deciding which movie to see to discussing alternative explanations for the results of a microbiology experiment. But, in practice, one can use these skills only if one has enough domain knowledge to do so. A biology student whose knowledge of microbiology is limited to knowing that cells have membranes and nuclei will not be able to understand a microbiology experiment, let alone construct arguments for or against alternative explanations of its results.

Thus, effective argumentation requires domain-specific knowledge. This may include knowledge of evidence typical of a domain (e.g., the ability to argue about evolution theory requires domain-specific knowledge of different types of evidence such as fossils, DNA comparisons, and so on), knowledge of relevant theories (e.g., knowledge of evolutionary theory), knowledge of how to connect theories and evidence (e.g., understanding how to use particular patterns of microevolutionary data to argue that particular changes in traits are caused by particular selection pressures), and knowledge of the specific criteria for evaluating claims, evidence, and warrants in the domain.

There is evidence that engagement in collaborative argumentation promotes the ability to engage in and evaluate domain specific argumentation (Sandoval & Millwood, 2005). For instance, Zohar and Nemet (2002) found that engaging in argumentation about ethical issues raised by genetics improved the ability to construct other genetics arguments. Chinn et al. (2000) found that engaging in effective collaborative about electric circuit experiments enabled fifth graders to better evaluate the quality of conclusions about such experiments.

Chinn (2006) has argued that there is an intermediate level of argument-relevant knowledge that falls in between very general knowledge of argument components such as counterarguments (which can be used in *all* argumentation) and specific knowledge about common flaws in a certain kind of microbiology experiment (which can be used only in one particular domain of argumentation). For instance, knowledge about sample size is relevant to reasoning about a wide variety of studies in the social sciences and biology, but is not relevant to all topics and situations. Similarly, knowledge about how differences in wording can change responses to questionnaires is useful in reasoning about a wide range of research—psychological studies, political polls, and a company's internal employee surveys. Walton's (1996) argumentation schemes are another example of general but not universal argument forms; the argument from signs can be used in many situations, but there are many other situations in which it cannot be used (e.g., the argument from signs probably plays no role in mathematical arguments). Thus, there is an intermediate level of knowledge that is needed for effective argumentation. Although such intermediate knowledge seems to be a promising target of instruction, there is little evidence to date on whether collaborative argumentation can promote skill with such intermediate-level reasoning skills.

Improved Knowledge Building Practices

So far, we have considered the role of argumentation in developing particular kinds of individual knowledge—such as content knowledge and general knowledge of how to argue. Other scholars have emphasized that argumentation is a social practice for constructing knowledge, and what students are learning is how to participate in and contribute to these practices. This is the perspective of knowledge building (Scardamalia & Bereiter, 2006) discussed in several other chapters in this volume (e.g., Bielaczyc et al., chapter 13 this volume; Chan, chapter 25 this volume). Students are learning to create knowledge in communities via a powerful tool for social knowledge creation.

SCAFFOLDING EFFECTIVE COLLABORATIVE ARGUMENTATION

In this section of the chapter, we discuss research that focuses on how to provide scaffolds within instruction so that students can learn more effectively from collaborative argumentation. We begin by looking at features of collaborative argumentation that are associated with greater learning, which helps us see what kinds of scaffolds should be used. We then turn to research on various methods of scaffolding collaborative argumentation.

Features of Collaborative Argumentation Associated with Greater Learning

One focus of empirical research has been to investigate features of collaborative argumentation that are associated with greater learning. For instance, Chinn et al. (2000) found that fourth graders learned more in collaborative argumentation about what to conclude from electric circuit experiments if their argumentation was deeper and more complex. Students who learned more were in groups that engaged in extensive counterarguments, coconstruction of arguments, and discussion of whether the reasons offered by participants were good reasons or not. Students in groups that engaged in simpler argumentation (such as students giving simple reasons for their claims but without engaging with each other's reasons) learned less. Other studies have yielded comparable results (e.g., Sampson & Clark, 2011).

Another general finding from this research is that learning is often greater if there has, in fact, been disagreement and argumentation to try to resolve the disagreement (e.g., Chinn et al., 2000; Perret-Clermont, 1980). Evidence also suggests that participants learn more when they set a goal to integrate their perspectives into a final solution that involves finding a compromise position or a position that integrates aspects of the initial opposing positions (Asterhan & Schwarz, 2007; Nussbaum & Schraw, 2007). When there is a focus on "defending one's position," learning is less likely, as participants may be more inflexible and less willing to try to understand and appreciate other perspectives (e.g., Clark, D'Angelo, & Menekse, 2009).

The value of identifying features of collaborative argumentation that are associated with greater learning is that researchers learn something about what should be promoted when designing learning environments. For instance, the Chinn et al. (2000) research described above suggests that designers should aim to create environments that strongly encourage deep rather than shallow discussions.

Scaffolding Understanding of the Basic Components of Argumentation

A large proportion of the instructional research on argumentation has focused on methods for teaching students the basic components of argumentation and scaffolding students as they engage in the basic processes of argumentation. For example, Kuhn and her colleagues (see Kuhn, 2010) have taught students basic components of dialectical argumentation, such as making and rebutting counterarguments. Students working in groups also complete diagrams in which they identify their key arguments, anticipate counterarguments and rebuttals to those counterarguments. They have found that these methods promote growth in students' ability to argue. Schworm and Renkl (2007) also found that explicitly teaching students about the components of arguments improved students' ability to evaluate argumentation. Clark and colleagues (2010) reviewed research on a variety of approaches to scaffolding scientific argumentation among multiple students in online learning environments to support the development of 21st-century skills. Results with such methods of explicit instruction have been mixed. Reznitskaya, Anderson, McNurlen et al. (2001), for example, found that explicit instruction in argument components did not improve learning (see also Reznitskaya, Anderson, & Kuo, 2007).

A number of researchers have employed diagrams to help students identify the key components of arguments. For instance, Suthers and Hundhausen (2003) used a computer-based tool to help students envision the components of arguments. This tool helped students identify the claims, data, and their interrelationships by connecting claims and data with links that indicate whether the data supports or contradicts the claims. Suthers and Hundhausen (2003) found that students using this tool focused more on evidence and wrote essays that showed greater mastery of key scientific ideas (Suthers, 2003). A variety of projects have used various graphs to help represent the key ideas presented in collaborative argumentation (e.g., Asterhan & Schwarz, 2007; Bell & Linn, 2000; see Scheuer et al., 2010).

Buckland and Chinn (2010) augmented diagrams like the one in Figure 18.1 by having students not only decide whether evidence supports or contradicts an explanation, but also record decisions about *how strongly* the evidence supports or contradicts the model. The need to make these judgments can lead students to have richer discussions about the quality of evidence and how tightly connected evidence is to the explanations they support or contradict.

Scaffolding Dialectical Processes

Researchers have also developed instructional scaffolds to assist learners with effective argumentation processes. For example, they have developed scripts (Fisher, Kollar, Stegman, & Wecker, in press) that learners follow to enhance argumentation. Kopp and Mandl (2011) documented the effectiveness of having students use the following general procedure to structure argumentation: First, they read information individually and extracted what was most important. Second, they exchanged information, writing proposed solutions in a computer application. Third, they reflected on their solutions individually. Finally, they discussed their solutions.

McAlister, Ravenscroft, and Scanlon (2004) developed a computer-based tool that encouraged students to use certain phrases such as: "I think…." "Why do you think that…?" "I disagree because…" as openers. These openers helped students stay focused on statements that are appropriate to productive argumentative discourse.

Nussbaum and Schraw (2007) confirmed the effectiveness of a diagram that directed students to list arguments and counterarguments, and then to integrate the arguments, directing them explicitly to consider which side is stronger, why it is stronger, and to consider whether there might be a compromise or creative solution.

Clark, D'Angelo, and Menekse (2009) found that sorting students into groups with students who had different initial ideas was more productive than randomly assigning students to groups, and also found that seeding discussions with a diverse set of candidate explanations was more productive than seeding discussions with the group members' own explanations.

Scaffolding Intermediate-Level and Domain-Specific Knowledge

The scaffolds we have discussed so far are designed for use across nearly any situation. If learners learn the components of arguments and good processes for engaging in dialectical argumentation, they can potentially use this knowledge in any situation. Some researchers have also developed scaffolds that target the intermediate and domain-specific levels of argumentative knowledge that we discussed earlier. To promote domain-specific argumentation, for example, Reiser et al. (2001) developed a computer-based tool called Explanation Constructor to support argumentation specifically about natural selection. A number of studies have documented the effectiveness of this tool (e.g., Sandoval & Millwood, 2005).

Other scholars have explored scaffolds of intermediate-level knowledge. For instance, Kopp and Mandl's (2011) scaffold demonstrated the effectiveness of a tool designed to facilitate argumentation by preservice teachers about the cause of a student's poor performance. The tool directed students to identify information about how the student compared with other students, and information about how his behavior in the class in question compared with the rest of his behavior. This information was used to try to facilitate collaborative argumentation to determine the cause of the student's problem. We regard this as a tool to promote intermediate-level knowledge of how to infer causes of people's behavior using comparisons with other people and with the person's own behavior in other situations. Such intermediate level knowledge should be helpful in a broad range of arguments about human behavior but not in other situations. Studies of argumentation in history have similarly promoted intermediate level knowledge by helping students learn to reason well about historical sources (VanSledright, 2002). Knowledge of how to evaluate sources is an intermediate-level knowledge that can be used in argumentation in a variety of settings.

Summary: Scaffolding Productive Collaborative Argumentation

All of the interventions discussed in this section are designed to promote productive argumentation. However, despite these successes, many researchers have noted that even with these scaffolds to encourage argumentation, much of the discourse that emerges when groups discuss turns out not to be argumentation. The proportion of talk that can be classified as argumentation (i.e., the dialectical give and take of reasons, evidence, etc.) is often a small proportion of the overall talk, and the quality is often low (see Andriessen, Baker, & Suthers, 2003; Schwarz, 2009). Thus, there remains much to do to improve scaffolds of collaborative argumentation.

ORCHESTRATING CLASSROOM LEARNING ENVIRONMENTS TO ENCOURAGE ARGUMENTATION

This final section of the chapter explores how multiple specific instructional scaffolds can be combined in complex classroom environments. Given the assumption that argumentation is an important part of inquiry in many fields, educators who have sought to promote inquiry in classrooms have often sought to build argumentation into their inquiry-based classroom interventions. However, it is very challenging to promote and sustain argumentation in classroom settings (Duschl & Osborne, 2002). Educators must develop learning environments that will motivate and scaffold students to engage in argumentation for extended periods of time throughout a multiweek inquiry unit. A discussion of methods to succeed in accomplishing these ends could fill a chapter in itself. In this final section, we will mention just a few of these methods and approaches and the challenges they are intended to address. This discussion builds upon the discussion in the previous section on specific scaffolds within instruction.

Choice of Problems

A problem that will sustain argumentation over an extended time will typically be a complex problem on which students are likely to take different perspectives and which cannot be answered quickly (cf. Hmelo-Silver & DeSimone, chapter 21 this volume; Krajcik & Blumenfeld, 2006). Real world problems or problems that are relevant to students' lives may also facilitate sustained argumentation.

Building Domain Knowledge

As we discussed earlier, argumentation requires substantial domain knowledge. On some topics, students may require little time building up this domain knowledge. Consider the situation, for example, in which elementary-school children discuss ethical issues raised by a story about a farm girl who has cared for an injured wild goose and must decide whether to let it go (Chinn et al., 2001). The story provides a great deal of relevant detail, and the students have their own experiences with pets and other situations with which they are familiar that they can use to support their positions in argumentation. In contrast, elementary-school students who are asked to argue about whether wolves should be reintroduced to the wild will not know enough about the relevant evidence or arguments; to engage students in argumentation, the designers must build activities into the instruction that provide a rich knowledge base that can then be used as evidence in group and class argumentation (Reznitskaya et al., 2009). Without sufficient domain knowledge, productive collaborative argumentation is unlikely.

Reducing Status Differences

A potential problem with all collaborative groups, including groups engaged in argumentation, is that groups may exacerbate status differences. Students in classes can often agree on who the high- and low-status students are in the class. Those who are believed to be high-status students participate more in collaborative groups than those who are thought to be low status (Webb, chapter 1 this volume). Cohen (1994a, 1994b) has described interventions that can help counteract this problem in the context of complex problems that require contributions from all students. Cohen recommended the multiple-ability treatment, in which teachers emphasize to students that solving complex problems requires many abilities, and that none of the students in any group has all the abilities that are needed, but that every student in every group has some of the necessary abilities. Cohen also recommended techniques to enhance the status of low-status students, such as teachers working independently with lower-status students to promote the needed knowledge and skills prior to collaborative argumentation and calling attention to productive contributions made by lower-status students.

Cognitive Roles

A number of researchers in the area of collaborative learning have recommended the use of cognitive roles within groups (e.g., Cohen, 1994a, 1994b). Herrenkohl and Guerra (1998) developed three cognitive roles for students to use when working in groups and when responding to group presentations made to the whole class after each investigation. The three roles were: (a) making a prediction and building a theory, (b) summarizing results of investigations, and (c) relating the results to the prediction and theory. In class discussions, the teacher worked with the class to develop questions that would be associated with each of these roles; Herrenkohl and Guerra (1998) provided evidence that these interactions enhanced the quality of the reasoning in the class argumentation that followed the presentations. Similarly, Weinberger, Ertl, Fischer, and Mandl (2005) demonstrated the value of assigning the roles of "case analyst" and "constructive critic" to students engaged in computer-supported collaborative learning.

Norms and Criteria

A number of scholars have emphasized the importance of developing appropriate classroom norms to foster argumentation. We have already mentioned some general norms, such as seeking to understand rather than to win the argument and treating others with respect. Educators also aim to promote norms that are specific to the disciplines that students are learning. For example, mathematics students may adopt a norm to give deductive reasons for their mathematical claims, science students may adopt a norm to give strong weight to empirical evidence in their arguments, and history students may adopt a norm to carefully consider source credibility with all sources.

One kind of disciplinary norm consists of the *criteria* used to judge ideas. For example, criteria for evaluating scientific models include the extent to which the model fits with a broad scope of evidence and the extent to which it coheres with other accepted models (Pluta, Chinn, & Duncan, 2011). Chinn, Duschl, Duncan, Buckland, and Pluta (2008) have focused on the use of criteria in developing scientific models. In their project, teachers lead their classes in developing class sets of criteria for evaluating models. For example, in one class, the criteria included that the model explains using words, pictures, and diagrams; that the evidence supporting the model is true; that the model explains *how* or *why*, and that it provides the steps in the process. During the year, each class refined their own criteria. Students regularly referred to these criteria when engaging in argumentation about which of two or more models were better. The criteria provided one focus that could sustain the argumentation, as students considered whether their models met the various criteria they had elected to adopt as their class norms.

Sampson has found similar results regarding fostering shared criteria in his research (Sampson, Grooms, & Walker, 2009).

CONCLUSION

This chapter has outlined the potential benefits of collaborative argumentation in terms of improved motivation, content learning, improved general argumentation skills, improved specific argumentation skills, and improved knowledge building practices. This chapter has also outlined strategies and approaches for scaffolding productive collaborative argumentation. Unfortunately, the proportion of talk that can be classified as argumentation is often a small proportion of the overall talk, and the quality is often low (see Andriessen et al., 2003; Schwarz, 2009). At the policy level, there is increasing awareness of the importance of increasing collaborative argumentation in classrooms. In U.S. science education, for example, the 1996 National Science Education standards (National Research Council [NRC], 1996) increased emphasis on argumentation as central to inquiry, and the revised framework for science education (NRC, 2011), which are aligned closely with the NRC's *Taking Science to School* report (Duschl, Schweingruber, & Shouse, 2007), increases this emphasis further. Similar emphasis is placed on collaborative argumentation in terms of "21st century skills" (NRC, 2009). Standards no longer focus on rote facts. Instead standards focus on conceptual knowledge, epistemic understanding, and the ability, skills, identity, and inclination of students to engage in intellectual inquiry. Research, professional development, and policies to increase and enhance the quality and quantity of collaborative argumentation in classrooms will prove central to achieving these goals.

REFERENCES

Andriessen, J. (2006). Arguing to learn. In R. K. Sawyer (Ed.), *The Cambridge handbook of the learning sciences* (pp. 443–459). Cambridge, England: Cambridge University Press.

Andriessen, J., Baker, M., & Suthers, D. (2003). Argumentation, computer support, an dthe educational context of confronting cognitions. In J. Andriessen, M. Baker, & D. Suthers (Eds.), *Arguing to learn: Confronting cognitions in computer-supported collaborative learning environments* (pp. 1–25). Dordrecht: Kluwer.

Asterhan, C. S. C., & Schwarz, B. B. (2007). The effects of monological and dialogical argumentation on concept learning in evolutionary theory. *Journal of Educational Psychology, 99*, 626–639.

Baker, M., Andriessen, J., Lund, K., van Amelsvoort, M., & Quignard, M. (2007). Rainbow: A framework for analyzing computer-mediated pedagogical debates. *International Journal of Computer-Supported Collaborative Learning, 2*, 315–357.

Bell, P., & Linn, M. C. (2000). Scientific arguments as learning artifacts: Designing for learning from the web with KIE. *International Journal of Science Education, 22*, 797–817.

Buckland, L. A., & Chinn, C. A. (2010, June). Model-evidence link diagrams: A scaffold for model-based reasoning. In *ICLS 2010: Proceedings of International Society of the Learning Sciences*. Raleigh, NC: Lulu.

Chinn, C. A. (2006). Learning to argue. In A. M. O'Donnell, C. E. Hmelo-Silver, & G. Erkens (Eds.), *Collaborative learning, reasoning, and technology* (pp. 355–383). Mahwah, NJ: Erlbaum.

Chinn, C. A., Anderson, R. C., & Waggoner, M. A. (2001). Patterns of discourse in two kinds of literature discussion. *Reading Research Quarterly, 36*, 378–411.

Chinn, C. A., Duschl, R. A., & Duncan, R. G., Buckland, L. A., Pluta, W. P. (2008, June). *A microgenetic classroom study of learning to reason scientifically through modeling and argumentation*. In *ICLS 2008: Proceedings of International Society of the Learning Sciences*. Raleigh, NC: Lulu

Chinn, C. A., O'Donnell, A. M., & Jinks, T. S. (2000). The structure of discourse in collaborative learning. *Journal of Experimental Education, 69*, 77–97.

Clark, D. B., D'Angelo, C. M., & Menekse, M. (2009). Initial structuring of online discussions to improve learning and argumentation: Incorporating students' own explanations as seed comments versus an augmented-preset approach to seeding discussions. *Journal of Science Education and Technology, 18*, 321–333.

Clark, D. B., & Sampson, V. (2007). Personally-seeded discussions to scaffold online argumentation. *International Journal of Science Education, 29*, 253–277.

Clark, D. B., & Sampson, V. (2008). Assessing dialogic argumentation in online environments to relate structure, grounds, and conceptual quality. *Journal of Research in Science Teaching, 45*, 293–321.

Clark, D. B., Sampson, V. D., Stegmann, K., Marttunen, M., Kollar, I., Janssen, J., … Laurinen, L. (2010). Scaffolding scientific argumentation between multiple students in online learning environments to support the development of 21st century skills. In B. Ertl (Ed.), E-Collaborative knowledge construction: Learning from computer-supported and virtual environments (pp. 1–39). New York: IGI Global.

Clark, D., Sampson, V., Weinberger, A., & Erkens, G. (2007). Analytic frameworks for assessing dialogic argumentation in online learning environments. *Educational Psychology Review, 19*, 343–374.

Cobb, P., McClain, K., & Gravemeijer, K. (2003). Learning about statistical covariation. *Cognition and Instruction, 21*, 1–78.

Cohen, E. G. (1994a). *Designing group work: Strategies for the heterogeneous classroom* (2nd ed.). New York: Teachers College Press.

Cohen, E. G. (1994b). Restructuring the classroom: Conditions for productive small groups. *Review of Educational Research, 64*, 1–35.

Dong, T., Anderson, R. C., Kim, I.-H., & Li, Y. (2008). Collaborative reasoning in China and Korea. *Reading Research Quarterly, 43*, 400–424.

Duschl, R. A. (2008). Quality argumentation and epistemic criteria. In S. Erduran & M. P. Jiménez-Aleixandre (Eds.), *Argumentation in science education* (pp. 159–175). Dordrecht: Springer.

Duschl, R. A., & Osborne, J. (2002). Supporting and promoting argumentation discourse in science education. *Studies in Science Education, 38*, 39–72.

Duschl, R. A., Schweingruber, H. A., & Shouse, A. W. (Eds.). (2007). *Taking science to school: Learning and teaching science in grades K-8*. Washington, DC: National Academics Press.

Erduran, S., Simon, S., & Osborne, J. (2004). Tapping into argumentation: Developments in the application of Toulmin's argument pattern for studying science discourse. *Science Education, 88*, 915–933.

Felton, M., & Kuhn, D. (2001). The development of argumentive discourse skill. *Discourse Processes, 32*, 135–153.

Fischer F., Kollar, I. Stegmann, K, & Wecker, C. (in press). Toward a script library of guidance in computer-supported collabortative learning. *Educationsl Psychologist*.

Goldman, A. I. (1999). *Knowledge in a social world*. Oxford, England: Oxford University Press.

Herrenkohl, L. R., & Guerra, M. R. (1998). Participant structures, scientific discourse, and student engagement in fourth grade. *Cognition and Instruction, 16*, 431–473.

Janssen, J., Erkens, G., & Kanselaar, G. (2007). Visualization of agreement and discussion processes during computer-supported collaborative learning. *Computers in Human Behavior, 23*, 1105–1125.

Jeong, A., Clark, D. B., Sampson, V. D., & Menekse, M. (2010). Sequentially analyzing dialogical scientific argumentation across asynchronous online discussion environments. In S. Puntambekar, G. Erkens, & C. Hmelo-Silver (Eds.), *Interactions in CSCL: Methodologies, approaches and issues* (pp. 207–234), Dordrecht, Netherlands: Springer.

Jermann, P., & Dillenbourg, P. (2003). Elaborating new arguments through a CSCL script. In J. B. Andriessen, M. Baker, & D. Suthers (Eds.), *Arguing to learn: Confronting cognitions in computer-supported collaborative learning enviornments* (pp. 205–226). Dordrecht, Netherlands: Kluwer.

Kopp, B., & Mandl, H. (2011). Fostering argument justification using collaboration scripts and content schemes. *Learning and Instruction, 21*, 636–649.

Krajcik, J. S., & Blumenfeld, P. C. (2006). Project-based learning. In R. K. Sawyer (Ed.), *The Cambridge handbook of the learning sciences* (pp. 317–333). Cambridge, England: Cambridge University Press.

Kuhn, D. (1991). *The skills of argument*. Cambridge, England: Cambridge University Press.

Kuhn, D. (2010). Teaching and learning science as argument. *Science Education, 94*, 810–824.

Kuhn, D., Goh, W., Iordanou, K., & Shaenfield, D. (2008). Arguing on the computer: A microgenetic study of developing argument skills in a computer-supported environment. *Child Development, 79*, 1310–1328.

Kuhn, D., & Udell, W. (2003). The development of argument skills. *Child Development, 74*, 1245–1260.

Lakatos, I. (1976). *Proofs and refutations: The logic of mathematical discovery*. Cambridge, England: Cambridge University Press.

Linnenbrink, E., & Pintrich, P. (2002). The role of motivational beliefs in conceptual change. In M. Limón & L. Mason (Eds.), *Reconsidering conceptual change: Issues in theory and practice* (pp. 115–135). Dordrecht, Netherlands: Kluwer.

MacArthur, C., Ferretti, R. P., & Okolo, C. M. (2002). On defending controversial viewpoints: Debates of sixth graders about the desirability of early 20th-century American immigration. *Learning Disabilities Research & Practice, 17,* 160–172.

McAlister, S., Ravenscroft, A., & Scanlon, E. (2004). Combining interaction and context design to support collaborative argumentation using a tool for synchronous CMC. *Journal of Computer Assisted Learning, 20,* 194–204.

Mercer, N. (2009). Developing argumentation: Lessons learned in the primary school. In N. M. Mirza & A.-N. Perret-Clermont (Eds.), *Argumentation and education* (pp. 177–194). Dordrecht, Netherlands: Springer.

Mirza, N. M., Perret-Clermont, A.-N., Tartas, T., & Iannaccone, A. (2009). Psychological processes in argumentation. In N. M. Mirza & A.-N. Perret-Clermont (Eds.), *Argumentation and education* (pp. 67–90). Dordrecht, Netherlands: Springer.

National Research Council. (2009, February, 5–6). *Exploring the intersection of science education and the development of 21st century skills* (National Research Council Workshop). Washington, DC: Author.

National Research Council. (2011). *Conceptual framework for new science education standards.* (National Academy of Sciences Board on Science Education). Washington, DC: Author.

National Research Council. (1996). *National science education standards.* Washington, DC: National Academy Press.

Nussbaum, E. M. (2011). Argumentation, dialogue theory, and probability modeling: Alternative frameworks for argumentation research in education. *Educational Psychologist, 46,* 84–106.

Nussbaum, E. M., & Bendixen, L. D. (2003). Approaching and avoiding arguments: The role of epistemological beliefs, need for cognition, and extraverted personality traits. *Contemporary Educational Psychology, 28,* 573–595.

Nussbaum, E. M., & Schraw, G. (2007). Promoting argument-counterargument integration in students' writing. *Journal of Experimental Education, 76,* 59–92.

Perret-Clermont, A.-N. (1980). *Social interaction and cognitive development in children.* London: Academic Press.

Pluta, W. J., Chinn, C. A., & Duncan, R. G. (2011). Learners' epistemic criteria for good scientific models. *Journal of Research in Science Teaching, 48,* 486–511.

Reiser, B. J., Smith, B. K., Tabak, I., Steinmuller, F., Sandoval, W. A., & Leone, A. J. (2001). BGuILE: Strategic and conceptual scaffolds for scientific inquiry in biology classrooms. In S. M. Carver & D. Klahr (Eds.), *Cognition and instruction: Twenty-five years of progress* (pp. 263–305). Mahwah, NJ: Erlbaum.

Reznitskaya, A. (in press). Dialogic classroom: Rethinking theory, research, and practice. *Educational Psychologist.*

Reznitskaya, A., Anderson, R. C., & Kuo, L.-J. (2007). Teaching and learning argumentation. *Elementary School Journal, 107,* 449–472.

Reznitskaya, A., Anderson, R. C., McNurlen, B., Nguyen-Jahiel, K., Archodidou, A., & Kim, S.-Y. (2001). Influence of oral discussion on written argument. *Discourse Processes, 32,* 155–175.

Reznitskaya, A., Kuo, L.-j., Clark, A.-M., Miller, B., Jadallah, M., Anderson, R. C., & Nguyen-Jahiel, K. (2009). Collaborative reasoning: A dialogic approach to group discussions. *Cambridge Journal of Education, 39,* 29–48.

Sampson, V., & Clark, D. B. (2008). Assessment of the ways students generate arguments in science education: Current perspectives and recommendations for future directions. *Science Education, 92,* 447–472.

Sampson, V., & Clark, D. B. (2009). The impact of collaboration on the outcomes of argumentation. *Science Education, 93,* 448–484.

Sampson, V. D., & Clark, D. B. (2011). Comparison of more and less successful groups in collaboration. *Research in Science Education, 41,* 63–75.

Sampson, V. D., Grooms, J., & Walker, J. (2009). Argument-driven inquiry as a way to help students learn how to participate in scientific argumentation and craft written arguments: An exploratory study. *Science Education, 76,* 42–47.

Sandoval, W. A., & Millwood, K. A. (2005). The quality of students' use of evidence in written scientific explanations. *Cognition and Instruction, 23,* 23–55.

Scardamalia, M., & Bereiter, C. (2006). Knowledge building. In R. K. Sawyer (Ed.), *The Cambridge handbook of the learning sciences* (pp. 97–115). Cambridge, England: Cambridge University Press.

Scheuer, O., Loll, F., Pinkwart, N., & McLaren, B. M. (2010). Computer-supported argumentation: A review of the state of the art. *Computer Supported Collaborative Learning, 5,* 43–102.

Schwarz, B. (2009). Argumentation and learning. In N. M. Mirza & A.-N. Perret-Clermont (Eds.), *Argumentation and education* (pp. 91–126). Dordrecht, Netherlands: Springer.

Schworm, S., & Renkl, A. (2007). Learning argumentation skills through the use of prompts for self-explaining examples. *Journal of Educational Psychology, 99*, 285–296.

Smith, K., Johnson, D. W., & Johnson, R. T. (1981). Can conflict be constructive? Controversy versus concurrence seeking in learning groups. *Journal of Educational Psychology, 73*, 651–663.

Stein, N. L., & Albro, E. R. (2001). The origins and nature of arguments: Studies in conflict understanding, emotion, and negotiation. *Discourse Processes, 32*, 113–133.

Suthers, D. (2003). Representational guidance for collaborative inquiry. In J. Andriessen, M. Baker, & D. Suthers (Eds.), *Arguing to learn: Confronting cognitions in computer-supported collaborative learning environments* (pp. 27–46). Dordrecht, Netherlands: Kluwer.

Suthers, D. D., & Hundhausen, C., D. (2003). An experimental study of the effects of representational guidance on collaborative learning processes. *Journal of the Learning Sciences, 12*, 183–218.

Toulmin, S. E. (1958). *The uses of argument.* Cambridge, England: Cambridge University Press.

van Eemeren, F. H., & Grootendorst, R. (2004). *A systematic theory of argumentation: The pragma-dialectical approach.* Cambridge, England: Cambridge University Press.

VanSledright, B. A. (2002). Fifth graders investigating history in the classroom: Results from a researcher-practitioner design experiment. *The Elementary School Journal, 103*, 131–160.

Vygotsky, L. S. (1981). The genesis of higher mental functions. In J. V. Wertsch (Ed.), *The concept of activity in Soviet psychology* (pp. 144–188). Armonk, NY: Sharpe.

Walton, D. N. (1989). *Informal logic: A handbook for critical argumentation.* Cambridge, England: Cambridge University Press.

Walton, D. N. (1996). *Argumentation schemes for presumptive reasoning.* Mahwah, NJ: Erlbaum.

Walton, D. N., Reed, C., & Macagno, F. (2008). *Argumentation schemes.* Cambridge, England: Cambridge University Press.

Weinberger, A., Ertl, B., Fisher, F., & Mandl, H. (2005). Epistemic and social scripts in computer-supported collaborative learning. *Instructional Science, 33*, 1–30.

Wiley, J., & Voss, J. F. (1999). Constructing arguments from multiple sources: Tasks that promote understanding and not just memory for text. *Journal of Educational Psychology, 91*, 301–311.

Zohar, A., & Nemet, F. (2002). Fostering students' knowledge and argumentation skills through dilemmas in human genetics. *Journal of Research in Science Teaching, 39*, 35–62.

19

ORGANIZING COLLABORATIVE LEARNING EXPERIENCES AROUND SUBJECT MATTER DOMAINS

The Importance of Aligning Social and Intellectual Structures in Instruction

LINDSAY L. CORNELIUS, LESLIE R. HERRENKOHL, AND JENNA WOLFSTONE-HAY

University of Washington

Outside of institutions of formal education, students participate in a variety of social practices in their communities, each, as Nasir, Rosebery, Warren, and Lee (2006) describe, involve "diverse repertoires of overlapping, complementary or even conflicting cultural practices" (p. 489). These authors advocate a position that students' ways of knowing and communicating are developing skills which they bring with them into the classroom, and which inform the ways in which they interact with the content of the curriculum and the social and intellectual practices of instruction. Subject matter areas, or disciplined ways of knowing,[1] also embody distinct social practices and ways of interacting which experts draw upon when engaging in their professional communities (Lemke, 2001). Learning scientists, for example, routinely engage in practices of reading others' research in peer-reviewed journals, using these findings to bolster their arguments for novel research, engaging with trusted colleagues to receive feedback on early versions of their work, and submitting finished papers to conferences or to relevant journals in their field. Discussions among learning scientists rely upon shared sets of terminology and references to works which are assumed to be widely read by members of the academic community. Additionally, learning scientists make particular assumptions about how learning ought to be studied and they design research to investigate aspects of learning with human subjects. As disciplines are applied to formal schooling contexts, these ways of engaging are often masked within a generic mode of instruction which Bruner (1960) referred to as the "middle language" of schooling practices. In school communities, that is, dialogue is often limited to students' reproduction of "right" answers and is similar across subject matters, not reflecting important differences in how knowledge is organized in respective fields (Schwab, 1978). Current trends in education, however, have advocated for bringing disciplinary engagement with the subject matter to the fore in curriculum and instruction (Engle & Conant, 2002; Hatano & Inagaki, 1991). Having students engage in curriculum which is organized around sets of ideas such as experts draw upon in their respective domains has been discussed in the learning sciences literature as necessary to promoting meaningful opportunities that can be transferred or adapted to new types of problems (National Research Council, 2007a).

In this chapter we will consider how collaborative learning coupled with rich contexts of disciplinary problems and questions has the potential to serve as a bridge between students' out-of-school and in-school lives, and to achieve important social and intellectual goals concomitantly. The framework we utilize in this chapter to engage with and organize this complex network of ideas is a model of instruction called project-based learning (PBL). PBL is an approach to instruction that makes explicit important features of the discipline being studied, and positions students as active contributors in the creation of their own knowledge (Krajcik & Blumenfeld, 2006). Krajcik and Blumenfeld propose four main theoretical bases for project-based learning: (a) active construction; (b) situated learning; (c) social interactions; and (d) cognitive tools. We consider these four points and their interconnections as a way to explore the dynamic interplay between collaborative learning and domain-specific instruction.

ACTIVE CONSTRUCTION

We approach the study of collaborative learning with the goal of promoting effective student learning. Research into how people learn has generated overwhelming evidence that students do not come to the classroom as blank slates to be written on, or empty vessels to be filled. Rather, students actively construct knowledge for themselves, utilizing their current forms of understanding to make sense of new material, narratives, and tools which are introduced into the classroom community. Instruction is therefore most effective when it explicitly engages students' prior thinking (National Research Council, 2007a) and builds upon forms of discourse that they utilize in their out-of-school interactions (Lee, 1995; Nasir et al., 2006). Using students' prior knowledge of real world situations has been described as a powerful resource for building new conceptions of the subject matter (Lemke, 1990; J. P. Smith, diSessa, & Roschelle, 1993).

Involving students in constructing their own knowledge and integrating their prior experiences requires curricula which motivate this type of engagement and allow students to become personally invested in the processes and products of their learning. Employing *driving questions* (Krajcik & Blumenfeld, 2006) and problematizing the subject matter (Warren & Rosebery, 1996) can provide the necessary framework and motivation. A driving question is defined by Krajcik and Blumenfeld as a question which "encompasses worthwhile content that is meaningful and anchored in a real-world situation" (2006, p. 320). Used as a beginning to knowledge building, this instructional practice helps to develop students' interests in the solution of problems that they find meaningful, organizes their engagement with the curriculum, and provides a coherent context for students to engage in a range of disciplinary practices and intellectual activities.

SITUATED LEARNING: DOMAIN-SPECIFIC KNOWLEDGE AS AN IMPORTANT CONTEXT FOR LEARNING

Where the tenet of *active construction* of knowledge can inform educators of how to effectively construct learning environments (e.g., by employing driving questions to motivate lessons), a focus on "situated learning" broadens the contexts that one needs to consider when thinking about the trajectory of learners over time in their learning communities. Situated learning as a theory refers to how people come to participate and learn in real-world situations, through a process that Lave and Wenger (1991) termed *legitimate peripheral participation.* This perspective on learning describes how novices become experts through their increased participation in a group's social and intellectual practices over time. Learning in this way is profound; it engages not just the learner's intellect, but his or her emotions and interests, and motivations to belong and to become. Nasir's research on African American students' participation in playing dominoes (2005) and basketball (2000) exemplifies how participants in these activities gained mathematical understanding through their engagement in games which they enjoyed and strived to become more expert players. Formal schooling environments, even when they promote students' active construction of knowledge, typically remove students from direct participation in the professional communities of practices that the curriculum attempts to represent through the school subjects. It therefore becomes necessary to innovate curriculum which brings these knowledge-making practices into the classroom in ways that represent the types of meaningful problems which experts in the domain think about and how they go about solving these problems.

Where prior knowledge is a starting point, the goals of instruction in moving toward these domain-specific knowledge practices include bringing students into contact with normative ways of interacting with content, creating arguments, evaluating evidence, and crafting products. Having access to these disciplinary ways of thinking provide learners with powerful frameworks to interpret their prior experiences and to integrate them with what is learned in the educational setting. Smith et al. (1993) find that the "knowledge of the discipline one is studying affects people's abilities to monitor their own understanding and evaluate others' claims effectively" (p. 12). Vygotsky (1978) similarly described that "learning is more than the acquisition of the ability to think; it is the acquisition of many specialized abilities for thinking about a variety of things" (p. 83). Hence, in the same way that informal learning can be situated, the construction of knowledge in school settings might be shaped to resemble situated thinking about important types of problems using strategies most effective to those ways of understanding the world.

Academic interest in the theory and practice of teaching disciplinary, or domain *specific*, ways of thinking, in contrast to domain *general* thinking practices,[2] has been developing over the past 50 years (see Hirschfield & Gelman, 1994). In education, Bruner (1960) sparked this movement toward domain specific practices in schools, as he argued that each subject has its own structure of knowledge which can guide students' interactions with the content at every level. Schwab's writings on the structure of disciplines (1962, 1978) similarly argued the point that knowledge is organized in ways which help us to define the scope of our questions and to provide guidance in choosing methods which might address unresolved problems that exist in its study. Research in education has since come to rely more and more on domain specific theory both to explain learning (Perkins & Salomon, 1989) and to organize instruction (Driver, Newton, & Osbourne, 2000; Lemke, 2001; Schulman & Quinlan, 1996; Stevens, Wineburg, Herrenkohl, & Bell 2005). The National Research Council (2007a) describes this as having a knowledge-centered focus on learning and instruction, where core concepts in the subject matter are emphasized by providing concrete cases and detailed knowledge to assist students' ability to achieve mastery of those core concepts.

Much of what defines a domain are the ways in which scholars working in that tradition think about the subject matter, create arguments, and the types of discourse they use to support those arguments. In history, for example, Lowenthal (2000) describes five "modes of thinking" which he sees as being specific to that domain: (a) having *familiarity* with a common set of references; (b) using *comparative judgment* to think about and critique differences between sources; (c) having an *awareness of manifold truths* (i.e., that different viewers are bound to see a past event differently); (d) keeping an *appreciation of authority* where sources are respected but not venerated; and (e) developing *hindsight*, in that interpretations of the past can change as new evidence becomes available. The development of disciplinary epistemologies or ways of conceptualizing knowledge within a given domain is the result of engaging in these types of practices and ways of thinking about the subject matter. Hofer's (2002) research found, for instance, that by college, students hold differing beliefs about the certainty and stability of knowledge across domains such as science and psychology. For students just beginning to engage in these practices for the first time, their ability to express such formal epistemologies around the subject matter may be limited. Evidence of a *practical* or *personal epistemology*, defined as students' general views about the nature of knowledge and knowing (Elby, 2009), can be gleaned from the ways in which they interact with knowledge during inquiry (Sandoval, 2005), even when students do not reflect explicitly on them.

There are important distinctions to note in how "domain" is defined by different theorists in the research on teaching and learning. Some scholars use the term *domain* to indicate subfields of conceptually coherent subject matter. Inagaki and Hatano's (2004) work, for instance, identifies how children organize their own understandings of the natural world into the domains of physics, psychology, and biology. Their work concludes that children use different causal devices to explain biological processes, and in this way differentiate between living versus nonliving things. These distinctions are, of course, relevant to the larger fields of study that they correspond to, and some researchers necessarily focus on the ways in which conceptual change must encompass strategic ways of thinking about particular types of problems within these content areas (diSessa, 1993).

For students' growing understanding of subject matter to be situated within contexts of disciplinary learning, it is also necessary to consider what level of specificity in domain-specific knowledge and practices is ideal for younger learners to engage with. In school subjects, there are often broad demarcations of domains such as science, social studies, and mathematics, though we know from the research literature that subfields within a domain can differ in their disciplinary practices and epistemologies. Samarapungavan, Westby, and Bodner (2006) have found, for instance, that the self-described work of chemists differed from normative views of science as a primarily theory-building pursuit. These distinctions may be more readily apparent and their epistemological underpinnings more accessible to exploration by students in the upper grades and at the university level, where content knowledge is typically already divided into subfields of inquiry (e.g., "social studies" in lower grades becomes economics, geography, and history in upper grades). At the elementary and middle levels, while these distinctions inform the big ideas and concepts that students engage with in exploring knowledge within the domains, introducing core sets of thinking practices that transverse the domain more broadly defined (e.g., science) have been more common in the literature (National Research Council, 2007b). Examples of this from science include research on developing students' ideas about theory building, revising ideas over time, and how models can be used to represent thinking (Beeth & Hewson, 1999; Kawasaki, Herrenkohl, & Yeary, 2004). In mathematics, research has explored how teachers can engage students in position-driven discussion of mathematical ideas (O'Connor, 2001) which develop their understandings of the relationship between conjecture and proof (Lampert, 1990). There is a usefulness in considering both these broader epistemologies and disciplinary practices that we would like to engage students in, along with the nuanced conceptual understandings of particular subfields within disciplines. For our purposes in this chapter, we focus on the larger distinctions between disciplines (e.g., science, history, mathematics) and consider the ways in which collaborative learning can be used to facilitate disciplinary epistemologies.

SOCIAL INTERACTIONS: COLLABORATIVE LEARNING AND THE DEVELOPMENT OF DISCIPLINARY EPISTEMOLOGIES

Sophisticated models of using collaboration in the classroom emphasize that this instructional tool involves much more than simply putting students together in a group, giving them a problem, and asking them to find solutions. Barron's (2003) work illuminates some potential roadblocks to effective collaboration, namely, that groups can fail not because of the lack of effective intellectual ideas and tools, but rather due to the fact that they are unable to negotiate the relational demands of working together in a group, such as responding to each other's ideas and integrating them when warranted. Effective collaboration, as defined by Hmelo-Silver and Barrows (2008), involves participants in sharing responsibility for learning, distributing expertise, and building on each other's ideas. These images of collaboration build off of Brown and Campione's (1994) and Rogoff's (1994) theoretical discussions of *communities of learners*, where students are positioned as active in building understandings and teachers serve as guides. One important feature of this model of collaboration is the notion of distributed expertise, where individual students within a classroom community are positioned as being experts on different topics or problem-solving skills, and are asked to leverage each others' abilities in developing collective products and solutions. Slavin's (1999) model of collaboration similarly emphasizes individual accountability, where each person's contribution is expected and assessed, and group goals, where the group collectively works toward some understanding or solution. Discourse is utilized in collaborative learning environments as a way of sharing and building knowledge, and as we will discuss later in depth, is also situated within different domains of knowledge and types of problems to be solved.

Collaboration within models of collective, classroom-based, and constructivist learning affords students both social and intellectual benefits.[3] Though not truly separable, we will consider each of these in turn. The social benefits of collaboration include increased opportunities for individual students to participate, equalizing status differences among students (Cohen, 1994; Cohen & Lotan, 1995); providing students with the chance to negotiate their ideas with each other (Warren & Rosebery, 1996); and emphasizing group goals along with individual accountability (Slavin, 1999). We represent these aspects of collaboration as a foundational set of relations in a classroom which must be developed, in some form, before successful collaboration in a domain can be achieved, though certainly they continue to develop through sustained disciplinary engagement. Students' experiences using discourses germane to normative disciplinary practices can, in turn, impact and become a site for exploring the social relations among students and teachers. For instance, using our previous example, if students were to engage in investigating problems as learning scientists do, they may begin to utilize terminology which they have encountered in seminal pieces of work in the field, and may frame their own investigations with human subjects around these ideas. The process of engaging in such research may raise questions for the community, collectively, about the role of the researcher in both collecting and sharing information with colleagues. Disagreements about what forms of knowledge "count" and could advance the collective understanding of a common set of issues, can thus lead to discussion and reflection on the ways in which the group itself is functioning as a community of learners (Rogoff, 1994). Wortham's (2004, 2006) account of students' discourse in a literature unit, and Lensmire's (2000) account of writers' workshops illustrate how social relationships in the classroom constitute and are reconstituted by the curriculum.

The intellectual benefits of collaborating within disciplinary structures of knowledge include increased opportunities for students to practice speaking, for example, the "language of science" (Lemke, 1990) as they interact with each other. Collaborative learning presents opportunities for students to assume ownership of ideas and to use persuasive discourse as a means of creating arguments that their peers will find compelling (Cornelius & Herrenkohl, 2004). This negotiation of ideas with peers helps to develop "epistemic motivation" (Hatano & Inagaki, 1991; Sandoval, 2005) to know and understand the subject matter. Students can learn about scholarly practice within the domain through the activity of using evidence and defending their ideas to one another.

There are ways to introduce disciplinary ideas and discourses into a classroom which do not necessarily involve collaboration among groups of students. Nathan and Kim (2009) for instance focus on one teacher's role as facilitator of whole class conversations and his central role in scaffolding disciplinary ways of thinking through skilled elicitations of students' ideas. Conversely, there are ways of providing collaboration opportunities for students that are not explicitly disciplinary. Cohen and colleagues (Cohen, 1994; Cohen & Lotan, 1995; Cohen, Lotan, Scarloss, & Arellano, 1999), for example, focus on the nature of students' engagement with each other during classroom tasks which have been differentiated to provide multiple ways for students to engage with the material, but which do not promote disciplinary epistemologies specifically.

Collaborative learning which integrates a concern for social relations among students with disciplinary considerations for learning, however, can achieve powerful results in getting students to think and act more like mature practitioners of a discipline. Researchers of inquiry based classroom curriculum agree that the productiveness of inquiry depends on the scaffolding that the teacher provides, for both the social and intellectual activity of the classroom. Students must be introduced to an idea of "rights and responsibilities" to define their own roles in relation to others during their inquiry. Teachers must also introduce students to the key features of thinking in a given discipline: the kinds of questions one asks, the methods one uses to answer those questions, and what counts as evidence in a given domain.

Cognitive Tools

Representing disciplinary practices and ways of thinking in the classroom is a complex process which requires more than a teacher's explanation of the key features of the discipline, or the students' developing efforts and abilities to work together to solve problems. To bring students closer to the work that experts in the field are doing, it is necessary to introduce cognitive tools that guide students' active construction of knowledge within domain-specific practices while also facilitating collaboration which is an essential feature of any community of practice. Sociocultural theories of teaching and learning emphasize that understanding learning requires an analysis of the "cultural tools" one is using and how they mediate social and intellectual activity (Wertsch, 1998). Uses of technology, prompts, and classroom texts, along with the forms of discourse and evoking common narratives constitute some of the many ways in which classroom activity is shaped toward particular ends.

There are many examples of tools and approaches that have been developed to support students to learn to embrace discipline specific thinking strategies and which often concomitantly support effective collaborative learning as students share their ideas and work to build a collective understanding of the subject matter. Approaches to literacy instruction like Palinscar and Brown's (1984) classic model of reciprocal teaching externalize strategies that expert readers used as a way to explicitly support and guide novice readers struggling to comprehend text. Model-based reasoning approaches in science support students in developing and testing models as forms of scientific understanding (Lehrer & Schauble, 2004; Penner, Giles, Lehrer, & Schauble, 1997; C. A. Smith, 2007; C. Smith, Snir, & Grosslight, 1992). Scaffolding students' participation in scientific inquiry and argumentation has also produced sets of instructional tools to guide students as they work to make connections between claims and evidence (Bell & Linn, 2000; Herrenkohl, Tasker, & White, 2001; Reiser et al., 2001; Sandoval, 2003; White, 1993; White & Frederiksen, 1998). History instruction has produced approaches that assist students to understand essential features of thinking historically such as asking and answering essential historical questions, finding and evaluating relevant sources to answer questions, reconciling conflicting accounts of events, and creating interpretative accounts by synthesizing the evidence (Levstik & Barton, 2005; Seixas, 1994; Stevens et al., 2004; VanSledright, 2002).

DIFFERENCES AND SIMILARITIES IN COLLABORATION ACROSS DOMAINS

The foregoing discussion of supporting social and intellectual goals concomitantly in the classroom by employing cognitive tools which support collaborative learning within domain-specific areas of inquiry begs some questions: Do forms of collaboration differ across subject matter? Are there ways of talking and working together that are more relevant to some domains than others? What kinds of differences in visual representations or prompts would we expect to see to support collaboration toward domain-specific goals? In the broad area of research on collaboration which can range from descriptions of collaborative learning in which developing professionals engage in the practices of their field (Hmelo-Silver & Barrows, 2008) to groups of children engaging in scientific inquiry for the first time (Herrenkohl & Guerra, 1998), we recognize that it can be difficult to generalize what types of supports might be needed. For this reason, we will treat our discussion of these issues as an exploration of possible theoretical connections between collaboration and domain-specific learning.

In this section, we explore these questions through considering two disciplines, science and history, which we have personally studied in elementary classrooms with the explicit purpose of comparing students' disciplinary epistemologies (Stevens et al., 2005). We compare, first, the research literatures on history and science teaching and learning, and explore potential similarities and differences in the types of collaboration being proposed. We then turn to our own research program to highlight the following:(a) the common supports that we used across disciplines; (b) the ways in which we adapted these supports to the discipline-specific ways of thinking we were hoping to communicate to students; and (c) how these structures supported differences and similarities in argumentation across subject matters. We will then turn to a discussion of how these linkages might be utilized for a deeper understanding of the conceptual connections between domain specific practices of disciplines with the domain general practices of collaborative learning used in educational settings.

Collaboration in Science

Collaboration in the science classroom is deeply interconnected with principles of inquiry-based learning which can guide students' investigations into scientific ideas. According to Lemke (2001), science is essentially a social process where "what matters to learning and doing science is primarily the socially learned cultural traditions of what kinds of discourses and representations are useful and how to use them" (p. 298). If we represent science in this way as a social process, it follows that students' learning in this discipline should also represent the process, instead of merely focusing on the products of scientific inquiry, as has historically been the case in many science classrooms. Creating opportunities for students to collaborate in this process provides them with the space for developing sophisticated discourses and representations that resemble the practices that scientists routinely engage in.

Several programs of research in science education have been pivotal in exploring how students' scientific understandings are facilitated by collaboration and discussion. Rosebery and Warren's work in the Cheche Konnen Center for Science Education Reform (Rosebery,Warren, & Connant, 1992; Warren & Rosebery, 1995), research on Sister Gertrude Hennessey's exceptional teaching practice (Beeth & Hewson, 1999), and Herrenkohl and colleagues' research in elementary science classrooms (Herrenkohl & Guerra, 1998; Herrenkohl, Palincsar, DeWater, & Kawasaki, 1999) have provided powerful examples for how these practices can be made accessible to students within their own collaborations in the classroom. Herrenkohl's work has focused on how to make the intellectual practices of scientists visible to students by asking them to take on these roles themselves, both in small-group work and in whole-class conversation. Three scientific intellectual roles that Herrenkohl introduced to students included having students think and ask questions about (a) predicting and theorizing; (b) summarizing results; and (c) relating predictions and theories to results. Rotating through these roles on different days helped students to monitor their own and their peers' thinking. Over time, students engaging in these discussions of theories and interpretation of evidence can develop a sophisticated epistemology of science by participating in science as a process of revision.

Effective communication among students in science also depends on their ability to visually represent complex ideas and findings to one another. Bell (2004) and Bell and Linn (2000) focus specifically on representations, or argument maps, that students created to develop their thinking. Such visual representations help students to see how various pieces of a scientific topic connect, and to understand how and where their peers' thinking departs from their own. Collaboration is greatly facilitated by having such common structures through which to compare differences in thinking.

Collaboration in science often involves engaging students in small-group work to complete their investigations, which is followed by discussion at the classroom level to present and discuss their findings. In science, theories may be developed directly from experimental evidence. Theories can also be created by evaluating evidence collected by other means. Engle and Conant's (2002) work in the Fostering Communities of Learners research program describes how students used a variety of sources to inform their thinking about endangered species, including a visit to the local aquarium. With this evidence in hand, students can then go about the task of reading and assessing the validity of others' scientific ideas and experiments.

Engaging students in genuine attempts at scientific inquiry can create the conditions for realizing that different explanations might come to bear on interpreting scientific data. Working collaboratively encourages students to push for greater clarity in their explanations. Palincsar and Herrenkohl (1999) define collaborative work as a process of convergence which can be "achieved through cycles of display, confirming and repairing shared meaning" (p. 152). Efforts to reconcile differences in explanations provide opportunities for students to revise their own thinking in light of better evidence, arguments, and theories. Collaboration in science thus requires scaffolded opportunities for discussion in both small groups and whole class discussions, as well as representations for making their thinking visible to themselves and to others.

Collaboration in History

As in science, educators of history often find themselves in an uphill battle of trying to convey their field as a process of knowing, as opposed to a collection of facts. Argumentation is central in creating and evaluating historical accounts (Hexter, 1971). Students engaging in historical analysis are every bit as much engaged in inquiry as they are in science because they must learn to evaluate sources of evidence, to reconcile differences in historical accounts, and imaginatively take into consideration the context in which pieces of evidence were created (National Center for History in the Schools, n.d.). While there are similarities between history and science in their requirements for evidence-based arguments (Stevens et al., 2005), Lowenthal (2000) argues that history is different from natural and social sciences in that it "has no technical jargon" (p. 63), rather it requires a set of skills that one needs to think about issues of context, truth, and evidence.

When students work collaboratively in historical inquiry they can, as in science, engage in processes of developing and revising their ideas and arguments over time. The function of collaboration is to get students to externalize their thinking by together negotiating their ideas and understandings of the texts. Bain's (2000) work in history instruction emphasizes that students benefit from participating in a classroom where historical accounts are jointly created and shared, stating that "participation in such a community creates opportunities for students to internalize the discipline's higher functions or expertise" (p. 336). Bain's approach to teaching history draws on Palincsar and Brown's (1984) model of reciprocal teaching and resembles Herrenkohl et al.'s (1999) work in science, where complex understandings of history are possible when students divide the task of creating a complete and complex historical analysis of a document or group of documents. Each student in the group asks questions concerning a particular practice in reading historical documents: source, intended audience, story line, corroboration, or purpose of source.

Historical inquiry in the classroom, as in science, can be facilitated by the use of visual representations for students to develop and communicate their ideas to one another. As we will discuss with respect to our own research in Promoting Argumentation, argument maps similar to Bell's (2004) were adapted to the history curriculum as a way for students to organize their evidence, see connections between evidence and particular arguments, and to map out a physical space in an historical account (a Montgomery, Alabama bus from the historical event involving Rosa Parks).

The literature in science and history instruction, then, point to some similar themes in promoting collaborative learning in the classroom including: (a) the centrality of inquiry-based explorations of the subject matter; (b) promoting evidence-based argumentation in students' interactions with each other; (c) giving students intellectual roles which represent disciplinary ways of thinking to assist collective knowledge building; and (d) the importance of providing students with visual ways to represent their ideas to one another. There were few differences noted in the collaborative aspects of engaging students in this literature, though we note that there are fewer works on collaboration specifically related to historical inquiry in the classroom to compare with science. We turn now to our own research, which explored these disciplines side by side, to consider whether there is anything unique about collaboration in each domain, and what effect there might be on student learning when a focus on developing disciplinary epistemologies is infused in a classroom environment that promotes collaboration.

OUR CROSS-DISCIPLINARY RESEARCH

Our research in Promoting Argumentation involved the comparative study of two school subjects, science and history (see Stevens et al., 2005). In this section, we will explore both the common collaborative structures which functioned across domains, and also the ways in which the disciplinary structures of these two subjects gave rise to emergent differences in students' approaches to collaborative work.

In Promoting Argumentation, we were primarily interested in how upper elementary students (Grades 5 and 6) could develop comparative disciplinary epistemologies across two subject matters. Across one school year, we engaged students in each area of inquiry, history and science, separately through two units of science and two units of history. A final unit combined scientific and historical inquiry in a unique way, to assess how students were becoming aware of when they were engaging in scientific versus historical ways of thinking. For the purposes of this chapter, we focus on the two main units in science and history, which took place around the middle of the school year: Sinking and Floating in science, and Rosa Parks in history. Each unit contained driving questions which shaped students' own investigations into the subject matter. Instruction was also provided in the beginning of each unit, to introduce ideas of what it might mean to think scientifically or historically. For example, in Sinking and Floating, a lesson called the Orange Experiment took place at the beginning of the unit. This lesson required students to make predictions about whether a whole orange and an orange slice would sink or float, develop theories to account for their predictions, and refine their theories based on the experimental evidence. In the history unit on Rosa Parks, a lesson called the Playground Fight involved students in thinking about an imagined fight scenario, which introduced them to ideas about differing points of view, gathering and interpreting multiple sources of evidence, and making a decision about what happened based on divergent sources. These introductory lessons laid the groundwork for students to engage in discipline specific inquiry in each of these subject matters by bringing awareness to issues of evidence and the interpretation of evidence in each domain.

Scaffolding Collaboration: Common Supports across Disciplines

There were several instructional supports and participant structures (Philips, 1983) which were utilized in both subjects and aligned with other findings from the literature on collaboration in each of these domains. In this section, we focus on the similarities in the structures and practices that we introduced into the classrooms. In the following section we will focus on how these were adapted to different disciplinary goals. First, there were three key participant structures which provided opportunities for collaboration: whole-class teacher-led instruction, small-group work (four to five students per group), and whole-class presentations in which each group shared their findings and were questioned by other groups that comprised the "audience." Second, in both subjects, students engaged in inquiry in their small groups with the support of SenseMaker boards, adapted from Bell's (2004) software designed to scaffold argumentation in science. White boards (approximately 2' x 3' in size) were used in place of the software in Promoting Argumentation to ensure that students in all of the schools had access to this cognitive tool. The design space of the boards was organized differently across subject matters, which will be discussed in depth in the following section. The SenseMaker boards functioned both as a space for the small groups to record and revise their thinking based on their collaborative inquiries, and as a means for presenting their findings to the whole class. A third instructional support was the introduction of intellectual audience roles similar to those devised by Herrenkohl and colleagues (Herrenkohl & Guerra, 1998; Herrenkohl et al., 1999) to support students in asking questions of each other that reflected disciplinary ways of thinking about theories and evidence. During whole-class presentations, each audience member was assigned an intellectual role, where each corresponded to key thinking practices in each discipline, and these roles rotated so that each student could participate within each role. A "questions chart" was generated by the whole class with the teacher's support at the beginning of presentations to ensure that students had examples of what types of questions could be asked within each role, and these charts were displayed so that students could draw on these ideas during the presentations. Intellectual audience roles and questions charts involved students in a form of whole-class collaboration which stressed their responsibility as audience members to understand the presenting groups' arguments and to make critiques if necessary. A fourth instructional support was a "theory chart." In each subject, chart paper was used to provide space for the class to record new theories following groups' presentations. The theory chart helped the class to collectively keep track of their ideas and, at the end of the unit, to evaluate which arguments held up best to the evidence which was presented and explored during the unit.

Differences in the Common Supports across Disciplines: SenseMaker Board

The science unit on Sinking and Floating engaged students in a sequence of four experiments, where each set of experiments was designed to test one variable at a time and think about whether a theory involving that variable could explain why things sink or float. The objects were similar across experiments (small objects of varying materials, sizes, and shapes). The SenseMaker board was designed so that students would first order their objects according to that particular variable (e.g., size from largest to smallest) and make predictions about whether each would sink or float. For each set of experiments, the small group was required to come up with a theory to explain their predictions, to record their results next to their predictions, and to note any changes to their theory after the experiment as they took into account their results. The design of the board promoted an iterative process of creating predictions and theories, collecting data, examining the data, and then reevaluating the theories.

In history, the SenseMaker boards were designed in two different ways, one for each question about the historical event involving Rosa Parks on the Montgomery, Alabama bus. The first question in the unit asked "Where did Rosa Parks sit on the bus?" For this question, an accurate diagram of the Montgomery city bus was placed in the center of the board. After reading through 15 pieces of evidence from an archive bin, students placed small sticky-notes corresponding to these pieces of evidence on the board surrounding the bus, indicating where they ascertained each text said that Rosa Parks sat. Pieces of evidence that were not relevant to the question could be placed in a section at the bottom of the board labeled "irrelevant." For the second question "Why did Rosa Parks stay in her seat?" the boards were organized such that there were two columns: on the left, students recorded the different arguments that they saw emerging from the sources in the archive bin, and on the right, they placed the sticky-notes to indicate which pieces of evidence supported those arguments. A space for documents which were irrelevant to the question was again provided at the bottom of the board.

Intellectual Audience Roles

To scaffold students' disciplinary epistemologies, different intellectual roles were provided for each subject. In science, these roles were: (a) predicting and theorizing; (b) summarizing results; and (c) relating predictions and theories to results. These roles were introduced just before whole-class presentations began and referred to aspects of the process that students had just engaged in with the first experiment, emphasizing the iterative nature of scientific inquiry. As a whole class, sample questions for the questions chart were generated. Predicting and theorizing questions included, for example, "How did you come up with your predictions?" or "If you thought it would sink, why?" Relating predictions and theories to results included questions like "If you predicted it sank, and it floated, why was that?"

In history, the intellectual roles were (a) sourcing; (b) cross-checking; and (c) imagining the setting. Some questions that were generated for sourcing included, "Was a piece of evidence believable?" or "Why was it written?" Unlike in science, these roles focused less on understanding the groups' own arguments, and more on understanding their use and understanding of the evidence.

These roles did not cover all of the key intellectual practices that we were interested in introducing to students during these two units. Rather, they focused on key processes involved in creating arguments or theories, and discussing the evidence in relation to them.

SIMILARITIES AND DIFFERENCES IN COLLABORATION ACROSS SUBJECT MATTERS

As we anticipated from the literature, and as we planned for in instruction, inquiry was central to students' interactions within both science and history. Driving questions provided by the curriculum framed the investigations in each subject, and students worked to craft their own arguments in response to these questions. The evidence-based argumentation which was promoted in both subjects was taken up by students. Through their inquiry, students were increasingly able to reflect upon what counts as good evidence or a good argument in each domain (Herrenkohl & Cornelius, in press). Additionally, the participant structures and instructional supports that we introduced during Promoting Argumentation produced similar forms of collaboration across science and history. In both subjects, students moved through a familiar sequence of whole-class, teacher-led discussions, to small-group investigations, to whole-class presentations, where groups' ideas were discussed and evaluated toward the goal of creating more robust arguments.

Though the SenseMaker boards provided similar opportunities for students to record, explore, and visually represent their knowledge, as we expected from the literature, there emerged some differences between the two domains with respect to students' understandings of the two disciplines. One difference that we noted was that the positions of students differed with respect to the subject matter. This was related to the types of evidence they were given to work with and the extent to which their own theories were developed from direct experimentation or involved evaluations of others' evidence. The framing of the theory building space on the boards in each unit, along with the use of intellectual audience roles, emphasized different intellectual processes in the use and evaluation of evidence in each domain. Science, on the one hand, was framed through the four experiments in Sinking and Floating as an iterative process, where students must continually revisit their theories in light of new evidence. The questions from the questions chart likewise alerted students to the importance of this intellectual practice, and led to questions in the general form of, "What do you think *now*?" Since we did not introduce any textual resources for students to explore others' thinking on what makes things sink or float, their task was to engage in this series of experiments to develop a theoretical account of Sinking and Floating that could account for the objects tested. Students' roles in this were, primarily, as creators of knowledge and owners of original theories.

Though the analysis of historical documents certainly involves processes of revising one's thinking in light of new evidence (Boix-Mansilla, 2000), this intellectual activity was not as central in students' discussions. Our research on how students, together with their teachers, created arguments across these two units found, in fact, that talk about revising arguments and metalevel discussion about conceptual change occurred about six times more frequently in science than in history, even though history was a much longer unit (Herrenkohl & Cornelius, in press). In history, the SenseMaker boards and intellectual roles focused students more on evaluating evidence and in thinking about how pieces of evidence must corroborate to create a valid historical account. Though students were required to create their own arguments in history as well, these ideas were to be based on the ideas of others: namely, the authors of various historical texts. The demands of historical thought therefore required that students work in the role of evaluators of knowledge, at the same time that they were working to create a narrative/argument of their own.

The specific differences that we found, however, may have also been related to the type of tasks that were given to the students our science unit. Specifically, Sinking and Floating involved firsthand investigations of the phenomenon. Secondhand investigations are also plausible and common ways for students to interact with scientific subject matter, especially when the content is such that it does not allow for students to manipulate objects directly (Palincsar & Magnusson, 2001). Our observations within another unit we implemented, Deformed Frogs, where students relied upon secondhand sources to interact with scientific arguments, suggested that there may be more similarities to history in terms of how students approach and evaluate evidence. When considering secondhand scientific evidence, the sources must be considered, cross-checked against each other, and the student must actively "imagine the setting" of the initial research experiment that is described: processes more akin to historical thinking.

A second, epistemological difference that emerged between the two domains in our research involved notions of "truth." Working with historical documents, which students came to understand as being written by individuals with a certain perspective or point of view, led to considerations of whether the truth could ever be known. Though notions of truth are arguably as relevant to the discipline of science as they are to history, our structuring of the two units may have made this issue more salient in Rosa Parks than in Sinking and Floating. Again, we believe this to be related to the fact that in science, students were engaged in building up their own theories based on raw data, whereas in history they were evaluating claims made by others. A science unit involving students in comparing others' theories and evidence might yield more discussions of truth than we observed across classrooms during Promoting Argumentation.

Though several of these key differences existed between students' engagement in the disciplinary practices of history and science, we found that many similar disciplinary practices also emerged (Herrenkohl & Cornelius, in press). For instance, key practices such as creating arguments, defining what it means to engage in argument building in each discipline, revising arguments based on evidence, and engaging in imaginative and analogous thinking were observed in both subjects. Through engaging collaboratively in the processes of theory building themselves, students were able to push each other to think about the explanatory nature of theories, to decide together what types of evidence should and should not be allowed, and to propose which conclusions were reasonable based on the evidence.

Our comparative approach to engaging students in disciplinary inquiry shows that collaborative structures, in form, do not need to differ widely from each other to engender students' thought and engagement with discipline specific ideas and knowledge making practices. In fact, we venture the hypothesis that having common participant structures and instructional/cognitive tools across school subject matters may be beneficial to students' learning, as they build up predictable routines that free up time and students' cognitive resources to focus on the exploration of the academic content (Tabak & Baumgartner, 2004). When students come to expect these types of relationships with their peers in creating knowledge, they can more easily focus on how their engagement with each other differs from subject to subject, as necessitated by the intellectual work required by each type of inquiry. Our students in Promoting Argumentation were well on their way to discerning the differences and similarities between different types of argumentation required in history and science, and by the end of the school year could reflect on how the work of scientists and historians might proceed.

DIRECTIONS FOR FUTURE RESEARCH

In this chapter, we framed a discussion of domain specific learning as a type of social practice that involves various repertoires and utilizes expert forms of knowledge, parallel to the social practices in which students engage in their out-of-school lives. We believe that future research needs to keep a wider view of the purpose of engaging in domain-specific, collaborative inquiry, to consider the possibilities students are given to develop intellective identities (Greeno, 2002) and to be mindful of who they are "becoming" as students in the process (Herrenkohl & Mertl, 2010). Our task as educators is to ensure that students' out-of-school experiences overlap with their school experiences as much as possible, to strengthen the meaning that students are able to make across the contexts of their lives.

Furthermore, we need to continue to pay attention to ways in which different students connect or fail to connect with different disciplinary ways of knowing and talking. Status differences among students profoundly influence the dynamics of collaboration in ways which can often be difficult for teachers to overcome (Cohen & Lotan, 1995; Lensmire, 2000; Paley, 1979, 1992; Wortham, 2004). Collaborative learning must be utilized in ways that address these status differences and which challenge the typical relationships between students, teachers, and subject matter (Cornelius & Herrenkohl, 2004). Introducing structured collaborative learning opportunities into the classroom environment within rich contexts of disciplinary problems and questions has the potential to achieve both these social and intellectual goals concomitantly and can ultimately lead to a far more important goal for the lives of students: their growing sense of competence and identification of themselves as powerful thinkers and learners.

NOTES

1. We use the terms *subject matter, discipline*, and *domain* interchangeably as they apply to classroom instruction.
2. Domain general approaches to thinking and learning have assumed that there are general cognitive processes which can brought to bear on any number of diverse tasks and which can be developed irrespective of the domain.
3. And arguably emotional benefits which we will consider in our directions for future research.

REFERENCES

Bain, R. B. (2000). Into the breach: Using research and theory to shape history instruction. In P. N. Stearns, P. C. Seixas, & S. S. Wineburg (Eds.), *Knowing, teaching, and learning history: National and international perspectives* (pp. 331–352). New York: New York University Press.

Barron, B. (2003). When smart groups fail. *Journal of the Learning Sciences, 12*(3), 307–359.

Beeth, M. E., & Hewson, P. W. (1999). Learning goals in an exemplary science teacher's practice: Cognitive and social factors in teaching for conceptual change. *Science Education, 83*(6), 738–760.

Bell, P. (2004). Supporting students' argument construction and collaborative debate in the science classroom. In M. C. Linn, E. A. Davis, & P. Bell (Eds.), *Internet environments for science education* (pp. 115–143). Mahwah, NJ: Erlbaum.

Bell, P., & Linn, M. C. (2000). Beliefs about science: How does science instruction contribute? In B. Hofer & P. Pintrich (Eds.), *Personal epistemology: The psychology of beliefs about knowledge and knowing* (pp. 321–346). Mahwah, NJ: Erlbaum.

Boix-Mansilla, V. (2000). Historical understanding: Beyond the past and into the present. In P. N. Stearns, P. C. Seixas, & S. S. Wineburg (Eds.), *Knowing, teaching, and learning history: National and international perspectives* (pp. 390–418). New York: New York University Press.

Brown, A. L., & Campione, J. C. (1994). Guided discovery in a community of learners. In K. McGilly (Ed.), *Classroom lessons: Integrating cognitive theory and classroom practice* (pp. 229–270). Cambridge, MA: MIT Press.

Bruner, J. (1960). *The process of education*. Cambridge, MA: Harvard University Press.

Cohen, E. G. (1994). *Designing groupwork: Strategies for the heterogeneous classroom*. New York: Teacher's College Press.

Cohen, E. G., & Lotan, R. A. (1995). Producing equal-status interaction in the heterogeneous classroom. *American Educational Research Journal, 32*(1), 99–120.

Cohen, E. G., Lotan, R. A., Scarloss, B. A., & Arellano, A. R. (1999). Complex instruction: Equity in cooperative learning classrooms. *Theory into Practice, 38*(2), 80–86.

Cornelius, L. L., & Herrenkohl, L. R. (2004). Power in the classroom: How the classroom environment shapes students' relationships with each other and with concepts. *Cognition and Instruction, 22*(4), 467–498.

diSessa, A. A. (1993). Toward an epistemology of physics. *Cognition and Instruction, 10*(2&3), 105–225.

Driver, R., Newton, P., & Osborne, J. (2000). Establishing the norms of scientific argumentation in classrooms. *Science Education, 84*, 287–312.

Elby, A. (2009). Defining personal epistemology: A response to Hofer & Pintrich (1997) and Sandoval (2005). *Journal of the Learning Science, 18*(1), 138–149.

Engle, R. A., & Conant, F. R. (2002). Guiding principles for fostering productive disciplinary engagement: Explaining an emergent argument in a community of learners' classroom. *Cognition and Instruction, 20*, 399–484.

Greeno, J. G. (2002). Students with competence, authority and accountability: Affording intellective identities in classrooms. New York: The College Board.

Hatano, G., & Inagaki, K. (1991). Sharing cognition through collective comprehension activity. In L. B. Resnick, J. M Levine, & S. D. Teasley (Eds.), *Perspectives on socially shared cognition* (pp. 331–348). Washington, DC: American Psychological Association:.

Herrenkohl, L. R., & Cornelius, L. L. (in press). Investigating elementary students' scientific and historical argumentation: A comparative approach.

Herrenkohl, L. R., & Guerra, M. R.(1998). Participant structures, scientific discourse and student engagement in fourth grade. *Cognition and Instruction, 16*, 431–473.

Herrenkohl, L. R., & Mertl, V. (2010). *How students come to be, know and do: A case for a broad view of learning.* New York: Cambridge University Press.

Herrenkohl, L. R., Palincsar, A. S., DeWater, L. S., & Kawasaki, K. (1999). Developing scientific communities in classrooms: A sociocognitive approach. *Journal of the Learning Sciences, 8*, 451–493.

Herrenkohl, L. R., Tasker, T., & White, B. (2011). Pedagogical practices to support classroom cultures of scientific inquiry. *Cognition and Instruction, 29*(1), 1–44.

Hexter, J. H. (1971). *The history primer.* New York: Basic Books.

Hirschfield, L. A., & Gelman, S. A. (1994). *Mapping the mind: Domain specificity in cognition and culture.* Cambridge, England: Cambridge University Press.

Hofer, B. K. (2002). Personal epistemology as a psychological and educational construct: An introduction. In B. K. Hofer & P. R. Pintrich (Eds.), *Personal epistemology: The psychology of beliefs about knowledge and knowing* (pp. 3–14). Mahwah, NJ: Erlbaum.

Hmelo-Silver, C. E., & Barrows, H. S. (2008). Facilitating collaborative knowledge building. *Cognition and Instruction, 26*, 48–94.

Inagaki, K., & Hatano, G. (2004). Vitalistic causality in young children's naïve biology. *Trends in Cognitive Sciences, 8*(8), 356–362.

Kawasaki, K., Herrenkohl, L. R., & Yeary, S. (2004). Theory building and modeling in a sinking and floating unit: A case study of third and fourth grade students' developing epistemologies of science. *International Journal of Science Education, 26*, 1–26.

Krajcik, J. S., & Blumenfeld, P. C. (2006). Project-based learning. In R. K. Sawyer (Ed.), *The Cambridge handbook of the learning science* (pp. 317–334). New York: Cambridge University Press.

Lampert, M. (1990). When the problem is not the question and the solution is not the answer: Mathematical knowing and teaching. *American Educational Research Journal, 27*, 29–63.

Lave, J., & Wenger, E. (1991). *Situated learning: Legitimate peripheral participation*. Cambridge, England: Cambridge University Press.

Lee, C. D. (1995). Signifying as a scaffold for literary interpretation. *Journal of Black Psychology, 21*(4), 357–381.

Lehrer, R., & Schauble, L. (2004). Modeling natural variation through distribution. *American Educational Research Journal, 41*(3), 635–679.

Lemke, J. (1990). *Talking science: Language, learning, and values*. Norwood, NJ: Ablex.

Lemke, J. (2001). Articulating communities: Sociocultural perspectives on science education. *Journal of Research in Science Teaching, 38*, 296–316.

Lensmire, T. (2000). *Powerful writing, responsible teaching.* New York: Teachers College Press.

Levstik, L. S., & Barton, K. C. (2005). *Doing history: Investigating with children in elementary and middle school.* Mahwah, NJ: Erlbaum.

Lowenthal, David (2000). Dilemmas and delights of learning history. In, P. N. Stearns, P. C. Seixas, & S. S. Wineburg (Eds.), *Knowing, teaching, and learning history: National and international perspectives* (pp. 63–82). New York: New York University.

Nasir, N. (2000). "Points Ain't Everything": Emergent goals and average and percent understandings in the play of basketball among African-American students. *Anthropology and Education Quarterly, 31*(3), 283–305.

Nasir, N. (2005). Individual cognitive structuring and the sociocultural context: Strategy shifts in the game of dominoes. *Journal of the Learning Sciences, 14*, 5–34.

Nasir, N. S., Rosebery, A. S., Warren, B., & Lee, C. D. (2006). Learning as a cultural process: Achieving equity through diversity. In. R. K. Sawyer (Ed.), *The Cambridge handbook of the learning science* (pp. 489–504). New York: Cambridge University Press.

Nathan, M. J., & Kim, S. (2009). Regulation of teacher elicitations in the mathematics classroom. *Cognition and Instruction, 27*(2), 91–120.

National Center for History in the Schools. (n.d.). Retrieved from http://nchs.ucla.edu/

National Research Council. (2007a). *How people learn: Brain, mind, experience, and school.* Washington, DC: National Academy Press.

National Research Council. (2007b). *Taking science to school: Learning and teaching science in grades K-8*. Washington, DC: National Academy Press.

O'Connor, M. C. (2001). "Can any fraction be turned into a decimal?" A case study of a mathematical group discussion. *Educational Studies in Mathematics, 46*, 143–185.

Paley, V. G. (1979). *White teacher.* Cambridge, MA: Harvard University Press.

Paley, V. G. (1992). *You can't say you can't play.* Cambridge, MA: Harvard University Press.

Palincsar, A. S., & Brown, A. L. (1984). Reciprocal teaching of comprehension-fostering and comprehension monitoring activities. *Cognition and Instruction, 1*, 117–175.

Palincsar, A. S., & Herrenkohl, L. R. (1999). Designing collaborative contexts: Lessons from three research programs. In A. M. O'Donnell & A. King (Eds.), *Cognitive perspectives on peer learning* (pp. 151–177). Mahwah, NJ: Erlbaum.

Palincsar, A. S. & Magnusson, S. J. (2001). The interplay of first-hand and text-based investigations to model and support the development of scientific knowledge and reasoning. In S. Carver & D. Klahr (Eds.), *Cognition and instruction: Twenty five years of progress* (pp. 151–194). Mahwah, NJ: Erlbaum.

Penner, D., Giles, N., Lehrer, R., & Schauble, L. (1997). Building functional models: Designing an elbow. *Journal of Research in Science Teaching, 34*(2), 125–143.

Perkins, D. N., & Salomon, G. (1989). Are cognitive skills context bound? *Educational Researcher, 18*(1), 16–25.

Philips, S. (1983). *The invisible culture: Communication in classroom and community on the Warm Springs Indian Reservation*. Prospect Heights, IL: Waveland Press.

Reiser, B. J., Tabak, I., Sandoval, W. A., Smith, B., Steinmueller, F., & Leone, T. J. (2001). BGuILE: Strategic and conceptual scaffolds for scientific reasoning in biology classrooms. In S. M. Carver & D. Klahr (Eds.), *Cognition and instruction: 25 years of progress* (pp. 263–305). Mahwah, NJ: Erlbaum.

Rogoff, B. (1994). Developing understanding of the idea of communities of learners. *Mind, Culture, & Activity: an International Journal, 1*(4), 209–229.

Rosebery, A., Warren, B., & Conant, F. (1992). Appropriating scientific discourse: Findings from language minority classrooms. *The Journal of the Learning Sciences, 2*, 61–94.

Samarapungavan, A., Westby, E. L., & Bodner, G. M. (2006). Contextual epistemic development in science: A comparison of chemistry students and research chemists. *Science Education, 90*, 468–495.

Sandoval, W. A. (2003). Conceptual and epistemic aspects of students' scientific explanations. *Journal of the Learning Science, 12*(1), 5–51.

Sandoval, W. A. (2005). Understanding students' practical epistemologies and their influence on learning through inquiry. *Science Education, 89,* 634–656.

Schulman, L. S., & Quinlan, K. M. (1996). The comparative psychology of school subjects. In D. C. Berliner, & R. C. Calfee (Eds.), *Handbook of educational psychology* (pp. 399–422). New York: Macmillan

Schwab, J. J., (1962). The concept of the structure of a discipline. *Educational Record, 43,* 197–205.

Schwab, J. J. (1978). Education and the structure of the disciplines. In J. J. Schwab, I. Westbury, & N. J. Wilkof (Eds.), *Science, curriculum, and liberal education: Selected essays* (pp. 229–274). Chicago, IL: University of Chicago Press.

Seixas, P. (1994). Students' understanding of historical significance. *Theory and Research in Social Education, 22,* 475–522.

Slavin, R. E. (1999). Comprehensive approaches to cooperative learning. *Theory into Practice, 38*(2), 74–79.

Smith, C. A. (2007). Bootstrapping processes in the development of students' commonsense matter theories: Using analogical mappings, thought experiments, and learning to measure to promote conceptual restructuring, *Cognition and Instruction, 24*(4), 337–398.

Smith, C., Snir, J., & Grosslight, L. (1992). Using conceptual models to facilitate conceptual change: The case of weight/density differentiation. *Cognition and Instruction, 9,* 221–283.

Smith, J. P. III., diSessa, A. A., & Roschelle, J. (1993). Misconceptions reconceived: A constructivist analysis of knowledge in transition. *Journal of the Learning Sciences, 3*(2), 115–163.

Stevens, R., Wineburg, S., Herrenkohl, L. R., & Bell, P. (2005). The comparative understanding of school subjects: Past, present, and future. *Review of Educational Research, 75*(2), 125–157.

Tabak, I., & Baumgartner, E. (2004). The teacher as partner: Exploring participant structures, symmetry, and identity work in scaffolding. *Cognition and Instruction, 22*(4), 393–429.

VanSledright, B. (2002). *In search of America's past: Learning to read history in elementary school.* New York: Teacher's College Press.

Vygotsky, L. S. (1978). *Mind in society: The development of higher psychological process* (M Cole, V. John-Steiner, S. Scriber, & E. Souberman, Eds.). Cambridge, MA: Harvard University Press.

Warren, B., & Rosebery, A. (1995). Equity in the future tense: Redefining relationships among teachers, students, and science in linguistic minority classrooms. In W. Secada, E. Fennema, & L. Adajian (Eds.), *New directions for equity in mathematics education* (pp. 298–328). New York: Cambridge University Press.

Warren, B., & Rosebery, A. (1996). "This question is just too, too easy!" Perspectives from the classroom on accountability in science. In L. Schauble & R. Glaser (Eds.), *Innovations in learning: New environments for education* (pp. 97–125). Mahwah: NJ: Erlbaum.

Wertsch, J. V. (1998). *Mind as action.* New York: Oxford University Press.

White, B. (1993). Causal models and intermediate abstractions: A missing link for successful science education? In R. Glaser (Ed.), *Advances in instructional psychology* (Vol. 4, pp. 177–252). Hillsdale, NJ: Erlbaum.

White, B., & Frederiksen, J. (1998). Inquiry, modeling, and metacognition: Making science accessible to all students. *Cognition and Instruction, 16*(1), 3–118.

Wortham, S. (2004). The interdependence of social identification and learning. *American Educational Research Journal, 41,* 715–750.

Wortham, S. (2006). *Learning identity: The joint emergence of social identification and academic learning.* New York: Cambridge University Press.

20

THE GROUP INVESTIGATION APPROACH TO COOPERATIVE LEARNING

SHLOMO SHARAN

Tel Aviv University, Israel

YAEL SHARAN

GRIP-Group Investigation Projects, Tel Aviv, Israel

IVY GEOK-CHIN TAN

Nanyang Technological University, Singapore

> Group Investigation is a … self-consistent educational method … concerned with getting the student to have planned experiences, reflect on them, and extend their meaning and usefulness through knowledge obtained from the experiences of other people. (Thelen, 1981, p. 5)

INTRODUCTION

Cooperative learning is a generic approach to teaching that has spawned a variety of methods to facilitate learning together in small groups so that everyone can participate in and contribute to attaining the group's goal. As students and teachers gain confidence in the practice of cooperative learning (CL), teachers introduce methods which call for increasingly diverse and complex learning skills and interaction among learners. One of these methods is Group Investigation (GI), where the content of the inquiry is determined in varying degrees by the diversity of students' interests, experiences, and knowledge (S. Sharan & Hertz-Lazarowitz, 1980; Y. Sharan & S. Sharan, 1992, 1999; Thelen, 1960, 1981).

Group Investigation is a cooperative learning method that integrates interaction and communication among learners with the process of academic inquiry. As learners take an active part in their inquiry in the course of a GI project, the classroom becomes a social system built on cooperation in learning within groups and on coordination of learning among groups. At first small groups of learners plan what they will study and how they will study. As the investigation progresses they divide the responsibilities for various aspects of the investigation, combining individual, pair, and group learning. When they complete their inquiry, group members integrate and summarize their findings and plan how to present them to their classmates. Throughout the process, teachers guide their students in the required social and learning skills.

Group Investigation is applicable in any content area, whenever a multifaceted problem is identified that has more than one answer or sources for its resolution. GI is also aimed at students of all ages, in all grades, including college and university classrooms.

Research on cooperative learning (CL) made its major debut in the relevant literature about 35 years ago when CL reemerged as a systematic pedagogy. Like most other concepts and methods in education, cooperative learning can be traced to ancient and modern thinkers and educators, as is described in the historical review by Hertz-Lazarowitz and Zelniker (1995). CL practice is consistently supported by research, with ongoing examination of the effectiveness of CL and constant revision and refinement of theory and cooperative procedures (Johnson & Johnson, 2009; S. Sharan, 1990; Slavin, 2010). An analysis of the literature on GI by Mitchell, Montgomery, Holder, and Stuart (2008) presents evidence of renewed interest in making the effects of GI known to a contemporary generation of teachers and researchers.

In this chapter we discuss the theoretical background of GI, present the steps of implementation, and review research from several decades of GI related studies.

GROUP INVESTIGATION'S DEBT TO JOHN DEWEY (1859–1952), HERBERT THELEN (1913–2008), AND KURT LEWIN (1890–1947)

Dewey, Thelen, and Lewin provided both the theoretical and practical foundations of Group Investigation; Dewey as early as the last decade of the 19th century (Archambault, 1964; Childs, 1951; Kilpatrick, 1951; Miel, 1952; Thelen, 1954). Dewey's and Thelen's seminal roles were discussed in earlier publications (S. Sharan, 1980; Y. Sharan, & S. Sharan, 1992). All developers of CL methods acknowledge their debt to the development and understanding of group dynamics by Kurt Lewin (1947a). After all, humans have interacted in small groups since time immemorial, and the dynamics of interaction in small groups have been recognized throughout history (Hare, 1962/1976; Hertz-Lazarowitz & Zelniker, 1995). Developers of methods other than GI trace their roots to various theories, such as social interdependence theory (Johnson & Johnson, 1975/1994), or to a neobehaviorist orientation and a motivational perspective, where some competition and the accumulation of rewards are incorporated (Slavin, 1983, 1995, 2010). Yet given that CL methods always include some form or degree of group interaction, lessons taught by the school of group dynamics are applicable to all forms of cooperative learning, whatever their primary theoretical orientation.

Dewey emphasized the social nature of schools, and also tried to influence schools to embody the principles of democracy. Dewey established what he called a Laboratory School at the University of Chicago in 1896 (Kilpatrick, 1951). First and foremost that meant, for Dewey, that students express their preferences in terms of what to learn and how they should proceed with their work or activities in school. The citizens in a democracy have the right to express their will to the authorities in power. He asserted that students' interest in their studies would be stimulated when given the opportunity to bear responsibility for directing their work in school. Self-direction is one of the prime motivators of human behavior. People are more motivated to carry out what *they* decide to do rather than when they are told what to do by others. A high level of motivation to learn is also accompanied by intellectual and emotional involvement in the content of what is being studied (Dewey, 1899/1943).

The title of Dewey's 1899 publication, *The School and Society*, suggests that he recognized the importance of the social and societal dimensions of education, no less than the cognitive-intellectual ones. Through its social character the school manifests its participation in life itself, rather than being a preparation for life. If schools are set apart from society they appear to be disconnected from the structure and values of society at large, as if the school was concentrated almost exclusively on the transmission of information. "A spirit of free communication, of interchange of ideas … becomes the dominating note … school life (thereby) organizes itself on a social basis …" (Dewey, 1899 cited in Archambault, 1964, pp. 301–302). To this very day, communication in most schools is carefully monitored and not "free" as Dewey wished, although, try as they may, schools consistently fail in their attempt to regulate communication among students during classroom sessions. As explained in greater detail later in this chapter, CL in general, and GI in particular, are based upon and seek to encourage communication among students as well as between students and teachers, as an essential instrument of learning.

The practical link between Dewey's and Lewin's theories and their application to classrooms was forged by Herbert Thelen, who developed Group Investigation as a systematic inquiry strategy for students learning together in small groups. Thelen's design combines the view of learning as the conduct of inquiry by cooperative small groups with the principles of effective group management, so that groups can successfully solve problems and make decisions based on all group members' contributions and views (Y. Sharan & S. Sharan, 1992; Thelen, 1960, 1981). GI is also compatible with Piaget's constructivist cognitive psychology that asserts that individuals actively build their notions of reality out of their own experiences. Learning *about* a subject is inadequate without providing the learner with an opportunity to actively experience how knowledge is generated. GI enables learners to seek information in cooperation with their peers, and together shape their information and ideas into meaningful constructs.

Why an Inquiry Approach to Learning?

The systematic application of an investigative approach to learning is one of the cardinal ways by which humanity has expanded its knowledge and understanding of itself, the world and the universe. Therefore it comes as no surprise that throughout the years educators in various countries and contexts have designed inquiry-based approaches to learning that go by different names (or even without a name), supported by experimental or action research, or sometimes by teachers' reports. For example, in England in the 1970s an "Environmental Studies Project" (Harris & Evans, 1972) invited students in the elementary grades to plan and carry out the investigation of phenomena in their surroundings that piqued their interest. Some 20 years later Peter Forrestal (1990) taught his English literature students in Australia to pose questions for inquiry and conduct a subsequent investigation. These two projects were not studied in the rigorous way expected today, but their descriptions serve as edifying examples of inquiry-based learning.

Today school systems in different countries have adopted problem solving approaches to learning that require team work; even businesses and industries have realized the benefit of such an approach to attaining their goals. Each variation on the process of engaging learners in the active pursuit and construction of knowledge may emphasize a different aspect of the investigative process. Detailed research into one inquiry model known as problem-based learning conducted by Hmelo-Silver and Barrows (2006, 2008) centers on components such as scaffolding, framing goals and strategies, the teacher's and facilitator's role, and the role of technology. Problem-based learning shares the general orientation toward learning by investigation, whereby students seek the ideas or information they need to solve a problem or answer questions that they themselves pose at the onset of a PBL project.

Authentic implementation of inquiry-based learning advances students' understanding of their lives in society and of the connection between their community and the world. With teachers providing direction, helping to clarify group problems, and providing access to resources both in and out of school, student groups will be able to pursue cooperative investigations with greater efficacy. This approach focuses on the group's cooperative planning of its investigation, setting its goals, delegating different tasks or roles to group members who to some degree must coordinate with their colleagues the manner and pace of their work. Advance group planning of goals, distribution of tasks and roles, and plans for continued coordination are early steps in the formation of an investigative group.

A unique feature of an investigation is that neither the teacher nor the students know at the outset the entire scope of knowledge they will gain in the process of investigating, organizing, and presenting their findings. The major part of the teacher's role is to serve as a resource person, not to serve as the primary font of prescribed knowledge. The point is not that the group members "discover" the basic idea or solution to the questions they posed (Shulman & Keislar, 1966) but that they build up knowledge from the information they are able to find in the sources available to them.

A major challenge to teachers who guide the investigation is the development of a classroom climate in which students have the confidence to ask questions about what they would like to know and understand about a topic. To do so, teachers should facilitate and guide their students in the development of all the interactive skills discussed below. In addition they alter the traditional nature of questions they ask, to which they know the answers, by posing questions that do not have one right or wrong answer, but generate a wide range of acceptable answers. These produce fewer predictable responses and enable students to include what they already know in their answers (Forrestal, 1990). Conditions that affect students' ability to ask questions and their ability to exercise other thinking and problem-solving skills have been studied by Gillies and associates (Gillies, 2000, 2002; Gillies & Asaduzzaman, 2009). Their findings emphasize the centrality of the teacher's role in structuring learning in cooperative groups so that students gain the maximum benefits from working together. This is further highlighted in the Gillies and Boyle study (2008) that illustrates the importance of training teachers in the types of mediated learning behaviors that challenge students' thinking and promote higher order thinking and reasoning so that they can model it in the classroom and then guide students in their application.

How Is Interaction Essential to Group Investigation?

GI takes place in a classroom organized as an inquiring community, which provides the social context for the process. At each stage of GI there are ample opportunities for interaction. In pairs and in small groups, learners discuss what they will investigate, how they will go about it, how they interpret their findings, and how they will present them to the class. Throughout the investigation learners share ideas and resources and provide mutual help and support

The cultivation and development of positive group norms that sustain constructive interaction and group productivity, with emphasis on mutual assistance among group members, have been discussed for decades in the literature on group dynamics (Hare, 1973; Hertz-Lazarowitz, 1989; Hill, 1969; Lewin, 1947b; Mann, 1967; R. Schmuck & P. Schmuck, 2001; Steiner, 1972; Tuckman, 1965). Groups function relatively well when their members wish to belong to the group and feel accepted by group members. Constructive communication with peers is most often accomplished when they anticipate that group members will listen to them sympathetically, without necessarily agreeing with everything they have to say. The absence of members' expectations for a favorable platform on which to express their ideas will naturally inhibit communication among group members and result in relatively sterile group activity.

Group members may display behaviors intended to enhance their status in the group and their relative influence over other group members. Positive group interaction requires that members relinquish a certain degree of autonomy and grant each other the right to participate in, and influence, the group's work and decisions. They must also recognize the group chairperson's authority in his or her effort to manage how the group conducts discussions and divides the work at each stage of the inquiry.

Before embarking on a GI project teachers find it helpful to demonstrate and practice interaction skills with the class. These skills are intended to make group members aware of *how* they behave as group members, and not concentrate solely on *what* they wish to say. To help teachers set the stage for successful interaction during an investigation, there is a varied and time honored pool of short term activities that develop the social and learning skills needed for successful group discussion and interaction, such as found in Cohen (1994) and in Kagan and Kagan (2009). All the basic cooperative learning skills offered by these sources (and many others) are part and parcel of the ongoing interaction among students in all cooperative learning methods, and especially during a GI project.

Each group in a GI project derives its goal directly from the design of the learning task, which is not related to any extrinsic reward that may trigger intergroup comparisons and competition. In order to allow for groups to base their goal on the learning task, it must be sufficiently complex to permit a variety of subtopics to be identified, or for different points of view to be expressed. Mutual assistance in the group is multilateral, and is made possible because everyone has something to contribute that is not studied by other group members. Group members also receive feedback about the extent to which they accepted the equitable distribution of time that allows everyone a chance to express their thoughts (Schmuck & Schmuck, 2001; Y. Sharan & S. Sharan, 1992).

IMPLEMENTING GROUP INVESTIGATION

A GI project is launched when the teacher poses a broad, multifaceted problem such as:

- How Did Explorers Change the World?
- What Makes a Poem a Poem?
- What and How Do Animals Eat?

Students plan which aspects of the problem to investigate and what resources to use. They ask questions about the topic, form groups to seek answers to their questions, and to interpret and integrate information in light of their knowledge, ideas, experiences, and abilities.

There are six stages that follow each other, each of which may require two, three, or more class sessions. The stages of GI, the students' and teacher's role in each stage, and examples of GI projects are presented in great detail in Y. Sharan (1995), and Y. Sharan and S. Sharan (1992, 1999).

Stages of Implementation of Group Investigation

1. Class determines subtopics of the problem and organizes into research groups;
2. Groups plan their investigations;
3. Groups carry out their investigations;
4. Groups plan their presentations;
5. Groups present their findings;
6. Teacher and students evaluate the projects.

Stage 1: Class Determines Subtopics and Organizes into Research Groups

At this stage the class explores possible subtopics for investigation. Each group selects one of the subtopics as the title of its investigation.

At the outset of the process the teacher's role is to:

a. present the whole class with a broad problem that generates many questions;
b. stimulate students' interest in investigating the problem.

A broad problem can have global relevance, as in: "Why do we want to explore outer space?" or regional relevance, as in, "How has the river affected our town?" or reflect the changing makeup of the local population, as in "How have recent settlers affected our town?" To begin learning about the scope of such problems and possible questions they generate, students are invited to look over a variety of sources, including films, newspapers, books, and of course to search the Internet. They are also encouraged to interview people who might have knowledge of the topic, visit a relevant site, and so forth. Exposure to diverse sources helps students identify a particular aspect of the subject that arouses their interest. That will help them to formulate specific questions for investigation.

Individually students write their questions, compare their lists in pairs, and finally in groups of four. All questions are presented to the class; the compiled list represents the interests of all students and so becomes the class's "capital—a form of wealth which carries with it a mounting expectation of further interesting investments" (Thelen, 1981, p. 153). The next step is for the class to sort the questions into several categories, which become the subtopics of the investigation. The final step at this stage can be carried out in one of two ways: groups are formed and each group chooses the subtopic it will investigate, or each student chooses a subtopic and groups are formed of students with the same interests.

Stage 2: Groups Plan Their Investigation.

At this stage each group plans its investigation, and each group member decides on which aspect of the group's subtopic he or she will focus. Using the class's list of questions as a base, group members choose one or two questions that best reflect their interests, and the group recorder notes all members' questions. Plans should include a statement of the steps each group member will take, what he or she will do to collect information, and where the information can be found. The teacher circulates among the groups and offers assistance where needed. As often happens when one looks for information, one source leads to another, so that the list of sources of information identified at this stage may not be final.

It is recommended that, in addition to the research groups, a group consisting of one representative from each small group serves on a "steering committee," which will coordinate all groups' presentations in stage 4.

Stage 3: Groups Carry Out Their Investigations

The number of class sessions at this stage depends on the scope of the investigation, the range of relevant resources, and their accessibility. Plans for collecting information may rely on a wide variety of sources, such as information on the Web, traditional library work, conducting a science experiment or a survey of opinions of people related to the topic, a visit to a museum, interviews with people who can shed light on the topic, and even someone's grandparents' stamp collection.

In a social studies investigation of the effects of migration on the community, students may find that adults in the community are among the more significant resources. An opportunity to visit diverse sites where adults practice their professions or carry out their business impresses students with the meaning of the topic for their lives in their society.

While carrying out their investigation students take notes and record the main ideas of what they read, see, or hear so they can share their findings with their group mates. Periodically in the course of the investigation groups discuss the investigation's meaning as it unfolds and strive to integrate the ideas they read about, the events they see, and the answers they find to the questions they ask. It is not uncommon, as groups become skilled in GI, for these discussions to generate new questions, which then lead to further investigation.

Stage 4: Groups Plan Their Presentations

Presentation of groups' findings to their class acknowledges their results as well as highlighting the contribution of each group's findings to the resolution of the whole-class problem. When presenting their findings students assume a new role, the role of teacher. To teach their classmates well, group members first summarize the answers to their questions, then plan cooperatively how best to convey the major findings of their investigation.

The first step in planning a presentation to an audience is for the group to identify the main ideas of its findings. The second step is to choose a way to present them clearly so that the audience can easily grasp them. Presentations may include a handout of sources and other evidence of the group's findings. There are multiple means for conveying their message, such as: an exhibit, a model, a skit, a quiz, a tour, a video presentation, and so forth. If the investigation included an experiment, groups may weigh the appropriateness of having the whole class conduct the same experiment as evidence of their claims.

Stage 5: Groups Present Their Findings

The class reconvenes for the groups' presentations after the steering committee and the teacher have set up and posted a schedule of presentations. After each presentation the class (the "audience") fills out a short feedback questionnaire. Questions might include: (a) What was the main idea of the presentation? (b) Did all members of the group participate? (c) How did the presentation help you understand the group's findings? Beforehand it is important to establish rules for making comments in a constructive way.

The teacher also fills out a questionnaire, in addition to her or his role as coordinator of the presentations. At the end of each presentation teachers lead a feedback discussion with the entire class. This is the students' opportunity to note how other groups organized and presented their findings, thereby broadening their perspective on the preparation of presentations. In that process, each group can became aware of its role as a resource for other groups who may wish to learn more about their specific area of investigation. When all presentations are completed the teacher leads the class in a discussion of how all of the groups' findings contributed to the resolution of the original class-wide problem, thus demonstrating how at the end of the project the class comes together as a group of groups.

Stage 6: Teacher and Students Evaluate Their Projects

Evaluation of GI focuses on the knowledge acquired in the course of the project, and on the individual and group experience of investigation. Traditional testing of facts is a distinctly limiting form of evaluation and out of character with the entire process of GI. There are several ways to evaluate the outcomes of students' learning in a GI project.

Students' feedback on the learning experience is one example of class-wide assessment (Birenbaum, 2003; Birenbaum & Dochy, 1996; Stiggens, 2000). Teachers and students can also collaborate by preparing a quiz that incorporates questions submitted by the students, based on their findings.

If teachers are constrained to test students so they can be given a grade, the test can consist of two questions submitted by each group. In a class with seven groups, for example, there would be 14 questions in the test. Each student is asked to respond to 12 questions, excluding the 2 submitted by his or her own group. The expectation is that before the test individual students review their own work and that of other groups. Of course teachers may also add 2 questions.

Another way of evaluating learning is to invite students to demonstrate their ability to draw conclusions from their inquiry and to apply their new knowledge to related problems or situations. To this end teachers could invite the class to publish a newspaper that includes all the group summaries, or, when appropriate, draft a bill to present to the mayor calling for changes in zoning policy. For individual evaluations students may be asked to write a letter describing a day in the life of a personage they investigated, or a letter from that person to a colleague or to someone who contested their work, or prepare a series of electronic messages that follow the work of a particular person, and so on. The teacher would stipulate in advance the type of facts and main ideas students are expected to demonstrate in individual and in group summarizing efforts.

The teacher's role in stage 6 is to:

a. Evaluate students' understanding of the main ideas learned in their investigation;
b. Evaluate students' knowledge of new facts and terms;
c. Evaluate how students integrated findings from all of the groups;
d. Facilitate individual, group, and class-wide reflections on the process and content of the investigation.

Throughout the investigation the teacher has many opportunities to observe students' academic performance, cooperative behaviors, and level of motivation. As they circulate among the groups teachers learn a great deal about how individuals and groups proceed, how well students are acquainted with the subject under study, how they conduct discussions with one another and in their groups, if everyone is participating, if they reveal a sufficiently high level of thinking about the subject matter, and so forth. Teachers can also discuss with individual students what they feel about the content of their investigation, what interests them, or even if anything surprised them. By circulating among the groups teachers also spot the need for help when it arises.

As in all cooperative learning situations, teachers facilitate students' reflections on the process of learning and of cooperating with their peers. Reflection informs practice. By reflecting on what one does and on students' reactions to the teacher's facilitation of the investigation, the teacher is better equipped to choose those actions that are best suited to the students' needs. Reflection also facilitates the transformation of practice: teachers and students learn how to weigh the effects of their experience in the classroom and with the help of the resulting conclusions, plan how to change their behaviors and actions accordingly (Y. Sharan, 2010).

Clearly teachers do not wait for the sixth stage of the project to evaluate their students. It is best to inform students at the onset of the project about the criteria for evaluation, and to let them be aware of the fact that the teacher observes them while they carry out their investigation. It is equally important for students to be told that teachers will not evaluate them on criteria or in ways not specified in advance.

The stages of GI, the teacher's and student's role at each stage are summarized in Table 20.1. The stages of GI are not meant to be followed mechanically. Mitchell, et al. (2008) observe that in situations where time is limited or when students may be too young or not have the requisite skills, the teacher may wish to provide more direction. Indeed it may take some time before students can carry out an elaborate investigative project. To set the stage for such a project teachers may organize short-term investigations on a narrow range of topics, each time giving students the opportunity to practice a different component of investigation, such as raising questions, searching for information in a variety of sources, and summarizing findings. In addition we would like to point out that GI is not an "exclusive" model, and at different stages of the investigation teachers often organize students in Jigsaw groups, and incorporate other CL structures (see the examples of GI projects in Y. Sharan, 1995; Y. Sharan & S. Sharan, 1992, 1994). There is even room for direct instruction, as, for example, when all groups have the same problem in organizing their information, or when it is helpful to teach the whole class some basic facts about the topic they are investigating to facilitate their understanding of the kind of information they need to collect and how to make sense of it.

Table 20.1 Stages of Group Investigation, Teacher's Role, and Students' Role

Stages of Group Investigation	What does the Teacher do?	What do the Students do?
I. Class determines sub-topics and organizes research groups	Leads exploratory discussions to choose sub-topics; facilitates organization of research	Generate questions of interest; sort them into categories; join a research group
II. Groups plan their investigation: what they will study; how they will carry out their investigation	Helps groups formulate their plan; helps maintain cooperative norms; helps find resources	Plan what to study; choose resources; assign roles and divide study tasks
III. Groups carry out their plans	Helps with study skills; continues to help maintain cooperative norms	Seek answers to their questions; locate information; integrate, summarize findings
IV. Groups plan their presentations	Organizes plans for presentations; coordinates plans with steering committee	Determine main ideas; plan how to transmit them and involve all group mates
V. Groups present their findings	Coordinates presentations; facilitates feedback	Present their findings; class gives feedback
VI. Teacher and students evaluate individuals, groups, and class	Evaluates learning of new information, higher level thinking, and cooperative behavior; facilitates reflection	Reflect on learning as investigators and on group processes

HOW EFFECTIVE IS GROUP INVESTIGATION?

Together the stages of the investigation constitute a model that is the subject of several experimental studies of the GI method in particular, and of cooperative learning methods in general (Hertz-Lazarowitz & Shachar, 1990; Johnson, Maruyama, Johnson, Nelson, & Skon, 1981; S. Sharan, 1980; S. Sharan & Hertz-Lazarowitz, 1980; S. Sharan & Rich, 1984; Slavin, 1980, 1983; Tan, Sharan, & Lee, 2006; Webb, 1982; Weigel, Wiser, & Cook, 1972). Most of the studies on GI were carried out in the period when many CL researchers were developing their own models. One of the factors that gave impetus to this flurry of development and research at the time was the desire to counter the prevailing climate in schools, which saw students solely as individuals and which ultimately failed to create schools that could effectively integrate students and raise their academic levels (Brody, 2011).

Evaluation of the effects of GI requires an experimental research design of assessment carried out before and after the implementation of GI, as well as the assessment of control classes. A unique feature of the intensive study of GI is that it involved all the teachers in whole-school experiments that lasted a year or two. Admittedly this design is quite daunting, particularly when the instructional method is new to teachers and demands drastic changes in their instructional behavior and requires extensive teacher training. These conditions were carried out in the extensive research studies on various aspects of GI, reported in the following publications: S. Sharan (1990); S. Sharan, Kussell, et al. (1984); S. Sharan & Shachar (1988); S. Sharan & Shaulov (1990); Y. Sharan & S. Sharan (1992). Data obtained in these studies about students' academic achievement, their spoken language, intrinsic motivation to learn, and their social interaction with one another, as well as about teachers' style of talking while teaching, indicate that the GI method exerts distinctly positive effects on both teachers and students. Findings show discernible improvement in classroom climate, with teachers reporting that students enjoy their classroom experience and seem to derive far greater personal meaning from it than in the traditionally taught class. What follows are several findings from this body of research.

Students' Language in the Cooperative Classroom

One experiment, by S. Sharan and Shachar (1988), assessed the effects of GI on students' achievement, social interaction, and verbal behavior among 351 students from different Jewish ethnic groups in Israel in nine eighth-grade classrooms. We will focus on the findings of the effects of GI on students' verbal behavior.

Carrying out a GI project requires constant conversations between group members. Assessment of students' spoken language at the end of several months demonstrated its significantly superior features compared to peers who had studied in traditionally taught classes. Both the social-interactive and cognitive intellectual features of the discussions carried out by young adolescent speakers were evaluated in this study. There were 197 students in the five classrooms taught by the GI method, and 154 pupils in four classes taught by the whole-class method; 27 groups of six students per group were selected at random from the nine classrooms. These groups engaged in two 15-minute discussions (one on a subject taken from their geography textbook, a second on a subject selected from their history book). The videotaped discussions were analyzed by two judges. Each group had 7 minutes "warm-up" time before actual filming began.

Data were collected by observers who recorded verbal events whose nature was decided upon in advance. Recordings were made at the start, in the middle, and toward the end of the classroom session. The geography discussion groups were given the following instructions:

> Check the atlas to find the largest concentrations of population in the United States. Discuss the following points:
>
> a. What are possible reasons why so many people live in these areas?
> b. What might be the consequences of the concentration of such large populations?
> c. Let's say your group is asked to advise the American government. Would you recommend that it adopt a policy of population dispersion? Discuss and explain your recommendations and have one group member summarize them in writing.

Three judges were trained to analyze the tapes according to several sets of criteria. The number of words spoken by students during the 30 minutes of their group's discussion was counted. Statistical analysis revealed that students in the GI group expressed more words than did their peers from the whole-class classes. The same was true for the number of turns they took to speak during the discussions, although the latter finding was true for students from Middle Eastern ethnic background but not for those from Western background; the latter took fewer turns in groups in the GI classes than they did in the classes taught by the whole-class method. Moreover, students from the GI classes, regardless of their ethnic-group membership, took the same number of speaking turns during the discussions, where there was a significant difference in favor of the Western compared to students of Mid-Eastern background in the frequency with which they took turns to speak in the whole-class method. In the original publication there are extended details about the students' ethnicity that served as one of the independent variables in the study (i.e., Jewish students whose parents or grandparents came to Israel from Western countries, and those Jewish students whose parents arrived in Israel from the Muslim countries of the Middle East).

ACADEMIC ACHIEVEMENT AND SOCIAL RELATIONS IN THE GROUP INVESTIGATION CLASSROOM

The general problem posed by another study was: "Another study investigated the difference between academic achievement and social relations in mixed ethnic classes that emphasized peer coopoeration versus traditional instruction" (Sharan, Kussell, et al., 1984, p. 15).

This study encompassed a number of independent and dependent variables that cannot be effectively discussed within the confines of this chapter; once again the reader is referred to the original publication. Here we will focus on the GI method and its effects on students. Some of the variables employed in the study reviewed here overlap those used in the above mentioned study by S. Sharan and Shachar (1988).

The study focused on the effects of two CL methods, group investigation and student-teams and academic divisions (STAD; Slavin, 1980), versus whole-class instruction, on three sets of dependent variables: achievement and English language and literature; cooperative and competitive behavior; and social attitudes. The report also presented an overview of cooperative versus traditional teaching and compared the findings for each of three different instructional approaches in terms of classroom climate, students' prosocial behavior, and the challenge of disseminating CL among teachers.

Results demonstrate that pupils in classes taught by GI registered greater improvement than their peers in the whole-class instruction classes on the total English Language test and on the Listening Comprehension section of the test. Pupils in the STAD classes also achieved higher scores than those in the whole-class instruction classes on the total test and on the Listening Comprehension section. These results emerged from both individual-level and group-level statistical analyses. Moreover, both ethnic groups (i.e., Jewish students from Western and from Mid-Eastern ethnic background) were affected similarly by the three instructional methods. Direct instruction proved less effective for teaching language skills than were the group methods.

The test for achievement in English literature consisted of questions classified by judges as low-level and high-level questions. The scores of students in classes taught with STAD and whole-class instruction declined from pre- to posttest administrations of the exam but remained unchanged in the GI classes. It must be noted that the two tests were not the same and were not of the same level of difficulty. These results may be interpreted to mean that pupils in the GI classes made more progress in their ability to respond to questions than did their peers taught by the other two methods. The opposite results were obtained with the low-level questions, where students in the STAD and whole-class instruction classes got higher scores than did students in the GI classes.

The distinction between high- and low-level questions was used in earlier research in Israel (S. Sharan, Hertz-Lazarowitz, & Ackerman, 1980). Cooperative learning in small groups yielded superior achievement on the high-level questions, but no differences were found on questions assessing low-level mental functioning according to Bloom's taxonomy. Similar findings were reported in the United States (Johnson, Skon, & Johnson, 1980).

Cooperative and Competitive Behavior

Though the central role of cooperation in contemporary society is acknowledged and documented (Johnson & Johnson, 1994; Pepitone, 1980; Piaget, 1948; Thelen, 1960), a great deal of research has classified cooperation as an independent variable, even in studies of cooperative learning.

In the present chapter cooperation is treated as a dependent variable, as it is in studies of the effects of students' ethnic identity on their behavior (Kagan, 1980; Kagan & Madsen, 1972; Madsen & Shapira, 1970; Shapira, 1976). One of the conclusions from this body of research is that children's personality characteristics interact with the structure of classroom instruction. Children who grow up in a cooperative society encounter great difficulty in adjusting to the competitive classroom that prevails in the United States, Israel, and other countries (Kagan, 1980). Without implying any causal relationships, research has shown that children from competitive cultures express high self-esteem when they live up to their competitive norms. In our time, "cooperative societies" are likely to be economically and industrially far less developed than allegedly competitive societies. There is also evidence to show that even children who are considered to be "competitive" in terms of their personal orientation adapt well to cooperatively run classrooms and, when asked, say that they prefer cooperative to competitive classmates (Blaney, Stephen, Rosenfield, Aronson, & Sikes, 1977).

STUDIES OF STUDENTS' PERCEPTIONS OF GI

In another study several hundred children in Grades 3 through 7, who participated in a 1½ year experiment to implement GI, were asked to write letters to the researchers about what they thought and felt about their experience (Hertz-Lazarowitz, Sharan, & Shachar, 1981). They mailed their letters directly to the researchers so no one in their schools—teachers or peers—would know what they wrote. Content analysis of the 400 letters identified 692 statements that were categorized and counted by independent judges. The category that appeared most frequently in the students' statements was that they liked studying in small groups because they could help each other; this promoted learning and prevented failure. The same study showed that the children made significantly more altruistic and cooperative decisions on a task that asked them to allocate resources to themselves and classmates (the "chocolate coin game"). Similar findings about students' preference for cooperative classrooms were reported by other investigators (Aronson, Bridgeman, & Geffner, 1978).

GROUP INVESTIGATION IN ETHNICALLY HETEROGENEOUS CLASSROOMS

Another problem posed by S. Sharan, Kussell, et al. (1984) was: Do three instructional methods—group investigation, student teams and academic divisions (Slavin, 1978, 1979), and whole-class instruction—exert differential effects on children›s cooperative behavior cross-ethnically and with same-ethnic peers? The focus of the study was on overt social behavior, rather than on attitudinal change or friendship patters as expressed in socio-metric measures (Hansell & Slavin, 1981).

Six-member groups of Jewish students (three from a Western background and three from a Mid-Eastern background) were selected at random from a given class and were allowed a maximum of 30 minutes to complete the construction of the figure of a man using Lego blocks. Some groups completed the task in less than the allotted time. Results recorded by observers indicate that the GI method generated more cooperative behavior during performance of the task than did either of the two other methods. STAD students displayed more cooperative behavior than did those in classes taught with the whole-class approach (nonverbal); and conversely, students in the GI and STAD classes were less competitive than those who studied in the classes taught by the whole-class method. Statistical analysis of data gathered with the Lego-man task shows that with the whole-class category competition is the dominant factor. No findings for ethnic group emerged in the data obtained with the chocolate-coin game.

From the findings reported in this study we learn that:

a. Whole-Class instruction produces more competitive behavior both within and between ethnic groups than do GI or STAD.
b. The GI method generates more cooperative exchanges among students from both ethnic groups and between ethnic groups than does the whole-class method.
c. GI promotes almost complete reciprocity in cooperation, whereas in classes taught with either STAD or the Whole-Class method, the Middle-Eastern background students, who were of lower social status than their Western background peers, directed twice as many cooperative acts to the Western background students than the latter did to their Mid-Eastern classmates. (S. Sharan, Raviv, Kussell, & Hertz-Lazarowitz, 1984, p. 96)

What accounts for the diverse effects of the GI and STAD methods on students' cooperative behavior? In our view the answer can be found in the manner in which the instructional methods structure students' relationships with one another. STAD structures interaction between group members so that students with a relatively higher level of academic success offer assistance to those with a lower level of achievement. That approach can easily create a "division-of-labor" within groups along ethnic lines. Minority-group students become *recipients* of help from the majority-group students, who are identified as *dispensers* of assistance (S. Sharan, 1980, p. 260). In any case, the relationships are not symmetrical, at least not in the findings reported in the study conducted in 1984 (see S. Sharan, Raviv et al., 1984, p. 97). STAD did not promote cross-ethnic cooperation, so that the status hierarchy in the classroom was not changed.

In contrast with STAD, GI assigns a portion of the task to different students without assigning them to a social role that may have implications for the minority-majority relationship between them. Moreover, helping a fellow student in a group is not a function of knowing more about the academic material that was presented earlier by the teacher. Each student investigates a particular subtopic in order to contribute his or her share to the final group product. All members acquire status in the group through reciprocal exchange rather than by dispensing or receiving assistance.

RECOMMENDATIONS FOR FURTHER RESEARCH

One recommendation for future research focuses on the school as an organization and on the professional staff, rather than on the students. A question that deserves a considerable investment of time and effort is: Just what are the organizational features of a school that will most likely be inclined to adopt instructional innovations in general, and the Group Investigation method in particular? Often school consultants spend months or even years working with one or several schools that agree to adopt a particular innovation in classroom teaching methods, only to learn that during the process the project is abandoned. The change is not just on the level of curricular contents (S. Sharan & Tan, 2008). One of the reasons why schools unexpectedly changed their minds is because the principal or teaching staff recognizes that the innovation requires genuine change in their professional behavior.

Secondary schools are particularly resistant to significant change. A very substantial percentage of them have not adopted any noteworthy change in decades. Why this is the case, and how to overcome the obstacles preventing change in instructional methods used by secondary schools, deserves more attention from educational authorities, from educators from a variety of disciplines, and from educational research. Findings from extensive research in this area will, we hope enable educators to focus on the most relevant factors impeding change and redirect resources and personnel accordingly. The current situation in respect to changing instructional methods in secondary schools brings to mind the title (and contents) of Sarason's classic work, *The Predictable Failure of Educational Change* (1990). Providing more of the same investments in change can lead only to the same results. Authentic and sustainable implementation of innovations such as the Group Investigation method of cooperative learning calls for an organizational approach to change that goes far beyond the functioning of students as individuals.

Another recommendation for research on the effects of GI is in the field of intercultural education, the urgent challenge that many schools face today. We believe that GI offers diverse learners the opportunity to harness their cultural differences in the pursuit of their learning goals (Y. Sharan, 1998). It would be helpful to study how a GI project in the intercultural classroom actively involves students' varied backgrounds and learning styles. Does the sharing of responsibilities for the investigation create conditions that help students of different backgrounds and abilities gain status and acceptance among their peers? Is GI or its components a good vehicle in today's intercultural classroom for helping students and teachers realize that the different interests, backgrounds, values, and abilities of group members are in fact the group's greatest asset and enrich the class's pool of resources for expanding knowledge? What adjustments and modifications can be made in the GI process in light of different cultural contexts?

CONCLUSION

In this chapter we have revisited the rationale and methodology of GI that grew out of Dewey's vision of learning as a process of inquiry in a social context. By encouraging learners to build on the knowledge they construct during the process of inquiry, Dewey may also be viewed as one of the early proponents of "constructivism" in the psychology of thinking and learning (Vygotsky, 1962, 1978). The belief in these views of learning, combined with the contributions by the group dynamics school of psychology, inspired Thelen to develop Group Investigation, a systematic model of inquiry-based learning. We have shown how GI is validated by the thorough research conducted by Sharan and his colleagues.

Though not always explicitly acknowledged, Dewey's vision of education continually resurfaces in different inquiry-based learning models, designed by practitioners and researchers. An intriguing example is the one presented by Murgatroyd (2010), who calls for teachers to present "wicked problems" to their students; that is, complex and challenging problems based on genuine community or organizational needs. While the inquiry into sources and the creation of possible solutions to these problems address curriculum needs, they go beyond them to enable students to "experience the fact that their knowledge and understanding can make a difference to a community" (Murgatroyd, 2010, p. 268). This goal is similar to several other projects and models: the "Environmental Studies Project" cited above, the more structured "Roots and Wings" project developed by Slavin and Madden (2001), the Complex Instruction model, developed at Stanford University (Cohen, 1994), "Coop-Coop" (Kagan & Kagan, 2009), and "Comprehension and Collaboration: Inquiry Circles in Action" (Harvey & Daniels, 2009). Each of the permutations of Dewey's vision of education has a unique focus, yet all seek to develop thinking and decision-making skills in the process of inquiry, to provide students with opportunities for finding creative solutions to real life problems, to nurture cooperation and mutual help, and to enlist the use of appropriate technology, all of which are as vital to society today (Sahlberg & Oldroyd, 2010) as when Thelen initially shaped Dewey's ideas into Group Investigation.

Group Investigation can now be seen as a classic model of inquiry-based learning that provides the basic guidelines for this approach to learning. It is our hope that the GI model will continue to evolve and enable teachers and students to experience the emotional involvement, the mental stimulation, and the cooperative behaviors that make it an authentic learning experience.

REFERENCES

Archambault, R. (Ed.). (1964). *John Dewey on education: Selected writings*. Chicago, IL: University of Chicago Press.

Aronson, E., Bridgeman, D., & Geffner, R. (1978). Interdependent interactions and prosocial behavior. *Journal of Research and Development in Education, 12,* 16–27.

Birenbaum, M. (2003). New insights into learning and teaching, and their implications for assessment. In M. Segers, F. Dochy, & E. Cascallar (Eds.), *Optimizing new methods of assessment: In search of qualities and standards* (pp. 13–36). Boston, MA: Kluwer.

Birenbaum, M., & Dochy, F. (Eds.). (1996). *Alternatives in assessment of achievements, learning processes and prior knowledge*. Boston, MA: Kluwer.

Blaney, N. T., Stephen, C., Rosenfield, D., Aronson, E., & Sikes, J. (1977). Interdependence in the classroom: A field study. *Journal of Educational Psychology, 69,* 139–146.

Brody, C. (2011). Cooperation in education: The promise, the challenges and possibilities for the future. *Experiments in Education*, S.I.T.U. Council of Educational Research. Chennai, India.

Childs, J. (1951). The educational philosophy of John Dewey. In P. Schilpp (Ed.), *The philosophy of John Dewey* (pp. 417–443). New York: Tudor.

Cohen, E. (1994). *Designing group work: Strategies for the heterogeneous classroom* (2nd ed.). New York: Teachers College Press.

Dewey, J. (1943). *The school and society* (rev. ed.). Chicago, IL: University of Chicago Press. (Original work published 1899)

Forrestal, P. (1990). Talking: Toward classroom action, In M. Brubacher, R. Payne, & K. Rickett (Eds.), *Perspectives in small group learning* (pp. 157–167). Oakville, ONT, Canada: Rubicon.

Gillies, R. (2000). The maintenance of cooperative and helping behavior in cooperative groups. *British Journal of Educational Psychology, 70,* 97–112.

Gillies, R. (2002). The residual effects of cooperative learning experiences: A two-year follow-up. *Journal of Educational Research, 96,* 15–22.

Gillies, R., & Asaduzzaman, K. (2009). Promoting reasoned argumentation, problem solving and learning during small-group work. *Cambridge Journal of Education, 39,* 7–27.

Gillies, R. M., & M. Boyle (2008) Teachers' discourse during cooperative learning and their perceptions of this pedagogical practice. *Teacher and Teacher Education, 24,* 1333–1348.

Hansell, S., & Slavin, R. (1981). Cooperative learning and the structure of inter-racial friendships. *Sociology of Education, 54,* 98–106.

Hare, A. P. (1973). Theories of group development and categories for interaction analysis. *Small Group Behavior, 4,* 259–304.

Hare, A. P. (1976). *Handbook of small group research*. New York: Free Press. (Original work published 1962)

Harris, M., & Evans, M. (Eds.). (1972). *Case studies: Schools Council Environmental Studies Project*. London: Hart-Davis Educational.

Harvey, S., & Daniels, H. (2009). *Comprehension and collaboration: Inquiry circles in action*. London: Heinemann.

Hertz-Lazarowitz, R. (1989). Cooperation and helping in the classroom. *International Journal of Educational Research, 13,* 113–119.

Hertz-Lazarowitz, R., & Shachar, H. (1990). Teachers' verbal behavior in cooperative and whole-class instruction. In S. Sharan (Ed.), *Cooperative learning: Theory and research* (pp. 77–94). New York: Praeger.

Hertz-Lazarowitz, R., Sharan, S., & Shachar, H. (1981). What children think about small-group learning. In S. Sharan & R. Hertz-Lazarowitz (Eds.), *Changing schools: The small-group teaching project in Israel* (pp. 293-311). Tel-Aviv University. (in Hebrew)

Hertz-Lazarowitz, R., & Zelniker, T. (1995). Cooperative learning in an Israeli context. *International Journal of Educational Research, 23,* 267–285.

Hill, W. (1969). *Learning through discussion*. Beverly Hills, CA: Sage.

Hlemo-Silver, C. E., & Barrows, H. S. (2006). Goals and strategies of a problem-based learning facilitator. *Interdisciplinary Journal of Problem-based Learning, 1,* 21–39.

Hlemo-Silver, C. E., & Barrows, H. S. (2008). Facilitating collaborative knowledge building. *Cognition and Instruction, 26*(1), 48–94.

Johnson, D., & Johnson, R. (1994). *Learning together and alone* (4th ed.). Boston, MA: Allyn & Bacon.

Johnson, D., & Johnson, R. (2009). An educational psychology success story: Social interdependence theory and cooperative learning. *Educational Researcher, 38,* 365–379.

Johnson, D., Maruyama, G., Johnson, R., Nelson, D., & Skon, L. (1981). Effects of cooperative, competitive and individualistic goal structures on achievement: A meta-analysis. *Psychological Bulletin, 89,* 47–62.

Johnson, D. W., Skon, L. & Johnson, R. (1980). Effects of cooperative, competitive and individualistic conditions on children's problem-solving performance. *American Educational Research Journal, 17*(1), 83–93.

Kagan, S. (1980). Cooperation-competition, culture and structural bias in classrooms. In S. Sharan, P. Hare, C. Webb, & R. Hertz-Lazarowitz (Eds.), *Cooperation in education* (pp. 197–211). Provo, UT: Brigham Young University Press,

Kagan, S., & Kagan, M. (2009) *Cooperative learning*. San Clemente, CA: Kagan.

Kagan, S., & Madsen, M. (1972). Experimental analyses of cooperation and competition of Anglo-American and Mexican children. *Developmental Psychology, 6,* 49–59.

Kilpatrick, W. (1951). Dewey's influence on education. In P. Schilpp (Ed.), *The philosophy of John Dewey* (pp. 447–473). New York: Tudor. Lewin, K. (1947a). Frontiers in group dynamics: Concepts, method, and reality in social science, social equilibria, and social change. *Human Relations, 1,* 5–42.

Lewin, K. (1947b). Group decision and social change. In E. Maccoby, T. Newcomb, & E. Hartley (Eds.), *Readings in social psychology* (3rd ed., pp. 197–211). New York: Holt, Rinehart & Winston.

Madsen, M., & Shapira, A. (1970). Cooperative and competitive behavior of urban Afro-American, Anglo-American, Mexican-American and Mexican village children. *Developmental Psychology, 3,* 16–20.

Mann, R. (1967). *Interpersonal styles and group development*. New York: Wiley.

Miel, A. (1952). *Cooperative procedures in learning*. New York: Teachers College Press.

Mitchell, M., Montgomery, H., Holder, M., & Stuart, D. (2008). Group investigation as a cooperative learning strategy: An integrated analysis of the literature. *Alberta Journal of Educational Research, 54,* 388–395.

Murgatroyd, S. (2010). "Wicked problems" and the work of the school. *European Journal of Education, 45*(2), 259–279.

Pepitone, E. (1980). *Children in cooperation and competition*. Lexington, MA: Lexington.
Piaget, J. (1948). *The moral judgement of the child*. Glencoe, IL: Free Press.
Sahlberg, P., & Oldroyd, D. (2010). Pedagogy for economic competitiveness and sustainable development. *European Journal of Education, 45*(2), 280–299.
Sarason, S. B. (1990). *The predictable failure of educational reform: Can we change course before it's too late?* San Francisco, CA: Jossey-Bass.
Schmuck, R., & Schmuck, P. (1974). *A humanistic psychology of education*. Palo Alto, CA: National Press Books.
Schmuck, R., & Schmuck, P. (2001). *Group processes in the classroom* (8th ed.). Boston, MA: McGraw Hill.
Shapira, A. (1976). Developmental differences in competitive behavior of kibbutz and city children in Israel. *Journal of Social Psychology, 98,* 19–26.
Sharan, S. (1980). Cooperative learning in small groups: Recent methods and effects on achievement, attitudes and ethnic relations. *Review of Educational Research, 50,* 241–271.
Sharan, S. (Ed.). (1990). *Cooperative learning: Theory and research*. New York: Praeger.
Sharan, S. (Ed.). (1999). *Handbook of cooperative learning methods*. Westport, CT: Greenwood.
Sharan, S., & Hertz-Lazarowitz, R. (1980). A group-investigation method of cooperative learning in the classroom. In S. Sharan, P. Hare, C. Webb, & R. Hertz-Lazarowitz (Eds.), *Cooperation in education* (pp. 14–46). Provo, UT: Brigham Young University.
Sharan, S., Hertz-Lazarowitz, R., & Ackerman, Z. (1980). Academic achievement of elementary school children in small-group versus whole-class instruction. *Journal of Experimental Education, 48,* 125–129.
Sharan, S., Kussell, P., Hertz-Lazarowitz, R., Bejarano, Y., Raviv, S., & Sharan, Y. (Eds.). (1984). *Cooperative learning in the classroom: Research in desegregated schools*. Hillsdale, NJ: Erlbaum.
Sharan, S., Raviv, S., Kussell, P., & Hertz-Lazarowitz, R. (1984). Cooperative and competitive behavior. In S. Sharan, P. Kussell, Y. Bejarano, S. Raviv, & Y. Sharan (Eds.), *Cooperative learning in the classroom: Research in desegregated schools* (pp. 73–106). Hillsdale, NJ: Erlbaum.
Sharan, S., & Rich, Y. (1984). Field experiments on ethnic integration in Israeli schools. In Y. Amir & S. Sharan (Eds.), *School desegregation: Cross-cultural perspectives* (pp. 189–217). Hillsdale, NJ: Erlbaum.
Sharan, S., & Shachar, H. (1988). *Language and learning in the cooperative classroom*. New York: Springer.
Sharan, S., & Shaulov, A. (1990). Cooperative learning, motivation to learn and academic achievement. In S. Sharan (Ed.), *Cooperative learning: Theory and research* (pp. 173–202). New York: Praeger.
Sharan, S., & Tan, G. C. I. (2008). *Organizing schools for productive learning*. New York: Springer.
Sharan, Y. (1995). Music of many voices: Group investigation in a cooperative high school classroom. In J. Pederson & A. Digby (Eds.), *Cooperative learning in the secondary school: Theory and practice* (pp. 313–339). New York: Garland.
Sharan, Y. (1998) Enriching the group and the investigation in the intercultural classroom. *European Journal of Intercultural Studies, 9*(2), 133–140.
Sharan, Y. (2010) Cooperative learning for academic and social gains: Valued pedagogy, problematic practice. *European Journal of Education, 45*(2), 300–310.
Sharan, Y., & Sharan, S. (1992). *Expanding cooperative learning through group investigation*. New York: Teachers College Press.
Sharan, Y., & Sharan, S. (1994). What do we want to study? How should we go about it? Group investigation in the cooperative social studies classroom. In R. Stahl (Ed.), *Cooperative learning in social studies: A handbook for teachers* (pp. 257–276). Menlo Park, CA: Addison-Wesley.
Sharan, Y., & Sharan, S. (1999). Group investigation in the cooperative classroom. In S. Sharan (Ed.), *Handbook of cooperative learning methods* (pp. 97–113). Westport, CT: Greenwood.
Shulman, L., & Keislar, E. (Eds.). (1966). *Learning by discovery: A critical appraisal*. New York: Rand McNally.
Slavin, R. E. (1978). Student teams and achievement divisions. *Journal of Research and Development in Education, 12,* 39–49.
Slavin, R. E. (1979). Effects of biracial learning teams on cross-racial friendships. *Journal of Educational Psychology, 71,* 381–387.
Slavin, R. E. (1983). *Cooperative learning*. New York: Longman.
Slavin, R. E. (1995). *Cooperative learning: Theory, research, and practice*. (2nd ed.). Boston, MA: Allyn & Bacon.
Slavin, R. E. (2010). Instruction based on cooperative learning. In R. Mayer (Ed.), *Handbook of research on learning and instruction*. London: Routledge.
Slavin, R. E., & Madden, N. (2001). Summary of research on Success for All and Roots and Wings. In R. E. Slavin & N. Madden (Eds.), *Success for all: Research and reform in elementary education*. Mahwah, NJ: Erlbaum.
Steiner, I. (1972). *Group process and productivity*. New York: Academic Press.
Stiggens, R. (2000). *Student-involved classroom assessment* (3rd ed.). New York: Prentice Hall.

Stubbs, M. (1982). *Discourse analysis: The sociolinguistic analysis of natural language*. Oxford, England: Blackwell.

Tan, G. C. I., Sharan, S. & Lee, K. E. C. (2006). *Group investigation and student learning: A cooperative learning experiment in Singapore schools*. Singapore: Marshall Cavendish.

Thelen, H. (1954). *Dynamics of groups at work*. Chicago, IL: University of Chicago.

Thelen, H. (1960). *Education and the human quest*. New York: Harper.

Thelen, H. (1981). *The classroom society*. London: Croom Helm.

Tuckman, B. (1965). Developmental sequence in small groups. *Psychological Bulletin, 63*, 384–399.

Vygotsky, L. (1962). *Thought and language*. Cambridge, MA: MIT Press.

Vygotsky, L. (1978). *Mind in society: The development of higher psychological processes*. Cambridge, MA: Harvard University Press.

Webb, N. (1982). Student interaction and learning in small groups. *Review of Educational Research, 52,* 421–445.

Weigel, R., Wiser, P., & Cook, S. (1972). The impact of cooperative learning experiences on cross-ethnic relations and attitudes. *Journal of Social Issues, 28,* 1–19.

21

PROBLEM-BASED LEARNING

An Instructional Model of Collaborative Learning

CINDY E. HMELO-SILVER
Rutgers University

CHRISTINA DeSIMONE
University of Ottawa

Problem-based learning (PBL) is a learner-centered pedagogical approach in which students engage in goal-directed inquiry. In PBL, students work collaboratively to learn through solving complex and ill-structured problems (Barrows, 2000; Hmelo-Silver, 2004). They engage in self-directed learning (SDL) and then apply their new knowledge to the problem and reflect on their learning of the content and strategies employed. The teacher's role changes from one of telling to one of facilitating the learning process. More specifically, the goals of PBL include helping students develop (a) flexible knowledge, (b) effective problem-solving skills, (c) SDL skills, and (d) effective collaboration skills.

PEDAGOGICAL GOALS OF PROBLEM-BASED LEARNING

The first goal of PBL, constructing flexible knowledge, refers to knowledge that is coherently organized around the deep principles in a domain (Chi, Feltovich, & Glaser, 1981). Learners need to understand when and why such knowledge is useful (Bransford, Brown, & Cocking, 2000). Flexible knowledge develops as people apply their knowledge in a range of problem situations (Cognition and Technology Group at Vanderbilt [CTGV], 1997; Kolodner, 1993).

For learners to develop usable knowledge and skills, learning should be situated in problem-solving contexts (e.g., Capon & Kuhn, 2004; Hmelo, 1998; Perfetto, Bransford, & Franks, 1983). Moreover, discussing problems in a PBL group prior to accessing information activates relevant prior knowledge and facilitates the construction of new knowledge (Schmidt, DeVolder, DeGrave, Moust, & Patel, 1989).

The second goal of developing effective problem-solving skills refers to the ability to exercise appropriate reasoning strategies. Different strategies may be appropriate for different domains and for different problems. For example, hypothetical-deductive reasoning is an appropriate strategy for medical problem solving whereas analogical or case-based reasoning may be appropriate in many design domains such as architecture

A third goal of PBL is to support the development of lifelong learning skills, which means helping students become self-regulated learners (Zimmerman, 2002). To accomplish this, learners must have a metacognitive awareness of what they do and do not understand. During the PBL process, students set learning goals for themselves as they identify what they need to learn, how to reach their goals, and evaluate whether or not their goals have been attained.

The fourth goal of PBL is learning to collaborate, which means productively participating in small groups. This encompasses establishing common ground, resolving discrepancies, negotiating the actions that a group is going to take, and coming to an agreement (Barron, 2002). PBL allows for an open exchange of ideas and engagement of all group members (Cohen, 1994; O'Donnell, 2006).

FEATURES OF PBL

There are several key features of PBL that help to support these goals. First and foremost is the student-centered tutorial process that is at the heart of problem-based learning.

The PBL Tutorial Process

Typically, the tutorial process begins by presenting a group of students with minimal information about a messy, ill-defined problem (Barrows, 2000). These problems may be presented as a narrative, a paper or computer-based problem simulation, or in a range of other formats (Hmelo-Silver, 2004). From the outset, students must engage in some form of inquiry to obtain additional problem information (Torp & Sage, 2002). For example, when middle school children were asked to build artificial lungs, they performed experiments to determine how much air the lungs had to displace (Hmelo, Holton, & Kolodner, 2000). For teacher education students, videos of classroom practice may provide rich problem contexts (Derry, Hmelo-Silver, Nagarajan, Chernobilsky, & Beitzel, 2006). As learners work through a problem, they may pause to reflect on the data they have collected so far, generate questions about that data, and hypothesize about underlying causal mechanisms that might help explain it. The students then identify concepts they need to learn more about in order to solve the problem (i.e., "learning issues"). After considering the problem with their naïve knowledge, the students divide and independently research the learning issues they have identified. They then regroup to share what they learned, reconsider their hypotheses, or generate new hypotheses in light of their new learning, as shown in the cycle displayed in Figure 21.1. When completing the task, learners reflect on the problem in order to abstract the lessons learned, as well as how they performed in self-directed learning and collaborative problem solving.

Typically, in the PBL model, students use whiteboards to help scaffold their problem solving (Hmelo-Silver, 2004). The whiteboard is divided into four columns: facts, ideas, action plans, and learning issues. These columns help the learners keep track of where they have been and where they are going. The four columns scaffold learning by helping to communicate and guide the learning process (Dillenbourg, 2002; Hmelo-Silver,

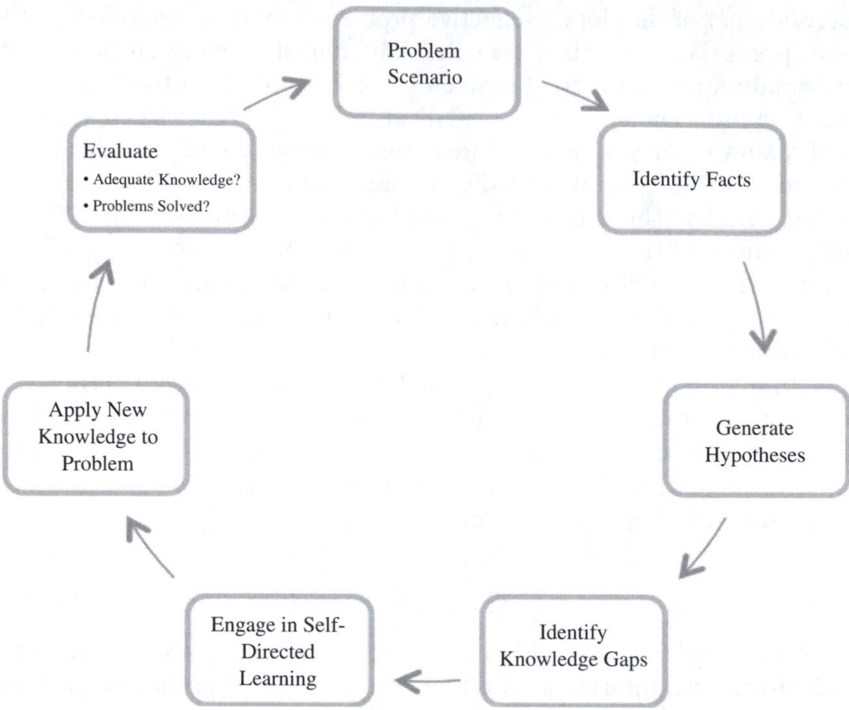

Figure 21.1 The PBL Cycle

2006). The whiteboard serves as a focus for students to negotiate ideas and co-construct knowledge.

The other key aspects of the PBL process, the problem, facilitation, collaboration, and reflection, are all embedded within the PBL tutorial and help provide a mechanism for PBL to achieve its goals.

The Role of the PBL Problem

Both research and practical experience provide suggestions for the characteristics of good problems (Cohen, 1994; Jonassen & Hung, 2008; Kolodner, Hmelo, & Narayanan, 1996). To promote flexible thinking and to be group-worthy, problems need to be complex, ill structured, and open ended; there should be multiple solution paths (Jonassen & Hung, 2008). To support intrinsic motivation, problems must be perceived as realistic by the students, resonate with their experiences, and motivate their need to know. When possible, problems should provide feedback that allows students to evaluate their success as learners, problem solvers, and collaborators. Such problems should foster conjecture and argumentation. Good problems help students become engaged in the PBL process right from the beginning based on their initial understanding. Generative problems often require multidisciplinary solutions. For example, planning a trip on the Appalachian Trail requires using knowledge from several content areas, which allows students to see how different categories of knowledge are useful tools for problem solving.

The ill-structured problems used in PBL can serve as the basis for high levels of problem-relevant collaborative interaction; however, groups may need good facilitation to make this interaction productive (Kapur & Kinzer, 2007; Van Berkel & Schmidt, 2000).

Although in studies of PBL, the predominant type of ill-structured problem has been diagnosis (e.g., medical students need to diagnose the cause of a patient's problem), other types of problems have been successfully used. Walker and Leary (2009) found that the greatest achievement effects were for problems that were classified as design problems and strategic performance problems. A design problem might ask learners to design artificial lungs or an instructional plan (e.g., Derry et al., 2006; Hmelo, Holton, & Kolodner, 2000). A strategic performance problem might ask learners to act in complex, real time situations in which they have to employ and adapt tactics as appropriate to situational demands (Walker & Leary, 2009). A teacher implementing a lesson and having to deal with student ideas on the fly would be an example of such a problem.

The Role of the Facilitator

PBL facilitators play a key role in modeling the problem solving and self-directed learning skills needed when self-assessing one's reasoning and understanding, consistent with a cognitive apprenticeship model of learning (Collins, 2006). Facilitators are expert learners, modeling good strategies for learning and thinking rather than providing content knowledge. As portrayed in the PBL process earlier, facilitators progressively fade their scaffolding as students become more experienced with PBL and take increased responsibility for their collaborative learning (Hmelo-Silver & Barrows, 2008). The facilitator agenda includes both moving the students through the stages of PBL and monitoring the collaborative learning process—assuring that all students are involved and encouraging them to make their own thinking visible and to comment on each other's ideas (Hmelo-Silver & Barrows, 2006, 2008; Koschmann, Myers, Feltovich, & Barrows, 1994). The PBL facilitator guides the development of higher order thinking skills by encouraging students (and the group) to justify their thinking, and externalizing self-reflection by directing appropriate questions to individuals. Expert facilitators accomplish their goals through the use of a variety of strategies (see Hmelo-Silver & Barrows, 2006 for a list of examples) that often involve the use of open-ended and metacognitive questioning (Hmelo-Silver & Barrows, 2008). These strategies build on student thinking and help catalyze and focus discussions in subtle but productive ways. Facilitators progressively fade their support as students assume more responsibility for their collaborative learning (Collins, 2006; Hmelo-Silver & Barrows, 2008).

Collaborative Learning in PBL

Learning in PBL is a fundamentally collaborative experience where problem solving and knowledge building require dialogue amongst group members. One assumption of PBL is that the small-group structure helps distribute the cognitive load among the members of the group, taking advantage of group members' distributed expertise by allowing the group members to become "experts" in particular topics. This expertise develops as learners divide up learning issues and conduct self-directed research that they share with the rest of the group. Thus, the whole group is needed to tackle problems that would normally be too difficult for each student alone (Pea, 1993; Salomon, 1993). Moreover, through this process of interaction and dialogue, learners (e.g., preservice teachers, medical students) in PBL become enculturated in their professional community. Through this process members learn the language, issues, and explore tools and resources available to them, which will help them solve relevant problems. Furthermore, research suggests that the small-group discussions and debate in PBL sessions enhance higher order thinking and promote shared knowledge construction (Blumenfeld, Marx, Soloway, & Krajcik, 1996; Vye, Goldman, Voss, Hmelo, & Williams, 1997).

In PBL groups, the students often work together to construct collaborative explanations, but collaboration in PBL does not necessarily come easily. In the traditional PBL model, a facilitator helps accomplish this. Hmelo-Silver, Chernobilsky, and Nagarajan (2009) presented a case study demonstrating that students can learn to collaborate better with reflection by the students and guidance by the facilitator. Emergent leadership in PBL groups can also be important for supporting collaboration as students take responsibility for facilitating themselves when PBL is implemented in larger classes (Gressick & Derry, 2010; Hmelo-Silver, Katic, Chernobilsky, & Nagarajan, 2007). In the absence of a dedicated facilitator, several techniques can foster productive collaboration. Scripted cooperation, reciprocal teaching, guided peer questioning, and the use of student roles have all been used to support effective collaborative learning with K–16 students and might offer possibilities for supporting collaboration in PBL (Herrenkohl & Guerra, 1998; King, 1999; O'Donnell, 1999; Palincsar & Herrenkohl, 1999; see O'Donnell and Hmelo-Silver Introduction this volume; Fischer et al., chapter 23 this volume).

Collaborative inquiry and problem solving does not necessarily happen without support (Ertmer & Simons, 2006; Schmidt, Loyens, & van Gog & Paas, 2007). Rather, this collaboration needs to be facilitated by PBL tutors who have both content knowledge and communication skills. Zhang, Lundeberg, McConnell, Koehler, and Eberhardt (2010) found that questioning assists teachers in the development of collaborative inquiry. In particular, questions such as those that ask for clarification, elaboration, and connection to classroom practice lead to better content understanding. In another study of PBL in teacher professional development, Zhang, Lundeberg, and Eberhardt (2011) demonstrated that questioning and revoicing were the most common strategies used by expert facilitators, but that often a combination of strategies was needed to help support the progression of ideas during collaborative discussions.

Reflection for Learning and Transfer

Reflection is a critical component of PBL and is important for constructing generalizable knowledge (Salomon & Perkins, 1989). This reflection must help the learner understand that the tasks they are doing are in the service of the questions they have asked, and that these questions arise from the learning goals they have set for themselves (Bereiter & Scardamalia, 1989). Reflection helps students: (a) relate their new knowledge to their prior understanding, (b) mindfully abstract knowledge in order to understand the "big ideas" of a domain, and (c) understand how strategies and content might be applied, extended, and constructed. PBL incorporates reflection throughout the tutorial process and when completing a problem. Students periodically reflect on the adequacy of their hypothesis list and their own knowledge relative to the problem. After each problem, students reflect on what they learned, how they functioned as part of a team, and their effectiveness as self-directed learners. As students make inferences that tie the general concepts and skills to the specifics of the problem that they are working on, they construct more coherent understanding (Chi, Bassock, Lewis, Reimann, & Glaser, 1989). The reflection process in PBL helps students make inferences, identify knowledge gaps, and prepares them for transfer.

Often groups need help to reflect on their learning (Hmelo-Silver, 2000). A dedicated facilitator can support student reflection, but in larger groups and with younger learners, there are other techniques that may be helpful. One approach to dealing with this is the use of structured journals (Puntambekar & Kolodner, 1998). Another approach is to mix both small-group and large-group discussion of process and content (De Simone, 2008, 2009).

RESEARCH ON PBL OUTCOMES

With an understanding of the features and affordances of PBL as a model of collaborative learning, we next consider what the research says with respect to its goals for PBL. We look in turn at how PBL helps develop (a) flexible knowledge, (b) effective problem-solving skills, (c) SDL skills, and (d) effective collaboration skills. We group these first goals together because they are often examined in the same research studies.

Flexible Knowledge and Problem Solving

In the medical context, PBL students perform equal to or slightly worse than traditional medical students on tests of basic sciences but consistently better on clinical medicine tests (Albanese & Mitchell, 1993; Goodman et al., 1991; Mennin, Friedman, Skipper, Kalishman, & Snyder, 1993; Schmidt, van der Molen, te Winkel, & Wijnan, 2009; Vernon & Blake, 1993). There are mixed results on problem-solving tasks (e.g., Hmelo, 1998; Patel, Groen, & Norman, 1993). Patel et al. (1993) asked traditional and PBL medical students to provide diagnostic explanations of a clinical problem. PBL students' explanations, although containing more errors, were also more elaborated than those of the medical students in traditional curricula. More recent results are more positive. When studied over the first year of medical school, students in a PBL curriculum were more likely to construct accurate hypotheses and use science concepts than students in a traditional curriculum (Hmelo, 1998). The accuracy effect appears to be robust. When students in PBL and traditional curricula were compared in terms of diagnostic accuracy for 30 case vignettes, PBL students were more accurate than students in a traditional curriculum (Schmidt, Machiels-Bongaerts et al., 1996). Thus, studies in medical schools tend to show that PBL students are able to construct knowledge, if tasks are used that tap knowledge in problem-solving contexts (e.g., Gijbels, Dochy, Van den Bossche, & Segers, 2005; Hmelo, 1998; Schmidt, Machiels-Bongaerts et al., 1996) rather than multiple-choice measures (Albanese & Mitchell, 1993; Goodman et al., 1991; Vernon & Blake, 1993).

Research on the use of PBL in teacher education has proliferated in the past 10 years. Teachers face complex and diverse pedagogical and classroom problems, and they tend to bring their personal experiences and beliefs to these problems and have yet to learn to draw upon research and theories of learning (Arvaja, Salovaara, Häkkinen, & Jävelä, 2007; O'Donnell, 2004). Because of its emphasis on inquiry and knowledge application, PBL can be used to assist preservice teachers in their pedagogical problem solving. There is research evidence demonstrating that in comparison to a group of preservice teachers who served as controls, those preservice teachers who learned through PBL were significantly better able to work through diagnosis-solution pedagogical problems (De Simone, 2008, 2009). Both of these studies repeatedly showed that preservice teachers were able to: (a) provide feasible solutions; (b) evaluate the solutions; and (c) use educational concepts as support for their analysis of the pedagogical situation. PBL can help teachers to make considered decisions and navigate through the teaching and learning issues that they confront.

In a study that demonstrated how technology could support PBL in teacher education, Derry, Hmelo-Silver, and colleagues (Derry, Hmelo-Silver, Nagarajan, Chernobilsky, & Beitzel, 2006; Hmelo-Silver, Derry, Bitterman, & Hatrak, 2009) conducted a 3-year study in educational psychology courses using a hybrid online and face-to-face PBL environment consisting of multimedia cases and an electronic notebook to highlight important issues and use as a springboard for discussion. These were compared to a standard comparison class using lectures and face-to-face interactions. The results demonstrated that those using the technology-supported hybrid PBL were better able to transfer educational psychology concepts to analysis of a novel video case than those who used a more traditional approach. The transfer of problem solving skills and concepts is a pivotal goal of learning and the results here suggest that PBL can meet that goal.

PBL has been applied in undergraduate education as well. In a study of a PBL engineering course in sustainable technology, students used PBL in multidisciplinary teams (Hmelo, Shikano et al., 1995). The students demonstrated a significant increase in both knowledge and problem solving. When PBL was used to teach statistical reasoning to undergraduates, Derry, Levin, Osana, Jones, and Peterson (2000) found that students showed significant learning gains for some, but not all, of the course content.

Although PBL appears to support learning in professional and undergraduate educational contexts, there has been less work with other populations, particularly younger learners. In work with gifted high school students, Gallagher and Stepien (1996) found that PBL students scored higher on a multiple-choice test than traditionally instructed students. Comparing traditional and problem-based instruction in high school economics, Mergendoller, Maxwell, and Bellisimo (2006) found that across multiple teacher and schools, students in the PBL course gained more knowledge than the students in a traditional course.

Another approach used design problems with a heterogeneous population of sixth grade students. Hmelo, Holton, and Kolodner (2000) developed a PBL unit that involved students designing artificial lungs and demonstrated that PBL students showed greater gains on both short answer tests and mental model analyses than students in comparison classrooms. However, students in the PBL class had some misunderstandings at the end of the 3-week unit. This suggests that adaptations such as additional scaffolding and just-in-time minilessons might be needed to use PBL in developmentally appropriate ways.

Becoming Self-Directed Learners

Proponents of PBL make claims about preparing lifelong learners by explicitly stressing self-directed learning (SDL) as part of the PBL design. Becoming a self-directed learner is a complex and multifaceted process, and students' SDL strategies evolve over time (Evensen; 2000; Evensen, Salisbury-Glennon, & Glenn, 2001). It is worth noting that SDL as defined in the PBL and adult learning research literature shares many characteristics with self-regulated learning (SRL); however, there are also some key differences (Loyens, Magda, & Rikers, 2008; Zimmerman & Lebeau, 2000). Loyens et al. argue that SDL is broader than SRL and is a design feature of learning environments that require full learner control on learner-defined tasks (but see Loyens et al., 2008 for a full discussion of the relationship between SDL and SRL).

Students' approaches to learning from problems differ qualitatively depending on their degree of self-regulation. Ertmer, Newby, and MacDougall (1996) found that students who were low self-regulated learners (SRL) had difficulty in adapting to the kind of learning required in PBL. Hmelo and Lin (2000) demonstrated that PBL students transferred the reasoning strategies from their problem solving into their SDL as they used their hypotheses to guide their SDL.

When comparing traditional and PBL medical students in terms of the learning resources used, Blumberg and Michael (1992) found that PBL students were more likely to use self-chosen learning resources whereas students in the other curriculum used faculty-chosen resources. In a technology-enhanced PBL course for preservice teachers, Jeong and Hmelo-Silver (2010) found that there was great variability in how preservice teachers used resources in their SDL. Students who used a range of resources and went beyond those resources that were most obvious, and processed those resources most deeply were most likely to demonstrate high achievement.

A recent review of the literature demonstrated that self-directed learning is a developmental process. Loyens, Magda, and Rikers (2008) found that across many studies of postsecondary students, students became more self-directed learners as they advanced in their PBL programs. The review also noted that although SDL processes can be learned, these skills don't necessarily develop without support. In a descriptive study of SDL as it occurred in a naturalistic context in a Singapore polytechnic school, Yew and Schmidt (2009) found that facilitators often provided support to help students plan their SDL research and reporting and make connections between ideas and the problem statement. This support generally took the form of open-ended questions that invited the students to identify what they would research and present as well as asking them how what they had learned would connect to the problem. More studies like these are needed to better understand how SDL unfolds as a collaborative, self-regulated, and constructive process.

Learning to Collaborate

Helping students to become effective collaborators is one of the main goals of PBL. Most of the research in this area has focused on the factors that affect how well students learn collaboratively. This is particularly important because group functioning affects learning outcomes and intrinsic motivation (Schmidt & Moust, 2000). They found that collaboration was affected by the quality of the problem and facilitator functioning.

Students in PBL curricula are aware of the importance of collaboration (DeGrave, Boshuizen, & Schmidt, 1996). Effective collaboration can lead to knowledge construction as students construct joint explanations. An analysis of PBL tutorial sessions found that student discourse often focused on responding to and refining ideas that had been proposed (Hmelo-Silver & Barrows, 2008). In PBL, students are encouraged to attend to collaboration processes through reflection and the interdependence of learning within the group. But students do not necessarily know how to deal effectively with the collaborative aspects of PBL (Abrandt Dahlgren & Dahlgren, 2002; Evensen et al., 2001).

We still need to better understand whether and how students in PBL learn to collaborate. There is evidence that students do work together to provide collaborative explanations (Hmelo-Silver & Barrows, 2008) as well as to coconstruct knowledge during self-directed learning (Yew & Schmidt, 2009). There is also evidence that the collaboration in tutorial groups is a key factor in student learning and motivation but that not all groups collaborate well (Derry et al., 2006). There has been progress in understanding the factors that affect the quality of collaboration. The quality of collaborative discussions is affected by the nature of the problem (e.g., structure, relevance, interest), the facilitator, the group composition and experience, and participation equity (Kapur & Kinzer, 2007; Zhang, Lundeberg, Koehler, & Eberhardt, 2008).

There is at least one recent study that addresses the issue of collaboration directly. In an adaptation of PBL called challenge-based learning, O'Mahony and colleagues (2012) compared collaborative discourse in a traditional and problem-based module for an aerospace workplace. The results demonstrated that the learners in the challenge-based course engaged in higher quality collaboration than students in the traditional course, and that this effect on participation persisted even when the instructor returned to a lecture mode. Their analyses demonstrated that the quality of the collaboration improved over time moving from the participants' initial efforts at establishing what they knew with the group to what O'Mahony et al. called knowledge-sharing exchanges. These were conversations in which group members asked questions of each other and worked collaboratively to address the questions. The results of this study suggest that through PBL experiences, students can learn to collaborate, although additional research is needed to study this in other settings.

To summarize, in answer to our question: Has PBL achieved its stated goals? There is increasing evidence that PBL is effective for problem solving and for constructing flexible knowledge. We also know that dialogue scaffolded by an expert PBL and content facilitator does facilitate collaborative inquiry, which is important for problem solving and transfer. We are still lacking an adequate research base regarding collaboration as an outcome of PBL but we do have evidence of promise. In the next section, we describe adaptations of PBL for different settings and how these adaptations can foster collaborative inquiry.

ADAPTATIONS OF PBL

The traditional model of PBL has been successful in the training of medical doctors. For this model, certain criteria must be met: PBL must be integrated across the curriculum; the focus must be on issues or problems instead of subjects; class sizes must be very small; and students must be high achievers. However, alternative models are needed when one or more of these factors are not present or other factors intervene resulting in resource challenges. An important issue in moving beyond this model of PBL is one of scale. The role of the facilitator is extremely important in modeling thinking skills and providing metacognitive scaffolding as well as providing support for collaboration.

Hmelo-Silver (2000) and De Simone (2008, 2009) have successfully managed to facilitate multiple groups using a wandering facilitation model, with facilitators rotating from group to group, adjusting the time spent with each of the groups in the classroom according to the needs of the group. By using large tear sheets hung on the classroom walls, they were able to dynamically assess the progress of each of the groups and adjust facilitation efforts accordingly.

Technology can also be used to extend skilled facilitation (Derry et al., 2006). Students may also be called upon to help facilitate themselves (Hmelo-Silver, Katic et al., 2007; Leary, Walker, Fitt, & Shelton, 2009). Indeed, Leary et al. (2009) have demonstrated that peer facilitation can lead to positive learning outcomes.

An example of technology used to support PBL can be found in the STELLAR project (Derry et al., 2006). Using STELLAR, Derry, Hmelo-Silver, and colleagues (2006) developed hybrid courses in educational psychology and the learning sciences for preservice teachers. The system included two major components:

1. The Knowledge Web (KWeb), a multimedia online resource that includes two integrated networks. One is the case library; a library of video cases representing teaching practices, and the second is a hypertext of conceptual knowledge from educational psychology.
2. PBL online: A site including scaffolding and tools to help groups carry out lesson design tasks. The tools included personal and collaborative workspaces, such as a group whiteboard (Figure 21.2) and threaded discussion.

The STELLAR environment provided preservice teachers with opportunities to engage with educational psychology concepts by using video cases as contexts for collaborative lesson design (Derry et al., 2006). STELLAR courses consist of three to four problem scenarios each lasting 2 to 3 weeks. A problem scenario includes both a videocase of a student or classroom as well as a problem statement that sets the students' goal to redesign the lesson or design a similar one, based on learning principles. These PBL modules present opportunities for discussion and (re)design of instruction based on video cases of classroom practice. The video cases were indexed to the KWeb, helping students identify fruitful learning issues.

The PBL online modules included tools that scaffold students' individual and group PBL activities (Collins, 2006; Hmelo-Silver, 2006). It broke the PBL process into 8 steps that guided students' collaborative problem solving (Dillenbourg, 2002) and directed them toward appropriate tools. These tools included a personal notebook to record initial observations; a threaded discussion, where students shared research; and a whiteboard where students posted and commented on proposals for lesson (re)designs. STELLAR embedded a domain-specific model of instructional planning in the tools (Wiggins & McTighe, 1998). For example, the whiteboard had separate tabs for identifying enduring understanding, evidence of understanding, and assessments. These same categories were used as prompts in the individual workspaces, communicating the instructional planning process with the intent of scaffolding the learners' activity throughout the PBL activity (Hmelo-Silver, 2006).

The second author has worked with preservice teachers in class sizes of 40 to 45 (De Simone, 2008, 2009). This is a large class for a group of novice PBL users. In this case, what made for an effective PBL implementation was initial modeling by an experienced PBL facilitator. We began the training by having preselected five high-performing students who the course instructor anticipated would readily engage in dialogue with one another as part of the PBL demonstration in front of the rest of the class. Then, as in the traditional PBL model, she presented students with a PBL problem and students generated learning issues, which were recorded on large sticky notes. Because of time restrictions, rather than having students pursue their inquiry, the facilitator served as their resource and helped students obtain the information needed to work through and analyze the problem. Because these students were new to PBL, the facilitator probed students with respect to educational psychology content and helped students with collaborative aspects of PBL inquiry. For example, she modeled how to summarize and check for understanding as well as how to record alternative points of view and consider all information before arriving at a conclusion. Finally, there was a period of self-reflection.

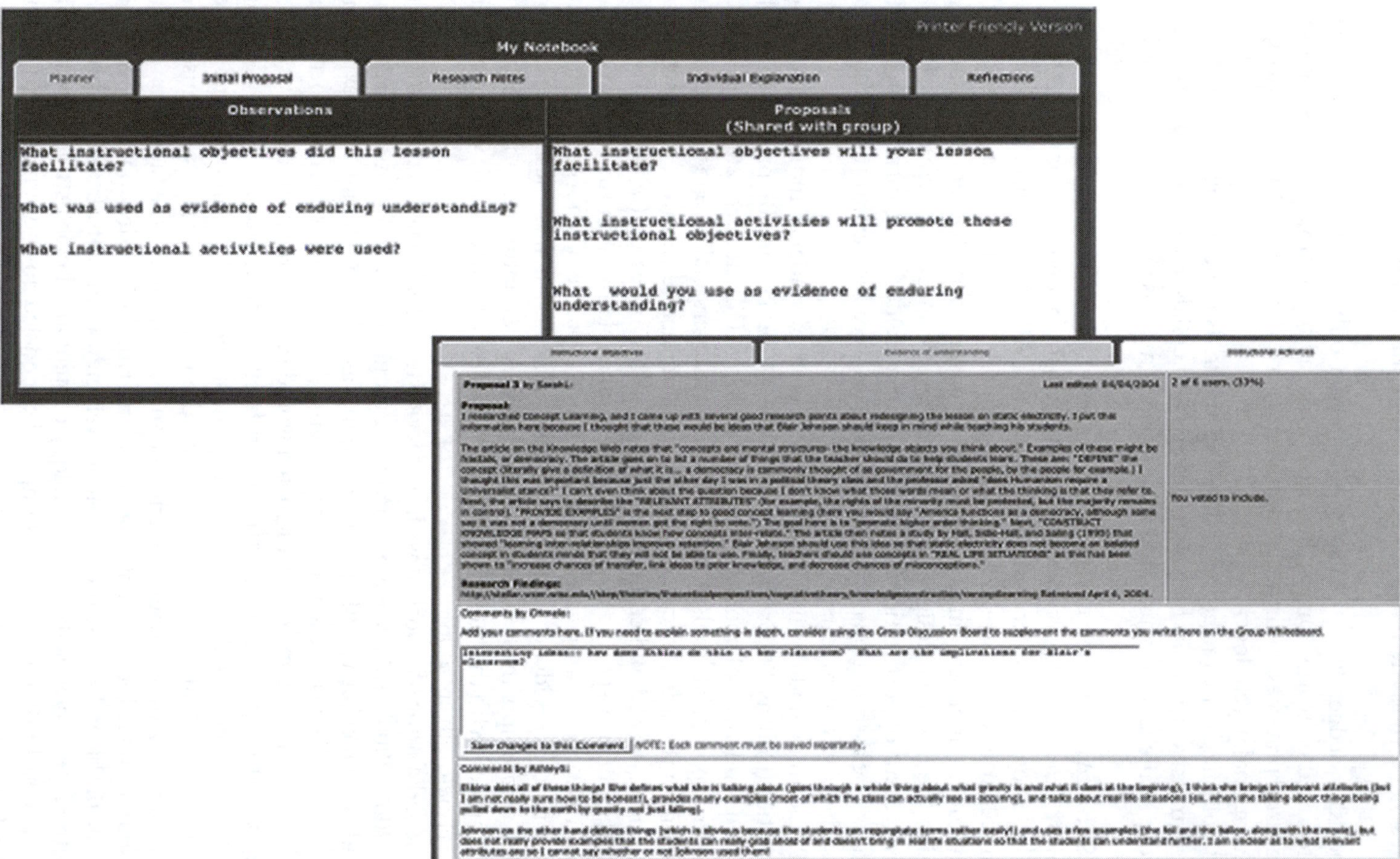

Figure 21.2 STELLAR Personal Notebook and Whiteboard

The facilitator probed group members' understanding of the PBL process and encouraged group members to ask further questions they might have about the content as it applied to the case. The rest of the class also had opportunities to ask questions about PBL process or content.

Subsequently, each newly trained person was assigned a small group where they modeled the PBL process. Expert facilitators rotated from group to group providing support and guidance as needed while students worked on a new problem. Groups were also given large sticky notes on which to write the facts and learning issues. Each group had a laptop computer to help with their SDL as well as a copy of their educational psychology text. Throughout the course process of helping students use PBL, the teacher conducted minilessons, which is a departure from the traditional model of PBL. Minilessons served the purpose of teaching a concept when the class as a whole needed the clarification or wanted to engage in a whole-class discussion. Conducting minilessons allowed students to listen to one another, discuss, and ask questions which could be shared with the rest of the class.

In addition, to foster collaboration among the PBL groups, the teacher provided group members with cue cards. Each cue card contained a question they could ask their group members in case they reached an impasse. The questions were guided by King's (1999) research on guided questioning. For example, one cue card asked a summarizing question such as "What are the main points so far?" Other cue cards presented a question that sought for clarification, such as "Can you provide me with another example?" "Would this be an example of what you are referring to?" and "I don't see how these two things relate? Can you explain it again?" Other recommended questions that picked up on a group member's idea, included: "Mike just said…what do we think about his idea given what is said in the case?" The purpose of these questions was to assist group members to probe one another's thinking by way of extending it. As group members became more comfortable asking each other questions, they were encouraged to further their dialogue by constructing their own probing questions that went beyond "yes" or "no" answers.

CONCLUSION

PBL is an approach to collaborative learning that situates learning in complex problems. It has been used for a range of grade levels and educational contexts. Although PBL uses complex problems as contexts for learning, there are a variety of supports for learning and collaboration that help students learn content, problem solving, and lifelong learning skills (Hmelo-Silver, Duncan, & Chinn, 2007). In addition to having a "groupworthy" problem, the facilitation helps keep the collaborative learning on track and supports productive collaboration. Representations such as the PBL whiteboard give the group a common focus for negotiation—it helps give the group a place to externalize their thinking and provides a concrete product for the group to jointly construct. We have illustrated two different adaptations of PBL in teacher education that provided additional supports for collaborative learning. Such supports include the use of technology-based scaffolding, peer facilitation, and just-in-time instruction. PBL can be challenging to manage because of large class size and varying levels of student commitment; it is nevertheless important to explore these adaptations to PBL as it is critical for these pedagogies to become adapted for all types of learners. Further research needs to examine how some of the instructional tools described elsewhere in this volume can support adaptation of PBL to the range of collaborative learning possibilities.

REFERENCES

Abrandt Dahlgren, M. & Dahlgren, L. O. (2002). Portraits of PBL: Students' experiences of the characteristics of problem-based learning in physiotherapy, computer engineering, and psychology. *Instructional Science. 30,* 111–127.

Albanese, M. A., & Mitchell, S. (1993). Problem-based learning: A review of literature on its outcomes and implementation issues. *Academic Medicine, 68,* 52–81.

Arvaja, M., Salovaara, H., Häkkinen, P., & Järvelä, S. (2007). Combining individual and group-level perspectives for studying collaborative knowledge construction in context. *Learning and Instruction, 17,* 448–459.

Barron, B. J. S. (2002). Achieving coordination in collaborative problem-solving groups. *Journal of the Learning Sciences. 9,* 403–437.

Barrows, H. S. (2000). *Problem-based learning applied to medical education.* Springfield, IL: Southern Illinois University Press.

Bereiter, C., & Scardamalia, M. (1989). Intentional learning as a goal of instruction. In L. B. Resnick (Ed.), *Knowing, learning, and instruction: Essays in honor of Robert Glaser* (pp. 361–392). Hillsdale NJ: Erlbaum.

Blumberg, P., & Michael, J. A. (1992). Development of self-directed learning behaviors in a partially teacher-directed problem-based learning curriculum. *Teaching and Learning in Medicine, 4,* 3–8.

Blumenfeld, P. C., Marx, R. W., Soloway, E., & Krajcik, J. S. (1996). Learning with peers: From small group cooperation to collaborative communities. *Educational Researcher, 25*(8), 37–40.

Bransford, J. D., Brown, A. L., & Cocking, R. (2000). *How people learn.* Washington, DC: National Academy Press.

Capon, N., & Kuhn, D. (2004). What's so good about problem-based learning? *Cognition and Instruction, 22,* 61–79.

Chi, M. T. H., Bassok, M., Lewis, M. W., Reimann, P., & Glaser, R. (1989). Self-explanations: How students study and use examples in learning to solve problems. *Cognitive Science, 13,* 145–182.

Chi, M. T. H., Feltovich, P., & Glaser, R. (1981). Categorization and representation of physics problems by experts and novices. *Cognitive Science, 5,* 121–152.

Cognition and Technology Group at Vanderbilt (CTGV). (1997). *The Jasper project: Lessons in curriculum, instruction, assessment, and professional development.* Mahwah NJ: Erlbaum.

Cohen, E. G. (1994). Restructuring the classroom: Conditions for productive small groups. *Review of Educational Research, 64,* 1–35.

Collins, A. (2006). Cognitive apprenticeship. In R. K. Sawyer (Ed.), *Cambridge handbook of the learning sciences* (pp. 47–60). New York: Cambridge University Press.

DeGrave, W. S., Boshuizen, H. P. A., & Schmidt, H. G. (1996). Problem-based learning: Cognitive and metacognitive processes during problem analysis. *Instructional Science, 24,* 321–341.

Derry, S. J., Hmelo-Silver, C. E., Nagarajan, A., Chernobilsky, E., & Beitzel, B. (2006). Cognitive transfer revisited: Can we exploit new media to solve old problems on a large scale? *Journal of Educational Computing Research, 35,* 145–162.

Derry, S. J., Levin, J. R., Osana, H. P., Jones, M. S., & Peterson, M. (2000). Fostering students' statistical and scientific thinking: Lessons learned from an innovative college course. *American Educational Research Journal, 37,* 747–773.

De Simone, C. (2008). Problem-based learning: A framework for prospective teachers' pedagogical problem solving. *Teacher Development*, 12, 179–191.

De Simone, C. (2009). Problem-based learning and prospective teachers: Implications for problem solving and practice. *Journal on Excellence in College Teaching, 20,* 143–159.

Dillenbourg, P. (2002). Over-scripting CSCL: The risks of blending collaborative learning with instructional design. In P. A. Kirschner (Ed.), *Three worlds of CSCL* (pp. 61–91). Heerlen, Netherlands: Open Universitat Nederland.

Ertmer, P. A., & Simons, K. D. (2006). Jumping the PBL implementation hurdle: Supporting the efforts of K-12 teachers. *Interdisciplinary Journal of Problem-based Learning, 1,* 1–15.

Ertmer, P., Newby, T., & MacDougall, M. (1996). Students' responses and approaches to case-based instruction: The role of reflective self-regulation. *American Educational Research Journal, 33,* 719–752.

Evensen, D. (2000). Observing self-directed learners in a problem-based learning context: Two case studies. In D. Evensen & C. E. Hmelo (Eds.), *Problem-based learning: A research perspective on learning interactions* (pp. 263–298). Mahwah, NJ: Erlbaum.

Evensen, D. H., Salisbury-Glennon, J., & Glenn, J. (2001). A qualitative study of 6 medical students in a problem-based curriculum: Towards a situated model of self-regulation. *Journal of Educational Psychology, 93,* 659–676.

Gallagher, S., & Stepien, W. (1996). Content acquisition in problem-based learning: Depth versus breadth in American studies. *Journal for the Education of the Gifted, 19*, 257–275.

Gijbels, D., Dochy, F., Van den Bossche, P., & Segers, M. (2005). Effects of problem-based learning: A meta-analysis from the angle of assessment. *Review of Educational Research, 75*, 27–61.

Goodman, L. J., Erich, E., Brueschke, E. E., Bone, R. C., Rose, W. H., Williams, E. J., & Paul, H. A. (1991). An experiment in medical education: A critical analysis using traditional criteria. *Journal of the American Medical Association, 265*, 2373–2376.

Gressick, J., & Derry, S. J. (2010). Distributed leadership in online groups. *International Journal of Computer Supported Collaborative Learning, 5*, 211–236.

Herrenkohl, L. R., & Guerra, M. R. (1998). Participant structures, scientific discourse, and student engagement in fourth grade. *Cognition and Instruction, 16*, 431–473.

Hmelo, C. E. (1998). Problem-based learning: Effects on the early acquisition of cognitive skill in medicine. *Journal of the Learning Sciences, 7*, 173–208.

Hmelo, C. E., Holton, D., & Kolodner, J. L. (2000). Designing to learn about complex systems. *Journal of the Learning Sciences, 9*, 247–298.

Hmelo, C. E., & Lin, X. (2000). The development of self-directed learning strategies in problem-based learning. In D. Evensen & C. E. Hmelo (Eds.), *Problem-based learning: Research perspectives on learning interactions* (pp. 227–250). Mahwah, NJ: Erlbaum.

Hmelo, C. E., Shikano, T., Bras, B., Mulholland, J., Realff, M., & Vanegas, J. (1995). A problem-based course in sustainable technology. In D. Budny, R. Herrick, G. Bjedov, & J. B. Perry (Eds.), *Frontiers in education 1995* [CD]. Washington, DC: American Society for Engineering Education.

Hmelo-Silver, C. (2000). Knowledge recycling: Crisscrossing the landscape of educational psychology in a problem-based learning course for preservice teachers. *Journal on Excellence in College Teaching, 11*, 41–56.

Hmelo-Silver, C. E. (2004). Problem-based learning: What and how do students learn? *Educational Psychology Review, 16*, 235–266.

Hmelo-Silver, C. E. (2006). Design principles for scaffolding technology-based inquiry. In A. M. O'Donnell, C. E. Hmelo-Silver, & G. Erkens (Eds.), *Collaborative learning, reasoning, and technology* (pp. 147-170). Mahwah, NJ: Erlbaum.

Hmelo-Silver, C. E., & Barrows, H. S. (2006). Goals and strategies of a problem-based learning facilitator. *Interdisciplinary Journal of Problem-Based Learning, 1*, 21–39.

Hmelo-Silver, C. E., & Barrows, H. S. (2008). Facilitating collaborative knowledge building. *Cognition and Instruction, 26*, 48–94.

Hmelo-Silver, C. E., Chernobilsky, E., & Nagarajan, A. (2009). Two sides of the coin: Multiple perspectives on collaborative knowledge construction in online problem-based learning. In K. Kumpulainen, C. E. Hmelo-Silver, & M. César (Eds.), *Investigating classroom interaction: Methodologies in action* (pp. 73–98). Boston, MA: Sense.

Hmelo-Silver, C. E., Derry, S. J., Bitterman, A. H., & Hatrak, N. (2009). Targeting transfer in a STELLAR PBL course for pre-service teachers. *Interdisciplinary Journal of Problem-Based Learning, 3*(2), 24–42.

Hmelo-Silver, C. E., Duncan, R. G., & Chinn, C. A. (2007). Scaffolding and achievement in problem-based and inquiry learning: A response to Kirschner, Sweller, and Clark (2006). *Educational Psychologist, 42*, 99–107.

Hmelo-Silver, C.E., Katic, E., Nagarajan, A., & Chernobilsky, E. (2007). Soft leaders, hard artifacts, and the groups we rarely see: Using video to understand peer learning processes. In R. Goldman, R. Pea, B. Barron, & S. Derry (Eds.), *Video research in the learning sciences* (pp. 255–270). Mahwah, NJ: Erlbaum.

Jeong, H., & Hmelo-Silver, C. E. (2010). Productive use of learning resources in an online problem-based learning environment. *Computers and Human Behavior, 26*, 84–99.

Jonassen, D., & Hung, W. (2008). All problems are not equal: Implications for problem-based learning. *Interdisciplinary Journal of Problem-Based Learning, 2*(2), 6–28.

Kapur, M., & Kinzer, C. K. (2007). Examining the effect of problem type in a synchronous computer-supported collaborative learning (CSCL) environment. *Educational Technology Research and Development, 55*, 439–459.

King, A. (1999). Discourse patterns for mediating peer learning. In A. M. O'Donnell & A. King (Eds.), *Cognitive perspectives on peer learning* (pp. 87–117). Mahwah, NJ: Erlbaum.

Kolodner, J. L. (1993). *Case-based reasoning.* San Mateo, CA: Morgan Kaufmann.

Kolodner, J. L., Hmelo, C. E., & Narayanan, N. H. (1996). Problem-based learning meets case-based reasoning. In D. C. Edelson & E. A. Domeshek (Eds.), *Proceedings of ICLS 96* (pp. 188–195). Charlottesville, VA: AACE.

Koschmann, T. D., Myers, A. C., Feltovich, P. J., & Barrows, H. S. (1994). Using technology to assist in realizing effective learning and instruction: A principled approach to the use of computers in collaborative learning. *Journal of the Learning Sciences, 3*, 225–262.

Leary, H., Walker, A. E., Fitt, H., & Shelton, B. E. (2009). *Expert versus novice tutors: Impacts on student outcomes in problem-based learning.* Paper presented at the Annual Meeting of the American Educational Research Association. San Diego, CA.

Loyens, S. M. M., Magda, J., & Rikers, R. M. J. P. (2008). Self-directed learning in problem-based and its relationships with self-regulated learning. *Educational Psychology Review, 20,* 411–427.

Mennin, S. P., Friedman, M., Skipper, B., Kalishman, S., & Snyder, J. (1993). Performances on the NBME I, II, and III by medical students in the problem-based and conventional tracks at the University of New Mexico. *Academic Medicine, 68,* 616–624.

Mergendoller, J. R., Maxwell, N. L., & Bellisimo, Y. (2006). The effectiveness of problem-based instruction: A comparative study of instructional method and student characteristics. *Interdisciplinary Journal of Problem-based Learning, 1,* 49–69.

O'Donnell, A. M. (1999). Structuring dyadic interaction through scripted cooperation. In A. M. O'Donnell & A. King (Eds.), *Cognitive perspectives on peer learning* (pp. 179–196). Mahwah, NJ: Erlbaum.

O'Donnell, A. M. (2004). Shared and unshared knowledge: The collaborative analysis of a classroom case by pre-service teachers. In J. van der Linden & P. Renshaw (Eds.), *Dialogic learning: Shifting perspectives to learning, instruction, and teaching* (pp. 233–250). Dordrecht, Netherlands: Kluwer Academic Press.

O'Donnell, A. M. (2006). The role of peers and group learning. In P. Alexander & P. Winne (Eds.), *Handbook of educational psychology* (2nd ed., pp. 781–202). Mahwah, NJ: Erlbaum.

O'Mahony, K., Vye, N. J., Bransford, J. D., Stevens, R., Lin, K., Ritchey, M. C., … Soleiman, M. K. (2012). Learning and collaboration in fast changing environments. *Journal of the Learning Sciences, 21,* 182–206.

Palincsar, A. S., & Herrenkohl, L. R. (1999). Designing collaborative contexts: Lessons from three research programs. In A. M. O'Donnell & A. King (Eds.), *Cognitive perspectives on peer learning* (pp. 151–178). Mahwah, NJ: Erlbaum.

Patel, V. L., Groen, G. J., & Norman, G.R. (1993). Reasoning and instruction in medical curricula. *Cognition & Instruction, 10,* 335–378.

Pea, R. D. (1993). Practices of distributed intelligence and designs for education. In G. Salomon & D. Perkins (Eds.), *Distributed cognitions* (pp. 47-87). New York: Cambridge University Press.

Perfetto, G. A., Bransford, J. D., & Franks, J. J. (1983). Constraints on access in a problem-solving context. *Memory & Cognition, 11,* 24–31.

Puntambekar, S., & Kolodner, J. L. (1998). The design diary: A tool to support students in learning science by design. In A. S. Bruckman, M. Guzdial, J. Kolodner, & A. Ram (Eds.), *Proceedings of ICLS 98* (pp. 230–236). Charlottesville, VA: AACE.

Salomon, G. (1993). No distribution without individual cognition: A dynamic interactional view. In G. Salomon & D. Perkins (Eds.), *Distributed cognitions* (pp. 111–38). New York: Cambridge University Press.

Salomon, G., & Perkins, D. N. (1989). Rocky roads to transfer: Rethinking mechanisms of a neglected phenomenon. *Educational Psychologist, 24,* 113–142.

Schmidt, H. G, DeVolder, M. L., De Grave, W. S., Moust, J. H. C., & Patel, V. L. (1989). Explanatory models in the processing of science text: The role of prior knowledge activation through small-group discussion. *Journal of Educational Psychology, 81,* 610–619.

Schmidt, H. G., Loyens, S. M. M., van Gog, T., & Paas, F. (2007). Problem-based learning is compatible with human cognitive architecture: Commentary on Kirschner, Sweller, & Clark (2006). *Educational Psychologist, 42,* 91–97.

Schmidt, H. G., Machiels-Bongaerts, M., Hermans, H., ten Cate, T. J., Venekamp, R., & Boshuizen, H. P. A. (1996). The development of diagnostic competence: Comparison of a problem-based, an integrated, and a conventional medical curriculum. *Academic Medicine, 71,* 658–664.

Schmidt, H. G., & Moust, J. H. C. (2000). Factors affecting small-group tutorial learning: A review of research. In D. Evensen & C. E. Hmelo (Eds.), *Problem-based learning: A research perspective on learning interactions* (pp. 19–51). Mahwah, NJ: Erlbaum.

Schmidt, H. G., van der Molen, H. T., te Winkel, W. R., & Wijnen, W. H. F. W. (2009). Constructivist, problem-based learning does work: A meta-analysis of curricular comparisons involving a single medical school. *Educational Psychologist, 44,* 227–249.

Torp, L., & Sage, S. (2002). *Problems as possibilities: Problem-based learning for k-12 education* (2nd ed.). Alexandria, VA: ASCD.

Van Berkel, H. J. M., & Schmidt, H. G. (2000). Motivation to commit oneself as a determinant of achievement in problem-based learning. *Higher Education, 40,* 231–242.

Vernon, D. T., & Blake, R. L. (1993). Does problem-based learning work? A meta-analysis of evaluative research. *Academic Medicine, 68,* 550–563.

Vye, N., Goldman, S., Voss, J., Hmelo, C., & Williams, S. (1997). Complex math problem- solving by individuals and dyads: When and why are two heads better than one? *Cognition and Instruction, 15,* 435–484.

Walker, A. E., & Leary, H. (2009). A problem based learning meta analysis: Differences across problem types, implementation types, disciplines, and assessment levels. *Interdisciplinary Journal of Problem-Based Learning, 3*, 12–43.

Wiggins, G., & McTighe, J. (1998). *Understanding by design*. Alexandria, VA: ASCD.

Yew, E. H. J., & Schmidt, H. G. (2009). Evidence for constructive, self-regulatory and collaborative processes in problem-based learning. *Advances in Health Sciences Education, 14*, 251–273.

Zhang, M., Lundeberg, M., & Eberhardt, J. (2011). Strategic facilitation of problem-based discussion for teacher professional development. *Journal of the Learning Sciences, 20*. doi: 10.1080/10508406.2011.553258

Zhang, M., Lundeberg, M., Koehler, M., & Eberhardt, J. (2008). *Conditions for collaborative knowledge construction of in-service science teachers in problem-based professional development*. Paper presented at the Annual Meeting of the National Association for Research in Science Teaching.

Zhang, M., Lundeberg, M., McConnell, T., Koehler, M., & Eberhardt, J. (2010). Using questioning to facilitate discussion of science teaching problems in teacher professional development. *Interdisciplinary Journal of Problem-Based Learning, 4*(1), 57–82.

Zimmerman, B. (2002). Becoming a self-regulated learner: An overview. *Theory Into Practice, 41*, 64–71

Zimmerman, B. J., & Lebeau, R. (2000). A commentary on self-directed learning. In D. Evensen & C. E. Hmelo (Eds.), *Problem-based Learning: A research perspective on learning interactions* (pp. 299–313). Mahwah, NJ: Erlbaum.

IV

Technology and Collaborative Learning

22

DESIGNING COLLABORATIVE LEARNING THROUGH COMPUTER SUPPORT

VANESSA P. DENNEN

Florida State University

CHRISTOPHER HOADLEY

New York University

INTRODUCTION

Collaborative learning with technology is more than the use of some tool; rather, it requires careful design of not only tools, but also the learning activities and settings in which those tools take place. Computer-supported collaborative learning is distinguished by the use of technology to support collaborative learning, as well as by a history of examining not only the design of technology tools but also by the design of learning environments, including such aspects as curriculum or even more emergent aspects such as facilitated student-driven inquiry. In this chapter, we discuss theories, principles, and techniques for designing computer-supported collaborative learning environments. In the next section, we examine the role of instructional theories and provide several examples. Following that, we examine some of the designed elements of CSCL and the settings in which it may be implemented. Finally, we discuss some of the design models used in creating CSCL environments.

THEORETICAL UNDERPINNINGS OF COLLABORATIVE LEARNING DESIGN

The first section of this volume has focused on understanding learning theories that attempt to explain collaborative learning. In this chapter, we acknowledge the role of these theories in designing CSCL, but we also begin to focus on instructional theories. Unlike learning theories, instructional theories may be silent on what learning involves or *how* a set of conditions leads to learning, but they must make a strong statement on what is to be done in order to foster a particular type of learning. Bruner (1966) initially proposed theories of instruction as requiring a mode of motivating a learner, a content structure and sequence, and an incentive structure for learners. However, in more recent work, especially in collaborative learning, the idea of a theory of instruction has evolved away from predefined content structures and sequences, and instead toward systems in which content is explored through defined processes, prioritizations of key generative concepts which might be realized differently when driven by knowledge-building principles (Scardamalia & Bereiter, 2006), or knowledge integration processes (Bell & Linn, 2000). Indeed, collaborative learning poses a challenge in some sense for the term *instruction* if, instead, the goal is to construct an environment where students learn from and with each other instead of through direct instruction by a teacher. The field of instructional systems design has broadened the sense of the term *instruction* explicitly to encompass some of these ideas (Reiser, 2012).

Collaborative learning design strategies are not contingent upon one specific learning theory. Designers may have theoretical preferences, but just having a theory is not adequate and design considerations are needed. In any instructional experience, it is likely that the participants are learning in a way that contains elements explained by a variety of learning theories. While a sociocultural learning theorist might explain the learning here in terms of Vygotsky's zone of proximal development (Vygotsky, 1974) or a sociocognitivist might explain it in terms of cognitive apprenticeship (Collins, Brown, & Newman, 1989), the information-processing theorists may focus on attention, memory, and cognitive load. It is unlikely that any one learning theory is the best way to explain every aspect of a learning situation. Even if one particular learning theory offers the most comfortable fit to explain some aspect of learning, other theories can often be used to explain the same outcomes and processes.

Although there are many instructional theories and approaches, it is useful to examine a few examples in order to better understand the role of instructional theories for designing collaborative learning. Below, we discuss four instructional theories as examples with relevance to design: Reciprocal teaching and the jigsaw approach; the problem-based learning model; the communities of practice model; and the knowledge-building communities model. Each of these models provides a vision for how to structure a collaborative learning environment such that it will lead to learning.

The jigsaw method (Aronson & Yates, 1983) and reciprocal teaching (Palincsar & Brown, 1984), both used extensively in the communities of learners model (Brown & Campione, 1996; see also Bielaczyc, Kapur, & Collins, chapter 13 this volume), are methods used to structure collaborative learning. In the jigsaw method, learners are given a problem requiring information that they themselves do not possess. The problem is broken down into different parts, and individual students from different groups are assigned to different areas in which they work in "expert" groups. Finally, the group reconvenes to share expertise across team members, and the problem can be solved only with the contributions of each member. Because each person's contribution is essential to the shared solution, learners are both motivated to develop their expertise and respected for that expertise.

Reciprocal teaching also involves students teaching other students in collaborative groups. In reciprocal teaching, students engage in cooperative activities in learning from text and employ four key strategies including summarizing, question generating, clarifying, and prediction. Initially, the teacher models the use of these reading strategies for students, and then the students take on the role of the teacher, leading the group to use these strategies to construct the text meaning. Students take turns leading the group with different pieces of text; the learners model, observe, and practice, working collaboratively with the teacher and peers.

Problem-based learning, first popularized by Barrows and Tamblyn (1980; see also Hmelo-Silver & DeSimone, chapter 21 this volume), is an instructional model in which students are expected to learn through group work in attempting to solve real-life problems with the support of a facilitator. A key part of the model is the idea that if students iteratively identify knowledge gaps required to solve the problem, and then attempt to remediate those gaps with reference to authoritative sources, the students will not only become exposed to content but will internalize it in a way that is highly practicable and not inert. In addition, PBL attempts to support the development of high-level lifelong learning skills and other appropriate problem-solving strategies that might be more transferable (Hmelo-Silver, 2004). PBL relies on collaboration among learner-peers as a key part of helping assemble problem-relevant information, identifying and negotiating strategies, and identifying knowledge gaps. In the PBL model, the teacher models problem-solving processes, supports knowledge finding and gap identification, and facilitates a process of not only problem solving but also reflection and knowledge construction (Hmelo-Silver, 2004; Hmelo-Silver & De Simone, chapter 21 this volume).

Communities of practice are social communities of individuals who share a set of core practices, rather than an interest or a background (Lave & Wenger, 1991; Orr, 1990). Lave and Wenger identified naturally occurring communities of practice, and demonstrated how individuals move from peripheral to central participation in the practices of the community, and used this notion to define learning as the adoption of social practices. Moving from naturally occurring communities of practice to deliberate ones, often fostered by technology, is a process Wenger, McDermott, and Snyder (2002) called "cultivation," in which learning is fostered by connecting individuals with similar problems to solve; sharing, documenting, and validating what they know and do; and applying these ideas to shared or individual problems, only to repeat the cycle again. Wenger advocated seven dimensions important for communities of practice: designing for evolution (allowing the community to evolve rather than trying to micromanage it), beginning dialogues between "inside" and "outside" perspectives, inviting multiple levels of participation, developing both private and public community spaces, providing incentives or value for participants, combining familiarity and excitement (or routine and novel practices), and establishing regular rhythms of activity within the community. The goal of a community of practice does not focus on supporting knowledge application; collaboration is for developing shared practice and for acculturating participants to become members of the community.

Another model focusing on community is the knowledge-building community (Scardamalia & Bereiter, 1994, 2006; see Chan, chapter 25 this volume). Rather than solving problems collaboratively or developing shared practices, like communities of practice, knowledge-building communities emphasize collective cognitive responsibility in which all participants share responsibility for advancing the community's collective knowledge, often mediated by Knowledge Forum, a computer-supported collaborative learning environment. Knowledge-building environments support intentional learning and epistemic agency as students collectively pursue knowledge (Scardamalia & Bereiter, 2006). Unlike traditional classrooms, knowledge-building communities are driven by the problems generated by the learners and emphasize the promotion of higher levels of collective epistemic agency among learners. Student-generated problems are objects of inquiry as students work collectively to generate explanations, supported with authoritative information, to continually improve their theories. For example, a learner could post a computer note with the scaffold, "I need to understand," followed by another student posting a note with the scaffolds "my theory" and "new information" to tackle the problem. Different computer notes may consist of questions, theories, results of an experiment, and additional questions, and students may put a scaffold "putting our knowledge together" to track how the community has made advances (see Chan, chapter 25 this volume). Knowledge-building communities have been explored in a wide range of school settings, in which teachers serve as coinvestigators and set broad parameters for the inquiry processes. The goal is to help learners work on creating and improving their knowledge, similar to scientists working on creating new knowledge; students are to become more responsible for managing their collaborative learning and democratizing knowledge, rather than focusing on authoritative sources for knowledge (Scardamalia, 2003).

What these four examples show is a variety of approaches for developing instruction, using collaborative learning in a way that might be supported by technology (though not all of these examples necessarily use technology). Typically, instructional designers are concerned with validating learning needs, learning goals, and objectives; with sequencing content and determining optimal presentation and engagement strategies for the content; and with providing learners with predefined assessment feedback to drive their learning. In contrast, these four examples demonstrate an openness toward learning goals and objectives; a willingness to let different forms of collaboration determine the sequence of ideas, usually building on prior conceptions of learners; and on using more social or open-ended forms of assessment. For example, assessment in a jigsaw classroom might rely on being able to explain a concept to peers or use it to help solve part of a joint problem; in a PBL classroom, sequencing might come from aspects of a particular authentic problem, and so on. Thus, one way to examine how to design CSCL environments is not to focus on the particular recommendations of one instructional theory (indeed, several of these theories are covered in much greater detail elsewhere in this handbook). Importantly, the design of CSCL is not to define a specific learning theory or a content domain to be covered and the optimal way to cover it. Instead, CSCL instructional theories often specify roles, norms, values, or other process-oriented aspects of the learning environment. The CSCL designer gives up control of many instructional choices that would be normal in the traditional design of a noncollaborative learning environment. In exchange, the designer can tap into powerful (if unpredictable) social processes to help drive learning. Below, we discuss some of the types of decisions that are within the purview of a designer of CSCL.

DESIGNED ELEMENTS OF COLLABORATIVE LEARNING

Collaborative learning designers, whether instructional designers and technologists creating materials and programs to be used by others, or classroom teachers who are preparing lessons for their own students, must consider various elements of the learning experience during their design process. Some of these are the standard elements one might expect to be designed for any instruction, whereas others are specific to the collaborative process and are intended to help ensure it is a productive and effective one. Although discussed separately for the sake of clarity, the elements are systemic and synergistic in nature; changes to one will impact the others, and the best designs are those that are able to make the elements work in harmony with each other. Below, we consider several designed elements of CSCL environments: (a) the learning goals, (b) the collaborative premise, (c) group assignment and composition, (d) assigned or emerging roles, (e) discourse norms or values, (f) collaboration scripts or sequences of activity, and (g) types of facilitation and motivational inputs such as incentives.

Learning Goals. Learning goals set the stage for the rest of the learning experience. Without clear learning goals, the rest of the learning experience is difficult to design. Ideally, learning goals are stated in terms of learner outcomes, not activities. From learning goals develops a sense of alignment for the rest of the learning experience; each subsequent element may be checked against the goals to ensure that the element—whether an activity, resource, or instruction—remains consistent with the goals. In CSCL, goals that go beyond the acquisition of fixed skills or propositional knowledge are important; for example, goals such as developing a capacity for inquiry, or content goals that may be more flexible than those a fixed curriculum would produce. A CSCL learning goal might be to understand systemic connections in ecosystems generally, as opposed to a more inflexible and objectively measurable learning goal such as being able to recall a list of the predators of one species in one specific ecosystem on a test.

Sometimes learning designers begin with a stated goal around which they must plan instruction, but at other times designers will begin with an idea for an activity that is interesting or compelling to them and may not have a stated goal. However, within any activity, implicit learning goals can be found. By making those implicit goals explicit, a designer can determine if the goals truly represent their intent and the needs of their learner audience, and whether or not a particular design is succeeding.

Collaborative Premise. The collaborative premise is the very reason for engaging learners in a collaborative process and should be made clear to the learners, who need to know why they are supposed to collaborate. The premise should express clearly what value might emerge from their collaborative work, why their interdependence will be an important part of the learning process or their personal incentive structures, in what ways they will be interdependent, and how the very act of collaboration relates to the learning goals. If these things cannot be articulated to the learners, then the collaborative premise is likely to be weak. Some approaches, such as PBL, gaming, and scenario-based learning, lend themselves directly to a premise; the collaboration might lead directly to a shared outcome or goal. Other instructional approaches might require more direct or intentional premise development; for example, if a teacher directs students to discuss a reading in an online discussion board without giving further guidance, the learners may wonder whether their goal is to summarize their thoughts, have their own questions (if any) answered, or create a shared understanding of key features of the reading. At times learners may be resistant, feeling that they could be more successful or efficient on their own. The collaborative premise, however, should motivate them to work together. This is related closely to other elements, such as group assignments, designed roles, and work processes.

Group Assignment and Composition. A group assignment should be a deliberate decision, typically specifying both the size and composition of collaborative groups. Size is critical because too small a group may result in limited opportunities for collaboration or too much work and too large a group may make it difficult for learners to form a collaborative vision (Strijbos, Martens, & Jochems, 2004). Additionally, group size may vary during the course of a collaborative learning project, with larger groups forming or smaller ones splintering off (and even individual time being encouraged or provided) as appropriate to the specific activity or task (Dillenbourg, 2002).

Group composition—specifically, the relative homogeneity or heterogeneity of a collaborative group—is also necessary to consider. Certain activities will work better when groups are of similar ability levels, while others will benefit from diverse abilities or talents (Blumenfeld, Marx, Soloway, & Krajcik, 1996; Webb, Nemer, Chizhik, & Sugrue, 1998). Even in a homogenous ability group, the zones of proximal development for individual learners will vary somewhat, and learners will need to be able to support each other's learning via peer scaffolding in order to collaborate successfully (Borthick & Jones, 2003). Other group composition factors to consider include age, gender (Dillenbourg, 2002), and even self-efficacy beliefs, which have been found to impact group motivation (S.-L.Wang & Lin, 2007).

If designers anticipate or plan for cross-cultural collaborative groups then this aspect of group composition should be considered during the design process. Cross-cultural groups may face initial challenges on the path to successful collaboration (Liu, Liu, Lee, & Magjuka, 2010; C. M. Wang, 2011). In particular, groups composed of culturally diverse learners may need specific guidance regarding roles, expectations, and how the group members might best work together.

In some circumstances a designer may decide not to specify group assignments for specific reasons (e.g., if one important learning goal is for learners to develop skills in leadership or team formation), but even within this realm, the decision to not specify group assignment will undoubtedly impact upon the collaboration, and the instructor will need to convey the parameters in which the group assignment is to take place.

Roles. Designed roles can provide learners with a structure or direction to guide their collaboration by telling learners what part each will play in the collaboration. Imagine five people placed in a group and provided with a general outcome, such as a written document. Given such an assignment, with no additional oversight or direction, the learners may embark on any number of paths to completion. They could take a divide and conquer approach, each working alone on a section of the end product. They could work on each part together, negotiating every decision along the way. Or they might have one or two group members take over and do the entire assignment, controlling the process and not providing opportunities for, or encouraging participation of, their fellow learners. These approaches vary in their efficiency as well as their degree of collaboration and the evenness of learning experience for different group members. Research by De Wever, Schellens, Van Keer, and Valcke (2008) showed that students, by and large, do take up roles as assigned to them, and the previously mentioned reciprocal teaching model has demonstrated some of the power of assigning teacher roles for supporting learning. Even when learners are not given differentiated roles, the teacher's overall expectations for their roles should be made clear.

Norms. Also important is stating expectations or establishing norms for the types of interactions learners are supposed to have. Interactions among learners should not be assumed, no matter how structured or suggestive the learning tools may be (Kreijns, Kirschner, & Jochems, 2003). Left to their own devices, without explicit expectations, learners may focus quite narrowly on their own contributions to the outcome and fail to engage fully or collaborate with their peers (Wheeler, Yeomans, & Wheeler, 2008). These participation expectations are best stated by the instructional designer, who holds the initial vision for the collaborative activity. An instructor may then alter them as necessary to fit a given context, but will at least be working from a plan.

Collaboration Scripts. One method that designers use to structure collaboration is the use of collaborative scripts (see Fischer, Kollar, Stegmann, Wecker, & Zottmann, chapter 22 this volume). Scripts vary in their specificity, but what they describe is an ordering of events or activities, usually implying roles that are to be taken during those events or activities. Some scripts are quite linear, specifying a fixed sequence of activities or tasks, sometimes even with gate-keeping functions that control when one activity may give way to the next: for example, the jigsaw teaching sequence. On the other hand, very loose scripts may allow spiral or looping orderings of activities or events, where learners may at any time decide to move in and out of information-gathering activities or agenda-setting activities or reflection activities. A general notion of a cycle of inquiry may be present, but it is not rigidly linear or even a cyclical sequence of tasks in time.

Facilitation and Motivation. Collaborative learning, although focused heavily on learner–learner interactions, is not teacherless learning. Teachers play an important role in the collaborative process, facilitating learners by monitoring their progress and providing support, guidance, and feedback as needed. Collaborative learning designs need to include guidance for teachers on both how best to facilitate the learning process for their students and how to adapt the learning tools and activities as needed in their own context (Dillenbourg, Järvelä, & Fischer, 2009). Interactions among learners need to be fostered (Kreijns et al., 2003), and the learning designer specifies what these interactions should look like and makes recommendations for how collaborative learners might be supported.

Designers also should consider motivational elements of the learning situation, both intrinsic motivation and extrinsic incentives. Motivational elements are not separate unto themselves, but rather may be integrated into various other elements of the design. For example, allowing learners to engage in self-selection when forming groups may be motivating (Q. Wang, 2009), although other grouping variables and how group composition might impact upon collaborative success should be considered as well. Competitive versus cooperative reward structures can be considered (Johnson, Johnson, & Stanne, 1986). Grading, of course, is not the only extrinsic motivation structure; agency or intrinsic motivation can be harnessed. For example, allowing collaborative groups to have some choice in the topics they work on can help increase their motivation (Q. Wang, 2009). Additionally, reputation is often cited as one of the motivators of participants in open-source communities. Finally, the instructors also play an important role in motivating learners, and they must be sufficiently able to support learners as they interact with and through collaborative technologies (Dennen & Bonk, 2007).

One last point bears emphasis: the choices made by the designer may be applied uniformly across learners, or applied differentially, but, regardless, learners differ from each other, and therefore variability should be expected in the impacts of design choices. Learning control is one such consideration. Not all learners should be able to have a high degree of control; the appropriateness and degree of learner control may vary according to the learner's age and expertise (Lowyck & Pöysä, 2001). In this case, variable levels of control might help to accommodate the needs of a wide range of learners, but even customizing the level of control is unlikely to produce homogenous outcomes. In short, variation among learners needs to be considered when designers make decisions about the collaboration aspects we have described above.

DESIGN FOR DIFFERENT SETTINGS

Designing collaborative learning requires a departure from more traditional instructional design in a variety of ways. Historically, instructional design has focused on learners as individuals and consequently has been concerned with individual outcomes, whereas collaborative learning also requires consideration of the group and its outcomes (Gros, 2001). These two processes need not be at odds. The collaborative process has necessitated a shift from thinking about instructional design as an activity with causal outcomes to an activity with probabilistic outcomes (Kirschner, Strijbos, Kreijns, & Beers, 2004). The uncertainty about outcomes is necessary given the uncertainty of human interactions.

Whatever one is designing and for whatever setting, context is a critical factor to consider. As Tessmer and Richey (1997, p. 88) pointed out, "Instructional designs can accommodate context, but cannot control it." In other words, the task at hand requires flexibility, as the designer negotiates between instructional ideals and real-world users and conditions. Further, what works in one setting may not work in another, creating what Alvino, Asensio-Perez, Dimitriadis, and Hernandez-Leo (2009) termed the script instantiation problem. This problem occurs when one designer tries to adopt another's CSCL scripts—although really the problem could affect the reuse of any designed instructional element—and fails to consider the differences fully in context from one setting to the next. This adoption process, in effect, recontextualizes the instruction and may result in a less effective learning experience or a drift from the learning objectives unless context-appropriate modifications are made.

This issue of control is not to be underestimated. Instructional designers may wish to feel that they have control over their designs, but the design cycle is not truly complete until the design is implemented and evaluated. Hoadley (2010) discussed this issue in the context of CSCL scripts, noting that the enactment of a design may not match the initial intent. In the end teachers and learners will adapt lesson plans, software programs, and learning materials to suit their own specific goals and purposes.

For designers, the most practical approach is probably to focus but not fixate on their goals. The end function that a collaborative learning design needs to serve has been stated quite clearly by Dillenbourg, Järvelä, and Fischer (2009, p. 6), "to create conditions in which effective group interactions are expected to occur." This statement fits collaborative learning in any setting, and thus across settings the designer must determine how the medium will impact or shape group interactions.

Face-to-Face Collaborative Settings

In a face-to-face setting, collaborative learning requires, at a minimum, a plan that details what should be learned (learning objectives), ground rules for how learners should interact, what types of activities may be used to achieve these objectives, and desired outcomes. The specification of process (activities) and product (outcomes) may vary in detail depending on the objectives, the learning domain, the learners, and the facilitator.

Computer-Supported Collaborative Settings

In the context of designing learning, computer-supported collaborative learning is a broad category. Although learning *with* (i.e., in face-to-face settings) and *through* (i.e., in computer-mediated settings) computers are both means through which CSCL may occur, they are sufficiently different practices and require separate discussion.

Learning with Computers. CSCL in face-to-face settings is dependent on the interplay of rules, roles, and tasks; collectively these elements should elicit a desired interaction among the learners (Zurita & Nussbaum, 2004). An additional actor in the collaborative context is the computer, and designers need to consider how interactions will be changed or shaped by the technology. For instance, technology maybe used to attempt to emulate or enhance typical face-to-face interaction, or may be used to try to subvert it in specific ways; for instance, technology might permit anonymity even in face-to-face settings (Hsi & Hoadley, 1997). The designer should specify when and how learners will make use of the computer, noting if they will need to share or take turns, select a person to use it, or if each learner will each have his or her own computer.

CSCL-specific tools are often designed to support the social processes on which successful collaborative learning is dependent. However, in practice, their designs often fall short (Kreijns et al., 2003). While tool design and features are important, they must be aligned effectively with a task, with learners following role-based guidelines and facilitated at a context-appropriate level.

Mobile computer supported collaborative learning (MCSCL) builds off the original concepts of CSCL with the addition of portability, allowing CSCL activities to take place in the field rather than just in classrooms and computer labs (see Looi, Wong, & Song, chapter 24 this volume). Mobile devices have been used to facilitate collaboration in a wide variety of contexts, with examples ranging from classrooms at all levels (Evans & Johri, 2008; Roschelle, Rafanan, Estrella, Nussbaum, & Claro, 2010) to museums and field experiences (Sharples, Arnedillo-Sánchez, Milrad, & Vavoula, 2009). Mobile devices have been suggested as a technology that might alleviate some of the limitations found in face-to-face CSCL activities (Roschelle & Pea, 2002; Zurita & Nussbaum, 2004). Of particular note is that all learners can have their own devices and, as a collaborative group, engage simultaneously with their devices and in face-to-face interactions with each other. Within a design context, this contrast between shared computer, individual computer, and mobile face-to-face CSCL activities once again highlights the key question for consideration: How will the technology impact upon interaction?

Learning through Computers. Designing for computer-mediated collaborative learning requires anticipating the needs of learners who may not be colocated and who may not be working in real time. These geographic and temporal differences result in slightly different design considerations, suggesting that computer-mediated learning requires more structure than any other form, particularly when it occurs asynchronously.

Social connectedness is a concern when learners are separated geographically from each other and do not know each other in another context. Their initial tendency may be to take on a strict task focus, although doing so may ultimately hurt their ability to succeed. Learner communication should not be limited to task-based discourse, and learning designs may need explicitly to encourage social interactions or let learners know that such interactions are acceptable (Kreijns et al., 2003). Sufficient exchange of personal information is necessary so that learners can establish a sense of each other and overcome the online environment's lack of nonverbal communication cues. Social interactions also help learners to establish online group norms (Slagter van Tryon & Bishop, 2009).

Computer-based interactions generate a tremendous amount of information that can be used within a learning design to help facilitate or encourage collaboration. Janneck (2010) recommended using tools to highlight parts of interactions that get lost in the online environment. For example, in a classroom learners can tell if others are paying attention, but online settings are typically bereft of such indicators. Providing information about who has accessed (and presumably read) a given message will help mimic some of the information available to face-to-face learners. Janneck also recommended against the heavy use of push technology, because providing learners with easy access to notifications and updates can encourage the development of reactive behavior as a norm.

A final point about learning through computers is that computer mediation may not be simply about mediating communication acts. Computers can mediate other important aspects of the learning environment in CSCL. For instance, Q. Wang (2009) suggested that CSCL tools should now include space for sharing files, extending their collaboration abilities beyond just discussion space to include shared artifacts as a core function. Similarly, other tools such as activity awareness, reputation or recommender systems, or adaptive scaffolding, might have great impact on CSCL environments without directly routing communication acts through the computer.

Trends and New Technologies. Looking ahead, collaborative learning designs must continue evolving to accommodate new technologies and learning modalities. For example, learners are being connected increasingly through smart phones (see Looi et al., chapter 24 this volume). The ubiquity of mobile phones worldwide suggests that it is a technology ready to be leveraged to support collaborative learning in a wide variety of contexts (Evans & Johri, 2008), and in particular to mediate collaboration among distance learners. Researchers are beginning to examine how CSCL scripts might be run on mobile phones (Dillenbourg & Crivelli, 2009), and how mobile phones might be leveraged to introduce CSCL into new settings. Similarly, the worlds of gaming and CSCL have found points of overlap (see Kafai & Fields, chapter 27 this volume). Various multiplayer games rely on collaborative principles and support informal learning, providing the inspiration for the development of collaborative learning games (Jong, Shang, & Lee, 2010; Monahan, McArdle, & Bertolotto, 2008; Scacchi, Nideffer, & Adams, 2008). With each of these advancements comes a potential new set of considerations, conditions and parameters to be considered when designing collaborative learning.

OTHER DESIGN PROCESSES AND MODELS

Collaborative learning designers may draw upon a variety of design processes and models to help guide and support their efforts. An instructional design approach to designing collaborative learning has been mentioned throughout this chapter, but participatory design and interface design also merit a mention in this context.

Historically, instructional design models such as Analysis, Design, Development, Implemention, Evaluation (ADDIE) (see Molenda, 2003 for a discussion of this model's origins and use) or the Dick and Carey model (Dick, Carey, & Carey, 2001) focused heavily on analyzing users and their needs, then meeting those needs through the design of materials, and, finally, by evaluating the designs (either formatively or summatively). However, other models for instructional design emphasize a more opportunistic or less top-down process. Merrill's Pebble in the Pond design method (Merrill, 2002) starts with a prototypical problem that learners should be able to solve, then generalizes to other similar problems, and finally works backwards to determine learning goals from the problems, instructional strategies for the learning goals, and finally designs intended to deliver those strategies.

While traditional instructional design processes consider the learner as the end-user, they do not typically involve the learner directly in the instructional design process as a collaborating designer (Carr-Chellman & Savoy, 2004). Participatory design processes purposefully involve stakeholders, in particular learners, in the design process. Carr-Chellman and Savoy spread design processes along a continuum, with traditional instructional design involving the least control, and emancipatory design of the sort described by Giroux or Friere as the most user control. Participatory design falls short of emancipatory design in that learners have an important role as members of the design team, but they are not the sole or most privileged members of that team. Representative learners may be members of a design team that plans learning activities in advance, or the design process can unfold over the course of the instruction with all learners serving as codesigners. Participatory design requires both time and trust within the learner-design team members, and thus is probably best undertaken on larger learning projects (Carroll, 2009). However, one can consider extended agenda setting, similar to the agenda set by knowledge-building communities, as a form of participatory learning design.

Instructional design and interface design are complementary processes, and people with expertise in both areas are needed when designing collaborative learning tools. Although traditionally the domain of programmers or ergonomists, interface design has become increasingly important for learning designers to understand. The best designed instruction and interactions may fail if embedded in a confusing interface (Kirschner et al., 2004). When designing tools that support or mediate learning it is important to draw upon the principles of interface design discussed by people such as Schneiderman (1997) and Cooper (1995; Cooper, Reimann, & Cronin, 2007) and even the multimedia design principles supported by Mayer (2009) along with engaging in cycles of usability testing (Dumas & Redish, 1999; Nielsen, 1999; Nielsen & Loranger, 2006) . Many of the design processes used in human–computer interface design have broad applicability to learning design, such as value-sensitive design (Friedman & Kahn, 2000), scenario-based design (Bardram, 2000), or rapid prototyping design (Hartson & Hix, 1989). Further, maintaining a focus on the technology and its affordances can help CSCL researchers work toward the recommendation made by Resta and Laferrière (2007) to focus on CSCL that is not benchmarked against face-to-face learning but rather takes full advantage of the unique offerings of the computer-based environment.

CONCLUSIONS

Collaborative learning design is a necessarily complex process; to treat it otherwise would be to neglect some of the core elements necessary to promote fruitful learning interactions. CSCL provides many important levers for designers to use to shape the learning environment, but it also introduces complexity (Table 22.1). Designers need to consider the full context—pedagogical, interpersonal, environmental, and technological—of the settings in which their learning activities, tools, and materials may be used. While the designer may espouse a particular learning theory or theories, this rarely provides much guidance for what is to be designed or how. Designers must select and carry out a design process through which they will select appropriate instructional strategies and make decisions regarding designed elements in the learning environment. In

Table 22.1: Summary of Design Issues for CSCL

Considerations	Design Models or Processes	Instructional Theories	Designed Elements
• Setting: Learning *with* or *through* computers, synchronous vs. asynchronous • Existing culture or norms • Prior knowledge and individual differences	• Learning design methods or techniques (e.g. Pebble in the pond, ADDIE, user-design, etc.) • Interface design methods or techniques (e.g., Participatory design, scenario-based design, rapid prototyping, etc.)	Examples include: • Communities of Practice • PBL • Jigsaw • Reciprocal teaching • Knowledge-building communities • (for more CSCL-relevant strategies, see Bonk & Dennen, 2003, pp. 338–340, Table 23.5 and Table 23.6)	• Learning goals • Collaborative premise • Group assignment and composition • Learner roles (assigned or emergent) • Discourse norms or values • Collaboration scripts or sequences of activity • Types of facilitation • Motivational inputs such as incentives

the end, most design processes will involve negotiation and trade-off among these elements and any practical constraints surrounding the learning situation. Outcomes in the design of CSCL are more varied and unpredictable than they would be with more traditional forms of instruction. However, a designer who is well versed in a variety of design processes and models and who approaches design with flexibility will be well prepared to handle the multifaceted decisions that may be required.

REFERENCES

Alvino, S., Asensio–Perez, J. I., Dimitriadis, Y., & Hernandez–Leo, D. (2009). Supporting the reuse of effective CSCL learning designs through social structure representations. *Distance Education, 30*(2), 239–258.

Aronson, E., & Yates, S. (1983). Cooperation in the classroom: The impact of the jigsaw method on inter-ethnic relations, classroom performance, and self-esteem. In H. H. Blumberg, A .P. Hare, V. Kent, & M. Davies (Eds.), *Small groups and social interactions* (Vol. 1, pp. 119–130). Hillsdale, NJ: Wiley.

Bardram, J. (2000). Scenario-based design of cooperative systems. *Group Decision and Negotiation, 9*(3), 237–250.

Barrows, H. S., & Tamblyn, R. M. (1980). *Problem-based learning: An approach to medical education*. New York: Springer.

Bell, P. L., & Linn, M. C. (2000). Scientific arguments as learning artifacts: designing for learning from the web with KIE. *International Journal of Science Education, 22*(8), 797–817.

Blumenfeld, P. C., Marx, R. W., Soloway, E., & Krajcik, J. (1996). Learning with peers: From small group cooperation to collaborative communities. *Educational Researcher, 25*(8), 37–40.

Bonk, C. J., & Dennen, V. P. (2003). Frameworks for research, design, benchmarks, training, and pedagogy in Web-based distance education. In M. G. Moore (Ed.), *Handbook of distance education* (pp. 331–348). Mahwah, NJ: Erlbaum.

Borthick, A. R., & Jones, D. R. (2003). Designing learning experiences within learners' zones of proximal development (ZPDs): Enabling collaborative learning on-site and online. *Journal of Information Systems, 17*(1), 107–134.

Bruner, J. S. (1966). *Toward a theory of instruction*. Cambridge, MA: Harvard University Press.

Carr-Chellman, A., & Savoy, M. (2004). User-design research. In D. H. Jonassen (Ed.), *Handbook of research on educational communication and technology* (2nd ed., pp. 701–716) (Association For Educational Communications and Technology). Mahwah, NJ: Erlbaum.

Carroll, J. M. (2009). The participant-observer in community-based learning as community bard. In J. M. Carroll (Ed.), *Learning in communities* (pp. 7–10). London: Springer-Verlag.

Collins, A., Brown, J. S., & Newman, S. E. (1989). Cognitive apprenticeship: Teaching the crafts of reading, writing, and mathematics. In L. B. Resnick (Ed.), *Knowing, learning, and instruction: Essays in honor of Robert Glaser* (pp. 453–494). Hillsdale, N.J.: Erlbaum.

Cooper, A. (1995). *About face: The essentials of user interface design*. New York: Wiley.

Cooper, A., Reimann, R., & Cronin, D. (2007). *About face 3: The essentials of interaction design*. Hoboken, NJ: Wiley.

Dennen, V. P., & Bonk, C. J. (2007). We'll leave the light on for you: Keeping learners motivated in online courses. In B. Khan (Ed.), *Flexible learning in an information society* (pp. 64–76). Hershey, PA: Information Science.

De Wever, B., Schellens, T., Van Keer, H., & Valcke, M. (2008). Structuring asynchronous discussion groups by introducing roles: Do students act in line with assigned roles? *Small Group Research, 39*(6), 770–794.

Dick, W., Carey, L., & Carey, J. O. (2001). *The systematic design of instruction* (5th ed.). New York: Longman.

Dillenbourg, P. (2002). Over-scripting CSCL: The risks of blending collaborative learning with instructional design. In P. Kirschner (Ed.), *Three worlds of CSCL: Can we support CSCL?* (pp. 61–91). Heerlen, Netherlands: Open Universiteit Nederland.

Dillenbourg, P., & Crivelli, Z. (2009). A model of collaborative learning scripts instantiated with mobile technologies. *International Journal of Mobile and Blended Learning, 1*(1), 36–48. doi: 10.4018/jmbl.2009010103

Dillenbourg, P., Järvelä, S., & Fischer, F. (2009). The evolution of research on computer-supported collaborative learning. In N. Balacheff, S. Ludvigsen, T. Jong, A. Lazonder, & S. Barnes (Eds.), *Technology-Enhanced learning* (pp. 3–19). Dordrecht, The Netherlands: Springer.

Dumas, J. S., & Redish, J. C. (1999). *A practical guide to usability testing*. Exeter, England: Intellect Books.

Evans, M., & Johri, A. (2008). Facilitating guided participation through mobile technologies: Designing creative learning environments for self and others. *Journal of Computing in Higher Education, 20*(2), 92–105. doi: 10.1007/s12528-008-9004-1

Friedman, B., & Kahn, P. H., Jr. (2000). A value-sensitive design approach to augmented reality. In W. E. Mackay (Ed.), *DARE 2000: Design of augmented reality environments* (pp. 163–164). Cambridge, MA: MIT Press.

Gros, B. (2001). Instructional design for computer-supported collaborative learning in primary and secondary school. *Computers in Human Behavior, 17*(5–6), 439–451. doi: 10.1016/s0747-5632(01)00016-4

Hartson, H. R., & Hix, D. (1989). Human-computer interface development: Concepts and systems for its management. *ACM Computing Surveys, 21*(1), 5–92. doi:10.1145/62029.62031

Hmelo-Silver, C. E. (2004). Problem-based learning: What and how do students learn? *Educational Psychology Review, 16*(3), 235–266.

Hoadley, C. (2010). Roles, design, and the nature of CSCL. *Computers in Human Behavior, 26*, 551–555. doi:10.1016/j.chb.2009.08.012

Hsi, S., & Hoadley, C. (1997). Productive discussion in science: Gender equity through electronic discourse. *Journal of Science Education and Technology, 10*(1), 23–36.

Janneck, M. (2010). Making the invisible visible: Design guidelines for supporting social awareness in distributed collaboration. In J. Cordeiro & J. Filipe (Eds.), *Web information systems and technologies* (Vol. 45, pp. 185–197). Berlin: Springer.

Johnson, R. T., Johnson, D. W., & Stanne, M. B. (1986). Comparison of computer-assisted cooperative, competitive, and individualistic learning. *American Educational Research Journal, 23*(3), 382–392.

Jong, M. S. Y., Shang, J., & Lee, F.-l. (2010). Constructivist learning through computer gaming. In M. R. Syed (Ed.), *Technologies shaping instruction and distance education: New studies and utilizations* (pp. 207–222). Hershey, PA: Information Science Reference. doi:10.4018/978-1-60566-934-2.ch014

Kirschner, P., Strijbos, J.-W., Kreijns, K., & Beers, P. J. (2004). Designing electronic collaborative learning environments. *Educational Technology Research and Development, 52*(3), 47–66.

Kreijns, K., Kirschner, P. A., & Jochems, W. (2003). Identifying the pitfalls for social interaction in computer-supported collaborative learning environments: A review of the research. *Computers in Human Behavior, 19*(3), 335–353. doi: 10.1016/s0747-5632(02)00057-2

Lave, J., & Wenger, E. (1991). *Situated learning: Legitimate peripheral participation*. New York: Cambridge University Press.

Liu, X., Liu, S., Lee, S.-H., & Magjuka, R. J. (2010). Cultural differences in online learning: International student perceptions. *Educational Technology & Society, 13*(3), 177–188.

Lowyck, J., & Pöysä, J. (2001). Design of collaborative learning environments. *Computers in Human Behavior, 17*(5–6), 507–516. doi: 10.1016/s0747-5632(01)00017-6

Mayer, R. E. (2009). *Multimedia learning* (2nd ed.). Cambridge, England: Cambridge University Press.

Merrill, M. D. (2002). A pebble in the pond model for instructional design. *Performance Improvement, 41*(7), 41–46.

Molenda, M. (2003). In search of the elusive ADDIE model. *Performance Improvement, 42*(5), 34–37.

Monahan, T., McArdle, G., & Bertolotto, M. (2008). Virtual reality for collaborative e-learning. *Computers & Education, 50*(4), 1339–1353. doi: 10.1016/j.compedu.2006.12.008

Nielsen, J. (1999). *Designing web usability.* Indianapolis, IN: New Riders.

Nielsen, J., & Loranger, H. (2006). *Prioritizing web usability.* Thousand Oaks, CA: New Riders.

Orr, J. E. (1990). Sharing knowledge, celebrating identity: Community memory in a service culture. In D. Middleton & D. Edwards (Eds.), *Collective remembering* (pp. 169–189). Newbury Park, CA: Sage.

Palincsar, A. S., & Brown, A. L. (1984). Reciprocal teaching of comprehension-fostering and comprehension-monitoring activities. *Cognition and Instruction, 1*(2), 117–175.

Reiser, R. A. (2012). What field did you say you were in? Defining and naming our field. In R. A. Reiser & J. V. Dempsey (Eds.), *Trends and issues in instructional design and technology* (3rd ed., pp. 1–7). New York: Pearson.

Resta, P., & Laferrière, T. (2007). Technology in support of collaborative learning. *Educational Psychology Review, 19*(1), 65–83. doi: 10.1007/s10648-007-9042-7

Roschelle, J. & Pea, R. (2002). A walk on the WILD side: How wireless handhelds may change CSCL. In G. Stahl (Ed.), *Computer Support for Collaborative Learning (CSCL) 2002* (pp. 51–60). Boulder, CO: International Society of the Learning Sciences.

Roschelle, J., Rafanan, K., Estrella, G., Nussbaum, M., & Claro, S. (2010). From handheld collaborative tool to effective classroom module: Embedding CSCL in a broader design framework. *Computers & Education, 55*(3), 1018–1026. doi://10.1016/j.compedu.2010.04.012

Scacchi, W., Nideffer, R., & Adams, J. (2008). A collaborative science learning game environment for informal science education: DinoQuest Online. In P. Ciancarini, R. Nakatsu, M. Rauterberg, & M. Roccetti (Eds.), *New frontiers for entertainment computing* (Vol. 279, pp. 71–82). Boston, MA: Springer.

Scardamalia, M. (2003). Knowledge Society Network (KSN): Toward an expert society for democratizing knowledge. *Journal of Distance Education, 17*(3), 63–66.

Scardamalia, M., & Bereiter, C. (1994). Computer support for knowledge-building communities. *Journal of the Learning Sciences, 3*(3), 265–283.

Schneiderman, B. (1997). *Designing the user interface: Strategies for effective human-computer interaction.* Boston, MA: Addison-Wesley Longman.

Sharples, M., Arnedillo-Sánchez, I., Milrad, M., & Vavoula, G. (2009). Mobile learning. In N. Balacheff, S. Ludvigsen, T. Jong, A. Lazonder, & S. Barnes (Eds.), *Technology-enhanced learning* (pp. 233–249). Dordrecht, The Netherlands: Springer.

Slagter van Tryon, P. J., & Bishop, M. J. (2009). Theoretical foundations for enhancing social connectedness in online learning environments. *Distance Education, 30*(3), 291–315.

Strijbos, J. W., Martens, R. L., & Jochems, W. M. G. (2004). Designing for interaction: Six steps to designing computer-supported group-based learning. *Computers & Education, 42*(4), 403–424. doi: 10.1016/j.compedu.2003.10.004

Tessmer, M., & Richey, R. C. (1997). The role of context in learning and instructional design. *Educational Technology Research and Development, 45*(2), 85–115.

Vygotsky, L. S. (1974). *Mind in society: The development of higher psychological processes* (M. Cole, Trans.). Cambridge, MA: Harvard University Press.

Wang, C. M. (2011). Instructional design for cross-cultural online collaboration: Grouping strategies and assignment design. *Australasian Journal of Educational Technology, 27*(2), 243–258.

Wang, Q. (2009). Design and evaluation of a collaborative learning environment. *Computers & Education, 53*(4), 1138–1146. doi: 10.1016/j.compedu.2009.05.023

Wang, S.-L., & Lin, S. S. J. (2007). The effects of group composition of self-efficacy and collective efficacy on computer-supported collaborative learning. *Computers in Human Behavior, 23*(5), 2256–2268. doi: 10.1016/j.chb.2006.03.005

Webb, N. M., Nemer, K. M., Chizhik, A. W., & Sugrue, B. (1998). Equity issues in collaborative group assessment: group composition and performance. *American Educational Research Journal, 35*(4), 607–651. doi: 10.3102/00028312035004607

Wenger, E., McDermott, R. A., & Snyder, W. (2002). *Cultivating communities of practice: A guide to managing knowledge.* Boston, MA: Harvard Business School Press.

Wheeler, S., Yeomans, P., & Wheeler, D. (2008). The good, the bad and the wiki: Evaluating student-generated content for collaborative learning. *British Journal of Educational Technology, 39*(6), 987–995. doi: 10.1111/j.1467-8535.2007.00799.x

Zurita, G., & Nussbaum, M. (2004). Computer supported collaborative learning using wirelessly interconnected handheld computers. *Computers & Education, 42*(3), 289–314. doi: 10.1016/j.compedu.2003.08.005

23

COLLABORATION SCRIPTS IN COMPUTER-SUPPORTED COLLABORATIVE LEARNING

FRANK FISCHER, INGO KOLLAR, KARSTEN STEGMANN, CHRISTOF WECKER, JAN ZOTTMANN

University of Munich, Germany

ARMIN WEINBERGER

Saarland University, Germany

Information and communication technologies are being used increasingly to support collaboration in formal and informal educational settings. Research on computer-supported collaborative learning (CSCL; Stahl, Koschmann, & Suthers, 2006) has investigated methods of employing computer technologies to facilitate collaborative processes in groups of learners, and are typical for the realization of advanced instructional approaches such as inquiry learning (Linn, Lee, Tinker, Husic, & Chiu, 2006) or knowledge building (Scardamalia & Bereiter, 2006). Although research has suggested the great potential for such challenging scenarios to increase the attractiveness and effectiveness of learning experiences (Scardamalia & Bereiter, 1996; Stahl, 2002; Strijbos, Kirschner, & Martens, 2004), many learners have difficulty exploiting these opportunities when simply assigned to groups and left to their own devices (e.g., Barron, 2003). This especially applies when learners have little knowledge of how to collaborate effectively with one another; that is, when they have low-structured internal collaboration scripts (Kollar, Fischer, & Slotta, 2007). In such cases, learners may be supported effectively by external computer-supported collaboration scripts, which specify, sequence, and distribute learning activities and roles among the learners of a group (Kollar, Fischer, & Hesse, 2006). Thus, collaboration scripts can be regarded as specific instances of collaboration-related scaffolds that provide interaction-related support rather than content-related support, which makes them a special kind of scaffold for collaborative learning. As an example of early face-to-face collaboration script approaches, the scripted cooperation approach (O'Donnell & Dansereau, 1992) first assigns the task of reading and summarizing a paragraph to one learner, second asks the other learner to review the summary, and third rotates these roles for the next paragraph. Further examples for collaboration scripts that have been designed to structure face-to-face collaboration are guided reciprocal peer questioning (King, 1998, 2007) and reciprocal teaching (Palincsar & Brown, 1984).

With the advent and continuous development of the Internet, scripting has recently been adapted to CSCL and has often been integrated into existing web-based learning environments that realize more general instructional approaches such as inquiry learning (Kollar et al., 2007) or problem-based learning (Weinberger, Ertl, Fischer, & Mandl, 2005) that have been criticized for often being too unstructured to be beneficial (see Kirschner, Sweller, & Clark, 2006). Adding collaboration scripts that structure the interactions that are supposed to occur during these learning scenarios directly addresses the criticisms that have been put forward by Kirschner and colleagues (2006) and others (e.g., Mayer, 2004).

One distinction that has repeatedly been made in research on computer-supported collaboration scripts refers to macro- and microscripting. The term *macroscripting* refers to managing classroom activities by organizing extended learning phases into sequences (e.g., individual analysis followed by class discussion and small-group reflection) without providing further guidance on how to act during these phases (see Dillenbourg & Hong, 2008; Dillenbourg & Tchounikine, 2007). One example is the ArgueGraph script developed by Dillenbourg and Jermann (2007), which first guides students to express individually their opinions on a controversial topic (e.g., drug use in sports) by filling in an online questionnaire. This is followed by a first plenary phase during which arguments that were expressed in the online questionnaire are discussed orally. After that, ArgueGraph uses a software algorithm that groups together students with divergent opinions and asks them to fill in the questionnaire again, with the task of coming to agreement concerning the different questions. Then, the dyads' answers are reviewed and discussed again in the plenary. Finally, the teacher may distribute assignments to individual students to sum up the discussion on single questions that were part of the questionnaire. While macroscripts provide a sequence of rather general phases to be followed in a complex learning setting (e.g., a classroom), microscripting refers to supporting very specific collaborative learning activities at the level of collaborative roles, turn-taking, and individual discourse contributions. For example, a microscript used by Weinberger et al. (2005) that was integrated into an asynchronous online discussion board prompted members of small groups to ask specific questions or provide counterarguments to the learning partner's contributions; for example, by using sentence openers (e.g., "What is still unclear to me in your analysis is …"). Certainly, macro- and microscripts may also be combined to possibly amplify each other's effects, and first studies in this direction are currently being conducted (e.g., Kollar, Wecker, Langer, & Fischer, 2011). Yet, one danger of designing and possibly combining different scripts and thus a central challenge in designing CSCL is to keep the balance between self-regulation and instructional guidance (Kollar & Fischer, 2006; Winne, Haldwin, & Perry, chapter 26 this volume). This means avoiding both "overscripting" (in the sense of guiding learners to follow preset sequences when they already possess well-developed collaboration skills or "internal scripts for collaboration"; see Stegmann, Mu, Gehlen-Baum, & Fischer, 2011; for a different notion of the overscripting concept, see Dillenbourg, 2002) and "underscripting" in terms of leaving too many degrees of freedom for inexperienced collaborative learners with poorly developed internal scripts (Kollar, Fischer, & Slotta, 2007; Stegmann, Mu et al., 2011; Weinberger, Stegmann, & Fischer,

2010). As will be described later, one way of reaching the balance between under- and overscripting may be to increase the flexibility of collaboration scripts.

Overall, this chapter reviews recent and current empirical research on CSCL scripting and has three parts: First, we give an overview of empirical research that has analyzed the general effectiveness of the collaboration script approach to facilitate CSCL. Second, we describe five issues that have developed out of this general research and that take a closer look at specific aspects of scripting CSCL. These include (a) cognitive explanations for the facilitating effects of CSCL scripts; (b) the interplay of internal and external scripts; (c) the fading out of external scripts; (d) opportunities for using technology to conceptualize, formalize, and implement external collaboration scripts; and (e) field research on the effects of CSCL scripts on various learning parameters and outcomes. Third, the discussion summarizes the current state of research and identifies open questions for future research on CSCL scripts.

TO WHAT EXTENT CAN EXTERNAL COLLABORATION SCRIPTS IMPROVE CSCL?

CSCL builds onto the notion of learning being an active and social process with learners sharing and jointly constructing knowledge. When learners collaborate over distance, it is challenging to engage them in establishing and maintaining a joint problem space to share and construct knowledge (Teasley & Roschelle, 1993). Providing learners with a software architecture that allows them to communicate with each other is usually not sufficient to establish rich argumentative interactions and responses to the problems typically encountered in collaborative learning, such as heterogeneous participation (e.g., free riding; Kerr & Bruun, 1983) and low-quality discourse (e.g., uncoordinated discourse; Barron, 2000; unsound argumentation; Kuhn, 1991). Scripting is an instructional approach that focuses on collaborative learners' activities and interaction patterns. Scripts provide learners with an interaction plan and thereby change their expectations with respect to interaction, coordinate their activities, and help them to engage in activities they would otherwise disregard or have difficulties with. Collaboration scripts have been applied in various types of CSCL environments, such as discussion boards (De Wever, van Keer, Schellens, & Valcke, 2010; Weinberger, Stegmann, Fischer, & Mandl, 2007), video conferences (Rummel & Spada, 2005; Weinberger, Ertl, et al., 2005), and 3D-game environments (Hämäläinen, Oksanen, & Häkkinen, 2008).

The empirical evidence concerning the effectiveness of the collaboration script approach is largely positive: Several experimental studies have shown that external collaboration scripts can improve (a) the balance between individual and collaborative activities (Hämäläinen et al., 2008; Rummel & Spada, 2005; Schoonenboom, 2008); (b) learners' engagement in online discussions (Schoonenboom, 2008; Weinberger, Stegmann et al., 2007); (c) the quality of discussions (De Wever et al., 2010; Stegmann, Weinberger, & Fischer, 2007; Weinberger, Ertl, et al., 2005; Weinberger, Stegmann, & Fischer, 2010); and (d) individual learning outcomes, in particular regarding domain-general knowledge (Kollar et al., 2007; Weinberger, Stegmann, & Fischer, 2010), including collaboration and argumentation skills (Rummel & Spada, 2005; Stegmann, Weinberger, & Fischer, 2007; Weinberger, Stegmann, & Fischer, 2010). For example, Schoonenboom (2008) designed a macroscript for a distance learning scenario that was designed to support grounding processes within the group (see also Kirschner, Beers, Boshuizen,

& Gijselaers, 2008; Pfister & Oehl, 2009) by instructing learners to provide input individually at first, then discuss the contributions, and finally build a consensus. Scripted learners contributed more messages regardless of whether the script was represented on a paper handout or integrated into a computer-supported communication interface as compared to learners not supported by the script. Learners followed the outlined script, and this in effect helped them share their individual knowledge and identify knowledge differences. Similarly, Hämäläinen and colleagues (2008) developed a macroscript for vocational education that guided learners to start a joint problem-solving task with an individual planning subtask, then jointly identify the problem, take over specific responsibilities and tools within the environment, and finally, face a challenge together putting the distributed expertise to use and complete the task. Based on qualitative analyses, learners were found to follow and benefit from the script by being guided toward shared problem solving.

In contrast to such macroscripts, microscripts provide more fine-grained guidance concerning the specific activities learners are supposed to engage in during the different phases of their collaboration. Microscript effects are typically very specific regarding the aspects of collaboration they foster: Quality of argumentation can, for example, be improved using specific external argumentation scripts (Kollar, Fischer, & Slotta, 2007; Stegmann, Weinberger, & Fischer, 2007; Weinberger, Stegmann, & Fischer, 2010). Similarly, De Wever, van Keer, Schellens, and Valcke (2009) developed a microscript that distributed roles in an asynchronous discussion board which led individuals in small groups to engage in the intended, role-congruent activities.

However, with respect to the acquisition of domain-specific knowledge (i.e., knowledge about the topic under discussion), only a few microscripts have proven effective, among them a peer-critiquing script (Weinberger, Ertl, et al., 2005) which supported individual analysis of authentic problem cases in an asynchronous, problem-oriented learning environment by introducing a "case analyst" role and constructive feedback by introducing a "critic" role (Figure 23.1). Furthermore, positive effects of a collaborative online search script supporting students' mutual monitoring and feedback have been observed both on the domain-general skill of web searching, as well as on

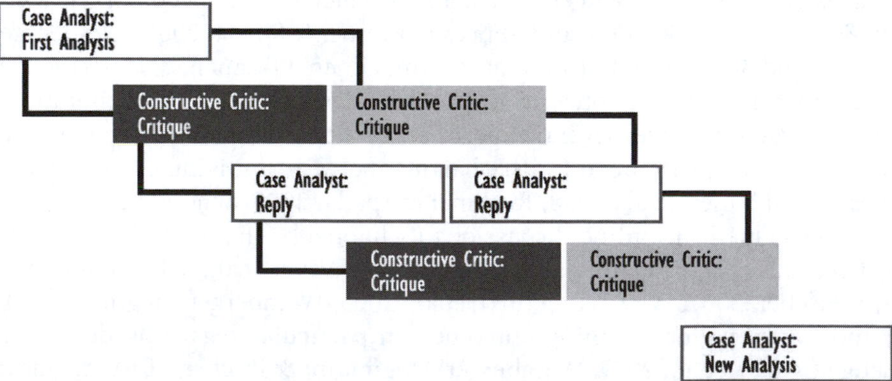

Figure 23.1 Peer-critique script for university students. Learners analyze three cases in groups of three. Each learner is a case analyst for one case and a constructive critic for the other cases; the figure displays roles and activities for one of the cases. Activities are supported by prompts which help learners to fulfill their roles (e.g., the sentence starter "What I miss in your analysis is . . ." for learners in the role of the critic).

domain-specific knowledge (Wecker, Kollar, Fischer, & Prechtl, submitted). Beyond the fact that both scripts (the one developed by Weinberger, Ertl et al., 2005, and the one used by Wecker et al., submitted) aim at increasing the quality of each individual's cognitive and metacognitive activities, the key to their success in fostering the acquisition of domain-specific knowledge may be that they have individuals of a group explicitly build onto their partners' contributions and thus increase the reciprocal elaboration of the learning content and the contributions of group members (transactivity; see Teasley, 1995).

However, external microscripts can also have negative side-effects. Mäkitalo, Weinberger, Häkkinen, Järvelä, and Fischer (2005) developed a task-specific collaboration script that was integrated in an asynchronous discussion board which turned out, on the one hand, to help groups solve complex problems, but on the other hand simultaneously impeded individual acquisition of knowledge on the topic at hand (Mäkitalo et al., 2005).

In sum, computer-supported collaboration scripts can be regarded as an effective instructional approach to facilitate CSCL. When designed carefully, scripts may help learners to engage more and more homogeneously in often neglected collaborative activities, such as constructing sound (counter-) arguments. However, as empirical evidence on negative side-effects of collaboration scripts has illustrated (see Mäkitalo et al., 2005), effective collaboration scripts need to be designed with a lot of care. Again, one delicate issue seems to be keeping the balance between over- and underscripting: while some guidance is usually necessary, especially when learners lack necessary collaboration skills, too much guidance may impede rather than facilitate collaboration. The latter may be especially true when the collaboration script activates inappropriate internal scripts (see Fischer, Kollar, Stegmann, & Wecker, in press). For example, an argumentation-related script may evoke internal scripts that aim at pushing through personal viewpoints for the sake of finding joint solutions and have biased information-processing and competition rather than collaboration as a consequence.

CURRENT ISSUES IN RESEARCH ON CSCL SCRIPTS

The research evidence for the effectiveness of collaboration scripts in facilitating CSCL has triggered a number of more specific research questions: How does cognitive processing mediate script effects on learning outcomes? How do internal and external scripts interact in CSCL? What are the opportunities for using technology to conceptualize, formalize, and implement external collaboration scripts in CSCL? Do script effects observed in the lab translate "into the wild"? These questions and related research are described in the next section.

How Does Cognitive Processing Mediate Script Effects on Learning Outcomes?

One general aim in providing learners with collaboration scripts is to improve the quality of their collaborative learning processes (e.g., by increasing the number and depth of explanations or thought-provoking questions), and, as described above, collaboration scripts can be tailored to facilitate the execution of such processes very specifically. From a cognitive perspective that views "learning" as a relatively persistent change in the long-term memory of an individual, the aim of providing learners with collaboration scripts is then to evoke certain collaboration processes that, in turn, go along with high-level individual cognitive processes. Thus, it seems likely that the effects of CSCL scripts on individual learning outcomes (i.e., acquisition of domain-specific and domain-general strategy knowledge) are mediated by individual cognitive processes. However, analyses that systematically measure and relate discourse quality, cognitive processes, and learning outcomes are rare (Schellens & Valcke, 2005). In a replication study on Weinberger, Stegmann, and Fischer's (2010) script for the construction of single arguments, Stegmann, Wecker, Weinberger, and Fischer (2012) used think-aloud methods to assess cognitive processes (in distributed and asynchronous collaborative learning settings) in addition to discourse quality. Findings showed that those scripts which effectively support discourse quality (in this case, argumentation) also lead learners to engage in deeper cognitive elaboration with respect to both the learning material and the contributions of their learning partners (e.g. Stegmann, Wecker et al., 2012). Case studies mapping cognitive and discourse processes on a time axis showed evidence of what can be called reorchestration of discourse and cognition: The peer critiquing script facilitated a pattern of discourse and cognition that resembled those of successful unscripted learners. The script enabled phases of intensive reflection on the learning material (with scaffolding contributions initiating a discussion) and phases of transactive discourse (with scaffolding contributions critiquing contributions of learning partners).

Furthermore, in a quantitative experimental setup implementing a different type of script (e.g., for argumentation), Weinberger, Stegmann, and Fischer (2010) found that in the same experimentally controlled period of time, the script deepened individual cognitive elaboration of knowledge substantially, but at the expense of breadth (i.e., the amount of aspects of the topic covered). In addition, this study showed that the positive effects of the CSCL script examined for learning processes and outcomes were *mediated* by the depth of cognitive elaboration of both the learning material and the ideas contributed by fellow learners.

How Do External and Internal Scripts Interact?

Although CSCL scripts may provide fairly fine-grained and detailed instruction on how a small group of learners should proceed during collaboration, the collaboration pattern that is actually observable will not be determined completely by the instruction provided in the external script. Instead, learners also bring internal scripts (Kollar et al., 2007) to a learning situation. Such scripts are acquired via repeated participation in collaborative activities and then activated in a new collaborative learning situation (Kolodner, 2007; Schank, 1999; for an overview of research on the development of internal scripts see Hudson, Fivush, & Kuebli, 1992). To investigate how differently well-structured external collaboration scripts interact with learners' predeveloped internal collaboration scripts, Kollar et al. (2007) conducted an experimental laboratory study with high-school biology students who collaborated in dyads in a web-based inquiry learning environment. Depending on the experimental condition, recurring discussion phases were scripted in one of two ways: in the high-structured external script condition, students received specific instruction (based on theoretical models of argumentation) on how to produce arguments and argument sequences. They were then asked to enter arguments in prespecified text boxes (Figure 23.2). In the low-structured version, the discussion between the learners was not structured any further. The degree of structure of learners' internal scripts was tested two weeks before the actual collaboration by asking students to find instances of good and poor argumentation in a fictitious protocol of a science-related

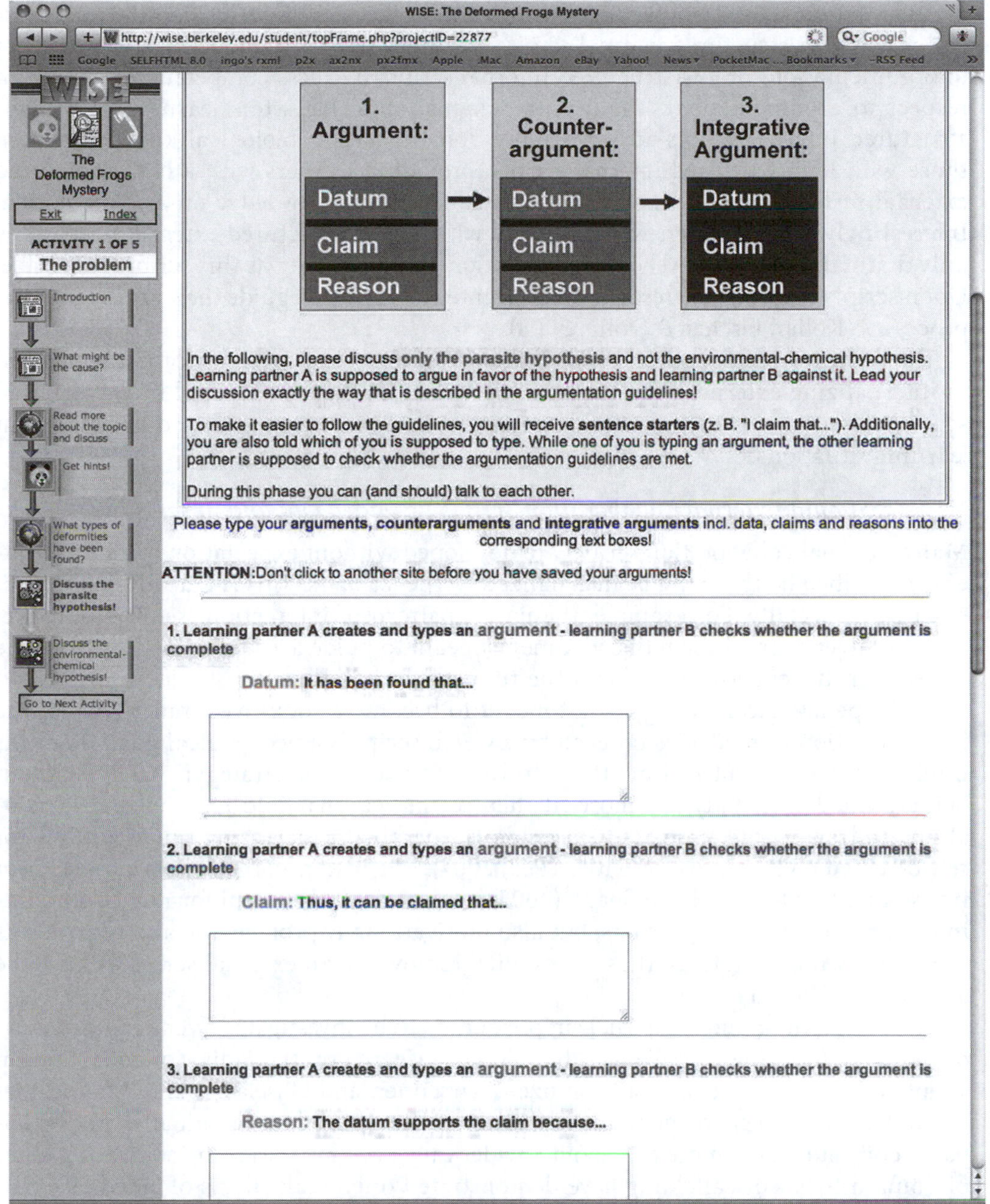

Figure 23.2 High-structured external collaboration script designed to support collaborative argumentation, implemented in the Web-based Inquiry Science Environment (WISE; for a recent review of WISE, please see Linn & Eylon, 2011). Following content-specific activities, learners are required to discuss the validity of two hypotheses against the background of various kinds of information. The script distributes the production of well-warranted arguments, counter-arguments, and integrative arguments among the two learning partners and organizes them into a sequence using appropriate prompts (e.g., "Therefore, it can be claimed..." to support the production of a claim).

argumentation. Based on performance on this test, learners were identified as holding either high-structured internal scripts (i.e., highly competent learners with respect to argumentation) or low-structured internal scripts (i.e., less competent learners with respect to argumentation). The results demonstrated that while learners with high-structured internal scripts acquired more domain-*specific* biological knowledge than those with low-structured internal scripts, providing learners with a high-structured external script helped them gain more domain-*general* knowledge on argumentation. Interestingly, when learners were provided with a high-structured external script, they only maintained a high level of argumentation quality as long as this script was visible. Upon script removal, they resorted to their internal scripts to guide their argumentation processes (Kollar, Fischer, & Slotta, 2008).

Thus, one interesting question for further research is how students can be supported in internalizing external scripts so that the strategies that are induced by the external script become part of their personal strategy repertoire and are activated in subsequent learning situations.

Should External Collaboration Scripts Be Faded Out and, if so, How?

Many external collaboration scripts are developed without expectations that the strategy prescribed by the script be internalized by the learners. This is true for many macroscripts especially. For example, the jigsaw pattern of interaction (see O'Donnell & Hmelo-Silver, Introduction this volume) is meant to guide learners to benefit from the interaction in "expert groups" and the tutoring activities in the "basic group." However, the pedagogical strategy is not meant to become a cognitive strategy. Yet, if the internalization of strategies induced by a CSCL script is a pedagogical goal, then this implies at some point in time the self-directed use of the strategy; that is, without being guided externally any more. It then seems reasonable to fade out (i.e., gradually withdraw) script prompts to provide learners with increasing opportunities for self-directed collaborative activities (Pea, 2004). For instance, the collaboration script investigated by Rummel and Spada (2005) was particularly useful for novice students in the first collaborative sessions, but also motivationally problematic and regarded as too rigid by these students, thus the gradual removal of an external script seems to be a plausible solution.

The fading in or out of external support needs to be investigated over extended periods of time (e.g., Kester & Paas, 2005). So far, research on the fading of collaboration scripts has been sparse. Beers, Boshuizen, Kirschner, and Gijselaers (2005) found that when the degree of coercion of a collaboration script was reduced gradually, the participants communicated more and about a wider range of topics. In some contrast, studies of domain-focused scaffolding have demonstrated only weak effects of faded (as compared to continuous) scaffolding and, further, have reported a decline in the quality of students' work during the fading process (e.g., McNeill, Lizotte, Krajcik, & Marx, 2006).

Similar results were found by Wecker et al. (submitted) during a 5-week quasi-experimental field study in an inquiry context in regular biology classes, in which the amount of instructional support during dyadic online searches for information that could be used as arguments for or against genetic engineering of crops was manipulated. While an unfaded collaboration script had a positive effect on both domain-specific knowledge and online search competence compared to unscripted collaboration, learners working with a faded collaboration script outperformed those who were not supported by a collaboration script only with respect to online search competence, but not with respect to domain-specific knowledge. Furthermore, there was no effect of fading on top of the effect of the collaboration script itself with respect to online search competence. This might be explained by the fact that the collaboration script embodied a collaborative strategy (of collaborative online search) that learners were expected to acquire as an individual strategy (of individual online search). It could be hypothesized that effective fading of a collaboration script would have to include aspects of "individualization" of the corresponding strategy; that is, that the targeted strategy might be acquired better when it is finally employed by individuals, and not in dyads.

A laboratory study in a higher education context, however, showed that fading out can also have a more substantial effect on learning (Wecker & Fischer, 2011). While writing criticisms of analyses of cases from educational practice based on the attribution theory of achievement motivation within an asynchronous CSCL environment, all learners received a collaboration script for the generation of counterarguments. The results showed that fading can actually be effective with respect to the acquisition of a domain-general competence such as argumentation when combined with distributed monitoring (i.e., feedback by a learning partner about the learner's adherence to the script). Process analyses revealed that distributed monitoring can keep the adherence to the script high during phases of fading, which proved to be crucial for the internalization of the strategy induced by the collaboration script. Hence, fading requires more than gradually removing instructional guidance. In addition, appropriate self-regulation has to be secured by means of appropriate support (see also Winne, Haldwin, & Perry, chapter 26 this volume). Learning partners can support their peers effectively with respect to this aspect of script internalization.

Additional support can also be offered through adaptive and adaptable scripts. Adaptive scripts are faded out and faded in with respect to the current quality of the supported activities; that is, the amount or depth of script support is adjusted constantly on an objective basis (Gweon, Rosé, Zaiss, & Carey, 2006, see also next section). In some contrast, adaptable scripts provide learners themselves with the opportunity to adjust the script to their own subjective needs (Wang, Kollar, Stegmann, & Fischer, 2011). Concerning the effectiveness of adaptive scripts, Gweon and colleagues (2006) compared learners supported by adaptive prompts with learners not receiving prompt support. The prompts aimed to support problem-solving activities of dyads within a synchronous online collaboration via screen sharing. Specific prompts only appeared if automated analyses of the collaborative learning process detected, for example, unelaborated feedback (e.g., "Wrong!"), executive feedback (i.e., providing correct solutions), or working independently on the problem (i.e., solving the problem without integrating contributions of the learning partner). The results showed that such adaptive prompts positively affected the problem-solving activities as well as learning. Similar results have been found in a study by Diziol, Walker, Rummel, and Koedinger (2010; see also Walker, Rummel, & Koedinger, 2011). With respect to adaptability of CSCL scripts, Wang et al. (2011) found preliminary evidence for its effectiveness. In their study, providing learners with the opportunity to switch certain parts of the script on and off (after having gained extensive experience with the complete script) led learners to acquire higher levels of individual and collaborative skills than did the provision of a nonadaptable script. Thus, making CSCL scripts adaptive or adaptable is a promising way to increase opportunities for self-regulation, and, in the end, learning.

What Are the Opportunities for Using Technology to Conceptualize, Formalize, and Implement External Collaboration Scripts in CSCL?

As the study by Gweon et al. (2006) exemplifies, scripting CSCL has become more and more of an interdisciplinary endeavor, involving cognitive psychology, computer science, linguistics, and education (Fischer, Kollar, Mandl, & Haake, 2007). Current interdisciplinary research on scripting focuses on two important issues.

1. In an attempt to draw CSCL scripts closer to educational practice, interdisciplinary teams (see Dillenbourg & Jermann, 2007; Miao, Harrer, Hoeksema, & Hoppe, 2007) try to make external scripts more flexible, adaptable, and reusable by building on a systematic conceptualization of components and mechanisms of CSCL scripts. According to Kobbe et al. (2007), the components of a collaboration script are *participants, activities, roles, resources,* and *groups*. The participants are learners, tutors, and teachers who participate actively in the learning session. Scripts often require a fixed number of participants per group. This requirement results from a specific number of other components like roles or resources. Activities are all (learning) activities defined by the script developer; for example, writing a counterargument or reviewing the contribution of a learning partner. Roles of an analyst or a constructive critic, for example, are often used to define clusters of a set of activities. Within the script, participants use, manipulate, or create resources, whereas roles specify a set of activities. Groups are used to specify participants who interact directly with each other. The mechanisms of CSCL scripts that manipulate the components are task distribution, group formation, and sequencing (Kobbe et al., 2007). The activities, roles, and resources described in a script may be distributed within a group. Some scripts use specific group formation mechanisms to facilitate learning processes; instead of self-organized groups, an algorithm is used to compose groups. Through sequencing, scripts often provide a temporal structure of components and mechanisms.

Conceptualizations like this allow users to represent scripts in graphical script editors and to formalize them in a machine-readable language (see Harrer, Malzahn, & Hoppe, 2007; Miao et al., 2007) so as to afford their reimplementation in different learning platforms. The MoCoLaDe tool (Harrer et al., 2007), for example, allows for formal modeling of collaboration scripts. It enables graphical notation of the components and mechanisms of scripts and produces a machine readable xml-file. Furthermore, with MoCoLaDe, collaboration scripts can be tested interactively by conducting simulations before actually implementing them for real collaborators. Web-based collaborative learning environments like CeLS (Collaborative e-Learning Structures; see Ronen, Kohen-Vacs, Harrer, & Kali, 2009) are able to interpret the formalized scripts. The functional framework XSS (eXtremely Simple Scripting; see Stegmann, Streng et al., 2009) is based on the conceptualization of Kobbe and colleagues (2007) and especially facilitates the development of collaboration scripts for different devices like smart phones or tabletop displays.

2. Script formalization is also a precondition for a second issue of current interdisciplinary research on CSCL scripts: the development of CSCL scripts that adapt constantly to the learners' development of internal scripts. Using methods of natural language processing (Rosé et al., 2008; Y. Wang, Rosé et al., 2007), researchers hope to assess the quality of the collaboration process automatically and to infer information about learners' internal scripts. Having an architecture that enables flexible and adaptive CSCL scripts is, however, only part of what is needed to provide real adaptive support to learners.

While the architecture may already enable teachers, tutors, and learners to adapt CSCL scripts, an adaptive CSCL script requires information on the collaboration process. For example, an adaptive script that supports argumentation will fade in if the actual argumentation in a group is identified as weak and fade out if argumentation has improved. Recent advances in the field of natural language processing show that algorithms can be developed to analyze the quality of online discussions with a high accuracy (Mu, Stegmann, Mayfield, Rosé, & Fischer, 2012; Rosé et al., 2008). The output of these analyses may be used to control components and mechanisms of CSCL scripts (e.g., Gweon et al., 2006). Thereby, the challenge is to train algorithms that segment and code collaboration processes with high objectivity, reliability, and validity, which are applicable not only to very specific datasets. Advances toward this goal were made by integrating context information like the position of a contribution within a thread in online discussions (e.g., Y. Wang, Rosé et al., 2007).

Do Scripts Work "In the Wild" as Well?

As described above, much empirical research on CSCL scripts has been conducted in the lab under rather controlled conditions. Thus, an important question is whether the effects of CSCL scripts can also be found "in the wild" in real educational contexts and over longer learning periods. In a field study in medical education (Zottmann, Dieckmann, Rall, Fischer, & Taraszow, 2006), an external script was implemented with the aim of raising the participants' activity in a full-scale simulator training in emergency medicine. These simulation-based trainings often include observational phases during which individual learners are watching others perform in the simulator. The script was designed to support learners in these observational phases and foster their acquisition of domain-general knowledge (e.g., heuristics to cope with critical incidents; see Rall & Gaba, 2005) besides factual medical knowledge. The collaboration script had substantial positive effects on processes of collaboration and learning with respect to both content and activity: scripted learners showed an increased focus on the heuristics under consideration. Moreover, the script led learners to a more accurate assessment of their own skills, reducing the danger of developing an illusion of competence without, however, actually facilitating the development of the skills.

In another field study, Demetriadis, Egerter, Hanisch, and Fischer (2011) investigated the effects of collaboration scripts in a learning environment where students worked together in small groups on programming problems in computer science that required both domain-specific and domain-general knowledge. Learners collaborating by aid of an external peer-review script spent significantly more time developing solutions and (self-) reported a higher learning gain than members of the control group. Scripted groups also acquired more knowledge about peer reviewing than groups from the control condition.

Field research on collaboration scripts has also been concerned with the long-term effects of scripts. The previously mentioned 5-week field study in an inquiry context (Wecker et al., submitted) investigated whether effects observed in lab studies would emerge in a pronounced way in real-life educational settings extending over longer periods of time. In this study, the collaboration script not only showed a positive effect on the acquisition of a domain-general competence (online search competence), but also with respect to domain-specific knowledge, which had not previously been observed in many short-term lab studies. To conclude, although field research on the effectiveness of scripts for facilitating CSCL is still limited, there are indications that they can produce positive learning effects "in the wild" as well.

CONCLUSIONS AND FUTURE RESEARCH

In this chapter we have (a) given an overview of general research on the effectiveness of the collaboration script approach to facilitate CSCL and (b) described several issues and empirical studies on more specific aspects of CSCL scripts that were triggered by this more general research. In this final section we draw some conclusions and point to current and future challenges for research on CSCL scripting. More specifically, we elaborate on five statements that can be concluded from the arguments made in this chapter: (a) Scripting does not kill "true" collaboration, it empowers learners. (b) Scripting sometimes needs to be structured to make learning harder. (c) There is a need for more adaptable and adaptive collaboration scripts. (d) There is a need to strengthen field research on CSCL scripts. (e) "Collaboration script" is an ideal boundary concept for interdisciplinary research. Each of these statements is elaborated upon in more detail below.

Scripting Does Not Kill "True" Collaboration—Scripting Empowers Learners

The reported empirical studies found that learners typically are not able to participate in computer-supported collaborative learning processes in a fruitful way *spontaneously*, which indicates that internal scripts on collaborative learning in these contexts are typically not well developed. Underscripted CSCL, therefore, fails to empower students and increase their levels of self-regulation. Of course, scripting temporarily reduces a learner's options to act in a specific instance (see also Pea, 2004), but there is (so far) no systematic empirical evidence for overscripting effects, at least if understood as reduced individual-cognitive learning outcomes due to too much external script support. Instead, scripts enable participation in high-level collaborative activities leading to higher levels of understanding. Purposefully scripted CSCL can thus ultimately increase the learner's degrees of freedom. This argumentation is related to the different notions of positive and negative freedom put forward by Berlin (1969). In his essay "Two Concepts of Liberty," he distinguished between the *freedom from* regulative influence of the environment (negative freedom) and the *freedom to* act in certain commonly valued ways (positive freedom). Applied to scripting, highly coercive microscripts may impose restrictive conditions (and thereby reduce choice/autonomy by decreasing *freedom from* regulative influence of others), but they may also enable learners to acquire knowledge and skills they can use to engage productively in new collaborative situations (and thereby provide *freedom to* participate successfully in collaboration). A potentially important but neglected factor related to the aspect of freedom and autonomy is the *learner's subjective interpretation* of the freedom or coercion that is offered or exerted by the collaborative learning task, thus subjective overscripting and underscripting. Motivational problems resulting from feelings of lacking freedom *from* constraints might be compensated by the motivational gain derived from the individual's understanding and insight into the potential increase in options or freedom *to* act (see Berlin, 1969). The role of participants' subjective task interpretations and their impact on motivation has not yet been studied systematically however.

Scripting Sometimes Needs to Be Structured to Make Learning Harder

With the notion of scripts helping to regulate or even taking over regulation of learning activities, scripts appear to be primarily oriented toward smoothing learners' interactions and reducing CSCL process losses (Strijbos, Martens, Jochems, & Broers, 2004). Although reducing process losses may be one valuable function of scripts (Weinberger, Stegmann, & Fischer, 2010), smooth collaboration does not always imply successful individual learning. In addition to supporting learners' performance, Reiser (2004) argued that scaffolds in the form of software tools can and should sometimes problematize important aspects of the content. In fact, think-aloud studies (see Stegmann, Wecker et al., 2012) found that external scripts that were effective with respect to individual knowledge acquisition problematized the task to create opportunities for individual cognitive elaboration preceding or following discourse engagement. For instance, scripts could suggest that learners construct thought-provoking questions (King, 1999), which is certainly often a hard task, but which is directly related to cognitive processes of learning.

There Is a Need for More Adaptable and Adaptive Collaboration Scripts

A widespread misconception of CSCL scripting is that it is about designing and investigating relatively rigid digital stencils for learners to ensure knowledge acquisition, but at the expense of naturally occurring processes (e.g., Laurillard, 2009) of divergence and convergence in a group. Rather, scripting approaches aim at providing temporary external regulation when collaboration-related self-regulation skills (i.e., internal collaboration scripts) are not accessible to the learners. They enable meaningful activities in situations where these activities are not occurring spontaneously. CSCL scripts, therefore, need to be geared to learners' (non-)existing internal scripts and anticipate the complex interplay of external and internal scripts. Moreover, with learners' internal scripts developing, external scripts should in turn fade out to facilitate script internalization. External scripts, therefore, need to be adaptable (i.e., modifiable by the learners, tutors, or teachers; see X. Wang, Kollar et al., 2011) or adaptive (i.e., automatically adjusted by a computer; see Gweon et al., 2006). This idea is at the very heart of the broader concept of scaffolding (Pea, 2004). However, the studies reviewed in this chapter show that getting rid of external scripts is not all that easy. Whereas laboratory studies yielded positive effects of fading, especially when the self-regulated application of strategies are monitored by peers (Wecker & Fischer, 2011), studies in field settings have not been able to produce fading effects systematically so far. To implement CSCL scripting, further research is needed urgently on both fading and the development of adaptable and adaptive digital technologies. Conceptual frameworks, studies, and technologies (e.g., Harrer et al., 2007; Kobbe et al., 2007; Miao et al., 2007) reported in this chapter have only been initial steps toward flexible scripting in computer-supported collaborative learning.

There Is a Need to Strengthen Field Research on CSCL Scripts

Do scripts survive their release (back) "into the wild" of educational practice? The reported field studies have provided some preliminary evidence that collaboration scripts can be used effectively in various domains and that the general pattern of results can be replicated under "real world" conditions. However, there is still a lot to be done to produce systematic evidence that these complex lab-grown instructional tools are effective means of improving CSCL in real educational practice in formal education in schools and universities. There, collaboration scripts need to be embedded into a broader instructional approach (e.g., inquiry learning, problem-based learning, expository teaching). Scripting research thus must take the classroom context into account and identify or develop classroom scripts that orchestrate learning and collaboration processes at individual, small-group, and plenary levels in appropriate ways (e.g., Kollar et al., 2011; Mäkitalo-Siegl, Kohnle, & Fischer, 2011). It is even more of a pioneering task to address the questions of the extent to which and the effects with which computer-supported collaboration scripts once released into the wild might even penetrate *informal* learning landscapes.

"Collaboration Script" Is an Ideal Boundary Concept for Interdisciplinary Research

Collaboration scripts have been developed and investigated by researchers from cognitive psychology, educational science, and computer science and thus the concept that lies at truly cross-section of collaborative learning, instruction, and technology (see Fischer et al., 2007). On the technical side, the automated analysis of discourse is an important precondition for the development of more adaptive external scripts. Although promising, the reported findings on this topic (e.g., Diziol et al., 2010; Gweon et al., 2006; Y. Wang, Rosé, et al., 2007) can only be considered as first steps. To take full advantage of automated analyses, machine-readability is another important precondition. Script formalization is a challenging interdisciplinary endeavor toward a psychologically valid and yet machine-readable description of essential script components.

REFERENCES

Barron, B. (2000). Achieving coordination in collaborative problem-solving groups. *Journal of the Learning Sciences, 9*(4), 403–436.

Barron, B. (2003). When smart groups fail. *Journal of the Learning Sciences, 12*(3), 307–359.

Beers, P. J., Boshuizen, H. P. A., Kirschner, P. A., & Gijselaers, W. H. (2005). Computer support for knowledge construction in collaborative learning environments. *Computers in Human Behavior, 21*, 623–643.

Berlin, I. (1969). Two concepts of liberty. In *Four essays on liberty* (pp. 118-172). Oxford, UK: Oxford University Press.

Demetriadis, S., Egerter, T., Hanisch, F., & Fischer, F. (2011). Peer review-based scripted collaboration to support domain-specific and domain-general knowledge acquisition in computer science. *Computer Science Education, 21*(1), 29–56.

De Wever, B., Van Keer, H., Schellens, T., & Valcke, M. (2009). Structuring asynchronous discussion groups: The impact of role assignment and self-assessment on students' levels of knowledge construction through social negotiation. *Journal of Computer Assisted Learning, 25*, 177–188.

De Wever, B., van Keer, H., Schellens, T., & Valcke, M. (2010). Roles as a structuring tool in online discussion groups: The differential impact of different roles on social knowledge construction. *Computers in Human Behavior, 26*(4), 516–523.

Dillenbourg P. (2002). Over-scripting CSCL: The risks of blending collaborative learning with instructional design. In P. A. Kirschner (Ed.), *Three worlds of CSCL* (pp. 61–91). Heerlen, The Netherlands: Open University Press.

Dillenbourg, P., & Hong, F. (2008). The mechanics of CSCL macro scripts. *International Journal of Computer Supported Collaborative Learning, 3*(1), 5–23.

Dillenbourg, P., & Jermann, P. (2007). Designing integrative scripts. In F. Fischer, H. Mandl, J. Haake, & I. Kollar (Eds.), *Scripting computer-supported communication of knowledge-cognitive, computational and educational perspectives* (pp. 275–301). New York: Springer.

Dillenbourg, P., & Tchounikine, P. (2007). Flexibility in macro-scripts for computer-supported collaborative learning. *Journal of Computer Assisted Learning, 23*, 1–13.

Diziol, D., Walker, E., Rummel, N., & Koedinger, K. (2010). Using intelligent tutor technology to implement adaptive support for student collaboration. *Educational Psychology Review, 22*(1), 89–102.

Fischer, F., Kollar, I., Mandl, H., & Haake, J. M. (Eds.). (2007). *Scripting computer-supported communication of knowledge-cognitive, computational, and educational perspectives.* New York: Springer.

Fischer, F., Kollar, I., Stegmann, K. & Wecker, C. (in press). Toward a script theory of guidance in computer-supported collaborative learning. *Educational Psychologist.*

Gweon, G., Rosé, C. P., Zaiss, Z., & Carey, R. (2006). Providing support for adaptive scripting in an on-line collaborative learning environment. *Proceedings of the SIGCHI conference on human factors in computing systems* (pp. 251–260). New York: ACM Press.

Hämäläinen, R., Oksanen, K., & Häkkinen, P. (2008). Designing and analyzing collaboration in a scripted game for vocational education. *Computers in Human Behavior, 24*(6), 2496–2506.

Harrer, A., Malzahn, N., & Hoppe, H. U. (2007). Graphical modeling and simulation of learning designs. In T. Hirashima, H. U. Hoppe, & S. S. Young (Eds.), *Supporting learning flow through integrative technologies* (pp. 291–294). Amsterdam, The Netherlands: IOS Press.

Hudson, J. A., Fivush, R., & Kuebli, J. (1992). Scripts and episodes: The development of event memory. *Applied Cognitive Psychology, 6*, 483–505.

Kerr, N. L., & Bruun, S. E. (1983). Dispensability of member-effort and group motivation loss: Free-rider effects. *Journal of Personality and Social Psychology, 44*, 78–94.

Kester, L., & Paas, F. (2005). Instructional interventions to enhance collaboration in powerful learning environments. *Computers in Human Behavior, 21*, 689–696.

King, A. (1998). Transactive peer tutoring: Distributing cognition and metacognition. *Educational Psychology Review, 10*, 57–74.

King, A. (1999). Discourse patterns for mediating peer learning. In A. M. O'Donnell & A. King (Eds.), *Cognitive perspectives on peer learning* (pp. 87–115). Mahwah, NJ: Erlbaum.

King, A. (2007). Scripting collaborative learning processes: A cognitive perspective. In F. Fischer, I. Kollar, H. Mandl, & J. M. Haake (Eds.), *Scripting computer-supported collaborative learning: Cognitive, computational, and educational perspectives* (pp. 13–37). New York: Springer.

Kirschner, P. A., Beers, P. J., Boshuizen, H. P. A., & Gijselaers, W. H. (2008). Coercing shared knowledge in collaborative learning environments. *Computers in Human Behavior, 24*(2), 403–420.

Kirschner, P. A., Sweller, J., & Clark, R. E. (2006). Why minimal guidance during instruction does not work: An analysis of the failure of constructivist, discovery, problem-based, experiential, and inquiry-based teaching. *Educational Psychologist, 41*(2), 75–86.

Kobbe, L., Weinberger, A., Dillenbourg, P., Harrer, A., Hämäläinen, R., Häkkinen, P., & Fischer, F. (2007). Specifying computer-supported collaboration scripts. *International Journal of Computer-Supported Collaborative Learning, 2*(2–3), 211–224.

Kollar, I., & Fischer, F. (2006). Supporting self-regulated learners for a while and what computers can contribute. *Journal of Educational Computing Research, 35*(4), 425–435.

Kollar, I., Fischer, F., & Hesse, F. W. (2006). Collaboration scripts—A conceptual analysis. *Educational Psychology Review, 18*(2), 159–185.

Kollar, I., Fischer, F., & Slotta, J. D. (2007). Internal and external scripts in computer–supported collaborative inquiry learning. *Learning & Instruction, 17*(6), 708–721.

Kollar, I., Fischer, F., & Slotta, J. D. (2008). Argumentation in web-based collaborative inquiry learning: Scripts for writing and scripts for talking aren't the same. In G. Kanselaar, V. Jonker, P. A. Kirschner, & F. Prins (Eds.), *International perspectives in the learning sciences: creating a learning world: Proceedings of the 8th International Conference for the Learning Sciences (ICLS) 2008* (Vol. 1, pp. 453–460). Utrecht, The Netherlands: ISLS.

Kollar, I., Wecker, C., Langer, S., & Fischer, F. (2011). Orchestrating web–based collaborative inquiry learning with small group and classroom scripts. In H. Spada, G. Stahl, N. Miyake, & N. Law (Eds.), *Connecting computer-supported collaborative learning to policy and practice: CSCL2011 Conference Proceedings* (Vol. 1, pp. 422–429). Hong Kong, China: ISLS.

Kolodner, J. L. (2007). The roles of scripts in promoting collaborative discourse in learning by design. In F. Fischer, H. Mandl, J. Haake, & I. Kollar (Eds.), *Scripting computer-supported collaborative learning—Cognitive, computational, and educational perspectives* (pp. 237–271). New York: Springer.

Kuhn, D. (1991). *The skills of argument*. New York: Cambridge University Press.

Laurillard, D. (2009). The pedagogical challenges to collaborative technologies. *International Journal of Computer-Supported Collaborative Learning, 4*(1), 5–20.

Linn, M. C., & Eylon, B.-S. (2011). *Science learning and instruction: Taking advantage of technology to promote knowledge integration*. New York: Routledge.

Linn, M.C., Lee, H.-S., Tinker, R., Husic, F., & Chiu, J. L. (2006). Teaching and assessing knowledge integration in science. *Science, 313,* 1049–1050.

Mäkitalo, K., Weinberger, A., Häkkinen, P., Järvelä, S., & Fischer, F. (2005). Epistemic cooperation scripts in online learning environments: Fostering learning by reducing uncertainty in discourse? *Computers in Human Behavior, 21*(4), 603–622.

Mäkitalo-Siegl, K., Kohnle, C., & Fischer, F. (2011). Computer-supported collaborative inquiry learning and classroom scripts: Effects on help-seeking processes and learning outcomes. *Learning and Instruction, 21*(2), 257–266.

Mayer, R. E. (2004). Should there be a three strikes rule against pure discovery learning? The case for guided methods of instruction. *American Psychologist, 59*(1), 14–19.

McNeill, K. L., Lizotte, D. J., Krajcik, J., & Marx, R. W. (2006). Supporting students' construction of scientific explanations by fading scaffolds in instructional materials. *Journal of the Learning Sciences, 15*(2), 153–191.

Miao, Y., Harrer, K., Hoeksema, K., & Hoppe, U. (2007). Modeling CSCL scripts—A reflection on learning design approaches. In F. Fischer, I. Kollar, H. Mandl, & J. M. Haake (Eds.), *Scripting computer-supported collaborative learning—Cognitive, computational and educational perspectives* (pp. 117–135). New York: Springer.

Mu, J., Stegmann, K., Mayfield, E., Rosé, C., & Fischer, F. (2012). The ACODEA framework: Developing classification schemes for fully automatic classification of online discussions. *International Journal of Computer-Supported Collaborative Learning, 7*(2), 285–304.

O'Donnell, A. M., & Dansereau, D. F. (1992). Scripted cooperation in student dyads: A method for analyzing and enhancing academic learning and performance. In R. Hertz-Lazarowitz & N. Miller (Eds.), *Interactions in cooperative groups: The theoretical anatomy of group learning* (pp. 120–141). Cambridge, UK: Cambridge University Press.

Palincsar, A. S., & Brown, A. (1984). Reciprocal teaching of comprehension-fostering and comprehension-monitoring activities. *Cognition and Instruction, 1*(2), 117–175.

Pea, R. D. (2004). The social and technological dimensions of scaffolding and related theoretical concepts for learning, education, and human activity. *Journal of the Learning Sciences, 13*(3), 423–451.

Pfister, H. R., & Oehl, M. (2009). The impact of goal focus, task type and group size on synchronous net-based collaborative learning discourses. *Journal of Computer Assisted Learning, 25*(2), 161–176.

Rall, M., & Gaba, D. M. (2005). Human performance and patient safety. In R. D. Miller (Ed.), *Miller's anesthesia* (pp. 3021–3072). Philadelphia, PA: Elsevier.

Reiser, B. J. (2004). Scaffolding complex learning: The mechanisms of structuring and problematizing student work. *Journal of the Learning Sciences, 13*(3), 273–304.

Ronen, M., Kohen-Vacs, D., Harrer, A., & Kali, Y. (2009). Modeling, creating and enacting online collaborative scripts. In A. Dimitracopoulou, C. O'Malley, D. Suthers, & P. Reimann (Eds.), *Computer supported collaborative learning practices: CSCL2009 Community events proceedings* (p. 218). Rhodes, Greece: ISLS.

Rosé, C. P., Wang, Y. C., Arguello, J., Stegmann, K., Weinberger, A., & Fischer, F. (2008). Analyzing collaborative learning processes automatically: Exploiting the advances of computational linguistics in computer-supported collaborative learning. *International Journal of Computer-Supported Collaborative Learning, 3,* 237–271.

Rummel, N., & Spada, H. (2005). Learning to collaborate. An instructional approach to promoting collaborative problem-solving in computer-mediated settings. *Journal of the Learning Sciences, 14*(2), 201–241.

Scardamalia, M., & Bereiter, C. (1996). Computer support for knowledge-building communities. In T. Koschmann (Ed.), *CSCL: Theory and practice of an emerging paradigm* (pp. 249–268). Mahwah, NJ: Erlbaum.

Scardamalia, M., & Bereiter, C. (2006). Knowledge building: Theory, pedagogy, and technology. In K. Sawyer (Ed.), *Cambridge handbook of the learning sciences* (pp. 97–118). New York: Cambridge University Press.

Schank, R. C. (1999). *Dynamic memory revisited.* New York: Cambridge University Press.

Schellens, T., & Valcke, M. (2005). Collaborative learning in asynchronous discussion groups: What about the impact on cognitive processing? *Computers in Human Behavior, 21,* 957–975.

Schoonenboom, J. (2008). The effect of a script and a structured interface in grounding discussions. *International Journal of Computer-Supported Collaborative Learning, 3*(3), 327–341.

Stahl, G. (2002). Rediscovering CSCL. In T. Koschmann, R. Hall, & N. Miyake (Eds.), *CSCL 2: Carrying forward the conversation* (pp. 169–181). New York: Springer.

Stahl, G., Koschmann, T., & Suthers, D. (2006). Computer-supported collaborative learning. In R. K. Sawyer (Ed.), *The Cambridge handbook of the learning sciences* (pp. 409–425). New York: Cambridge University Press.

Stegmann, K., Mu, J., Gehlen–Baum, V., & Fischer, F. (2011). The myth of over-scripting: Can novices be supported too much? In H. Spada, G. Stahl, N. Miyake, & N. Law (Eds.), *Connecting computer-supported col-*

laborative learning to policy and practice: CSCL2011 Conference Proceedings (Vol. 1, pp. 406–413). Hong Kong, China: ISLS.

Stegmann, K., Streng, S., Halbinger, M., Koch, J., Fischer, F., & Hussmann, H. (2009). eXtremely Simple Scripting (XSS): A framework to speed up the development of computer-supported collaboration scripts. In A. Dimitracopoulou, C. O'Malley, D. Suthers, & P. Reimann (Eds.), *Computer supported collaborative learning practices: CSCL2009 community events proceedings* (pp. 195–197). Rhodes, Greece: ISLS.

Stegmann, K., Wecker, C., Weinberger, A., & Fischer, F. (2012). Collaborative argumentation and cognitive elaboration in a computer-supported collaborative learning environment. *Instructional Science, 40*(2), 297–323.

Stegmann, K., Weinberger, A., & Fischer, F. (2007). Facilitating argumentative knowledge construction with computer-supported collaboration scripts. *International Journal of Computer-Supported Collaborative Learning, 2*(4), 421–447.

Strijbos, J. W., Kirschner, P. A., & Martens, R. (2004). What we know about CSCL … and what we do not know (but need to) know about CSCL. In J. W. Strijbos, P. A. Kirschner, & R. Martens (Eds.), *What we know about CSCL and implementing it in higher education* (pp. 245–259). Boston, MA: Kluwer.

Strijbos, J. W., Martens, R. L., Jochems, W. M. G., & Broers, N. J. (2004). The effect of functional roles on group efficiency: Using multilevel modeling and content analysis to investigate computer-supported collaboration in small groups. *Small Group Research, 35*, 195–229.

Teasley, S. D. (1995). The role of talk in children's peer collaborations. *Developmental Psychology, 31*(2), 207–220.

Teasley, S. D., & Roschelle, J. (1993). Constructing a joint problem space: The computer as a tool for sharing knowledge. In S. P. Lajoie & S. J. Derry (Eds.), *Discourse, tools, and reasoning: Essays on situated cognition* (pp. 229–258). Berlin, Germany: Springer.

Walker, E., Rummel, N., & Koedinger, K. (2011). Adaptive support for CSCL: Is it feedback relevance or increased student accountability that matters? In H. Spada, G. Stahl, N. Miyake, & N. Law (Eds.), *Connecting computer-supported collaborative learning to policy and practice: CSCL2011 Conference Proceedings* (Vol. 1, pp. 334–341). Hong Kong, China: ISLS.

Wang, X., Kollar, I., Stegmann, K., & Fischer, F. (2011). Adaptable scripting in computer–supported collaborative learning to foster knowledge and skill acquisition. In H. Spada, G. Stahl, N. Miyake, & N. Law (Eds.), *Connecting computer-supported collaborative learning to policy and practice: CSCL2011 Conference Proceedings* (Vol. 1, pp. 382–389). Hong Kong, China: ISLS.

Wang, Y., Rosé, C. P., Joshi, M., Fischer, F., Weinberger, A., & Stegmann, K. (2007). Context based classification for automatic collaborative learning process analysis. *Proceeding of the 2007 Conference on Artificial Intelligence in Education: Building Technology Rich Learning Contexts that Work* (pp. 662–664). Amsterdam, Netherlands: IOS.

Wecker, C. & Fischer, F. (2011). From guided to self-regulated performance of domain-general skills: The role of peer monitoring during the fading of instructional scripts. *Learning and Instruction, 21*(6), 746–756.

Wecker, C., Kollar, I., Fischer, F., & Prechtl, H. (submitted). *Fostering scientific literacy in the classroom with continuous and faded computer-supported collaboration scripts.*

Weinberger, A., Ertl, B., Fischer, F., & Mandl, H. (2005). Epistemic and social scripts in computer-supported collaborative learning. *Instructional Science, 33*(1), 1–30.

Weinberger, A., Stegmann, K., & Fischer, F. (2010). Learning to argue online: Scripted groups surpass individuals (unscripted groups do not). *Computers in Human Behavior, 26*(4), 506–515.

Weinberger, A., Stegmann, K., Fischer, F., & Mandl, H. (2007). Scripting argumentative knowledge construction in computer-supported learning environments. In F. Fischer, I. Kollar, H. Mandl, & J. Haake (Eds.), *Scripting computer-supported communication of knowledge—Cognitive, computational and educational Perspectives* (pp. 191–211). New York: Springer.

Zottmann, J., Dieckmann, P., Rall, M., Fischer, F., & Taraszow, T. (2006). Fostering simulation-based learning in medical education with collaboration scripts. *Simulation in Healthcare, 1*(3), 193.

24

MOBILE COMPUTER-SUPPORTED COLLABORATIVE LEARNING

CHEE-KIT LOOI, LUNG-HSIANG WONG, AND YANJIE SONG

National Institute of Education, Singapore

INTRODUCTION

Computer-supported collaborative learning (CSCL) researchers have explored the types of interaction that are necessary in a collaborative team in order to produce positive learning outcomes. These include such interactions as data and idea exchanges, explanations, argumentations, conflict resolution, knowledge construction, and artifact coconstruction. The researchers have also designed learning environments and scripts which scaffold these interactions. Collaborative activities are now integrated into curricular activity systems, learning activity workflows, or pedagogical scenarios that include individual, small-group, and class-wide activities occurring in a variety of settings (e.g., classroom, home, workplace, field trips, off-campus community) and modes (e.g., face-to-face or remote; synchronous or asynchronous).

From the perspective of mobile learning (m-learning), the premise is that learners are mobile, mobile technologies are ubiquitous and ready-at-hand, and learners can learn and collaborate in context. The unique technology characteristic of "mobility" offers opportunities for learners to share and construct knowledge readily in different settings and modes. Historically, mobile technologies were introduced into education in the last decade of the 20th century, and mobile technology educational applications have taken shape at the beginning of 21st century throughout the world. Mobile-computer supported learning (mCSCL) was "discovered" among these applications at an early stage, focusing on notions of collaboration enabled by mobile devices (e.g., Colella, 2000; Soloway et al., 2001; Zurita & Nussbaum, 2004).

Researchers have also designed and tested various forms of mCSCL to support collaboration in and out of classrooms and in online learning communities. In classrooms, tools such as classroom response systems, participatory simulations, and collaborative scaffolding have been designed and adopted in mCSCL activities for enhancing interactivity, augmenting collaborative spaces, and enhancing negotiation about meaning (e.g., Davis, 2003; Klopfer, Squire, & Jenkins, 2008; Nussbaum et al., 2009). Outside the classroom, various tools on the mobile devices have been used for groups' situated, experiential, and inquiry learning in field trips or outdoor mCSCL activities (e.g., Chen, Kao, & Sheu, 2003; Rogers & Price, 2009; Wong, Chen, Looi, & Zhang, 2010). Mobile device tools have also been employed to bridge indoor and outdoor mCSCL activities, and cross the boundary between formal and informal learning (e.g., Looi, Seow, et al., 2010; Vavoula, Sharples, Rudman, Meek, & Lonsdale, 2009).

This chapter provides a summary of research and development in the emerging field of CSCL using mobile technologies, known in the literature as mCSCL (mobile CSCL). In exploring the synergies between CSCL approaches and m-learning approaches, we will review m-learning definitions and the nascent work in theorizing them. We will discuss the characteristics and affordances of mobile technologies, mCSCL pedagogical practices, and methodological issues.

EVOLUTION OF DEFINITIONS OF M-LEARNING

In parallel with the increase in mobile educational applications is the growth of different understandings of m-learning. According to Quinn (2001, p. 21), "m-learning is e-learning through mobile computational devices"; likewise, Hoppe, Joiner, Milrad, and Sharples (2003) defined it as "e-learning using mobile devices and wireless transmission" (p. 255). Both of these definitions convey the message that m-learning is an extension of "e-learning." O'Malley et al. (2003) defined m-learning as "any sort of learning that happens when the learner is not at a fixed, predetermined location, or learning that happens when the learner takes advantage of the learning opportunities offered by mobile technologies" (p. 9). This definition, taking into consideration the "mobility" offered by mobile technologies, has a broader view than the previous ones.

Barbosa, Geyer, and Barbosa (2005) contended that m-learning is about increasing learners' capabilities to move their own learning environments physically as they move. With m-learning, the learning environment is no longer fixed to one particular location (e.g., physical classroom) or digital context (e.g., e-learning portal) but moves to wherever the learner is, hence enabling the surroundings to transform into the learning environment. This definition and characterization recognizes the importance of learning environments that transcend physical settings, emphasizing the "mobility" of m-learning in context. From these definitions, it can be noted that m-learning is evolving from a focus on intersecting mobile computing with e-learning to a focus on the "mobility" of learning in context, reflecting the shift of m-learning educational research from a technological focus to foregrounding a social, situated, and "just-in-time and -place" learning. Nevertheless, these definitional concepts barely touch on how to theorize m-learning in education.

EXPLORING WAYS TO THEORIZE M-LEARNING

Recognizing the undertheorization of m-learning, Sharples, Taylor, and Vavoula (2007) paved the way in developing a theory of m-learning that reconceptualized learning by encompassing both learning supported by the mobile technology and learning characterized by the mobility of people and knowledge. They argued that, in order to create a theory of m-learning, it should be distinguished from other forms of learning by showing: (a) that learners learn across space as they take ideas and learning resources obtained in one location and apply or develop them in another, learners learn across time by revisiting knowledge acquired earlier in a different context, which provides a framework for lifelong learning, learners move from topic by topic by managing a range of personal learning projects rather than sticking to a single curriculum, and learners move in and out of engagement with technology; (b) how impromptu sites of learning are created out of offices, classrooms, and lecture halls; (c) a social-constructivist approach that views learning as an active process of building knowledge and skills through practice in a supportive community; and (d) the ubiquitous use of personal and shared technologies. Based on these criteria, the authors defined m-learning as "the processes of coming to know through conversations across multiple contexts amongst people and personal interactive technologies" (p. 225).

Thus m-learning is reconceptualized as a process of coming to know through conversation/communication across continually reconstructed contexts. The authors used activity theory (Engeström, 1987) as a framework, this typically being used to understand human activity in context (Cole & Engestrom, 2007). It assumes human cognition and behavior as embedded in collectively organized, artifact-mediated activity systems (Cole & Engestrom, 2007; Engestrom, 1987; Leont'ev, 1978). Learning is conceptualized as interactions and negotiations between individuals, humans, or nonhumans (e.g., mobile technologies), which occur in the form of evolving states of knowing as they are shaped by continuously negotiated goals in the changing contexts. The mobile technology provides a shared conversational learning space on the move, which can be used not only for single learners but also for learning groups and communities. The technology can also be utilized to demonstrate ideas or proffer advice, as with the Internet or through specific tools to negotiate agreements, such as concept maps and visualization tools. Other studies (e.g., Liaw, Hatala, & Huang, 2010; Wali, Winters, & Oliver, 2008; Waycott, Jones, & Scanlon, 2005; Zurita & Nussbaum, 2007) have also grounded and conceptualized m-learning using activity theory.

Laurillard (2007) proposed using a conversational framework to investigate how mobile technologies can contribute to the learning process. Regarding collaboration, the conversational framework holds that learners will be motivated to improve their collaborative practices if they can share their products with peers, and to enhance their conceptual understanding if they can reflect on their experiences by discussing their products with peers. Such a view is congruent with that advocated in So, Seow, and Looi (2009) and Wong, Chen, and Jan (2012), that students' contextualized artifacts created in situ (e.g., during a teacher-facilitated field trip) have the potential to go beyond facilitating just-in-time knowledge sharing to mediating future knowledge coconstructions. This requires that the teacher set up motivating collaborative and competitive tasks for the students, who will be motivated by the prospect of contributing to a product or artifact as part of the learning process. A typical collaborative m-learning activity can provide more opportunities for digitally facilitated site-specific collaboration, and for ownership and control over what the learners do jointly, because the mobile devices digitally facilitate the link between the students and the data/products on the spot. However, Sharples et al. (2007) posited that, because the Conversational Framework describes conversations for learning situated in one physical location, it does not address adequately the challenging issues of the constantly negotiated communication and interaction in the continually changing context in mCSCL.

Notwithstanding these theorizations of m-learning in the context of an activity system and Conversational Framework, large numbers of mCSCL studies have adopted "folk theories" based on commonsense assumptions in interpreting the results of interventions for collaborative learning, as if there were no need for theory (Stahl & Hesse, 2010), while much less research has attempted to delve into and refine theoretical perspectives specific to mCSCL. It is high time to rediscover mCSCL. What does mCSCL mean? What are the pedagogies and methodological issues of mCSCL? These are the questions that confront us, and that are hard for us to answer, yet need to be discussed.

MCSCL

What Does mCSCL Stand For?

Does mCSCL stand for "mobile + CSCL"? Our answer is "Yes" and "No." The evolution of mobile technology is believed to be part of the fourth wave computer technology that will deliver anywhere, anytime learning (Pownell & Bailey, 2002). Thus, if we try to understand the acronyms of mCSCL literally, our answer is "Yes": it stands for mobile-computer supported collaborative learning. However, if we attempt to understand practices of mCSCL, our answer is "No": it does not simply mean that the differences in the practices of CSCL and mCSCL lie in the word *mobile* added to the front of CSCL, but lie in the changing practices that "mobile" technologies have contributed to.

Characteristics and Affordances of Mobile Technologies

To understand the changes regarding mCSCL practices caused by mobile technologies, it is important to be clear about the characteristics and affordances of the technologies that are new and different from computer (desktop and laptop) technologies. Many researchers have expressed the belief that mobile technologies can potentially have a great impact on the ways of practice as a result of their portability/mobility, immediate accessibility, and connectivity (Klopfer, Yoon, & Rivas, 2004; Norris & Soloway, 2004; Segall, Doolen, & Porter, 2005). In particular, the portability of mobile devices is considered to be a significant factor that contributes to collaborative learning because it can help students to coordinate and interact in joint projects and share resources over the mobile devices more readily (So, Seow & Looi, 2009; Zurita & Nussbaum, 2004). The immediate accessibility offered by mobile devices is considered to be one of the greatest benefits for both teachers and students (Ally, McGreal, Schafer, Tin, & Cheung, 2008). Using the devices, data can be collected, stored, and organized easily, and the information can be searched, posted, and shared instantly (Ally et al., 2008; Crowe & van't Hooft, 2006; Sharples et al., 2007).

Another characteristic of mobile devices is connectivity. Now the evolution of computing, using mobile devices with new types of wireless connectivity, allows collaborative learning to happen anytime, anywhere. This changes the rules of technology use, both in and out of the classroom. With connectivity, communication between students and the tutor, and among peers, is enhanced via a package of communication tools such as short messaging service (SMS), e-mails, phone calls, communication systems, and the Internet (e.g., Markett, Arnedillo-Sanchez, Weber, & Tangney, 2006); valuable information and resources can be shared via file exchanges between mobile devices using Bluetooth or Infrared port "just-in-time" (e.g., Lai & Wu, 2006); and coconstruction of knowledge among students and online learning communities can be improved via online chat tools such as MSN messaging and forums (So, Seow, & Looi, 2010). Although interactivity, individuality, and context sensitivity (e.g., Cui & Bull, 2005; Markett et al., 2006) have also been considered to be characteristics of mobile devices, mobility, accessibility, and connectivity are the essential features that make all other characteristics possible. In addition, interactivity is not unique to mobile technologies.

Affordances coexist with constraints (Conole & Dyke, 2004). Mobile technology educational research has also revealed a host of technical constraints. The main constraints include the small screen sizes of mobile devices, a lack of standard platforms among different devices, problems in browsing websites, lack of ubiquitous connectivity, difficulties in writing input, and lack of computational power.

The affordances and constraints of mobile technologies influence the possibilities for collaboration. Different types of mobile devices offer different form factors and mobility affordances. The mobility of a device and its weight (from hand-held smart phones to tablets to Netbooks to notebooks), along with the form factor of mobile devices, afford and constrain the potential for CSCL. However, a small screen size does not have to be a barrier to collaborative work. For example, small screen displays do afford multiple users viewing their displays and seem to support more cooperative styles of working when partners have their own activities to complete, but come together periodically to share digital information (Stanton & Neale, 2002). mCSCL software tools can have forms of interface design that allow children to collaborate around a mobile device or devices which coordinate the interaction among them and enable them to share their responses and other information (Zurita & Nussbaum, 2004). In particular, Rogers, Connelly, Hazlewood, and Tedesco (2010) viewed the small form factor as an opportunity to facilitate new learning models or habits—with the devices to be used for short bursts of time (e.g., entering and comparing data, looking up and reviewing information, brief communication and sharing of artifacts with peers and remote people) to support foregrounded physical activities in situ.

The mobile devices of relatively smaller form factors may still make the relatively "complex" and in-depth knowledge synthesis and knowledge coconstruction activities rather tedious if the learners are using mobile devices solely to perform these tasks. For example, it is difficult even for a single learner to create a concept map with more than 20 nodes using a smart phone, not to mention if a collaborative concept mapping task is to be carried out by a group of students through their smart phones. With this, Wong and Looi (2011) advocated a "division of labor" strategy, with each student keeping one smart phone and one netbook or laptop at hand to handle the needs of various formal and informal, planned and incidental learning tasks. The small size and light weight of smart phones make them the perfect tool for students to perform quick and rapid learning tasks on the move, including scripted or spontaneous communication or collaboration among members of the learning community (students, teachers, etc.). Whenever students have the chance to sit down (either during a field trip, on public transport, in the library, in the park, or at home), the netbook or laptop (or perhaps school or home PC) will compensate for the limitations of the smart phones by supporting them in carrying out more "complex" learning tasks such as detailed data analysis, learning collaboratively in 3D virtual environments, and knowledge building. Examples of prior mCSCL studies that adopted similar strategies were reported in So, Seow, and Looi (2008), Thompson and Stewart (2007), and Wong, Chin, Tan, and Liu (2010), with students making use of lightweight mobile devices for personal or collaborative in situ learning activities, and school or home computers for extended knowledge coconstruction over a relatively longer period of time.

MCSCL PEDAGOGICAL DESIGN AND PRACTICES

This section summarizes current mCSCL pedagogical design and practices by categorizing them into three main types: in-class mCSCL, out-of-class mCSCL, and mCSCL that bridges both in-class and out-of-class activities. We also discuss the notion of a curricular activity system that might comprise learning activities of these three main types put together coherently to realize some curricular goals.

In-Class mCSCL Pedagogical Practices

Roschelle (2003), focusing on the "key [classroom] communication issues" (p. 262) of mobile technologies that may affect pedagogic practices, classified collaborative activities into three types: classroom response systems (e.g., Davis, 2003), participatory simulations (e.g., Colella, 2000; Soloway et al., 2001), and collaborative data gathering (e.g., Vahey & Crawford, 2002). A classroom response system allows a teacher to pose a short answer or a multiple-choice question. The system instantly collects and aggregates all students' responses through their handheld devices (such as clickers, graphing calculators, WinCE handhelds, or special-purpose infrared beaming units). Facilitated through a 1:1 setting, a participatory simulation enables students to act as agents in simulations in which overall patterns emerge from local decisions and information exchanges. The system computes the simulation of a scientific phenomenon such as swarming ants, traffic jams, or the spread of disease. In collaborative data gathering activities, students use probes to gather and graph data from live experiments.

Looking back on Roschelle's publication almost a decade later, we found his classification is far from being exhaustive given the more diversified innovative designs in this area that emerged after the paper was published. Nevertheless, Roschelle had indeed highlighted three specific classroom-based mCSCL models that were developed in the early days of m-learning research which are otherwise impossible or tedious to be implemented without the deployment of mobile technology (specifically, a 1:1 setting is essential to facilitate the first two models). Conversely, in advocating their approach to future classrooms organized around wireless internet learning devices (WILD), Roschelle and Pea (2002) argued that CSCL should leverage application-level affordances such as augmenting physical spaces, leveraging topological spaces, aggregating coherently across all students, as well as the physical affordances of mobile devices.

One important study of in-class mCSCL tackled the use of mobile connected devices in classrooms for teaching young children how to collaborate (Nussbaum, Alvarez et al., 2009). In the CollPad system, students were given language and mathematics tasks they had to solve by working in fixed groups of three, with each student being equipped with a PDA. Figure 24.1 shows a pedagogical flow in which groups of three students, each working out their own solutions to a mathematics problem, collaborated and sought consensus with each other in the group and later in the class, with the teacher mediating and guiding classroom discussions.

In Syllable-mCSCL, a Spanish vocabulary-learning game for young children, the students were given language tasks that they had to solve by working in groups of three. A syllable is assigned by the system to each group member's mobile device (e.g., "si," "la,"

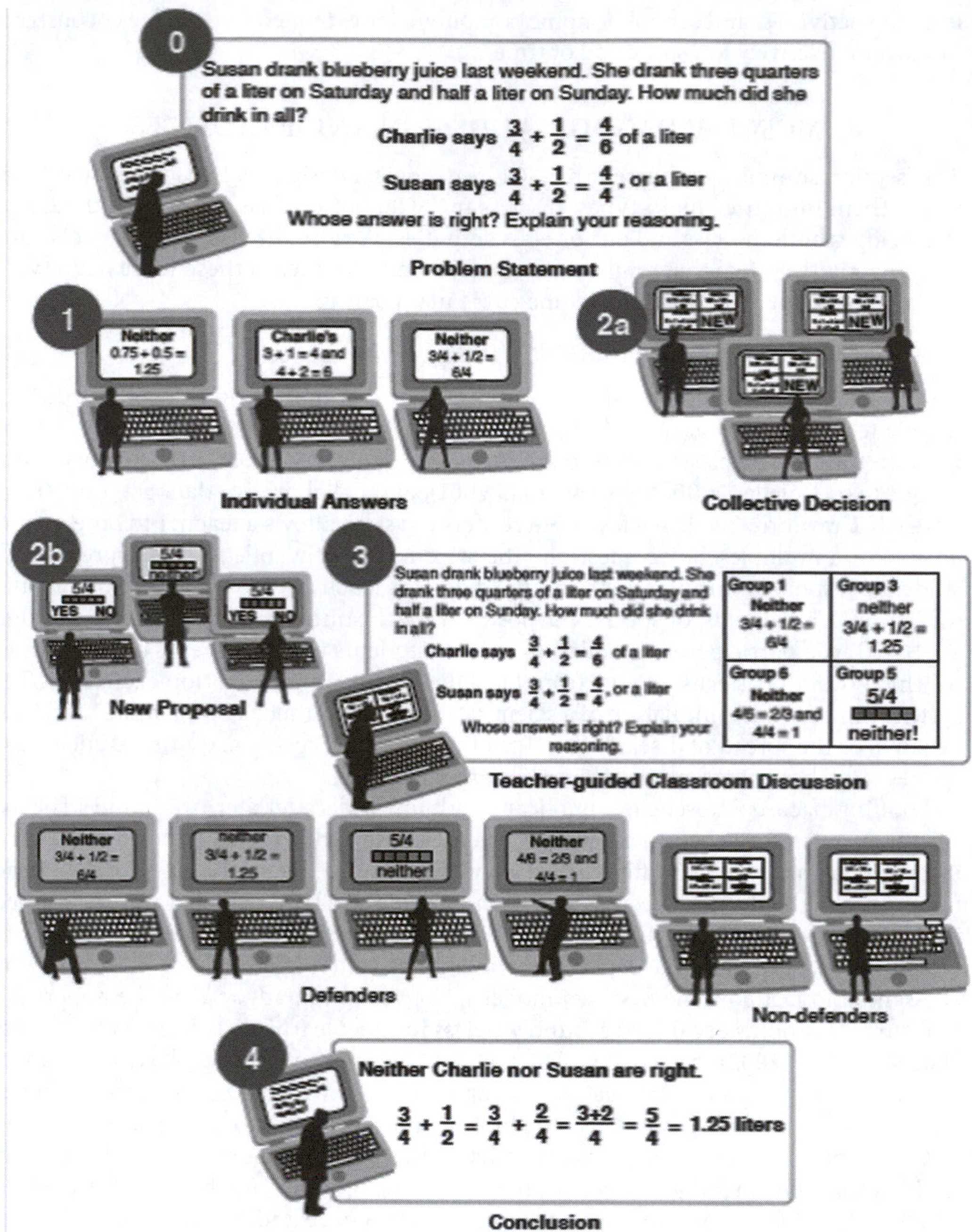

Figure 24.1 CollPad system for mCSCL (we thank Miguel Nussbaum of providing this figure).

and "bi") and the three students within the group need to determine the sequences of the syllables to form correct Spanish words (e.g., "silabi"). In the process, they have to exhibit a certain level of interaction and communication in order to complete the group tasks. The authors reported that the use of wireless networks in the classroom opened up many educational possibilities and that mobile devices advanced various components of collaborative learning, namely the learning material organization, social negotiation space, communication between team members, coordination between activity states, and the possibilities for interactivity and mobility of team members (Kreijns et al., 2002).

These mCSCL practices extend the idea of mobile technology mediated learning with the collaborative scaffolding in order to include both social and epistemic collaboration scripts encouraging small-group participation (Nussbaum et al., 2009). The design of collaborative scaffolding encourages social interactions, facilitates joint problem solving, leads to richer knowledge construction, takes into account different and emerging roles, joint group goals and actions, and facilitates verbal explanations.

Inspired by Zurita and Nussbaum's body of work, Boticki, Looi, and Wong (2011) designed and developed Form-A-One (FAO), a game-based mCSCL approach with the salient characteristics of spontaneous group formation and the dynamic balance between collaboration and competition. The FAO approach was instantiated in two domains—mathematics and Chinese Language learning. In the mathematics game, each student receives a different fraction and has to find other students with fractions to form a whole of one. In the Chinese Language game (Wong, Boticki, Sun, & Looi, 2011), each student receives a different component of a Chinese character, and has to find other students with components that form legitimate Chinese characters (Figure 24.2). Students have to achieve local goals (maximizing individual group size) and a global goal (minimizing the number of peers who are unable to form groups or even disbanding groups to form new combinations with others).

The Zurita and Nussbaum mCSCL learning model and Boticki, Looi, and Wong's FAO are based on the common idea of disseminating domain-specific components to

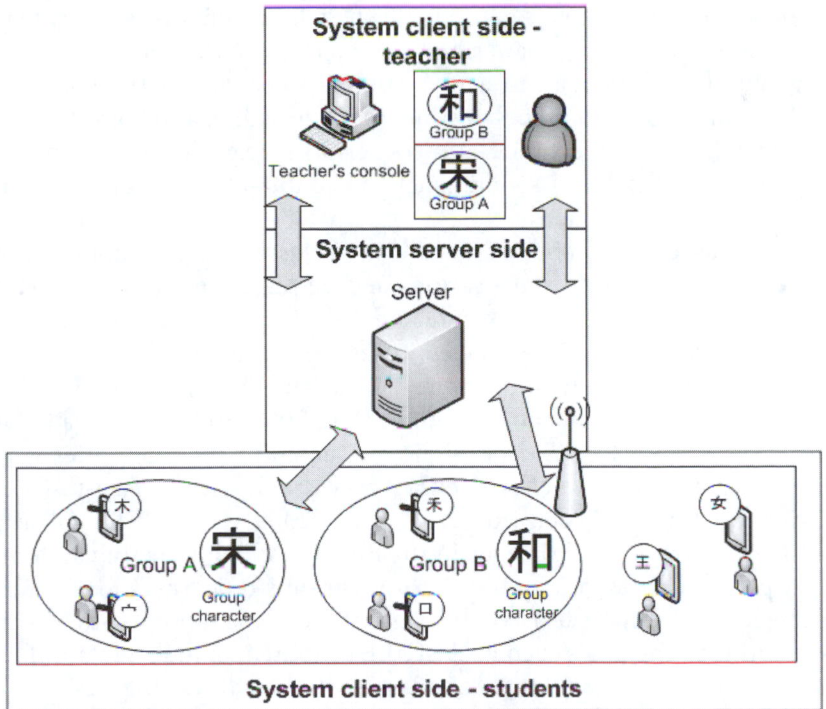

Figure 24.2 Students collaborating to form Chinese characters in mCSCL.

individual students through their mobile devices and requiring them to piece the components together to achieve certain objectives. Indeed, both learning models can also be implemented through non-mCSCL means, such as using cards or paper tokens or using stable technologies (e.g., personal computers) in 1:1 settings. However, it is the mCSCL solution that brings together the mutually exclusive but complementary advantages of the two alternative settings. The mCSCL solutions may free students and teachers from dealing with cumbersome physical resources and, instead allows them to focus on the sociocognitive process, or (for teachers) orchestrating the learning process "globally," as well as ensuring a mixture of face-to-face and mobile technology mediated communication for greater social interactivity.

In-class mCSCL typically augments the conventional face-to-face communication and collaboration of physical classrooms with a layer of networked communication through devices. Face-to-face collaboration is not necessarily obsolete as a result, but its forms might be changed or simplified. For example, in FAO games (Boticki et al., 2011), although a student can identify and invite peers to form a group via the device, more sophisticated negotiations (e.g., for optimizing the groupings), as well as the teacher's domain-specific scaffolding, may still need to be carried out face-to-face when such needs arise. In collaboration over mobile devices, the device can serve as a cognitive tool, as a productive tool, as a data retrieval or context sensing tool, or provide the means to use existing collaboration tools like Web 2.0, SMS/MMS, IM, or Group Scribbles.

Out-of-Class mCSCL Activities

Congruent with the notion of situated, experiential, social, and inquiry views of learning, field trips and outdoor activities are well-established activities for many schools. With the incorporation of mobile equipment, the trip facilitators, such as teachers, are in a better position to strike a balance between ensuring a learner-centered experience (e.g., using mobile technologies to access context-sensitive multimedia information, reflective data collection and processing, augmented reality, and communication with peers or teachers) and external moderation or scripting (e.g., field trip management and scaffolding), through flexibility, spontaneity, and adaptability in mobile settings (Frohberg, 2006).

In the social aspect of mobile-assisted out-of-class learning, mobile technologies provide a vehicle for multiple conversations to take place, and more opportunities for students and their instructors to verbalize and reflect upon their inquiries (Chan et al., 2006; Rogers & Price, 2009). Nevertheless, museum visitors or learners using mobile devices tend to focus their attention more on the mobile devices than on interacting with the physical environment and each other (Hsi, 2003; Spikol & Milrad, 2008).

Therefore, researchers have been designing situated mCSCL activities with explicit requirements for collaborative efforts, either over the device via face-to-face communication, such as Ambient Wood (Rogers & Price, 2009) and LET'S GO! (Maldonado & Pea, 2010), or through the device, as in the Bird-Watching Learning system (Chen et al. 2003). A particular design requires separate groups of learners located at different parts of a site (or at multiple sites) to collect and share information on-the-fly in order to achieve certain learning goals such as AMULETS (Kurti, Spikol, & Milrad, 2008) and Laborador Trail (Wong, Chen, Looi, & Zhang, 2010). Such learning designs, which are made possible by the mobile technology, are rooted in the notions of distributed cognition (Hutchins, 2000) and positive interdependence (Johnson & Johnson, 1992). For example, in the AMULETS activity, students in the outdoor group can explore the old city area of Vaxjö, Sweden, and collect cultural, historical, and geographical data (such as photos of ancient buildings) with their smart phones. The data can then be transmitted to the indoor group of students stationed in a local museum and equipped with laptops for further processing.

Similarly, in Labrador Trail, where students visit some World War II military infrastructure within Labrador Park, Singapore, several scripted tasks are introduced to reinforce mCSCL activities throughout the field trip. One such example pertains to a hole in the ceiling of a restored tunnel where former soldiers inside the tunnel could transfer ammunition by means of a hanging rope to their counterparts who were operating a battery on top of the tunnel. Two different student groups, who have not been told about the functionality of the hole, are led to the battery and the tunnel respectively. They are asked to take videos and share with each other via a moblog in order to piece their observations together and deduce the use of the hole. It is the collaborative inquiry process that both designs bring forward to the students in order to foster their awareness and capabilities in collaboratively collecting, analyzing, and synthesizing data and knowledge, with the aid of the mobile technology.

Bridging In-Class and Out-of-Class mCSCL Activities

Bridging the sharp boundary between formal and informal learning, as elaborated by Chan et al. (2006), is "to extend formal learning time, usually limited to the classroom, into informal learning time, to embrace opportunities for out-of-school learning driven by the personal interests of students" (p. 6). In delineating the boundary, some literature looks exclusively at the physical context—learning that occurs out of the classroom or school compound, including teacher-planned field trips, which is considered informal learning (e.g., Spikol & Milrad, 2008; Vavoula et al., 2009). Other literature has looked into who is in control of the learning goals and content—only student-initiated learning or incidental (unintended) learning is regarded as informal learning (Looi, Zhang et al., 2011), while teacher-planned field trips can be characterized as "formal learning in informal settings." Mann and Reimann (2007) referred to the two types of informal learning as "non-curriculum-oriented informal learning" and "curriculum-oriented informal learning."

Examples of mCSCL activities bridging formal and informal learning are students carrying out teacher-instructed learning activities beyond the formal class time or teacher-led outdoor learning activities at their own convenience, such as online discussions (e.g., Huang, 2007), ongoing game playing (e.g., Metcalf, Milrad, Cheek, Raasch, & Hamilton, 2008), or data collection or artifact creation (largely incidental encounters or improvisations), sharing or peer reviews in daily life (e.g., Wong, Chin et al., 2010).

A seamless learning environment bridges private and public learning spaces where learning happens as both individual and collective efforts and across different contexts (such as in-school versus after-school, formal versus informal). Two seamless learning studies: SEAMLESS Project (Looi, Seow et al., 2010; Zhang et al., 2010) and "Move, Idioms!" (Wong, Chin et al., 2010; Wong & Looi, 2010) have focused on the *mobilization* of the formal science curriculum and Chinese idiom learning (with a "seamless language learning" construct) respectively. Student learning experiences have been designed in the form of cross-context learning flows that reinforce or encourage small student group collaborations in classroom or field trip settings, student–parent interaction or collaboration such as artifact cocreation or "teaching the parents" activities (Looi, Zhang, et al., 2011), and online peer reviews. The mobile devices mediate all the activities by assuming the role of a personal "learning hub" (Looi, Wong, et al., 2009) to support students' seamless learning experiences, including their blending into various social learning spaces. From the seamless learner's point of view, the individual experiences seamlessness when switching contexts between different learning activities (Wong, 2012; Wong & Looi, 2011).

Curricular Activity Systems that Incorporate mCSCL

We use the notion of a curricular activity system as the minimal unit of "impactful, adoptable" packaging of technology for a school (Roschelle, Knudsen, & Hegedus, 2010). In such an activity system, the activities are designed for teachers and students to enact and participate in. The responsibility for supporting such activities is distributed across technologies, software, paper curricula, teacher guides, and teacher professional development workshops. The designers of a curricular activity system seek to engineer an aligned set of related components that support the desired curricular activities coherently. Thus teacher professional development, curriculum materials, software documents, and so on are all designed together with a system perspective toward enabling classroom realization of the intended activities. It is in this context that we look at learning designs that incorporate mCSCL activities. Curricular activity systems in the classroom may include elements of in-class mCSCL, out-of-class mCSCL as well as seamless mCSCL, thus broadening the notion of curricular activity systems to learning activity systems where the context may also be out-of-class.

In a curricular or learning flow system, the mCSCL component may enable initial in-context interaction, and content delivery and creation that can stimulate further meaning-making (Kukulska-Hulme, Sharples, Milrad, Arnedillo-Sanchez, & Vavoula, 2009). For example, the mCSCL component allows the learner to tag areas of interest and create context annotations that can lead to further follow-up learning using desktop PCs in fixed spaces.

One approach to designing curricular activity systems that incorporate mCSCL is to situate the use of mobile technologies to support various forms of cooperative/collaborative learning like jigsaw, brainstorming, reciprocal teaching, problem-based learning and other collaborative scripts. Here, we take mCSCL-based jigsaw, arguably the best-known collaborative script, to exemplify how the synthesis of m-learning and "conventional" collaborative learning scripts can take place to varied extents. Jigsaw shares some common features with distributed inquiry in which students need to exchange information to achieve certain learning objectives. Distributed inquiry requires different student groups to play different roles. In AMULETS, one group collects data in the outdoor setting and another processes the collected data in the indoor setting (Kurti, Milrad, & Spikol, 2008). In the Labrador Trail, the students exchange and discuss information in order to synthesize knowledge (Wong et al., 2010). In jigsaw activities, an individual who returns to her home group after working with her expert group only has access to a subset of the information necessary to solve the problem, and the entire group needs to piece up and process the information together (Aronson, 1978).

In the various studies on mCSCL-based jigsaw that were conducted in the past decade, the roles played by the mobile technology varied considerably. In Liu et al. (2003), and

Lai and Wu's (2006) designs, the mobile devices were used merely for Internet search, or creating and exchanging student artifacts, while the group discussions have been carried out face-to-face within the traditional classroom. In the jigsaw-scripted mCSCL field trip design of AnswerTree (Moore, Goulding, Brown, & Swan, 2009), students who explore different areas of a wood communicate with each other via phone calls and text messages. The Mobile Jigsaw project (Thompson & Stewart, 2007) aims to facilitate students to collect information about their local environment and which pertains to the topics assigned to their respective expert groups in order to create a database of plant species for subsequent home-group learning.

The diversified ways in which the "m" is incorporated into these mCSCL-mediated jigsaw activities can probably offer a "miniature" view of the roles that the mobile technologies play in facilitating CSCL in learning activities—as a reference tool and productivity tool (which does not foreground the collaborative aspect of the learning script) to authentic data capturing/repository and synchronous/asynchronous communication tools. mCSCL offers the potential for further collaborative knowledge construction but we argue that this aspect has not been analyzed well in typical m-learning literature, as m-learning researchers usually put greater emphasis on studying the aspects of mobility, context-awareness, or personalization in their designs.

New Methodological Challenges for mCSCL Research

This section discusses new methodological challenges regarding methodological design and analysis in mCSCL research. In mCSCL educational research, a large number of mCSCL research studies have adopted quantitative approaches. Research methods used in these studies have employed instruments of pre- and posttests and questionnaire surveys with a small number of participants (e.g., Huizenga, Admiraal, Akkerman, & ten Dam, 2009; Lan, Sung, & Chang, 2007; Yin, Ogata, & Yano, 2007). Surveys with closed questions, seeking to understand the behaviors or attitudes of participants toward mobile technology educational applications, have been prevalent (e.g., Corlett, Sharples, Bull, & Chan, 2005; Lai & Wu, 2006). However, it has been claimed that open-ended questionnaire items have far greater credibility in terms of the results they produce than quantitative ones based on survey data (Patton, 2002). Some studies have claimed to have adopted mixed research methods, but, in fact, a questionnaire survey has been the dominant means of data collection (e.g., Motiwalla, 2007). Moreover, if only a few participants have been involved in a study, it challenges the value of conducting surveys as one of the mixed methods (e.g., Swan, van't Hooft, Kratcoski, & Unger, 2007).

Some studies have addressed research problems through qualitative approaches, but, in many cases, the studies have been carried out over short periods of time, and only used single data collection instruments, such as interviews, or video data (e.g., Lan, Sung, & Chang, 2007). Therefore, the credibility of the research may be challenged due to lack of data triangulation (e.g., Creswell, 2008).

Traxler and Kukulska-Hulme (2005) pointed out that "many of the trials and pilots themselves rest on a 'common sense' view of learning" (p. 7) without using much theoretical justification or coherence to support the research methods or techniques. Although the research findings have generally been positive, this may result partly from a "strong novelty effect" which refers to the phenomenon of participants being highly motivated to use new technologies to support their studies due to great interest and curiosity in using these technologies (Thornton & Houser, 2005, p. 224) or the "Hawthorne effect"

(Swan et al., 2005, p. 110) which refers to the phenomenon that participants report what they think researchers expect to hear or see, not what is actually happening.

Generally speaking, currently, well-designed research studies on mCSCL are still scant. Methodologies adopted in much of the current mCSCL educational research rely largely on small-scale, short-term trials or pilot studies using quantitative approaches. Studies using qualitative approaches exist but usually these have been carried out over short periods of time, and data collection methods have been limited to using interviews as major means of data collection. These issues are also prevalent in research on other forms of m-learning and on other technology supported learning environments. New methodological issues arise with the emerging research area of mCSCL.

For mCSCL studies that bridge formal and informal contexts, new methodological challenges emerge such as the need for data collection methods that can capture mCSCL processes and outcomes in continually moving and re-constructed contexts. Learners may carry and use their 1:1 mobile devices as their personalized devices to do a range of activities, only some of which may be relevant for the analysis of mCSCL interactions. The characteristics of mCSCL data may be their lightweight nature when captured on mobile devices or their potential to be distributed over interactions spanning digital and face-to-face, and artifacts that are spread out in the switching contexts in which the learner happens to be. The distributed and sparse nature of interactions through and over mobile devices poses a challenge for tracing the uptake of ideas and idea development processes.

Learners may become more and more engaged in personalized learning as part of a bigger context of learning flow. How does such personalized learning contribute to mCSCL? What may be the qualitative research methods available for such analysis? How do we analyze individual learning, group learning, and community learning in the learner generated contexts? These are the new conceptual and methodological challenges for studies in mCSCL.

Nevertheless, current studies have paved the way for further research on mCSCL by adopting methodologies such as design-based research (DBR) (e.g., Lan et al., 2009; Roschelle, Rafanan, Estrella, Nussbaum, & Claro, 2010). DBR refers to an iterative process of designing, experimenting, reflecting upon, and redesigning the learning model and applications, and to integrating design principles with technological affordances to render plausible solutions. While experimental design (experimental vs. control) is more useful for lab-based studies, DBR examines school and classroom practices which are situated in complex learning environments where it is difficult to hold variables constant. Typically, design-based researchers have tried to optimize as much of the design as possible and to observe how the different variables and elements are working out (Barab & Squire, 2004; Collins, Joseph, & Bielacyzc, 2004). For instance, Wong, Boticki, et al. (2011) described the first DBR cycle of their mCSCL study where the (class-)cultural, behavioral, cognitive, and subject matter-specific factors were observed in the preliminary trial runs of the game-based learning activities. These factors informed the rigorous revision of their game rules, CSCL scaffolds, and software user interface design. The DBR methodology allows researchers to collect and analyze data to multiple mCSCL factors simultaneously and to use the rich data to improve a design iteratively than might be accomplished through systematic experimentation on each individual factor (Design-Based Research Collective, 2003).

CONCLUSION

mCSCL, as a specialization of the field of CSCL, alleviates the condition of fixed times, spaces, locations, and topics for doing collaboration activities. By employing mobile devices, learning becomes personal and mobile, and students are able to participate in collaborative learning activities whenever and wherever they want to (Looi, Seow, et al., 2010). Students leverage on their own mobility and the mobility of the devices in order to coordinate collaboration and to construct or build knowledge over the wirelessly connected devices. Some prior mCSCL designs have incorporated knowledge construction components that either take place after certain teacher-facilitated field trips or intertwine with learners' informal learning activities (typically carried out in their own time). Such integrative activities are usually performed by using school or home computers instead, in order to overcome the form factor constraint caused by the complexity of the tasks.

We also emphasize the embedding of mCSCL activities in a broader curricular or learning flow system in which mCSCL supports in-context interaction and context delivery and creation, as well as time and space for personalized and social learning. As our review shows, there are in-class mCSCL studies in which the learning design and practices do foreground collaborative learning as a process and outcome of learning. The current studies for m-learning, which incorporate a strong element of mCSCL for out-of-class and for bridging both in-class and out-of-class, do not seem to necessarily foreground analysis of collaborative learning processes and outcomes. We argue that such a phenomenon can be attributed to the underlying difference between the major interests of the researchers in m-learning and the CSCL communities; general m-learning researchers usually focus on the study of learning mobility, contextualization/situated-*ness* of learning, or personalization of learning as their overarching research inquiries.

This phenomenon is also due partially to difficulties in tracking and collecting CSCL data when learning takes place on the move or across a long period of time in constantly switching contexts. Therefore, mCSCL is usually incorporated as a significant component of these studies but the collected data are rarely analyzed in a rigorous manner (e.g., discourse analysis or social network analysis) as typical CSCL research does. Herein lies a research challenge for mCSCL. It is our hope that this book chapter can stimulate a dialogue between the m-learning and CSCL research communities. The m-learning community can extend its focus on the mobility of the learning environment to generating and analyzing productive collaborative human interactions resulting from such mobility. The CSCL community can start to investigate new methodologies and approaches to study an amalgam of data sources that arise in different contexts, modalities, and time periods.

REFERENCES

Ally, M., McGreal, R., Schafer, S., Tin, T., & Cheung, B. (2008). Use of a mobile digital library for mobile learning. In G. Needham & M. Ally (Eds.), *Mlibraries: Libraries on the move to provide virtual access* (pp. 217–277). London: Facet.

Aronson, E. (1978). Interdependent interactions and prosocial behavior. *Research and Development in Education, 12*(1), 16–27.

Barab, S., & Squire, K. (2004). Design-based research: Putting a stake in the ground. *The Journal of the Learning Sciences, 13*(1), 1–14.

Barbosa, D. N. F., Geyer, C, F. R., & Barbosa, J. L. V. (2005). Globaledu—An architecture to support learning in a pervasive computing environment. In A. Rettberg & C. Bobda (Eds.), *New trends and technologies in computer-aided learning for computer aided design* (pp. 1–10), New York: SpringerLink.

Boticki, I., Looi, C.-K., & Wong, L.-H. (2011). Supporting mobile collaborative activities through scaffolded flexibile grouping. *Educational Technology & Society, 14*(3), 190–202.

Chan, T. W., Roschelle, J., Hsi, S., Kinshuk, Sharples, M., Brown, T., … Hoppe, U. (2006). One-to-one technology enhanced learning: An opportunity for global research collaboration. *Research and Practice in Technology Enhanced Learning, 1*(1), 3–29.

Chen, Y.-S., Kao, T.-C., & Sheu, J.-P. (2003). A mobile learning system for scaffolding bird-watching learning. *Journal of Computer Assisted Learning, 19*(3), 347–359.

Cole, M., & Engestrom, Y. (2007). Cultural-historical approaches to designing for development. In J. Valsiner & A. Rosa (Eds.), *The Cambridge handbook of sociocultural psychology* (pp. 484–507). New York: Cambridge University Press.

Colella, V. (2000). Participatory simulations: Building collaborative understanding through immersive dynamic modeling. *The Journal of the Learning Sciences, 9*(4), 471–500.

Collins, A., Joseph, D., & Bielaczyc, K. (2004). Design research: Theoretical and methodological issues. *The Journal of the Learning Sciences, 13*(1), 15–42.

Conole, G., & Dyke, M. (2004). Discussion: Understanding and using technological affordances: A response to Boyle and Cook. *ALT-J, 12*(3), 301–308.

Corlett, D., Sharples, M., Bull, S., & Chan, T. (2005). Evaluation of a mobile learning organiser for university students. *Journal of Computer Assisted Learning, 21*(3), 162–170.

Creswell, J. W. (2008). *Educational research: planning, conducting, and evaluating quantitative and qualitative research* (3rd ed.). Upper Saddle River, NJ: Pearson/Merrill Prentice Hall.

Crowe, A., & van't Hooft, M. (2006). Technology and the prospective teacher: Exploring the use of the TI-83 handheld devices in social studies education. *Contemporary Issues in Technology and Teacher Education, 6*(1), 99–119.

Cui, Y., & Bull, S. (2005). Context and learner modelling for the mobile foreign language learner. *System, 33*(2), 353–367.

Davis, S. (2003). Observations in classrooms using a network of handheld devices. *Journal of Computer Assisted Learning, 19*(3), 298–307.

Design-Based Research Collective (2003). Design-based research: an emerging paradigm for educational inquiry. *Educational Researcher, 32*(1), 5–8.

Engestrom, Y. (1987). *Learning by expanding: An activity-theoretical approach to developmental research*. Helsinki, Finland: Orienta-Konsultit Oy.

Frohberg, D. (2006, September). Mobile learning is coming of age: What we have and what we still miss. *Proceedings of the DELFI*, Darmstadt, Germany.

Hoppe, H. U., Joiner, R., Milrad, M., & Sharples, M. (2003). [Guest editorial] Wireless and mobile technologies in education. *Journal of Computer Assisted Learning, 19*(3), 255–259.

Hsi, S. (2003). A study of user experiences mediated by nomadic web content in a museum. *Journal of Computer Assisted Learning, 19*(3), 308–319.

Huang, H.-J. (2007). *A study on a hybrid seamless collaborative learning environment with active push e-mail technology* (Unpublished Master's thesis). National Central University, Jhongli, Taiwan.

Huizenga, J., Admiraal, W., Akkerman, S., & ten Dam, G. (2009). Mobile game-based learning in secondary education: Engagement, motivation and learning in a mobile city game. *Journal of Computer Assisted Learning, 25*(4), 332–344.

Johnson, D., & Johnson, R. (1992). Positive interdependence: Key to effective cooperation. In R. Hertz-Lazarowitz & N. Miller (Eds.), *Interaction in cooperative groups: The theoretical anatomy of group learning* (pp. 174–199). New York: Cambridge University Press.

Klopfer, E., Squire, K., & Jenkins, H. (2008). Environmental detectives: The development of an augmented reality platform for environmental simulations. *Educational Technology Research and Development, 56*(2), 203–228.

Klopfer, E., Yoon, S., & Rivas, L. (2004). Comparative analysis of Palm and wearable computers for participatory simulations. *Journal of Computer Assisted Learning, 20*(5), 347–359.

Kreijns, K., Kirschner, P., & Jochems, W. (2002). The sociability of computer-supported collaborative learning environments. *Educational Technology & Society, 5*(1), 8–25.

Kukulska-Hulme, A., Sharples, M., Milrad, M., Arnedillo-Sánchez, I., & Vavoula, G. (2009). Innovation in mobile learning: A European perspective. *International Journal of Mobile and Blended Learning, 1*(1), 13–35.

Kurti, A., Spikol, D., & Milrad, M. (2008). Bridging outdoors and indoors educational activities in schools with the support of mobile and positioning technologies. *International Journal of Mobile Learning and Organisation, 2*(2), 166–186.

Lai, C.-Y., & Wu, C.-C. (2006). Using handhelds in a jigsaw cooperative learning environment. *Journal of Computer Assisted Learning, 22*(4), 284–297.

Lan, Y.-J., Sung, Y.-T., & Chang, K.-E. (2007). A mobile-device-supported peer-assisted learning system for collaborative early EFL reading. *Language Learning & Technology, 11*(3), 130–151.

Lan, Y.-J., Sung, Y.-T., & Chang, K.-E. (2009). Let us read together: Development and evaluation of a computer-assisted reciprocal early English reading system. *Computers & Education, 53*(4), 1188–1198.

Laurillard, D. (2009). The pedagogical challenges to collaborative technologies. *International Journal of Computer-Supported Collaborative Learning, 4*(1), 5–20.

Leont'ev, A. N. (1978). *Activity, consciousness, personality.* Englewood Cliffs, NJ: Prentice Hall.

Liaw, S.-S., Hatala, M., & Huang, H.-M. (2010). Investigating acceptance toward mobile learning to assist individual knowledge management: Based on activity theory approach. *Computers & Education, 54(*2), 446–454.

Liu, T.-C., Wang, H.-Y., Liang, J.-K., Chan, T.-W., Ko, H.-W., & Yang, J.-C. (2003). Wireless and mobile technologies to enhance teaching and learning. *Journal of Computer Assisted Learning, 19*(3), 371–382.

Looi, C.-K., Seow, P., Zhang, B., So, H. J., Chen, W., & Wong, L.-H. (2010). Leveraging mobile technology for sustainable seamless learning: A research agenda. *British Journal of Educational Technology, 41*(2), 154–169.

Looi, C.-K., Wong, L.-H., So, H.-J., Seow, P., Toh, Y., Norris, C., … Soloway, E. (2009). Anatomy of a mobilized lesson: Learning my way. *Computers & Education, 53*(4), 1120–1132.

Looi, C.-K., Zhang, B., Chen, W., Seow, P., Chia, G., Norris, C., & Soloway, E. (2011). 1:1 mobile inquiry learning experience for primary science students: A study of learning effectiveness. *Journal of Computer Assisted Learning, 27*(3), 269–287.

Maldonado, H., & Pea, R. (2010, April). LET's GO! to the Creek: Co-design of water quality inquiry using mobile science collaboratories. *Proceedings of the IEEE International Conference on Wireless, Mobile, and Ubiquitous Technologies in Education 2010* (pp. 81–87), Kaohsiung, Taiwan.

Mann, S., & Reimann, P. (2007, October). Mobile technology as a mediating tool for learning in the convergences from technology, collaboration and curriculum perspectives. *Proceedings of the International Conference on Mobile Learning 2007* (pp. 144–148), Melbourne, Australia.

Markett, C., Arnedillo Sanchez, I., Weber, S., & Tangney, B. (2006). Using short message service to encourage interactivity in the classroom. *Computers & Education, 46*(3), 280–293.

Metcalf, D., Milrad, M., Cheek, D., Raasch, S., & Hamilton, A. (2008, March). My Sports Pulse: Increasing student interest in STEM disciplines through sports themes, games and mobile technologies. *Proceedings of the IEEE International Conference on Wireless, Mobile, and Ubiquitous Technology in Education 2008* (pp. 23–30), Beijing, China.

Moore, A., Goulding, J., Brown, E., & Swan, J. (2008, October). AnswerTree—A hyperplace-based game for collaborative mobile learning. *Proceedings of mLearn 2009*, Orlando, FL.

Motiwalla, L. F. (2007). Mobile learning: A framework and evaluation. *Computers & Education, 49*(3), 581–596.

Norris, C., & Soloway, E. (2004). Envisioning the handheld-centric classroom. *Educational Computing Research, 30*(4), 281–294.

Nussbaum, M., Alvarez, C., McFarlane, A., Gomez, F., Claro, S., & Radovic, D. (2009). Technology as small group face-to-face Collaborative Scaffolding. *Computers & Education, 52*(1), 147–153.

O'Malley, C., Vavoula, G., Glew, J. P., Taylor, J., Sharples, M., & Lefrere, P. (2003). *Guidelines for learning/teaching/tutoring in a mobile environment* (No. MOBIlearn/UoN, UoB, OU/D4.1/1.0). London: Open University

Patton, M. Q. (2002). *Qualitative research and evaluation methods* (3rd ed.). Thousand Oaks, CA.: Sage.

Pownell, D., & Bailey, G. D. (2002). Are you ready for handhelds? Using a rubric for handheld planning and implementation. *Learning & Leading with Technology, 30*(2), 50–55.

Quinn, C. (2001). Get ready for m-learning. *Training and Development, 20*(2), 20–21.

Rogers, Y., Connelly, K., Hazlewood, W., & Tedesco, L. (2010). Enhance learning: A study of how mobile devices can facilitate sense making. *Personal and Ubiquitous Computing, 14*(2), 111–124.

Rogers, Y., & Price, S. (2009). How mobile technologies are changing the way children learn. In A. Druin (Ed.), *Mobile technology for children* (pp. 3–22). Boston, MA: Morgan Kaufmann.

Roschelle, J., & Pea, R. (2002). A walk on the WILD side: How wireless handhelds may change computer-supported collaborative learning. *Cognition and Technology, 1*(1), 145–168.

Roschelle, J., S. (2010). From handheld collaborative tool to effective classroom module: Embedding CSCL in a broader design framework. *Computers & Education, 56*(3), 1018–1026.

Roschelle, J., Knudsen, J. & Hegedus, S. (2010). From new technological infrastructures to curricular activity systems: Advanced designs for teaching and Learning. In M. Jacobson & P. Reimann, (Eds.), *Designs for learning environments of the future* (pp. 233–262). New York: Springer.

Roschelle, J., Rafanan, K., Estrella, G., Nussbaum, M., & Claro, S. (2010). From handheld collaborative tool to effective classroom module: Embedding CSCL in a broader design framework. *Computers & Education, 55*(3), 1018–1026.

Segall, N., Doolen, T. L., & Porter, J. D. (2005). A usability comparison of PDA-based quizzes and paper-and-pencil quizzes. *Computers & Education, 45*(4), 417–432.
Sharples, M., Taylor, J., & Vavoula, G. (2007). A theory of learning for the mobile age. In R. Andrews & C. Haythornthwaite (Eds.), *The Sage handbook of e-learning research* (pp. 221–247). London: Sage.
So, H.-J., Seow, P., & Looi, C.-K. (2009). Location matters: Leveraging knowledge building with mobile devices and Web 2.0 technology. *Interactive Learning Environment, 17*(4), 367–382.
Soloway, E., Norris, C., Blumenfeld, P., Fishman, B., Krajcik, J., & Marx, R. (2001). Devices are ready-at-hand. *Communications of the ACM, 44*(6), 15–20.
Spikol, D., & Milrad, M. (2008). Physical activities and playful learning using mobile games. *Research and Practice in Technology Enhanced Learning, 3*(3), 275–295.
Stahl, G., & Hesse, F. (2010). Beyond folk theories of CSCL. *International Journal of Computer-Supported Collaborative Learning, 5*, 355–358.
Stanton, D., & Neale, H. (2002). *Designing mobile technologies to support collaboration* (Technical Report Equator-02-028). Equator. Retrieved from http://www.equator.ac.uk/papers/Abstracts.
Swan, K., van't Hooft, M., Kratcoski, A., & Unger, D. (2005). Uses and effects of mobile computing devices in K-8 classrooms. *Research on Technology in Education, 38*(1), 99–112.
Thompson, K., & Stewart, K. (2007, April). The mobile jigsaw—A collaborative learning strategy for mlearning about the environment. *Proceedings of mLearn 2007*, Melbourne, Australia.
Traxler, J., & Kukulska-Hulme, A. (2005, October). Evaluating mobile learning: Reflections on current practice. *Proceedings of mLearn 2005*, Cape Town, South Africa.
Thornton, P., & Houser, C. (2005). Using mobile phones in English education in Japan. *Journal of Computer Assisted Learning, 21*(3), 217–228.
Vahey, P., & Crawford, V. (2002). *Palm education: Final report*. Menlo Park, CA: SRI International.
Vavoula, G., Sharples, M., Rudman, P., Meek, J., & Lonsdale, P. (2009). Myartspace: Design and evaluation of support for learning with multimedia phones between classrooms and museums. *Computers & Education, 53*(2), 286–299.
Wali, E., Winters, N., & Oliver, M. (2008). Maintaining, changing and crossing contexts: An activity theoretic reinterpretation of mobile learning. *ALT-J, Research in Learning Technology, 16*(1), 41–57.
Waycott, J., Jones, A., & Scanlon, E. (2005). PDAs as lifelong learning tools: An activity theory based analysis. *Learning, Media and Technology, 30*(2), 107–130.
Wong, L. H. (2012). A learner-centric view of mobile seamless learning. *British Journal of Educational Technology, 43*(1), E19-E23.
Wong, L. H., Boticki, I., Sun, J., & Looi, C. K. (2011). Improving the scaffolds of a mobile-assisted Chinese character forming game via a design-based research cycle. *Computers in Human Behavior, 27*(5), 1783–1793.
Wong, L. H., Chen, W., & Jan, M. (2012). How artefacts mediate small group co-creation activities in a mobile-assisted learning environment? *International Journal of Computer Assisted Learning, 28*(5), 411–424.
Wong, L. H., Chen, W., Looi, C. K., & Zhang, B. H. (2010). Analysis of attributes of mobile learning activities: Two case studies of m-learning design. *China Educational Technology, 2010*(2), 7–15.
Wong, L.-H., Chin, C.-K., Tan, C.-L., & Liu, M. (2010). Students' personal and social meaning making in a Chinese idiom mobile learning environment. *Educational Technology & Society, 13*(4), 15–26.
Wong, L.-H., & Looi, C.-K. (2010). Vocabulary learning by mobile-assisted authentic content creation and social meaning-making: Two case studies. *Journal of Computer Assisted Learning, 26*(5), 421–433.
Wong, L. H., & Looi, C.-K. (2011). What seams do we remove in mobile assisted seamless learning? A critical review of the literature. *Computers & Education, 57*(4), 2364–2381.
Yin, C., Ogata, H., & Yano, Y. (2007). Participatory simulation framework to support learning computer science. *International Journal of Mobile Learning and Organisation, 1*(3), 288–304.
Zhang, B. H, Looi, C.-K., Wong, L.-H., Seow, P., Chia, G., Chen, W., So, H. J., Norris, C., & Soloway, E. (2010). Deconstructing and reconstructing: Transforming primary science learning via a mobilized curriculum, *Computers & Education, 55*(4), 1504–1523.
Zurita, G., & Nussbaum, M. (2004). Computer supported collaborative learning using wirelessly interconnected handheld computers. *Computers & Education, 42*(3), 289–314.
Zurita, G., & Nussbaum, M. (2007). A conceptual framework based on activity theory for mobile CSCL. *British Journal of Educational Technology, 38*(2), 211–235.

25

COLLABORATIVE KNOWLEDGE BUILDING

Towards a Knowledge Creation Perspective

CAROL K. K. CHAN
University of Hong Kong

INTRODUCTION

Helping students to engage in collaborative inquiry and work creatively with ideas is now a major educational goal. Despite widespread interest in inquiry learning and computer-supported learning, most schools continue to focus on surface forms of constructivist learning, with students busily engaged in gathering information from the Web and completing tasks (Scardamalia & Bereiter, 2003); for example, inquiry learning is often limited to predetermined goals, sequences of activities, and fixed standards that focus on skills rather than creating knowledge, which is the goal of real scientific inquiry (Chinn & Malhotra, 2002). Sustained and emergent inquiry that aims at *knowledge creation*, much valued in scientific and innovative communities, poses major challenges for theories and designs for collaborative learning.

A major research theme in computer-supported collaborative learning (CSCL) and the learning sciences examines how students, supported by technology, engage in inquiry, problem solving, and collaboration (Jacobson & Reimann, 2010; Koschmann, Hall, & Miyake, 2002; Stahl, 2006). Learning collaboratively has been theorized in terms of knowledge acquisition, acculturation, and knowledge creation (Paavola, Lipponen, & Hakkarainen, 2004). "Knowledge building" is an educational model of the productive knowledge work typical of scientific, research, and innovative communities. Children can collaboratively create and improve ideas that add value to the community in a way that is similar to scientists working to generate new knowledge (Bereiter, 2002; Scardamalia & Bereiter, 2003, 2006). Much of this work takes place in a computer-supported learning environment called Knowledge Forum®, which is designed to support the improvement of ideas, synthesis, and developing higher levels of conceptualization.

Scardamalia and Bereiter (2006) suggested that they were the first to use the term *knowledge building* in education, but found it in 125,000 Web documents in this domain in 2005. The term is now used frequently in the research literature on CSCL, where it generally refers to computer-supported and collaborative meaning-making processes by which groups construct understanding (Stahl, 2006). In recent years, these authors have begun to use the term *knowledge building* synonymously with *knowledge creation* to focus attention on the model (Bereiter & Scardamalia, 2008, p. 87). Knowledge building, conceived as knowledge creation, focuses on how people work together to advance the state of knowledge of the community (Scardamalia & Bereiter, 2003). These authors advocate an education agenda that students need if they are to develop a knowledge-creating culture to extend the frontiers of knowledge of the community. The need for knowledge creation is recognized in many fields, and collaborative learning designs for the knowledge era need to support students to work with knowledge productively and creatively.

This chapter focuses on the model of knowledge building, developed by Scardamalia and Bereiter since the 1980s, which can be defined as "the production of knowledge that adds value to the community" (Scardamalia & Bereiter, 2003, p. 1370). Knowledge building and Knowledge Forum were a forerunner of CSCL and have continued to develop since the 1980s; knowledge building is considered one of the major models of the learning sciences (Sawyer, 2006). There has been seminal publication of the framework (see Bereiter, 2002; Scardamalia & Bereiter, 1994, 2006) together with substantial evidence from empirical studies conducted in different countries (see Knowledge Building Exchange http://kbc2.edu.hku.hk). Despite much interest, thus far, there has been no integrative review of this model encompassing theory, analysis, design, and impact. This chapter aims to provide a comprehensive review, with a focus on knowledge creation, and to examine research issues relevant to CSCL. Following a historical introduction and overview of Knowledge Forum, the following questions will be addressed: (a) What is knowledge building from the lens of knowledge creation? (b) How can knowledge building be analyzed with a focus on knowledge-creation processes? (c) Can a model focusing on collective knowledge bring about educational benefits for individuals? (d) How is knowledge creation designed and supported in classrooms? (e) What are the roles of technology and communities in knowledge creation? The chapter closes with research directions and implications. In this chapter, the term *knowledge creation* will be used synonymously with *knowledge building* when referring to this research model.

HISTORICAL BACKGROUND AND KNOWLEDGE FORUM

The theoretical ideas of knowledge creation originated from cognitive studies on writing in the early 1980s that contrasted "knowledge telling," a linear process regurgitating what one already knows, versus "knowledge transformation," a recursive process with dialectics between the content and rhetorical spaces that transform one's knowledge (Bereiter & Scardamalia, 1987). In the 1980s, research on intentional learning examined student agency and constructive learning efforts over and above what is needed for task completion (Bereiter & Scardamalia, 1993). Cognitive research examines the nature of expertise and knowledge structure (Chi, Glaser, & Farr, 1988), but Bereiter and Scardamalia (1993) investigated the process of expertise and how people advance their expertise via progressive problem solving; building new knowledge involves students viewing their knowledge as something problematic that needs to be explained (Chan, Burtis, & Bereiter, 1997). For intentional and expert learning to take place, students need to execute high-level cognitive processes on their own and the community must become a sustaining force for knowledge advances. A new kind of learning environment was needed, with students exerting high-level agency supported by community processes, to counteract the familiar teacher-directed process.

In 1983, against this background, a prototype environment, Computer-Supported Intentional Learning Environments (CSILE) was developed for a university course. By 1986, a networked version was being used in an elementary school. CSILE continued to evolve; in 1997, it was replaced by Knowledge Forum, which was designed to make knowledge-creation processes accessible to children and to foster the creation and continual improvement of public knowledge (see http://www.knowledgeforum.com).

CSILE/Knowledge Forum is a networked environment that provides a communal knowledge space where students share their ideas and theories and work on improving them for theory building, not just information sharing. Primarily, students write (author and coauthor) computer notes consisting of questions, explanations, evidence, experiments, or reference materials that can be "contributed" (posted) as text or graphics. A major feature is the "view," which is the shared workspace where students contribute and build on others' notes (Figure 25.1). A Knowledge Forum database spanning over weeks or months typically consists of a number of views for different inquiry problems (or curriculum topics) created during the course of study. Students post notes consisting of their ideas and questions; these may develop into different theories and conceptual themes, and they can be represented graphically in the view. As an example, Figure 25.1 shows a "plate tectonics" view in which students started with a problem on how continents move apart; the squares are note icons, and the lines between the notes show the links among students' responses to each another. Many different notes are posted and students, working with their teacher, have organized disparate notes into several conceptual and inquiry themes—continental drift, sea-floor spreading, earth structure, and fossil evidence—that can be taken up in new views for deeper inquiry into the key problem. Computer notes can be moved from one view to another so that the same idea (e.g., information, evidence) can be examined from different contexts and perspectives.

As an example, with more notes on these different inquiry themes, the teacher may have discussions with students about what new areas of inquiry are needed and, with that, new views on "fossils" or "earth structure" may be created and students can further their inquiry in these areas. It is also possible that different groupings of students may specialize in different inquiry themes, taking responsibility for different views. Such an arrangement is akin to scientific inquiry in which researchers identify different themes and different research labs then delve deeper into these different issues. Views are connected and "rise-above" views can be formed to support the superordination of higher-level ideas. An example of a "rise-above" view can be "Landforms and Processes," in which students may consider the research evidence from other views to address the more central problem.

When writing computer notes or building on (responding to) others' notes, students can add scaffolds (metacognitive prompts) to support idea generation and theory improvement. Figure 25.2 shows a computer note posted by a student as she wonders about the relations between plate tectonics and continental drift. Students can start a note through the flexible use of Knowledge Forum scaffolds. The scaffolds, which include stems such as "I need to understand," "my theory," "new information," "a better theory," and "putting our knowledge together," reflect the centrality of theory development in knowledge building.

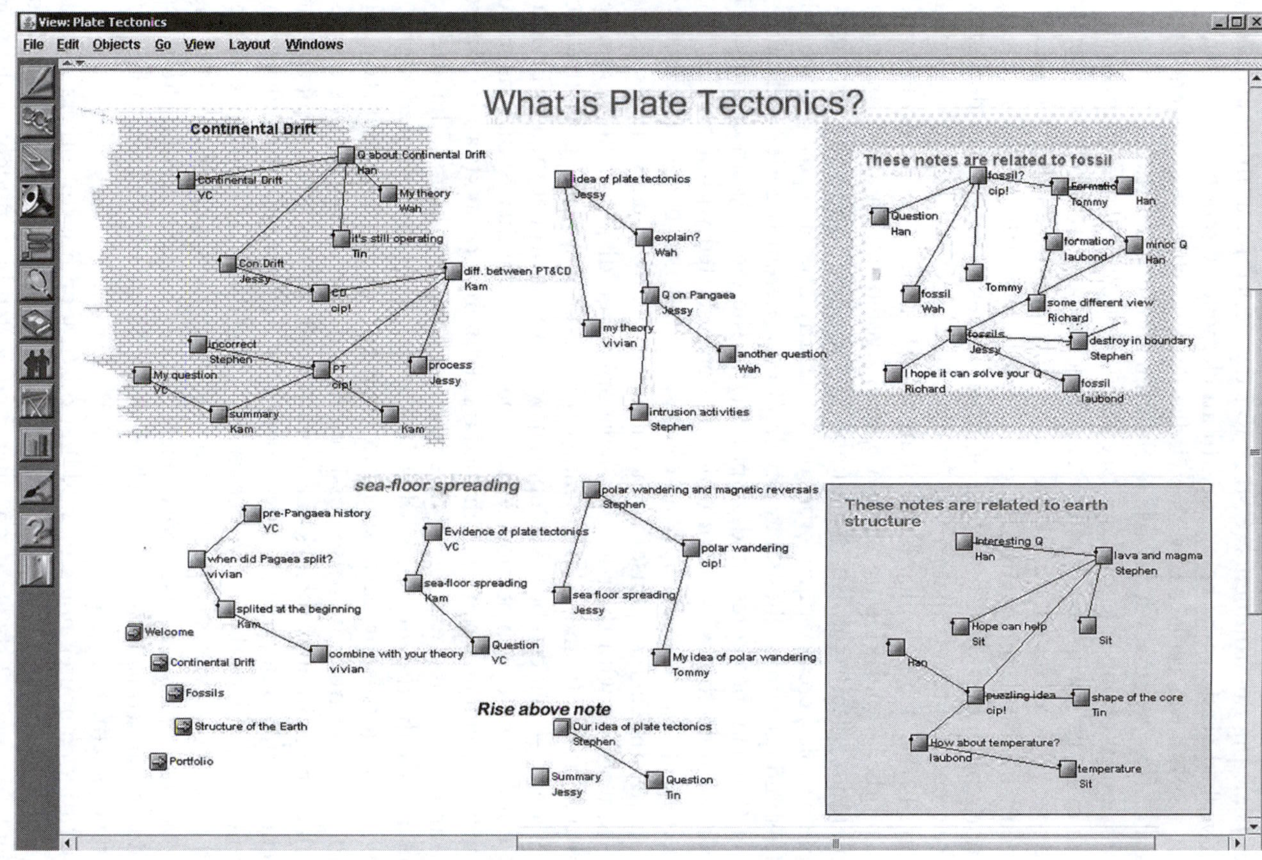

Figure 25.1 A view on Knowledge Forum for Collective Inquiry.

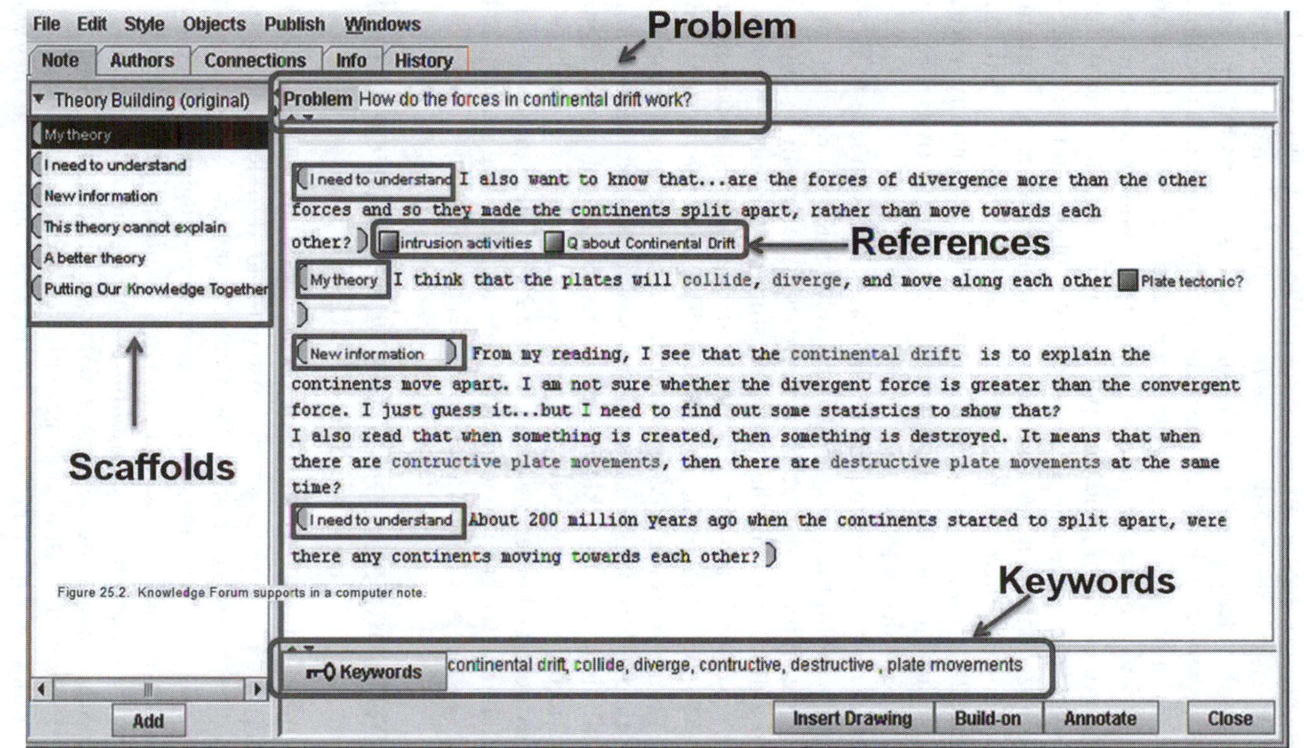

Figure 25.2 Knowledge Forum supports in a computer note.

Another feature is a *problem* prompt that helps to scaffold a problem-oriented rather than a topical approach to the discourse. A problem is usually more general than the questions for which students use the "I Need to Understand" scaffold; this functionality allows students to search to find out who in the community is working on similar problems. Other features include *keywords* to highlight domain vocabulary and for searches into similar ideas; *annotations* for individual students rather than the whole community; and *graphics* to illustrate the ideas, within a note. It is also possible to cite the contributions of others as happens in a scientific community; for example, when one student writes a note, she may add *reference links* to other notes that explain plate tectonics and continental drift, and then put forth her integrated idea (theory). Finally, the *rise-above note* can be used to synthesize contributions and introduce higher levels of conceptualization; the notes that are used in this process are subsumed by the rise-above note and are therefore no longer viewable in their original context in the view (e.g., Figure 25.1: "Our idea of plate tectontics"). The community space is designed not only for interaction, but also for enhanced community activity and improvement around shared knowledge objects.

Typically, students start their inquiry in the classroom with face-to-face discussion, then record and work on their ideas collaboratively on Knowledge Forum. Classroom inquiry frames the online work that, in turn, enriches classroom discourse. Using both the online and offline aspects of the discourse, students formulate problems (e.g., why do rainbows have colors?), advance theories, examine different ideas and models, and identify relevant information in the process of revising their theories. Students may also work in small groups on some occasions and in whole-class mode on others, conducting experiments to test theories, reading to understand difficult information, and using "knowledge-building talks" to tackle problems emerging from forum discourse. Knowledge Forum is accompanied by a set of *analytic tools* that index contributions, interactions, connectedness, and other measures (Figure 25.3). These indices provide not only research data for analysis, but also formative feedback, enabling students to assess their own contributions (see sections on analysis and technology).

KNOWLEDGE BUILDING AS KNOWLEDGE CREATION: THEORIES AND PRINCIPLES

In the CSCL and learning sciences literature, knowledge building often refers to collaborative learning and group processes to construct shared understanding supported by technology. Although this is educationally valuable, it may not include notions *of knowledge creation*. Knowledge building, with a focus on knowledge creation, places emphasis on the production and advancement of knowledge; knowledge creation is common in scientific, research, and innovative communities whose goal is to create and expand public knowledge. Scardamalia and Bereiter (2003) postulate that, just as scientists develop inventions, artifacts, and tools, school-aged children can generate ideas and theories as epistemic inventions, which can be inquired about and examined, as they work together to advance the collective knowledge of the community. Knowledge-creating dynamics include students taking agency generating knowledge problems, producing tentative theories and explanations with sustained efforts to improve them, supported by progressive discourse on Knowledge Forum (Bereiter & Scardamalia, 2008).

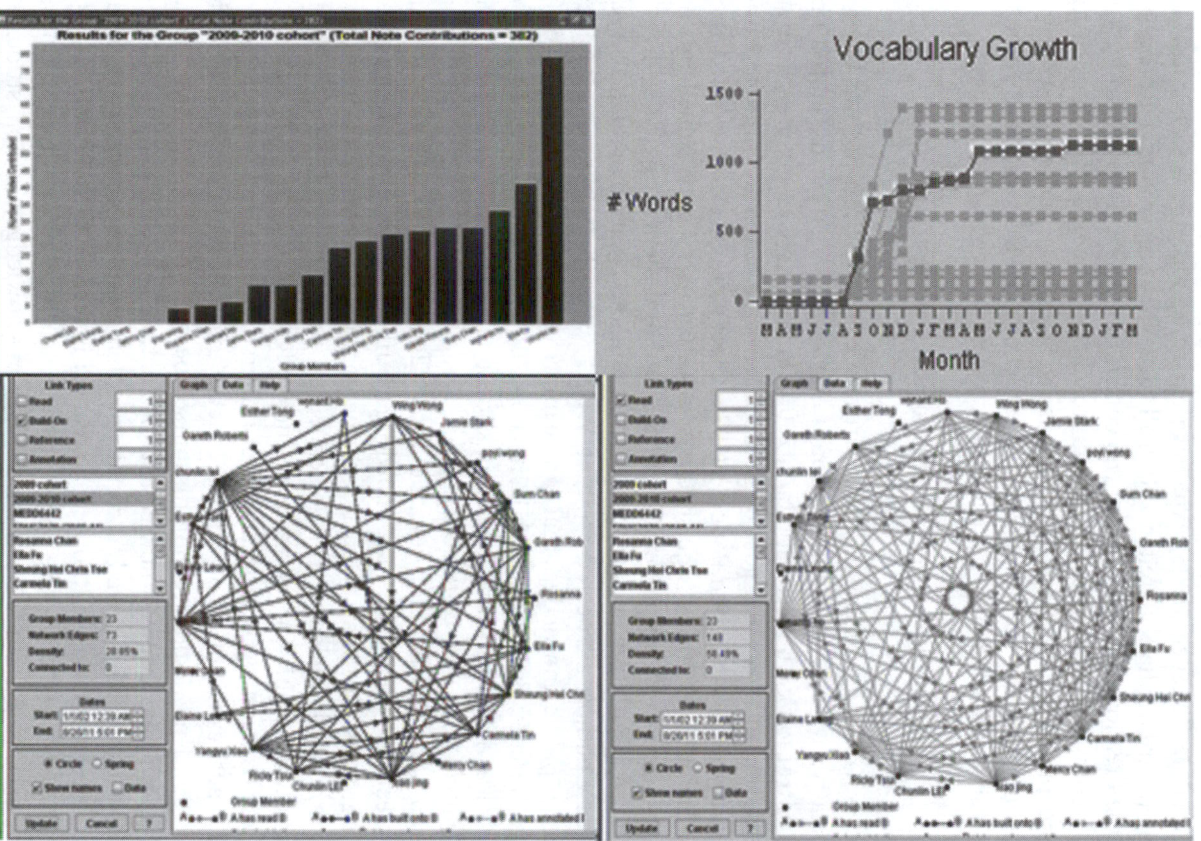

Figure 25.3 Assessment tools for Knowledge Forum: note contribution (top left), vocabulary growth (top right), note build-on density (bottom left), and note-reading density (bottom right).

This section focuses on examining the knowledge-building model, highlighting aspects of knowledge creation. Sfard (1998) distinguished between two views of learning, the acquisition of knowledge and participation in the practices of a community. Paavola et al. (2004) postulated a third view they called *knowledge creation* that integrates the first two views: they analyzed three models including the knowledge-creation company (Nonaka & Takeuchi, 1995), expansive learning (Engeström, 1999), and knowledge building (Scardamalia & Bereiter, 2003); all three focus on innovative processes of inquiry for the creation of knowledge in the community. Expansive learning, knowledge-creation company, and other current approaches focus on sociocultural activity, materials, and practices (Hakkarainen, Paavola, & Seitamaa-Hakkarainen, chapter 3 this volume), but the Scardamalia and Bereiter model of knowledge creation emphasizes epistemic and sociocognitive dynamics for collective cognitive responsibility.

Theoretical and Epistemological Foundation

Learning versus Knowledge Building. There are now major theoretical shifts from individual to social views of learning; how groups engage in constructing shared understanding is central to CSCL research (Stahl, 2006). Schooling is often about individual learning, however, and even the goal of group learning is often to improve students' individual outcomes. Drawing on Popper's (1979) theory of objective knowledge, Scardamalia and Bereiter (1994) distinguished between "learning" and "knowledge building." Learning refers to the improvement of the mind and mental capacities (World 2), whereas knowledge building refers to the improvement and creation of *public knowledge* (World 3). These authors advocated bringing World 3 into the classroom: The ideas of students can be "public knowledge" that can be improved by their own collective efforts (Scardamalia, Bereiter, & Lamon, 1994). In knowledge building classrooms, children are not merely learning or acquiring existing knowledge; they are *working to extend the frontiers of knowledge of their community.*

How Scardamalia and Bereiter describe knowledge building highlights a focus on knowledge creation. They note that knowledge building goes beyond constructing understanding; while that may be part of it, the goal is to add value to, improve, and advance community knowledge. This is echoed by research that distinguishes three modes of knowledge-building discourse: knowledge sharing as information flow, knowledge construction as coconstruction of understanding, and knowledge creation as the social practices within a community that advance the frontiers of its knowledge (van Aalst, 2009). Knowledge-creation discourse goes beyond the cognitive aspects of problem solving; it may embed knowledge construction but additionally reifies how a community comes to be interested in certain problems and how collective knowledge is advanced. A key emphasis of knowledge creation is *theory building*, which supports the advance of public and collective knowledge in scientific communities. Importantly, although emphasis is given to *collective* knowledge in knowledge creation, students also learn *individually.* The notion of knowledge creation that examines sustained pursuit for advancing public knowledge may help to address questions about the nature of these models (e.g., fostering communities of learning versus knowledge building; see Scardamalia & Bereiter, 2007) and enrich conceptualizations of learning communities (Hakkarainen, 2009).

Belief Mode vs. Design Mode. How are complex new concepts developed? How do people learn something more complex than what they already know? Bereiter and Scardamalia (2006) postulated a distinction between belief mode and design mode. Current education practice primarily emphasizes the former; for example, how children make claims, justify their beliefs, and use reasoning and evidence to support their arguments. Argumentation, construed as debates and persuasion, although popular in schools, may not generate new knowledge. While there is much interest in argumentation, it would be useful to consider other forms of discourse that have potential for the creation of new knowledge. Scardamalia and Bereiter (2006) asserted that an understanding of discourse beyond "discussion" and "argumentation" is needed. Design mode involves viewing ideas as conceptual artifacts and continually improving on them for theory building (Bereiter & Scardamalia, 2006). Drawing on Thagard's research (1989), Bereiter and Scardamalia postulated that knowledge creation dynamics involve constructing theories for "explanatory coherence"—how students theorize, construct explanation, and account for conflicting evidence, much as scientists build theories. In design-mode thinking, each cycle opens up problems to new possibilities; when a problem is solved, efforts are reinvested to tackle deeper problems, for bootstrapping and for knowledge advancement (Bereiter & Scardamalia, 1993). In addition to belief-mode thinking (e.g., "what are the reasons?" or "what is the evidence?"), these authors call attention to the role of design-mode thinking (e.g., "What is this idea good for?" or "How can this idea be improved upon?") in theory revision. While these researchers have raised concerns, different forms of argumentation, persuasion-based and inquiry-based, have been identified (Chinn & Clark, chapter 18 this volume). Persuasion discourse is limiting for new ideas but inquiry-oriented collaborative argumentation may align more with knowledge generation. The differences and dialectics of belief-mode and design-mode thinking may shed light on different forms of knowledge building in CSCL and need to be examined further.

Knowledge-Building Principles

Scardamalia (2002) has postulated a system of 12 principles to characterize and design knowledge building. This chapter outlines the most often examined ones, from the lens of knowledge creation, and relates them to other approaches.

Epistemic Agency. Metacognition, reflection, and agency are emphasized in inquiry and collaborative models (e.g., problem-based learning; Hmelo-Silver & De Simone, chapter 21 this volume); epistemic agency includes these while emphasizing *dialectics of personal and collective agency.* Scardamalia (2002) noted that epistemic agency involves students setting forth their ideas and negotiating a fit between their personal ideas and ideas of others, using contrasting models to spark and sustain knowledge advances. There is now increased interest in social metacognition in CSCL; for example, the self-regulation of one's own cognition, regulation with others, and collective regulation (Winne, Hadwin, & Perry, chapter 26 this volume). While there are similarities with other approaches that focus on sociometacognitive processes, there are also differences. CSCL research examines shared goals and understandings, while epistemic agency involves students having an overall sense of purpose and commitment to making their ideas better collectively beyond completing tasks.

Idea Improvement. Contrary to school practice, which sets curriculum, standards, and objectives as end-states, knowledge creation focuses on scientific progress and the sustained pursuit of ideas. Although student ideas improve over time with strong design in CSCL and learning sciences, what distinguishes improvable ideas is the notion of *intentionality* and explicit goals of the community to *pursue* idea improvement, which makes knowledge-creation efforts closer to goals and dynamics in research communities (Scardamalia, 2002). This principle emphasizes metacognitive and epistemic components, with students examining what is known, what needs to be known, and why and how a given idea can be improved upon. Key to the principle of improvable ideas is the epistemic understanding that ideas are knowledge objects that can be explored, examined, and improved upon, and this may also involve the volition to engage in complex knowledge work discussed in the framework of epistemic cognition (Chinn, Buckland, & Samarapungavan, 2010).

Constructive Use of Authoritative Information. A common challenge with online discussion in CSCL is fragmented discourse and "everyday talk" (Hewitt, 2005). *Constructive uses of authoritative information* underscores that students should consider "authoritative sources" of the discipline, such as empirical evidence, experiments, and academic resources, but examine them critically in the context of what they know and the relevance to their problem solving. In practice, student discourse is frequently devoid of such sources or they are treated uncritically. Constructive use of authoritative information may address problems of "everyday talk" as students bring information directly to bear on the problems to enrich the discourse. CSCL research also examines and scaffolds students to search for new information; in knowledge creation, constructive use of information is needed for *theory revision.* Participants in the community have a responsibility to enrich the pool of information necessary for community advances, and that brings them closer to the kind of knowledge creation practice of scholarly and research communities.

Community Knowledge. The participants' commitment to advance community knowledge is central to knowledge creation. Creative work with knowledge involves not only personal learning, but also communal work on problems the community deems important. Working together allows improved ideas and theories to diffuse through the communal knowledge space; community knowledge is extendable to connected communities and multiple communities through technology (Scardamalia, 2002). Community knowledge resembles CSCL's emphasis on group cognition—the whole is more than the sum of the parts (Stahl, 2006). While CSCL research also examines collective work beyond small groups supported by technology (e.g., Wikis; Cress & Kimmerle, 2008), community knowledge goes beyond representing the *current* state of knowledge and includes theory building and design-mode efforts to *advance* the current state of knowledge.

Taken together, these principles may shed light on examining and scaffolding for productive discourse in CSCL. A common challenge in CSCL and online forums is that putting students together may not bring about productive collaboration (Kreijins, Kirschner, & Jochems, 2003); students may consider collaboration as knowledge sharing rather than knowledge-creating efforts to advance the quality of their discourse (van Aalst, 2006). Using a knowledge-creation perspective, students can engage in *epistemic agency*, reflecting on personal and collective knowledge, and comparing different ideas (models) to spark advances. Such agency is possible only with the epistemic belief that *all ideas are improvable* as objects of inquiry via collective efforts. Students need to take on epistemic and metacognitive roles, considering gaps in discourse and how ideas can be improved. It is important to be aware of the cutting-edge of the discipline—students need to make *constructive use of information* for explanation, evidence, and theory revision for the community. The goals are collective advancement and the creation of useful *community knowledge* which facilitates further knowledge creation. These principles illuminate knowledge creation dynamics with implications for advancing CSCL.

This knowledge-building model, with a focus on knowledge creation, has similarities to other prominent models of collaborative inquiry, including project-based learning (Krajcik & Blumenfeld, 2006), Learning by Design (Kolodner et al., 2003), and Problem-Based Learning (Hmelo-Silver & De Simone, chapter 21 this volume), all of which focus on problems or questions as a starting point, and the centrality of discourse, metacognition, inquiry, and problem solving. However, there are also differences. At a more general level, these approaches are sophisticated and invaluable pedagogical models that examine and scaffold deep understanding, collaboration, and knowledge construction. Knowledge creation is a pedagogical model, but it is also a more general model that seeks to characterize and explain phenomena and processes observed among innovative communities for knowledge production. When comparing these models as pedagogical models, they also differ. Primarily these approaches focus on small groups, whereas knowledge creation emphasizes the class community (see section on "Classroom Design and Pedagogy for Knowledge Creation"). As these inquiry-based approaches emphasize knowledge, inquiry skills, and epistemic growth, knowledge creation focuses on advancing community knowledge. As well, less attention is given to structured inquiry and curricular goals, with a strong emphasis on emergent processes. Knowledge creation places centrality on student agency and the sustained pursuit of idea improvement and collective advances; problems generate new problems and knowledge generates new knowledge (Bereiter & Scardamalia, 2010). There may be different views as to whether an educational model needs to be dependent on technology; in this model, theory, pedagogy, and technology are integral to one another. The following sections review empirical studies in this research tradition. This chapter focuses on research that is congruent with the conceptualization of knowledge building as knowledge creation.

ANALYZING KNOWLEDGE BUILDING: SCIENTIFIC PROCESSES OF KNOWLEDGE CREATION

Different approaches have been employed to analyze the nature, evidence, and development of knowledge building focusing on knowledge-creation processes. In comparison to most analyses in the field of CSCL, data sources are usually based on student work for a prolonged period, from a few weeks to a few months, and sometimes spanning several years.

Contribution, Interactions, and Connectedness on Knowledge Forum: Sociocognitive–Behavioral Indices

Sociocognitive and technological processes are intertwined (Scardamalia, 2002). Students' contributions, participation, and networking patterns on Knowledge Forum can be examined using server log data from a set of analytic tools (Figure 25.3); these indices can be generated for individuals, discussion views, and the classroom community. A set of commonly used "Basic Knowledge-Building indices" (e.g., numbers of notes written/read, scaffolds, revisions, keywords, references) from the Analytic Toolkit (Burtis, 1998) measure participation and contribution patterns. The numbers of authored and coauthored notes illustrate contributions to the knowledge space and the use of scaffolds and revisions reflects metacognition and recursive processes. These quantitative indices have shown changes in participation over time, and demonstrate correlations with note quality and domain understanding (Lee, Chan, & van Aalst, 2006; van Aalst & Chan, 2007). Another major set of analyses involves indices derived from Social Network Analysis (SNA; e.g., who read and build onto whose notes, note-reading and note-linking percentage and density, in-degree and out-degree, and clique) that examine the extent of "community awareness" and "community connectedness" and dynamic patterns of collaboration. SNA has been used to examine participation patterns to illustrate changing patterns toward collective cognitive responsibility (Zhang, Scardamalia, Reeve, & Messina, 2009) and knowledge networking among researchers (Hong, Scardamalia, & Zhang, 2010). Analyses that employ these indices provide basic measures of interaction and connectedness. For example, Zhang et al. used SNA to examine participation patterns in three different pedagogical designs, and found that the design in which the teacher was least central was the most effective in terms of knowledge advancement and the diffusion of new knowledge. Although measures from SNA do not assess the quality of ideas or interactions, there is no basis for community knowledge advances without a high level of connectedness. Assessing changes in quantitative indices provides useful background information to guide further qualitative analyses.

Quality of Notes: Conceptual and Epistemological Processes

A key approach to analyzing knowledge creation with a focus on theory building pertains to how children can engage in scientific research similar to that of scientists in pursuit of scientific advances. Oshima, Scardamalia, and Bereiter (1996) compared CSILE Grade 5 students who had low and high degrees of conceptual progress; the more advanced students focused on *problem-centered knowledge*, whereas their counterparts pursued *topical knowledge*. Hakkarainen (2003, 2004) analyzed the quality of CSILE notes (idea units) in terms of explanatory-driven inquiry: how students generate and improve their intuitive theories as they formulate problems, develop hypotheses, and generate explanations. These analyses indicate that the discourse of CSILE students changes over time, from fact-based to explanatory-based inquiry. Several mechanisms were identified, including generating research questions, using scientific information, and comparing one's own naïve models with scientific models. Such analyses emphasize epistemological inquiries, going beyond superficial distinctions coding "what" versus "how and why" questions. Lee et al. (2006) focused on epistemic quality, identifying depth of inquiry and depth of explanation that distinguished between general questions and those that identified gaps in understanding with hypotheses, conjectures, and the formulation of explanations; more sophisticated explanations include the synthesis of different ideas, which is similar to metadiscourse. Analyses have shown that epistemic levels of questions and explanations are correlated with domain knowledge (Lee et al., 2006). Although analyses of questions are commonly examined as collaborative processes, these analyses reflect concerns for epistemic inquiry—questions are analyzed in terms of varying depths as conceptual artifacts subject to inquiry and explanation.

Quality of Discourse: Conceptual, Epistemological, and Sociocognitive Processes

Researchers have examined how students engage in progressive discourse to explain natural phenomena. Bereiter, Scardamalia, Cassells, and Hewitt (1997) analyzed Grade 5 students' group-notes on Knowledge Forum and identified four themes characterizing collective inquiry as *scientific progress*: mutual advances in understanding, empirical testability, expanding the basis for discussion, and commitment to openness. In the light of controversies surrounding postmodernism, these researchers argued that scientific inquiry is neither *relative* nor a grand march toward some *truth* or accepted scientific theory; rather, it is characterized by continual efforts to improve on existing theories. Although these students may not be creating scientific knowledge, they are engaged in the kinds of productive discourse that demonstrate commitment toward scientific progress for knowledge creation.

Whereas earlier analyses examined idea units or individual notes, now considered limited on their own for collective cognition, parallel with changes in CSCL (Puntambekar, Erkens, & Hmelo-Silver, 2011), current work focuses on the analyses of connected discourse. A major approach adopted by many researchers in this tradition involves using a set of knowledge-building principles to analyze the discourse (Scardamalia, 2002). One analytic tool is the use of *inquiry threads*, conceptual clusters focusing on problems that demonstrate idea development (Zhang, Scardamalia, Lamon, Messina, & Reeve, 2007); analyses include examining the problems students are working on, and the epistemic complexity and sophistication of their scientific explanations. Qualitative and quantitative analyses demonstrate how Grade 4 students are engaged in the sustained pursuit of ideas, illustrating the principles of authentic problems, idea improvement, community knowledge, and constructive uses of information. Another approach examines e-portfolio with metadiscourse, in which high school students create a rise-above note that documents how their collective knowledge has advanced (E. Y. C. Lee et al., 2006; van Aalst & Chan, 2007). Similar to inquiry threads, e-portfolios were analyzed to illustrate idea development important for knowledge creation; the portfolio narratives range from general descriptions to analysis of processes and metadiscourses, and demonstrate the interaction of individual and collective understanding.

The notion of knowledge creation has been examined directly in research that identified three different kinds of discourse modes—knowledge sharing, knowledge construction, and knowledge creation—among Canadian high-school students working on Knowledge Forum (van Aalst, 2009). Students worked in four groups and they collectively inquired into infectious diseases. Analyses were conducted for different discourse moves pertaining to information, questions, ideas, emergence, metadiscourse, and social dynamics. Comparing different groups working on Knowledge Forum, the researcher found that student groups identified as making more knowledge gains (through group summary notes) made more discourse moves coded as social processes and community dynamics compared to their counterparts.

Classroom Discourse: Sociocognitive, Sociocultural, and Other Processes

Classroom discourse and process can illuminate the broader aspects of collaboration and show how authentic knowledge work can take place in classroom. Caswell and Bielaczyc (2001) examined how Knowledge Forum alters the relations between children and scientific knowledge—children see themselves as contributors to knowledge in a community. Zhang and Sun (2011) analyzed online and offline discourse to examine reading for idea improvement and constructive use of authoritative information. Other studies have examined different processes relevant for understanding knowledge-creation discourse, such as metaprocedural comments and collective regulation (Cohen & Scardamalia, 1998); semantic analyses and idea diversity (Teplovs & Scardamalia, 2007); and lexical process in domain-specific vocabulary and epistemic verbs (Sun, Zhang, & Scardamalia, 2010).

Analyses of knowledge creation have encompassed different approaches, often used in combination, and both individual and collective processes have been examined. Current CSCL schemes for analyzing collaboration generally focus on interaction processes and pay relatively less attention to the conceptual quality of ideas. On the other hand, analysis of knowledge creation, as described, while encompassing sociometacognitive processes, tends to focus on conceptual-epistemological aspects. More broadly, to enrich research on the analyses of collaboration, it may be helpful to examine how analytic schemes can be developed to examine more closely the intertwined relationships between collaborative interaction and conceptual quality of ideas.

EVALUATING THE EDUCATIONAL EFFECTS OF KNOWLEDGE CREATION

Since the model of knowledge creation emphasizes collective and community advances, there may be questions as to whether this model has educational benefits for individual students. This section reports on empirical research that illustrates the educational benefits for students experiencing knowledge creation in different areas.

Scientific Inquiry, Reflection, Epistemic, and Conceptual Understanding

The previous section has suggested that even young students can engage in scientific inquiry and knowledge work, including formulation of problems, generation of models and theories, and sustained pursuit of knowledge. Evaluation studies have shown that CSILE students outperform non-CSILE students in scientific understanding; they construct deeper explanations with coherent accounts rather than merely listing facts, and their understanding is not hampered by misconceptions in the CSILE database (Scardamalia et al., 1994). Research comparing Grade 5 students working in the face-to-face condition versus the CSILE condition has shown that students make more group-regulated metacomments in CSILE-supported discourse compared to more self-regulation comments without CSILE (Cohen & Scardamalia, 1998). Research has indicated that CSILE students are more reflective in their portfolios, while interviews have revealed beliefs about learning with higher epistemic levels compared to non-CSILE students (Scardamalia et al., 1994). In a design-based study, students in CSILE classrooms were shown to move from listing information to formulating better theories (Hewitt, 2002). Research on conceptual change indicated that high-school chemistry students working on knowledge building shifted to higher levels of epistemic beliefs compared to their counterparts (Chan & Lam, 2010).

While focusing on design and process, researchers have also obtained outcome measures using portfolio notes (Zhang et al., 2007) and demonstrating substantial pre- and posttest gains on scientific concepts (Oshima et al., 2004; van Aalst & Truong, 2011).

Few studies have included comparison groups, but there are exceptions: several studies have shown that students working on Knowledge Forum outperformed other students on domain understanding (Lee et al., 2006; van Aalst & Chan, 2007). There is also some evidence linking collective and individual advances; analyses of collective inquiry threads demonstrating the use of problems and explanations have been related to individual student's scientific knowledge in personal portfolio notes (Zhang et al., 2007). Furthermore, the extent to which students engage in collective agency and social metacognition (reflection on principles, metadiscourse) while working on Knowledge Forum has been found to predict their individual achievement in essay writing (E. Y. C. Lee et al., 2006) and gains in epistemic and conceptual-change scores (Chan & Lam, 2010).

Reading Processes, Textual, and Graphical Literacy

While this research model has been used primarily in science domains, research has also shown positive benefits in language and literacy. CSILE students were found to outperform their non-CSILE peers in reading difficult scientific texts, have more sophisticated beliefs about learning, and show deeper text understanding (Scardamalia et al., 1994). Recent research has examined the reciprocal advantages of literacy and knowledge work, and how literacy is best developed in academic discourse. Collaborative reading, transformative writing, and dialogic literacy are important for generating new knowledge and supporting high-level literacy (Zhang & Sun, 2011). In analyses of textual literacy—including the amount of writing, distinctiveness and frequency of words used, domain-specific vocabulary, and *epistemic* words (e.g., wonder, hypothesize, experiment, explain)—students who used Knowledge Forum consistently performed above their grade levels (Sun, Zhang, & Scardamalia, 2010).

In Knowledge Forum, students can use graphics within their notes and views to represent their ideas; graphical literacy refers to their ability to use visual and communication skills in building knowledge. Grade 3 and 4 students with Knowledge Forum experiences have demonstrated greater graphical literacy than do their Grade 6 counterparts, producing graphical representation of knowledge with more dynamic information, interpretive summaries and advanced causal explanations (Gan, Scardamalia, Hong, & Zhang, 2010).

Curriculum Standards and Educational Attainment

Although knowledge-building environments are not designed primarily to improve test scores, there is evidence that they do have positive benefits. Evaluation studies have shown that CSILE students outperformed comparison groups on standardized tests on language and literacy, with these advantages persisting over years (Scardamalia et al., 1994). However, there have been no differences reported in standardized math test scores; as discussed above, reading and writing undertaken in Knowledge Forum account for the advantages. As the knowledge-creation approach has spread to Asian countries, researchers have assessed student knowledge using national curriculum standards (Oshima et al., 2004). Students have outperformed their counterparts on public examination results when their teacher has integrated the sociometacognitive aspects of the knowledge-creation approach with the sociocultural milieu of the Asian classroom (Chan, 2008).

Equity Issues and Different Learners

It is commonly believed by educators that inquiry approaches benefit only high-achieving students, despite evidence to the contrary (Zohar & Dori, 2003). The knowledge-creation approach stresses community advancement, emphasizing that all students can contribute. In a study of social studies students, for instance, Niu and van Aalst (2009) reported similar progress with knowledge-building principles among both regular and honors high school students. Similarly, So, Seah, and Toh-Heng (2010) demonstrated that both high- and low-achieving students in an elementary classroom in Singapore made gains assessed with knowledge tests based on the National Curriculum Standards when using Knowledge Forum. Moss and Beatty (2010) explained scaffolding in terms of the principle of democratizing knowledge and showed how low-achieving Grade 6 students incorporated and reinterpreted the mathematics solutions presented by their high-achieving peers.

Although most research has been conducted with Canadian elementary science students, this model has been examined in a variety of research contexts for different learners in different cultures, including preschool children (Pelletier, Reeve & Halewood, 2006), Aboriginal students (McAuley, 2009), tertiary students (de Jong, Veldhuis-Diermanse, & Lutgens, 2002), nursing community practitioners (Russell & Perris, 2003); and students in Asian classrooms (E. Y. C. Lee et al., 2006; Oshima et al., 2004).

This section has reviewed studies reporting various educational benefits. Compared to other technology-enhanced inquiry-based programs (e.g., H. S. Lee, Linn, Varma, & Liu, 2010), this research tradition has made less progress evaluating children's learning of specific science content. While some questions may be raised as to whether this model, which emphasizes emergent and collective processes, is an effective way of learning science content, a different view is to consider what science learning encompasses; innovative programs may have different theoretical goals reflecting knowledge acquisition, acculturation, and knowledge creation (Chan & van Aalst, 2008). As the research program focuses on process and designs, most of the studies have not included comparison groups. Moreover, it is useful to note that it is insufficient to just assign students to work on Knowledge Forum when examining the effectiveness of the program; all the reported studies have involved careful curricular designs aligned with the goals of knowledge creation. There has been considerable interest in using the technology of Knowledge Forum, often in interventions of short duration, and the results can be disappointing without sustained implementation (Hurme & Järvelä, 2005). For advances to occur, classroom and technological designs need to be aligned with principles of knowledge creation.

CLASSROOM DESIGN AND PEDAGOGY FOR KNOWLEDGE CREATION

How can knowledge creation be designed and supported in classrooms? Knowledge-creation pedagogy focuses on open and emergent approaches and design-based research that support improvable designs and practices (Collins, Joseph, & Bielaczyc, 2004). Rich descriptions of classroom work are reported in another chapter (Bielaczyc, Kapur, & Collins, chapter 13 this volume).

Task-Based versus Idea-Centered Approaches

A major theme in supporting creative knowledge work in the classroom is to shift focus from *tasks* to *ideas*—Knowledge Forum is designed to give a central role to student ideas. As discussed earlier, students put forth ideas and problems and propose theories to explain them; they continually improve on these theories by making constructive use of information and working for collective advances. Hewitt (2002) reported an expert teacher's changing designs and identified several ways in which this teacher scaffolded idea development: problem-centered collaboration; productive queries; making student thinking central; iterative progression of learning; and a focus on understanding. Idea-centered approaches need to be accompanied by a *progressive curriculum*. Caswell and Bielaczyc (2001) described how students collectively pursued inquiry beyond the goals defined by the curriculum in ways that resemble the trajectory of Darwin's inquiries. Scardamalia (2002) noted that students working on inquiry are often engaged in task completion without *intentionality* or goals. Caswell and Bielaczyc explicitly presented the notion of idea improvement to Grade 5 and 6 students ("Ideas are pretty neat things. We've all got ideas and the thing about ideas is that they can be improved," 2001, p. 288); even young students can take on agency to pursue idea improvement.

Fixed Groups versus Emergent Groups and Communities

Knowledge building is often examined in small groups in CSCL; it is useful to examine how to scaffold authentic knowledge work that emerges beyond fixed groupings. Zhang et al. (2009) reported a 3-year study of how a teacher changed his collaborative design with progress toward knowledge creation. In Year 1 students worked in fixed groups, in Year 2 they worked in interactive groups, and in Year 3 the whole class worked collectively in opportunistic ways to inquire into emerging problems. Knowledge Forum affordances such as views and rise-above supports make it more possible for students to come together as opportunistic groups working on emerging problems. Social network analyses showed that the teacher was central in Year 1 but, by Year 3, was just a member of the community. These longitudinal findings show that the shifts toward flexible groups are associated with more knowledge advances. Such pedagogy and design, with emergent goals and problems, also reflect the knowledge-creation dynamics in scientific communities. One implication for CSCL pedagogy is that there can be more flexible use of small groups, emergent groups, and the whole class for knowledge diffusion in the community.

Procedure-Based versus Principle-Based Design

How do teachers go about understanding knowledge creation so they can implement and sustain the pedagogy in the classroom? A major problem in implementing innovation is that teachers often follow surface procedures while distorting the underlying key principles (Brown & Campione, 1996). Scardamalia and Bereiter (2006) advocated the importance of a principle-based approach rather than one that focuses on procedures, routines, and sequences of activities. In such an approach, teachers are encouraged to inquire into classroom practice from the lens of knowledge-building principles, which is consistent with the notion of adaptive expertise (Lin, Schwartz, & Hatano, 2005). Knowledge Forum provides a workspace for the realization of these principles;

students work with their teacher in flexible ways rather than follow structured guides and scripted activities (Reeve, Messina, & Scardamalia, 2008).

Oshima et al. (2004), comparing activity structures common in Japanese classroom with more open, emergent designs, reported gains in deeper student understanding. Van Aalst and Chan (2007) used four knowledge-building principles in e-portfolio assessment and asked high school students to document their own trajectories of growth; students developed insights into the nature of knowledge-building discourse because these principles provide criteria for monitoring their work (see Winne et al., chapter 26 this volume). Students using principles demonstrated more knowledge gains than did their counterparts. At the school level for teacher development, Zhang, Hong, Scardamalia, Teo, and Morley (2011) examined principle-based innovation over 8 years and explored how teachers focused on principles as they continually improved their practice. While this model originated in Canadian classrooms, there are now examples of how it can be implemented by teachers new to the approach (van Aalst & Truong, 2011). A principle-based approach may also address the question of appropriating collaboration, technology, and innovation across cultural contexts; surface activities may vary, but deep principles are needed to inform the designs (Chan, 2011).

Knowledge creation is a complex approach and the focus on ideas and principles rather than scripted activities makes it even more challenging. Pedagogy and technology design should align with the theoretical foundation of the model (Hong & Sullivan, 2009). Given the epistemic focus, principles, rather than procedures, are needed to allow for emergent processes in knowledge creation. Current controversies exist regarding structured instruction versus inquiry-based learning (Hmelo-Silver, Duncan, & Chinn, 2007; Kirschner, Sweller, & Clark, 2006). It may be useful to consider different goals of the pedagogical models; for learning of content and skills, more structure may be useful, but less structured pedagogy may be more appropriate for emergent processes; and there may be a continuum for different approaches. Moreover, knowledge-creation pedagogy, as well as other models, also requires consideration of the broader sociocultural dynamics of classroom implementation. Bielaczyc (2006) discussed creating a social infrastructure framework to support knowledge creation in the classroom, and this can be applicable to other CSCL models (see also Bielaczyc et al., chapter 13 this volume).

TECHNOLOGY FOR KNOWLEDGE CREATION AND KNOWLEDGE COMMUNITIES

Technology Embedded in Theory and Pedagogy

The earlier section has introduced the features of Knowledge Forum; this section focuses on key themes that characterize the design of technology environments in support of knowledge creation (Scardamalia, 2004; Scardamalia & Bereiter, 2003).Whereas many CSCL environments focus on knowledge construction, networking, and communication, CSILE/Knowledge Forum is designed to *embed* theory and pedagogy to support advances in ideas and theories. Unlike CSCL environments using fixed inquiry guides, Knowledge Forum uses an *open* environment with flexible and opportunistic prompts for emergent goals; for example, "scaffolds" have epistemic purposes different from sentence openers in many CSCL environments. The communal knowledge space supports students' work on theory improvement: "Citing" and "referencing" others' notes is key to scholarly work; these trajectories and historical records provide accounts of children's growth of ideas (analogous to evolution of ideas in science). Unlike threaded discourse, Knowledge Forum notes "live" in different views that allow students to represent knowledge and reformulate ideas in different ways. Research on e-portfolios capitalizes on such affordances (i.e., "reference links") to characterize and to scaffold collective knowledge (van Aalst & Chan, 2007). Knowledge Forum technology emphasizes superordination and higher level structure to support emergence and bootstrapping. Opportunistic searching and linking of ideas, persons, and groups help participants connect with others and to identify the cutting-edge of inquiry in the community.

In terms of further development of Knowledge Forum, Bereiter and Scardamalia (2011) highlighted several recurrent themes: (a) one discourse, multiple access points; (b) metadiscourse as discourse about discourse (where are we heading?); (c) Web objects as objects of inquiry; (d) supports for tagging, citing, and referencing work for the evolution of ideas; (e) developing idea tools and idea spaces, for collective advances; and (f) support for rise-above, ubiquitous theory building and self-organization. Although Knowledge Forum supports many advanced processes, some teachers and students may not understand the affordances and continuing classroom design studies are needed. In light of new technological advances in CSCL, how Knowledge Forum will continue to develop also poses fruitful and challenging questions for further inquiry.

Technology for Concurrent, Embedded, and Transformative Assessment

How does technology designed for assessing knowledge-creation processes both examine and scaffold the process? Knowledge Forum technology includes analytic tools and assessment tools, including Analytic Toolkit (Burtis, 1998) and Java-based Applet tools for analyzing contribution, interaction, and connectedness (Figure 25.3). While usage statistics are common for online forums, these tools are premised on the principle of concurrent, embedded, and transformative assessment. Assessments are "concurrent" in that they provide instantaneous feedback; are "embedded" into the pedagogy; and are "transformative" in that they can change the process (Scardamalia, 2002). Knowledge-creation communities assess and monitor their own progress as well as difficulties so as to chart new advances (van Aalst, chapter 16 this volume). CSCL assessment technology usually involves the researchers designing tools to analyze student discourse after the study has been completed. Knowledge Forum assessment tools, however, are designed to be used not only by researchers for analysis but also by teachers and students, who use the tools and indices formatively for monitoring progress for new cycles of improvable work. As an example, students working with their teacher can use the indices (e.g., use of scaffold; who has read whose notes) to reflect and to monitor how they have been making progress individually and collectively and what changes are needed for advances. While these assessment tools are specific to Knowledge Forum, the idea can be relevant to designing other CSCL tools for students to monitor their collaboration and metacognition.

There is other work analyzing knowledge creation using technology; for example, automatic coding and visualization techniques (Law, Yuen, Wong, & Leng, 2011). Teplovs and Scardamalia (2007), using Knowledge Visualizer, investigated the use of latent semantic techniques and visualization tools to identify notes with semantically linked ideas for examining idea diversity. Other ongoing development continues to focus on designing assessment tools that both "examine" and "transform" the process. Van

Aalst and colleagues (2012) have developed the Knowledge Connection Analyzer which allows participants (teachers and students) to query their work including the prompts: (a) Are we collaborating? (b) Are we putting our knowledge together? (c) How do our ideas develop over time? (d) What is happening to my idea? Development of these and other tools may support students to monitor, regulate, and take collective responsibility for advancing their knowledge work. A broader question for CSCL tool development is to consider how tools can be designed to be employed by participants themselves, thus allowing both *assessing* and *scaffolding* collaboration in knowledge communities.

Knowledge Networks and Communities for Knowledge Creation

Collaboration, conceptualized as knowledge creation, provides the opportunity to understand how knowledge can be created and sustained in knowledge communities supported with technology. Laferrière et al. (2010) examined knowledge-creation partnerships and designed school innovation with networks of schools using the research model. Chan (2011) discussed how knowledge creation can be sustained in a teacher network supported by Knowledge Forum, with the teachers working as a knowledge-creating community to create community knowledge that helps them to pursue further knowledge.

A major initiative for developing knowledge-creation communities is the Knowledge Society Network (KSN), based at the University of Toronto, which consists of a worldwide knowledge innovation network and is supported by Knowledge Forum's flexible structure and affordances. The model of knowledge creation is now implemented in many countries. KSN participants include researchers, scientists, engineers, teachers, policymakers, and professionals from various sectors; they research on knowledge creation in their own sites, while contributing to the meta database as members of a knowledge creation community. A key goal of the KSN is to realize the vision of knowledge creation in multiple networked communities. Hong, Scardamalia, and Zhang (2010) have analyzed the growth of the KSN network over a period of 4 years, identifying a variety of network patterns for sustained knowledge innovation. There are major barriers and sustainability challenges; nonetheless, it demonstrates Knowledge Forum's potential to support theories of knowledge creation with symmetrical community advances.

RESEARCH DIRECTIONS AND CONCLUDING REMARKS

The importance of working collaboratively with knowledge is now recognized widely in the knowledge era (e.g., Organisation for Economic Co-Operation and Development [OECD], 2004), and designing collaborative learning supported by technology is a major research theme. This chapter has reviewed the knowledge-building model from the perspective of knowledge creation. A key theoretical focus of this educational model is to examine and foster the goals and dynamics for generating and advancing community knowledge, similar to those in scientific and innovative communities, and Knowledge Forum is designed to support the knowledge-creation processes. A review of the literature suggests that students from different ages and different cultures are able to move beyond surface forms of constructivism and engage in knowledge-creation dynamics. There is also some evidence of educational gains in scientific inquiry, reflection, epistemic understanding, textual and graphical literacy, and educational attainment. This model is commonly known as knowledge building, but examining the model from the lens of knowledge creation may suggest areas of further research.

There are now increasing research interests in knowledge building in CSCL, referring generally to how students collaborate to construct knowledge and to learn in groups. Knowledge building as knowledge creation, focusing on sustained theory-building efforts and community dynamics, may help to address issues related to the complex process of creative work with ideas in knowledge communities; further work can be conducted on different and related approaches and models of knowledge building (also see Hakkarainen et al., chapter 3 this volume). Research on CSCL has examined the importance of collective cognition mostly in small groups, usually over short time spans, and knowledge creation may examine further how collective cognition can be developed, sustained, and *advanced* in communities. Conceptualizing knowledge building more broadly and examining collaboration as knowledge creation will raise new questions for CSCL theories and designs.

This chapter has reviewed different approaches to analyzing knowledge building, focusing on knowledge creation processes. While there are some illuminating accounts, stronger evidence of knowledge creation is needed. Development of this model necessitates more analysis of what constitutes knowledge-creation discourse, as well as the identification of indicators and discourse mechanisms in emergent processes, meta-discourse, and social dynamics. A broader question for CSCL methodology is to examine the analyses of collaborative interactions with the conceptual quality of idea development.

Knowledge-creation pedagogy emphasizes ideas, emergence, and principles. This research model has now been implemented in many different countries and contexts, but it is one that is difficult to implement well without a deep understanding of its epistemology. The creation of new ideas is key, but scaffolding for emergence and self-organization needs further investigation across different research settings and contexts. In light of the debates between structured instruction versus inquiry learning, the polarized tensions, such as principles versus procedures, can be examined more closely, and to explore their dialectics to shed light on technology-enhanced designs for different goals and forms of collaboration.

The review shows positive educational benefits of knowledge creation but that there also is a need to develop stronger evidence. More broadly, for this model and others in CSCL, the dynamics of how collective knowledge can be diffused in the community need to be investigated further. This model emphasizes the roles of technology that need to *embed* theory and pedagogy, and highlights the design of CSCL assessment technology that both *examines* and *scaffolds* collaboration. The nature and dynamics of knowledge creation also need to be tested in networks and communities supported by technologies that go beyond classrooms to knowledge communities and international networks. These challenges and directions suggest many fruitful areas of research that may enrich theories and practices of CSCL, as researchers both examine knowledge creation and work to create knowledge.

REFERENCES

Bereiter, C. (2002). *Education and mind in the knowledge age.* Mahwah, NJ: Erlbaum.

Bereiter, C., & Scardamalia, M. (1987). *The psychology of written composition.* Hillsdale, NJ: Erlbaum.

Bereiter, C., & Scardamalia, M. (1993). *Surpassing ourselves: An inquiry into the nature and implications of expertise*. Chicago, IL: Open Court.

Bereiter, C., & Scardamalia, M. (2003). Learning to work creatively with knowledge. In E. De Corte, L. Verschaffel, N. Entwistle, & J. van Merrienboer (Eds.), *Powerful learning environments: Unravelling basic components and dimensions* (pp. 55–68). Oxford, England: Elsevier Science.

Bereiter, C., & Scardamalia, M. (2006). Education for the knowledge age: Design-centered models of teaching and instruction. In P. A. Alexander & P. H. Winne (Eds.), *Handbook of educational psychology* (pp. 695–713). Mahwah, NJ: Erlbaum.

Bereiter, C., & Scardamalia, M. (2008). Towards a research-based innovation. *Innovating to learn, learning to innovate* (pp. 67–88). Centre for Educational Research and Innovation, Paris: Organisation of Economic Co-Operation and Development.

Bereiter, C., & Scardamalia, M. (2010). Can children really create knowledge? *Canadian Journal of Learning and Technology, 36*(1). Retrieved from http://www.cjlt.ca/index.php/cjlt/article/view/585/289.

Bereiter, C., & Scardamalia, M. (2011, July). Advancing the design of knowledge building technology. Paper presented at the 2011 Knowledge Building Summer Institute and CSCL Post-Conference, Guangzhou, China.

Bereiter, C., Scardamalia, M., Cassells, C., & Hewitt, J. (1997). Postmodernism, knowledge building, and elementary science. *Elementary School Journal, 97*, 329–340.

Bielaczyc, K. (2006). Designing social infrastructure: Critical issues in creating learning environments with technology. *Journal of the Learning Sciences, 15*, 301–329.

Brown, A., & Campione, J. (1996). Psychological theory and the design of innovative environments: On procedures, principles and systems. In L. Schauble & R. Glaser (Eds.), *Innovation in learning: New environments for education* (pp. 289–325). Mahwah, NJ: Erlbaum.

Burtis, P. J. (1998). Analytic toolkit for Knowledge Forum. Retrieved from http://kf.oise.utoronto.ca/atk/cgis/atkdoc.html.

Caswell, B., & Bielaczyc, K. (2001). Knowledge forum: Altering the relationship between students and scientific knowledge. *Education, Communication and Information, 1*, 281–305.

Chan, C. K. K. (2008). Pedagogical transformation and knowledge building for the Chinese learner. *Evaluation and Research in Education, 21*, 235–251.

Chan, C. K. K. (2011). Bridging research and practice: Implementing and sustaining knowledge building in Hong Kong classrooms. *International Journal of Computer-Supported Collaborative Learning, 6*, 147–186.

Chan, C., Burtis, P. J., & Bereiter, C. (1997). Knowledge-building as a mediator of conflict in conceptual change. *Cognition and Instruction, 15*, 1–40.

Chan, C. K. K., & Lam, I. C.K. (2010). Conceptual change and epistemic growth through reflective assessment in computer-supported knowledge building. In K. Gomez, L. Lyons, & J. Radinsky (Eds.), *Learning in the disciplines: Proceedings of the 9th International Conference of the Learning Sciences 2010* (pp. 1063–1070). Chicago, IL: ISLS.

Chan, C. K .K., & van Aalst, J. (2008). Collaborative inquiry and knowledge building in networked multimedia environments. In J. Voogt & G. Knezek (Eds.), *International handbook of information technology in primary and secondary education* (pp. 299–316). Dordrecht, Netherlands: Springer.

Chi, M. T. H., Glaser, R., & Farr, M. J. (Eds). (1988). *The nature of expertise*. Mahwah, NJ: Erlbaum.

Chinn, C. A., Buckland, L. A., & Samarapungavan, A. (2010). Expanding the dimensions of epistemic cognitions: Arguments from philosophy and psychology. *Educational Psychologist, 46*, 141-167.

Chinn, C. A., & Malhotra, B. A. (2002). Epistemologically authentic reasoning in schools: A theoretical framework for evaluating inquiry tasks. *Science Education, 86*, 175–218.

Cohen, A. L., & Scardamalia, M. (1998). Discourse about ideas: Monitoring and regulation in face-to-face and computer-mediated learning environments. *Interactive Learning Environments, 6*, 114–142.

Collins, A., Joseph, D., & Bielaczyc, K. (2004). Design research: Theoretical and methodological issues. *Journal of the Learning Sciences, 13*, 15–42.

Cress, U., & Kimmerle, J. (2008). A systemic and cognitive view on collaborative knowledge building with wikis. *International Journal of Computer-Supported Collaborative Learning, 3*, 105–122.

De Jong, F. C. M., Veldhuis-Diermanse, E., & Lutgens, G. (2002). Computer-supported collaborative learning in university and vocational education. In T. Koschmann, R. Hall, & M. Miyake (Eds.), *CSCL2: Carrying forward the conversation* (pp. 111–128). Mahwah, NJ: Erlbaum.

Engeström, Y. (1999). Activity theory and individual and social transformation. In Y. Engeström, R. Miettinen, & R.-L. Punamäki (Eds.), *Perspectives on activity theory* (pp. 19–38). Cambridge, England: Cambridge University Press.

Gan, Y. C., Scardamalia, M., Hong, H. Y., & Zhang, J.(2010).Making thinking visible: Growth in graphical literacy, Grades 3 to 4. *Canadian Journal of Learning and Technology, 36*(1). Retrieved from http://www.cjlt.ca/index.php/cjlt/article/view/581/284.

Hakkarainen, K. (2003). Emergence of progressive-inquiry culture in computer-supported collaborative learning. *Learning Environments Research, 6*, 199–220.

Hakkarainen, K. (2004). Pursuit of explanation within a computer-supported classroom. *International Journal of Science Education, 26*, 979–996.

Hakkarainen, K. (2009). A knowledge-practice perspective on technology-mediated learning. *International Journal of Computer-Supported Collaborative Learning, 4*, 213–231.

Hewitt, J. (2002). From a focus on tasks to a focus on understanding: The cultural transformation of a Toronto classroom. In T. Koschmann, R. Hall, & M. Miyake (Eds.), *CSCL2: Carrying forward the conversation* (pp. 11–41). Mahwah, NJ: Erlbaum.

Hewitt, J. (2005). Towards an understanding of how threads die in asynchronous computer conferences. *Journal of the Learning Sciences, 14*, 567–579.

Hmelo-Silver, C. E., Duncan, R. G., & Chinn, C. A. (2007). Scaffolding and achievement in problem-based and inquiry learning: A response to Kirschner, Sweller, and Clark. *Educational Psychologist, 42*, 99–107.

Hong, H. Y., Scardamalia, M., & Zhang, J. (2010). Knowledge Society Network: Toward a dynamic, sustained network for building knowledge. *Canadian Journal of Learning and Technology, 36*(1). http://www.cjlt.ca/index.php/cjlt/article/view/579/282.

Hong, H. Y., & Sullivan, F. R. (2009). Towards an idea-centred, principle-based design approach to support learning as knowledge creation. *Educational Technology Research and Development, 57*, 613–627.

Hurme, T. R., & Järvelä, S. (2005). Students' activity in computer-supported collaborative problem solving in mathematics. *International Journal of Computers for Mathematical Learning, 10*, 49–73.

Jacobson, M. J., & Reimann, P. (Eds.). (2010). *Designs for learning environments of the future: International perspectives from the learning sciences*. New York: Springer.

Kirschner, P., Sweller, J., & Clark, R. (2006). Why minimal guidance during instruction does not work: An analysis of the failure of constructivist, discovery, problem-based, experiential, and inquiry-based teaching. *Educational Psychologist, 41*, 75–86.

Knowledge Building Exchange. Retrieved from http://kbc2.edu.hku.hk.

Kolodner, J. L., Camp, P. J., Crismond, D., Fasse, B., Gray, J., Holbrook, J., ... Ryan, M. (2003). Problem-based learning meets case-based reasoning in the middle-school science classrooms: Putting learning by design (tm) into practice. *Journal of the Learning Sciences, 12*, 495–547.

Koschmann, T., Hall, R., & Miyake, N. (Eds.) (2002). *CSCL2: Carrying forward the conversation*. Mahwah, NJ: Erlbaum.

Krajcik, J. S., & Blumenfeld, P.C. (2006). Project-based learning. In R. K. Sawyer (Ed.), *The Cambridge handbook of the learning sciences* (pp. 317–333). New York: Cambridge University Press.

Kreijins, K., Kirschner, P. A., & Jochems, W. (2003). Identifying the pitfall for social interactions in computer-supported collaborative learning environments. A review of the research. *Computers in Human Behavior, 19*, 335–353.

Laferrière, T., Montane, M., Gros, B., Alvarez, I., Bernaus, M., Breuleux, A., & Lamon, M. (2010). Partnership for knowledge building: An emerging model. *Canadian Journal of Learning Technology, 36*(1). Retrieved from http://www.cjlt.ca/index.php/cjlt/article/view/578/280.

Law, N., Yuen, J., Wong, W. O. W., & Leng, J. (2011). Understanding knowledge building trajectory through visualizations of multiple automated analyses. In S. Puntambekar, G. Erkens, & C. E. Hmelo-Silver (Eds.), *Analyzing interactions in CSCL: Methods, approaches and issues* (pp. 47–82). Dordrecht, Netherlands: Springer.

Lee, E. Y. C., Chan, C., & van Aalst, J. (2006). Students assessing their own collaborative knowledge building. *International Journal of Computer-Supported Collaborative Learning, 1*, 277–307.

Lee, H. S., Linn, M., Varma, K., & Liu, O. L. (2010). How do technology-enhanced inquiry science units impact classroom learning? *Journal of Research in Science Teaching, 47*, 71–90.

Lin, X., Schwartz, D. L., & Hatano, G. (2005). Towards teachers' adaptive metacognition. *Educational Psychologist, 40*, 245–255.

McAuley, A. (2009). Knowledge building in an aboriginal context. *Canadian Journal of Learning and Technology, 35*(1). Retrieved from http://www.cjlt.ca/index.php/cjlt/article/viewArticle/514/244

Moss, J., & Beatty, R. (2010). Knowledge building and mathematics: Shifting the responsibility for knowledge advancement and engagement. *Canadian Journal of Learning and Technology, 36*(1). Retrieved from http://www.cjlt.ca/index.php/cjlt/article/view/575/277

Niu, H., & van Aalst, J. (2009). Participation in knowledge-building discourse: An analysis of online discussions in mainstream and honours social studies. *Canadian Journal of Learning and Technology, 35*(1). Retrieved from http://www.cjlt.ca/index.php/cjlt/article/viewArticle/515/245.

Nonaka, I., & Takeuchi, H. (1995). *The knowledge creating company: How Japanese companies create the dynamics of innovation*. New York: Oxford University Press.

Organisation for Economic Co-Operation and Development (OECD). (2004). *Innovation in the knowledge economy: Implications for education and learning*. Paris: Author.

Oshima, J., Oshima, R., Murayama, I., Inagaki, S., Takenaka, M., Nakayama, H., & Yamaguchi, E. (2004). Design experiments in Japanese elementary science education with computer support for collaborative learning: hypothesis testing and collaborative construction. *International Journal of Science Education, 26*, 1199–1221.

Oshima, J., Oshima, R., Murayama, I., Inagaki, S., Takenaka, M., Yamamoto, T., … Nakayama, H. (2006). Knowledge-building activity structures in Japanese elementary science pedagogy. *International Journal of Computer-Supported Collaborative Learning, 1*, 229–246.

Oshima, J., Scardamalia, M., & Bereiter, C. (1996). Collaborative learning processes associated with high and low conceptual process. *Instructional Science, 24*, 125–155.

Paavola, S., Lipponen, L., & Hakkarainen, K. (2004). Models of innovative knowledge communities and three metaphors of learning. *Review of Educational Research, 74*, 557–576.

Pelletier, J., Reeve, R., & Haleward. C. (2006). Young children"s knowledge building and literacy development through Knowledge Forum. *Early Education and Development, 17*, 323–346.

Popper, K. R. (1979). *Objective knowledge: An evolutionary approach*. Oxford, England: Oxford University Press.

Puntambekar, S., Erkens, G., & Hmelo-Silver, C. (Eds.). (2011). *Analyzing interactions in CSCL: Methods, approaches and issues*. Dordrecht, Netherlands: Springer.

Reeve, R., Messina, R., & Scardamalia, M. (2008). Wisdom in an elementary school. In M. Ferrari & G. Potworowski (Eds.), *Teaching for wisdom* (pp. 79–92). Dordrecht, Netherlands: Springer.

Russell, A., & Perris, K. (2003). Telementoring in community nursing: A shift from dyadic to communal models of learning and professional development. *Mentoring and Tutoring, 11*, 227–237.

Sawyer, R. K. (Ed.). (2006). The Cambridge handbook of the learning sciences. New York: Cambridge University Press.

Scardamalia, M. (2002). Collective cognitive responsibility for the advancement of knowledge. In B. Smith (Ed.), *Liberal education in a knowledge society* (pp. 67–98). Chicago, IL: Open Court.

Scardamalia, M. (2004). CSILE/Knowledge Forum®. In A. Kovalchick & K. Dawson (Eds.), *Education and technology: An encyclopedia* (pp. 183–192). Santa Barbara, CA: ABC-CLIO.

Scardamalia, M. (Ed.). (2010). Knowledge Building. [Special Issue] *Canadian Journal of Learning and Technology, 35*(1).

Scardamalia, M., & Bereiter, C. (1994). Computer support for knowledge building communities. *Journal of the Learning Sciences, 3*, 265–283.

Scardamalia, M. & Bereiter. C. (2003). Knowledge building. In J. W. Guthrie (Ed.), *Encyclopedia of education* (2nd ed., pp. 1370–1373). New York: Macmillan.

Scardamalia, M., & Bereiter, C. (2006). Knowledge building: Theory, pedagogy, and technology. In R. K. Sawyer (Ed.), *The Cambridge handbook of the learning sciences* (pp. 97–115). New York: Cambridge University Press.

Scardamalia, M., & Bereiter, C. (2007). Fostering communities of learners and knowledge building: An interrupted dialogue. In J. C. Campione, K. E. Metz, & A. S. Palincsar (Eds.), *Children's learning in the laboratory and in the classroom: Essays in honor of Ann Brown* (pp. 197–212). Mahwah, NJ: Erlbaum.

Scardamalia, M., Bereiter, C., & Lamon, M. (1994). The CSILE project: Trying to bring the classroom into World 3. In K. McGilley (Ed.), *Classroom lessons: Integrating cognitive theory and classroom practice* (pp. 201–228). Cambridge, England: Cambridge University Press.

Sfard, A. (1998). On two metaphors for learning and the danger of choosing just one. *Educational Researcher, 27*(2), 4–13.

So, H. J., Seah, L. H., & Toh-Heng, H. L. (2010). Designing collaborative knowledge building environments accessible to all learners: Impact and design challenges. *Computers & Education, 54*, 479–490.

Stahl, G. (2006). *Group cognition: Computer support for building collaborative knowledge*. Cambridge, MA: MIT.

Sun, Y., & Zhang, J., & Scardamalia, M. (2010). Knowledge building and vocabulary growth over two years: Grades 3 and 4. *Instructional Science, 38*(2), 147–171.

Teplovs, C., & Scardamalia, M. (2007, July). *Visualization for knowledge building assessment*. Paper presented at the conference of Computer-Supported Collaborative Learning, New Brunswick, NJ.

Thagard, *P. (1989). Explanatory coherence. Behavior and Brain Sciences, 12,* 435–502.

van Aalst, J. (2006). Rethinking the nature of online work in asynchronous learning networks. *British Journal of Educational Technology, 37,* 279–288.

van Aalst, J. (2009). Distinguishing knowledge-sharing, knowledge-construction, and knowledge-creation discourses. *International Journal of Computer-Supported Collaborative Learning, 4,* 259–287.

van Aalst, J., & Chan, C. K. K. (2007). Student-directed assessment of knowledge building using electronic portfolios. *Journal of the Learning Sciences, 16,* 175–220.

van Aalst, J., Chan, C.K.K., Tian, S. W., Teplovs, C., Chan, Y. Y., & Wan, W. S. (2012). The knowledge connections analyzer. In J. van Aalst, K. Thompson, M. J. Jacobson, & P. Reimann (Eds.), *The future of learning: Proceedings of the 10th international conference of the learning sciences (ICLS 2012), Volume 2* (pp. 361–365). Sydney, Australia: ISLS.

van Aalst, J., & Truong, M. S. (2011). Promoting knowledge creation discourse in an Asian primary five classroom: Results from an inquiry into life cycles. *International Journal of Science Education, 33,* 487–515.

Zhang, J., Hong, H. Y., Scardamalia, M., Teo, C. L., & Morley, E. A. (2011). Sustaining knowledge building as a principle-based innovation at an elementary school. *Journal of the Learning Sciences, 20,* 262–307.

Zhang, J., Scardamalia, M., Lamon, M., Messina, R., & Reeve, R. (2007). Socio-cognitive dynamics of knowledge building in the work of 9- and 10-year-olds. *Educational Technology Research & Development, 55*(2), 117_145.

Zhang, J., Scardamalia, M., Reeve, R., & Messina, R. (2009). Designs for collective cognitive responsibility in knowledge-building communities. *Journal of the learning sciences, 18,* 7–44.

Zhang, J., & Sun, Y. (2011). Reading for idea advancement in a Grade 4 knowledge building community. *Instructional Science, 39,* 429–452.

Zohar, A., & Dori, Y. J. (2003). Higher order thinking skills and low achieving students—Are they mutually exclusive? *Journal of the Learning Sciences, 12,* 145–182.

26

METACOGNITION AND COMPUTER-SUPPORTED COLLABORATIVE LEARNING

PHILIP H. WINNE

Simon Fraser University

ALLYSON F. HADWIN

University of Victoria

NANCY E. PERRY

University of British Columbia

Research on metacognition evolved from seminal papers by Hart and Flavell (Schwartz & Perfect, 2010; Winne & Nesbit, 2010). Hart (1965, 1967) investigated whether people could judge accurately what they know. He asked people questions about common knowledge. If they could not recall the answer, he asked them to estimate the likelihood they would recognize the answer among options in a multiple-choice question. In general, people were quite good at these tasks. Flavell (1971, 1979) urged investigations into what people perceived about (a) their memories and (b) operations they used to remember. He further theorized that people could inspect features of their knowledge, tasks they undertook, and methods for working on tasks. With information gleaned from these metacognitive activities and feedback about differences between goals and plans, he conjectured that people could choose or create more effective methods for making progress.

Models of metacognition and research that builds on those models open new lenses for examining how participants perceive and work in computer-supported collaborative learning (CSCL). We survey this area and suggest prospects for future research. Specifically, we begin by reviewing components of metacognition in solo activity and then distinguish it from co- and shared metacognition and regulation that ideally occur during collaborative activity. Then, we discuss factors implicated in promoting metacognition in collaboration and conclude with ideas for advancing research on the roles of metacognition in CSCL.

METACOGNITIVE MONITORING

Metacognition is commonly described as thinking about how one thinks, and characterizing cognitive products that cognitive operations create. For example, after studying the law of supply and demand, a learner might question the benefits of extra work to generate her own everyday examples of the law. Generating this question about benefits and answering it are elements of metacognitive monitoring. To monitor, features of a target are compared to a set of standards. In this case, the target is the cognitive work to generate examples of supply and demand; the standards refer to returns to the learner on that investment of effort, likely measured in terms of estimated memorability.

In addition to considering the general efficiency of generating examples when trying to learn abstract principles such as the law of supply and demand, metacognitive monitoring can also focus on a particular instance of cognition, how a particular example was generated. The products of metacognitive monitoring, in both cases, are metacognitive "knowledge." We have marked the word *knowledge* with scare quotes in the preceding sentence because, while that term is widely used, information generated by metacognitive monitoring sometimes does not meet everyday requirements for knowledge, namely, that knowledge is durable, retrievable, and accurate. In this case, the word *information* is more appropriate than knowledge (see Winne, 2010).

In analyzing metacognition that occurs in solo and collaborative learning, it is helpful to differentiate topics of metacognition. In our example, particular cognitive operations or tactics that generate examples or that lead to recalling examples, as well as the examples themselves, are located at what is termed the *object level*. People can apply cognition to their mental representations of these "objects." The learner can monitor attributes of cognitive tactics used to generate examples relative to standards such as effort and the likelihood operations yield cogent examples. The examples per se can be monitored relative to standards such as completeness and clarity. These monitoring operations occur at the *metalevel* because they are not the objects examined but, rather, they examine information about the objects (Nelson & Narens, 1990).

It is unfortunate, in our view, that the word *level* was used to differentiate object from meta. Level invites interpretations that metacognition is somehow a "higher" or more complex form of cognition than "normal" cognition. We hold a different view. Cognitive operations people apply are fundamentally the same at the object level and the metalevel. People have only one toolkit of basic or primitive cognitive operations. The difference between the object level and metalevel is not the operations applied to information; rather, what differs are the topics on which learners cognitively operate. The understanding a learner generates about a concept such as how evaporation occurs is information at the object level. The learner's estimate of how well evaporation is understood is information at the metalevel.

People use information in the world to design routines for learning (or scripts or production systems depending on one's choice of models of cognition) and for other cognitively demanding tasks. These routines are refined successively based on the results of using them. An example is learning to use mnemonic devices that improve memory. The first letter of colors in the visible spectrum can form a mnemonic—ROY G BIV—that encodes the colors' names in the order of their wavelengths (from longer to shorter). This schema for a first letter mnemonic can be adapted to music (Every Good Boy Does Fine and FACE for the notes on the lines and spaces of the treble clef) and geometry

(Chief SOH CAH TOA for the trigonometric relations of sine, cosine, and tangent). This view of cognition is optimistic because it allows that learners' cognitive and metacognitive capabilities can improve by experience.

METACOGNITIVE CONTROL

Learners use the results of metacognitive monitoring to guide choices about how to proceed in a current task and to plan for future tasks. Our economics student may opt to slog on, generating even more examples of the law of supply and demand, or he might choose another tactic—searching for examples in the Internet—because he predicts it is more efficient and just as effective. Exercising options is metacognitive control.

A second way to exercise metacognitive control is to change features in the external environment that constrain or support how one is working on a task. For example, our learner might shift from working solo and initiate an online chat to involve a peer in generating examples. A third expression of metacognitive control is selecting content for input to cognitive operations. Our learner might estimate that a better route to learning is to study his group's wiki rather than independently constructing possibly erroneous examples. A fourth way to exercise metacognitive control is changing cognitive operations (e.g., switching from generating examples to spaced rehearsals of the statement of the law).

When learners apply metacognition to monitor activity that leads to adapting tactics, reshaping environmental factors, selecting content, or revising standards for metacognitive monitoring, they can exercise metacognition "in the moment" if they aim to alter fine-grained features of engagement in a current task. Metacognition may, instead, lay a foundation for wholesale perceptions of this task or tasks like this, general beliefs and goals, and large-grained strategies for working on tasks in the same category as a current task. When fine-grained or large-grained adaptations concern how to carry out learning, learners are engaged in self-regulated learning (SRL).

METACOGNITIVE KNOWLEDGE

In the context of collaboration, metacognition concerns information about features in the collaborative work setting as well as views about her attributes and those of her collaborators. Standards can be set for five categories of information handily summarized by the acronym COPES (Winne, 2001; Winne & Hadwin, 1998), as we list below. To be considered metacognitive knowledge, information about these features must be durable and retrievable. Fleeting thoughts and one-time perceptions are not knowledge.

1. *Conditions* shape how learners approach their tasks. These might include the group's composition and whether the environment provides access to useful resources or the software is familiar. Some conditions may be malleable but may require some time for changes to be realized; for example, a learner's domain knowledge, epistemological beliefs, and skills for learning.
2. *Operations* manipulate information. Cognitive operations are internal to each learner. Round-robin reviews of progress at the end of each group session are an example of a group operation. Examples of standards for operations include load (effort applied) and the probability of an operation generating a particular product.

3. *Products* are information that operations create. Standards for products can be set externally, by a teacher or by each group member or negotiated by the group. For example, a group might set standards for its second meeting to (a) finalize the list of resources they will use and (b) ensure each member makes an equal contribution to group work.
4. *Evaluations* assign values to differences identified by metacognitive monitoring. For example, effort required to generate examples (an operation) can be valued as a sign of productive work or low ability (attribution theory; or, making frequent contributions to a chat may be motivating because it provides an arena for demonstrating competence or for deepening understanding by leveraging others' contributions (goal orientation; see Winne & Hadwin, 2008).
5. *Standards* can themselves be monitored. A person or group might examine standards for a project and conclude they are vague or picayune.

Calibration

The success of adaptive metacognition depends on two issues. First, metacognitive monitoring must be accurate: what the learner judges to be the case must match what is the case. The accuracy of this match is called calibration. Second, if metacognitive monitoring is well calibrated, the successful learner must accurately forecast outcomes that will be generated for each option that is available for expressing metacognitive control. These are outcome expectations.

In various contexts for solo learning, undergraduates can be quite poorly calibrated in judging what they have learned by studying. Not only are they inaccurate, but they are also inaccurate in a way that hampers development of knowledge in the domain of study (the object level). Specifically, overconfidence—predicting more knowledge than one has—characterizes learners with less achievement, underconfidence—predicting less knowledge than one has—is typically found among learners with higher achievement. The overconfident learner chooses a poor course of action (metacognitive control) in not changing tactics for studying or restudying when this would be beneficial. The underconfident learner suffers an opportunity cost either by spending unnecessary time restudying when new material could be studied or by changing tactics unnecessarily.

In the case of outcome expectations, learners and collaborators who have broad knowledge of tactics and strategies need to make optimal choices in changing conditions, operations, and standards in relation to products they forecast to be most useful to their task. Currently, we know little about collaborators' outcome expectations regarding group processes. While the theory is well structured, data to test it are meager (cf. Peterson & Schrieber, 2006).

METACOGNITION IN COLLABORATIVE TASKS: SELF-REGULATION, COREGULATION, SHARED REGULATION

In this section, we extend the view of metacognition from a solo cognitive activity to a collaborative context. Ideal collaboration is work that is coordinated and interdependent. In collaborative activities, learners strive to achieve a shared goal or solve a shared problem (Roschelle & Teasley, 1995). In contrast to cooperative work, where labor is divided among group members, genuine collaboration involves dynamic, mutually interdependent interaction intended to move the group toward a shared goal in a joint task (Dillenbourg, 1999). A collaborative team leverages individuals' unique and distributed knowledge and expertise to achieve a product that could not be achieved by individuals alone (Johnson & Johnson, 1999).

Success in collaborations depends on: (a) strategies and self-regulatory skills individuals contribute to the group, (b) support members provide to one another that facilitates individuals' self-regulatory competence (coregulation), and (c) shared or collective regulation of learning that involves metacommunicative awareness and successful coordination of strategies (Barron, 2003). From this perspective, collaborative work fuses individuals' distributed metacognitive work with shared and coordinated metacognitive work of the group.

Individuals in a group can metacognitively monitor and control their own personal knowledge and operations. This is metacognition in the service of self-regulation (Hadwin, Järvelä, & Miller, 2011). It maintains each individual's active and strategic involvement in the collaborative task.

However, collaborative work entails interdependence. Thus, each group member's participation depends on coordinated metacognitive knowledge, monitoring, and control exercised by team members. If one participant is off-track or not calibrated well in metacognitive monitoring or metacognitive control, this compromises collaborative work. Students coregulate learning by temporarily guiding, prompting, or assisting each other to accurately monitor and control cognitive work that contributes to the group product. Coregulation occurs, for example, when one participant prompts or questions another about metacognitive topics at the metalevel; or, when one student adopts another's metacognitive stance and makes a judgment about the peer's learning or thinking (Hadwin, Järvelä, & Miller, 2011). Coregulation implies reciprocity—group members assist each other to calibrate or realign one another's metacognition in the service of regulating contributions to the collaborative task. Thus, they distribute responsibility to optimize each group member's metacognitive activity and calibration.

Full collaboration implies meta-awareness of the coordinated whole. Successful groups are not only metacognitively aware of what individual group members are doing, they also unite their individual metacognitive information and control to negotiate consensus about task perceptions, goals, knowledge about group process, evaluations of collective progress and outcomes, and regulatory decisions about how to stay or get back on track. In addition to solo metacognition and coregulation of group members' metacognitive processes, shared metacognition underlies planning, monitoring, evaluating and regulating "in unison" (Hadwin, Järvelä, & Miller, 2011). Shared metacognition builds communal awareness of the conditions, operations, products, evaluations, and standards bearing on group processes and products. Metacognition that underlies shared regulation shifts the plane from "I" or "you" to how well "we" are working to accomplish "our" goal.

Fundamental Metacognitive Processes in Collaborative Tasks

Three central questions relate to metacognitive events in collaborative tasks: (a) What is monitored? (b) How are goals/standards for monitoring determined? (c) What is metacognitively controlled or regulated? Elaborations of these questions, in Table 26.1, provide a useful frame for comparing metacognition in self-regulation, coregulation, and shared regulation of learning when tasks are collaborative. Regulation occurs when metacognitive knowledge, monitoring, and control fuel individual or collective large-scale adaption of task perceptions, goals, plans, strategies, or approaches within one task or from one task to another.

Research on Metacognition in Collaboration

Metacognition per se and computer supports for metacognition are beginning to be examined in CSCL environments. Manlove, Lazonder, and De Jong (2006) examined solo metacognitive processes in collaborative work. Group members worked at separate work stations using Co-Lab (a collaborative computer based learning environment) and a process coordinator (PC) tool for setting, monitoring, and evaluating goals. For half the students, the PC tool was enhanced by providing a hierarchy of preset goals from which to choose, hints and explanations, and a template for the final report. The PC tool supported solo metacognition and a chat tool created a collaborative space for emergent regulatory conversation. Traces of planning, monitoring, and regulating were logged separately for each team member during the collaborative task, then aggregated across participants to examine relationships between collective (or averaged) metacognition and the quality group products.

Students who used the enhanced PC tool for planning, monitoring, and regulating engagement in the collaborative task: (a) collectively engaged in more planning, but not monitoring or evaluating activities, than students for whom tools were merely available, and (b) collectively performed better on a collaborative modeling task. In contrast to hypotheses, correlations between aggregate frequencies of planning, monitoring, and regulating and collaborative task performance were weak for both conditions and surprisingly higher for groups using the unenhanced PC tool. Importantly, Manlove et al. also coded and analyzed chat dialogues for instances of regulative talk. Participants who used the enhanced PC tool apparently had less need for regulatory talk in the chats. These data also afforded the researchers opportunities to uncover instances of coregulation in the group.

Iiskala, Vauras, and Lehtinen (2004) and Vauras, Iiskala, Kajamies, Kinnunen, and Lehtinen (2003) made important contributions in studies that examined metacognitive and cognitive interactions at the interindividual level (coregulation in collaboration). Grade 4 dyads were videotaped during a computer-based problem-solving game to study how peers mediate each other's regulated learning and metacognition. These researchers operationalized instances of metacognition as exchanges in which individuals monitored and regulated each others' contributions to a shared task. They used the term *socially shared regulation* to emphasize: (a) egalitarian distribution of monitoring across participants, and (b) the task as a joint problem-solving activity completed together rather than solo.

Metacognitive monitoring and control in this study tended to focus on participants' monitoring and controlling each others' perceptions or coming to understand each others' thinking and decisions, not monitoring and controlling shared knowledge and beliefs about the task and processes. From our perspective (see Table 26.1), this implies coregulation because participants assisted each other to accurately monitor and control the cognitive work they contributed to the group.

Examining socially shared metacognition has posed challenges for researching: (a) what is consistent across group members in terms of their distributed metacognition within the group, and (b) what is communal or shared in terms of group planning and regulation. A specific challenge is separating the individual from the collective, and

Table 26.1 Contrasting Self-Regulation, Co-Regulation, and Shared-Regulation of Metacognition in Collaborative Tasks

	Self-Regulated Learning in a Collaborative Task	**Co-Regulated Learning in a Collaborative Task**	**Shared Regulation of Learning in a Collaborative Task**
What is metacognitively monitored? • Task knowledge • Self knowledge • Goals and plans • Strategy knowledge • Strategy use	• My perceptions about the task (what we are supposed to do) • Strategies I know/use for this task • Progress toward goals and standards I hold for this task • How I think we should approach this task • Ways my actions influence the task	• Each of my team members' perceptions of this task • Strengths and strategies each team member knows/uses for this task • Goals and standards each team member holds for this task and progress toward those goals • Plans each team member has for this task and their work • Ways our actions and interactions influence each other and the task	• Common and negotiated perceptions of this task • Knowledge about our collective strengths and weaknesses for this task • Goals and standards we negotiate together for this task • Alignment between collective and individual goals • Strategies we choose to guide our collaborative process • Ways our actions influence our status and effectiveness as a team
How are standards for metacognitive monitoring determined?	Individuals hold personal standards against which they monitor their own progress	Individuals hold standards for themselves and others against which they monitor each other's progress	Collective standards are negotiated to align and maximize individual standards and monitor progress as a collective
What is metacognitively controlled or regulated? • Task knowledge • Self knowledge • Goals and plans • Strategy knowledge • Strategy use	• My perceptions about the task • My strategy knowledge • My strategy use • My goals and standards for this task • My plans for working together • Perceptions and evaluations of my progress • Calibration of self-monitoring	• Each other's task perceptions • Each other's strategy knowledge • Each other's strategy use • Each other's goals and standards for this task and for contributing to this task • Each other's plans for this task and for contributing to this task • Awareness of other's roles and actions in this task • Perceptions and evaluations of each other's progress • Calibration of other-monitoring	• Our negotiations of a common task perceptions • The common perceptions we hold for this task • Knowledge of this group's strengths and weaknesses with respect to this task • Shared goals • Alignment of individual task perceptions and goals • Our use of team processes and strategies for succeeding with this task • Knowledge about strategies we have used together and their effectiveness • Perceptions and evaluations of our collective progress toward the goals/standards we have negotiated for this task • Calibration of collective monitoring

shared metacognitive activity from shared cognitive and problem solving activities. For example, when collaboration is prompted with scaffolds such as "I need to understand ...," "My theory ...," or "A better theory ..." shared cognition for constructing knowledge in a domain is supported. In contrast, scaffolds such as "Our goal is ...," "We need to understand why we are doing this problem," or "Our best strategy might be ..." focus on developing shared metacognitive knowledge about the task, goals, and strategies.

Students clearly engage metacognitive processes in the context of collaborative problem solving (Hurme & Järvelä, 2005) when constituent metacognitive knowledge and metacognitive skills are distributed among individuals (Hurme, Palonen, & Järvelä, 2006). However, in group problem solving, different types of metacognitive events emerge, including metacognition becoming shared, metacognition becoming visible but not shared, and individuals sharing metacognition by attempting to regulate joint activity (Hurme, Merenluoto, Salonen, & Järvelä, submitted).

Hurme, Merenluoto, and Järvelä (2009) examined shared metacognition when groups of three preservice primary teachers worked together to solve mathematical tasks. Students worked online using an asynchronous learning environment (WorkMates) and exchanged text messages. Messages were coded for evidence of metacognitive activity when three criteria were met, namely when a message was: (a) related to and focused on earlier discussion; (b) intended to interrupt, change, or promote the progression of joint problem solving; and (c) explicit about reasoning for considering an alternative. From the perspective of Hurme et al. (submitted), metacognition was shared when individual metacognition was made explicit to the group and intended to shift the group's collective approach. In other words, as per Table 26.1, what was controlled or regulated was group planning. The group problem solving process was monitored but what fueled a shift in the group's plan was a team member self-monitoring her strategy and sharing results with the group. That is, shared metacognition built on individuals' metacognition.

In contrast to this approach to examining shared regulation, Hadwin, Malmberg, Järvelä, Järvenoja, and Vainionpää (2010) examined shared metacognition in the context of task perceptions and goals for collaborative work. Participants included three triads of graduate students collaborating on three consecutive online collaborative tasks using the nStudy software (Winne, Hadwin, & Beaudoin, 2010). Shared task perceptions and shared goals were examined by contrasting: (a) notes co-constructed about planning and reflection that were submitted by each group at the beginning of each task, and (b) convergence among group members' individual reflective statements about goals they held for the task they had just completed. Findings indicated that shared metacognition was rarely achieved and did not evolve across tasks. In this study, juxtaposing co-constructed goal statements for the task with data about each group member's individual goal for the task was useful in revealing shared metacognition.

PROMOTING METACOGNITION IN COLLABORATION

We posit that researchers and practitioners need to attend to several factors that potentially afford and constrain metacognition and collaboration: task structures, technological tools, and interpersonal support.

Tasks

To prompt and support metacognition and regulation, tasks need to be at an intermediate level of difficulty. This affords and requires mindful attention to task demands and collaborators' characteristics, as well as thoughtful use and evaluation of tactics and strategies selected to close gaps between current conditions and goals. Classroom research has linked appropriately complex tasks to opportunities for and evidence of metacognition and regulation of learning (Many, Fyfe, Lewis, & Mitchell, 1997; Perry, Phillips, & Hutchinson, 2006; Perry, VandeKamp, Mercer, & Nordby, 2002; Walker, Pressick-Kilborn, Arnold, & Sainsbury, 2004). Perry and colleagues characterized tasks as complex when they addressed multiple goals, focused on large chunks of meaning, and extended over time. Such tasks engage learners in a variety of cognitive and metacognitive processes and afford creating a broad range of products as evidence of learning (Bruning, Schraw, & Ronning, 1995; McCaslin & Good, 1996; Turner, 1997). Succeeding at challenging tasks is motivating—it increases self-efficacy and the likelihood that learners will persist in the face of difficulty. Perry's research links teachers' design and the implementation of complex tasks to metacognition and the regulation of learning in solo and collaborative settings.

Walker et al. (2004) examined an intervention designed to promote metacognitive monitoring, collaborative learning, and regulation of learning in a context of teacher-scaffolded instruction. Learners were Grade 5 students studying society and the environment by engaging in projects using information and communication technologies (ICT) to search for information on the Internet. Data included assessments of students' ability to plan a research project and use ICT, and teacher achievement ratings of students' products. Assessments of planning and ICT use included assessments of metacognitive knowledge monitoring. Observations recorded teacher scaffolding, collaborative group functioning, and regulatory discourse. Compared with students in control classrooms, those in the intervention were characterized as "advantaged" in terms of their achievement, ICT skills, planning skills, and accuracy in metacognitive knowledge monitoring. Moreover, observations of collaborative group functioning illustrated collaborative monitoring and evaluation of the quality of work against agreed-upon standards, plus coregulatory actions that promoted persistence and sharing ideas to overcome challenges.

We note that tasks characterized as collaborative in the CSCL literature reflect a continuum of communication between and among learners. At one end of the continuum, collaboration involves consulting or coregulating as group members complete individual tasks, as was the case in the study reported by Choi, Land, and Turgeon (2005). At the other end, learners work together to develop shared understandings of task conditions and standards, and to coconstruct processes and products that complete tasks, as in Hadwin et al.'s (2010) study. Shared metacognition and shared regulation to optimize performance and problem solving are unlikely or, at least, not assured in the first case, but are required in the second case. Also, complex tasks that challenge learners' individual zones of proximal development in intellectually rigorous activities (Englert & Mariage, 2003; McCaslin & Good, 1996) are more likely to prompt interdependence among group members that engenders metacognition and self- and shared regulation than unidimensional task structures.

Hurme and Jarvela (2005) studied metacognition and CSCL as students worked on "projects" in geometry and probability. Participants were 16 students (aged 13) in a secondary school classroom in Finland. Working in dyads, students used Knowledge Forum (KF), the current version of the earlier Computer-Supported Intentional Learning Environment (Chan, chapter 25 this volume; Scardamalia & Bereiter, 1996) that includes a discussion forum where participants can post text and graphical notes, and comment (build) on their partners' notes. Students in dyads posted solutions to problems as notes, commented on the correctness of their partners' solutions, and discussed alternative solutions or paths to solutions. The teacher instructed the students to make their thinking as visible as possible and was available to facilitate networked discussions if needed, but the researchers commented that "her role was minor in the discussions" (p. 52).

Hurme and Jarvela (2005) were interested in how students shared knowledge and regulated cognition during CSCL. They found that the students shared math concepts as well as strategies and heuristics for solving math problems. Evidence of metacognitive knowledge and metacognitive monitoring was found in networked notes, although there was more evidence of metacognitive knowledge than metacognitive monitoring. Perhaps students did not need to monitor—which raises the question of whether the problems were challenging enough to prompt monitoring—or the knowledge was easier to make visible than to monitor. It is also possible that the students needed more explicit prompting to monitor, either from the teacher or by the software. We will take up this topic again when we discuss interpersonal support for metacognition in collaboration.

The researchers noted an important constraint on students' collaboration in these projects: mathematical symbols could not be entered into notes in Knowledge Forum. The researchers speculated that this limitation of the software was likely to have prompted the students to add narrative detail to their notes, which affords metacognition but may also have decreased their use of mathematical symbols, the language of math, and the accuracy of arguments in shared notes. Hurme and Jarvela characterized the majority of students' exchanges as "mainly 'everyday talk' rather than attempts to argue using mathematical concepts" (p. 68). This aligns with other research—left on their own, most students do not develop optimal self-regulation (Zimmerman, 2008), which may signal the need for more explicit scaffolding of self- and shared regulation, as we have already suggested. Finally, Hurme and Jarvela noted there was no evidence students used collaborations to improve problem solving. Depending on their goals (i.e., communication in the service of completing independent or shared tasks), this may not be a limitation as shared metacognition and regulation need not always enhance individual regulation and performance. Their report is unclear about whether every student was expected to provide a solution to the problems or could share solutions. A focus for future research on metacognition in collaboration should be to understand and clarify outcomes for individuals and groups, and key elements for accurate calibration. Researchers should also attend to differences in synchronous versus asynchronous collaborations. Collaborations were asynchronous in the Hurme and Jarvela study. Tools that allow synchronous collaboration through, for example, online chats and discussion forums and shared workspaces, would seem to be ideal for shared metacognition and regulation (e.g., Virtual School; Carroll, Neale, Isenhour, Rosson, & McCrickard, 2003), but shared metacognition and regulation may also be supported in asynchronous environments such as wiki spaces and discussion forums when collaborators are prompted specifically to negotiate and reach consensus about metacognitive aspects of the task such as task perceptions and task goals.

Technological Tools

The CSCL literature invites a critical question: "Are technological tools instrumental to learners' metacognition or collaboration and, if so, how?" In Walker et al. (2004), support for metacognition and collaboration was provided through teacher–student and student–student interactions but we cannot identify how software contributed to this. In a study reported by Hurme and Jarvela (2005), students communicated about their projects using software, but their metacognitive and collaborative activity may have been just as rich had they engaged in face-to-face discussions. Again, it was the teachers' instructions that prompted the students' metacognitive activity.

Soller, Martinez, Jermann, and Muehlenbrock (2005) identified three classes of tools for supporting metacognition in collaboration: mirroring systems, metacognitive systems, and guiding systems. Mirroring systems (e.g., ART/SAILE; Goodman, Geier, Haverty, Linton, & McCready, 2001) collect and aggregate data during students' collaborations and reflect it back to them (e.g., as a graphical representation). These systems are designed to raise learners' awareness of their thoughts and actions, but the locus for metacognitive engagement and regulation lies in students, or teachers, who must monitor differences metacognitively between products and standards, then exercise metacognitive control to change conditions, operations or standards so the goal can be met. Metacognitive systems (e.g., Sharlock II; Ogata, Matsuura, & Yano, 2000) display standards for desired interaction along with information about the current state of collaborations. With these data, collaborators can monitor and adjust their interactions. Again, the locus for metacognition and potential regulation is with students, teachers, or coaches. Guiding systems (e.g., DEGREE; Barros & Jerdejo, 2000) perform all the phases in a typical regulatory loop. These systems record and analyze data as collaboration occurs and evaluate whether the form of current interactions will achieve the desired goal. As possible, they offer advice or guidance about how interactions can be adapted. Finally, they evaluate outcomes from their interventions and begin again in the first phase of the loop. According to Soller et al. (2005), an ideal system might be one that progressively moves the locus for regulation from the system to the students—a transformation from guiding tool to metacognitive tool and then to mirroring tool. We suggest that an ideal tool would adjust these levels of support in just-in-time fashion aligned to the state of the learners' metacognitive and collaborative activites. Virtual School is an example of a system that takes steps in this direction (Carroll et al., 2003). We also note that ideal systems will not only achieve this flexibility but also, unobtrusively, collect data that researchers need to advance the field (Winne, 2006, 2010).

Interpersonal Support and Scaffolding

In much of the research we have cited, software was neither a necessary factor nor a sufficient factor in accounting for observed metacognition and collaboration. Usually, instrumental support came from teachers or peers. For example, Walker et al. (2004) reported that teachers provided extensive scaffolding that led to outcomes. Hurme and Jarvela (2005) made little mention of teacher support in their study, but the classroom in which they were working appeared to be focused on complex tasks, higher order learning, and collaboration (projects for pairs and small groups), and the teacher explicitly prompted students to be metacognitive. Less clear is whether the teacher in this classroom monitored and scaffolded metacognition and collaboration after initial instruction.

Hurme and Jarvela (2005) offered more extensive analyses and examples of how students supported one another's metacognition in collaboration than Walker et al. (2004), while both studies had positive results concerning learners' collaborative monitoring and coconstruction of standards and strategies. However, Hurme and colleagues (Hurme & Jarvela, 2005; Hurme, Merenluoto, & Jarvela, 2009; Hurme, Palonen, & Jarvela, 2006) expressed disappointment that much of what they observed involved "everyday talk" with low levels of metacognitive activity (e.g., planning). One reason for this may be the typically low levels of support for metacognition and collaboration that students received in CSCL environments from teachers or software. We observed that instructions about metacognition were vague (e.g., make your thinking visible) and students received little or no guiding feedback from teachers or from software about the quality of their interactions or their progress on tasks. Metacognition and regulation were left to "unfold."

A reliable finding is that productive communication, metacognition, and regulation are unlikely without the support that helps collaborators forge effective participation structures. Makitalo-Siegl, Kohnle, and Fischer (2011) demonstrated this in their study of how high and low levels of teachers' scaffolding affected secondary school students' help-seeking and science learning. Students who received high levels of scaffolding required less help and learned more. Left on their own, learners seemed less inclined or less capable of monitoring and regulating their engagement metacognitively by refining perceptions of tasks, adapting goals, or revising plans for learning. Pressures for grades, lack of feedback about procedures, and low accuracy in tracking how they work (Winne & Jamieson-Noel, 2002) limit opportunities for students to improve learning and collaboration. Thus, they work below optimal levels (Winne & Jamieson-Noel, 2003) as they try to discover how well they are doing and what worked well versus not so well (Hadwin & Winne, 2012).

A challenge for CSCL research is to design software systems to support metacognition and collaboration in ways that parallel or extend what effective teachers and competent peers do. Soller et al. (2005, p. 274) characterize this challenge as one of "(a) defining, as best possible, a model of desired interaction, and (b) designing algorithms that measure the degree to which the current model of interaction meets the requirements of the desired model, which [is often] uncertain and unstable." They go on to argue models of "productive interaction" derived from understandings about factors that affect learning positively. Judgments concerning these qualities of students' interactions require skilled subjectivity (see Brown & Campione, 1994) which software may not be able to achieve.

While software can prompt collaborators about metacognitive matters, for example standards for examining a group process, software almost surely cannot match people's ability to shape both group processes and collaborators' thinking about those events. Systems like those described by Carroll et al. (2003) and Soller et al. (2005) may scaffold metacognition but, for the present, productive interventions in students' metacognition about CSCL probably require melding guidance from mentors and software (Dennen & Hoadley, chapter 22 this volume). To examine metacognition fully in collaborative enterprises, researchers should gather data from all parties, including mentors, in both collaborative and solo settings.

ADVANCING RESEARCH ON ROLES AND EFFECTS OF METACOGNITION IN CSCL

Software technologies offer many benefits. They can help collaborators search for and organize information solo and collaboratively, and prompt learners to consider features of their work metacognitively across levels of self, co-, and shared regulation. Today's technologies also can, unobtrusively, log data about almost every observable facet of these events in formats that are ready immediately for further, sometimes automated, analysis. Researching metacognition and its roles in computer-supported collaborative learning still poses challenges because it is very difficult to operationally define and record two key complex metacognitive events—monitoring and decision making that underlie metacognitive control—without knowing something about the standard(s)/goal(s) and the judgment(s) individuals make about progress.

Here, we have space to examine briefly three issues important for future research on this topic: modeling metacognition, analyzing *trace* data about metacognition and supporting collaboration in collaborative settings. Before addressing these, however, we note three requirements for progressive research programs on the forms and roles of metacognition in CSCL. First, to exercise metacognition, collaborators must have *options* for managing solo and collaborative work. Options for operating on information, establishing collaborative agendas and procedures and so forth may be trained by a researcher or simply "brought" to the setting by the collaborators. Second, productive regulation requires *feedback* about the topic(s) and task(s) on which learners collaborate as well as the features of collaboration itself (Butler & Winne, 1995; Winne, 2011). Feedback may be provided by software without mediation by a researcher (other than having designed the software in the first place) but tracking feedback among collaborators and between collaborators and their mentors should not be overlooked. Third, the collaborative environment must at least afford and preferably support *collaborators' experimentation* with options for carrying out their individual and shared work. This extends beyond merely trying out various options. It means at least having genuine opportunities plus explicit permission to redesign and even evolve replacements for initial forms of the conditions, operations, and standards that characterize a collaborative enterprise. Even more helpful would be support in the form of tools that help collaborators design experiments, and track and analyze data they generate as they put self-, co-, and shared regulation into practice.

Modeling Metacognition

Metacognitive monitoring requires collaborators to: (a) perceive task conditions accurately, including their collaborators' mental states; (b) assemble a set of standards, which are negotiated in fully collaborative work, against which products and processes at the object level are examined; and (c) ascertain differences accurately between features and standards. To exercise metacognitive control, collaborators must: (a) search memory and perhaps external resources for operations—cognitive and group processes—beyond those already used; (b) generate outcome expectations about the products each (set) of the operation(s) yields; (c) metacognitively monitor whether an expected product's profile is a better match to standards than the product generated by past or possible future candidate operations; and (d) if there is no clearly superior candidate for what to do, weigh the pros and cons of the possible candidates and operations to decide what to do.

Modeling metacognition fully requires data about all these topics. Gress, Fior, Hadwin, and Winne (2010) catalogued methods used in CSCL research published between 1999 and 2006. Varieties of self-reports (surveys, interviews), discussions and dialogues, and collaborators' feedback to instructors were overwhelmingly dominant. Self-report data from surveys and think-aloud protocols contribute to modeling metacognition in

CSCL because information gathered using these methods may match what collaborators have "in mind" as they work. We write "may match" because there are many reasons to question the veridicality of self-reports—biases and heuristics shape recall and on-the-spot interpretations (see Baron, 2008) in ways that render them inaccurate in various ways, even when self-reports are gathered as think-aloud concurrent with collaborators' work (see Winne, 2011, 2010; Winne, Jamieson-Noel, & Muis, 2002; Winne & Perry, 2000). Rather than relying on collaborators' interpretations of behavior, researchers need data that describe behavior per se. For example, did the collaborators negotiate a shared goal? What did the collaborators do to negotiate a shared goal?

Analyzing Trace Data about Metacognition

Suppose a CSCL environment provides a tool for collaborators to apply various tags to information they contribute to a chat (e.g., Winne & Beaudoin, 2009). During a chat, Lucy tags Sara's contribution, "Let's survey parents" with "vague goal." Lucy's tag traces metacognitive monitoring of Sara's input. The particular tag she chose among several available tags (e.g., "important," "review for work agenda") reveals the standard she used to monitor. Applying a tag rather than doing something else (e.g., making a note, surfing for a published parent survey) identifies how Lucy exercised selective metacognitive control.

Trace data are observable markers of cognitive events generated as collaborators study solo and work together (see Winne, 2011). Carefully designed features of an interface and cognitive tools allow trace data to be gathered unobtrusively. Gress et al. (2008) reported that traces were used infrequently in CSCL research. We recommend more use of trace data because they complement other kinds of data and do not suffer the shortcomings just described for self report data.

Trace data about metacognition in CSCL can be modeled by an *If–Then* pattern (see Winne, 2010). For example, *If* a contribution to a chat is judged a vague goal and Lucy tags it "vague goal," Sara might *Then* respond, "Why do you think so?" as a request for Lucy to share the standards she used to monitor metacognitively the earlier suggestion to survey parents.

Patterns of *If–Then* traces can be analyzed in two steps. First, traces are listed in order of their occurrence. This creates a timeline (see Figure 26.1). Second, a matrix is created that can represent transitions across adjacent traces. Each row of the matrix identifies one kind of trace logged by CSCL software; for example a contribution to a chat: "Check facts." Columns of the matrix are the transpose of rows. A tally in a cell of the matrix describes a transition from (a) the first trace in the sequence, identified by the cell's row, an *If*; to (b) the next trace represented by the cell's column, a *Then*. For example, *If* the first trace is an A (in Figure 26.1), *Then* the second trace is a B. Therefore, a tally is made in cell [A,B] to represent the transition from A to B. Trace B now takes on the role of the first trace at this point in the sequence, an *If*. It is followed by a *Then*, which is trace D in Figure 26.1. A tally is recorded in cell [B,D]. Trace D is now the *If*, and so on.

The sum of tallies across a row describes the incidence of each trace in the corpus of data. Figure 26.1 shows that trace A occurred 3 times. This sum can be normed (divided) by the total of tallies in all row totals to represent the percentage of all traces that were observed in that category. Norming a cell's tally by dividing it by the sum of tallies across cells in a row describes the conditional probability of the column trace (*Then*) given the row trace (*If*). For example, the conditional probability of D given B,

Event Sequence: A B D B C E D B C E D A C E D A B C F ...

Transition Matrix

	A	B	C	D	E	F	sum
A		//	/				3
B			///	/			4
C					///	/	4
D	//	//					4
E				///			3
F							0
							18

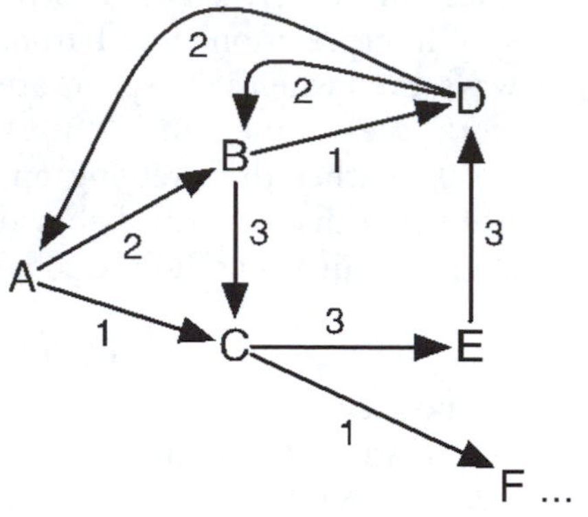

Figure 26.1 A sequence of events, the transition matrix, and a graphical display of the pattern represented by the sequence.

Pr[D|B] = 0.25. Generalizing, whenever the group produces a trace of type B (an *If*), odds are 0.25 the next trace will be a D (a *Then*).

A "picture" of a transition matrix (technically, a graph; Figure 26.1) can depict how a group expresses metacognitive activity. Weights (numbers) on the edges (arrows) of this graph show the frequency of a transition corresponding to cells with tallies in the transition matrix. Several quantitative indexes can be computed using these data. They describe, for example, the degree to which different contexts (*Ifs*) trigger the same expression of metacognitive control (*Then*). See Winne et al. (2002) for elaboration. Future CSCL research should investigate patterns of metacognition underlying collaborators' self-, co-, and shared regulation of work. Trace data and trace-based descriptions about patterns of collaboration may also be a rich source of feedback to collaborators. More than simple frequency counts, patterns represent context that must be tracked to examine metacognitively what might be changed to improve work (Winne, 2011).

Focusing Collaborators' Metacognition on Facets of Tasks

As noted earlier, we found few CSCL systems that truly support metacognition in collaborative activities. The COPES schema introduced earlier maps categories about which basic support might be provided. Helping collaborators identify factors of conditions and consider how conditions might affect collaborative work might be accomplished in various ways; for example, a warm-up checklist or a wrap-up exercise where collaborators are invited to consider conditions. A "smart" system might track features in online chats where the group "thrashes" as traced by scripted contributions (e.g., chosen from a dropdown list; see Beaudoin & Winne, 2009) like "What do you mean?" or "How did you get that" appearing with high conditional probability in relation to the topic of collaboration. Operations might be brought to the fore by training collaborators to use a branching script for collaboration, which can then become an object of metacognitive enquiry. In short, providing tools that directly invite metacognition, such as tags, and signaling simple activities that entail metacognitively examining the collaborative process will generate data needed to explore roles for metacognition in CSCL at the same time that variations in these scaffolds might be the focus of experiments on how they affect the quality and efficiency of collaboration. Capabilities of modern software to log extensive, fine-grained, time-stamped data about how collaboration unfolds in the context of options such tools afford (e.g., see Carroll et al., 2003; Soller et al., 2005) hold significant promise to widen and deepen research on CSCL as well as learning through CSCL.

REFERENCES

Baron, J. (2008). *Thinking and deciding.* New York: Cambridge University Press.

Barron, B. (2003). When smart groups fail. *Journal of the Learning Sciences, 12,* 307–359.

Barros, B., & Jerdejo, M. F. (2000). Analyzing student interaction processes in order to improve collaboration: The DEGREE approach. *International Journal of Artificial Intelligence in Education, 11,* 221–241.

Beaudoin, L. P., & Winne, P. H. (2009, June). *nStudy: An internet tool to support learning, collaboration and researching learning strategies.* Paper presented at the Canadian e-Learning Conference, Vancouver.

Brown, A. L., & Campione, J. C. (1994). Guided discovery in a community of learners. In K. McGilly (Ed.), *Classroom lessons: Integrating cognitive theory with classroom practice* (pp. 229–270). Cambridge, MA: MIT Press.

Bruning, R. H., Schraw, G. J., & Ronning, R. R. (1995). *Cognitive psychology and instruction.* Englewood Cliffs, NJ: Merrill.

Butler, D. L., & Winne, P. H. (1995). Feedback and self-regulated learning: A theoretical synthesis. *Review of Educational Research, 65,* 245–281.

Carroll, J. M., Neale, D. C., Isenhour, M. B., Rosson, D., & McCrickard, D. S. (2003). Notification and awareness: Synchronizing task-oriented collaborative activity. *International Journal of Human-Computer Studies, 58,* 605–632.

Choi, I., Land, S., & Turgeon, A. (2005). Scaffolding peer questioning strategies to facilitate metacognition during online small group discussion, *Instructional Science, 33,* 483–511.

Dillenbourg, P. (1999). Introduction: What do you mean by "collaborative learning"? In P. Dillenbourg (Ed.), *Collaborative learning: Cognitive and computational approaches* (pp. 1–19). Amsterdam, Netherlands: Pergamon.

Englert, C. S., & Mariage, T. (2003). The sociocultural model in special education interventions: Apprenticing students in higher-order thinking. In H. Lee Swanson, K. R. Harris, & S. Graham (Eds.), *Handbook of learning disabilities* (pp. 450–467). New York: Guilford.

Flavell, J. H. (1979). Metacognitive and cognitive monitoring: A new area of cognitive developmental inquiry. *American Psychologist, 34,* 906–911.

Flavell, J. H. (1971). First discussant's comments: What is memory development the development of? *Human Development, 14,* 272–278.

Goodman, B., Geier, M., Haverty, L., Linton, F., & McCready, R. (2001). A framework for asynchronous collaborative learning and problem solving. In J. D. Moore, C. Redfield, & W. L. Johnson (Eds.), *Artificial intelligence in education: AI-ED in the wired and wireless future* (pp. 188–199). Amsterdam, Netherlands: IOS.

Gress, C. L. Z., Fior, M., Hadwin, A. F., & Winne, P. H. (2010). Measurement and assessment in computer supported collaborative learning. *Computers in Human Behavior, 26,* 806–814.

Hadwin, A.F., Järvelä, S., & Miller, M. (2011). Self-regulated, co-regulated and socially shared regulation of learning. In B. J. Zimmerman & D. H. Schunk (Eds.), *Handbook of self-regulated learning and performance* (pp. 65–84). New York: Routledge.

Hadwin, A. F., Malmberg, J., Järvelä, S., Jarvenoja, H., & Vainiopää, M. V. (2010, May). *Exploring socially-shared metacognition in the context of shared task perceptions and goals.* Paper presented at the 4th Biennial Meeting of the EARLI special interest group 16 Metacognition. Muenster, Germany.

Hadwin, A. F., & Winne, P. H. (2012). Promoting learning skills in undergraduate students. In M. J. Lawson & J. R. Kirby (Eds.), *The quality of learning: Dispositions, instruction and mental structures* (pp. 201–227). New York: Cambridge University Press.

Hart, J. T. (1965). Memory and the feeling-of-knowing experience. *Journal of Educational Psychology, 56,* 208–216.

Hart, J. T. (1967). Memory and the memory-monitoring process. *Journal of Verbal Learning and Verbal Behavior, 6,* 685–691.

Hurme, T. R., & Jarvela, S. (2005). Students' activity in computer-supported collaborative problem solving in mathematics. *International Journal of Computers for Mathematical Learning, 10,* 49–73.

Hurme, T-R., Merenluoto, K., & Jarvela, S (2009). Socially shared metacognition of pre-service primary teachers in a computer supported mathematics course and their feelings of task difficulty: A case study. *Educational Research and Evaluation, 15,* 503–524.

Hurme, T-R., Merenluoto, K., Salonen, P., & Järvelä, S. (2009). Regulation of group problem solving—A case for socially shared metacognition. Unpublished manuscript.

Hurme, T. R., Palonen, T., & Järvelä, S. (2006). Metacognition in joint discussions: An analysis of the patterns of interaction and the metacognitive content of the networked discussions in mathematics. *Metacognition and Learning, 1,* 181–120.

Iiskala, T., Vauras, M., & Lehtinen, E. (2004). Socially-shared metacognition in peer learning? *Hellenic Journal of Psychology, 2,* 147–178.

Johnson, D. W., & Johnson, R. (1999). Making cooperative learning work. *Theory Into Practice, 38*(2), 67–73.

Makitalo-Siegl, K., Kohnle, C., & Fischer, F. (2011). Computer-supported collaborative inquiry learning and classroom scripts: Effects on help-seeking processes and learning outcomes. *Learning and Instruction, 21,* 257–266.

Manlove, S., Lazonder, A. W., & De Jong, T. (2006). Regulative support for collaborative scientific inquiry learning. *Journal of Computer Assisted Learning, 22,* 87–98.

Many, J. E., Fyfe, R., Lewis, G., & Mitchell, E. (1996). Traversing the topical landscape: Exploring students' self-directed reading-writing-research processes. *Reading Research Quarterly, 31,* 12–35.

McCaslin, M., & Good, T. L. (1996). The informal curriculum. In D. C. Berliner & R. C. Calfee (Eds.), *Handbook of educational psychology* (pp. 622–670). New York: Simon & Schuster Macmillan.

Nelson, T. O., & Narens, L. (1990). Metamemory: A theoretical framework and new findings. In G. Bower (Ed.), *The psychology of learning and motivation: Advances in research and theory* (Vol. 26, pp. 125–141). San Diego, CA: Academic Press.

Ogata, H., Matsuura, K., & Yano, Y. (2000). *Active knowledge awareness map: Visualizing learners' activities in a web based CSCL environment.* Paper presented at the International Workshop on New Technologies in Collaborative Learning, Tokushima, Japan.

Perry, N., Phillips, L., & Hutchinson, L. (2006). A comparison of experienced and beginning teachers' support for self-regulated learning. *Elementary School Journal, 106,* 237–254.

Perry, N., VandeKamp, K. O., Mercer, L. K., & Nordby, C. J. (2002). Investigating teacher–student interactions that foster self-regulated learning. *Educational Psychologist, 37,* 5–15.

Peterson, S. E., & Schreiber, J. B. (2006). An attributional analysis of personal and interpersonal motivation for collaborative projects. *Journal of Educational Psychology, 98,* 777–787.

Roschelle, J., & Teasley, S. (1995). The construction of shared knowledge in collaborative problem solving. In C. O'Malley (Ed.), *Computer supported collaborative learning* (pp. 69–97). Heidelberg, Germany: Springer.

Scardamalia, M., & Bereiter, C. (1996). Adaptation and understanding: A case for new cultures of schooling. In S. Vosniadau, E. DeCorte, R. Glaser, & H. Mandl (Eds.), *International perspectives on the design of technology-supported learning environments* (pp. 149–164). Mahwah, NJ: Erlbaum.

Schwartz, B. L., & Perfect, T. J. (2010). Introduction: Toward an applied metacognition. In T. J. Perfect & B. L. Schwartz (Eds.), *Applied metacognition* (pp. 1–14). New York: Cambridge University Press.

Soller, A., Martinez, A., Jermann, P., & Muehlenbrock, M. (2005). From mirroring to guiding: A review of state of the art technology for supporting collaborative learning. *International Journal of Artificial Intelligence in Education, 15,* 261–290.

Turner, J. C. (1997). Starting right: Strategies for engaging young literacy learners. In J. T. Guthrie & A. Wigfield (Eds.), *Reading engagement: Motivating readers through integrated instruction* (pp. 183–204). Newark, DL: International Reading Association.

Vauras, M., Iiskala, T., Kajamies, A., Kinnunen, R., & Lehtinen, E. (2003). Shared-regulation and motivation of collaborating peers: A case analysis. *Psychologia, 46,* 19–37.

Walker, R. A., Pressick-Kilborn, K., Arnold, L. S., & Sainsbury, E.J. (2004). Investigating motivation in context: Developing sociocultural perspectives. *European Psychologist, 9,* 245–256.

Winne, P. H. (2001). Self-regulated learning viewed from models of information processing. In B. J. Zimmerman & D. H. Schunk (Eds.), *Self-regulated learning and academic achievement: Theoretical perspectives* (2nd ed., pp. 153–189). Mahwah, NJ: Erlbaum.

Winne, P. H. (2006). How software technologies can improve research on learning and bolster school reform. *Educational Psychologist, 41,* 5–17.

Winne, P. H. (2010). Improving measurements of self-regulated learning. *Educational Psychologist, 45,* 267–276.

Winne, P. H. (2011). A cognitive and metacognitive analysis of self- regulated learning. In B. J. Zimmerman & D. H. Schunk (Eds.), *Handbook of self-regulation of learning and performance* (pp. 15–32). New York: Routledge.

Winne, P. H., & Hadwin, A. F. (1998). Studying as self-regulated learning. In D. J. Hacker, J. Dunlosky, & A. C. Graesser (Eds.), *Metacognition in educational theory and practice* (pp. 277–304). Mahwah, NJ: Erlbaum.

Winne, P. H., & Hadwin, A. F. (2008). The weave of motivation and self-regulated learning. In D. H. Schunk & B. J. Zimmerman (Eds.), *Motivation and self-regulated learning: Theory, research, and applications* (pp. 297–314). Mahwah, NJ: Erlbaum.

Winne, P. H., & Hadwin, A. F., & Beaudoin, L. (2010). *nStudy: A web application for researching and promoting self-regulated learning* (version 2.0) [computer program]. Simon Fraser University, Burnaby, BC, Canada.

Winne, P. H., & Jamieson-Noel, D. L. (2002). Exploring students' calibration of self-reports about study tactics and achievement. *Contemporary Educational Psychology, 27*, 551–572.

Winne, P. H., & Jamieson-Noel, D. L. (2003). Self-regulating studying by objectives for learning: Students' reports compared to a model. *Contemporary Educational Psychology, 28*, 259–276.

Winne, P. H., Jamieson-Noel, D. L., & Muis, K. (2002). Methodological issues and advances in researching tactics, strategies, and self-regulated learning. In P. R. Pintrich & M. L. Maehr (Eds.), *Advances in motivation and achievement: New directions in measures and methods* (Vol. 12, pp. 121–155). Greenwich, CT: JAI Press.

Winne, P. H., & Nesbit, J. C. (2010). The psychology of school performance. *Annual Review of Psychology, 61*, 653–678.

Winne, P. H., & Perry, N. E. (2000). Measuring self-regulated learning. In M. Boekaerts, P. Pintrich, & M. Zeidner (Eds.), *Handbook of self-regulation* (pp. 531–566). Orlando, FL: Academic Press.

Zimmerman, B. J. (2008). Investigating self-regulation and motivation: Historical background, methodological developments, and future prospects. *American Educational Research Journal, 45*, 166–183.

27

COLLABORATION IN INFORMAL LEARNING ENVIRONMENTS

Access and Participation in Youth Virtual Communities

YASMIN B. KAFAI

University of Pennsylvania

DEBORAH A. FIELDS

Utah State University

Many after-school centers, community technology centers, and summer camps designed for youth have begun to incorporate technology. For instance, the Fifth Dimension and the Boys and Girls Clubs provide access to computer game play or learning of technical skills (e.g., Cole, 2006; Hay & Barab, 2001; Hirsch, 2005; Zhao, Mishra, & Girod, 2000). Some sites, such as the Computer Clubhouse (Kafai, Peppler, & Chapman, 2009), have further adopted an explicit focus on providing access to technology in underserved communities by engaging youth in collaborative design activities. Not only have learning technologies become part of informal learning environments, they have also become informal sites of learning in their own rite, virtual communities accessible to millions of youth around the world anywhere they can gain Internet access. Recent developments suggest that new virtual locations such as games, virtual worlds, and social networks have become as important for informal learning as their more physically based counterparts (Ito et al., 2008).

What does this mean for studying and understanding computer-supported collaboration in informal learning environments? Many challenges documented in well-researched, local informal learning environments still apply; for instance, the balance of youth working individually on a project over an extended period of time or the community engaging in holistic collaborative activities together. The support of peer teaching and mentoring relationships also continues to be important (Vadeboncoeur, 2007). Free choice and will, the ability of youth to choose the activities in which they engage, for how long and when, continue to be hallmarks of informal learning for designers of virtual and local learning communities alike (Bell, Lewenstein, Shouse, & Feder, 2009). Yet there are also new issues to study. What are the challenges of promoting collaboration not only in local community settings but also within virtual settings? What difficulties do youth face in achieving membership in virtual learning communities? What kinds of opportunities are there for collaboration, participation, and membership, not only within local or virtual settings but also *across* them?

In this chapter, we will focus on collaboration in informal learning environments with youth virtual communities and examine access and participation across online and local venues. We will do so by focusing on two cases: Whyville, a tween play virtual world which offers millions of registered players opportunities to engage in science games and activities (Kafai, 2010), and Scratch, an open source design network, with millions of software games, animations, and graphics programmed and shared by hundreds of thousands of young programmers (Resnick et al., 2009). These two virtual learning environments are representative in terms of the size of the youth virtual communities found in many other virtual worlds but differ in the types of collaboration they promote. The main activity in Whyville is socializing with others (though there are many other activities) while the primary activity in Scratch is programming and sharing projects with others. We will examine how youth negotiate access to these virtual communities to illustrate how collaborations take place across online and offline spaces. We will conclude by outlining challenges for future research and the design of collaboration in informal virtual learning environments.

COLLABORATIVE LEARNING IN INFORMAL YOUTH COMMUNITIES

Researchers have long argued that informal learning environments offer promising opportunities for youth because they serve as an important middle ground between home and school, providing comfortable, supportive, and safe spaces for youth to explore new ideas and develop new skills that are outside the scope of the current schooling curriculum (Hirsch, 2005). More importantly, they often engage youth in different forms of collaborative interactions with peers or mentors not found in traditional school settings (Vadeboncoeur, 2007). Many after-school centers also use computers to support collaborations offline and online. For instance, the Computer Clubhouse village connects local clubhouses to a worldwide network of other clubhouses and allows members to exchange ideas and share their projects (Kafai, Peppler, & Chapman, 2009). In the Fifth Dimension, a local network allows participating youth to connect and play games with each other (Cole, 2006). While not an exclusive feature, many of these virtual communities also provide contexts where youth regularly act as content creators and programmers (Jenkins, Clinton, Purushotm, Robison, & Weigel, 2006).

Being on the Internet is an increasingly important part of youths' social lives as they initiate, navigate, and develop relationships through participation in e-mail, chat, blogs, and social networking sites (e.g., Lenhart & Madden, 2007; Tapscott, 2008). Virtual communities provide them with the opportunity to explore new social arenas and have been called the digital publics because they provide a "youth space, a place to gather and see and be seen by peers" (Boyd, 2006). One striking feature of these virtual communities is their massive scale and the collaboration that can take place among hundreds, if not thousands, of members. Consider multiplayer online role-playing game communities where millions of players organize themselves in guilds to participate in quests (Gee, 2003) or the interactions of members of fan fiction sites where thousands of writers create new stories and participants provide constructive feedback (Black, 2008). Thus youths' ability to access and participate in these massive community collectives is of great interest to researchers of informal collaborative learning.

The research on online gaming communities has made the most inroads in how players collaborate in cross-functional teams when engaging in quests and learning how to problem solve and coordinate their activities (e.g., Gee, 2003; Steinkuehler, 2006; Taylor, 2006). Most gaming studies have focused on college youth and adults while largely ignoring younger players. Yet even a casual observer will notice how rapidly teens have adopted social networking sites like MySpace and Friendster as their own for continuing friendships and developing casual relationships (Buckingham & Willett, 2006; Mazzarella, 2005). Virtual worlds also offer social settings in which players can engage with others. The size, in numbers, of participating members in these online communities is indeed impressive, especially considering that the possibility to interact with hundreds of thousands, if not millions, of others across geographical boundaries is unprecedented in history. This is particularly true for youth who might have connected at most with hundreds or thousands of others in their local communities and schools. Research is now showing that participation in these online communities is a rich social playground where youth socialize with others, including many they know as friends locally (Ito et al., 2008).

In order to understand better what it means for youth to collaborate in these informal virtual learning environments, we have selected two cases for further review. The first informal learning community is a virtual world, called Whyville.net. Virtual worlds such as Whyville, Habbo Hotel, Neopets, Toontown, and Second Life, are populated by millions of players and who participate in simulated experiences, meet others via their avatars, and engage in collaborative play. The second informal learning community is an online design community called Scratch.mit.edu. In Scratch, hundreds of thousands of young designers create and program their own software and share them with others worldwide. Both of these virtual communities have become popular among youth, judging by their growing membership, and allow players to contribute content of their own—avatar or media designs.

In our review we will also examine a feature that has received relatively little attention, namely the mix of collaborative interactions across the virtual communities themselves and in the offline contexts of after-school clubs or programs through which they are accessed. While there are relatively few studies about either online or offline contexts, little is known about the potential for accessing both local and virtual communities in combination or the challenges of negotiating membership and fostering collaboration across these spaces. Previous research on cybercafés, popular in gaming communities outside the United States, has indicated that most, if not all, of the informal learning cited by cybercafé players is related directly to the physical presence of other players in the same space (Lin, 2008). For instance, observations have found players walking around and watching other people play, checking out the patches and new computer codes others have downloaded for a game, asking about adjustments to computers, and watching their strategies in various games (Beavis, Nixon, & Atkinson, 2005). Thus, in our case studies, we examine the interaction between online and offline collaborations among youth. Our focus will be on how peer collaboration supports youth in gaining access into large-scale communities and participating in activities with others.

COLLABORATION IN AN INFORMAL VIRTUAL PLAY COMMUNITY

Whyville.net is a massive, free virtual world (in 2005, at the time of our study, it had 1.5 million registered players and currently it lists 6.5 million players) that encourages youth aged 8 to 16 to play casual science games in order to earn a virtual salary (in "clams"), which they can then spend on buying and designing parts for their avatars (virtual characters), projectiles to throw at other players, and other goods such as cars and plots of land. On a typical day in Whyville, players log on to Whyville, check their ymail messages and bank statements, adjust their looks using a feature called "Pick Your Nose," then alternate between socializing and earning clams, perhaps with a shopping break at Akbar's Face Mall. Earning clams is accomplished by playing science games, profiting from the trading of face parts, or designing and selling face parts, the latter of which is quite difficult and is usually taken up after several weeks of participation (Kafai, Fields, & Cook, 2010).

When we studied social interactions in Whyville, we conducted observations at one after-school club to get a sense of how that social setting structured play and participation in Whyville online and offline (for more detail on data collection and analyses, see Kafai, 2010). The after-school club was visited by about 20 youth aged 9 to 12 years for an hour most weekdays from January to March 2005. In addition, we received tracking data from 438 online and after-school players that gave us comprehensive logfiles of every click and chat exchange. We used these logfile data for case studies of players or practices by creating minute-by-minute summaries of all clicks (see Kafai & Fields, 2012). We also studied *The Whyville Times*, an archive with over 9,000 articles written by youth themselves, in addition to hundreds of cheat sites that were outside of the Whyville site.

Peer Collaboration in Gaining Access

One of our primary questions is concerned with gaining access in youth virtual communities. How do kids learn to become a part of a new virtual world, a new culture where people look like two-dimensional avatars, chat through typing, and have millions of potential peers with whom to navigate relationships? We found that youth drew together a variety of resources to learn to be a part of these worlds, and that the relative openness of the shared social spaces they occupied—both virtual and local—was important for facilitating this learning. Here we illustrate some of the variety of techniques the youth used in learning from others and the affordances of different kinds of spaces in facilitating such collaborative learning. We found that using the perspective of the openness of tools and social interactions (Hutchins, 1995) helps to consider the learning opportunities available to youth in informal virtual environments.

Youth in the after-school club used a range of practices to learn to become a part of Whyville. They drew on observation of other club members, observation of others in Whyville, exploring and experimenting in the virtual community, and drawing on outside sites with helpful information (see section below on cheat sites). In the club, conversation and help-giving practices were ubiquitous as members shopped together, traded with each other, dressed and evaluated their avatars, flirted, and even threw (virtual) mudballs at each other. Yet to truly understand their learning, we had to study their interactions across the communities they occupied in accessing Whyville. To illuminate this, here we highlight how youth in the club learned a specific practice that could only spread socially—teleporting. In Whyville, teleporting is a secret way to gain access to select spaces in the virtual world including the Moon, Mars, and Jupiter that are not written about in any instructions. It requires typing a specific command, "teleport moon," with correct spelling and syntax, but unlike most chat in Whyville which appears in bubbles above the avatars' heads, the teleport command is not visible because the avatar is transported to the said location before the command can appear in chat. This makes teleporting a unique case for looking at collaborative learning in a virtual world (see Fields & Kafai, 2009).

In learning to teleport, we found that club members took advantage of the different spaces, people, and times available to them across Whyville, the club, and even home and classroom spaces. They observed and talked with Whyvillians in the virtual setting of Whyville through chat and whispers, the whispers being private one-on-one conversations. They also used the local setting of the after-school club to call out for help, look at others' computers, shout out something funny, and generally observe the other club members' interactions in Whyville. In fact, we found that the discovery of teleporting cascaded quickly through the local community once it was discovered by a few (Fields & Kafai, 2009). Consider how Briana helped Gabe (username WOW4) to teleport while chatting in Whyville with a friend from school (Marv/dudeman93) who was not present in the club. Marv greeted Gabe by his last name (Smith). Gabe called over to Briana in the club to identify the avatar who knew him, which she did, "That's Marv." Marv suggested that Gabe meet him at the moon, which prompted Gabe to ask Briana how to do this, and she introduced him to the idea of teleporting and how to spell and type it.

While this excerpt captured just a brief instance of peer helping (Ching & Kafai, 2008), it is indicative of the ways in which the youth drew collaborative resources together to learn to navigate a virtual world like Whyville. As in this example, collaborative interactions connected across online and offline spaces in the club, at home and in the virtual world of Whyville between the three youth. Indeed at the very moment portrayed in this excerpt, the three spaces overlapped merging into one joint interaction space. Overall we found that for both relatively simple practices like teleporting, or in another case, throwing projectiles (Fields & Kafai, 2010a), as well as more complicated practices like learning to dress one's avatar in socially appropriate ways (Fields & Kafai, 2012; Kafai, Fields, & Cook, 2010), the youth utilized social interactions with club members both locally and in Whyville as well as Whyvillians with whom they were not familiar locally. Once they had a grasp of the idea, they experimented with these practices, discovering new places and developing their own styles of exploring looks, relationships, and ways of acting in Whyville.

This example also demonstrates how the relatively open spaces (Hutchins, 1995) of the club—the computer screens easily visible to others, the opportunity to move about to look at others' computers, and the ability to overhear club members talking out loud—facilitated the casual leaning over and offering of the type of periodic and in-time assistance that we have found, in other research, to be instrumental for new players to learn more advanced forms of participation (Ching & Kafai, 2008). Research on the importance of cybercafés and shared play in college dorms for older youth and adults gaming in virtual spaces (Lin, 2008, Lindtner et al, 2008) supports our assertion that in studying collaborative learning in virtual spaces, we must pay attention to local spaces of coplay as well.

We have focused on the relatively simple yet purely socially learned practice of teleporting to make a case for youth drawing on resources across people and spaces, both locally and virtually. Through their analysis of chat in the *World of Warcraft*, Nardi, Ly, and Harris (2007) also found that players learned through spontaneous, contextual conversations "driven by small events" that enabled fact finding, development of tactics or strategies, and working out the moral order of the game (p. 9). This places small, single-player games within the worlds (such as most of Whyville's salary-raising science games) as one of the least likely places for collaborative learning, because they allow only one player to be in the game "space" at a time: players cannot observe what others are doing, ask questions without leaving the game, or share information in the virtual environment. Still, there are other, asynchronous forms of collaborative learning for Whyville, as we will discuss below.

Peer Collaboration in Community Knowledge Building Sites

In addition to resources in a local club and a virtual environment, outside websites serve as important sites of collaboration. Here we direct our attention to the dynamics of virtual sites of knowledge building seemingly peripheral to the central sites of study. For both Whyville and Scratch, youth have created cheat sites, forums, and wikis that build knowledge among participants about participation in the primary virtual worlds. Commercially developed online games like the *World of Warcraft* and *Civilization* formally sponsor these types of sites as forums where players share knowledge about the best builds for certain characters, guild formation, and strategies for winning (Squire, 2008; Steinkuehler & Duncan, 2009). Steinkuehler and Duncan argue that one such forum for the *World of Warcraft* sponsors broad participation in scientific epistemology as players problem solve and share solutions. In contrast to the in-the-moment peer collaborative learning discussed above, this is more centralized collective knowledge building, what some would call collective intelligence (Levy, 1997; McGonigal, 2008; Jenkins et al., 2006).

The unofficial, youth-generated cheat sites associated with Whyville provide further illustration of community-driven discussion forums and resources. These sites have a disputed relationship with the main Whyville community because they share cheats for the science games that are supposedly one of the primary areas of learning on Whyville. Developing the cheats requires collaborative sharing and problem solving, and the better designed the game, the more likely the development of a cheat will sponsor valued science learning. Elsewhere we have suggested "transgressive design" (Kafai & Fields, 2009) as a way to consider designing games with cheats in mind, such that players learn by developing cheats. For instance, Whyville's Spin Game promotes theory development about how to make different kinds of objects spin faster. The best "cheat" for this game is a theory about what makes things spin faster rather than a simplistic list of answers. Cheats may also include pictures, screenshots, scientific diagrams, and even videos of how to accomplish certain strategies for completing a game. Thus they bear similarities to the knowledge building practices discussed by Scardamalia and Bereiter (2006).

We observed that the highest quality cheat sites for Whyville were created collaboratively (see Fields & Kafai, 2010b). Out of more than 200 cheat sites (many youth had partially completed sites or even copied other sites), the most visited cheat sites were those that had a large following that contributed knowledge as needed to help their peers in Whyville. When new games came out on Whyville, the site owners of our focus site, GameSite.net, issued calls for action, sometimes including large (virtual) cash prizes, and consolidated findings from numerous players. This involved a more asynchronous form of peer collaboration than the kind of peer learning discussed earlier in the club and Whyville. The solutions were collectively gathered from a distributed group of invested players and centrally archived so that thousands could access the shared knowledge. Further, they included not just solutions for salary raising science games, but also more culturally oriented knowledge about where to shop, how to look "good," and how to act in Whyville. Thus these sites acted as cultural, collaborative repositories of gaming capital—a concept developed by Consalvo (2007). They provide youth with an opportunity to build and share their learning with others in the community in a more lasting way than in-the-moment conversations.

We find cheat sites provoking because they are initiated by youth for youth, outside the official space of a virtual world or game. In an analysis of children's virtual worlds, Grimes (2008) points out that most children's commercial virtual worlds are relatively impoverished compared to their teenage or adult counterparts in opportunities for player creativity and collaboration. Cheats and cheat sites, particularly those that promote collaboration, are sites of agency where youth can push back on the virtual worlds made for them and are potential sites of creativity, knowledge building, and critical engagement. Although the value of cheating in games may be contested, player participation in the design and use of cheat sites can be considered a valuable activity, its implications reaching far beyond the original site. Future research should focus on how such educational sites can be incorporated as extensions of the primary virtual environment.

COLLABORATION IN AN INFORMAL VIRTUAL DESIGN COMMUNITY

In our second example we illustrate issues of access and participation in the massive open source community Scratch.mit.edu. More specifically, we examine how participants gain access and interact with others online and how small groups of individuals that have commonly met one another in the online environment engage in the production of Scratch projects. Scratch is a media-rich programming language that allows youth to design, share, and remix software programs in the form of games, stories, and animations (Resnick et al., 2009). Since its public launch in May of 2007, the Scratch website (http://scratch.mit.edu) has been the primary means for users to share their work with one another.

With over 700,000 thousand registered contributors and over 1.5 million projects shared to date, the Scratch website is a vibrant online community with over 1,000 new projects being uploaded every day. It is possible to use Scratch as an individual programming tool or in traditional small-group formats (e.g., pair programming) but the website further facilitates broader types of collaboration in remixing and open-source like sharing of programs with others. In the following section, we summarize a series of independent studies that highlight the complexities of collaborating in the local and online communities of Scratch. We start with research that took place in 2008 in an after-school club where youth aged 11 to 13 used Scratch to design software such as games, music videos, or animations of their own choosing (Kafai, Fields, & Burke, 2010) complemented with observations of Scratch use in community centers (Kafai, Peppler, & Chapman, 2009).

Peer Collaboration in Gaining Access

Within the Scratch community, the move toward membership in a large-scale virtual community like Scratch.mit.edu can be a complex interplay between how young software designers develop personal agency with programming and gain status as experts amongst their peers. As part of a 4-month long ethnographic study (Kafai, Fields, & Burke, 2010), we followed two 12-year old participants, Lucetta and Matthew, as they learned the programming software Scratch and then joined Scratch.mit.edu both in an after-school club and later in a class. Initially in the club, much to our surprise neither Lucetta, Matthew, nor their peers were interested in joining the larger Scratch online community. Despite efforts by club leaders to introduce members to the range of projects on the website and the opportunities to meet others who enjoyed Scratch, club members stayed local in their participation, using Scratch on the club computers and at home, but ignoring the larger virtual community. One of the primary reasons for this appeared to be a reluctance to share imperfect and unfinished projects with what seemed to the club members as a more competent programming community.

Interest in the virtual community perked when one mischievous club member copied a program by Lucetta and put it on the website declaring it as his own. Spurred by indignation at this travesty, which was later reinterpreted as a validation of Lucetta's design, the club began exploring the site, "friending" each other, posting their projects, talking about giving "credit" to others' influences on their designs, and eventually downloading and remixing other Scratchers' projects. However, Lucetta's initial reaction of indignation highlights an important aspect of online collaborations, that of trust and recognition. While collaborative learning has always struggled with how contributions can be achieved and recognized by all members, in online communities such as Scratch where program code and graphics are shared freely and can be repurposed with the click of a button, this is much harder to accomplish. Others, such as Perkel (2008), have written about this violation of trust and point to it as a crucial issue in joining large-scale communities.

Still, once they overcame their hesitation in joining the online Scratch community, we found that the web community furthered both Lucetta's and Matthew's pursuit of Scratch. Lucetta friended other users, commented on projects, and uploaded her own projects, taking advantage of the social community on the site. This fit her cooperative social style, mixing with others while sharing an interest in Scratch. In contrast, Matthew embraced the potential of downloading and remixing projects that would otherwise have been out of his range of abilities, though there were other aspects of participation that he did not take up such as sharing his own projects for validation and feedback from the community. Overall, these findings suggest that establishing membership in a larger programming community, while promising, is not as easily achieved as we had hoped. Moving toward membership in a virtual project sharing community is a complex interplay between how young designers develop personal agency with programming, gain status as experts amongst their peers, and perceive the relative status of the virtual community.

Peer Collaboration on the Community Site

While the previous study provided us with some insights into what motivated youth to access the virtual community of Scratch or turned them off, in the following sections we want to turn to the dynamics of the larger site and how collaboration is structured across its many members. We do know that once members have joined the Scratch online community, their participation profiles in terms of contributions and feedback vary quite dramatically. For instance, in a study of 65 Israeli Scratch designers, Zuckerman, Blau, and Monroy-Hernandez (2009) found that 3% of users were most active, followed by 15% active and 82% moderate users in making contributions to the site (a finding very reminiscent of the Whyville site where 7% of youth were core players, 30% semicore players, and 63% peripheral players; see Giang, Kafai, Fields, & Searle, 2012). The most active Scratch users contributed 43% of all content, whereas active users contributed 25% and moderate users only 33%. These distributions are also correlated positively with the number of friends on the site and number of downloads as well as other forms of community feedback on the site.

The practice of remixing Scratch projects, taking someone else's program, and modifying code or graphics is common in peer-production communities like Scratch. This is yet a further type of collaboration available in local and virtual communities in addition to the earlier discussed synchronous or asynchronous collaboration. In fact, over 28% of all projects posted on the website are remixes of existing Scratch projects, up from 10 to 15% since the site's launch (Monroy-Hernández & Hill, 2010), and this number has been increasing steadily since its launch. It has been argued that remixing is a key practice in today's networked culture that started in the music industry and has migrated into other media domains (Jenkins, 2006). It provides an opportunity to build on or experiment with another's work, though youths' views on remixing vary widely from considering it cheating/copying (like Lucetta did above) to seeing it as an opportunity for learning and building on another's work. Crediting ownership is an important and contested aspect of remixing, something that has drawn a great deal of conversation in the Scratch community.

A study that examined the relationship between remixes, age, and other factors found that younger participants complained more often about remixes than older contributors, and that the complexity of the project played a role in these complaints, as well as how close the remix was to the original project (Hill, Monroy-Hernandez, & Olson, 2010). Design features in the online Scratch community also influenced the popularity of remixing. After tweaking by the designers to highlight "Top Remixed Projects" on the home page, the number of remixed projects went up significantly (Monroy-Hernandez & Hill, 2010). Further, many youth-created projects were intended specifically to be used as tools for others to remix and build on (as is the case with projects like side-scrolling game engines). These design changes, along with digital tools that allow Scratchers to trace the multiple versions of projects across designers, supported a broader and more accepted culture of remixing in the virtual community.

Codesigning programs is another form of collaborative participation in the Scratch site. For instance, there were spontaneously formed small groups like the Green Bear Group originally formed by three youth aged 8, 13, and 15 and later joined by over a dozen other members (Aragon, Poon, Monroy-Hernandez, & Aragon, 2009). Members posted their projects on a gallery and voted on which projects to develop further as a collaborative since each member brought different skills such as music, graphics, or editing to the group. Based on an analysis of comments on the gallery as well as a survey, the researchers found that 19% of the comments related directly to the job that needed to get done, 49% to socioemotional aspects such as socializing and personal discussions, and 32% to contextual aspects such as arranging how to organize work, system administration, and hardware issues. Thus supporting collaborative design and remixing in both virtual and local communities, and even across these communities, is an enticing subject for future design and research.

RESEARCH OPPORTUNITIES AND CHALLENGES

Our investigation of access and participation provided us with rich material to reflect on the opportunities and challenges ahead in studying online collaborations between massive numbers of youths in informal learning environments. Part of the challenge is that these virtual communities are ever changing since they are designed environments populated by real participants who contribute through their own content and social participation. We have organized our discussion around the following themes that are key to documenting, analyzing, and understanding collaboration in informal online learning environments: collaboration, mixing settings, research, and design.

Conceptualizing Collaboration

In this chapter we have discussed a few different types of collaboration facilitated by participation in virtual communities: informal peer pedagogy, youth-designed knowledge building sites, and project sharing and remixing. One of the themes across our cases was that of access and participation. How do youth become members of these virtual communities and to what degree do they take up (presumably) valued collaborative practices that are a part of membership? The noted participation gap (Jenkins et al, 2006) between intense and casual users in places like Whyville and Scratch counters the oft-told stories of youth as digital natives (e.g., Prensky, 2001). Rather, as seen in the local participants of our clubs and in the level of participation in virtual sites, only a select percentage of youth become the more sophisticated core members of such participation (e.g., Hargittai, 2010). We should not take for granted that youth will feel comfortable or motivated to participate in virtual communities that promote the forms of learning that we value. We ourselves were surprised when the youth in the local afterschool Scratch club seemed uninterested in online participation for several weeks. Our cases suggest that understanding the particular culture of a virtual world and feelings of competence may play an important role in which youth become core members and how they participate.

In particular we need further study of the possibilities of collaboration within massive communities. While there are hundreds of studies on online or offline collaboration in relatively small groups, often of dyads and triads, fewer studies have tackled online collaboration in larger groups such as a study of university classes participating in wiki activities (e.g., Rick & Guzdial, 2006). Collaborative interactions in massive virtual communities have different constraints and affordances due to their numbers of participants, the structures of their groups with the concurrent asynchronous and synchronous nature of interactions, and the ongoing persistence of online life. We need to know when and how smaller groups come into play, who decides to join, and how these groups continue working together. The traditional collaboration research (Cohen, 1994) provides us with little information about the dynamics of unstructured group collaborations prevalent in many massive communities. We can say that one aspect of collective learning is to assume multiple roles; these roles are not prescribed, though members are valued and recognized in the community for their particular abilities. Such changes in participation (Rogoff, 1995) are also part of communities of practice and often assumed for successful collaboration in small groups.

Mixed Spaces

We need to consider carefully how we examine collaboration as it happens between multiple participants and multiple spaces. Unlike a more physically bounded after-school club or classroom space, we know that online communities exist across multiple spaces. For instance, we found that the youth could be in the club, in one of many spaces in Whyville, and of course at home where there were potentially many other influences outside the range of our data collection (e.g., siblings, Instant Messaging, phone calls). Our study demonstrated that most of the club members used the multiple social spaces available to them to learn how to teleport. This included meeting friends from school in Whyville, confirming that "virtual" does not necessarily mean unrelated to "physical" social settings.

We also need to understand better the processes of knowledge sharing and diffusion of specific ideas and practices across local and virtual communities (Fields & Kafai, 2009). We found that the club members marshaled a number of resources and strategies to share knowledge. But we did not observe sharing between groups; rather, the sharing and diffusion of the practice of teleporting took place within an amorphous group of tweens loosely defined by the common goal of participating in Whyville that included not only the club but also some classrooms and Whyvillians at large. In these virtual and physical communities, knowledge sharing took place in the group but individual efforts and experimentation played an equally significant role in the adoption of new gaming practices. In addition, we know from cheat sites that collaboration does not just happen within a particular virtual world or game but also happens on the margins or outside. In fact, one could argue that the collaborations observed in discussion forums or cheat sites often represent in-depth engagement with activities and content. We also note that in our two case studies the collaborations were not directed by a central adult figure. Instead, facilitated by the open space and atmosphere of the club, members relied on "overheard" conversations (visible or audible), invitations to social activities, and direct help from their peers.

This also suggests that the boundaries we have drawn between online and offline spaces are quite blurry. Other researchers, such as Leander (2008) and Hine (2000), have argued that it is impossible to create clear boundaries between online and offline activities; certainly, our participants did not seem to care much about such a distinction in their interactions. Some of our observations in the after-school club where the youth participated in Whyville provided further evidence in support of merged realities. While cheat sites provided asynchronously accumulated knowledge about the site, the youth continued to learn through their peers about insider knowledge. One implication of this is that virtual spaces can expand the opportunities for peer-to-peer learning and that, where virtual spaces are introduced, studies of learning should encompass multiple spaces of collaboration—not bifurcating the physical from the virtual or even a virtual setting from associated affinity spaces like cheat sites or forums (Gee, 2004).

Research Approaches

Finally, we need to expand our repertoire of research methods for describing and analyzing collective learning. Observations of studies of gaming and social network communities reveal an unhealthy split in either quantitative or qualitative research approaches (Williams, 2005). For instance, survey methods and statistical data mining drive many efforts in coming to grips with what engages members in these communities. At the other end, we have detailed ethnographies of single massive communities that inform us of cultural practices and activities with fine-grained detail. Of course, others have complained about this dichotomy and argued for a mixed methods approach. In our view it is not just about juxtaposing data sources and analytical methods but also developing ways that integrate both approaches in a productive manner.

Many of our insights about collaboration across real and virtual spaces would have not been possible had we had only one single data source, either the tracking data, the video record, or the observation. As a case in point, we have suggested and employed connected ethnographies that make use of the data mining and reduction in large data sets to identify particular participants based on their contribution profiles and to cross-reference and develop these through in-depth ethnographies (Fields & Kafai, 2012; Kafai & Fields, 2012). Such analyses leverage the explanatory potential of each method and allow us to contextualize cases within larger community trends. By conducting a connective ethnography (Leander, 2008), we were able to tie together different threads that situated Gabe's experience of learning how to teleport and captured Briana's provision of casual assistance. Collaborating in virtual informal learning environments encompasses many of such supportive moments, whether in the spaces of a physical location such as an after-school club, the virtual space of Whyville, or the project-sharing site of Scratch. We have also employed connective ethnography successfully in analyzing even more complex Whyville practices, such as projectile throwing (Fields & Kafai, 2010a) and flirting (Giang et al., 2012), that involve complex social practices and nuances. Other analyses, such as social network analyses, would be excellent ways to further informal learning to expand the range of collaborative and collective activities for learning.

Technical Designs

Technical designs are equally important in studying and promoting collaborative interactions in informal learning environments. The virtual spaces of massive networked communities are artifacts, meaning that structures and features are designed by programmers and modified through community use. Changes in the technical design of a site can alter the ways in which participants collaborate in virtual settings, such as how the Scratch site's featuring remixes on the front page increased the number of remixes. Of course, this top-down change is only one way that virtual environments change; participants interact with the design of virtual sites, creating unexpected effects. From a systems design perspective, there are multiple feedback mechanisms and documentation notes that can be integrated and made accessible to participants and these are ripe for research. For instance, we do not understand well which features lead members to contribute productively to large efforts and which ones might hinder such contributions (Benkler, 2010). This involves an analysis of motivation, social interaction, and design choices, such as how much of this control is ceded to participants, is something that needs to be considered in the setup of these communities as well as the technical prerequisites of lay designers themselves, in particular when we talk about younger participants.

CONCLUSIONS

Research on informal learning in computer-supported collaborative learning (CSCL) provides evidence of new forms of collaborations and cross-spatial interactions. We illustrated how youth learned in various collaborative formats, from individual peer teaching to accessing online cheat sites with community knowledge, collaborating with others, and how these groups continued working together across virtual and physical settings. Further research needs to examine several crucial issues for understanding and designing such informal learning communities, including the emergence of leadership, distribution among members, division of labor, and how different roles are being assigned or taken on to fill a perceived need within the community, and the distribution of knowledge among members of the community and how expertise grows over time in these informal communities, if indeed it does. Additionally, new research methods can help us to document and analyze the forms of collaborative and collective interactions by coordinating data records from videos, tracking data, field notes, and interviews.

ACKNOWLEDGMENTS

The writing of this chapter was supported by a grant from the National Science Foundation (NSF-CDI-1027736) to Mitchel Resnick, Yasmin Kafai, and Yochai Benkler. The views expressed are those of the authors and do not necessarily represent the views of the National Science Foundation or the University of Pennsylvania.

REFERENCES

Aragon, C., Poon, S., Monroy-Hernandez, A., & Aragon, D. (2009). A tale of two online communities: Fostering collaboration and creativity in scientists and children. In M. Gross, H. Johnson, J. Ox, & R, Wakkary (Eds.), *Proceedings of the ACM Creativity and Cognition Conference* (pp. 9–18). New York: ACM Press.

Beavis, C., Nixon, H., & Atkinson, S. (2005). LAN cafes: Cafes, places of gathering, or sites of informal teaching and learning? *Education, Communication, Information, 5*(1), 41–60.

Bell, P., Lewenstein, B, Shouse, A. W., & Feder, M. A. (Eds.). (2009). *Learning science in informal environments: People, places, and pursuits* (Committee on Learning Science in an Informal Environment). Washington, DC: National Research Council.

Benkler, Y. (2010). Law, policy, and cooperation. In E. Balleisen & D. Moss (Eds.), *Government and markets: Toward a new theory of regulation* (pp. 299–334). New York: Cambridge University Press.

Black, R. W. (2008). *Adolescents and online fan fiction*. New York: Peter Lang.

Boyd, D., (2006, February). *Identity production in a networked culture: Why youth heart MySpace*. Paper presented at the American Association for the Advancement of Science. St. Louis, Missouri. Retrieved September 13, 2012, from http://www.danah.org/papers/AAAS2006.html

Buckingham, D., & Willett, R. (2006). *Digital generations: Children, young people, and new media*. Mahwah, NJ: Erlbaum.

Ching, C., & Kafai, Y. (2008). Peer pedagogy: Student collaboration and reflection in a learning through design project. *Teachers College Record, 110*(12), 2601–2632.

Cohen, E. G. (1994). Restructuring the classroom: Conditions for productive small groups. *Review of Educational Research, 64*, 1–35.

Cole, M. (2006). *The fifth dimension: An after-school program built on diversity*. New York: Russell Sage Foundation.

Consalvo, M. (2007). *Cheating*. Cambridge, MA: MIT Press.

Fields, D. A., & Kafai, Y. B. (2009). A connective ethnography of peer knowledge sharing and diffusion in a tween virtual world. *International Journal of Computer Supported Collaborative Learning, 4*(1), 47–68.

Fields, D. A., & Kafai, Y. B. (2010a). Stealing from Grandma or generating cultural knowledge? Contestations and effects of cheating in Whyville. *Games and Culture,* 5(1), 64–87.

Fields D. A., & Kafai, Y. B. (2010b). Knowing and throwing mudballs, hearts, pies, and flowers: A connective ethnography of gaming practices. *Games and Culture, 5*(1), 88–115.

Fields, D. A. & Kafai, Y. B. (2012). Navigating life as an avatar: The shifting identities-in-practice of a girl player in a tween virtual world. In C. C. Ching & B. Foley (Eds.), *Constructing identity in a digital world.* (pp. 222–250). Cambridge, England: Cambridge University Press.

Gee, J. P. (2003). *What video games have to teach us about learning and literacy.* New York: Palgrave Macmillan.

Gee, J. P. (2004). *Situated language and learning: A critique of traditional schooling.* New York: Routledge.

Giang, M., Kafai, Y. B., Fields, D. A. & Searle, K. (2012). Social interactions in virtual worlds: Patterns and profiles of tween relationship play. In J. Fromme & A. Unger (Eds.), *Computer games/player/game cultures: A handbook on the state and perspectives of digital games studies* (pp. 543–556). New York: Springer Verlag.

Grimes, S. (2008). Saturday morning cartoons go MMOG. *Media International Australia, 126,* 120–131.

Hargittai, E. (2010). Digital na(t)ives? Variation in Internet skills and uses among members of the "net generation." *Sociological Inquiry, 80*(1), 92–113.

Hay, K. E., & Barab, S. A. (2001). Constructivism in practice: A comparison and contrast of apprenticeship and constructionist learning environments. *Journal of the Learning Sciences, 10*(3), 281–322.

Hill, M. B., Monroy-Hernández, A., & Olson, K. (2010). *Responses to remixing on a social media sharing website.* Paper presented at the Fourth International AAAI Conference on Weblogs and Social Media.

Hine, C. (2000). *Virtual ethnography.* London: Sage.

Hirsch, B. (2005). *A place to call home: After-school programs for urban youth.* Washington, DC: American Psychological Association Press.

Hutchins, E. (1995). *Cognition in the wild.* Cambridge, MA: MIT Press.

Ito, M., Baumer, S., Bittanti, M., Boyd, D., Cody, R., Herr, B., … Tripp, L. (2008). *Hanging out, messing around, geeking out: Living and learning with new media.* Cambridge, MA: MIT Press.

Jenkins, H. (2006). *Convergence culture: Where old and new media collide.* New York: New York University Press.

Jenkins, H., Clinton. K., Purushotm, R., Robison, A., & Weigel, M. (2006). *Confronting the challenges of participation culture: Media education for the 21st century* (White Paper). Chicago, IL: The John D. and Catherine T. MacArthur Foundation.

Kafai, Y. B. (2010). The world of Whyville: Living, playing, and learning in a tween virtual world. *Games and Culture, 5*(1), 3–135.

Kafai, Y. B. & Fields, D. A. (2012). October). Connecting Play: Understanding Multimodal Participation in Virtual Worlds. In *Proceedings of the 14th International Conference on Multimodal Interaction,* Santa Monica, CA. New York: ACM Press.

Kafai, Y. B., Fields, D. A., & Burke, W. Q (2010). Entering the clubhouse: Case studies of young programmers joining the Scratch community. *Journal of Organizational and End User Computing, 22*(2), 21–35.

Kafai, Y. B., Fields, D. A., & Cook, M. S. (2010). Your second selves: Player designed avatar designs. *Games and Culture, 5*(1), 23–42.

Kafai, Y. B., Peppler, K. & Chapman, R. (2009). *The computer clubhouse: Constructionism and creativity in youth communities.* New York: Teachers College Press.

Leander, K. M. (2008). Toward a connective ethnography of online/offline literacy networks. In D. Leu, J. Cairo, M. Knobel, & C. Lankshear (Eds.), *Handbook of research on new literacies* (pp. 33–65). New York: Erlbaum.

Lenhart, A., & Madden, M. (2007). *Social networking websites and teens: An overview.* Washington, DC: Pew Internet and American Life Project.

Levy, P. (1997). *Collective intelligence: Mankind's emerging world in cyberspace.* Cambridge, MA: Plenum.

Lin, H. (2008). A cultural geography of gaming experiences in homes, cybercafés and dormitories. In Y. B. Kafai, C. Heeter, J. Denner, & J. Sun (Eds.), *Beyond Barbie and Mortal Kombat* (pp. 54–67). Cambridge: MIT Press.

Lindtner, S., Nardi, B., Wang, Y., Mainwaring, S., Jing, H., & Liang, W. (2008). A hybrid cultural ecology: World of Warcraft in China. In B. Begole & D. MacDonald (Eds.), *Proceedings of the 2008 ACM Conference on Computer Supported Cooperative Work* (pp. 371–382). New York: ACM Press.

Mazzarella, S. (2005). *Girl wide web: Girls, the Internet, and the negotiation of identity.* New York: Peter Lang.

McGonigal, J. (2008). Why I love bees: A case study in collective intelligence gaming. In K. Salen (Ed.), *The ecology of games: Connecting youth, games and learning* (pp. 199–228). Cambridge, MA: MIT Press.

Monroy-Hernandez, A., & Hill, B. M. (2010, February). Cooperation and attribution in an online community of young creators. In *Conference on Computer Supported Cooperative Work.* Retrieved from http://research.microsoft.com/en-us/um/redmond/groups/connect/cscw_10/docs/p469.pdf.

Nardi, B. A., Ly, S., & Harris, J. (2007). Learning conversation in World of Warcraft. In *Proceedings of the 40th Annual Hawaii International Conference on System Sciences* (p. 79) Washington, DC: IEEE Computer Society.
Perkel, D. (2008). No I don't feel complimented: A young artist's take on copyright. *Digital Youth Research.* Retrieved from http://digitalyouth.ischool.berkeley.edu/node/105.
Prensky, M. (2001). Digital natives, digital immigrants. *On the Horizon, 9*(5), 1–6.
Resnick, M., Maloney, J., Hernandez, A. M., Rusk, N., Eastmond, E., Brennan, K., ... Kafai, Y. B. (2009). Scratch: Programming for everyone. *Communications of the ACM, 52*(11), 711–721.
Rick, J. & Guzdial, M. (2006). Situating CoWeb: A scholarship of application. *International Journal of Computer-Supported Collaborative Learning, 1*(1), 89–115.
Rogoff, B. (1995). Observing socio-cultural activity on three planes: Participatory appropriation and apprenticeship. In J.V. Wertsch, P. Del Rio, & A. Alvarez (Eds.), *Sociocultural studies of the mind* (pp. 139–163). Cambridge, England: Cambridge University Press.
Scardamalia, M., & Bereiter, C. (2006). Knowledge building: Theory, pedagogy, and technology. In K. Sawyer (Ed.), *Cambridge handbook of the learning sciences* (pp. 97–118). New York: Cambridge University Press.
Squire, K. (2008). Civilization III as a world history sandbox. In *Civilization and its discontents: Virtual history. Real fantasies.* Milan, Italy: Ludilogica Press.
Steinkuehler, C. A. (2006). Massively multiplayer online video gaming as participation in a discourse. *Mind, Culture, and Activity, 13*(1), 38–52.
Steinkuehler, C. A., & Duncan, S. (2009). Scientific habits of mind in virtual worlds. *Journal of Science Education & Technology, 17*(6), 530–543.
Tapscott, D. (2008). *Grown up digital: How the net generation is changing your world.* New York: McGraw-Hill.
Taylor, T. L. (2006). *Play between worlds.* Cambridge, MA: MIT Press.
Vadeboncoeur, J. A. (2007). Engaging young people: Learning in informal contexts. *Review of Research in Education, 30,* 239–278. Washington, DC: AERA.
Williams, D. (2005). Bridging the methodological divide in game research. *Simulation & Gaming, 36*(4), 1–17.
Zhao, Y., Mishra, P., & Girod, M. (2000). A clubhouse is a clubhouse is a clubhouse. *Computers in Human Behavior, 16,* 287–300.
Zuckerman, O., Blau, I., & Monroy-Hernadez, A. (2009). Children's participation patterns in online communities: An analysis of Israeli learners in the Scratch online community. *Interdisciplinary Journal of E-Learning and Learning Objects, 5,* 263–274.

28

COLLABORATION, TECHNOLOGY, AND CULTURE

JIANWEI ZHANG

University at Albany, State University of New York

INTRODUCTION AND OVERVIEW

Culture has a deep impact on how people learn and interact, what type of learning is highly valued, and what technological uses are preferred (Chan, 2008; Nisbett, 2003; Tweed & Lehman, 2002; Watkins & Biggs, 1996; Zhang, 2007). Thus, understanding cross-cultural differences in learning and fostering cross-cultural interaction and reflection has become an important research topic. The significance of this topic is heightened by international assessments that place some nations ahead of others on various measures (Organisation for Economic Co-Operation and Development [OECD], 2010; Stigler & Hiebert, 1999). Research on collaborative learning and related computer support is rooted in a sociocultural perspective and has involved an international community of researchers. Computer-mediated communication and learning environments provide unprecedented opportunities for learners from different cultures to interact and collaborate, and for researchers to investigate such cross-cultural interaction and collaboration (Kim & Bonk, 2002; Lin & Schwartz, 2003). Therefore, researchers in the field of collaborative learning call for systematic efforts to investigate the impact of culture on the design and implementation of collaborative learning and cultural transformation underpinning classroom innovation (Vatrapu & Suthers, 2007, 2009; Zhang, 2010). The purpose of this chapter is to identify focal issues in this research area, synthesize conceptual underpinnings and empirical findings that can be built upon, and highlight educational implications and directions for future research.

The concept of culture is famous for being difficult to define and having diverse meanings. Vatrapu and Suthers (2007) reviewed the different definitions and identified Hofstede's (2001) as the most appropriate for cross-cultural research on collaborative learning and technology. According to Hofstede (2001), culture is "the collective programming of the mind that distinguishes the members of one group or category of people from another" (p. 9). Interpreting culture as the collective programming of the mind—or cultural schema—aligns with the Vygotskian sociocultural perspective of the social formation of the mind (Wertsch, 1985). This collective programming is coconstructed by members through participating in shared cultural practices. It manifests as shared values, norms, and thinking styles of a cohort group (e.g., a community or a nation) that rises above members' heterogeneity within the group. Culture, thus, represents the group members' collective particularity (Vatrapu & Suthers, 2007) that does not exclude individual variation and diversity. Characteristics identified at a collective and cultural level cannot be uniformly attributed to each of the individuals, who may simultaneously engage in and interact with multiple cultural communities and, thereby, constantly reconstruct their identity through lived cultural experience (Gutiérrez & Correa-Chavez, 2006).

This chapter synthesizes research that intersects with several scholarly areas including computer-supported collaborative learning (CSCL) and collaborative work (CSCW), computer-mediated communication (CMC), cross-cultural psychology, and cultural studies of education. It begins with examining cross-cultural variations, focusing on how learning, communication, and collaboration are conceived and approached in different cultures that have distinct beliefs, values, and traditions. In light of the cultural diversity and variation reviewed, the second section synthesizes research on cross-cultural learning and collaboration to enhance intercultural enrichment and complementarity for learners' mutual benefit. Finally, cultures, although relatively stable at the national level, are in state of constant evolution (Hofstede, 2001). The 21st century is witnessing social and cultural transformations characteristic of globalization, participatory networking, creativity, and flexibility in both public and personal realms, posing new challenges and demands to education (Florida, 2002; Lei & Zhang, 2010). Addressing these challenges, research on collaborative learning has generated various pedagogical and technology innovations to evolve creative learning communities among students as well as teachers. Implementing these innovations in different cultural contexts for deep change requires adapting cultural beliefs (e.g., views of knowledge) underlying educational practice and responding to culture-specific conditions and challenges. Thus, the third section of this chapter discusses ways to foster collaborative knowledge building in different cultural contexts for educational change, underlining a principle-based approach to classroom innovation.

CROSS-CULTURAL VARIATIONS IN LEARNING INTERACTION AND COLLABORATION

Cultures vary along a number of dimensions (e.g., Hofstede, 2001; Nisbett, 2003), which have significant influences on learning, communication, and collaboration. The cultural dimensions provide a framework to analyze and characterize cultural differences without implying any evaluative judgment. This section reviews research related to four dimensions, each of which represents a continuum instead of a dichotomy: individualism–collectivism, power distance, analytical and holistic thinking, and high- and low-context communication.

Individualism–Collectivism

Individualist cultures (e.g., the United States) emphasize independence, agency, and choice of individuals with loose social ties; whereas collectivist cultures (e.g., East Asian societies) emphasize interdependence and value collective over individual interest. Compared to individualist cultures, collectivist societies give more weight to social expectations, norms, and rules in education (Li, 1996) and tend to discourage individual initiative, interest, and distinctiveness (Nisbett, 2003). Students are urged to acquire socially recognized knowledge and moral principles and transform their thinking and behaviors accordingly (Tweed & Lehman, 2002; Zhang, 2007). Collectivist thinking is conducive to collaborative learning as it encourages students to contribute to shared goals and activities and learn with and from peers (Freedman & Liu, 1996). As Tang (1996) observed, although formal small-group learning is relatively new in China, informal collaborative learning has long been practiced in Chinese classrooms. These informal collaborative learning practices occur despite the pressure of high-stake examinations that increase student competition.

Studies have compared learner collaboration and communication in collectivist and individualist cultures. Participants from collectivist cultures are more relation-oriented and accustomed to face-protection and politeness strategies to minimize imposition and avoid hurting others' feelings with negative comments. In contrast, students from individualist cultures are more outcome- and task-oriented, paying more attention to the clarity and efficiency of communication and completion of tasks (Kim et al., 1996). In a study by Kim and Bonk (2002), American and Korean college students coengaged in online discussions about school-related problems. The Korean students contributed more postings to share personal feelings in support of positive relationships. Their American counterparts were more task-oriented and pragmatic, focusing on developing solutions to the problems. Similar patterns were found in an experimental study by Setlock and colleagues (Setlock, Fussell, & Neuwirth, 2004), who investigated collaborative decision making in a face-to-face or instant messaging (IM) environment. Participants were paired in such a way as to create three cultural groupings: American-American (AA), Chinese-Chinese (CC), and American-Chinese (AC). Content analysis of conversations showed that the CC pairs used more "we" pronouns—as opposed to "I" pronouns—and more social language to show respect and politeness such as through inviting partner's input. Further, two argumentation strategies were identified (Stewart, Setlock, & Fussell, 2004): (a) a quick agreement process for the AA pairs, who tended to state personal claims and negotiate solutions that they could quickly agree upon; and (b) a slow agreement process for the CC pairs, who devoted more discourse moves to offering reasons for claims and understanding their different perspectives. Similar observations were reported by Seo and colleagues (Seo, Miller, Schmidt, & Sowa, 2008), who analyzed student discourse in an online course that was shared between an American and a Hong Kong university. The Hong Kong students posted more messages to invite peers' opinions, whereas the U.S. students made more claims about their own views.

Power Distance

Associated with the degree of collectivism–individualism, cultures also vary in power distance—the extent to which members of a society accept and expect that power be distributed unequally. Societies with large power distances tend to accept a hierarchical order in which everybody has a place without needing further justification. Those with small power distances strive for equal power and demand justification for inequalities (Hofstede, 2001). Asian societies are characteristic of a larger power distance (Bond & Hwang, 1990). Accordingly, Asian schools tend to place more emphasis on respectfulness, strictness, and discipline (Aldridge & Fraser, 2000; Jin & Cortazzi, 1998) often at the cost of children's independence and creativity (Ho & Kang, 1984; Zhao, 2009). As several studies have suggested, Chinese students tend to be more respectful of their teachers than Western students (e.g., British and Australian; Aldridge & Fraser, 2000; Jin & Cortazzi, 1998); and are more likely to see text and the instructor as authoritative sources of knowledge (Lei & Zhang, 2010; Pratt & Wong, 1999). They prefer first to understand what these sources offer before questioning, commenting, and criticizing. In contrast, Western students and educators tend to attach greater importance to questioning and criticizing early in the learning process (Tweed & Lehman, 2002). In a study on computer-supported learning interactions among middle school students, Freedman and Liu (1996) found that Asian American students asked fewer questions to challenge peers and teachers and were less likely to use exploratory, trial-and-error inquiry strategies. There has also been evidence presented that students from high power distance cultures prefer to work in more structured learning environments with clear objectives and guidance (Pratt & Wong, 1999). Therefore, in computer-supported collaborative learning, Hong Kong students' discourse spaces tend to be more structured, such as based on topics and subtopics, as opposed to student-directed, less structured, and emergent discourse often found in North American contexts (Chan, 2008). In face-to-face and online social interaction, East Asians are more sensitive to distance in power among participants, and when such power distance exists, they are more likely to use indirect conversation strategies to show respect, avoid negative comments, and protect the face of the participants who have a higher power status (e.g., teachers, seniors, experts, leaders) (cf. Brew & Cairns, 2004).

Analytical and Holistic, Dialectal Thinking

People from different cultural traditions show different thinking styles in viewing and reasoning about the world, which have a deep impact on student learning and discourse. For example, different thinking styles have been observed between Asians and Westerners (Nisbett, 2003). Inheriting Eastern philosophy (e.g., Confucianism, Taoism, Buddhism), East Asians see the world as a complex and interconnected whole in constant flux, which can be best understood using a holistic approach though personal experience, reflection, and wisdom (Nisbett, 2003). Thus, they attend more to environments, contexts, and relationships and are reluctant to simplify the whole as isolated objects. Westerners, inheriting the philosophy of the Ancient Greeks, are more used to analytical thinking, which compartmentalizes the world into a limited number of discrete objects and then categorizes the objects based on clear logical rules (Nisbett, 2003).

Such different thinking styles favor different approaches to curriculum, teaching, and learning interactions (Stigler & Hiebert, 1999; Watanabe, 1998). When it comes to collaborative learning in particular, the different thinking styles lead to different ways to deal with conflicting perspectives and arguments, which are essential to productive discourse (Andriessen, 2006). When confronted with conflicting propositions, Americans and other Westerners are more likely to use a logical approach to reject one of the propositions in support of the other to avoid a possible contradiction. As a result, argumentation and debate form a pervasive pattern of discourse across social sectors including academia, often resulting in polarized views. East Asians often favor a dialectical approach to conflicting perspectives to find truth in both sides in search of the Middle Way (Nisbett, 2003). As a result, they tend to avoid direct arguments, and when disagreements emerge, they are inclined to connect with others' goals instead of merely focusing on their own (Hample, 2005; Stewart et al., 2004). Grounded in an analytical thinking style, argumentative writing and discourse typically follows a rhetoric structure that involves background, problem, hypothesis or proposition, means of testing, evidence to support an argument and refute possible counter arguments, and conclusions. This structure is familiar to Western students but foreign and challenging to many Asian students who have been cultivated with dialectical thinking (Nisbett, 2003).

Collaborative learning designs need to take into account such cultural differences to engage students in productive reasoning and discourse. On one hand, researchers and educators need to tackle the challenge to help students from non-Western cultures appropriate argumentative discourse. On the other hand, it is also important to capitalize on the value of collectivist, dialectical thinking in resolving arguments and constructing intersubjective understanding. In the experimental study mentioned previously, Stewart and colleagues (2004) engaged American and Chinese college students in collaborative decision making, either face-to-face or via instant messaging. In their conversations, the American participants devoted more discourse moves to making personal claims, followed by quick convergence to achieve their instrumental goals (i.e., resolving the task) without necessarily changing their personal understanding. The Chinese participants devoted more discourse moves to offering reasons for different claims, making clear where they disagreed, and connecting the different perspectives to achieve cooperative goals. This complex process of argumentation led to true consensus and transformed individual understanding. Thus, collaborative learning designs need to accommodate and integrate the different patterns of discourse, rooted in different cultural traditions, to complement and enrich each other for knowledge advancement.

Low- and High-Context Cultures

Another cultural dimension pertaining to collaboration and communication is low versus high context. Communication in low-context cultures (e.g., Germany, the United States, and other Western nations) requires coding meanings in words in favor of explicit rational information (Hall, 1976; Lustig & Koester, 1999). In contrast, communication in high-context cultures, such as Arabic countries, China, India, and Japan, relies heavily on physical and social contexts (e.g., social cues, vocal tones, relationships) to achieve mutual understanding, with relatively less information explicitly encoded in words. The low-context communication in Western societies aligns with the analytic thinking style that dissects the world into increasingly differentiated objects, each having particular attributes which can be captured in language (Nisbett, 2003).

Several studies have examined computer-mediated communication and collaboration among participants from high- and low-context cultures. Setlock and colleagues (2004) investigated collaborative decision making in different cultural groups working either face-to-face or via instant messaging. Participants were paired to create three cultural groupings: American-American (AA), Chinese-Chinese (CC), and American-Chinese (AC). The CC pairs talked more face-to-face than via instant messaging in which nonverbal cues were absent. They also engaged in more extensive conversational grounding than the AA pairs to build mutual understanding about the task and context in the first phase. Using a similar research design, Vatrapu (2008) examined collaborative problem solving among different cultural dyads supported by a knowledge mapping and inquiry environment. Compared to the Chinese participants, the American dyads created more messages in online discussions, consistent with a low-context communication style that explicitly codes meanings in words. Focusing on cultural preferences of communication media, Massey and colleagues (Massey, Montoya-Weiss, Hung, & Ramesh, 2001) found that Asian participants were less satisfied with asynchronous communication tools, such as online forums, in which they could not receive continuous and instant feedback. There is also evidence showing more frequent use of visual and audio components in online communication among Asian participants than in Western cultures (Choi, Lee, Kim, & Jeon, 2005; Kayan, Fussell, & Setlock, 2006).

In sum, cross-cultural differences identified along the various dimensions have a visible impact on student learning interaction and collaboration in both face-to-face and online environments. Research to identify and evaluate productive patterns of collaborative learning needs to consider both culture-bound and culture-neutral aspects to understand the cultural meaning of the discourse patterns for the participants involved. Designs of collaborative learning environments need to adapt to learners' diverse cultural profiles in order to best support their communication, collaboration, and learning. The cultural dimensions provide a framework to characterize learners' cultural profiles and create learner cultural models that can be embedded in collaborative learning systems. Various survey tools have been developed to characterize learners' cultural attributes and preferences on an individual basis (Vatrapu, 2008) instead of simply based on student ethnicity and nationality. Drawing on such learner data, collaboration systems may provide learners with culturally adaptive communication tools and scaffolds (e.g., prompts) of collaboration (Economides, 2008).

CROSS-CULTURAL LEARNING AND COLLABORATION

Capitalizing on the Benefits of Cross-Cultural Learning and Collaboration

Bringing together diverse views is helpful for problem solving and deep understanding. "We would expect that for most problems one would be better off having a mix of people from different cultures than having people who are all from one culture" (Nisbett, 2003, p. 217). Education in the age of globalization needs to create cross-cultural and multicultural learning experiences for students, supported by information and communication technologies. Existing research suggests important benefits to be gained from carefully designed cross-cultural collaboration and interaction (Levin & Cohen, 1985; Lin & Schwartz, 2003). In a culturally diverse learning community, students can access diverse perspectives, styles of thinking, and approaches to learning, and further connect to diverse social practices in different cultures. Such benefits have been demonstrated through the pioneering work of Levin and Cohen (1985), who engaged students from California, Illinois, Japan, Mexico, and Israel in a collaborative project to tackle the problems of water shortage. Through sharing and analyzing local actions and strategies to address water shortage, the students expanded their understanding, identified unique strategies used in other cultures, and recommended these strategies to their local communities.

In addition to cognitive benefits, interacting with peers from different cultures may trigger deep reflection upon one's identity and practice, leading to transformative learning. Lin and Schwartz (2003) asked American and Chinese students and teachers to design an "ideal student" for their classes. The American participants listed more behavioral properties (e.g., following rules), while those from China valued more learning-related properties (e.g., explaining clearly). The realization of such difference was so striking to the American teachers that they immediately started to reflect on their practice and ways to change it. Focusing on advancing collaborative knowledge building in classrooms, the author of this chapter (see Zhang, 2010) coordinated a multiyear initiative that involved teachers from different cultures and nations to share classroom practices, with researchers applying various analyses to produce feedback data. Observing and discussing diverse classroom strategies adopted by international colleagues, benchmarked by evidence of student engagement and progress, helped the teachers to reflect on their practices, identify common and unique challenges, and codevelop effective classroom designs. In a design experiment analyzed by Lai and Law (2006), two elementary teachers, from Hong Kong and Toronto, respectively, engaged their students in collaborative knowledge building about civilizations supported by Knowledge Forum. Through reading online discussions, the Hong Kong students noticed that their Toronto partners generated more questions and disagreements. Discussing and reflecting on this difference helped the Hong Kong students to improve their engagement, leading to more active problematizing moves in the subsequent online discourse.

Cross-cultural collaboration is challenging and requires learners to be sensitive to their partners' cultural expectations and reflective about their engagement. Culture, as collective programming of mind (Hofstede, 2001), provides a set of cognitive schemas related to various social situations. While engaging in collaborative learning with such schemas, participants interpret the interaction context and develop intuitions about what language and actions might be appropriate or inappropriate and how their partners may respond. In collaborative learning among learners with different cultural beliefs and expectations, learners may find that their partners' behaviors and responses violate their expectations. Without reflective adjustment, such cultural misalignment may cause frustration, misunderstanding and lack of trust. In a study by Prasolova-Forland, Wyeld, and Chang (2008), students from Australia, Norway, and Taiwan engaged in collaborative tower design in a 3D virtual environment. Through engaging in and reflecting on their online interaction, the Norwegian and Australian students learned adaptive strategies (e.g., talking about personal issues before getting to the task) to collaborate with their Taiwanese partners, who came from a high-context culture. However, misunderstandings emerged between the Norwegian and Australian students, who each complained about the other being too dominating or bossy.

Further addressing the challenge of cultural gaps to enable productive and enjoyable collaboration requires training and scaffolding of intercultural competence (Lustig & Koester, 1999). With intercultural competence, learners recognize that people growing up in different environments carry different "mental software" (Hofstede, 2001). They develop sensitivity to cultural differences along with knowledge and skills about the specific cultures they are interacting with, including the values, symbols, rituals, habits of thinking, and so forth. Such competence helps students from different cultures to engage in reflective and creative interaction to facilitate a new system of orientation as their shared, emergent "interculture" (Rathje, 2007). The willingness to understand and learn from other cultures can be enhanced through humanizing cultural exchanges (Macrae, Stangor, & Hewstone, 1996), so that participants will perceive their peers as persons from different cultures instead of based upon cultural stereotypes. In a study by Lin and Schwartz (2003), a group of Hong Kong students was asked to comment on stories written by their American peers. Their comments and feedback were more positive and encouraging when they had the opportunity to read not only the stories but also information about the authors' personal thoughts (e.g., how their stories had been created).

IMPLEMENTING COLLABORATIVE KNOWLEDGE BUILDING IN DIFFERENT CULTURES FOR EDUCATIONAL CHANGE

Cultures in the 21st century are witnessing transformations characteristic of globalization, networking, participation, creativity, and flexibility in economic, sociopolitical, and personal life, with collaborative and creative knowledge practices pervading most social sectors (Florida, 2002; Lei & Zhang, 2010). Collaborative learning research suggests new models of schooling in the 21st century with the focus on engaging students in collaborative knowledge building supported by new technologies. Enacting collaborative knowledge building requires students and teachers to embrace a set of new cultural beliefs that depart from traditional schooling (Bielaczyc & Collins, 1999): knowledge as improvable ideas instead of end answers; learning as sustained inquiry for deep understanding (Hakkarainen, Lipponen, & Jarvela, 2002; Hewitt, 2002); students as coinvestigators with their teacher to advance collective knowledge in a community (Scardamalia & Bereiter, 2006; Stahl, 2006; Tabak & Baumgartner, 2004). Transforming education in line with these new beliefs and perspectives represents a global challenge; however, some of these beliefs might be more foreign and challenging for some cultures than for others. For example, a constructivist, democratic view of knowledge is more foreign for teachers from Eastern societies, who may be more receptive to the notion of collective and shared knowledge. Therefore, fostering educational change through collaborative knowledge building requires creating culturally adaptive innovations that build on unique cultural values and practices and address context-specific challenges. Instead of simply adopting standard procedures of collaborative learning, teachers need to work as designers and innovators to construct pedagogical understanding and develop classroom designs and practices accordingly in their local contexts (Barab & Luehmann, 2003; Zhang, 2010).

Collaborative learning programs cannot simply be disseminated to different schools and cultures through wholesaling a standard set of activity procedures and tools, which often only results in surface changes (Brown & Campione, 1996; Zhang, 2010). Appreciating the complexity involved in the transformation of cultural beliefs and practices, recent research has underlined a principle-based approach to classroom innovation (Brown & Campione, 1996; Zhang, 2010). A principle-based innovation defines a set of core educational values and principles to inform teachers' pedagogical understanding and decision making. Instead of implementing pre-scripted activities, teachers are in a position to make reflective interpretations, discretionary judgments, and adaptive classroom decisions, supported by technological tools, sample lessons and assessments, and other resources (Zhang, 2010; Zhang, Hong, Scardamalia, Teo, & Morley, 2011). They work with principles of collaborative learning and knowledge building as instructional design parameters to create and improve specific classroom procedures and generate principled reflections, insights, and classroom strategies to address common and local challenges. Among collaborative learning programs, knowledge building pedagogy supported by Knowledge Forum technology, developed by Scardamalia and Bereiter (2006), is a principle-based innovation that has attracted the most intensive international efforts, involving researchers, educators, and policymakers from over 20 nations

(Hong, Scardamalia, & Zhang, 2010). A number of studies have investigated teachers' enactment of knowledge building/Knowledge Forum in different cultural contexts (e.g., Chai & Tan, 2009; Chan, 2011; Oshima et al., 2006; Zhang et al., 2011). These studies shed light on the possibility and processes for teachers to engage in principle-based innovation to address cultural challenges for deep change. Three of the processes are elaborated below.

Improving Pedagogical Understanding and Design through Collaborative Experimentation and Reflection

A challenge to educational transformation comes from traditional educational beliefs and understandings that prevent educators from seeing and accepting new possibilities. Principle-based innovation addresses this challenge by encouraging teachers to expose, reflect on, and improve their pedagogical understandings while developing and experimenting with specific classroom procedures and strategies. A recent study investigated the implementation and improvement of knowledge building/Knowledge Forum (Scardamalia & Bereiter, 2006) as a principle-based innovation in a Canadian elementary school over a decade (Zhang et al., 2011). The teachers, working as a community, reflected continually on core issues related to classroom practice (e.g., nature of knowledge and learning, teacher–learner relationships) in light of the principles of knowledge building as they codeveloped and tested specific classroom designs. The principles highlight student epistemic agency in dealing with problems of goals, motivation, evaluation, and long-range planning—problems that are normally left to teachers (Scardamalia & Bereiter, 2006). The teachers reflect on and deepen their understanding of what epistemic agency means in relation to their practice and what level of agency can be enabled among a particular group of children, leading to specific classroom strategies to turn over more control to students. Flexible collaboration structures are developed to encourage students to group and regroup in the service of their emergent inquiry needs, with students engaged in codesigning classroom activities for productive knowledge building (see Zhang, Scardamalia, Reeve, & Messina, 2009). Through reflective observations of students' work, the teachers are impressed by the level of thinking and collaboration that their students are capable of, leading to increased trust in student agency and further efforts to turn over high-level control to students. Such principle-based understanding, experimentation, and reflection, advanced through teachers' collaborative sharing and dialogues, lead to sustained improvement of knowledge-building practice evidenced with student engagement and outcomes (Zhang et al., 2011). Related studies in Hong Kong, Taiwan, and Singapore have concurred with the above findings, suggesting that engaging teachers in collaborative communities to enact and reflect continually on principle-based practice of knowledge building leads to a transformation of their pedagogical beliefs (e.g., learner agency) and improvement of classroom practice (Chai & Tan, 2009; Chan, 2011; Chang & Hong, 2010).

Addressing Challenges and Constraints from a Coherence Systems Perspective

Enacting collaborative knowledge building faces specific challenges and constraints in different classroom settings and cultural contexts, ranging from traditional beliefs, mandatory examinations, rigid bureaucratic administration, time pressure, lack of technological resources and support, and so forth. Instead of being overwhelmed by such challenges and constraints, teachers need to understand that they are working within a complex system that requires progressive problem solving to develop coherent solutions to interrelated problems (Zhang et al., 2011). They "need to be able to manage situations in which new knowledge about what to do must be created on the spot" (Lampert, 1999, p.168) in their context of teaching. As noted earlier, students from Eastern cultures often hold an authoritative view of knowledge and expect the teacher to provide more information and guidance (Tweed & Lehman, 2002). This view poses a challenge to the enactment of collaborative knowledge building that requires students to take on high-level control. Chan (2008) documented efforts made by a Hong Kong teacher to address the above and other challenges to implement collaborative knowledge building using Knowledge Forum. To help students become comfortable with expressing their own ideas and contributing to knowledge building discourse, the teacher first incorporated the strategy of students commenting on others' ideas into routine schoolwork. For example, students presented textbook readings followed by peer questioning and commenting. Such initial experience helped students to build confidence, skills, and understanding needed to contribute to knowledge building discourse, online and offline.

Building on Existing Cultural Practices for Opportunities of Innovation

To evolve creative learning communities in cultural and school contexts, educators may identify potential components within their current practices as anchors for new practices to be held onto, and redesign these cultural practices for knowledge building. In the aforementioned study by Chan (2008), the teacher from Hong Kong connected knowledge building and Knowledge Forum (Scardamalia & Bereiter, 2006) to two components pivotal to Chinese classrooms, homework and assessment. He modified student homework assignments to include discussions of core concepts in Knowledge Forum. As a part of the students' final assessment and grading, he asked them to submit a portfolio that summarized the best instances of their knowledge building discourse based on a set of principle-based criteria (e.g., progressive problem solving, van Aalst & Chan, 2007). These strategies helped to foster students' collaborative knowledge building leading to positive learning results. In another example, Oshima and colleagues (2006) conducted a design experiment to transform Japanese classrooms into knowledge building communities. As a part of their culture, Japanese teachers widely adopt a set of activity structures established through repeated research lessons (Rohlen & LeTendre, 1995). Oshima and colleagues identified such activity structures as a cultural practice to build onto while making the activities more idea-centered for collective knowledge building. For instance, as a lesson activity, teachers often begin their classes by reviewing what students have learned and making the transition from this to the new topic. This activity was adapted through incorporating authentic explanatory problems (e.g., would a dense block of newspaper burn and why?) to stimulate student ideas and explanations. These ideas were shared and advanced as the focus of the community, tested and refined through group investigations, and contributed as objects of continual discourse in Knowledge Forum.

In brief, evolving a new education framework centered at collaborative knowledge building requires extended efforts to adapt and accommodate the cultural assumptions underlying teaching and learning practices and address contextual challenges (Zhang, 2007). To support such efforts, a principle-based approach engages teachers to work as collaborative pedagogical knowledge builders to deepen and adapt their pedagogical understanding continually and develop increasingly effective classroom procedures and technology applications in their contexts. Systematic changes are needed to redesign educational goals, curriculum, and assessment and provide resources and support for teacher innovation (Law, 2008).

CONCLUDING REMARKS

Collaboration and learning are cultural activities. The development of 21st-century pedagogies and technologies will not wipe out the cultural differences, but will likely increase the differences on the basis of preexisting cultural values and practices (cf. Hofstede, 2001). Research on the processes and designs of collaborative learning has typically been conducted in specific, mostly Western, cultural settings. Reexamining such processes and designs in cross-cultural contexts helps to validate existing findings, explicate and investigate cultural presumptions and practices, and further inform new research themes. Understanding learners' different cultural profiles related to collaborative learning will further inform culturally adaptive designs of learning environments and systems that can attune to the needs of different learners and support intercultural interactions.

Cultural studies of collaborative learning in computer-supported environments is a relatively new theme. In future cross-cultural research on collaborative learning, researchers need to increase the sample size and time span and integrate multifaceted analyses to obtain reliable and rich results. There is also a need to conduct longitudinal studies of classroom change employing collaborative learning pedagogies and technologies to provide elaborated accounts of teacher transformation and innovation in specific school and cultural contexts. Design-based studies can be further conducted to create favorable contexts for collaborative and creative classroom practices to evolve and thrive in different contexts. Advancements in pedagogical knowledge and practice generated by educators can be shared across classrooms and cultures through online networks for sustained improvement and innovation.

REFERENCES

Aldridge, J. M., & Fraser, B.J. (2000). A cross-cultural study of classroom learning environments in Australia and Taiwan. *Learning Environments Research, 3,* 101–134.

Andriessen, J. (2006). Arguing to learn. In R. K. Sawyer (Ed.), *The Cambridge handbook of the learning sciences* (pp. 443–459). Cambridge, England: Cambridge University Press.

Barab, S. A., & Luehmann, A. L. (2003). Building sustainable science curriculum: Acknowledging and accommodating local adaptation. *Science Education, 87,* 454–467.

Bielaczyc, K., & Collins, A. (1999). Learning communities in classrooms: A reconceptualization of educational practice. In C. M. Reigeluth (Ed.), *Instructional-design theories and models: A new paradigm of instructional theory* (pp. 269–292). Mahwah, NJ: Erlbaum.

Bond, M. H., & Hwang, K. K. (1990). The social psychology of the Chinese people. In M. H. Bond (Ed.), *The psychology of the Chinese people* (pp. 213–266). Hong Kong: Oxford University Press.

Brew, F. P., & Cairns, D. R. (2004). Do culture or situational constraints determine choice of direct or indirect styles in intercultural workplace conflicts? *International Journal of Intercultural Relations, 28,* 331–352.

Brown, A. L., & Campione, J. (1996). Psychological theory and the design of innovative learning environments: On procedures, principles, and systems. In L. Schauble & R. Glaser (Eds.), *Innovations in learning: New environments for education* (pp. 289–325). Mahwah, NJ: Erlbaum.

Chai, C. S., & Tan, S. C. (2009). Professional development of teachers for computer-supported collaborative learning: A knowledge-building approach. *Teachers College Record, 111*(5), 1296–1327.

Chan, C. K. K. (2008). Pedagogical transformation and knowledge-building for the Chinese learner. *Evaluation and Research in Education, 21,* 235–251.

Chan, C. K. K. (2011). Bridging research and practice: Implementing and sustaining knowledge building in Hong Kong classrooms. *International Journal of Computer-Supported Collaborative Learning, 6*, 147–186.

Chang, Y. H., & Hong, H.-Y. (2011, April). *Facilitating belief change among prospective science teachers through knowledge building.* Paper presented at the annual conference of American Educational Research Association (AERA), New Orleans, Louisiana.

Choi, B., Lee, I., Kim, J., & Jeon, Y. (2005, April). *A qualitative cross-national study of cultural influences on mobile data service design.* Paper presented at the ACM conference on Computer Human Interaction (CHI 2005), Portland, Oregon.

Economides, A. A. (2008). Culture-aware collaborative learning. *Multicultural Education & Technology Journal, 2*, 243–267.

Florida, R. (2002). *The rise of the creative class.* New York: Basic Books.

Freedman, K., & Liu, M. (1996). The importance of computer experience, learning processes, and communication patterns in multicultural networking. *Educational Technology Research and Development, 44*, 43–59.

Gutiérrez, K., & Correa-Chavez, M. (2006). What to do about culture? *Lifelong Learning in Europe, 3*, 152–159.

Hakkarainen, K., Lipponen, L., & Järvelä, S. (2002). Epistemology of inquiry and computer-supported collaborative learning. In T. Koschmann, R. Hall, & N. Miyake (Eds.), *CSCL 2: Carrying forward the conversation* (pp. 129–156). Mahwah, NJ: Erlbaum.

Hall, E. T. (1976). *Beyond culture.* Garden City, NY: Anchor/Doubleday.

Hample, D. (2005). *Arguing: Exchanging reasons face-to-face.* Mahwah, NJ: Erlbaum.

Hewitt, J. (2002). From a focus on task to a focus on understanding: The cultural transformation of a Toronto classroom. In. T. Koschmann, R. Hall, & N. Miyake (Eds.), *CSCL2: Carrying forward the conversation* (pp. 11–41). Mahwah, NJ: Erlbaum.

Ho, D. Y. F., & Kang, T.K. (1984). Intergenerational comparisons of child-rearing attitudes and practices in Hong Kong. *Developmental Psychology, 20*, 1004–1016.

Hofstede, G. (2001). *Culture's consequences: Comparing values, behaviors, institutions, and organizations across nations* (2nd ed). Thousand Oaks, CA: Sage.

Hong, H.-Y., Scardamalia, M., & Zhang, J. (2010). Knowledge Society Network (KSN): Toward a dynamic, sustained network for building knowledge. *Canadian Journal of Learning and Technology, 36*(1). Retrieved from http://www.cjlt.ca

Jin, L., & Cortazzi, M. (1998). Dimensions of dialogue: Large classes in China. *International Journal of Educational Research, 29*, 739–761.

Kayan, S., Fussell, S., & Setlock, L. (2006). Cultural differences in the use of instant messaging in Asia and North America. In P. Hinds & D. Martin (Eds.), *Proceedings of the 2006 ACM Conference on Computer Supported Cooperative Work* (pp. 525–528). New York: ACM Press.

Kim, K. J., & Bonk, C. J. (2002). Cross-cultural comparisons of online collaboration among preservice teachers in Finland, Korea, and the United States. *Journal of Computer-Mediated Communication, 8*(1). Retrieved September 10, 2012, from http://jcmc.indiana.edu/vol8/issue1/kimandbonk.html

Kim, M. S., Hunter, J. E., Miyahara, A., Horvath, A., Bresnahan, M., & Yoon, H. (1996). Individual vs. cultural level dimensions of individualism and collectivism: Effects on preferred conversation styles. *Communication Monographs, 63*, 29–49.

Lai, M., & Law, N. (2006). Peer scaffolding of knowledge building through collaborative groups with differential learning experiences. *Journal of Educational Computing Research, 35*(2), 123–144.

Lampert, M. (1999). Knowing teaching from the inside out: Implications of inquiry in practice for teacher education. In G. Griffen (Ed.), *The education of teachers: 98th Yearbook of the National Society for the Study of Education, Part 1* (pp. 167–184). Chicago, IL: University of Chicago Press.

Law, N. (2008, June). *Ecologies that foster intentional learning for the pursuit of excellence in the 21st century.* Invited keynote presentation at the International Conference of the Learning Sciences, Utrecht, Netherlands.

Lei, J., & Zhang, J. (2010). Challenges and future directions in Sinic Education. In Y. Zhao (Ed.), *Handbook of Asian education: A cultural approach* (pp. 134–156). New York: Routledge.

Levin, J., & Cohen, M. (1985). The world as an international science laboratory: Electronic networks for science instruction and problem solving. *Journal of Computers in Mathematics and Science Teaching, 4*, 33–35.

Li, X.-M. (1996). *Good writing in cross-cultural context.* Albany, NY: SUNY Press.

Lin, X., & Schwartz, D. (2003). Reflection at the crossroads of cultures. *Mind, Culture, and Activity, 10*, 9–25.

Lustig, M. W., & Koester, J. (1999). *Intercultural competence: Interpersonal communication across cultures.* New York: Harper Collins.

Macrae, C. N., Stangor, C., & Hewstone, M. (Eds.). (1996). *Stereotypes and stereotyping.* New York: Guilford.

Massey, A., Montoya-Weiss, M., Hung, C., & Ramesh, V. (2001). When culture and style aren't about clothes: Perceptions of task-technology "fit" in global virtual teams. In T. Rodden, C. Ellis, & I. Zigurs (Eds.), *Proceeding of ACM Group 2001* (pp. 207–213). New York: ACM Press.

Nisbett, R. (2003). *The geography of thought: How Asians and Westerners think differently … and why.* New York: Free Press.

Organisation for Economic Co-operation and Development (OECD). (2010). *PISA 2009 results: What students know and can do: Student performance in reading, mathematics and science* (Vol. 1). Paris: Author.

Oshima, J., Oshima, R., Murayama, I., Inagaki, S., Takenaka, M., Yamamoto, T., … Nakayama, H. (2006). Knowledge-building activity structures in Japanese elementary science pedagogy. *International Journal of Computer-Supported Collaborative Learning, 1,* 229–246

Prasolova-Førland, E., Wyeld, T. G., & Chang, T-W. (2008). Constructing a virtual tower of Babel: A case study in cross-cultural collaboration across three continents. In T. G. Wyeld, S. Kenderdine, & M. Docherty (Eds.), *Proceedings of Virtual Systems and MultiMedia 2007* (pp. 143–153). New York: Springer.

Pratt, D. D., & Wong, K. M. (1999). Chinese conceptions of "effective teaching" in Hong Kong: Towards culturally sensitive evaluation of teaching. *International Journal of Lifelong Education, 18,* 241–258.

Rathje, S. (2007). Intercultural competence: The status and future of a controversial concept. *Language and Intercultural Communication, 7,* 254–266.

Rohlen, T., & LeTendre, G. (Eds.). (1995). *Teaching and learning in Japan.* New York: Cambridge University Press.

Scardamalia, M., & Bereiter, C. (2006). Knowledge building: Theory, pedagogy, and technology. In R. K. Sawyer (Ed.), *Cambridge handbook of the learning sciences* (pp. 97–115). New York: Cambridge University Press.

Seo, K., Miller, P. C., Schmidt, C., & Sowa, P. (2008, October). Creating synergy between collectivism and individualism in cyberspace: A comparison of online communication patterns between Hong Kong and U.S. students. *Journal of Intercultural Communication,* 18. Retrieved from http://www.immi.se/intercultural/nr18/kay.htm

Setlock, L. D., Fussell, S. R., & Neuwirth, C. (2004). Taking it out of context: collaborating within and across cultures in face-to-face settings and via instant messaging. In J. Herbsleb & G. Olson (Eds.), *Proceedings of the 2004 ACM Conference on Computer Supported Cooperative Work* (pp. 604–613). New York: ACM Press.

Stahl, G. (2006). *Group cognition: Computer support for building collaborative knowledge.* Cambridge, MA: MIT Press.

Stewart, C. O., Setlock, L. D., & Fussell, S. R. (2004). Conversational argumentation in decision making: Chinese and U.S. participants in face-to-face and instant-messaging interactions. *Discourse Processes, 44*(2), 113–139.

Stigler, J. W., & Hiebert, J. (1999). *The teaching gap: Best ideas from the world's teachers for improving education in the classroom.* New York: Free Press.

Tabak, I., & Baumgartner, E. (2004). The teacher as partner: Exploring participant structures, symmetry and identity work in scaffolding. *Cognition and Instruction, 22*(4), 393–429.

Tang, C. (1996). Collaborative learning: The latent dimension in Chinese students' learning. In D. A. Watkins & J. B. Briggs (Eds.), *The Chinese learner: Cultural, psychological and contextual influences* (pp. 183–204). Hong Kong: Comparative Education Research Center, University of Hong Kong.

Tweed, R. G., & Lehman, D. R. (2002). Learning considered within a cultural context: Confucian and Socratic Approaches. *American Psychologist, 57*(2), 89–99.

van Aalst, J., & Chan, C.K..K. (2007). Student-directed assessment of knowledge building using electronic portfolios in Knowledge Forum. *Journal of the Learning Sciences, 16,* 175–220.

Vatrapu, R. (2008). Cultural considerations in computer supported collaborative learning. *Research and Practice in Technology Enhanced Learning, 3*(2), 159–201.

Vatrapu, R., & Suthers, D. (2007, January). *Culture and computers: A review of the concept of culture and implications for intercultural collaborative online learning.* Paper presented at The First International Workshop on Intercultural Collaboration (IWIC2007), Kyoto, Japan.

Vatrapu, R., & Suthers, D. (2009, February). *Technological intersubjectivity in computer supported intercultural collaboration.* Paper presented at the International Workshop on Intercultural Collaboration (IWIC 2009), Palo Alto, CA.

Watanabe, M. (1998). *Styles of reasoning in Japan and the United States: Logic of education in two cultures.* Paper presented at the American Sociological Association, San Francisco, CA.

Watkins, D. A., & Biggs, J. B. (Eds.). (1996). *The Chinese learner: Cultural, psychological and contextual influences.* Hong Kong: Comparative Education Research Center, University of Hong Kong.

Wertsch, J. (1985). *Vygotsky and the social formation of mind.* Cambridge, MA: Harvard University Press.

Zhang, J. (2007). A cultural look at information and communication technologies in Eastern education. *Educational Technology Research and Development, 55,* 301–314.

Zhang, J. (2010). Technology-supported learning innovation in cultural contexts. *Educational Technology Research and Development, 58* (2), 229–243.

Zhang, J., Hong, H.-Y., Scardamalia, M., Teo, C., & Morley, E. (2011). Sustaining knowledge building as a principle-based innovation at an elementary school. *Journal of the Learning Sciences, 20,* 262–307.

Zhang, J., Scardamalia, M., Reeve, R., & Messina, R. (2009). Designs for collective cognitive responsibility in knowledge building communities. *Journal of the Learning Sciences, 18*, 7–44.

Zhao, Y. (2009). *Catching up or leading the way: American education in the age of globalization*. Alexandria, VA: ASCD.

INDEX

Page numbers in italic refer to figures or tables.